SECOND EDITION

MySQL High Availability

Charles Bell, Mats Kindahl, and Lars Thalmann

WITHDRAWN

Beijing · Cambridge · Farnham · Köln · Sebastopol · Tokyo

MySQL High Availability, Second Edition

by Charles Bell, Mats Kindahl, and Lars Thalmann

Copyright © 2014 Charles Bell, Mats Kindahl, Lars Thalmann. All rights reserved.

Printed in the United States of America.

Published by O'Reilly Media, Inc., 1005 Gravenstein Highway North, Sebastopol, CA 95472.

O'Reilly books may be purchased for educational, business, or sales promotional use. Online editions are also available for most titles (*http://my.safaribooksonline.com*). For more information, contact our corporate/institutional sales department: 800-998-9938 or *corporate@oreilly.com*.

Editor: Andy Oram
Production Editor: Nicole Shelby
Copyeditor: Jasmine Kwityn
Proofreader: Linley Dolby

Indexer: Lucie Haskins
Cover Designer: Karen Montgomery
Interior Designer: David Futato
Illustrator: Rebecca Demarest

June 2010:   First Edition

April 2014:   Second Edition

Revision History for the Second Edition:

2014-04-09:   First release

See *http://oreilly.com/catalog/errata.csp?isbn=9781449339586* for release details.

ISBN: 978-1-449-33958-6

[LSI]

Table of Contents

Part I.   High Availability and Scalability

Part II.   Monitoring and Managing

Foreword for the Second Edition

In 2011, Pinterest started growing. Some say we grew faster than any other startup to date. In the earliest days, we were up against a new scalability bottleneck every day that could slow down the site or bring it down altogether. We remember having our laptops with us everywhere. We slept with them, we ate with them, we went on vacation with them. We even named them. We have the sound of the SMS outage alerts imprinted in our brains.

When the infrastructure is constantly being pushed to its limits, you can't help but wish for an easy way out. During our growth, we tried no less than five well-known database technologies that claimed to solve all our problems, but each failed catastrophically. Except MySQL. The time came around September 2011 to throw all the cards in the air and let them resettle. We re-architected everything around MySQL, Memcache, and Redis with just three engineers.

MySQL? Why MySQL? We laid out our biggest concerns with any technology and started asking the same questions for each. Here's how MySQL shaped up:

- Does it address our storage needs? Yes, we needed mappings, indexes, sorting, and blob storage, all available in MySQL.

- Is it commonly used? Can you hire somebody for it? MySQL is one of the most common database choices in production today. It's so easy to hire people who have used MySQL that we could walk outside in Palo Alto and yell out for a MySQL engineer and a few would come up. Not kidding.

- Is the community active? Very active. There are great books available and a strong online community.

- How robust is it to failure? Very robust! We've never lost any data even in the most dire of situations.

- How well does it scale? By itself, it does not scale beyond a single box. We'd need a sharding solution layered on top. (That's a whole other discussion!)

- Will you be the biggest user? Nope, not by far. Bigger users included Facebook, Twitter, and Google. You don't want to be the biggest user of a technology if you can help it. If you are, you'll trip over new scalability problems that nobody has had a chance to debug yet.

- How mature is it? Maturity became the real differentiator. Maturity to us is a measure of the blood, sweat, and tears that have gone into a program divided by its complexity. MySQL is reasonably complex, but not nearly so compared to some of the magic autoclustering NoSQL solutions available. Additionally, MySQL has had 28 years of the best and the brightest contributing back to it from such companies as Facebook and Google, who use it at *massive* scale. Of all the technologies we looked at, by our definition of maturity, MySQL was a clear choice.

- Does it have good debugging tools? As a product matures, you naturally get great debugging and profiling tools since people are more likely to have been in a similar sticky situation. You'll find yourself in trouble at 3 A.M. (multiple times). Being able to root cause an issue and get back to bed is better than rewriting for another technology by 6 A.M.

Based on our survey of 10 or so database technologies, MySQL was the clear choice. MySQL is great, but it kinda drops you off at your destination with no baggage and you have to fend for yourself. It works very well and you can connect to it, but as soon as you start using it and scaling, the questions starting flying:

- My query is running slow, now what?
- Should I enable compression? How do I do it?
- What are ways of scaling beyond one box?
- How do I get replication working? How about master-master replication?
- REPLICATION STOPPED! NOW WHAT?!
- What are options for durability (fsync speeds)?
- How big should my buffers be?
- There are a billion fields in *mysql.ini*. What are they? What should they be set to?
- I just accidentally wrote to my slave! How do I prevent that from happening again?
- How do I prevent running an UPDATE with no where clause?
- What debugging and profiling tools should I be using?
- Should I use InnoDB, MyISAM, or one of several other flavors of storage engine?

The online community is helpful for answering specific questions, finding examples, bug fixes, and workarounds, but often lacks a strong cohesive story, and deeper discussions about architecture are few and far between. We knew how to use MySQL at small scale, but this scale and pace were insane. *High Availability MySQL* provided insights that allowed us to squeeze more out of MySQL.

One new feature in MySQL 5.6, Global Transaction Handlers, adds a unique identifier to every transaction in a replication tree. This new feature makes failover and slave promotion far easier. We've been waiting for this for a long time and it's well covered in this new edition.

During our grand re-architecture to a sharded solution, we referred to this book for architectural decisions, such as replication techniques and topologies, data sharding alternatives, monitoring options, tuning, and concerns in the cloud. It gave us a deeper understanding of how MySQL works underneath the hood, which allowed us to make better informed choices around the high level queries, access patterns, and structures we'd be using, as well as iterate on our design afterward. The resulting MySQL architecture still serves Pinterest's core data needs today.

—Yashwanth Nelapati and Marty Weiner
Pinterest
February 2014

Foreword for the First Edition

A lot of research has been done on replication, but most of the resulting concepts are never put into production. In contrast, MySQL replication is widely deployed but has never been adequately explained. This book changes that. Things are explained here that were previously limited to people willing to read a lot of source code and spend a lot of time—including a few late-night sessions—debugging it in production.

Replication enables you to provide highly available data services while enduring the inevitable failures. There are an amazing number of ways for things to fail, including the loss of a disk, server, or data center. Even when hardware is perfect or fully redundant, people are not. Database tables will be dropped by mistake. Applications will write incorrect data. Occasional failure is assured. But with reasonable preparation, recovery from failure can also be assured. The keys to survival are redundancy and backups. Replication in MySQL supports both.

But MySQL replication is not limited to supporting failure recovery. It is frequently used to support read scale-out. MySQL can efficiently replicate to a large number of servers. For applications that are read-mostly, this is a cost-effective strategy for supporting a large number of queries on commodity hardware.

And there are other interesting uses for MySQL replication. Online data definition language (DDL) is a very complex feature to implement in a relational database management system. MySQL does not support online DDL, but through the use of replication, you can implement something that is frequently good enough. You can get a lot done with replication if you are willing to be creative.

Replication is one of the features that made MySQL wildly popular. It is also the feature that allows you to convert a popular MySQL prototype into a successful business-critical deployment. Like most of MySQL, replication favors simplicity and ease of use. As a consequence, it is occasionally less than perfect when running in production. This book explains what you need to know to successfully use MySQL replication. It will help you to understand how replication has been implemented, what can go wrong, how to prevent problems, and how to fix them when—despite your best attempts at prevention—they crop up.

MySQL replication is also a work in progress. Change, like failure, is also assured. MySQL is responding to that change, and replication continues to get more efficient, more robust, and more interesting. For instance, row-based replication is new in MySQL 5.1.

While MySQL deployments come in all shapes and sizes, I care most about data services for Internet applications and am excited about the potential to replicate from MySQL to distributed storage systems like HBase and Hadoop. This will make MySQL better at sharing the data center.

I have been on teams that support important MySQL deployments at Facebook and Google. I've encountered many of the problems covered in this book and have had the opportunity and time to learn solutions. The authors of this book are also experts on MySQL replication, and by reading this book you can share their expertise.

—Mark Callaghan

Preface

The authors of this book have been creating parts of MySQL and working with it for many years. Dr. Charles Bell is a senior developer leading the MySQL Utilities team. He has also worked on replication and backup. His interests include all things MySQL, database theory, software engineering, microcontrollers, and three-dimensional printing. Dr. Mats Kindahl is a principal senior software developer currently leading the MySQL High Availability and Scalability team. He is architect and implementor of several MySQL features. Dr. Lars Thalmann is the development director and technical lead of the MySQL Replication, Backup, Connectors, and Utilities teams, and has designed many of the replication and backup features. He has worked on the development of MySQL clustering, replication, and backup technologies.

We wrote this book to fill a gap we noticed among the many books on MySQL. There are many excellent books on MySQL, but few that concentrate on its advanced features and applications, such as high availability, reliability, and maintainability. In this book, you will find all of these topics and more.

We also wanted to make the reading a bit more interesting by including a running narrative about a MySQL professional who encounters common requests made by his boss. In the narrative, you will meet Joel Thomas, who recently decided to take a job working for a company that has just started using MySQL. You will observe Joel as he learns his way around MySQL and tackles some of the toughest problems facing MySQL professionals. We hope you find this aspect of the book entertaining.

Who This Book Is For

This book is for MySQL professionals. We expect you to have basic knowledge of SQL, MySQL administration, and the operating system you are running. We provide introductory information about replication, disaster recovery, system monitoring, and other key topics of high availability. See Chapter 1 for other books that offer useful background information.

How This Book Is Organized

This book is divided into two parts. Part I encompasses MySQL high availability and scale-out. Because these depend a great deal on replication, a lot of this part focuses on that topic. Part II examines monitoring and performance concerns for building robust data centers.

Part I, High Availability and Scalability

Chapter 1, *Introduction*, explains how this book can help you and gives you a context for reading it.

Chapter 2, *MySQL Replicant Library*, introduces a Python library for working with sets of servers that is used throughout the book.

Chapter 3, *MySQL Replication Fundamentals*, discusses both manual and automated procedures for setting up basic replication.

Chapter 4, *The Binary Log*, explains the critical file that ties together replication and helps in disaster recovery, troubleshooting, and other administrative tasks.

Chapter 5, *Replication for High Availability*, shows a number of ways to recover from server failure, including the use of automated scripts.

Chapter 6, *MySQL Replication for Scale-Out*, shows a number of techniques and topologies for improving the read scalability of large data sets.

Chapter 7, *Data Sharding*, shows techniques for handling very large databases and/or improving the write scalability of a database through sharding.

Chapter 8, *Replication Deep Dive*, addresses a number of topics, such as secure data transfer and row-based replication.

Chapter 9, *MySQL Cluster*, shows how to use this tool to achieve high availability.

Part II, Monitoring and Managing

Chapter 10, *Getting Started with Monitoring*, presents the main operating system parameters you have to be aware of, and tools for monitoring them.

Chapter 11, *Monitoring MySQL*, presents several tools for monitoring database activity and performance.

Chapter 12, *Storage Engine Monitoring*, explains some of the parameters you need to monitor on a more detailed level, focusing on issues specific to MyISAM or InnoDB.

Chapter 13, *Replication Monitoring*, offers details about how to keep track of what masters and slaves are doing.

Chapter 14, *Replication Troubleshooting*, shows how to deal with failures and restarts, corruption, and other incidents.

Chapter 15, *Protecting Your Investment*, explains the use of backups and disaster recovery techniques.

Chapter 16, *MySQL Enterprise Monitor*, introduces a suite of tools that simplifies many of the tasks presented in earlier chapters.

Chapter 17, *Managing MySQL Replication with MySQL Utilities*, introduces the MySQL Utilities, which are a new set of tools for managing MySQL Servers.

Appendixes

Appendix A, *Replication Tips and Tricks*, offers a grab bag of procedures that are useful in certain situations.

Appendix B, *A GTID Implementation*, shows an implementation for handling failovers with transactions if you are using servers that don't support GTIDs.

Conventions Used in This Book

The following typographical conventions are used in this book:

Plain text
: Indicates menu titles, table names, options, and buttons.

Italic
: Indicates new terms, database names, URLs, email addresses, filenames, and Unix utilities.

`Constant width`
: Indicates command-line options, variables and other code elements, the contents of files, and the output from commands.

`Constant width bold`
: Shows commands or other text that should be typed literally by the user.

`Constant width italic`
: Shows text that should be replaced with user-supplied values.

 This element signifies a tip or suggestion.

This element signifies a general note.

 This element indicates a warning or caution.

Using Code Examples

Supplemental material (code examples, exercises, etc.) is available for download at at http://bit.ly/mysqllaunch.

This book is here to help you get your job done. In general, if example code is offered with this book, you may use it in your programs and documentation. You do not need to contact us for permission unless you're reproducing a significant portion of the code. For example, writing a program that uses several chunks of code from this book does not require permission. Selling or distributing a CD-ROM of examples from O'Reilly books does require permission. Answering a question by citing this book and quoting example code does not require permission. Incorporating a significant amount of example code from this book into your product's documentation does require permission.

We appreciate, but do not require, attribution. An attribution usually includes the title, author, publisher, and ISBN. For example: "*MySQL High Availability*, by Charles Bell, Mats Kindahl, and Lars Thalmann. Copyright 2014 Charles Bell, Mats Kindahl, and Lars Thalmann, 978-1-44933-958-6."

If you feel your use of code examples falls outside fair use or the permission given above, feel free to contact us at *permissions@oreilly.com*.

Safari® Books Online

 Safari Books Online (*www.safaribooksonline.com*) is an on-demand digital library that delivers expert content in both book and video form from the world's leading authors in technology and business.

Technology professionals, software developers, web designers, and business and creative professionals use Safari Books Online as their primary resource for research, problem solving, learning, and certification training.

Safari Books Online offers a range of product mixes and pricing programs for organizations, government agencies, and individuals. Subscribers have access to thousands of books, training videos, and prepublication manuscripts in one fully searchable database from publishers like O'Reilly Media, Prentice Hall Professional, Addison-Wesley Professional, Microsoft Press, Sams, Que, Peachpit Press, Focal Press, Cisco Press, John Wiley & Sons, Syngress, Morgan Kaufmann, IBM Redbooks, Packt, Adobe Press, FT Press, Apress, Manning, New Riders, McGraw-Hill, Jones & Bartlett, Course Technology, and dozens more. For more information about Safari Books Online, please visit us online.

How to Contact Us

Please address comments and questions concerning this book to the publisher:

O'Reilly Media, Inc.
1005 Gravenstein Highway North
Sebastopol, CA 95472
800-998-9938 (in the United States or Canada)
707-829-0515 (international or local)
707-829-0104 (fax)

We have a web page for this book, where we list errata, examples, and any additional information. You can access this page at *http://bit.ly/mysql_high_availability*.

To comment or ask technical questions about this book, send email to: *bookques tions@oreilly.com*.

For more information about our books, courses, conferences, and news, see our website at: *http://www.oreilly.com*.

Acknowledgments

The authors would like to thank our technical reviewers of this and the previous edition: Mark Callahan, Morgan Tocker, Sveta Smirnova, Luis Soares, Sheeri Kritzer Cabral, Alfie John, and Colin Charles. Your attention to detail and insightful suggestions were invaluable. We could not have delivered a quality book without your help.

We also want to thank our extremely talented colleagues on the MySQL team and in the MySQL community who have provided comments, including Alfranio Correia, Andrei Elkin, Zhen-Xing He, Serge Kozlov, Sven Sandberg, Luis Soares, Rafal Somla, Li-Bing Song, Ingo Strüwing, Dao-Gang Qu, Giuseppe Maxia, and Narayanan Venkateswaran for their tireless dedication to making MySQL the robust and powerful tool it is today. We especially would like to thank our MySQL customer support professionals, who help us bridge the gap between our customers' needs and our own desires to improve the product. We would also like to thank the many community members who so selflessly devote time and effort to improve MySQL for everyone.

Finally, and most important, we would like to thank our editor, Andy Oram, who helped us shape this work, for putting up with our sometimes cerebral and sometimes over-the-top enthusiasm for all things MySQL. A most sincere thanks goes out to the entire O'Reilly team and especially our editor for their patience as we struggled to fit so many new topics into what was already a very large book.

Charles would like to thank his loving wife, Annette, for her patience and understanding when he was spending time away from family priorities to work on this book. Charles would also like to thank his many colleagues on the MySQL team at Oracle who contribute their wisdom freely to everyone on a daily basis. Finally, Charles would like to thank all of his brothers and sisters in Christ who both challenge and support him daily.

Mats would like to thank his wife, Lill, and two sons, Jon and Hannes, for their unconditional love and understanding in difficult times. You are the loves of his life and he cannot imagine a life without you. Mats would also like to thank his MySQL colleagues inside and outside Oracle for all the interesting, amusing, and inspiring times together —you are truly some of the sharpest minds in the trade.

Lars would like to thank his amazing girlfriend Claudia; he loves her beyond words. He would also like to thank all of his colleagues, current and past, who have made MySQL such an interesting place to work. In fact, it is not even a place. The distributed nature of the MySQL development team and the open-mindedness of its many dedicated developers are truly extraordinary. The MySQL community has a special spirit that makes working with MySQL an honorable task. What we have created together is remarkable. It is amazing that it started with such a small group of people and managed to build a product that services so many of the Fortune 500 companies today.

## PART I

High Availability and Scalability

One of the key database features that supports both high availability and scalability in an application is replication. Replication is used to create redundancy in the database layer as well as to make copies of the database available for scaling the reads. Part I covers how you can use replication to ensure high availability and how you can scale your system.

## CHAPTER 1

Introduction

Joel looked through the classified ads for a new job. His current job was a good one, and the company had been very accommodating to him while he attended college. But it had been several years since he graduated, and he wanted to do more with his career.

"This looks promising," he said, circling an advertisement for a computer science specialist working with MySQL. He had experience with MySQL and certainly met the academic requirements for the job. After reading through several other ads, he decided to call about the MySQL job. After a brief set of cursory questions, the human resources manager granted him an interview in two days' time.

Two days and three interviews later, he was introduced to the company's president and chief executive officer, Robert Summerson, for his final technical interview. He waited while Mr. Summerson paused during the questions and referred to his notes. So far, they were mostly mundane questions about information technology, but Joel knew the hard questions about MySQL were coming next.

Finally, the interviewer said, "I am impressed with your answers, Mr. Thomas. May I call you Joel?"

"Yes, sir," Joel said as he endured another uncomfortable period while the interviewer read over his notes for the third time.

"Tell me what you know about MySQL," Mr. Summerson said before placing his hands on his desk and giving Joel a very penetrating stare.

Joel began explaining what he knew about MySQL, tossing in a generous amount of the material he had read the night before. After about 10 minutes, he ran out of things to talk about.

Mr. Summerson waited a couple of minutes, then stood and offered Joel his hand. As Joel rose and shook Mr. Summerson's hand, Summerson said, "That's all I need to hear, Joel. The job is yours."

"Thank you, sir."

Mr. Summerson motioned for Joel to follow him out of his office. "I'll take you back to the HR people so we can get you on the payroll. Can you start two weeks from Monday?"

Joel was elated and couldn't help but smile. "Yes, sir."

"Excellent." Mr. Summerson shook Joel's hand again and said, "I want you to come prepared to evaluate the configuration of our MySQL servers. I want a complete report on their configuration and health."

Joel's elation waned as he drove out of the parking lot. He didn't go home right away. Instead, he drove to the nearest bookstore. "I'm going to need a good book on MySQL," he thought.

So, you have decided to take on a large installation and take care of its operation. Well, you are up for some very interesting—as well as rewarding—times.

Compared to running a small site, supporting a large venture requires planning, fore-sight, experience, and even more planning. As a database administrator for a large venture, you are required to—or will be required to—do things like the following:

- Provide plans for recovery of business-essential data in the event of a disaster. It is also likely that you will have to execute the procedure at least once.
- Provide plans for handling a large customer/user base and monitoring the load of each node in the site in order to optimize it.
- Plan for rapid scale-out in the event the user base grows rapidly.

For all these cases, it is critical to plan for the events in advance and be prepared to act quickly when necessary.

Because not all applications using big sets of servers are websites, we prefer to use the term *deployment*—rather than the term *site* or *website*—to refer to the server that you are using to support some kind of application. This could be a website, but could just as well be a customer relationship management (CRM) system or an online game. The book focuses on the database layer of such a system, but there are some examples that demonstrate how the application layer and the database layer integrate.

You need three things to keep a site responsive and available: backups of data, redundancy in the system, and responsiveness. The backups can restore a node to the state it was in before a crash, redundancy allows the site to continue to operate even if one or more of the nodes stops functioning, and the responsiveness makes the system usable in practice.

There are many ways to perform backups, and the method you choose will depend on your needs.[1] Do you need to recover to an exact point in time? In that case, you have to ensure that you have all that is necessary for performing a point-in-time recovery (PITR). Do you want to keep the servers up while making a backup? If so, you need to ensure that you are using some form of backup that does not disturb the running server, such as an online backup.

Redundancy is handled by duplicating hardware, keeping several instances running in parallel, and using replication to keep multiple copies of the same data available on several machines. If one of the machines fails, it is possible to switch over to another machine that has a copy of the same data.

Together with replication, backup also plays an important role in scaling your system and adding new nodes when needed. If done right, it is even possible to automatically add new slaves at the press of a button, at least figuratively.

What's This Replication Stuff, Anyway?

If you're reading this book, you probably have a pretty good idea of what replication is about. It is nevertheless a good idea to review the concepts and ideas.

Replication is used to clone all changes made on a server—called the *master server* or just *master*—to another server, which is called the *slave server* or just *slave*. This is normally used to create a faithful copy of the master server, but replication can be used for other purposes as well.

The two most common uses of replication are to create a backup of the main server to avoid losing any data if the master crashes and to have a copy of the main server to perform reporting and analysis work without disturbing the rest of the business.

For a small business, this makes a lot of things simpler, but it is possible to do a lot more with replication, including the following:

Support several offices
It is possible to maintain servers at each location and replicate changes to the other offices so that the information is available everywhere. This may be necessary to protect data and also to satisfy legal requirements to keep information about the business available for auditing purposes.

Ensure the business stays operational even if one of the servers goes down
An extra server can be used to handle all the traffic if the original server goes down.

---

1. You are not restricted to using a single backup method; you can just as well use a mix of different methods depending on your needs. For each case, however, you have to make a choice of the most appropriate method to do the backup.

Ensure the business can operate even in the presence of a disaster

Replication can be used to send changes to an alternative data center at a different geographic location.

Protect against mistakes ("oopses")

It is possible to create a *delayed slave* by connecting a slave to a master such that the slave is always a fixed period—for example, an hour—behind the master. If a mistake is made on the master, it is possible to find the offending statement and remove it before it is executed by the slave.

One of the two most important uses of replication in many modern applications is that of *scaling out*. Modern applications are typically very read-intensive; they have a high proportion of reads compared to writes. To reduce the load on the master, you can set up a slave with the sole purpose of answering read queries. By connecting a load balancer, it is possible to direct read queries to a suitable slave, while write queries go to the master.

When using replication in a scale-out scenario, it is important to understand that MySQL replication traditionally has been *asynchronous*[2] in the sense that transactions are committed at the master server first, then replicated to the slave and applied there. This means that the master and slave may not be consistent, and if replication is running continuously, the slave will lag behind the master.

The advantage of using asynchronous replication is that it is faster and scales better than synchronous replication, but in cases where it is important to have current data, the asynchrony must be handled to ensure the information is actually up-to-date.

Scaling out reads is, however, not sufficient to scale all applications. With growing demands on larger databases and higher write load, it is necessary to scale more than just reads. Managing larger databases and improving performance of large database systems can be accomplished using techniques such as *sharding*. With sharding, the database is split into manageable chunks, allowing you to increase the size of the database by distributing it over as many servers as you need as well as scaling writes efficiently.

Another important application of replication is ensuring high availability by adding redundancy. The most common technique is to use a *dual-master setup* (i.e., using replication to keep a pair of masters available all the time, where each master mirrors the other). If one of the masters goes down, the other one is ready to take over immediately.

In addition to the dual-master setup, there are other techniques for achieving high availability that do not involve replication, such as using shared or replicated disks.

---

2. There is an extension called *semisynchronous replication* as well (see "Semisynchronous Replication" on page 257), but that is a relatively new addition. Until MySQL 5.7.2 DMR, it externalized the transaction before it was replicated, allowing it to be read before it had been replicated and acknowledged requiring some care when being used for high availability.

Although they are not specifically tied to MySQL, these techniques are important tools for ensuring high availability.

So, Backups Are Not Needed Then?

A backup strategy is a critical component of keeping a system available. Regular backups of the servers provide safety against crashes and disasters, which, to some extent, can be handled by replication. Even when replication is used correctly and efficiently, however, there are some things that it cannot handle. You'll need to have a working backup strategy for the following cases:

Protection against mistakes
> If a mistake is discovered, potentially a long time after it actually occurred, replication will not help. In this case, it is necessary to roll back the system to a time before the mistake was introduced and fix the problem. This requires a working backup schedule.
>
> Replication provides some protection against mistakes if you are using a time-delayed slave, but if the mistake is discovered after the delay period, the change will have already taken effect on the slave as well. So, in general, it is not possible to protect against mistakes using replication only—backups are required as well.

Creating new servers
> When creating new servers—either slaves for scale-out purposes or new masters to act as standbys—it is necessary to make a backup of an existing server and restore that backup image on the new server. This requires a quick and efficient backup method to minimize the downtime and keep the load on the system at an acceptable level.

Legal reasons
> In addition to pure business reasons for data preservation, you may have legal requirements to keep data safe, even in the event of a disaster. Not complying with these requirements can pose significant problems to operating the business.

In short, a backup strategy is necessary for operating the business, regardless of any other precautions you have in place to ensure that the data is safe.

What's With All the Monitoring?

Even if you have replication set up correctly, it is necessary to understand the load on your system and to keep a keen eye on any problems that surface. As business requirements shift due to changing customer usage patterns, it is necessary to balance the system to use resources as efficiently as possible and to reduce the risk of losing availability due to sudden changes in resource utilization.

There are a number of different things that you can monitor, measure, and plan for to handle these types of changes. Here are some examples:

- You can add indexes to tables that are frequently read.
- You can rewrite queries or change the structure of databases to speed up execution time.
- If locks are held for a long time, it is an indication that several connections are using the same table. It might pay off to switch storage engines.
- If some of your scale-out slaves are hot-processing a disproportionate number of queries, the system might require some rebalancing to ensure that all the scale-out slaves are hit evenly.
- To handle sudden changes in resource usage, it is necessary to determine the normal load of each server and understand when the system will start to respond slowly because of a sudden increase in load.

Without monitoring, you have no way of spotting problematic queries, hot slaves, or improperly utilized tables.

Is There Anything Else I Can Read?

There is plenty of literature on using MySQL for various jobs, and also a lot of literature about high-availability systems. Here is a list of books that we strongly recommend if you are going to work with MySQL:

MySQL by Paul DuBois (Addison-Wesley)
> This is *the* reference to MySQL and consists of 1,200 pages (really!) packed with everything you want to know about MySQL (and probably a lot that you don't want to know).

High Performance MySQL, Third Edition by Baron Schwartz, Peter Zaitsev, and Vadim Tkachenko (O'Reilly)
> This is one of the best books on using MySQL in an enterprise setting. It covers optimizing queries and ensuring your system is responsive and available.

Scalable Internet Architectures by Theo Schlossnagle (Sams Publishing)
> Written by one of the most prominent thinkers in the industry, this is a must for anybody working with systems of scale.

The book uses a Python library developed by the authors (called the *MySQL Python Replicant*) for many of the administrative tasks. MySQL Python Replicant is available on Launchpad (*http://bit.ly/mysqllaunch*).

Conclusion

In the next chapter, we will start with the basics of setting up replication, so get a comfortable chair, open your computer, and we'll get started.

Joel was adjusting his chair when a knock sounded from his door.

"Settling in, Joel?" Mr. Summerson asked.

Joel didn't know what to say. He had been tasked to set up a replication slave on his first day on the job and while it took him longer than he had expected, he had yet to hear his boss's feedback about the job. Joel spoke the first thing on his mind: "Yes, sir, I'm still trying to figure out this chair."

"Nice job with the documentation, Joel. I'd like you to write a report explaining what you think we should do to improve our management of the database server."

Joel nodded. "I can do that."

"Good. I'll give you another day to get your office in order. I expect the report by Wednesday, close of business."

Before Joel could reply, Mr. Summerson walked away.

Joel sat down and flipped another lever on his chair. He heard a distinct click as the back gave way, forcing him to fling his arms wide. "Whoa!" He looked toward his door as he clumsily picked up his chair, thankful no one saw his impromptu gymnastics. "OK, that lever is now off limits," he said.

## CHAPTER 2

MySQL Replicant Library

Joel opened his handy text file full of common commands and tasks and copied them into another editor, changing the values for his current need. It was a series of commands involving a number of tools and utilities. "Ah, this is for the birds!" he thought. "There has got to be a better way."

Frustrated, he flipped open his handy *MySQL High Availability* tome and examined the table of contents. "Aha! A chapter on a library of replication procedures. Now, this is what I need!"

Automating administrative procedures is critical to handling large deployments, so you might be asking, "Wouldn't it be neat if we could automate the procedures in this book?" In many cases, you'll be happy to hear that you can. This chapter introduces the MySQL Replicant library, a simple library written by the authors for managing replication. We describe the basic principles and classes, and will extend the library with new functionality in the coming chapters.

The code is available at Launchpad (*http://bit.ly/mysqllaunch*), where you can find more information and download the source code and documentation.

The Replicant library is based around the idea of creating a model of the connections between servers on a computer (any computer, such as your laptop), like the model in Figure 2-1. The library is designed so you can manage the connections by changing the model. For example, to reconnect a slave to another master, just reconnect the slave in the model, and the library will send the appropriate commands for doing the job.

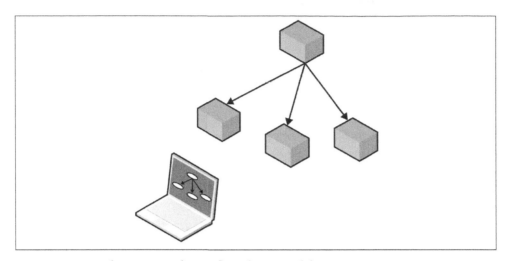

Figure 2-1. A replication topology reflected in a model

Besides the simple replication topology shown in Figure 2-1, two other basic topologies include tree topologies and dual masters (used for providing high availability). Topologies will be covered in more depth in Chapter 6.

To make the library useful on a wide variety of platforms and for a wide variety of deployments, it has been constructed with the following in mind:

- The servers are likely to run on a variety of operating systems, such as Windows, Linux, and flavors of Unix such as Solaris or Mac OS X. Procedures for starting and stopping servers, as well as the names of configuration files, differ depending on the operating system. The library should therefore support different operating systems and it should be possible to extend it with new operating systems that are not in the library.

- The deployment is likely to consist of servers running different versions of MySQL. For example, while you are upgrading a deployment to use new versions of the server, it will consist of a mixture of old and new versions. The library should be able to handle such a deployment.

- A deployment consists of servers with many different roles, so it should be possible to specify different roles for the servers. In addition, it should be possible to create new roles that weren't anticipated at the beginning. Also, servers should be able to change roles.

- It is necessary to be able to execute SQL queries on each server. This functionality is needed for configuration as well as for extracting information necessary to manage the deployment. This support is also used by other parts of the system to implement their jobs—for example, to implement a slave promotion.

- It is necessary to be able to execute shell commands on each machine. This is needed to perform some administrative tasks that cannot be done using the SQL interface. This support is also used by, for example, the operating system part of the library to manage the servers.

- It should be possible to add and remove options from the server's configuration file.

- The library should support a deployment with multiple servers on a machine. This requires the ability to recognize different configuration files and database files used by different MySQL servers on a single machine.

- There should be a set of utilities for performing common tasks such as setting up replication, but it should also be possible to extend the library with new utility functions that were not anticipated at the beginning.

The interface hides these complexities as much as possible and presents a simple interface in Python. Python was chosen by the authors because it is concise, easy to read, available on all operating systems that run MySQL, and increasingly popular for general-purpose scripting. You can see an example of how to define a topology in Example 2-1.

Example 2-1. Using the library to construct a topology

```
from mysql.replicant.server import Server, User
from mysql.replicant.machine import Linux
from mysql.replicant.roles import Master, Final

# The master that we use
MASTER = Server('master', server_id=1, ❶
                sql_user=User("mysql_replicant"), ❷
                ssh_user=User("mats"), ❸
                machine=Linux(), ❹
                host="master.example.com", port=3307, ❺
                socket='/var/run/mysqld/mysqld.sock')

# Slaves that we keep available
SLAVES = [ ❻
    Server('slave1', server_id=2,
           sql_user=User("mysql_replicant"),
           ssh_user=User("mats"),
           machine=Linux(),
           host="slave1.example.com", port=3308),
    Server('slave2', server_id=3,
           sql_user=User("mysql_replicant"),
           ssh_user=User("mats"),
           machine=Linux(),
           host="slave2.example.com", port=3309),
    Server('slave3', server_id=4,
           sql_user=User("mysql_replicant"),
           ssh_user=User("mats"),
           machine=Linux(),
```

```
                host="slave3.example.com", port=3310),
    ]

# Create the roles for these servers
master_role = Master(User("repl_user", "xyzzy")) ❼
slave_role = Final(MASTER) ❽

# Imbue the servers with the roles
master_role.imbue(MASTER) ❾
for slave in SLAVES:
    slave_role.imbue(slave)

# Convenience variable of all servers
SERVERS = [MASTER] + SLAVES
```

❶ The first step is to create a server object containing all the information about how to access the server. This server will be used as master, but this statement does nothing specific to configure it as a master. That is done later when *imbuing* the server with a role.

❷ When configuring the server, you need to include information on how to connect to the server to send SQL commands to it. For this example, we have a dedicated replicant user that is used to access the server. In this case, there is no password, but one could be set up when constructing the User instance.

❸ You will also need access to the machine where the server is running, to do such things as shut it down or access the configuration file. This line grants access to the user who will connect to the machine.

❹ Because servers are started and stopped in different ways on different kinds of operating systems, you must indicate the operating system the server is running on. In this case, Linux is used for all servers.

❺ This is where information about the host the server is running on goes. host and port are used when connecting to a remote machine, and socket is used when connecting on the same machine. If you will connect only remotely, you can omit socket.

❻ This constructs a list of servers that will be slaves. As for the master, it gives basic connection information but has nothing specific about slaves.

❼ To configure servers, the servers are *imbued* with *roles*. This statement constructs a Master role containing the replication user that will be used by slaves to connect to the server.

❽ This specifies the Final slave role, which does not run a binary log on the server, so cannot be promoted to a master later.

❾ These statements imbue all the servers with their roles. The effect is to update the configuration of each server so that it can be used in that role. If necessary (e.g., if the configuration file has to be changed), the statements will also restart the servers.

The previous example imbued all the server with their roles, and after you have started all the servers, Example 2-2 shows how you can use the library to redirect all slaves to use a new master.

Example 2-2. Using the library to redirect slaves

```
import my_deployment

from mysql.replicant.commands import change_master

for slave in my_deployment.slaves:
    slave.stop()
    change_master(slave, my_deployment.master)
    slave.start()
```

We have deliberately kept this example simple, and therefore have omitted some important steps. As the code stands, it stops replication in its tracks and is likely to lose transactions if executed on an active server. You will see how to change masters properly in Chapter 5.

The following sections show the code that makes such applications possible. To avoid cluttering the code more than necessary, we have removed some error checking and other defensive measures needed to have a stable and safe library. You will find the complete code for the library at Launchpad (*http://bit.ly/mysqllaunch*).

Basic Classes and Functions

The first things you need in order to use the library are some basic definitions for frequently used concepts. We need exceptions to be able to report errors, and we need some simple objects for representing positions and user information.

The complete list of exceptions can be found in the library. All the exceptions inherit from a common base class `Error` defined in the library, as is customary. The exceptions that you will see in later chapters include the following:

`EmptyRowError`
    This exception is thrown when an attempt is made to select a field from a query that did not return any rows.

`NoOptionError`
    This exception is raised when `ConfigManager` does not find the option.

SlaveNotRunningError
    This exception is raised when the slave is not running but was expected to run.

NotMasterError
    This exception is raised when the server is not a master and the operation is therefore illegal.

NotSlaveError
    This exception is raised when the server is not a slave and the operation is therefore illegal.

There is also a set of classes for representing some common concepts that will be used later in the book:

Position *and* GTID
    These classes represent a binlog position consisting of a filename and a byte offset within the file, or a global transaction identifier (introduced in MySQL 5.6). A representation method prints out a parsable representation of the binlog positions so that they can be put in secondary storage or if you just want to look at them.

    To compare and order the positions, the class defines a comparison operator that allows the positions to be ordered.

    Note that when global transaction identifiers are not used, positions can be different on different servers, so it is not useful to compare positions from different servers. For that reason, an exception will be thrown if an attempt is made to compare different kinds of positions.

User
    This class represents a user with a name and a password. It is used for many types of accounts: a MySQL user account, a shell user account, and the replication user (which we will introduce later).

Supporting Different Operating Systems

To work with different operating systems, you can use a set of classes that abstract away the differences. The idea is to give each class methods for each of the required tasks that are implemented differently by different operating systems. At this time, all we need are methods to stop and start the server:

Machine
    This class is the base class for a machine and holds all the information that is common to this kind of machine. It is expected that a machine instance has at least the following members:

    Machine.defaults_file
        The default location of the *my.cnf* file on this machine

---

```
Machine.start_server( server )
```
Method to start the server

```
Machine.stop_server( server )
```
Method to stop the server

Linux
This class handles a server running on a Linux machine. It uses the init(8) scripts stored under */etc/init.d* to start and stop the server.

Solaris
This class handles servers running on a Solaris machine and uses the svadm(1M) command to start and stop the server.

Servers

The Server class defines all the primitive functions that implement the higher-level functions we want to expose in the interface:

```
Server(name, ...)
```
The Server class represents a server in the system; there is one object for each running server in the entire system. Here are the most important parameters (for a full list, consult the project page on Launchpad):

name
This is the name of the server, and is used to create values for the pid-file, log-bin, and log-bin-index options. If no name parameter is provided, it will be deduced from the pid-file option, the log-bin option, the log-bin-index option, or as a last resort, using the default.

host, port, and socket
The host where the server resides, the port for connecting to the server as a MySQL client, and the socket through which to connect if on the same host.

ssh_user and sql_user
A combination of user and password that can be used for connecting to the machine or the server. These users are used to execute administrative commands, such as starting and stopping the server and reading and writing the configuration file, or for executing SQL commands on the server.

machine
An object that holds operating system–specific primitives. We chose the name "machine" instead of "os" to avoid a name conflict with the Python standard library os module. This parameter lets you use different techniques for starting and stopping the server as well as other tasks and operating system–specific parameters. The parameters will be covered later.

server_id

An optional parameter to hold the server's identifier, as defined in each server's configuration file. If this option is omitted, the server identifier will be read from the configuration file of the server. If there is no server identifier in the configuration file either, the server is a vagabond and does not participate in replication as master or slave.

config_manager

An optional parameter to hold a reference to a configuration manager that can be queried for information about the configuration for the server.

`Server.connect()` *and* `Server.disconnect()`

Use the `connect` and `disconnect` methods to establish a connection to the server before executing commands in a session and disconnect from the server after finishing the session, respectively.

These methods are useful because in some situations it is critical to keep the connection to the server open even after an SQL command has been executed. Otherwise, for example, when doing a `FLUSH TABLES WITH READ LOCK`, the lock will automatically be released when the connection is dropped.

`Server.ssh(`*command, args...*`)` *and* `Server.sql(`*command, args...*`)`

Use these to execute a shell command or an SQL command on the server.

The `ssh` and `sql` methods both return an iterable. `ssh` returns a list of the lines of output from the executed command, whereas `sql` returns a list of objects of an internal class named Row. The Row class defines the `__iter__` and `next` methods so that you iterate over the returned lines or rows, for example:

```
for row in server.sql("SHOW DATABASES"):
    print row["Database"]
```

To handle statements that return a single row, the class also defines a `__getitem__` method, which will fetch a field from the single row or raise an exception if there is no row. This means that when you know your return value has only one row (which is guaranteed for many SQL statements), you can avoid the loop shown in the previous example and write something like:

```
print server.sql("SHOW MASTER STATUS")["Position"]
```

`Server.fetch_config()` *and* `Server.replace_config()`

The methods `fetch_config` and `replace_config` fetch the configuration file into memory from the remote server to allow the user to add or remove options as well as change the values of some options. For example, to add a value to the `log-bin` and `log-bin-index` options, you can use the module as follows:

```
from my_deployment import master

config = master.fetch_config()
```

```
config.set('log-bin', 'capulet-bin')
config.set('log-bin-index', 'capulet-bin.index')
master.replace_config(config)
```

Server.start() *and* Server.stop()

> The methods start and stop forward information to the machine object to do their jobs, which depend on the operating system the server is using. The methods will either start the server or shut down the server, respectively.

Server Roles

Servers work slightly differently depending on their roles. For example, masters require a replication user for slaves to use when connecting, but slaves don't require that user account unless they act as a master and have other slaves connecting. To capture the configuration of the servers in a flexible manner, classes are introduced for representing different *roles*.

When you use the imbue method on a server, the appropriate commands are sent to the server to configure it correctly for that role. Note that a server might change roles in the lifetime of a deployment, so the roles given here just serve to configure the initial deployment. However, a server always has a designated role in the deployment and therefore also has an associated role.

When a server changes roles, it might be necessary to remove some of the configuration information from the server, so therefore an unimbue method is also defined for a role and used when switching roles for a server.

In this example, only three roles are defined. Later in the book, you will see more roles defined. For example, you will later see how to create nonfinal slaves that can be used as secondaries or relay servers. The following three roles can be found in the MySQL Replicant library:

Role

> This is the base class of all the roles. Each derived class needs to define the methods imbue and (optionally) unimbue to accept a single server to imbue with the role. To aid derived classes with some common tasks, the Role class defines a number of helper functions, including the following:

Role.imbue(*server*)

> This method imbues the server with the new role by executing the appropriate code.

Role.unimbue(*server*)

> This method allows a role to perform cleanup actions before another role is imbued.

`Role._set_server_id(`*`server, config`*`)`
> If there is no server identifier in the configuration, this method sets it to `server.server_id`. If the configuration has a server identifier, it will be used to set the value of `server.server_id`.

`Role._create_repl_user(`*`server, user`*`)`
> This method creates a replication user on the server and grants it the necessary rights to act as a replication slave.

`Role._enable_binlog(`*`server, config`*`)`
> This method enables the binary log on the server by setting the `log-bin` and `log-bin-index` options to appropriate values. If the server already has a value for `log-bin`, this method does nothing.

`Role._disable_binlog(server, config)`
> This method disables the binary log by clearing the `log-bin` and `log-bin-index` options in the configuration file.

`Vagabond`
> This is the default role assigned to any server that does not participate in the replication deployment. As such, the server is a "vagabond" and does not have any responsibilities whatsoever.

`Master`
> This role is for a server that acts as a master. The role will set the server identifier, enable the binary log, and create a replication user for the slaves. The name and password of the replication user will be stored in the server so that when slaves are connected, the class can look up the replication username.

`Final`
> This is the role for a (final) slave (i.e., a slave that does not have a binary log of its own). When a server is imbued with this role, it will be given a server identifier, the binary log will be disabled, and a `CHANGE MASTER` command will be issued to connect the slave to a master.

Note that we stop the server before we write the configuration file back to it, and restart the server after we have written the configuration file. The configuration file is read only when starting the server and closed after the reading is done, but we play it safe and stop the server before modifying the file.

One of the critical design decisions here is not to store any state information about the servers that roles apply to. It might be tempting to keep a list of all the masters by adding them to the role object, but because roles of the servers change over the lifetime of the deployment, the roles are used only to set up the system. Because we allow a role to contain parameters, you can use them to configure several servers with the same information.

```
import my_deployment

from mysql.replicant.roles import Final

slave_role = Final(master=my_deployment.master)
for slave in my_deployment.slaves:
    slave_role.imbue(slave)
```

Conclusion

In this chapter you have seen how to build a library for making administration of your servers easy. You have also seen the beginning of the MySQL Replicant library that we will be developing throughout this book.

Joel finished testing his script. He was pretty confident he had all of the parts in place and that the resulting command would save him a lot of time in the future. He clicked Enter.

A few moments later, his script returned the data he expected. He checked his servers thinking this was too easy, but he found everything he wanted to do had been done. "Cool, that was easy!" he said, and locked his screen before heading to lunch.

## CHAPTER 3

MySQL Replication Fundamentals

Joel jumped as a sharp rap on his door announced his boss's unapologetic interruption. Before Joel could say "come in," the boss stepped into his doorway and said, "Joel, we're getting complaints that our response time is getting slow. See what you can do to speed things up. The administrator told me there are too many read operations from the applications. See what you can do to offload some of that."

Before Joel could respond, Mr. Summerson was out the door and on his way elsewhere. "I suppose he means we need a bigger server," Joel thought.

As if he had read Joel's mind, Mr. Summerson stuck his head back in the doorway and said, "Oh, and by the way, the startup we bought all the equipment from had a bunch of servers we haven't found any use for yet. Can you take a look at those and see what you can do with them? OK, Joel?" Then he was gone again.

"I wonder if I'll ever get used to this," Joel thought as he pulled his favorite MySQL book off the shelf and glanced at the table of contents. He found the chapter on replication and decided that might fit the bill.

MySQL replication is a very useful tool when used correctly, but it can also be a source of considerable headaches when it experiences a failure or when it is configured or used incorrectly. This chapter will cover the fundamentals of using MySQL replication by beginning with a simple setup to get you started and then introducing some basic techniques to store in your "replication toolkit."

This chapter covers the following replication use cases:

High availability through hot standby
> If a server goes down, everything will stop; it will not be possible to execute (perhaps critical) transactions, get information about customers, or retrieve other important data. This is something that you want to avoid at (almost) any cost, because it can

severely disrupt your business. The easiest solution is to configure an extra server with the sole purpose of acting as a hot standby, ready to take over the job of the main server if it fails.

Report generation

Creating reports from data on a server will degrade the server's performance, in some cases significantly. If you're running lots of background jobs to generate reports, it's worth creating an extra server just for this purpose. You can get a snapshot of the database at a certain time by stopping replication on the report server and then running large queries on it without disturbing the main business server. For example, if you stop replication after the last transaction of the day, you can extract your daily reports while the rest of the business is humming along at its normal pace.

Debugging and auditing

You can also investigate queries that have been executed on the server—for example, to see whether particular queries were executed on servers with performance problems, or whether a server has gone out of sync because of a bad query.

Basic Steps in Replication

This chapter will introduce several sophisticated techniques for maximizing the efficiency and value of replication, but as a first step, we will set up the simple replication shown in Figure 3-1—a single instance of replication from a master to a slave. This does not require any knowledge of the internal architecture or execution details of the replication process (we'll explore these before we take on more complicated scenarios).

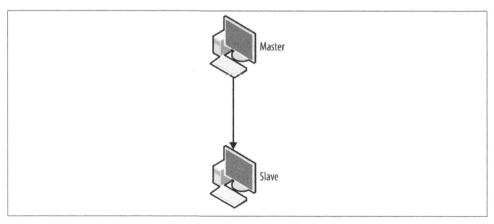

Figure 3-1. Simple replication

Setting up basic replication can be summarized in three easy steps:

1. Configure one server to be a master.

2. Configure one server to be a slave.

3. Connect the slave to the master.

Unless you plan replication from the start and include the right configuration options in the *my.cnf* files, you will have to restart each server to carry out steps 1 and 2.

 To follow the procedures in this section, it is easiest if you have a shell account on the machine with privileges to change the *my.cnf* file as well as an account on the server with ALL privileges granted.[1]

You should be very restrictive in granting privileges in a production environment. For precise guidelines, consult "Privileges for the User Configuring Replication" on page 27.

Configuring the Master

To configure a server so that it can act as master, ensure the server has an active *binary log* and a unique server ID. We will examine the binary log in greater detail later, but for now it is sufficient to say that it keeps a record of all the changes the master has made so that they can be repeated on the slave. The server ID is used to distinguish two servers from each other. To set up the binary log and server ID, you have to take the server down and add the log-bin, log-bin-index, and server-id options to the *my.cnf* configuration file as shown in Example 3-1. The added options are in boldface.

Example 3-1. Options added to my.cnf to configure a master

```
[mysqld]
user           = mysql
pid-file       = /var/run/mysqld/mysqld.pid
socket         = /var/run/mysqld/mysqld.sock
port           = 3306
basedir        = /usr
datadir        = /var/lib/mysql
tmpdir         = /tmp
log-bin        = master-bin
log-bin-index  = master-bin.index
server-id      = 1
```

The log-bin option gives the base name for all the files created by the binary log (as you will see later, the binary log consists of several files). If you create a filename with an extension to log-bin, the extension will be ignored and only the file's base name will be used (i.e., the name without the extension).

---

1. On Windows, the *command-line prompt* (CMD) or PowerShell can be used in place of the Unix "shell."

The log-bin-index option gives the name of the binary log index file, which keeps a list of all binlog files.

Strictly speaking, it is not necessary to give a name in the log-bin option. The default value is *hostname*-bin. The value for *hostname* is taken from the option for pid-file, which by default is the name of the host (as given by the gethostname(2) system call). If an administrator later changes the machine's hostname, the binlog files will change names as well, but they will be tracked correctly in the index file. However, it is a good idea to create a name that is unique for the MySQL server and not tied to the machine the server is running on because it can be confusing to work with a series of binlog files that suddenly change name midstream.

If no value is provided for log-bin-index, the default value will be the same base name as for the binlog files (*hostname*-bin if you don't give a default for log-bin). This means that if you do not provide a value for log-bin-index, the index file will change its name when you change the name of the host. So if you change the name of the host and start the server, it will not find the index file and therefore assume that it does not exist, and this will give you an empty binary log.

Each server is identified by a unique server ID, so if a slave connects to the master and has the same server-id as the master, an error will be generated indicating that the master and the slave have the same server ID.

Once you have added the options to the configuration file, start the server again and finish its configuration by adding a replication user.

After you make the change to the master's configuration file, restart the master for the changes to take effect.

The slave initiates a normal client connection to the master and requests the master to send all changes to it. For the slave to connect, a user with special replication privileges is required on the master. Example 3-2 shows a standard mysql client session on the master server, with commands that add a new user account and give it the proper privilege.

Example 3-2. Creating a replication user on the master

```
master> CREATE USER repl_user;
Query OK, 0 rows affected (0.00 sec)
master> GRANT REPLICATION SLAVE ON *.*
    -> TO repl_user IDENTIFIED BY 'xyzzy';
Query OK, 0 rows affected (0.00 sec)
```

There is nothing special about the REPLICATION SLAVE privilege except that the user can retrieve the binary log from the master. It is perfectly viable to have a normal user account and grant that user the REPLICATION SLAVE privilege. It is, however, a good idea to keep the replication slave user separate from the other users. If you do that, you can remove the user if you need to disallow certain slaves from connecting later.

Configuring the Slave

After configuring the master, you must configure the slave. As with the master server, you need to assign each slave a unique server ID. You may also want to consider adding the names of the relay log and the relay log index files to the *my.cnf* file (we will discuss the relay log in more detail in "Replication Architecture Basics" on page 228) using the options `relay-log` and `relay-log-index`. The recommended configuration options are given in Example 3-3, with the added options highlighted.

Example 3-3. Options added to my.cnf to configure a slave

```
[mysqld]
user            = mysql
pid-file        = /var/run/mysqld/mysqld.pid
socket          = /var/run/mysqld/mysqld.sock
port            = 3306
basedir         = /usr
datadir         = /var/lib/mysql
tmpdir          = /tmp
server-id       = 2
relay-log-index = slave-relay-bin.index
relay-log       = slave-relay-bin
```

Like the `log-bin` and `log-bin-index` options, the defaults for the `relay-log` and `relay-log-index` options depend on the hostname. The default for `relay-log` is *host name*-`relay-bin` and the default for `relay-log-index` is *hostname*-`relay-bin.index`. Using the default introduces a problem in that if the hostname of the server changes, it will not find the relay log index file and will assume there is nothing in the relay logfiles.

After editing the *my.cnf* file, restart the slave server for the changes to take effect.

Privileges for the User Configuring Replication

To configure the connection of the slave to the master for replication, it is necessary to have an account with certain privileges, in addition to a shell account with access to critical files. For security reasons, it is usually a good idea to restrict the account used for configuring the master and slave to just the necessary privileges. To create and drop users, the account needs to have the CREATE USER privilege. To grant the REPLICATION

SLAVE to the replication account, it is necessary to have the REPLICATION SLAVE privilege with the GRANT OPTION.

To perform further replication-related procedures (shown later in this chapter), you need a few more options:

- To execute the FLUSH LOGS command (or any FLUSH command), you need the RELOAD privilege.
- To execute SHOW MASTER STATUS and SHOW SLAVE STATUS, you need either the SUPER or REPLICATION CLIENT privilege.
- To execute CHANGE MASTER TO, you need the SUPER privilege.

For example, to give *mats* sufficient privileges for all the procedures in this chapter, issue the following:

```
server> GRANT REPLICATION SLAVE, RELOAD, CREATE USER, SUPER
    ->     ON *.*
    ->     TO mats@'192.168.2.%'
    ->     WITH GRANT OPTION;
```

Connecting the Master and Slave

Now you can perform the final step in setting up basic replication: directing the slave to the master so that it knows where to replicate from. To do this, you need four pieces of information about the master:

- A hostname
- A port number
- A user account on the master with replication slave privileges
- A password for the user account

You already created a user account with the right privileges and a password when configuring the master. The hostname is given by the operating system and can't be configured in the *my.cnf* file, but the port number can be assigned in *my.cnf* (if you do not supply a port number, the default value of 3306 will be used). The final two steps necessary to get replication up and running are to direct the slave to the master using the CHANGE MASTER TO command and then start replication using START SLAVE:

```
slave> CHANGE MASTER TO
    ->     MASTER_HOST = 'master-1',
    ->     MASTER_PORT = 3306,
    ->     MASTER_USER = 'repl_user',
    ->     MASTER_PASSWORD = 'xyzzy';
Query OK, 0 rows affected (0.00 sec)
```

```
slave> START SLAVE;
Query OK, 0 rows affected (0.15 sec)
```

Congratulations! You have now set up your first replication between a master and a slave! If you make some changes to the database on the master, such as adding new tables and filling them in, you will find that they are replicated to the slave. Try it out! Create a test database (if you do not already have one), create some tables, and add some data to the tables to see that the changes replicate over to the slave.

Observe that either a hostname or an IP address can be given to the MASTER_HOST parameter. If a hostname is given, the IP address for the hostname is retrieved by calling gethostname(3), which, depending on your configuration, could mean resolving the hostname using a DNS lookup. The steps for configuring such lookups are beyond the scope of this book.

A Brief Introduction to the Binary Log

What makes replication work is the *binary log* (or just *binlog*), which is a record of all changes made to the database on a server. You need to understand how the binary log works in order to have control over replication or to fix any problems that arise, so we'll give you a bit of background in this section.

Figure 3-2 shows a schematic view of the replication architecture, containing a master with a binary log and a slave that receives changes from the master via the binary log. We will cover the replication architecture in detail in Chapter 8. When a statement is about to finish executing, it writes an entry to the end of the binary log and sends the statement parser a notification that it has completed the statement.

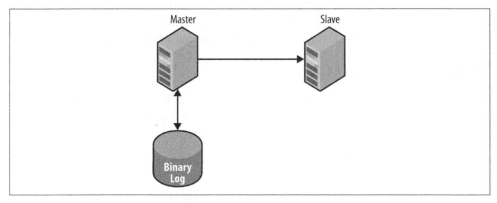

Figure 3-2. Role of the binary log in replication

Usually only the statement that is about to finish executing is written to the binary log, but there are some special cases where other information is written—either in addition to the statement or instead of the statement. It will soon be clear why this is so, but for the time being, you can pretend that only the statements that are being executed are being written to the binary log.

What's Recorded in the Binary Log

The purpose of the binary log is to record changes made to the tables in the database. The binary log can then be used for replication, as well as for point-in-time-recovery (PITR) , discussed in Chapter 15) and in some limited cases for auditing.

Note that the binary log contains only *changes* made to the database, so for statements that do not change any data in the database, no entry is written to the binary log.

Traditionally, MySQL replication records changes by preserving the SQL statement that made the change. This is called *statement-based replication*. Because statement-based replication re-executes the statements on the slave, the result on the slave can differ from the master if the context of the master and slave are not exactly the same. This is the reason why as of version 5.1, MySQL also offers *row-based replication*. In contrast to statement-based replication, row-based replication individually records each change to a row in the binary log. In addition to being more convenient, row-based replication can offer some speed advantages in certain situations.

To imagine the difference, consider a complex update that uses a lot of joins or WHERE clauses. Instead of re-executing all the logic on the slave in statement-based replication, all you really need to know is the state of the row after the change. On the other hand, if a single update changes 10,000 rows, you'd rather record just the statement instead of 10,000 separate changes as row-based replication does.

We will cover row-based replication in Chapter 8, explaining its implementation and its use. In the examples that follow, we'll focus on statement-based replication because it's easier to understand with respect to database management activities.

Watching Replication in Action

Using the replication example from the previous section, let's take a look at the binlog events for some simple statements. Let's start by connecting a command-line client to the master and executing a few commands to get a binary log:

```
master> CREATE TABLE tbl (text TEXT);
Query OK, 0 rows affected (0.04 sec)

master> INSERT INTO tbl VALUES ("Yeah! Replication!");
Query OK, 1 row affected (0.00 sec)

master> SELECT * FROM tbl;
+--------------------+
| text               |
```

```
+--------------------+
| Yeah! Replication! |
+--------------------+
1 row in set (0.00 sec)

master> FLUSH LOGS;
Query OK, 0 rows affected (0.28 sec)
```

The FLUSH LOGS command forces the binary log to rotate, which will allow us to see a "complete" binlog file in all its glory. To take a closer look at this file, use the SHOW BINLOG EVENTS command, as shown in Example 3-4.

Example 3-4. Checking what events are in the binary log

```
master> SHOW BINLOG EVENTS\G
*************************** 1. row ***************************
   Log_name: mysql-bin.000001
        Pos: 4
 Event_type: Format_desc
  Server_id: 1
End_log_pos: 107
       Info: Server ver: 5.5.34-0ubuntu0.12.04.1-log, Binlog ver: 4
*************************** 2. row ***************************
   Log_name: mysql-bin.000001
        Pos: 107
 Event_type: Query
  Server_id: 1
End_log_pos: 198
       Info: use `test`; CREATE TABLE tbl (text TEXT)
*************************** 3. row ***************************
   Log_name: mysql-bin.000001
        Pos: 198
 Event_type: Query
  Server_id: 1
End_log_pos: 266
       Info: BEGIN
*************************** 4. row ***************************
   Log_name: mysql-bin.000001
        Pos: 266
 Event_type: Query
  Server_id: 1
End_log_pos: 374
       Info: use `test`; INSERT INTO tbl VALUES ("Yeah! Replication!")
*************************** 5. row ***************************
   Log_name: mysql-bin.000001
        Pos: 374
 Event_type: Xid
  Server_id: 1
End_log_pos: 401
       Info: COMMIT /* xid=188 */
*************************** 6. row ***************************
   Log_name: mysql-bin.000001
        Pos: 401
```

```
    Event_type: Rotate
      Server_id: 1
    End_log_pos: 444
          Info: mysql-bin.000002;pos=4
6 rows in set (0.00 sec)
```

In this binary log, we can now see six events: a format description event, three query events, one XID event, and a rotate event. The query event is how statements executed against the database are normally written to the binary log, the XID event is used for transaction management, whereas the format description and rotate events are used by the server internally to manage the binary log. We will discuss these events in more detail in Chapter 8, but for now, let's take a closer look at the columns given for each event:

Event_type

    This is the type of the event. We have seen three different types here, but there are many more. The type of the event denotes what information is transported to the slave. Currently—in MySQL 5.1.18 to 5.5.33—there are 27 events (several of them are not used, but they are retained for backward compatibility), and in 5.6.12 there are 35, but this is an extensible range and new events are added as required.

Server_id

    This is the server ID of the server that created the event.

Log_name

    This is the name of the file that stores the event. An event is always contained in a single file and will never span two files.

Pos

    This is the position of the file where the event starts (i.e., the first byte of the event).

End_log_pos

    This gives the position in the file where the event ends and the next event starts. This is one higher than the last byte of the event, so the bytes in the range Pos to End_log_pos − 1 are the bytes containing the event and the length of the event can be computed as End_log_pos – Pos.

Info

    This is human-readable text with information about the event. Different information is printed for different events, but you can at least count on the query event to print the statement that it contains.

The first two columns, Log_name and Pos, make up the *binlog position* of the event and will be used to indicate the location or position of an event. In addition to what is shown here, each event contains a lot of other information—for example, a timestamp, which is the number of seconds since the Epoch (a classic Unix moment in time, 1970-01-01 00:00:00 UTC).

The Binary Log's Structure and Content

As we explained, the binary log is not actually a single file, but a set of files that allow for easier management (such as removing old logs without disturbing recent ones). The binary log consists of a set of binlog files with the real contents as well as a binlog index file, which keeps track of which binlog files exist. Figure 3-3 shows how a binary log is organized.

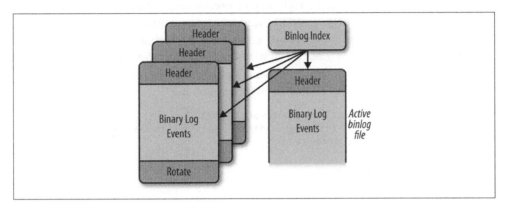

Figure 3-3. Structure of the binary log

One binlog file is the *active binlog file*. This is the file that is currently being written to (and usually read from as well).

Each binlog file starts with a *format description event* and ends with a *rotate event*. The format description log event contains, among other things, the version of the server that produced the file and general information about the server and binary log. The rotate event tells where the binary log continues by giving the filename of the next file in the sequence.

Each file is organized into binary log events, where each event makes a standalone, atomic piece of the binary log. The format description log event contains a flag that marks the file as properly closed. While a binlog file is being written, the flag is set, and when the file is closed, the flag is cleared. This way, it is possible to detect corrupt binlog files in the event of a crash and allow replication to recover.

If you try to execute additional statements at the master, you will observe something strange—no changes are seen in the binary log:

```
master> INSERT INTO tbl VALUES ("What's up?");
Query OK, 1 row affected (0.00 sec)

master> SELECT * FROM tbl;
+--------------------+
| text               |
```

```
+-------------------+
| Yeah! Replication! |
| What's up?         |
+-------------------+
1 row in set (0.00 sec)

master> SHOW BINLOG EVENTS\G
same as before
```

What happened to the new event? Well, as you already know, the binary log consists of several files, and the SHOW BINLOG EVENTS statement shows only the contents of the *first* binlog file. This is contrary to what most users expect, which is to see the contents of the active binlog file. If the name of the first binlog file is *master-bin.000001* (containing the events shown previously), you can take a look at the events in the next binlog file, in this case named *master-bin.000002*, using the following:

```
master> SHOW BINLOG EVENTS IN 'master-bin.000002'\G
*************************** 1. row ***************************
   Log_name: mysql-bin.000002
        Pos: 4
 Event_type: Format_desc
  Server_id: 1
End_log_pos: 107
       Info: Server ver: 5.5.34-0ubuntu0.12.04.1-log, Binlog ver: 4
*************************** 2. row ***************************
   Log_name: mysql-bin.000002
        Pos: 107
 Event_type: Query
  Server_id: 1
End_log_pos: 175
       Info: BEGIN
*************************** 3. row ***************************
   Log_name: mysql-bin.000002
        Pos: 175
 Event_type: Query
  Server_id: 1
End_log_pos: 275
       Info: use `test`; INSERT INTO tbl VALUES ("What's up?")
*************************** 4. row ***************************
   Log_name: mysql-bin.000002
        Pos: 275
 Event_type: Xid
  Server_id: 1
End_log_pos: 302
       Info: COMMIT /* xid=196 */
4 rows in set (0.00 sec)
```

You might have noticed in Example 3-4 that the binary log ends with a rotate event and that the Info field contains the name of the next binlog file and position where the events start. To see which binlog file is currently being written, you can use the SHOW MASTER STATUS command:

```
master> SHOW MASTER STATUS\G
*************************** 1. row ***************************
            File: master-bin.000002
        Position: 205
    Binlog_Do_DB:
Binlog_Ignore_DB:
1 row in set (0.00 sec)
```

Now that you've finished taking a look at the binary log, stop and reset the slave and drop the table:

```
master> DROP TABLE tbl;
Query OK, 0 rows affected (0.00 sec)

slave> STOP SLAVE;
Query OK, 0 rows affected (0.08 sec)

slave> RESET SLAVE;
Query OK, 0 rows affected (0.00 sec)
```

After that, you can drop the table and reset the master to start fresh:

```
master> DROP TABLE tbl;
Query OK, 0 rows affected (0.00 sec)

master> RESET MASTER;
Query OK, 0 rows affected (0.04 sec)
```

The RESET MASTER command removes all the binlog files and clears the binlog index file. The RESET SLAVE statement removes all files used by replication on the slave to get a clean start.

Neither the RESET MASTER nor the RESET SLAVE command is designed to work when replication is active, so:

- When executing the RESET MASTER command (on the master), make sure that no slaves are attached.
- When executing the RESET SLAVE command (on the slave), make sure that the slave does not have replication active by issuing a STOP SLAVE command.

We will cover the most basic events in this chapter, but for the complete list with all its gory details, refer to the MySQL Internals Manual (*http://bit.ly/mysql-manual*).

Adding Slaves

Now that you know a little about the binary log, we are ready to tackle one of the basic problems with the way we created a slave earlier. When we configured the slave, we provided no information about where to start replication, so the slave will start reading the binary logs on the master from the beginning. That's clearly not a very good idea if the master has been running for some time: in addition to making the slave replay quite a lot of events just to ramp up, you might not be able to obtain the necessary logs, because they might have been stored somewhere else for safekeeping and removed from the master (we'll discuss that more in Chapter 15 when we talk about backups and PITR).

We need another way to create new slaves—called *bootstrapping a slave*—without starting replication from the beginning.

The CHANGE MASTER TO command has two parameters that will help us here: MASTER_LOG_FILE and MASTER_LOG_POS. (Starting with MySQL 5.6, there is another, even easier way to specify positions: Global Transaction Identifiers, or GTIDs. Read more about them in Chapter 8.) You can use these to specify the binlog position at which the master should start sending events instead of starting from the beginning.

Using these parameters to CHANGE MASTER TO, we can bootstrap a slave using the following steps:

1. Configure the new slave.
2. Make a backup of the master (or of a slave that has been replicating the master). See Chapter 15 for common backup techniques.
3. Write down the binlog position that corresponds to this backup (in other words, the position following the last event leading up to the master's current state).
4. Restore the backup on the new slave. See Chapter 15 for common restore techniques.
5. Configure the slave to start replication from this position.

Depending on whether you use the master or a slave as a baseline in step 2, the procedure differs slightly, so we will start by describing how to bootstrap a new slave when you only have a single server running that you want to use as master—this is called *cloning the master*.

Cloning the master means taking a snapshot of the server, which is usually accomplished by creating a backup. There are various techniques for backing up the server, but in this chapter, we have decided to use one of the simpler techniques: running *mysqldump* to create a logical backup. Other options are to create a physical backup by copying the database files, online backup techniques such as MySQL Enterprise Backup, or even volume snapshots using Linux LVM (Logical Volume Manager). The various techniques will be described fully in Chapter 15, along with a discussion of their relative merits.

Cloning the Master

The *mysqldump* utility has options that allow you to perform all the steps in this section in a single step, but to explain the necessary operations, we will perform all the steps here individually. You will see a more compact version later in this section.

To clone the master, as shown in Figure 3-4, start by creating a backup of the master. Because the master is probably running and has a lot of tables in the cache, it is necessary to flush all tables and lock the database to prevent changes before checking the binlog position. You can do this using the FLUSH TABLES WITH READ LOCK command:

```
master> FLUSH TABLES WITH READ LOCK;
Query OK, 0 rows affected (0.02 sec)
```

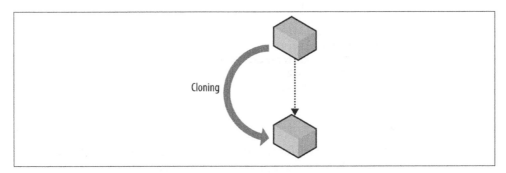

Figure 3-4. Cloning a master to create a new slave

Once the database is locked, you are ready to create a backup and note the binlog position. Note that at this point you should *not* disconnect *mysql* from the server as that will release the lock that you just took. Because no changes are occurring on the master, the SHOW MASTER STATUS command will correctly reveal the current file and position in the binary log. We will go through the details of the SHOW MASTER STATUS and the SHOW MASTER LOGS commands in Chapter 8.

```
master> SHOW MASTER STATUS\G
*************************** 1. row ***************************
            File: master-bin.000042
        Position: 456552
    Binlog_Do_DB:
Binlog_Ignore_DB:
1 row in set (0.00 sec)
```

The position of the next event to write is master-bin.000042, 456552, which is where replication should start, given that everything before this point will be in the backup. Once you have jotted down the binlog position, you can create your backup. The easiest way to create a backup of the database is to use *mysqldump*:

```
$ mysqldump --all-databases --host=master-1 >backup.sql
```

Because you now have a faithful copy of the master, you can unlock the tables of the database on the master and allow it to continue processing queries:

```
master> UNLOCK TABLES;
Query OK, 0 rows affected (0.23 sec)
```

Next, restore the backup on the slave using the *mysql* utility:

```
$ mysql --host=slave-1 <backup.sql
```

You have now restored the backup of the master on the slave and can start the slave. Recalling the binlog position of the master that you wrote down previously, configure the slave using CHANGE MASTER TO and start the slave:

```
slave> CHANGE MASTER TO
    ->     MASTER_HOST = 'master-1',
    ->     MASTER_PORT = 3306,
    ->     MASTER_USER = 'slave-1',
    ->     MASTER_PASSWORD = 'xyzzy',
    ->     MASTER_LOG_FILE = 'master-bin.000042',
    ->     MASTER_LOG_POS = 456552;
Query OK, 0 rows affected (0.00 sec)

slave> START SLAVE;
Query OK, 0 rows affected (0.25 sec)
```

It is possible to have *mysqldump* perform many of the previous steps automatically. To make a logical backup of all databases on a server called *master*, enter:

```
$ mysqldump --host=master -all-databases \
> --master-data=1 >backup-source.sql
```

The --master-data=1 option makes *mysqldump* write a CHANGEMASTER TO statement with the file and position in the binary log, as given by SHOW MASTER STATUS.

You can then restore the backup on a slave using:

```
$ mysql --host=slave-1 <backup-source.sql
```

Note that you can only use --master-data=1 to get a CHANGE MASTER TO statement for the master. When cloning the slave later, it is necessary to perform all the steps given in the following section.

Congratulations! You have now cloned the master and have a new slave up and running. Depending on the load of the master, you might need to allow the slave to catch up from the position you jotted down, but that requires far less effort than starting from the beginning.

Depending on how long the backup took, there might be a lot of data to catch up to, so before bringing the slave online, you might want to read through "Managing Consistency of Data" on page 177.

Cloning a Slave

Once you have a slave connected to the master, you can use the slave instead of the master to create new slaves. That way, you can create a new slave without bringing the master offline. If you have a large or high-traffic database, the downtime could be considerable, considering both the time to create the backup and the time for the slaves to catch up.

The process of cloning a slave is illustrated in Figure 3-5 and is basically the same as for a master, but it differs in how you find the binlog position. You also need to take into consideration that the slave you are cloning from is replicating a master.

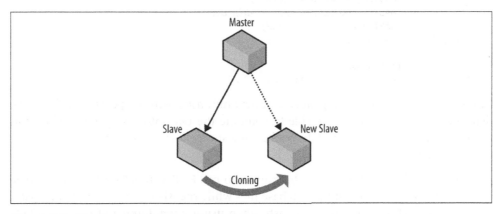

Figure 3-5. Cloning a slave to create a new slave

The first thing you have to do before starting a backup is to stop the slave so that no more changes occur on it. If replication is running while you create the backup, you will have an inconsistent backup image if changes are made to the database while it is being backed up. The exception is if you use some form of online backup method—such as MySQL Enterprise Backup—in which case you do not need to stop the slave before creating the backup. Here is what you will see when you stop the slave:

```
original-slave> STOP SLAVE;
Query OK, 0 rows affected (0.20 sec)
```

After the slave is stopped, you can flush the tables as before and create the backup. Because you created a backup of the slave (not the master), use the SHOW SLAVE STA TUS command instead of SHOW MASTER STATUS to determine where to start replication. The output from this command is considerable, and it will be covered in detail in Chapter 8, but to get the position of the next event in the binary log of the master that the slave will execute, note the value of the fields Relay_Master_Log_File and Ex ec_Master_Log_Pos:

```
original-slave> SHOW SLAVE STATUS\G
    ...
Relay_Master_Log_File: master-bin.000042
    ...
  Exec_Master_Log_Pos: 546632
```

After creating the backup and restoring it on the new slave, configure replication to start from this position and start the new slave:

```
new-slave> CHANGE MASTER TO
        -> MASTER_HOST = 'master-1',
        -> MASTER_PORT = 3306,
        -> MASTER_USER = 'slave-1',
        -> MASTER_PASSWORD = 'xyzzy',
        -> MASTER_LOG_FILE = 'master-bin.000042',
        -> MASTER_LOG_POS = 546632;
Query OK, 0 rows affected (0.19 sec)

new-slave> START SLAVE;
Query OK, 0 rows affected (0.24 sec)
```

Cloning the master and cloning the slave differ only on some minor points, which means that our Python library will be able to combine the two into a single procedure for creating new slaves by creating the backup at a source server and connecting the new slave to a master.

A common technique for making backups is to call FLUSH TABLES WITH READ LOCK and then to create a copy of the database files while the MySQL server is locked with the read lock. This is usually much faster than using *mysqldump*, but FLUSH TABLES WITH READ LOCK is *not safe for use with InnoDB!*

FLUSH TABLES WITH READ LOCK does lock the tables, preventing any new transactions from starting, but there are several activities going on in the background that FLUSH TABLES WITH READ LOCK does not prevent.

Use one of the following techniques to create a backup of InnoDB tables safely:

- Shut down the server and copy the files. This can be an advantage if the database is big, as restoring data with *mysqldump* can be slow.

- Use *mysqldump* after performing FLUSH TABLES WITH READ LOCK (as we did earlier). The read lock is preventing changes while the data is read. The database may be locked for a long time if there is a lot of data to be read. Note, however, that it is possible to take a consistent snapshot using the --single-transaction option, but this is only possible when using InnoDB tables. For more information, see "The mysqldump Utility" on page 560.

- Use a snapshot solution such as LVM (on Linux) or ZFS (on Solaris) while locking the database with FLUSH TABLES WITH READ LOCK.

- Use MySQL Enterprise Backup (or XtraBackup) to do an online backup of MySQL.

Scripting the Clone Operation

The Python library clones a master simply by copying the database from the master using the `Server` object that represents the master. To do this, it uses a `clone` function, which you will see in Example 3-6.

Cloning a slave is similar, but the backup is taken from one server, while the new slave connects to another server to perform replication. It is easy to support cloning both a master and a slave by using two different parameters: a `source` parameter that specifies where the backup should be created and a `use_master` parameter that indicates where the slave should connect after the backup is restored. A call to the `clone` method looks like the following:

```
clone(slave = slave[1], source = slave[0], use_master = master)
```

The next step is to write some utility functions to implement the cloning function, which will also come in handy for other activities. Example 3-5 shows the following functions:

`fetch_master_pos`
Fetches the binlog position from a master (i.e., the position of the next event the master will write to the binary log).

`fetch_slave_pos`
Fetches the binlog position from a slave (i.e., the position of the next event to read from the master).

`replicate_from`
Accepts as arguments a slave, a master, and a binlog position, and directs the slave to replicate from the master starting with the given position.

The `replicate_from` function reads the field `repl_user` from the master to get the name and password of the replication user. If you look at the definition of the `Server` class, you'll find that there is no such field. It is added by the `Master` role when the server is imbued.

Example 3-5. Utility functions to fetch the master and slave positions of a server

```
_CHANGE_MASTER_TO = """CHANGE MASTER TO
    MASTER_HOST=%s, MASTER_PORT=%s,
    MASTER_USER=%s, MASTER_PASSWORD=%s,
    MASTER_LOG_FILE=%s, MASTER_LOG_POS=%s"""

def replicate_from(slave, master, position):
    slave.sql(_CHANGE_MASTER_TO, (master.host, master.port,
                                  master.repl_user.name,
                                  master.repl_user.passwd,
                                  position.file, position.pos))
```

```
def fetch_master_pos(server):
    result = server.sql("SHOW MASTER STATUS")
    return Position(server.server_id, result["File"], result["Position"])

def fetch_slave_pos(server):
    result = server.sql("SHOW SLAVE STATUS")
    return Position(server.server_id, result["Relay_Master_Log_File"],
                    result["Exec_Master_Log_Pos"])
```

These are all the functions needed to create the clone function. To clone a slave, the calling application passes a separate use_master argument, causing clone to direct the new slave to that master for replication. To clone a master, the calling application omits the separate use_master argument, causing the function to use the "source" server as a master.

Because there are many ways to create a backup of a server, Example 3-6 restricts the method to one choice, using *mysqldump* to create a logical backup of the server. Later, we will demonstrate how to generalize the backup procedure so that you can use the same basic code to bootstrap new slaves using arbitrary backup methods.

Example 3-6. Function to clone either the master or the slave

```
def clone(slave, source, use_master = None):
    from subprocess import call
    backup_file = open(server.host + "-backup.sql", "w+")
    if master is not None:
        source.sql("STOP SLAVE")
    lock_database(source)
    if master is None:
        position = fetch_master_position(source)
    else:
        position = fetch_slave_position(source)
    call(["mysqldump", "--all-databases", "--host='%s'" % source.host],
         stdout=backup_file)
    if master is not None:
        start_slave(source)
    backup_file.seek()                          # Rewind to beginning
    call(["mysql", "--host='%s'" % slave.host], stdin=backup_file)
    if master is None:
        replicate_from(slave, source, position)
    else:
        replicate_from(slave, master, position)
    start_slave(slave)
```

Performing Common Tasks with Replication

Each of the common use cases for replication—scale-out, hot standbys, and so forth—involve their own implementation details and possible pitfalls. We'll show you how to perform some of these tasks and how to enhance the Python library to support them.

Passwords are omitted from the examples in this section. When configuring the accounts to control the servers, you can either allow access only from certain hosts that control the deployment (by creating accounts such as mats@'192.168.2.136'), or you can supply passwords to the commands.

Reporting

Most businesses need a lot of routine reports: weekly reports on the items sold, monthly reports on expenses and revenues, and various kinds of heavy data mining to spot trends or identify focus groups for the marketing department.

Running these queries on the master can prove to be troublesome. Data-mining queries can require a lot of computing resources and can slow down normal operations only to find out that, say, a focus group for left handed scissors might not be worthwhile to conduct. In addition, these reports are typically not very urgent (compared to processing normal transactions), so there is no need to create them as quickly as possible. In other words, because these reports are not time-critical, it does not matter much if they take two hours to complete instead of one.

A better idea is to dust off a spare server (or two, if you have enough reporting requirements) and set it up to replicate from the master. When you need to do the reporting, you can stop replication, run your reporting applications, then start replication again, all without disturbing the master.

Reporting often needs to cover a precise interval, such as a summary of all sales for the day, so it is necessary to stop replication at the right moment so you don't get any sales for the following day in the report. Because there is no way to stop the slave when it sees an event with a certain date or time, it has to be done some other way.

Let's pretend that reports are needed once each day, and that all transactions from midnight to midnight shall be included. It is necessary to stop the reporting slave at midnight so that no events from after midnight are executed on the slave and all events from before midnight are executed on the slave. The intention is not to do this manually, so let's consider how we can automate the procedure. The following steps will accomplish what we want:

1. Just before midnight, perhaps five minutes before midnight, stop the reporting slave so that no events come from the master.

2. After midnight, check the binary log on the master and find the last event that was recorded before midnight. Obviously, if you do this before midnight, you might not have seen all events for the day yet.

3. Record the binlog position of this event and start the slave to run until this position.

4. Wait until the slave has reached this position and stopped.

The first issue is how to schedule the jobs correctly. There are different ways to do this, depending on the operating system. Although we won't go into all the details here, you can see how to schedule tasks for Unix-like operating systems, such as Linux, in "Scheduling tasks on Unix" on page 48.

Stopping the slave is as simple as executing STOP SLAVE and noting the binlog position *after* the slave is stopped:

```
slave> STOP SLAVE;
Query OK, 0 rows affected (0.25 sec)

slave> SHOW SLAVE STATUS\G
   ...
Relay_Master_Log_File: capulet-bin.000004
   ...
  Exec_Master_Log_Pos: 2456
1 row in set (0.00 sec)
```

The remaining three steps are executed before the actual reporting starts and usually as part of the script that does the actual reporting. Before outlining the script, let's consider how to perform each step.

To read the contents of the binary log, invoke a utility called *mysqlbinlog*. This will be introduced in detail later, but this utility is used in the second step. The *mysqlbinlog* utility has the two handy options, --start-datetime and --stop-datetime, which you can use to read only a portion of the binary log. So to get all events from the time that you stopped the slave to just before midnight, use the following command:

```
$ mysqlbinlog --force --read-from-remote-server --host=reporting.bigcorp.com \
>     --start-datetime='2009-09-25 23:55:00' \
>     --stop-datetime='2009-09-25 23:59:59' \
>     binlog files
```

The timestamp stored in each event is the timestamp when the statement started executing, not the timestamp when it was written to the binary log. The --stop-datetime option will stop emitting events on the *first* timestamp after the date/time supplied, so it is possible that there is an event that started executing before the date/time but was written to the binary log after the date/time. Such an event is not included in the range given.

Because the master is writing to the binary logs at this time, it is necessary to supply the --force option. Otherwise, *mysqlbinlog* will refuse to read the open binary log. To execute this command, it is necessary to supply a set of binlog files to read. Since the names of these files are dependent on configuration options, the names of these files have to be fetched from the server. After that, it is necessary to figure out the range of binlog files that needs to be supplied to the *mysqlbinlog* command. Getting the list of binlog filenames is easy to do with the SHOW BINARY LOGS command:

```
master> SHOW BINARY LOGS;
+---------------------+-----------+
| Log_name            | File_size |
+---------------------+-----------+
| capulet-bin.000001  |     24316 |
| capulet-bin.000002  |      1565 |
| capulet-bin.000003  |       125 |
| capulet-bin.000004  |      2749 |
+---------------------+-----------+
4 rows in set (0.00 sec)
```

In this case, there are only four files, but there could potentially be quite a lot more. Scanning a large list of files that were written before the slave was stopped is just a waste of time, so it is a good idea to try to reduce the number of files to read in order to find the correct position to stop at. Because you recorded the binlog position in the first step, when the slave was stopped, it is an easy matter to find the name of the file where the slave stopped and then take that name and all the following names as input to the *mysqlbinlog* utility. Typically, this will only be one file (or two in the event that the binary log was rotated between stopping the slave and starting the reporting).

When executing the `mysqlbinlog` command with just a few binlog files, you will get a textual output for each with some information about the event:

```
$ mysqlbinlog --force --read-from-remote-server --host=reporting.bigcorp.com \
>      --start-datetime='2009-09-25 23:55:00'
>      --stop-datetime='2009-09-25 23:59:59' \
>      capulet-bin.000004
/*!40019 SET @@session.max_insert_delayed_threads=0*/;
/*!50003 SET @OLD_COMPLETION_TYPE=@@COMPLETION_TYPE,COMPLETION_TYPE=0*/;
DELIMITER /*!*/;
# at 4
#090909 22:16:25 server id 1  end_log_pos 106   Start: binlog v 4, server v...
ROLLBACK/*!*/;
      .
      .
      .
# at 2495
#090929 23:58:36 server id 1  end_log_pos 2650  Query   thread_id=27    exe...
SET TIMESTAMP=1254213690/*!*/;
SET /*!*/;
INSERT INTO message_board(user, message)
      VALUES ('mats@sun.com', 'Midnight, and I'm bored')
/*!*/;
```

The interesting part here is the `end_log_pos` of the last event in the sequence (in this case, 2650), because this is where the next event after midnight will be written.

If you were paying attention to the output from the previous command, you saw that there is no information about which binlog file this byte position is referring to, and it is necessary to have a file to find the event. If a single file is supplied to the `mysqlbin` log command, the filename is obvious, but if two files are supplied, it is necessary to figure out if the last event for the day is in the first or the second file.

If you look at the line containing the end_log_pos, you will also see that the event type is there. Because every binlog file starts with a format description event—a line for such an event appears in the previous output—you can check these events to determine the location of the event you want. If there are two format description events in the output, the event is in the second file, and if there is just one, it is in the first file.

The final step before starting the reporting work is to start replication and stop it at exactly the position where the event after midnight will be written (or has already been written, should that be the case). To do this, you can use the lesser-known syntax START SLAVE UNTIL. This command accepts a master logfile and a master log position where the slave should stop, and then starts the slave. When the slave reaches the given position, it will automatically stop:

```
report> START SLAVE UNTIL
    ->      MASTER_LOG_POS='capulet-bin.000004',
    ->      MASTER_LOG_POS=2650;
Query OK, 0 rows affected (0.18 sec)
```

Like the STOP SLAVE command (without the UNTIL), the START SLAVE UNTIL command will return immediately—not, as could be expected, when the slave has reached the position where it should stop. So commands issued after START SLAVE UNTIL continue to be executed as long as the slave is running. To wait for the slave to reach the position you want it to stop at, use the MASTER_POS_WAIT function, which will block while waiting for the slave to reach the given position:

```
report> SELECT MASTER_POS_WAIT('capulet-bin.000004',  2650);
Query OK, 0 rows affected (231.15 sec)
```

At this point, the slave has stopped at the last event for the day, and the reporting process can start analyzing the data and generating reports.

Handling reporting in Python

Automating this in Python is quite straightforward; Example 3-7 shows the code for stopping reporting at the right time.

The fetch_remote_binlog function reads a binary log from a remote server using the mysqlbinlog command. The contents of the file(s) will be returned as an iterator over the lines of the file. To optimize the fetches, you can optionally provide a list of files to scan. You can also pass a start date/time and a stop date/time to limit the date/time range of the result. These will be passed to the *mysqlbinlog* program.

The find_datetime_position function does the work of scanning the binlog lines to find the last end_log_pos as well as keeping track of how many start events have been observed. It also contacts the reporting server to find out where it stopped reading the binlog file and then contacts the master to get the binlog files and find the right one to start the scan from.

Example 3-7. Python code for running replication to a datetime

```python
def fetch_remote_binlog(server, binlog_files=None,
                        start_datetime=None, stop_datetime=None):
    from subprocess import Popen, PIPE
    if not binlog_files:
        binlog_files = [
            row["Log_name"] for row in server.sql("SHOW BINARY LOGS")]

    command = ["mysqlbinlog",
               "--read-from-remote-server",
               "--force",
               "--host=%s" % (server.host),
               "--user=%s" % (server.sql_user.name)]
    if server.sql_user.passwd:
        command.append("--password=%s" % (server.sql_user.passwd))
    if start_datetime:
        command.append("--start-datetime=%s" % (start_datetime))
    if stop_datetime:
        command.append("--stop-datetime=%s" % (stop_datetime))
    return iter(Popen(command + binlog_files, stdout=PIPE).stdout)

def find_datetime_position(master, report, start_datetime, stop_datetime):
    from itertools import dropwhile
    from mysql.replicant import Position
    import re

    all_files = [row["Log_name"] for row in master.sql("SHOW BINARY LOGS")]
    stop_file = report.sql("SHOW SLAVE STATUS")["Relay_Master_Log_File"]
    files = list(dropwhile(lambda file: file != stop_file, all_files))
    lines = fetch_remote_binlog(server, binlog_files=files,
                                start_datetime=start_datetime,
                                stop_datetime=stop_datetime)
    binlog_files = 0
    last_epos = None
    for line in lines:
        m = re.match(r"#\d{6}\s+\d?\d:\d\d:\d\d\s+"
                     r"server id\s+(?P<sid>\d+)\s+"
                     r"end_log_pos\s+(?P<epos>\d+)\s+"
                     r"(?P<type>\w+)", line)
        if m:
            if m.group("type") == "Start":
                binlog_files += 1
            if m.group("type") == "Query":
                last_epos = m.group("epos")
    return Position(files[binlog_files-1], last_epos)
```

You can now use these functions to synchronize the reporting server before the actual reporting job:

```
master.connect()
report.connect()
pos = find_datetime_position(master, report,
                            start_datetime="2009-09-14 23:55:00",
                            stop_datetime="2009-09-14 23:59:59")
report.sql("START SLAVE UNTIL MASTER_LOG_FILE=%s, MASTER_LOG_POS=%s",
           (pos.file, pos.pos))
report.sql("DO MASTER_POS_WAIT(%s,%s)", (pos.file, pos.pos))


    .
    .
code for reporting
    .
    .
```

As you can see, working with replication is pretty straightforward. This particular example introduces several of the critical concepts that we will be using later when talking about scale-out: how to start and stop the slave at the right time, how to get information about binlog positions or figure it out using the standard tools, and how to integrate it all into an automated solution for your particular needs.

Scheduling tasks on Unix

To easiest way ensure the slave is stopped just before midnight and the reporting is started after midnight is to set up a job for *cron(8)* that sends a stop slave command to the slave and starts the reporting script.

For example, the following *crontab(5)* entries would ensure that the slave is stopped before midnight, and that the reporting script to roll the slave forward is executed, say, five minutes after midnight. Here we assume that the `stop_slave` script will stop the slave, and the `daily_report` will run the daily report (starting with the synchronization described earlier):

```
# stop reporting slave five minutes before midnight, every day
55 23 * * * $HOME/mysql_control/stop_slave

# Run reporting script five minutes after midnight, every day
5 0 * * * $HOME/mysql_control/daily_report
```

Assuming that you put this in a crontab file, *reporttab*, you can install the crontab file using the `crontab reporttab` command.

Scheduling tasks on Windows

To start the Task Scheduler in Windows, open the search feature (Windows key+R) and enter *taskschd.msc*. Depending on your security settings and version of Windows, you may need to respond to the User Account Control (UAC) dialog box to continue. To create a new task trigger by time, choose Create Basic Task from the Action pane. This opens the Create Basic Task Wizard, which will guide you through the steps to create a simple task. On the first pane of the wizard, name the task and provide an optional description, then click Next.

The second pane allows you to specify the frequency of the firing of the task. There are many options here for controlling when the task runs: a single run, daily, weekly, and even when you log on or when a specific event occurs. Click Next once you've made your choice. Depending on the frequency you chose, the third pane will allow you to specify the details (e.g., date and time) of when the task fires. Click Next once you have configured the trigger timing options.

The fourth pane is where you specify the task or action to occur when the task event occurs (when the task fires). You can choose to start a program, send an email message, or display a message to the user. Make your selection and click Next to move to the next pane. Depending on the action you chose on the previous pane, here you can specify what happens when the task fires. For example, if you chose to run an application, you enter the name of the application or script, any arguments, and which folder the task starts in.

Once you have entered all of this information, click Next to review the task on the final pane. If you're satisfied all is set correctly, click Finish to schedule the task. You can click Back to return to any of the previous screens and make changes. Finally, you have the option to open the Properties page after you click Finish if you want to make additional changes to the task.

Conclusion

In this chapter, we have presented an introduction to MySQL replication, including a look at why replication is used and how to set it up. We also took a quick look into the binary log. In the next chapter, we examine the binary log in greater detail.

Joel finished giving Mr. Summerson his report on how he was going to balance the load across four new slaves, along with plans for how the topology could be expanded to handle future needs.

"That's fine work, Joel. Now explain to me again what this slave thing is."

Joel suppressed a sigh and said, "A slave is a copy of the data on the database server that gets its changes from the original database server called the master…"

## CHAPTER 4

The Binary Log

"Joel?"

Joel jumped, nearly banging his head as he crawled out from under his desk. "I was just rerouting a few cables," he said by way of an explanation.

Mr. Summerson merely nodded and said in a very authoritative manner, "I need you to look into a problem the marketing people are having with the new server. They need to roll back the data to a certain point."

"Well, that depends…" Joel started, worried about whether he had snapshots of old states of the system.

"I told them you'd be right down."

With that, Mr. Summerson turned and walked away. A moment later a woman stopped in front of his door and said, "He's always like that. Don't take it personally. Most of us call it a drive-by tasking." She laughed and introduced herself. "My name's Amy. I'm one of the developers here."

Joel walked around his desk and met her at the door. "I'm Joel."

After a moment of awkward silence Joel said, "I, er, better get on that thing."

Amy smiled and said, "See you around."

"Just focus on what you have to do to succeed," Joel thought as he returned to his desk to search for that MySQL book he bought last week.

The previous chapter included a very brief introduction to the binary log. In this chapter, we will fill in more details and give a more thorough description of the binary log structure, the replication event format, and how to use the *mysqlbinlog* tool to investigate and work with the contents of binary logs.

The binary log records changes made to the database. It is usually used for replication, and the binary log then allows the same changes to be made on the slaves as well. Because the binary log normally keeps a record of all changes, you can also use it for auditing purposes to see what happened in the database, and for point-in-time recovery (PITR) by playing back the binary log to a server, repeating changes that were recorded in the binary log. (This is what we did in "Reporting" on page 43, where we played back all changes done between 23:55:00 and 23:59:59.)

The binary log contains information that could change the database. Note that statements that could *potentially* change the database are also logged, even if they don't actually do change the database. The most notable cases are those statements that optionally make a change, such as DROP TABLE IF EXISTS or CREATE TABLE IF NOT EXISTS, along with statements such as DELETE and UPDATE that have WHERE conditions that don't happen to match any rows on the master.

SELECT statements are not normally logged because they do not make any changes to any database. There are, however, exceptions.

The binary log records each transaction in the order that the commit took place on the master. Although transactions may be interleaved on the master, each appears as an uninterrupted sequence in the binary log, the order determined by the time of the commit.

Structure of the Binary Log

Conceptually, the binary log is a sequence of *binary log events* (also called *binlog events* or even just *events* when there is no risk of confusion). As you saw in Chapter 3, the binary log actually consists of several files, as shown in Figure 4-1, that together form the binary log.

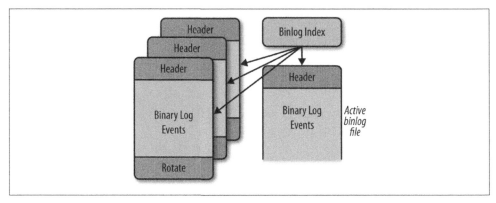

Figure 4-1. The structure of the binary log

The actual events are stored in a series of files called *binlog files* with names in the form *host-bin.000001*, accompanied by a *binlog index file* that is usually named *host-bin.index* and keeps track of the existing binlog files. The binlog file that is currently being written to by the server is called the *active* binlog file. If no slaves are lagging, this is also the file that is being read by the slaves. The names of the binlog files and the binlog index file can be controlled using the log-bin and log-bin-index options, which you are familiar with from "Configuring the Master" on page 25. The options are covered in more detail later in this chapter.

The index file keeps track of all the binlog files used by the server so that the server can correctly create new binlog files when necessary, even after server restarts. Each line in the index file contains the name of a binlog file that is part of the binary log. Depending on the MySQL version, it can either be the full name or a name relative to the data directory. Commands that affect the binlog files, such as PURGE BINARY LOGS, RESET MASTER, and FLUSH LOGS, also affect the index file by adding or removing lines to match the files that were added or removed by the command.

As shown in Figure 4-1, each binlog file is made up of binlog events, with the Format_description event serving as the file's header and the Rotate event as its footer. Note that a binlog file might not end with a rotate event if the server was interrupted or crashed.

The Format_description event contains information about the server that wrote the binlog file as well as some critical information about the file's status. If the server is stopped and restarted, it creates a new binlog file and writes a new Format_description event to it. This is necessary because changes can potentially occur between bringing a server down and bringing it up again. For example, the server could be upgraded, in which case a new Format_description event would have to be written.

When the server has finished writing a binlog file, a Rotate event is added to end the file. The event points to the next binlog file in sequence by giving the name of the file as well as the position to start reading from.

The Format_description event and the Rotate event will be described in detail in the next section.

With the exception of control events (e.g., Format_description, Rotate, and Incident), events of a binlog file are grouped into units called *groups*, as seen in Figure 4-2. In transactional storage engines, each group is roughly equivalent to a transaction, but for nontransactional storage engines or statements that cannot be part of a transaction, such as CREATE or ALTER, each statement is a group by itself.[1]

---

1. In some special cases, covered in "How nontransactional statements are logged" on page 88, nontransactional statements can be part of a group.

In short, each group of events in the binlog file contains either a single statement not in a transaction or a transaction consisting of several statements.

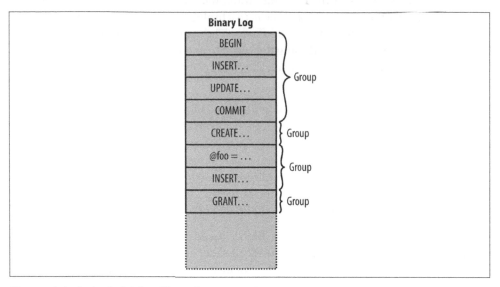

Figure 4-2. A single binlog file with groups of events

Each group is executed entirely or not at all (with the exception of a few well-defined cases). If, for some reason, the slave stops in the middle of a group, replication will start from the beginning of the group and not from the last statement executed. Chapter 8 describes in detail how the slave executes events.

Binlog Event Structure

MySQL 5.0 introduced a new binlog format: binlog format 4. The preceding formats were not easy to extend with additional fields if the need were to arise, so binlog format 4 was designed specifically to be extensible. This is still the event format used in every server version since 5.0, even though each version of the server has extended the binlog format with new events and some events with new fields. Binlog format 4 is the event format described in this chapter.

Each binlog event consists of four parts:

Common header

The common header is—as the name suggests—common to all events in the binlog file.

The common header contains basic information about the event, the most important fields being the event type and the size of the event.

Post header

The post header is specific to each event type; in other words, each event type stores different information in this field. But the size of this header, just as with the common header, is the same throughout a given binlog file. The size of each event type is given by the `Format_description` event.

Event body

After the headers comes the event body, which is the variable-sized part of the event. The size and the end position is listed in the common header for the event. The event body stores the main data of the event, which is different for different event types. For the `Query` event, for instance, the body stores the query, and for the `User_var` event, the body stores the name and value of a user variable that was just set by a statement.

Checksum

Starting with MySQL 5.6, there is a checksum at the end of the event, if the server is configured to generate one. The checksum is a 32-bit integer that is used to check that the event has not been corrupted since it was written.

A complete listing of the formats of all events is beyond the scope of this book, but because the `Format_description` and `Rotate` events are critical to how the other events are interpreted, we will briefly cover them here. If you are interested in the details of the events, you can find them in the MySQL Internals Manual.

As already noted, the `Format_description` event starts every binlog file and contains common information about the events in the file. The result is that the `Format_descrip tion` event can be different between different files; this typically occurs when a server is upgraded and restarted. The `Format_description_log_event` contains the following fields:

Binlog file format version

This is the version of the binlog file, which should not be confused with the version of the server. MySQL versions 3.23, 4.0, and 4.1 use version 3 of the binary log, while MySQL versions 5.0 and later use version 4 of the binary log.

The binlog file format version changes when developers make significant changes in the overall structure of the file or the events. In MySQL version 5.0, the start event for a binlog file was changed to use a different format and the common headers for all events were also changed, which prompted the change in the binlog file format version.

Server version

This is a version string denoting the server that created the file. This includes the version of the server as well as additional information if special builds are made. The format is normally the three-position version number, followed by a hyphen and any additional build options. For example, "5.5.10-debug-log" means debug build version 5.5.10 of the server.

Common header length

This field stores the length of the common header. Because it's here in the For mat_description, this length can be different for different binlog files. This holds for all events except the Format_description and Rotate events, which cannot vary.

Post-header lengths

The post-header length for each event is fixed within a binlog file, and this field stores an array of the post-header length for each event that can occur in the binlog file. Because the number of event types can vary between servers, the number of different event types that the server can produce is stored before this field.

 The Rotate and Format_description log events have a fixed length because the server needs them before it knows the size of the common header length. When connecting to the server, it first sends a Format_description event. Because the length of the common header is stored in the Format_description event, there is no way for the server to know what the size of the common header is for the Ro tate event unless it has a fixed size. So for these two events, the size of the common header is fixed and will never change between server versions, even if the size of the common header changes for other events.

Because both the size of the common header and the size of the post header for each event type are given in the Format_description event, extending the format with new events or even increasing the size of the post headers by adding new fields is supported by this format and will therefore not require a change in the binlog file format.

With each extension, particular care is taken to ensure that the extension does not affect interpretation of events that were already in earlier versions. For example, the common header can be extended with an additional field to indicate that the event is compressed and the type of compression used, but if this field is missing—which would be the case if a slave is reading events from an old master—the server should still be able to fall back on its default behavior.

Event Checksums

Because hardware can fail and software can contain bugs, it is necessary to have some way to ensure that data corrupted by such events is not applied on the slave. Random failures can occur anywhere, and if they occur inside a statement, they often lead to a syntax error causing the slave to stop. However, relying on this to prevent corrupt events from being replicated is a poor way to ensure integrity of events in the binary log. This policy would not catch many types of corruptions, such as in timestamps, nor would it work for row-based events where the data is encoded in binary form and random corruptions are more likely to lead to incorrect data.

To ensure the integrity of each event, MySQL 5.6 introduced replication event checksums. When events are written, a checksum is added, and when the events are read, the checksum is computed for the event and compared against the checksum written with the event. If the checksums do not match, execution can be aborted before any attempt is made to apply the event on the slave. The computation of checksums can potentially impact performance, but benchmarking has demonstrated no noticeable performance degradation from the addition and checking of checksums, so they are enabled by default in MySQL 5.6. They can, however, be turned off if necessary.

In MySQL 5.6, checksums can be generated when changes are written either to the binary log or to the relay log, and verified when reading events back from one of these logs.

Replication event checksums are controlled using three options:

`binlog-checksum=`*`type`*
> This option enables checksums and tells the server what checksum computation to use. Currently there are only two choices: CRC32 uses ISO-3309 CRC-32 checksums, whereas NONE turns off checksumming. The default is CRC32, meaning that checksums are generated.

`master-verify-checksum=`*`boolean`*
> This option controls whether the master verifies the checksum when reading it from the binary log. This means that the event checksum is verified when it is read from the binary log by the dump thread (see "Replication Architecture Basics" on page 228), but before it is sent out, and also when using SHOW BINLOG EVENTS. If any of the events shown is corrupt, the command will throw an error. This option is off by default.

`slave-sql-verify-checksum=`*`boolean`*
> This option controls whether the slave verifies the event checksum after reading it from the relay log and before applying it to the slave database. This option is off by default.

If you get a corrupt binary log or relay log, *mysqlbinlog* can be used to find the bad checksum using the --verify-binlog-checksum option. This option causes *mysqlbinlog* to verify the checksum of each event read and stop when a corrupt event is found, which the following example demonstrates:

```
$ client/mysqlbinlog --verify-binlog-checksum master-bin.000001
    .
    .
    .
```

```
# at 261
#110406  8:35:28 server id 1  end_log_pos 333 CRC32 0xed927ef2...
SET TIMESTAMP=1302071728/*!*/;
BEGIN
/*!*/;
# at 333
#110406  8:35:28 server id 1  end_log_pos 365 CRC32 0x01ed254d  Intvar
SET INSERT_ID=1/*!*/;
ERROR: Error in Log_event::read_log_event(): 'Event crc check failed!...
DELIMITER ;
# End of log file
ROLLBACK /* added by mysqlbinlog */;
/*!50003 SET COMPLETION_TYPE=@OLD_COMPLETION_TYPE*/;
```

Logging Statements

Starting with MySQL 5.1, row-based replication is also available, which will be covered in "Row-Based Replication" on page 97.

In statement-based replication, the actual executed statement is written to the binary log together with some execution information, and the statement is re-executed on the slave. Because not all events can be logged as statements, there are some exceptions that you should be aware of. This section will describe the process of logging individual statements as well as the important caveats.

Because the binary log is a common resource—all threads write to it—it is critical to prevent two threads from updating the binary log at the same time. To handle this, a lock for the binary log—called the LOCK_log mutex—is acquired just before each group is written to the binary log and released just after the group has been written. Because all session threads for the server can potentially log transactions to the binary log, it is quite common for several session threads to block on this lock.

Logging Data Manipulation Language Statements

Data manipulation are usuallylanguage (DML) statements are usually DELETE, INSERT, and UPDATE statements. To support logging changes in a consistent manner, MySQL writes the binary log while transaction-level locks are held, and releases them after the binary log has been written.

To ensure that the binary log is updated consistently with the tables that the statement modifies, each statement is logged to the binary log during statement commit, just before the table locks are released. If the logging were not made as part of the statement, another statement could be "injected" between the changes that the statement introduces to the database and the logging of the statement to the binary log. This would mean that the statements would be logged in a different order than the order in which they took effect in the database, which could lead to inconsistencies between master and slave. For instance, an UPDATE statement with a WHERE clause could update different rows on the slave because the values in those rows might be different if the statement order changed.

Logging Data Definition Language Statements

Data definition language (DDL) statements affect a schema, such as CREATE TABLE and ALTER TABLE statements. These create or change objects in the filesystem—for example, table definitions are stored in *.frm* files and databases are represented as filesystem directories—so the server keeps information about these available in internal data structures. To protect the update of the internal data structure, it is necessary to acquire an internal lock (called LOCK_open) before altering the table definition.

Because a single lock is used to protect these data structures, the creation, alteration, and destruction of database objects can be a considerable source of performance problems. This includes the creation and destruction of temporary tables, which is quite common as a technique to create an intermediate result set to perform computations on.

If you are creating and destroying a lot of temporary tables, it is often possible to boost performance by reducing the creation (and subsequent destruction) of temporary tables.

Logging Queries

For statement-based replication, the most common binlog event is the Query event, which is used to write a statement executed on the master to the binary log. In addition to the actual statement executed, the event contains some additional information necessary to execute the statement.

Recall that the binary log can be used for many purposes and contains statements in a potentially different order from that in which they were executed on the master. In some cases, part of the binary log may be played back to a server to perform PITR, and in some cases, replication may start in the middle of a sequence of events because a backup has been restored on a slave before starting replication.

In all these cases, the events are executing in different *contexts* (i.e., there is information that is implicit when the server executes the statement but that has to be known to execute the statement correctly). Examples include:

Current database
> If the statement refers to a table, function, or procedure without qualifying it with the database, the current database is implicit for the statement.

Value of user-defined variable
> If a statement refers to a user-defined variable, the value of the variable is implicit for the statement.

Seed for the RAND *function*

The RAND function is based on a pseudorandom number function, meaning that it can generate a sequence of numbers that are reproducible but appear random in the sense that they are evenly distributed. The function is not really random, but starts from a seed number and applies a pseudorandom function to generate a deterministic sequence of numbers. This means that given the same seed, the RAND function will always return the same number. However, this makes the seed implicit for the statement.

The current time

Obviously, the time the statement started executing is implicit. Having a correct time is important when calling functions that are dependent on the current time— such as NOW and UNIX_TIMESTAMP—because otherwise they will return different results if there is a delay between the statement execution on the master and on the slave.

Value used when inserting into an AUTO_INCREMENT *column*

If a statement inserts a row into a table with a column defined with the AUTO_INCREMENT attribute, the value used for that row is implicit for the statement because it depends on the rows inserted before it.

Value returned by a call to LAST_INSERT_ID

If the LAST_INSERT_ID function is used in a statement, it depends on the value inserted by a previous statement, which makes this value implicit for the statement.

Thread ID

For some statements, the thread ID is implicit. For example, if the statement refers to a temporary table or uses the CURRENT_ID function, the thread ID is implicit for the statement.

Because the context for executing the statements cannot be known when they're replayed—either on a slave or on the master after a crash and restart—it is necessary to make the implicit information explicit by adding it to the binary log. This is done in slightly different ways for different kinds of information.

In addition to the previous list, some information is implicit to the execution of triggers and stored routines, but we will cover that separately in "Triggers, Events, and Stored Routines" on page 70.

Let's consider each of the cases of implicit information individually, demonstrate the problem with each one, and examine how the server handles it.

Current database

The log records the current database by adding it to a special field of the Query event. This field also exists for the events used to handle the LOAD DATA INFILE statement, discussed in "LOAD DATA INFILE Statements" on page 65, so the description here applies to that statement as well. The current database also plays an important role in filtering on the database and is described later in this chapter.

Current time

Five functions use the current time to compute their values: NOW, CURDATE, CURTIME, UNIX_TIMESTAMP, and SYSDATE. The first four functions return a value based on the time when the statement *started* to execute. In contrast, SYSDATE returns the value when the function is executed. The difference can best be demonstrated by comparing the execution of NOW and SYSDATE with an intermediate sleep:

```
mysql> SELECT SYSDATE(), NOW(), SLEEP(2), SYSDATE(), NOW()\G
*************************** 1. row ***************************
SYSDATE(): 2013-06-08 23:24:08
    NOW(): 2013-06-08 23:24:08
 SLEEP(2): 0
SYSDATE(): 2013-06-08 23:24:10
    NOW(): 2013-06-08 23:24:08
1 row in set (2.00 sec)
```

Both functions are evaluated when they are encountered, but NOW returns the time that the statement started executing, whereas SYSDATE returns the time when the function was executed.

To handle these time functions correctly, the timestamp indicating when the event *started* executing is stored in the event. This value is then copied from the event to the slave execution thread and used as if it were the time the event started executing when computing the value of the time functions.

Because SYSDATE gets the time from the operating system directly, it is not safe for statement-based replication and will return different values on the master and slave when executed. So unless you really want to have the actual time inserted into your tables, it is prudent to stay away from this function.

Context events

Some implicit information is associated with statements that meet certain conditions:

- If the statement contains a reference to a user-defined variable (as in Example 4-1), it is necessary to add the value of the user-defined variable to the binary log.
- If the statement contains a call to the RAND function, it is necessary to add the pseudorandom seed to the binary log.
- If the statement contains a call to the LAST_INSERT_ID function, it is necessary to add the last inserted ID to the binary log.

- If the statement performs an insert into a table with an AUTO_INCREMENT column, it is necessary to add the value that was used for the column (or columns) to the binary log.

Example 4-1. Statements with user-defined variables

```
SET @value = 45;
INSERT INTO t1 VALUES (@value);
```

In each of these cases, one or more *context events* are added to the binary log before the event containing the query is written. Because there can be several context events preceding a Query event, the binary log can handle multiple user-defined variables together with the RAND function, or (almost) any combination of the previously listed conditions. The binary log stores the necessary context information through the following events:

User_var

Each such event records the name and value of a single user-defined variable.

Rand

Records the random number seed used by the RAND function. The seed is fetched internally from the session's state.

Intvar

If the statement is inserting into an autoincrement column, this event records the value of the internal autoincrement counter for the table before the statement starts.

If the statement contains a call to LAST_INSERT_ID, this event records the value that this function returned in the statement.

Example 4-2 shows some statements that generate all of the context events and how the events appear when displayed using SHOW BINLOG EVENTS. Note that there can be several context events before each statement.

Example 4-2. Query events with context events

```
master> SET @foo = 12;
Query OK, 0 rows affected (0.00 sec)

master> SET @bar = 'Smoothnoodlemaps';
Query OK, 0 rows affected (0.00 sec)

master> INSERT INTO t1(b,c) VALUES
    ->   (@foo,@bar), (RAND(), 'random');
Query OK, 2 rows affected (0.00 sec)
Records: 2  Duplicates: 0  Warnings: 0

master> INSERT INTO t1(b) VALUES (LAST_INSERT_ID());
Query OK, 1 row affected (0.00 sec)

master> SHOW BINLOG EVENTS FROM 238\G
```

```
*************************** 1. row ***************************
   Log_name: mysqld1-bin.000001
        Pos: 238
 Event_type: Query
  Server_id: 1
End_log_pos: 306
       Info: BEGIN
*************************** 2. row ***************************
   Log_name: mysqld1-bin.000001
        Pos: 306
 Event_type: Intvar
  Server_id: 1
End_log_pos: 334
       Info: INSERT_ID=1
*************************** 3. row ***************************
   Log_name: mysqld1-bin.000001
        Pos: 334
 Event_type: RAND
  Server_id: 1
End_log_pos: 369
       Info: rand_seed1=952494611,rand_seed2=949641547
*************************** 4. row ***************************
   Log_name: mysqld1-bin.000001
        Pos: 369
 Event_type: User var
  Server_id: 1
End_log_pos: 413
       Info: @`foo`=12
*************************** 5. row ***************************
   Log_name: mysqld1-bin.000001
        Pos: 413
 Event_type: User var
  Server_id: 1
End_log_pos: 465
       Info: @`bar`=_utf8 0x536D6F6F74686E6F6F6...
*************************** 6. row ***************************
   Log_name: mysqld1-bin.000001
        Pos: 465
 Event_type: Query
  Server_id: 1
End_log_pos: 586
       Info: use `test`; INSERT INTO t1(b,c) VALUES (@foo,@bar)...
*************************** 7. row ***************************
   Log_name: mysqld1-bin.000001
        Pos: 586
 Event_type: Xid
  Server_id: 1
End_log_pos: 613
       Info: COMMIT /* xid=44 */
*************************** 8. row ***************************
   Log_name: mysqld1-bin.000001
        Pos: 613
```

```
   Event_type: Query
    Server_id: 1
End_log_pos: 681
         Info: BEGIN
*************************** 9. row ***************************
   Log_name: mysqld1-bin.000001
         Pos: 681
   Event_type: Intvar
    Server_id: 1
End_log_pos: 709
         Info: LAST_INSERT_ID=1
*************************** 10. row ***************************
   Log_name: mysqld1-bin.000001
         Pos: 709
   Event_type: Intvar
    Server_id: 1
End_log_pos: 737
         Info: INSERT_ID=3
*************************** 11. row ***************************
   Log_name: mysqld1-bin.000001
         Pos: 737
   Event_type: Query
    Server_id: 1
End_log_pos: 843
         Info: use `test`; INSERT INTO t1(b) VALUES (LAST_INSERT_ID())
*************************** 12. row ***************************
   Log_name: mysqld1-bin.000001
         Pos: 843
   Event_type: Xid
    Server_id: 1
End_log_pos: 870
         Info: COMMIT /* xid=45 */
12 rows in set (0.00 sec)
```

Thread ID

The last implicit piece of information that the binary log sometimes needs is the thread ID of the MySQL session handling the statement. The thread ID is necessary when a function is dependent on the thread ID—such as when it refers to CONNECTION_ID—but most importantly for handling temporary tables.

Temporary tables are specific to each thread, meaning that two temporary tables with the same name are allowed to coexist, provided they are defined in different sessions. Temporary tables can provide an effective means to improve the performance of certain operations, but they require special handling to work with the binary log.

Internally in the server, temporary tables are handled by creating obscure names for storing the table definitions. The names are based on the process ID of the server, the thread ID that creates the table, and a thread-specific counter to distinguish between different instances of the table from the same thread. This naming scheme allows tables from different threads to be distinguished from each other, but each statement can access its proper table only if the thread ID is stored in the binary log.

Similar to how the current database is handled in the binary log, the thread ID is stored as a separate field in every Query event and can therefore be used to compute thread-specific data and handle temporary tables correctly.

When writing the Query event, the thread ID to store in the event is read from the pseudo_thread_id server variable. This means that it can be set before executing a statement, but only if you have SUPER privileges. This server variable is intended to be used by *mysqlbinlog* to emit statements correctly and should not normally be used.

For a statement that contains a call to the CONNECTION_ID function or that uses or creates a temporary table, the Query event is marked as thread-specific in the binary log. Because the thread ID is always present in the Query event, this flag is not necessary but is mainly used to allow *mysqlbinlog* to avoid printing unnecessary assignments to the pseudo_thread_id variable.

LOAD DATA INFILE Statements

The LOAD DATA INFILE statement makes it easy to fill tables quickly from a file. Unfortunately, it is dependent on a certain kind of context that cannot be covered by the context events we have discussed: files that need to be read from the filesystem.

To handle LOAD DATA INFILE, the MySQL server uses a special set of events to handle the transfer of the file using the binary log. In addition to solving the problem for LOAD DATA INFILE, this makes the statement a very convenient tool for transferring large amounts of data from the master to the slave, as you will see soon. To correctly transfer and execute a LOAD DATA INFILE statement, several new events are introduced into the binary log:

Begin_load_query
> This event signals the start of data transfer in the file.

Append_block
> A sequence of one or more of these events follows the Begin_load_query event to contain the rest of the file's data, if the file was larger than the maximum allowed packet size on the connection.

Execute_load_query
> This event is a specialized variant of the Query event that contains the LOAD DATA INFILE statement executed on the master.

> Even though the statement contained in this event contains the name of the file that was used on the master, this file will not be sought by the slave. Instead, the contents provided by the preceding Begin_load_query and Append_block events will be used.

For each LOAD DATA INFILE statement executed on the master, the file to read is mapped to an internal file-backed buffer, which is used in the following processing. In addition, a unique file ID is assigned to the execution of the statement and is used to refer to the file read by the statement.

While the statement is executing, the file contents are written to the binary log as a sequence of events starting with a Begin_load_query event—which indicates the beginning of a new file—followed by zero or more Append_block events. Each event written to the binary log is no larger than the maximum allowed packet size, as specified by the max-allowed-packet option.

After the entire file is read and applied to the table, the execution of the statement terminates by writing the Execute_load_query event to the binary log. This event contains the statement executed together with the file ID assigned to the execution of the statement. Note that the statement is not the original statement as the user wrote it, but rather a recreated version of the statement.

 If you are reading an old binary log, you might instead find Load_log_event, Execute_log_event, and Create_file_log_event. These were the events used to replicate LOAD DATA INFILE prior to MySQL version 5.0.3 and were replaced by the implementation just described.

Example 4-3 shows the events written to the binary log by a successful execution of a LOAD DATA INFILE statement. In the Info field, you can see the assigned file ID—1, in this case—and see that it is used for all the events that are part of the execution of the statement. You can also see that the file *foo.dat* used by the statement contains more than the maximum allowed packet size of 16384, so it is split into three events.

Example 4-3. Successful execution of LOAD DATA INFILE

```
master> SHOW BINLOG EVENTS IN 'master-bin.000042' FROM 269\G
*************************** 1. row ***************************
   Log_name: master-bin.000042
        Pos: 269
 Event_type: Begin_load_query
  Server_id: 1
End_log_pos: 16676
       Info: ;file_id=1;block_len=16384
*************************** 2. row ***************************
   Log_name: master-bin.000042
        Pos: 16676
 Event_type: Append_block
  Server_id: 1
End_log_pos: 33083
       Info: ;file_id=1;block_len=16384
*************************** 3. row ***************************
```

```
   Log_name: master-bin.000042
        Pos: 33083
 Event_type: Append_block
  Server_id: 1
End_log_pos: 33633
       Info: ;file_id=1;block_len=527
*************************** 4. row ***************************
   Log_name: master-bin.000042
        Pos: 33633
 Event_type: Execute_load_query
  Server_id: 1
End_log_pos: 33756
       Info: use `test`; LOAD DATA INFILE 'foo.dat' INTO...;file_id=1
4 rows in set (0.00 sec)
```

Binary Log Filters

It is possible to filter out statements from the binary log using two options: binlog-do-db and binlog-ignore-db (which we will call binlog-*-db, collectively). The binlog-do-db option is used when you want to filter only statements belonging to a certain database, and binlog-ignore-db is used when you want to ignore a certain database but replicate all other databases.

These options can be given multiple times, so to filter out both the database one_db and the database two_db, you must give both options in the *my.cnf* file. For example:

```
[mysqld]
binlog-ignore-db=one_db
binlog-ignore-db=two_db
```

The way MySQL filters events can be quite a surprise to unfamiliar users, so we'll explain how filtering works and make some recommendations on how to avoid some of the major headaches.

Figure 4-3 shows how MySQL determines whether the statement is filtered. The filtering is done on a statement level—either the entire statement is filtered out or the entire statement is written to the binary log—and the binlog-*-db options use the *current* database to decide whether the statement should be filtered, not the database of the tables affected by the statement.

To help you understand the behavior, consider the statements in Example 4-4. Each line uses bad as the current database and changes tables in different databases.

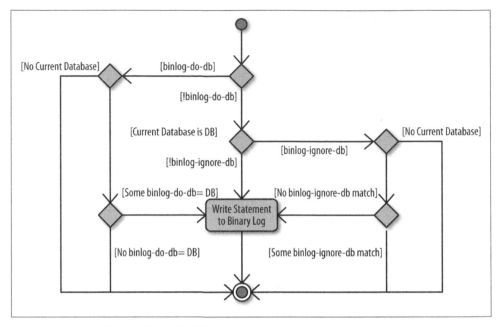

Figure 4-3. Logic for binlog-*-db filters

Example 4-4. Statements using different databases

```
USE bad; INSERT INTO t1 VALUES (1),(2);❶
USE bad; INSERT INTO good.t2 VALUES (1),(2);❷
USE bad; UPDATE good.t1, ugly.t2 SET a = b;❸
```

❶ This line changes a table in the database named bad since it does not qualify the table name with a database name.

❷ This line changes a table in a different database than the current database.

❸ This line changes two tables in two different databases, neither of which is the current database.

Now, given these statements, consider what happens if the bad database is filtered using binlog-ignore-db=bad. None of the three statements in Example 4-4 will be written to the binary log, even though the second and third statements change tables on the good and ugly database and make no reference to the bad database. This might seem strange at first—why not filter the statement based on the database of the table changed? But consider what would happen with the third statement if the ugly database was filtered instead of the bad database. Now one database in the UPDATE is filtered out and the other isn't. This puts the server in a catch-22 situation, so the problem is solved by just filtering on the current database, and this rule is used for all statements (with a few exceptions).

To avoid mistakes when executing statements that can potentially be filtered out, make it a habit not to write statements so they qualify table, function, or procedure names with the database name. Instead, whenever you want to access a table in a different database, issue a USE statement to make that database the current database. In other words, instead of writing:

```
INSERT INTO other.book VALUES ('MySQL', 'Paul DuBois');
```

write:

```
USE other; INSERT INTO book VALUES ('MySQL', 'Paul DuBois');
```

Using this practice, it is easy to see by inspection that the statement does not update multiple databases simply because no tables should be qualified with a database name.

This behavior does not apply when row-based replication is used. The filtering employed in row-based replication will be discussed in "Filtering in Row-Based Replication" on page 286, but since row-based replication can work with each individual row change, it is able to filter on the actual table that the row is targeted for and does not use the current database.

So, what happens when both binlog-do-db and binlog-ignore-db are used at the same time? For example, consider a configuration file containing the following two rules:

```
[mysqld]
binlog-do-db=good
binlog-ignore-db=bad
```

In this case, will the following statement be filtered out or not?

```
USE ugly; INSERT INTO t1 VALUES (1);
```

Following the diagram in Figure 4-3, you can see that if there is at least a binlog-do-db rule, all binlog-ignore-db rules are ignored completely, and since only the good database is included, the previous statement will be filtered out.

Because of the way that the binlog-*-db rules are evaluated, it is pointless to have both binlog-do-db and binlog-ignore-db rules at the same time. Since the binary log can be used for recovery as well as replication, the recommendation is *not* to use the binlog-*-db options and instead filter out the event on the slave by using replicate-* options (these are described in "Filtering and skipping events" on page 255). Using the binlog-*-db option would filter out statements from the binary log and you will not be able to restore the database from the binary log in the event of a crash.

Triggers, Events, and Stored Routines

A few other constructions that are treated specially when logged are *stored programs*—that is, triggers, events, and stored routines (the last is a collective name for stored procedures and stored functions). Their treatment with respect to the binary log contains some elements in common, so they will be covered together in this section. The explanation distinguishes statements of two types: statements that define, destroy, or alter stored programs and statements that invoke them.

Statements that define or destroy stored programs

The following discussion shows triggers in the examples, but the same principles apply to definition of events and stored routines. To understand why the server needs to handle these features specially when writing them to the binary log, consider the code in Example 4-5.

In the example, a table named `employee` keeps information about all employees of an imagined system and a table named `log` keeps a log of interesting information. Note that the `log` table has a `timestamp` column that notes the time of a change and that the `name` column in the `employee` table is the primary key for the table. There is also a `status` column to tell whether the addition succeeded or failed.

To track information about employee information changes—for example, for auditing purposes—three triggers are created so that whenever an employee is added, removed, or changed, a log entry of the change is added to a log table.

Notice that the triggers are after triggers, which means that entries are added only if the executed statement is successful. Failed statements will not be logged. We will later extend the example so that unsuccessful attempts are also logged.

Example 4-5. Definitions of tables and triggers for employee administration

```
CREATE TABLE employee (
    name CHAR(64) NOT NULL,
    email CHAR(64),
    password CHAR(64),
    PRIMARY KEY (name)
);

CREATE TABLE log (
    id INT AUTO_INCREMENT,
    email CHAR(64),
    status CHAR(10),
    message TEXT,
    ts TIMESTAMP,
    PRIMARY KEY (id)
);

CREATE TRIGGER tr_employee_insert_after AFTER INSERT ON employee
```

```
FOR EACH ROW
   INSERT INTO log(email, status, message)
     VALUES (NEW.email, 'OK', CONCAT('Adding employee ', NEW.name));

CREATE TRIGGER tr_employee_delete_after AFTER DELETE ON employee
FOR EACH ROW
   INSERT INTO log(email, status, message)
     VALUES (OLD.email, 'OK', 'Removing employee');

delimiter $$
CREATE TRIGGER tr_employee_update_after AFTER UPDATE ON employee
FOR EACH ROW
BEGIN
  IF OLD.name != NEW.name THEN
    INSERT INTO log(email, status, message)
      VALUES (OLD.email, 'OK',
               CONCAT('Name change from ', OLD.name, ' to ', NEW.name));
  END IF;
  IF OLD.password != NEW.password THEN
    INSERT INTO log(email, status, message)
      VALUES (OLD.email, 'OK', 'Password change');
  END IF;
  IF OLD.email != NEW.email THEN
    INSERT INTO log(email, status, message)
      VALUES (OLD.email, 'OK', CONCAT('E-mail change to ', NEW.email));
  END IF;
END $$
delimiter ;
```

With these trigger definitions, it is now possible to add and remove employees as shown in Example 4-6. Here an employee is added, modified, and removed, and as you can see, each of the operations is logged to the log table.

The operations of adding, removing, and modifying employees may be done by a user who has access to the employee table, but what about access to the log table? In this case, a user who can manipulate the employee table should *not* be able to make changes to the log table. There are many reasons for this, but they all boil down to trusting the contents of the log table for purposes of maintenance, auditing, disclosure to legal authorities, and so on. So the DBA may choose to make access to the employee table available to many users while keeping access to the log table very restricted.

Example 4-6. Adding, removing, and modifying users

```
master> SET @pass = PASSWORD('xyzzy');
Query OK, 0 rows affected (0.00 sec)

master> INSERT INTO employee VALUES ('mats', 'mats@example.com', @pass);

Query OK, 1 row affected (0.00 sec)

master> UPDATE employee SET name = 'matz'
```

```
    -> WHERE email = 'mats@example.com';
Query OK, 1 row affected (0.00 sec)
Rows matched: 1  Changed: 1  Warnings: 0

master> SET @pass = PASSWORD('foobar');
Query OK, 0 rows affected (0.00 sec)

master> UPDATE employee SET password = @pass
    -> WHERE email = 'mats@example.com';
Query OK, 1 row affected (0.00 sec)
Rows matched: 1  Changed: 1  Warnings: 0

master> DELETE FROM employee WHERE email = 'mats@example.com';
Query OK, 1 row affected (0.00 sec)

master> SELECT * FROM log;
+----+------------------+------------------------------+---------------------+
| id | email            | message                      | ts                  |
+----+------------------+------------------------------+---------------------+
|  1 | mats@example.com | Adding employee mats         | 2012-11-14 18:56:08 |
|  2 | mats@example.com | Name change from mats to matz | 2012-11-14 18:56:11 |
|  3 | mats@example.com | Password change              | 2012-11-14 18:56:41 |
|  4 | mats@example.com | Removing employee            | 2012-11-14 18:57:11 |
+----+------------------+------------------------------+---------------------+
4 rows in set (0.00 sec)
```

The INSERT, UPDATE, and DELETE in the example can generate a warning that it is unsafe to log when statement mode is used. This is because it invokes a trigger that inserts into an autoincrement column. In general, such warnings should be investigated.

To make sure the triggers can execute successfully against a highly protected table, they are executed as the user who defined the trigger, not as the user who changed the contents of the employee table. So the CREATE TRIGGER statements in Example 4-5 are executed by the DBA, who has privileges to make additions to the log table, whereas the statements altering employee information in Example 4-6 are executed through a user management account that only has privileges to change the employee table.

When the statements in Example 4-6 are executed, the employee management account is used for updating entries in the employee table, but the DBA privileges are used to make additions to the log table. The employee management account cannot be used to add or remove entries from the log table.

As an aside, Example 4-6 assigns passwords to a user variable before using them in the statement. This is done to avoid sending sensitive data in plain text to another server.

Security and the Binary Log

In general, a user with `REPLICATION SLAVE` privileges has privileges to read everything that occurs on the master and should therefore be secured so that the account cannot be compromised. Details are beyond the scope of this book, but here are some examples of precautions you can take:

- Make it impossible to log in to the account from outside the firewall.
- Track all login attempts for accounts with `REPLICATION SLAVE` privileges, and place the log on a separate secure server.
- Encrypt the connection between the master and the slave using, for example, MySQL's built-in Secure Sockets Layer (SSL) support.

Even if the account has been secured, there is information that does not have to be in the binary log, so it makes sense not to store it there in the first place.

One of the more common types of sensitive information is passwords. Events containing passwords can be written to the binary log when executing statements that change tables on the server and that include the password required for access to the tables.

A typical example is:

```
UPDATE employee SET pass = PASSWORD('foobar')
   WHERE email = 'chuck@example.com';
```

If replication is in place, it is better to rewrite this statement without the password. This is done by computing and storing the hashed password into a user-defined variable and then using that in the expression:

```
SET @password = PASSWORD('foobar');
UPDATE employee SET pass = @password WHERE email = 'chuck@example.com';
```

Since the `SET` statement is not replicated, the original password will not be stored in the binary log, only in the memory of the server while executing the statement.

As long as the *password hash*, rather than the plain-text password, is stored in the table, this technique works. If the raw password is stored directly in the table, there is no way to prevent the password from ending up in the binary log. But storing hashes for passwords is a standard good practice in any case, to prevent someone who gets his hands on the raw data from learning the passwords.

Encrypting the connection between the master and the slave offers some protection, but if the binary log itself is compromised, encrypting the connection doesn't help.

If you recall the earlier discussion about implicit information, you may already have noticed that both the user executing a line of code and the user who defines a trigger are implicit. As you will see in Chapter 8, neither the definer nor the invoker of the trigger is critical to executing the trigger on the slave, and the user information is effectively ignored when the slave executes the statement. However, the information *is* important when the binary log is played back to a server—for instance, when doing a PITR.

To play back a binary log to the server without problems in handling privileges on all the various tables, it is necessary to execute all the statements as a user with SUPER privileges. But the triggers may not have been defined using SUPER privileges, so it is important to recreate the triggers with the correct user as the trigger's definer. If a trigger is defined with SUPER privileges instead of by the user who defined the trigger originally, it might cause a privilege escalation.

To permit a DBA to specify the user under which to execute a trigger, the CREATE TRIGGER syntax includes an optional DEFINER clause. If a DEFINER is not given to the statements—as is the case in Example 4-7—the statement will be rewritten for the binary log to add a DEFINER clause and use the current user as the definer. This means that the definition of the insert trigger appears in the binary log, as shown in Example 4-7. It lists the account that created the trigger (root@localhost) as the definer, which is what we want in this case.

Example 4-7. A CREATE TRIGGER statement in the binary log

```
master> SHOW BINLOG EVENTS FROM 92236 LIMIT 1\G
*************************** 1. row ***************************
   Log_name: master-bin.000038
        Pos: 92236
 Event_type: Query
  Server_id: 1
End_log_pos: 92491
       Info: use `test`; CREATE DEFINER=`root`@`localhost` TRIGGER ...
1 row in set (0.00 sec)
```

Statements that invoke triggers and stored routines

Moving over from definitions to invocations, we can ask how the master's triggers are handled during replication. Well, actually they're not handled at all.

The statement that invokes the trigger is logged to the binary log, but it is not linked to the particular trigger. Instead, when the slave executes the statement, it automatically executes any triggers associated with the tables affected by the statement. This means that there can be different triggers on the master and the slave, and the triggers on the master will be invoked on the master while the triggers on the slave will be invoked on the slave. For example, if the trigger to add entries to the log table is not necessary on the slave, performance can be improved by eliminating the trigger from the slave.

Still, any context events necessary for replicating correctly will be written to the binary log before the statement that invokes the trigger, even if it is just the statements in the trigger that require the context events. Thus, Example 4-8 shows the binary log after executing the INSERT statement in Example 4-5. Note that the first event writes the INSERT ID for the log table's primary key. This reflects the use of the log table in the trigger, but it might appear to be redundant because the slave will not use the trigger.

You should, however, note that using different triggers on the master and slave—or no trigger at all on either the master or slave—is the exception and that the INSERT ID is necessary for replicating the INSERT statement correctly when the trigger is both on the master and slave.

Example 4-8. Contents of the binary log after executing INSERT

```
master> SHOW BINLOG EVENTS FROM 93340\G
*************************** 1. row ***************************
   Log_name: master-bin.000038
        Pos: 93340
 Event_type: Intvar
  Server_id: 1
End_log_pos: 93368
       Info: INSERT_ID=1
*************************** 2. row ***************************
   Log_name: master-bin.000038
        Pos: 93368
 Event_type: User var
  Server_id: 1
End_log_pos: 93396h
       Info: @`pass`=_utf8 0x2A3942353030333433424335324...
utf8_general_ci
*************************** 3. row ***************************
   Log_name: master-bin.000038
        Pos: 93396
 Event_type: Query
  Server_id: 1
End_log_pos: 93537
       Info: use `test`; INSERT INTO employee VALUES ...
3 rows in set (0.00 sec)
```

Stored Procedures

Stored functions and stored procedures are known by the common name *stored routines*. Since the server treats stored procedures and stored functions very differently, stored procedures will be covered in this section and stored functions in the next section.

The situation for stored routines is similar to triggers in some aspects, but very different in others. Like triggers, stored routines offer a DEFINER clause, and it must be explicitly added to the binary log whether or not the statement includes it. But the invocation of stored routines is handled differently from triggers.

To begin, let's extend Example 4-6, which defines tables for employees and logs, with some utility routines to work with the employees. Even though this can be handled with standard INSERT, DELETE, and UPDATE statements, we'll use stored procedures to demonstrate some issues involved in writing them to the binary log. For these purposes, let's extend the example with the functions in Example 4-9 for adding and removing employees.

Example 4-9. Stored procedure definitions for managing employees

```
delimiter $$
CREATE PROCEDURE employee_add(p_name CHAR(64), p_email CHAR(64),
                              p_password CHAR(64))
   MODIFIES SQL DATA
BEGIN
   DECLARE l_pass CHAR(64);
   SET l_pass = PASSWORD(p_password);
   INSERT INTO employee(name, email, password)
     VALUES (p_name, p_email, l_pass);
END $$

CREATE PROCEDURE employee_passwd(p_email CHAR(64),
                                 p_password CHAR(64))
   MODIFIES SQL DATA
BEGIN
   DECLARE l_pass CHAR(64);
   SET l_pass = PASSWORD(p_password);
   UPDATE employee SET password = l_pass
    WHERE email = p_email;
END $$

CREATE PROCEDURE employee_del(p_name CHAR(64))
   MODIFIES SQL DATA
BEGIN
   DELETE FROM employee WHERE name = p_name;
END $$
delimiter ;
```

For the `employee_add` and `employee_passwd` procedures, we have extracted the encrypted password into a separate variable for the reasons already explained, but the `employee_del` procedure just contains a DELETE statement, since nothing else is needed. A binlog entry corresponding to one function is:

```
master> SHOW BINLOG EVENTS FROM 97911 LIMIT 1\G
*************************** 1. row ***************************
   Log_name: master-bin.000038
        Pos: 97911
 Event_type: Query
  Server_id: 1
End_log_pos: 98275
       Info: use `test`; CREATE DEFINER=`root`@`localhost`PROCEDURE ...
1 row in set (0.00 sec)
```

As expected, the definition of this procedure is extended with the DEFINER clause before writing the definition to the binary log, but apart from that, the body of the procedure is left intact. Notice that the CREATE PROCEDURE statement is replicated as a Query event, as are all DDL statements.

In this regard, stored routines are similar to triggers in the way they are treated by the binary log. But invocation differs significantly from triggers. Example 4-10 calls the procedure that adds an employee and shows the resulting contents of the binary log.

Example 4-10. Calling a stored procedure

```
master> CALL employee_add('chuck', 'chuck@example.com', 'abrakadabra');
Query OK, 1 row affected (0.00 sec)

master> SHOW BINLOG EVENTS FROM 104033\G
*************************** 1. row ***************************
   Log_name: master-bin.000038
        Pos: 104033
 Event_type: Intvar
  Server_id: 1
End_log_pos: 104061
       Info: INSERT_ID=1
*************************** 2. row ***************************
   Log_name: master-bin.000038
        Pos: 104061
 Event_type: Query
  Server_id: 1
End_log_pos: 104416
       Info: use `test`; INSERT INTO employee(name, email, password)
             VALUES ( NAME_CONST('p_name',_utf8'chuck' COLLATE ...),
             NAME_CONST('p_email',_utf8'chuck@example.com' COLLATE ...),
             NAME_CONST('pass',_utf8'*FEB349C4FDAA307A...' COLLATE ...))
2 rows in set (0.00 sec)
```

In Example 4-10, there are four things that you should note:

- The CALL statement is not written to the binary log. Instead, the statements executed as a *result* of the call are written to the binary log. In other words, the body of the stored procedure is unrolled into the binary log.

- The statement is rewritten to not contain any references to the parameters of the stored procedure—that is, p_name, p_email, and p_password. Instead, the NAME_CONST function is used for each parameter to create a result set with a single value.

- The locally declared variable pass is also replaced with a NAME_CONST expression, where the second parameter contains the encrypted password.

- Just as when a statement that invokes a trigger is written to the binary log, the statement that calls the stored procedure is preceded by an `Intvar` event holding the insert ID used when adding the employee to the `log` table.

Since neither the parameter names nor the locally declared names are available outside the stored routine, `NAME_CONST` is used to associate the name of the parameter or local variable with the constant value used when executing the function. This guarantees that the value can be used in the same way as the parameter or local variable. However, this change is not significant; currently it offers no advantages over using the parameters directly.

Stored Functions

Stored functions share many similarities with stored procedures and some similarities with triggers. Similar to both stored procedures and triggers, stored functions have a `DEFINER` clause that is normally (but not always) used when the `CREATE FUNCTION` statement is written to the binary log.

In contrast to stored procedures, stored functions can return scalar values and you can therefore embed them in various places in SQL statements. For example, consider the definition of a stored routine in Example 4-11, which extracts the email address of an employee given the employee's name. The function is a little contrived—it is significantly more efficient to just execute statements directly—but it suits our purposes well.

Example 4-11. A stored function to fetch the name of an employee

```
delimiter $$
CREATE FUNCTION employee_email(p_name CHAR(64))
    RETURNS CHAR(64)
    DETERMINISTIC
BEGIN
    DECLARE l_email CHAR(64);
    SELECT email INTO l_email FROM employee WHERE name = p_name;
    RETURN l_email;
END $$
delimiter ;
```

This stored function can be used conveniently in other statements, as shown in Example 4-12. In contrast to stored procedures, stored functions have to specify a characteristic—such as `DETERMINISTIC`, `NO SQL`, or `READS SQL DATA`—if they are to be written to the binary log.

Example 4-12. Examples of using the stored function

```
master> CREATE TABLE collected (
    ->    name CHAR(32),
    ->    email CHAR(64)
    -> );
```

```
Query OK, 0 rows affected (0.09 sec)

master> INSERT INTO collected(name, email)
    -> VALUES ('chuck', employee_email('chuck'));
Query OK, 1 row affected (0.01 sec)

master> SELECT employee_email('chuck');
+------------------------+
| employee_email('chuck') |
+------------------------+
| chuck@example.com      |
+------------------------+
1 row in set (0.00 sec)
```

When it comes to calls, stored functions are replicated in the same manner as triggers: as part of the statement that executes the function. For instance, the binary log doesn't need any events preceding the INSERT statement in Example 4-12, but it will contain the context events necessary to replicate the stored function inside the INSERT.

What about SELECT? Normally, SELECT statements are not written to the binary log since they don't change any data, but a SELECT containing a stored function, as in Example 4-13, is an exception.

Example 4-13. Example of stored function that updates a table

```
CREATE TABLE log(log_id INT AUTO_INCREMENT PRIMARY KEY, msg TEXT);

delimiter $$
CREATE FUNCTION log_message(msg TEXT)
  RETURNS INT
  DETERMINISTIC
BEGIN
  INSERT INTO log(msg) VALUES(msg);
  RETURN LAST_INSERT_ID();
END $$
delimiter ;

SELECT log_message('Just a test');
```

When executing the stored function, the server notices that it adds a row to the log table and marks the statement as an "updating" statement, which means that it will be written to the binary log. So, for the slightly artificial example in Example 4-13, the binary log will contain the event:

```
*************************** 7. row ***************************
   Log_name: mysql-bin.000001
        Pos: 845
 Event_type: Query
  Server_id: 1
End_log_pos: 913
       Info: BEGIN
```

```
*************************** 8. row ***************************
  Log_name: mysql-bin.000001
       Pos: 913
Event_type: Intvar
 Server_id: 1
End_log_pos: 941
      Info: LAST_INSERT_ID=1
*************************** 9. row ***************************
  Log_name: mysql-bin.000001
       Pos: 941
Event_type: Intvar
 Server_id: 1
End_log_pos: 969
      Info: INSERT_ID=1
*************************** 10. row ***************************
  Log_name: mysql-bin.000001
       Pos: 969
Event_type: Query
 Server_id: 1
End_log_pos: 1109
      Info: use `test`; SELECT `test`.`log_message`(_utf8'Just a test' COLLATE...
*************************** 11. row ***************************
  Log_name: mysql-bin.000001
       Pos: 1105
Event_type: Xid
 Server_id: 1
End_log_pos: 1132
      Info: COMMIT /* xid=237 */
```

Stored Functions and Privileges

The CREATE ROUTINE privilege is required to define a stored procedure or stored function. Strictly speaking, no other privileges are needed to create a stored routine, but since it normally executes under the privileges of the definer, defining a stored routine would not make much sense if the definer of the procedure didn't have the necessary privileges to read to or write from tables referenced by the stored procedure.

But replication threads on the slave execute without privilege checks. This leaves a serious security hole allowing any user with the CREATE ROUTINE privilege to elevate her privileges and execute any statement on the slave.

In MySQL versions earlier than 5.0, this does not cause problems, because all paths of a statement are explored when the statement is executed on the master. A privilege violation on the master will prevent a statement from being written to the binary log, so users cannot access objects on the slave that were out of bounds on the master. However, with the introduction of stored routines, it is possible to create conditional execution paths, and the server does not explore all paths when executing a stored routine.

Since stored procedures are unrolled, the exact statements executed on the master are also executed on the slave, and since the statement is logged only if it was successfully executed on the master, it is not possible to get access to other objects. Not so with stored functions.

If a stored function is defined with SQL SECURITY INVOKER, a malicious user can craft a function that will execute differently on the master and the slave. The security breach can then be buried in the branch executed on the slave. This is demonstrated in the following example:

```
CREATE FUNCTION magic()
  RETURNS CHAR(64)
  SQL SECURITY INVOKER
BEGIN
  DECLARE result CHAR(64);
  IF @@server_id <> 1 THEN
     SELECT what INTO result FROM secret.agents LIMIT 1;
     RETURN result;
  ELSE
     RETURN 'I am magic!';
  END IF;
END $$
```

One piece of code executes on the master (the ELSE branch), whereas a separate piece of code (the IF branch) executes on the slave where the privilege checks are disabled. The effect is to elevate the user's privileges from CREATE ROUTINE to the equivalent of SUPER.

Notice that this problem doesn't occur if the function is defined with SQL SECURITY DEFINER, because the function executes with the user's privileges and will be blocked on the slave.

To prevent privilege escalation on a slave, MySQL requires SUPER privileges by default to define stored functions. But because stored functions are very useful, and some database administrators trust their users with creating proper functions, this check can be disabled with the log-bin-trust-function-creators option.

Events

The events feature is a MySQL extension, not part of standard SQL. Events, which should not be confused with binlog events, are handled by a stored program that is executed regularly by a special event scheduler.

Similar to all other stored programs, definitions of events are also logged with a DEFIN ER clause. Since events are invoked by the event scheduler, they are always executed as the definer and do not pose a security risk in the way that stored functions do.

When events are executed, the statements are written to the binary log directly.

Since the events will be executed on the master, they are automatically disabled on the slave and will therefore not be executed there. If the events were not disabled, they would be executed twice on the slave: once by the master executing the event and replicating the changes to the slave, and once by the slave executing the event directly.

 Because the events are disabled on the slave, it is necessary to enable these events if the slave, for some reason, should lose the master.

So, for example, when promoting a slave as described in Chapter 5, don't forget to enable the events that were replicated from the master. This is easiest to do using the following statement:

```
UPDATE mysql.events
    SET Status = ENABLED
    WHERE Status = SLAVESIDE_DISABLED;
```

The purpose of the check is to enable only the events that were disabled when being replicated from the master. There might be events that are disabled for other reasons.

Special Constructions

Even though statement-based replication is normally straightforward, some special constructions have to be handled with care. Recall that for the statement to be executed correctly on the slave, the context has to be correct for the statement. Even though the context events discussed earlier handle part of the context, some constructions have additional context that is not transferred as part of the replication process.

The LOAD_FILE function

The LOAD_FILE function allows you to fetch a file and use it as part of an expression. Although quite convenient at times, the file has to exist on the slave server to replicate correctly since the file is *not* transferred during replication, as the file to LOAD DATA INFILE is. With some ingenuity, you can rewrite a statement involving the LOAD_FILE function either to use the LOAD DATA INFILE statement or to define a user-defined variable to hold the contents of the file. For example, take the following statement that inserts a document into a table:

```
master> INSERT INTO document(author, body)
    ->     VALUES ('Mats Kindahl', LOAD_FILE('go_intro.xml'));
```

You can rewrite this statement to use LOAD DATA INFILE instead. In this case, you have to take care to specify character strings that cannot exist in the document as field and line delimiters, since you are going to read the entire file contents as a single column.

```
master> LOAD DATA INFILE 'go_intro.xml' INTO TABLE document
    ->     FIELDS TERMINATED BY '@*@' LINES TERMINATED BY '&%&'
    ->     (author, body) SET author = 'Mats Kindahl';
```

An alternative is to store the file contents in a user-defined variable and then use it in the statement.

```
master> SET @document = LOAD_FILE('go_intro.xml');
master> INSERT INTO document(author, body) VALUES
    ->    ('Mats Kindahl, @document);
```

Nontransactional Changes and Error Handling

So far we have considered only transactional changes and have not looked at error handling at all. For transactional changes, error handling is pretty uncomplicated: a statement that tries to change transactional tables and fails will not have any effect at all on the table. That's the entire point of having a transactional system—so the changes that the statement attempts to introduce can be safely ignored. The same applies to transactions that are rolled back: they have no effect on the tables and can therefore simply be discarded without risking inconsistencies between the master and the slave.

A specialty of MySQL is the provisioning of nontransactional storage engines. This can offer some speed advantages, because the storage engine does not have to administer the transactional log that the transactional engines use, and it allows some optimizations on disk access. From a replication perspective, however, nontransactional engines require special considerations.

The most important aspect to note is that replication cannot handle arbitrary nontransactional engines, but has to make some assumptions about how they behave. Some of those limitations are lifted with the introduction of row-based replication in version 5.1 —a subject that will be covered in "Row-Based Replication" on page 97—but even in that case, it cannot handle arbitrary storage engines.

One of the features that complicates the issue further, from a replication perspective, is that it is possible to mix transactional and nontransactional engines in the same transaction, and even in the same statement.

To continue with the example used earlier, consider Example 4-14, where the log table from Example 4-5 is given a nontransactional storage engine while the *employee* table is given a transactional one. We use the nontransactional MyISAM storage engine for the log table to improve its speed, while keeping the transactional behavior for the employee table.

We can further extend the example to track unsuccessful attempts to add employees by creating a pair of insert triggers: a before trigger and an after trigger. If an administrator sees an entry in the log with a status field of FAIL, it means the before trigger ran, but the after trigger did not, and therefore an attempt to add an employee failed.

Example 4-14. Definition of log and employee tables with storage engines

```
CREATE TABLE employee (
    name CHAR(64) NOT NULL,
    email CHAR(64),
    password CHAR(64),
    PRIMARY KEY (email)
```

```
) ENGINE = InnoDB;

CREATE TABLE log (
    id INT AUTO_INCREMENT,
    email CHAR(64),
    message TEXT,
    status ENUM('FAIL', 'OK') DEFAULT 'FAIL',
    ts TIMESTAMP,
    PRIMARY KEY (id)
) ENGINE = MyISAM;

delimiter $$
CREATE TRIGGER tr_employee_insert_before BEFORE INSERT ON employee
FOR EACH ROW
BEGIN
  INSERT INTO log(email, message)
    VALUES (NEW.email, CONCAT('Adding employee ', NEW.name));
  SET @LAST_INSERT_ID = LAST_INSERT_ID();
END $$
delimiter ;

CREATE TRIGGER tr_employee_insert_after AFTER INSERT ON employee
FOR EACH ROW
    UPDATE log SET status = 'OK' WHERE id = @LAST_INSERT_ID;
```

What are the effects of this change on the binary log?

To begin, let's consider the INSERT statement from Example 4-6. Assuming the statement is not inside a transaction and AUTOCOMMIT is 1, the statement will be a transaction by itself. If the statement executes without errors, everything will proceed as planned and the statement will be written to the binary log as a Query event.

Now, consider what happens if the INSERT is repeated with the same employee. Since the email column is the primary key, this will generate a duplicate key error when the insertion is attempted, but what will happen with the statement? Is it written to the binary log or not?

Let's have a look…

```
master> SET @pass = PASSWORD('xyzzy');
Query OK, 0 rows affected (0.00 sec)

master> INSERT INTO employee(name,email,password)
    ->     VALUES ('chuck','chuck@example.com',@pass);
ERROR 1062 (23000): Duplicate entry 'chuck@example.com' for key 'PRIMARY'
master> SELECT * FROM employee;
+-------+-------------------+---------------------------------------------+
| name  | email             | password                                    |
+-------+-------------------+---------------------------------------------+
| chuck | chuck@example.com | *151AF6B8C3A6AA09CFCCBD34601F2D309ED54888   |
+-------+-------------------+---------------------------------------------+
1 row in set (0.00 sec)
```

```
master> SHOW BINLOG EVENTS FROM 38493\G
*************************** 1. row ***************************
   Log_name: master-bin.000038
        Pos: 38493
  Event_type: User var
   Server_id: 1
 End_log_pos: 38571
        Info: @`pass`=_utf8 0x2A313531414636423843333413641413...
*************************** 2. row ***************************
   Log_name: master-bin.000038
        Pos: 38571
  Event_type: Query
   Server_id: 1
 End_log_pos: 38689
        Info: use `test`; INSERT INTO employee(name,email,password)...
2 rows in set (0.00 sec)
```

As you can see, the statement is written to the binary log even though the employee table is transactional and the statement failed. Looking at the contents of the table using the SELECT reveals that there is still a single employee, proving the statement was rolled back—so why is the statement written to the binary log?

Looking into the log table will reveal the reason.

```
master> SELECT * FROM log;
+----+-----------------+------------------------+--------+---------------------+
| id | email           | message                | status | ts                  |
+----+-----------------+------------------------+--------+---------------------+
|  1 | mats@example.com | Adding employee mats   | OK     | 2010-01-13 15:50:45 |
|  2 | mats@example.com | Name change from ...   | OK     | 2010-01-13 15:50:48 |
|  3 | mats@example.com | Password change        | OK     | 2010-01-13 15:50:50 |
|  4 | mats@example.com | Removing employee      | OK     | 2010-01-13 15:50:52 |
|  5 | mats@example.com | Adding employee mats   | OK     | 2010-01-13 16:11:45 |
|  6 | mats@example.com | Adding employee mats   | FAIL   | 2010-01-13 16:12:00 |
+----+-----------------+------------------------+--------+---------------------+
6 rows in set (0.00 sec)
```

Look at the last line, where the status is FAIL. This line was added to the table by the before trigger tr_employee_insert_before. For the binary log to faithfully represent the changes made to the database on the master, it is necessary to write the statement to the binary log if there are any nontransactional changes present in the statement or in triggers that are executed as a result of executing the statement. Since the statement failed, the after trigger tr_employee_insert_after was not executed, and therefore the status is still FAIL from the execution of the before trigger.

Since the statement failed on the master, information about the failure needs to be written to the binary log as well. The MySQL server handles this by using an error code field in the Query event to register the exact error code that caused the statement to fail. This field is then written to the binary log together with the event.

The error code is not visible when using the `SHOW BINLOG EVENTS` command, but you can view it using the *mysqlbinlog* tool, which we will cover later in the chapter.

Logging Transactions

You have now seen how individual statements are written to the binary log, along with context information, but we did not cover how transactions are logged. In this section, we will briefly cover how transactions are logged.

A transaction can start under a few different circumstances:

- When the user issues `START TRANSACTION` (or `BEGIN`).
- When `AUTOCOMMIT=1` and a statement accessing a transactional table starts to execute. Note that a statement that writes only to nontransactional tables—for example, only to MyISAM tables—does not start a transaction.
- When `AUTOCOMMIT=0` and the previous transaction was committed or aborted either implicitly (by executing a statement that does an implicit commit) or explicitly by using `COMMIT` or `ROLLBACK`.

Not every statement that is executed after the transaction has started is part of that transaction. The exceptions require special care from the binary log.

Nontransactional statements are by their very definition not part of the transaction. When they are executed, they take effect immediately and do not wait for the transaction to commit. This also means that it is not possible to roll them back. They don't affect an open transaction: any transactional statement executed after the nontransactional statement is still added to the currently open transaction.

In addition, several statements do an implicit commit. These can be separated into three groups based on the reason they do an implicit commit.

Statements that write files
Most DDL statements (`CREATE`, `ALTER`, etc.), with some exceptions, do an implicit commit of any outstanding transaction before starting to execute and an implicit commit after they have finished. These statements modify files in the filesystem and are for that reason not transactional.

Statements that modify tables in the mysql database
All statements that create, drop, or modify user accounts or privileges for users do an implicit commit and cannot be part of a transaction. Internally, these statements modify tables in the *mysql* database, which are all nontransactional.

In MySQL versions earlier than 5.1.3, these statements did not cause an implicit commit, but because they were writing to nontransactional tables, they were treated as nontransactional statements. As you will soon see, this caused some inconsistencies, so implicit commits were added for these statements over the course of several versions.

Statements that require implicit commits for pragmatic reasons
Statements that lock tables, statements that are used for administrative purposes, and LOAD DATA INFILE cause implicit commits in various situations because the implementation requires this to make them work correctly.

Statements that cause an implicit commit are clearly not part of any transaction, because any open transaction is committed before execution starts. You can find a complete list of statements that cause an implicit commit in the online MySQL Reference Manual.

Transaction Cache

The binary log can have statements in a different order from their actual execution, because it combines all the statements in each transaction to keep them together. Multiple sessions can execute simultaneous transactions on a server, and the transactional storage engines maintain their own transactional logs to make sure each transaction executes correctly. These logs are not visible to the user. In contrast, the binary log shows all transactions from all sessions in the order in which they were committed as if each executed sequentially.

To ensure each transaction is written as a unit to the binary log, the server has to separate statements that are executing in different threads. When committing a transaction, the server writes all the statements that are part of the transaction to the binary log as a single unit. For this purpose, the server keeps a *transaction cache* for each thread, as illustrated in Figure 4-4. Each statement executed for a transaction is placed in the transaction cache, and the contents of the transaction cache are then copied to the binary log and emptied when the transaction commits.

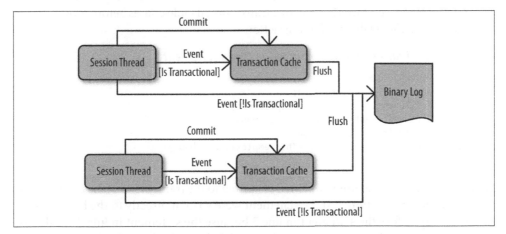

Figure 4-4. Threads with transaction caches and a binary log

Statements that contain nontransactional changes require special attention. Recall from our previous discussion that nontransactional statements do not cause the current transaction to terminate, so the changes introduced by the execution of a nontransactional statement have to be recorded somewhere without closing the currently open transaction. The situation is further complicated by statements that simultaneously affect transactional and nontransactional tables. These statements are considered transactional but include changes that are not part of the transaction.

Statement-based replication cannot handle this correctly in all situations, so a best-effort approach has been taken. We'll describe the measures taken by the server, followed by the issues you have to be aware of in order to avoid the replication problems that are left over.

How nontransactional statements are logged

When no transaction is open, nontransactional statements are written to the binary log at the end of execution of the statement and do not "transit" in the transaction cache before ending up in the binary log. If, however, a transaction is open, the rules for how to handle the statement are as follows:

1. Rule 1: If the statement is marked as transactional, it is written to the transaction cache.

2. Rule 2: If the statement is not marked as transactional and there are no statements in the transaction cache, the statement is written directly to the binary log.

3. Rule 3: If the statement is not marked as transactional, but there are statements in the transaction cache, the statement is written to the transaction cache.

The third rule might seem strange, but you can understand the reasoning if you look at Example 4-15. Returning to our `employee` and `log` tables, consider the statements in Example 4-15, where a modification of a transactional table comes before modification of a nontransactional table in the transaction.

Example 4-15. Transaction with nontransactional statement

```
1    START TRANSACTION;
2    SET @pass = PASSWORD('xyzzy');
3    INSERT INTO employee(name,email,password)
     VALUES ('mats','mats@example.com', @pass);
4    INSERT INTO log(email, message)
     VALUES ('root@example.com', 'This employee was bad');
5    COMMIT;
```

Following rule 3, the statement on line 4 is written to the transaction cache even though the table is nontransactional. If the statement were written directly to the binary log, it would end up before the statement in line 3 because the statement in line 3 would not end up in the binary log until a successful commit in line 5. In short, the slave's log would end up containing the comment added by the DBA in line 4 before the actual change to the employee in line 3, which is clearly inconsistent with the master. Rule 3 avoids such situations. The left side of Figure 4-5 shows the undesired effects if rule 3 did not apply, whereas the right side shows what actually happens thanks to rule 3.

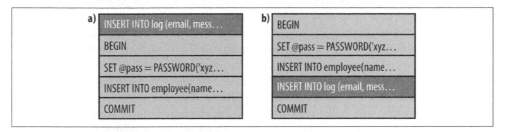

Figure 4-5. Alternative binary logs depending on rule 3

Rule 3 involves a trade-off. Because the nontransactional statement is cached while the transaction executes, there is a risk that two transactions will update a nontransactional table on the master in a different order from that in which they are written to the binary log.

This situation can arise when there is a dependency between the first transactional and the second nontransactional statement of the transaction, but this cannot generally be handled by the server because it would require parsing each statement completely, including code in all triggers invoked, and performing a dependency analysis. Although technically possible, this would add extra processing to *all* statements during an open transaction and would therefore affect performance, perhaps significantly. Because the problem can almost always be avoided by designing transactions properly and ensuring that there are no dependencies of this kind in the transaction, the overhead was not added to MySQL.

How to avoid replication problems with nontransactional statements

The best strategy for avoiding problems is not to use nontransactional tables. However, if they are required by the application, a strategy for avoiding the dependencies discussed in the previous section is to ensure that statements affecting nontransactional tables are written first in the transaction. In this case, the statements will be written directly to the binary log, because the transaction cache is empty (refer to rule 2 in the preceding section). The statements are known to have no dependencies.

If you need any values from these statements later in the transaction, you can assign them to temporary tables or variables. After that, the real contents of the transaction can be executed, referencing the temporary tables or variables.

Writing Non-Transactional Statements Directly

Starting with MySQL 5.6, it is possible to force nontransactional statements to be written directly to the binary log by using the option `binlog_direct_non_transactional_up dates`. When this option is enabled, all nontransactional statements will be written to the binary log *before* the transaction where they appear instead of inside the transaction, even when the nontransactional statement appears after a transactional statement. This option changes the behavior only in statement-based replication. In row-based replication, the rows for the nontransactional statement are *always* written before the transaction. This will work because row-based replication does not execute the statements, but just changes the data in the table. Hence, the nontransactional "statement" will not have any dependencies at all and can be safely written before the transaction.

As an example, if the transaction in Example 4-15 is executed with `binlog_di rect_non_transactional_updates` disabled (which is the default), statements are written to the binary log in the order shown by Figure 4-6.

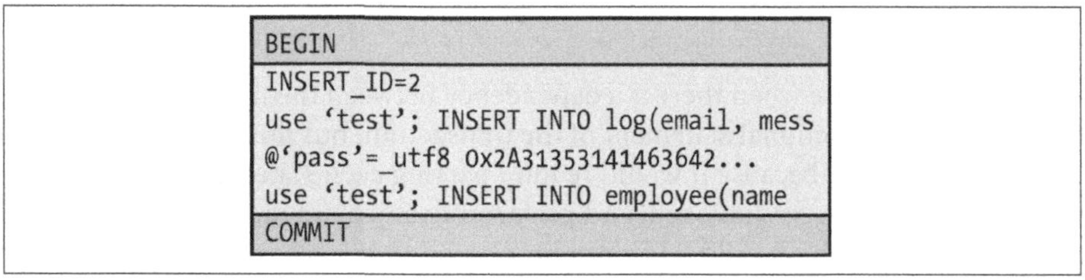

```
BEGIN
INSERT_ID=2
use 'test'; INSERT INTO log(email, mess
@'pass'=_utf8 0x2A31353141463642...
use 'test'; INSERT INTO employee(name
COMMIT
```

Figure 4-6. Order of statements from Example 4-15 in natural order

If, instead, `binlog_direct_non_transactional_updates` is enabled, the sequence of events will be in the order shown in Figure 4-7. Here, a separate transaction created for the write to the `log` table, which is then written before the transaction containing transactional statements.

```
BEGIN
INSERT_ID=2
use 'test'; INSERT INTO log(email, mess
COMMIT
BEGIN
@'pass'= _latin1 0x2A31353141463642
use 'test'; INSERT INTO employee (name
COMMIT
```

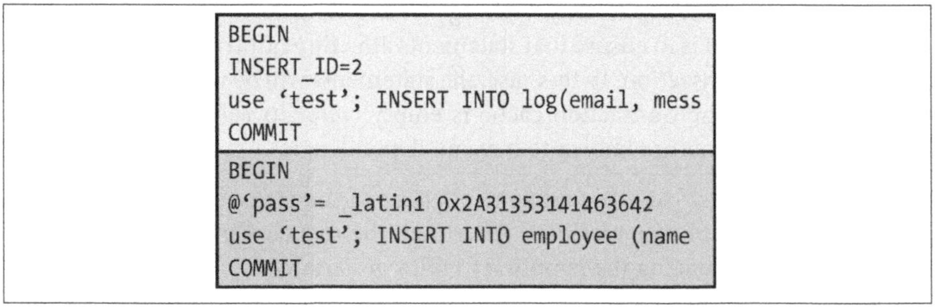

Figure 4-7. Order of statements from Example 4-15 in safe order

Because the nontransactional statement is written before the transaction, it is critical that there are no dependencies on the statements executed before the nontransactional statement in the transaction. If this is something that you need, you should consider using row-based replication instead.

Distributed Transaction Processing Using XA

MySQL version 5.0 lets you coordinate transactions involving different resources by using the X/Open Distributed Transaction Processing model, XA. Although currently not very widely used, XA offers attractive opportunities for coordinating all kinds of resources with transactions.

In version 5.0, the server uses XA internally to coordinate the binary log and the storage engines.

A set of commands allows the client to take advantage of XA synchronization as well. XA allows different statements entered by different users to be treated as a single transaction. On the other hand, it imposes some overhead, so some administrators turn it off globally.

Instructions for working with the XA protocol are beyond the scope of this book, but we will give a brief introduction to XA here before describing how it affects the binary log.

XA includes a *transaction manager* that coordinates a set of *resource managers* so that they commit a global transaction as an atomic unit. Each transaction is assigned a unique XID, which is used by the transaction manager and the resource managers. When used internally in the MySQL server, the transaction manager is usually the binary log and the resource managers are the storage engines. The process of committing an XA transaction is shown in Figure 4-8 and consists of two phases.

In phase 1, each storage engine is asked to prepare for a commit. When preparing, the storage engine writes any information it needs to commit correctly to safe storage and then returns an OK message. If any storage engine replies negatively—meaning that it cannot commit the transaction—the commit is aborted and all engines are instructed to roll back the transaction.

After all storage engines have reported that they have prepared without error, and before phase 2 begins, the transaction cache is written to the binary log. In contrast to normal transactions, which are terminated with a normal Query event with a COMMIT, an XA transaction is terminated with an Xid event containing the XID.

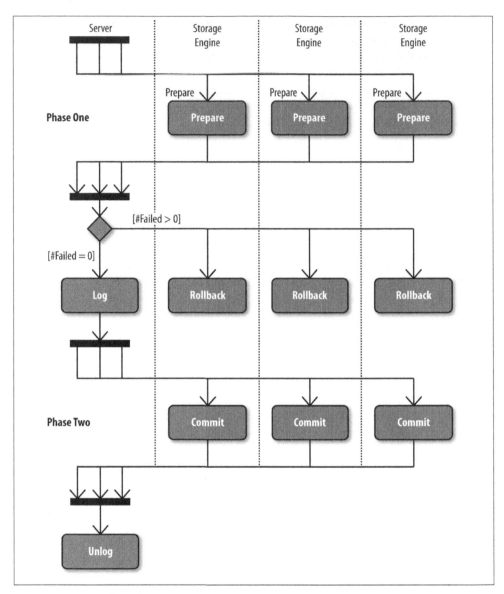

Figure 4-8. Distributed transaction commit using XA

In phase 2, all the storage engines that were prepared in phase 1 are asked to commit the transaction. When committing, each storage engine will report that it has committed the transaction in stable storage. It is important to understand that the commit cannot fail: once phase 1 has passed, the storage engine has guaranteed that the transaction can be committed and therefore is not allowed to report failure in phase 2. A hardware failure can, of course, cause a crash, but since the storage engines have stored the information in durable storage, they will be able to recover properly when the server restarts. The restart procedure is discussed in the section "The Binary Log and Crash Safety" on page 100.

After phase 2, the transaction manager is given a chance to discard any shared resources, should it choose to. The binary log does not need to do any such cleanup actions, so it does not do anything special with regard to XA at this step.

In the event that a crash occurs while committing an XA transaction, the recovery procedure in Figure 4-9 will take place when the server is restarted. At startup, the server will open the last binary log and check the Format_description event. If the binlog-in-use flag is set (described in "Binlog File Rotation" on page 101), it indicates that the server crashed and XA recovery has to be executed.

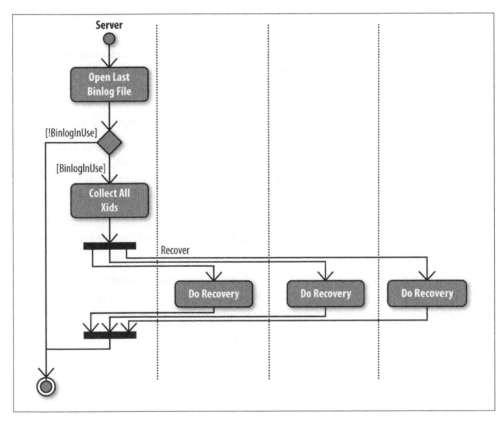

Figure 4-9. Procedure for XA recovery

The server starts by walking through the binary log that was just opened and finding the XIDs of all transactions in the binary log by reading the Xid events. Each storage engine loaded into the server will then be asked to commit the transactions in this list.

For each XID in the list, the storage engine will determine whether a transaction with that XID is prepared but not committed, and commit it if that is the case. If the storage engine has prepared a transaction with an XID that is *not* in this list, the XID obviously did not make it to the binary log before the server crashed, so the transaction should be rolled back.

Binary Log Group Commit

Writing data to disk takes time; quite a lot actually. The performance of disk is orders of magnitude slower than main memory, where disk access times is counted in milliseconds, main memory access is counted in nanoseconds. For that reason, operating systems have elaborate memory management systems for keeping part of the files in memory and not performing more writes to disk than necessary. Since database systems have to be safe from crashes, it is necessary to force the data to be written to disk when a transaction is committed.

To avoid the performance impact resulting if each transaction has to be written to disk, multiple independent transactions can be grouped together and written to disk as a single unit, which is called *group commit*. Because the disk write time is mainly a consequence of the time it takes to move the disk head to the correct position on the disk, and not the amount of data written, this improves performance significantly.

It is, however, not sufficient to commit the transaction data in the storage engine efficiently, the binary log also has to be written efficiently. For that reason, *binary log group commit* was added in MySQL 5.6. With this, multiple independent transactions can be committed as a group to the binary log, improving performance significantly.

In order for online backup tools like MySQL Enterprise Backup to work correctly, it is important that transactions are written to the binary log in the same order as they are prepared in the storage engine.

The implementation is built around a set of *stages* that each transaction has to pass through before being fully committed, you can see an illustration in Figure 4-10. Each stage is protected by a mutex so there can never be more than one thread in each stage.

Each stage handles one part of the commit procedure. The first stage flushes the transaction caches of the threads to the file pages, the second stage executes a sync to get the file pages to disk, and the last stage commits all transactions.

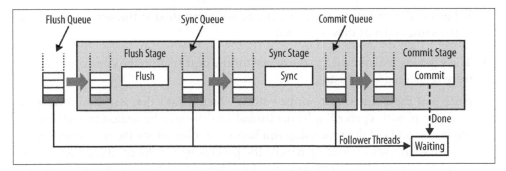

Figure 4-10. Binary log group commit architecture

To move sessions between stages in an ordered manner, each stage has an associated queue where sessions can queue up for processing. Each stage queue is protected by a mutex that is held briefly while manipulating the queue. You can see the names of the mutexes for each stage in Table 4-1, in case you want to use the performance schema to monitor performance of the commit phase.

Table 4-1. Binlog group commit stages and their mutexes

Stage	Stage mutex	Stage queue mutex
Flush	LOCK_log	LOCK_flush_queue
Sync	LOCK_sync	LOCK_sync_queue
Commit	LOCK_commit	LOCK_commit_queue

Sessions normally run in separate threads, so any session thread that wants to commit a transaction enqueues the session in the flush stage queue. A session thread then proceeds through each stage in the following way:

1. If the session thread is enqueued to a *non-empty* stage queue, it is a *follower* and will go and wait for its transaction to be committed by some other session thread.

2. If the session thread enqueued to an *empty* stage queue, it is a *(stage) leader* and will bring all the sessions registered for the stage through the stage.

3. The leader empties all the sessions of the queue in a single step. The order of the sessions will be maintained, but after this step, new sessions can enqueue to the stage queue.

4. The stage processing is done as follows:

   - For the flush queue, the transaction of each session will be flushed to the binary log in the same order as they enqueued to the flush queue.

   - For the sync stage, an `fsync` call is executed.

- For the commit stage, the transactions are committed in the storage engines in the same order as they registered.

5. The sessions are enqueued to the queue for the next stage in the same order as they were registered for this stage.

   Note that the queue might not be empty, which means that a session thread has "caught up" with a preceding leader thread. In this case, the session thread that was the leader and did the processing will become a follower for the next stage and let the leader already queued up handle the processing for the combined sets of sessions. Note that a leader can become a follower, but a follower can never become a leader.

As explained, new leader threads merge their session queues with older threads that are in the middle of commit procedures. This lets the system adapt dynamically to changing situations. Normally, the sync stage is the most expensive stage, so many batches of sessions will pass through the flush stage and "pile up" in the sync stage queue, after which a single leader thread will bring all the sessions through that stage. However, if battery-backed caches are used, `fsync` calls are very cheap, so in that case, sessions *might* not pile up at this stage.

Transactions have to be committed in order so that online backup methods (such as XtraBackup or MySQL Enterprise Backup) work correctly. For this reason, the commit stage commits the transactions in the same order as they are written to the binary log.

However, it is also possible to commit transactions in parallel in the commit stage. This means that the commits are done in an arbitrary order. This does not affect correctness in normal operations, but it means that you should not take an online backup while doing parallel commits.

Benchmarks did not show any measurable improvement in performance when committing transactions in parallel, so the default is to always commit in order. This is also the recommended setting, unless you have special needs (or just want to test it).

You can control whether transactions should be ordered using `binlog_order_com mits`. If this is set to `OFF`, transactions are committed in parallel and the last stage is skipped (the threads commit themselves in an arbitrary order instead of waiting for the leader).

The flush stage includes an optimization when reading sessions from the queue. Instead of entering the flush stage and taking the entire queue for processing, the leader "skims" one session at a time from the queue, flushes it, and then repeats the procedure. The idea behind this optimization is that as long as there are sessions enqueueing, there is no point in advancing to the queue stage, and since flushing the transaction to the binary log takes time, performing it on each session provides an opportunity for more sessions that need committing to enqueue themselves. This optimization showed significant performance improvements in throughput. But because it can affect latency, you can control how long the leader thread will keep "skimming" sessions from the flush queue using the `binlog_max_flush_queue_time`, which takes the number of microseconds that the leader should skim the queue. Once the timer expires, the entire queue will be grabbed and the leader reverts to executing the procedure described in the preceding list for the stage. This means that the time given is not the maximum latency of a transaction: the leader will have to flush all the transactions that are registered for the queue before moving to the sync stage.

Row-Based Replication

The primary goal of replication is to keep the master and the slave synchronized so they have the same data. As you saw earlier, replication offers a number of special features to ensure the results are as close as possible to being identical on master and slave: context events, session-specific IDs, etc.

Despite this, there are still some situations that statement-based replication can't currently handle correctly:

- If an UPDATE, DELETE, or INSERT statement contains a LIMIT clause, it may cause problems if a database crashes during execution.
- If there is an error during execution of a nontransactional statement, there is no guarantee that the effects are the same on the master and the slave.
- If a statement contains a call to a UDF, there is no way to ensure the same value is used on the slave.
- If the statement contains any nondeterministic function—such as USER, CURRENT_USER, or CONNECTION_ID—results may differ between master and slave.
- If a statement updates two tables with autoincrement columns, it will not work correctly, because only a single last insert ID can be replicated, which will then be used for both tables on the slave, while on the master, the insert ID for each table will be used individually.

In these cases, it is better to replicate the actual data being inserted into the tables, which is what *row-based replication* does.

Instead of replicating the statement that performs the changes, row-based replication replicates each row being inserted, deleted, or updated separately, with the values that were used for the operation. Since the row that is sent to the slave is the same row that is sent to the storage engine, it contains the actual data being inserted into the table. Hence there are no UDFs to consider, no autoincrement counters to keep track of, and no partial execution of statements to take into consideration—just data, plain and simple.

Row-based replication opens up an entirely new set of scenarios that you just cannot accomplish with statement-based replication. However, you must also be aware of some differences in behavior.

When choosing between statement-based and row-based replication, consider the following:

- Do you have statements that update a lot of rows, or do the statements usually only change or insert a few rows?

  If the statement changes a lot of rows, statement-based replication will have more compact statements and may execute faster. But since the statement is executed on the slave as well, this is not always true. If the statement has a complex optimization and execution plan, it might be faster to use row-based replication, because the logic for finding rows is much faster.

  If the statement changes or inserts only a few rows, row-based replication is potentially faster because there is no parsing involved and all processing goes directly to the storage engine.

- Do you need to see which statements are executed? The events for handling row-based replication are hard to decode, to say the least. In statement-based replication, the statements are written into the binary log and hence can be read directly.[2]

- Statement-based replication has a simple replication model: just execute the same statement on the slave. This has existed for a long time and is familiar to many DBAs. Row-based replication, on the other hand, is less familiar to many DBAs and can therefore potentially be harder to fix when replication fails.

- If data is different on master and slave, executing statements can yield different results on master and slave. Sometimes this is intentional—in this case, statement-based replication can and should be used—but sometimes this not intentional and can be prevented through row-based replication.

Enabling Row-based Replication

You can control the format to use when writing to the binary log using the option `binlog-format`. This option can take the values `STATEMENT`, `MIXED`, or `ROW` (see "Options for Row-Based Replication" on page 120 for more information), which comes both as a global variable and session variable. This makes it possible for a session to temporarily switch replication format (but you need `SUPER` privileges to change this variable, even the session version). However, to ensure that row-based replication is used when starting

---

2. MySQL 5.6 supports logging the statement that generated the rows to the binary log together with the rows. See the note in "Options for Row-Based Replication" on page 120.

the server, you need to stop the master and update the configuration file. Example 4-16 shows the addition needed to enable row-based replication.

Example 4-16. Options to configure row-based replication

```
[mysqld]
user           = mysql
pid-file       = /var/run/mysqld/mysqld.pid
socket         = /var/run/mysqld/mysqld.sock
port           = 3306
basedir        = /usr
datadir        = /var/lib/mysql
tmpdir         = /tmp
log-bin        = master-bin
log-bin-index  = master-bin.index
server-id      = 1
binlog-format  = ROW
```

Using Mixed Mode

Mixed-mode replication is recommended for MySQL version 5.1 and later, but the default value for the `binlog-format` option is `STATEMENT`. This might seem odd, but that decision was made to avoid problems for users who upgrade from versions 5.0 or earlier. Because those versions had no row-based replication and users had to use statement-based replication, the MySQL developers did not want servers to make a sudden switch. If the servers suddenly started sending out row-based replication events when they were upgraded, the deployment would likely be a mess. To reduce the number of factors that an upgrading DBA has to consider, the default for this option remains `STATEMENT`.

However, if you use one of the template files distributed with MySQL version 5.1, you will notice the `binlog-format` option has the value `MIXED`, per the recommendation.

The principles behind mixed-mode replication are simple: use statement-based replication normally and switch to row-based replication for unsafe statements. We have already examined the kinds of statements that can lead to problems and why. To summarize, mixed-mode currently switches to row-based replication if:

- The statement calls any of the following:
  — The `UUID` function
  — A user-defined function
  — The `CURRENT_USER` or `USER` function
  — The `LOAD_FILE` function
- Two or more tables with an `AUTO_INCREMENT` column are updated in the same statement.
- A server variable is used in the statement.

- The storage engine does not allow statement-based replication (e.g., the MySQL Cluster engine).

This list is, by necessity, incomplete: it is being extended as new constructions are discovered unsafe. For a complete and accurate list, refer to the online MySQL Reference Manual.

Binary Log Management

The events mentioned thus far represent some real change of data that occurred on the master. However, things can happen that do not represent any change of data on the master but can affect replication. For example, if the server is stopped, it can potentially affect replication. No events can, of course, be written to the binary log when the server is not running, but this means that if anything is changed in the datafile, it will *not* be represented in the binary log. A typical example of this is restoring a backup, or otherwise manipulating the datafiles. Such changes are not replicated simply because the server is not running. However, the fact that the server stopped is sometimes represented in the binary log using a binary log event precisely to be able to recognize that there can be a "gap" in the binary log where things *could* have happened.

Events are needed for other purposes as well. Because the binary logs consist of multiple files, it is necessary to split the groups at convenient places to form the sequence of binlog files. To handle this safely, special events (*rotate events*) are added to the binary log.

The Binary Log and Crash Safety

As you have seen, changes to the binary log do not correspond to changes to the master databases on a one-to-one basis. It is important to keep the databases and the binary log mutually consistent in case of a crash. In other words, there should be no changes committed to the storage engine that are not written to the binary log, and vice versa.

Nontransactional engines introduce problems right away. For example, it is not possible to guarantee consistency between the binary log and a MyISAM table because MyISAM is nontransactional and the storage engine will carry through any requested change long before any attempt to log the statement.

But for transactional storage engines, MySQL includes measures to make sure that a crash does not cause the binary log to lose too much information.

As we described in "Logging Statements" on page 58, events are written to the binary log before releasing the locks on the table, but after all the changes have been given to the storage engine. So if there is a crash before the storage engine releases the locks, the server has to ensure that any changes recorded to the binary log are actually in the table on the disk before allowing the statement (or transaction) to commit. This requires coordination with standard filesystem synchronization.

Because disk accesses are very expensive compared to memory accesses, operating systems are designed to cache parts of the file in a dedicated part of the main memory—usually called the *page cache*—and wait to write file data to disk until necessary. Writing to disk becomes necessary when another page must be loaded from disk and the page cache is full, but it can also be requested by an application by doing an explicit call to write the pages of a file to disk.

Recall from the earlier description of XA that when the first phase is complete, all data has to be written to durable storage—that is, to disk—for the protocol to handle crashes correctly. This means that every time a transaction is committed, the page cache has to be written to disk. This can be very expensive and, depending on the application, not always necessary. To control how often the data is written to disk, you can set the `sync-binlog` option. This option takes an integer specifying how often to write the binary log to disk. If the option is set to 5, for instance, the binary log will be written to disk on every fifth commit group of statements or transactions. The default value is 0, which means that the binary log is not explicitly written to disk by the server, but happens at the discretion of the operating system.

 Note that since the introduction of binary log group commit in MySQL version 5.6, there is a sync with each commit group and not with each transaction or statement. This means that with `sync-binlog=1` several transactions will be written to disk in a batch. You can read more about binary log group commit in "Binary Log Group Commit" on page 94.

For storage engines that support XA, such as InnoDB, setting the `sync-binlog` option to 1 means that you will not lose any transactions under normal crashes. For engines that do not support XA, you might lose at most one transaction.

If, however, every group is written to disk, it means that the performance suffers, usually a lot. Disk accesses are notoriously slow and caches are used for precisely the purpose of improving the performance because they remove the need to always write data to disk. If you are prepared to risk losing a few transactions or statements—either because you can handle the work it takes to recover this manually or because it is not important for the application—you can set `sync-binlog` to a higher value or leave it at the default.

Binlog File Rotation

MySQL starts a new file to hold binary log events at regular intervals. For practical and administrative reasons, it wouldn't work to keep writing to a single file—operating systems have limits on file sizes. As mentioned earlier, the file to which the server is currently writing is called the *active* binlog file.

Switching to a new file is called *binary log rotation* or binlog file rotation, depending on the context.

Four main activities cause a rotation:

The server stops
> Each time the server starts, it begins a new binary log. We'll discuss why shortly.

The binlog file reaches a maximum size
> If the binlog file grows too large, it will be automatically rotated. You can control the size of the binlog files using the `binlog-cache-size` server variable.

The binary log is explicitly flushed
> The `FLUSH LOGS` command writes all logs to disk and creates a new file to continue writing the binary log. This can be useful when administering recovery images for PITR. Reading from an open binlog file can have unexpected results, so it is advisable to force an explicit flush before trying to use binlog files for recovery.

An incident occurred on the server
> In addition to stopping altogether, the server can encounter incidents that cause the binary log to be rotated. These incidents sometimes require special manual intervention from the administrator, because they can leave a "gap" in the replication stream. It is easier for the DBA to handle the incident if the server starts on a fresh binlog file after an incident.

The first event of every binlog file is the `Format_description` event, which describes the server that wrote the file along with information about the contents and status of the file.

Three items are of particular interest here:

The `binlog-in-use` *flag*
> Because a crash can occur while the server is writing to a binlog file, it is critical to indicate when a file was closed properly. Otherwise, a DBA could replay a corrupted file on the master or slave and cause more problems. To provide assurance about the file's integrity, the `binlog-in-use` flag is set when the file is created and cleared after the final event (`Rotate`) has been written to the file. Thus, any program can see whether the binlog file was properly closed.

Binlog file format version
> Over the course of MySQL development, the format for the binary log has changed several times, and it will certainly change again. Developers increment the version number for the format when significant changes—notably changes to the common headers—render new files unreadable to previous versions of the server. (The current format, starting with MySQL version 5.0, is version 4.) The binlog file format

version field lists its version number; if a different server cannot handle a file with that version, it simply refuses to read the file.

Server version

This is a string denoting the version of the server that wrote the file. The server version used to run the examples in this chapter was "5.5.31-0ubuntu0.12.04.1," for instance. As you can see, the string is guaranteed to include the MySQL server version, but it also contains additional information related to the specific build. In some situations, this information can help you or the developers figure out and resolve subtle bugs that can occur when replicating between different versions of the server.

To rotate the binary log safely even in the presence of crashes, the server uses a write-ahead strategy and records its intention in a temporary file called the *purge index file* (this name was chosen because the file is used while purging binlog files as well, as you will see). Its name is based on that of the index file, so for instance if the name of the index file is *master-bin.index*, the name of the purge index file is *master-bin.~rec~*. After creating the new binlog file and updating the index file to point to it, the server removes the purge index file.

 In versions of MySQL earlier than 5.1.43, rotation or binlog file purging could leave orphaned files; that is, the files might exist in the filesystem without being mentioned in the index file. Because of this, old files might not be purged correctly, leaving them around and requiring manual cleaning of the files from the directory.

The orphaned files do not cause a problem for replication, but can be considered an annoyance. The procedure shown in this section ensures that no files are orphaned in the event of a crash.

In the event of a crash, if a purge index file is present on the server, the server can compare the purge index file and the index file when it restarts and see what was actually accomplished compared to what was intended.

Before MySQL version 5.6 it was possible that the binary log could be left partially written. This could occur if only a part of the cache was written to the binary log before the server crashed. With MySQL version 5.6, the binary log will be trimmed and the partially written transaction removed from the binary log. This is safe because the transaction is not committed in the storage engine until it was written completely to the binary log.

Incidents

The term "incidents" refers to events that don't change data on a server but must be written to the binary log because they have the potential to affect replication. Most incidents don't require special intervention from the DBA—for instance, servers can stop and restart without changes to database files—but there will inevitably be some incidents that call for special action.

Currently, there are two incident events that you might discover in a binary log:

Stop

> Indicates that the server was stopped through normal means. If the server crashed, no stop event will be written, even when the server is brought up again. This event is written in the old binlog file (restarting the server rotates to a new file) and contains only a common header; no other information is provided in the event.

> When the binary log is replayed on the slave, it ignores any Stop events. Normally, the fact that the server stopped does not require special attention and replication can proceed as usual. If the server was switched to a new version while it was stopped, this will be indicated in the next binlog file, and the server reading the binlog file will then stop if it cannot handle the new version of the binlog format. In this sense, the Stop event does not represent a "gap" in the replication stream. However, the event is worth recording because someone might manually restore a backup or make other changes to files before restarting replication, and the DBA replaying the file could find this event in order to start or stop the replay at the right time.

Incident

> An event type introduced in version 5.1 as a generic incident event. In contrast with the Stop event, this event contains an identifier to specify what kind of incident occurred. It is used to indicate that the server was forced to perform actions that almost guarantee that changes are missing from the binary log.

> For example, incident events in version 5.1 are written if the database was reloaded or if a nontransactional event was too big to fit in the binlog file. MySQL Cluster generates this event when one of the nodes had to reload the database and could therefore be out of sync.

> When the binary log is replayed on the slave, it stops with an error if it encounters an Incident event. In the case of the MySQL Cluster reload event, it indicates a need to resynchronize the cluster and probably to search for events that are missing from the binary log.

Purging the Binlog File

Over time, the server will accumulate binlog files unless old ones are purged from the filesystem. The server can automatically purge old binary logs from the filesystem, or you can explicitly tell the server to purge the files.

To make the server automatically purge old binlog files, set the expire-logs-days option—which is available as a server variable as well—to the number of days that you want to keep binlog files. Remember that as with all server variables, this setting is not preserved between restarts of the server. So if you want the automatic purging to keep going across restarts, you have to add the setting to the *my.cnf* file for the server.

To purge the binlog files manually, use the PURGE BINARY LOGS command, which comes in two forms:

PURGE BINARY LOGS BEFORE *datetime*
> This form of the command will purge all files that are before the given date. If *datetime* is in the middle of a logfile (which it usually is), all files before the one holding *datetime* will be purged.

PURGE BINARY LOGS TO '*filename*'
> This form of the command will purge all files that precede the given file. In other words, all files before *filename* in the output from SHOW MASTER LOGS will be removed, leaving *filename* as the first binlog file.

Binlog files are purged when the server starts or when a binary log rotation is done. If the server discovers files that require purging, either because a file is older than expire-logs-days or because a PURGE BINARY LOGS command was executed, it will start by writing the files that the server has decided are ripe for purging to the purge index file (for example, *master-bin.~rec~*). After that, the files are removed from the filesystem, and finally the purge index file is removed.

In the event of a crash, the server can continue removing files by comparing the contents of the purge index file and the index file and removing all files that were not removed because of a crash. As you saw earlier, the purge index file is used when rotating as well, so if a crash occurs before the index file can be properly updated, the new binlog file will be removed and then re-created when the rotate is repeated.

The mysqlbinlog Utility

One of the more useful tools available to an administrator is the client program *mysqlbinlog*. This is a small program that can investigate the contents of binlog files as well as relay logfiles (we will cover the relay logs in Chapter 8). In addition to reading binlog files locally, *mysqlbinlog* can also fetch binlog files remotely from other servers.

The *mysqlbinlog* is a very useful tool when investigating problems with replication, but you can also use it to implement PITR, as demonstrated in Chapter 3.

The *mysqlbinlog* tool normally outputs the contents of the binary log in a form that can be executed by sending them to a running server. When statement-based replication is employed, the statements executed are emitted as SQL statements. For row-based replication, which will be introduced in Chapter 8, *mysqlbinlog* generates some additional data necessary to handle row-based replication. This chapter focuses entirely on statement-based replication, so we will use the command with options to suppress output needed to handle row-based replication.

Some options to *mysqlbinlog* will be explained in this section, but for a complete list, consult the online MySQL Reference Manual (*http://bit.ly/msbinlog-util*).

Basic Usage

Let's start with a simple example where we create a binlog file and then look at it using *mysqlbinlog*. We will start up a client connected to the master and execute the following commands to see how they end up in the binary log:

```
mysqld1> RESET MASTER;
Query OK, 0 rows affected (0.01 sec)

mysqld1> CREATE TABLE employee (
    ->     id INT AUTO_INCREMENT,
    ->     name CHAR(64) NOT NULL,
    ->     email CHAR(64),
    ->     password CHAR(64),
    ->     PRIMARY KEY (id)
    -> );
Query OK, 0 rows affected (0.00 sec)

mysqld1> SET @password = PASSWORD('xyzzy');
Query OK, 0 rows affected (0.00 sec)

mysqld1> INSERT INTO employee(name,email,password)
    ->     VALUES ('mats','mats@example.com',@password);
Query OK, 1 row affected (0.01 sec)

mysqld1> SHOW BINARY LOGS;
+--------------------+-----------+
| Log_name           | File_size |
+--------------------+-----------+
| mysqld1-bin.000038 |       670 |
+--------------------+-----------+
1 row in set (0.00 sec)
```

Let's now use *mysqlbinlog* to dump the contents of the binlog file *master-bin.000038*, which is where all the commands ended up. The output shown in Example 4-17 has been edited slightly to fit the page.

Example 4-17. Output from execution of mysqlbinlog

```
$ sudo mysqlbinlog                         \
>     --short-form                         \
>     --force-if-open                      \
>     --base64-output=never                \
>     /var/lib/mysql1/mysqld1-bin.000038
1 /*!40019 SET @@session.max_insert_delayed_threads=0*/;
```

```
 2 /*!50003 SET @OLD_COMPLETION_TYPE=@@COMPLETION_TYPE,COMPLETION_TYPE=0*/;
 3 DELIMITER /*!*/;
 4 ROLLBACK/*!*/;
 5 use test/*!*/;
 6 SET TIMESTAMP=1264227693/*!*/;
 7 SET @@session.pseudo_thread_id=999999999/*!*/;
 8 SET @@session.foreign_key_checks=1, @@session.sql_auto_is_null=1,
       @@session.unique_checks=1, @@session.autocommit=1/*!*/;
 9 SET @@session.sql_mode=0/*!*/;
10 SET @@session.auto_increment_increment=1,
       @@session.auto_increment_offset=1/*!*/;
11 /*!\C utf8 *//*!*/;
12 SET @@session.character_set_client=8,@@session.collation_connection=8,
       @@session.collation_server=8/*!*/;
13 SET @@session.lc_time_names=0/*!*/;
14 SET @@session.collation_database=DEFAULT/*!*/;
15 CREATE TABLE employee (
16     id INT AUTO_INCREMENT,
17     name CHAR(64) NOT NULL,
18     email CHAR(64),
19     password CHAR(64),
20     PRIMARY KEY (id)
21 ) ENGINE=InnoDB
22 /*!*/;
23 SET TIMESTAMP=1264227693/*!*/;
24 BEGIN
25 /*!*/;
26 SET INSERT_ID=1/*!*/;
27 SET @`password`:=_utf8 0x2A31353141463... COLLATE `utf8_general_ci`/*!*/;
28 SET TIMESTAMP=1264227693/*!*/;
29 INSERT INTO employee(name,email,password)
30     VALUES ('mats','mats@example.com',@password)
31 /*!*/;
32 COMMIT/*!*/;
33 DELIMITER ;
34 # End of log file
35 ROLLBACK /* added by mysqlbinlog */;
36 /*!50003 SET COMPLETION_TYPE=@OLD_COMPLETION_TYPE*/;
```

To get this output, we use three options:

short-form

> With this option, *mysqlbinlog* prints only information about the SQL statements issued, and leaves out comments with information about the events in the binary log. This option is useful when *mysqlbinlog* is used only to play back the events to a server. If you want to investigate the binary log for problems, you will need these comments and should not use this option.

force-if-open

> If the binlog file is not closed properly, either because the binlog file is still being written to or because the server crashed, *mysqlbinlog* will print a warning that this

binlog file was not closed properly. This option prevents the printing of that warning.

`base64-output=never`

This prevents *mysqlbinlog* from printing base64-encoded events. If *mysqlbinlog* has to print base64-encoded events, it will also print the `Format_description` event of the binary log to show the encoding used. For statement-based replication, this is not necessary, so this option is used to suppress that event.

In Example 4-17, lines 1–4 contain the preamble printed in every output. Line 3 sets a delimiter that is unlikely to occur elsewhere in the file. The delimiter is also designed to appear as a comment in processing languages that do not recognize the setting of the delimiter.

The rollback on line 4 is issued to ensure the output is not accidentally put inside a transaction because a transaction was started on the client before the output was fed into the client.

We can skip momentarily to the end of the output—lines 33–35—to see the counterpart to lines 1–4. They restore the values set in the preamble and roll back any open transaction. This is necessary in case the binlog file was truncated in the middle of a transaction, to prevent any SQL code following this output from being included in a transaction.

The `USE` statement on line 5 is printed whenever the database is changed. Even though the binary log specifies the current database before each SQL statement, *mysqlbinlog* shows only the changes to the current database. When a `USE` statement appears, it is the first line of a new event.

The first line that is guaranteed to be in the output for each event is `SET TIMESTAMP`, as shown on lines 6 and 23. This statement gives the timestamp when the event started executing in seconds since the epoch.

Lines 7–14 contain general settings, but like `USE` on line 5, they are printed only for the first event and whenever their values change.

Because the `INSERT` statement on lines 29–30 is inserting into a table with an autoincrement column using a user-defined variable, the `INSERT_ID` session variable on line 26 and the user-defined variable on line 27 are set before the statement. This is the result of the `Intvar` and `User_var` events in the binary log.

If you omit the `short-form` option, each event in the output will be preceded by some comments about the event that generated the lines. You can see these comments, which start with hash marks (#) in Example 4-18.

Example 4-18. Interpreting the comments in mysqlbinlog output

```
$ sudo mysqlbinlog                      \
>     --force-if-open                   \
>     --base64-output=never             \
>     /var/lib/mysql1/mysqld1-bin.000038
       .
       .
       .
1  # at 386
2  #100123  7:21:33 server id 1  end_log_pos 414    Intvar
3  SET INSERT_ID=1/*!*/;
4  # at 414
5  #100123  7:21:33 server id 1  end_log_pos 496    User_var
6  SET @`password`:=_utf8 0x2A313531...838 COLLATE `utf8_general_ci`/*!*/;
7  # at 496
8  #100123  7:21:33 server id 1  end_log_pos 643
   Query    thread_id=6     exec_time=0     error_code=0
9  SET TIMESTAMP=1264227693/*!*/;
10 INSERT INTO employee(name,email,password)
11   VALUES ('mats','mats@example.com',@password)
12 /*!*/;
13 # at 643
14 #100123  7:21:33 server id 1  end_log_pos 670    Xid = 218
15 COMMIT/*!*/;
16 DELIMITER ;
17 # End of log file
18 ROLLBACK /* added by mysqlbinlog */;
19 /*!50003 SET COMPLETION_TYPE=@OLD_COMPLETION_TYPE*/;
```

The first line of the comment gives the byte position of the event, and the second line contains other information about the event. Consider, for example, the INSERT statement line:

```
# at 496
#100123  7:21:33 server id 1  end_log_pos 643    Query    thread_id=6
    exec_time=0     error_code=0
```

The various parts of the comments have the following meanings:

at 496

> The byte position where the event starts (i.e., the first byte of the event).

100123 7:21:33

> The timestamp of the event as a datetime (date plus time). This is the time when the query started executing or when the events were written to the binary log.

server_id 1

> The server ID of the server that generated the event. This server ID is used to set the pseudo_thread_id session variable, and a line setting this variable is printed if the event is thread-specific and the server ID is different from the previously printed ID.

end_log_pos 643

The byte position of the event that follows this event. By taking the difference between this value and the position where the event starts, you can get the length of the event.

Query

The type of event. In Example 4-18, you can see several different types of events, such as User_var, Intvar, and Xid.

The fields after these are event-specific, and hence different for each event. For the Query event, we can see two additional fields:

thread_id=6

The ID of the thread that executed the event. This is used to handle thread-specific queries, such as queries that access temporary tables.

exec_time=0

The execution time of the query in seconds.

Example 4-17 and Example 4-18 dump the output of a single file, but *mysqlbinlog* accepts multiple files as well. If several binlog files are given, they are processed in order.

The files are printed in the order you request them, and there is no checking that the Rotate event ending each file refers to the next file in sequence. The responsibility for ensuring that these binlog files make up part of a real binary log lies on the user.

Thanks to the way the binlog files binlog files are given, they will be processed in are named, submitting multiple files to *mysqlbinlog*—such as by using * as a file-globbing wildcard—is usually not a problem. However, let's look at what happens when the binlog file counter, which is used as an extension to the filename, goes from 999999 to 1000000:

```
$ ls mysqld1-bin.[0-9]*
mysqld1-bin.000007  mysqld1-bin.000011  mysqld1-bin.000039
mysqld1-bin.000008  mysqld1-bin.000035  mysqld1-bin.1000000
mysqld1-bin.000009  mysqld1-bin.000037  mysqld1-bin.999998
mysqld1-bin.000010  mysqld1-bin.000038  mysqld1-bin.999999
```

As you can see, the last binlog file to be created is listed before the two binlog files that are earlier in binary log order. So it is worth checking the names of the files before you use wildcards.

Since your binlog files are usually pretty large, you won't want to print the entire contents of the binlog files and browse them. Instead, there are a few options you can use to limit the output so that only a range of the events is printed.

start-position=*bytepos*

The byte position of the first event to dump. Note that if several binlog files are supplied to *mysqlbinlog*, this position will be interpreted as the position in the *first* file in the sequence.

If an event does not start at the position given, *mysqlbinlog* will still try to interpret the bytes starting at that position as an event, which usually leads to garbage output.

`stop-position=`*bytepos*
> The byte position of the last event to print. If no event ends at that position, the last event printed will be the event with a position that precedes *bytepos*. If multiple binlog files are given, the position will be the position of the *last* file in the sequence.

`start-datetime=`*datetime*
> Prints only events that have a timestamp at or after *datetime*. This will work correctly when multiple files are given—if all events of a file are before the *datetime*, all events will be skipped—but there is no checking that the events are printed in order according to their timestamps.

`stop-datetime=`*datetime*
> Prints only events that have a timestamp before *datetime*. This is an exclusive range, meaning that if an event is marked `2010-01-24 07:58:32` and that exact datetime is given, the event will *not* be printed.
>
> Note that since the timestamp of the event uses the start time of the statement but events are ordered in the binary log based on the commit time, it is possible to have events with a timestamp that comes *before* the timestamp of the preceding event. Since *mysqlbinlog* stops at the first event with a timestamp outside the range, there might be events that aren't displayed because they have timestamps before *date time*.

Reading remote files

In addition to reading files on a local filesystem, the *mysqlbinlog* utility can read binlog files from a remote server. It does this by using the same mechanism that the slaves use to connect to a master and ask for events. This can be practical in some cases, since it does not require a shell account on the machine to read the binlog files, just a user on the server with `REPLICATION SLAVE` privileges.

To handle remote reading of binlog files, include the `read-from-remote-server` option along with a host and user for connecting to the server, and optionally a port (if different from the default) and a password.

When reading from a remote server, give just the name of the binlog file, not the full path.

So to read the `Query` event from Example 4-18 remotely, the command would look something like the following (the server prompts for a password, but it is not output when you enter it):

```
$ sudo mysqlbinlog
>     --read-from-remote-server
>     --host=master.example.com
```

```
>    --base64-output=never
>    --user=repl_user --password
>    --start-position=294
>    mysqld1-bin.000038
Enter password:
/*!50530 SET @@SESSION.PSEUDO_SLAVE_MODE=1*/;
/*!40019 SET @@session.max_insert_delayed_threads=0*/;
/*!50003 SET @OLD_COMPLETION_TYPE=@@COMPLETION_TYPE,COMPLETION_TYPE=0*/;
DELIMITER /*!*/;
# at 294
#130608 22:09:19 server id 1  end_log_pos 0  Start: binlog v 4, server v 5.5.31
 -0ubuntu0.12.04.1-log created 130608 22:09:19
# at 294
#130608 22:13:08 server id 1  end_log_pos 362  Query thread_id=53 exec_time=0
 error_code=0
SET TIMESTAMP=1370722388/*!*/;
SET @@session.pseudo_thread_id=53/*!*/;
SET @@session.foreign_key_checks=1, @@session.sql_auto_is_null=0...
SET @@session.sql_mode=0/*!*/;
SET @@session.auto_increment_increment=1, @@session.auto_increment_offset...
/*!\C utf8 *//*!*/;
SET @@session.character_set_client=33,@@session.collation_connection=33...
SET @@session.lc_time_names=0/*!*/;
SET @@session.collation_database=DEFAULT/*!*/;
BEGIN
/*!*/;
# at 362
#130608 22:13:08 server id 1  end_log_pos 390  Intvar
SET INSERT_ID=1/*!*/;
# at 390
#130608 22:13:08 server id 1  end_log_pos 472  User_var
SET @`password`:=_utf8 0x2A313531414636423834333413641413039434643434244333...
# at 472
#130608 22:13:08 server id 1  end_log_pos 627  Query thread_id=53 exec_time=0
use `test`/*!*/;
SET TIMESTAMP=1370722388/*!*/;
INSERT INTO employee(name, email, password)
  VALUES ('mats', 'mats@example.com', @password)
/*!*/;
# at 627
#130608 22:13:08 server id 1  end_log_pos 654  Xid = 175
COMMIT/*!*/;
DELIMITER ;
# End of log file
ROLLBACK /* added by mysqlbinlog */;
/*!50003 SET COMPLETION_TYPE=@OLD_COMPLETION_TYPE*/;
/*!50530 SET @@SESSION.PSEUDO_SLAVE_MODE=0*/;
```

Reading raw binary logfiles

The *mysqlbinlog* utility is very useful for investigating binary logs, but it can also be used
for taking backups of binlog files. This is very useful when you do not have access to

the machine using normal shell but have REPLICATION SLAVE privileges. In this case, you can read the binary logfiles from the server, but they should not be parsed and rather just saved to files.

The normal way to use *mysqlbinlog* for taking a backup of binlog files remotely is:

```
mysqlbinlog --raw --read-from-remote-server \
   --host=master.example.com --user=repl_user \
   master-bin.000012 master-bin.000013 ...
```

In this example, the binlog files *master-bin.000012* and *master-bin.000013* will be read and saved in the current directory. Note that you have to use `--read-from-remote-server` together with `--raw`. Using `--raw` without `--read-from-remote-server` is pointless since that would be the same as using a plain file copy. The most interesting options to control the behavior of *mysqlbinlog* are described below. You can find a detailed description of how to use *mysqlbinlog* for backups at the MySQL Reference Manual (*http://bit.ly/backup-files*).

`--result-file=prefix`

This option gives the prefix to use when constructing the files to write to. The prefix can be a directory name (with trailing slash), or any other prefix. It defaults to the empty string, so if this option is not used, files will be written using the same name as they have on the master.

`--to-last-log`

Normally, only the files given on the command line are transferred, but if this option is provided, only the starting binary log file has to be given. After that, *mysqlbinlog* will transfer all files after the first one.

`--stop-never`

Do not stop reading after reaching end of file of the last log: keep waiting for more input. This option is useful when taking a backup that is to be used for point-in-time recovery. See "Backup and MySQL Replication" on page 570 for a detailed treatment of backing up for point-in-time recovery.

Interpreting Events

Sometimes, the standard information printed by *mysqlbinlog* is not sufficient for spotting a problem, so it is necessary to go into the details of the event and investigate its content. To handle such situations, you can pass the hexdump option to tell *mysqlbinlog* to write the actual bytes of the events.

Before going into the details of the events, here are some general rules about the format of the data in the binary log:

Integer data

Integer fields in the binary log are printed in little-endian order, so you have to read integer fields backward. This means that, for example, the 32-bit block 03 01 00 00 represents the hexadecimal number 103.

String data

String data is usually stored both with length data and null-terminated. Sometimes, the length data appears just before the string and sometimes it is stored in the post header.

This section will cover the most common events, but an exhaustive reference concerning the format of all the events is beyond the scope of this book. Check the Binary Log section (*http://bit.ly/binarylog*) in the MySQL Internals Manual for an exhaustive list of all the events available and their fields. The most common of all the events is the Query event, so let's concentrate on it first. Example 4-19 shows the output for such an event.

Example 4-19. Output when using option --hexdump

```
$ sudo mysqlbinlog                       \
>       --force-if-open                  \
>       --hexdump                        \
>       --base64-output=never            \
>       /var/lib/mysql1/mysqld1-bin.000038
    .
    .
    .
```

```
1  # at 496
2  #100123  7:21:33 server id 1  end_log_pos 643
3  # Position  Timestamp  Type   Master ID       Size       Master Pos    Flags
4  #     1f0 6d 95 5a 4b  02    01 00 00 00   93 00 00 00   83 02 00 00   10 00
5  #     203 06 00 00 00 00 00 00 00   04 00 00 1a 00 00 00 40 |................|
6  #     213 00 00 01 00 00 00 00 00   00 00 00 06 03 73 74 64 |.............std|
7  #     223 04 08 00 08 00 08 00 74   65 73 74 00 49 4e 53 45 |.......test.INSE|
8  #     233 52 54 20 49 4e 54 4f 20   75 73 65 72 28 6e 61 6d |RT.INTO.employee|
9  #     243 65 2c 65 6d 61 69 6c 2c   70 61 73 73 77 6f 72 64 |.name.email.pass|
10 #     253 29 0a 20 20 56 41 4c 55   45 53 20 28 27 6d 61 74 |word....VALUES..|
11 #     263 73 27 2c 27 6d 61 74 73   40 65 78 61 6d 70 6c 65 |.mats...mats.exa|
12 #     273 2e 63 6f 6d 27 2c 40 70   61 73 73 77 6f 72 64 29 |mple.com...passw|
13 #     283 6f 72 64 29                                        |ord.|
14 #     Query   thread_id=6    exec_time=0     error_code=0
   SET TIMESTAMP=1264227693/*!*/;
   INSERT INTO employee(name,email,password)
     VALUES ('mats','mats@example.com',@password)
```

The first two lines and line 14 are comments listing basic information that we discussed earlier. Notice that when you use the hexdump option, the general information and the event-specific information are split into two lines, whereas they are merged in the normal output.

Lines 3 and 4 list the common header:

Timestamp
> The timestamp of the event as an integer, stored in little-endian format.

Type
> A single byte representing the type of the event. Some event types are given in the MySQL Internals Manual (*http://bit.ly/intern-man*) but to get the values for your specific server you need to look in the source code (in the file *sql/log_event.h*).

Master ID
> The server ID of the server that wrote the event, written as an integer. For the event shown in Example 4-19, the server ID is 1.

Size
> The size of the event in bytes, written as an integer.

Master Pos
> The same as end_log_pos (i.e., the start of the event following this event).

Flags
> This field has 16 bits reserved for general flags concerning the event. The field is mostly unused, but it stores the binlog-in-use flag. As you can see in Example 4-19, the binlog-in-use flag is set, meaning that the binary log is not closed properly (in this case, because we didn't flush the logs before calling *mysqlbinlog*).

After the common header come the post header and body for the event. As already mentioned, an exhaustive coverage of all the events is beyond the scope of this book, but we will cover the most important and commonly used events: the Query and Format_description log events.

Query event post header and body

The Query event is by far the most used and also the most complicated event issued by the server. Part of the reason is that it has to carry a lot of information about the context of the statement when it was executed. As already demonstrated, integer variables, user variables, and random seeds are covered using specific events, but it is also necessary to provide other information, which is part of this event.

The post header for the Query event consists of five fields. Recall that these fields are of fixed size and that the length of the post header is given in the Format_description event for the binlog file, meaning that later MySQL versions may add additional fields if the need should arise.

Thread ID
> A four-byte unsigned integer representing the thread ID that executed the statement. Even though the thread ID is not always necessary to execute the statement correctly, it is always written into the event.

Execution time

The number of seconds from the start of execution of the query to when it was written to the binary log, expressed as a four-byte unsigned integer.

Database name length

The length of the database name, stored as an unsigned one-byte integer. The database name is stored in the event body, but the length is given here.

Error code

The error code resulting from execution of the statement, stored as a two-byte unsigned integer. This field is included because, in some cases, statements have to be logged to the binary log even when they fail.

Status variables length

The length of the block in the event body storing the status variables, stored as a two-byte unsigned integer. This status block is sometimes used with a `Query` event to store various status variables, such as `SQL_MODE`.

The event body consists of the following fields, which are all of variable length.

Status variables

A sequence of status variables. Each status variable is represented by a single integer followed by the value of the status variable. The interpretation and length of each status variable value depends on which status variable it concerns. Status variables are not always present; they are added only when necessary. Some examples of status variables follow:

`Q_SQL_MODE_CODE`

The value of `SQL_MODE` used when executing the statement.

`Q_AUTO_INCREMENT`

This status variable contains the values of `auto_increment_increment` and `auto_increment_offset` used for the statement, assuming that they are not the default of 1.

`Q_CHARSET`

This status variable contains the character set code and collation used by the connection and the server when the statement was executed.

Current database

The name of the current database, stored as a null-terminated string. Notice that the length of the database name is given in the post header.

Statement text

The statement that was executed. The length of the statement can be computed from the information in the common header and the post header. This statement is normally identical to the original statement written, but in some cases, the statement is rewritten before it is stored in the binary log. For instance, as you saw earlier in this chapter, triggers and stored procedures are stored with `DEFINER` clauses specified.

Format description event post header and body

The `Format_description` event records important information about the binlog file format, the event format, and the server. Because it has to remain robust between versions—it should still be possible to interpret it even if the binlog format changes—there are some restrictions on which changes are allowed.

One of the more important restrictions is that the common header of both the `Format_description` event and the `Rotate` event is fixed at 19 bytes. This means that it is not possible to extend the event with new fields in the common header.

The post header and event body for the `Format_description` event contain the following fields:

Binlog file version
> The version of the binlog file format used by this file. For MySQL versions 5.0 and later, this is 4.

Server version string
> A 50-byte string storing server version information. This is usually the three-part version number followed by information about the options used for the build, "5.5.31-0ubuntu0.12.04.1," for instance.

Creation time
> A four-byte integer holding the creation time—the number of seconds since the epoch—of the first binlog file written by the server since startup. For later binlog files written by the server, this field will be zero.
>
> This scheme allows a slave to determine that the server was restarted and that the slave should reset state and temporary data—for example, close any open transactions and drop any temporary tables it has created.

Common header length
> The length of the common header for all events in the binlog file *except* the `Format_description` and `Rotate` events. As described earlier, the length of the common header for the `Format_description` and `Rotate` events is fixed at 19 bytes.

Post-header lengths
> This is the only variable-length field of the `Format_description` log event. It holds an array containing the size of the post header for each event in the binlog file as a one-byte integer. The value 255 is reserved as the length for the field, so the maximum length of a post header is 254 bytes.

Binary Log Options and Variables

A set of options and variables allow you to configure a vast number of aspects of binary logging.

Several options control such properties as the name of the binlog files and the index file. Most of these options can be manipulated as server variables as well. Some have already been mentioned earlier in the chapter, but here you will find more details on each:

expire-log-days=*days*

> The number of days that binlog files should be kept. Files that are older than the specified number will be purged from the filesystem when the binary log is rotated or the server restarts.
>
> By default this option is 0, meaning that binlog files are never removed.

log-bin[=*basename*]

> The binary log is turned on by adding the log-bin option in the *my.cnf* file, as explained in Chapter 3. In addition to turning on the binary log, this option gives a base name for the binlog files; that is, the portion of the filename before the dot. If an extension is provided, it is removed when forming the base name of the binlog files.
>
> If the option is specified without a *basename*, the base name defaults to *host*-bin where *host* is the base name—that is, the filename without directory or extension— of the file given by the pid-file option, which is usually the hostname as given by *gethostname(2)*. For example, if pid-file is */usr/run/mysql/master.pid*, the default name of the binlog files will be *master-bin.000001*, *master-bin.000002*, etc.
>
> Since the default value for the pid-file option includes the hostname, it is strongly recommended that you give a value to the log-bin option. Otherwise the binlog files will change names when the hostname changes (unless pid-file is given an explicit value).

log-bin-index[=*filename*]

> Gives a name to the index file. This can be useful if you want to place the index file in a different place from the default.
>
> The default is the same as the base name used for log-bin. For example, if the base name used to create binlog files is master-bin, the index file will be named *master-bin.index*.
>
> Similar to the situation for the log-bin option, the hostname will be used for constructing the index filename, meaning that if the hostname changes, replication will break. For this reason, it is strongly recommended that you provide a value for this option.

---

log-bin-trust-function-creators

When creating stored functions, it is possible to create specially crafted functions that allow arbitrary data to be read and manipulated on the slave. For this reason, creating stored functions requires the SUPER privilege. However, since stored functions are very useful in many circumstances, it might be that the DBA trusts anyone with CREATE ROUTINE privileges not to write malicious stored functions. For this reason, it is possible to disable the SUPER privilege requirement for creating stored functions (but CREATE ROUTINE is still required).

binlog-cache-size=*bytes*

The size of the in-memory part of the transaction cache in bytes. The transaction cache is backed by disk, so whenever the size of the transaction cache exceeds this value, the remaining data will go to disk.

This can potentially create a performance problem, so increasing the value of this option can improve performance if you use many large transactions.

Note that just allocating a very large buffer might not be a good idea, because that means that other parts of the server get less memory, which might cause performance degradation.

max-binlog-cache-size=*bytes*

Use this option to restrict the size of each transaction in the binary log. Since large transactions can potentially block the binary log for a long time, they will cause other threads to convoy on the binary log and can therefore create a significant performance problem. If the size of a transaction exceeds *bytes*, the statement will be aborted with an error.

max-binlog-size=*bytes*

Specifies the size of each binlog file. When writing a statement or transaction would exceed this value, the binlog file is rotated and writing proceeds in a new, empty binlog file.

Notice that if the transaction or statement exceeds max-binlog-size, the binary log will be rotated, but the transaction will be written to the new file in its entirety, exceeding the specified maximum. This is because transactions are never split between binlog files.

sync-binlog=*period*

Specifies how often to write the binary log to disk using *fdatasync(2)*. The value given is the number of transaction commits for each real call to *fdatasync(2)*. For instance, if a value of 1 is given, *fdatasync(2)* will be called for each transaction commit, and if a value of 10 is given, *fdatasync(2)* will be called after each 10 transaction commits.

A value of zero means that there will be no calls to *fdatasync(2)* at all and that the server trusts the operating system to write the binary log to disk as part of the normal file handling.

read-only

Prevents any client threads—except the slave thread and users with SUPER privileges —from updating any data on the server (this does not include temporary tables, which can still be updated). This is useful on slave servers to allow replication to proceed without data being corrupted by clients that connect to the slave.

Options for Row-Based Replication

Use the following options to configure row-based replication:

binlog-format

The binlog-format option can be set to use one of the following modes:

STATEMENT

This will use the traditional statement-based replication for all statements.

ROW

This will use the shiny new row-based replication for all statements that insert or change data (data manipulation language, or DML, statements). However, statement-based replication must still be used for statements that create tables or otherwise alter the schema (data definition language, or DDL, statements).

MIXED

This is intended to be a safe version of statement-based replication and is the recommended mode to use with MySQL version 5.1 and later. In mixed-mode replication, the server writes the statements to the binary log as statements, but switches to row-based replication if a statement is considered unsafe through one of the criteria we have discussed in this chapter.

The variable also exists as a global server variable and as a session variable. When starting a new session, the global value is copied to the session variable and then the session variable is used to decide how to write statements to the binary log.

binlog-max-row-event-size

Use this option to specify when to start a new event for holding the rows. Because the events are read fully into memory when being processed, this option is a rough way of controlling the size of row-holding events so that not too much memory is used when processing the rows.

binlog-rows-query-log-events *(new in MySQL 5.6)*

This option causes the server to add an informational event to the binary log before the the row events. The informational event contains the original query that generated the rows.

Note that, because unrecognized events cause the slave to stop, any slave server before MySQL 5.6.2 will not recognize the event and hence stop replicating from the master. This means that if you intend to use an informational event, you need to upgrade all slaves to MySQL 5.6.2 (or later) before enabling `binlog-rows-query-log-events`.

Starting with MySQL 5.6.2, informational events can be added for other purposes as well, but they will not cause the slave to stop. They are intended to allow information to be added to the binary log for those readers (including slaves) that can have use for it, but they should not in any way change the semantics of execution and can therefore be safely ignored by slaves that do not recognize them.

Conclusion

Clearly, there is much to the binary log—including its use, composition, and techniques. We presented these concepts and more in this chapter, including how to control the binary log behavior. The material in this chapter builds a foundation for a greater understanding of the mechanics of the binary log and its importance in logging changes to data.

Joel opened an email message from his boss that didn't have a subject. "I hate it when people do that," he thought. Mr. Summerson's email messages were like his taskings—straight and to the point. The message read, "Thanks for recovering that data for the marketing people. I'll expect a report by tomorrow morning. You can send it via email."

Joel shrugged and opened a new email message, careful to include a meaningful subject. He wondered what level of detail to include and whether he should explain what he learned about the binary log and the *mysqlbinlog* utility. After a moment of contemplation, he included as many details as he could. "He'll probably tell me to cut it back to a bulleted list," thought Joel. That seemed like a good idea, so he wrote a two-sentence summary and a few bullet points and moved them to the top of the message. When he was finished, he sent it on its way to his boss. "Maybe I should start saving these somewhere in case I have to recount something," he mused.

## CHAPTER 5

Replication for High Availability

Joel was listening to his iPod when he noticed his boss standing directly in front of his desk. He took off his headphones and said, "Sorry, sir."

Mr. Summerson smiled and said, "No problem, Joel. I need you to figure out some way to ensure we can keep our replicated servers monitored so that we don't lose data and can minimize downtime. We're starting to get some complaints from the developers that the system is too inflexible. I can deal with the developers, but the support people tell me that when we have a failure it takes too long to recover. I'd like you to make that your top priority."

Joel nodded. "Sure, I'll look at load balancing and improving our recovery efforts in replication."

"Excellent. Give me a report on what you think we need to do to solve this problem."

Joel watched his boss leave his office. "OK, let's find out what this high availability chapter has to say," he thought, as he opened his favorite MySQL book.

Buying expensive machines known for their reliability and ensuring that you have a really good UPS in case of power failures should give you a highly available system. Right?

Well, high availability is actually not that easy to achieve. To have a system that is truly available all the time, you have to plan carefully for any contingency and ensure that you have redundancy to handle failing components. True high availability—a system that does not go down even in the most unexpected circumstances—is hard to achieve and very costly.

The basic principles for achieving high availability are simple enough; implementing the measures is the tricky part. You need to have three things in place for ensuring high availability:

Redundancy

If a component fails, you have to have a replacement for it. The replacement can be either idly standing by or part of the existing deployment.

Contingency plans

If a component fails, you have to know what to do. This depends on which component failed and how it failed.

Procedure

If a component fails, you have to be able to detect it and then execute your plans swiftly and efficiently.

If the system has a single component whose failure will cause the entire system to fail, the system has a *single point of failure*. If a system has a single point of failure, it puts a severe limit on your ability to achieve high availability, which means that one of your first goals is to locate these single points of failure and ensure you have redundancy for them.

Redundancy

To understand where redundancy might be needed, you have to identify every potential point of failure in the deployment. Even though it sounds easy—not to mention a tad tedious and boring—it requires some imagination to ensure that you really have found them all. Switches, routers, network cards, and even network cables are single points of failure. Outside of your architecture, but no less important, are power sources and physical facilities. But what about services needed to keep the deployment up? Suppose all network management is consolidated in a web-based interface? Or what if you have only one staff person who knows how to handle some types of failure?

Identifying the points of failure does not necessarily mean that you have to eliminate them all. Sometimes it is just not possible for economical, technical, or geographic reasons, but being aware of them helps you with planning.

Some things that you should consider, or at least make a conscious decision about whether to consider, are cost of duplicating components, the probability of failure for different components, the time to replace a component, and risk exposure while repairing a component. If repairing a component takes a week and you are running with the spare as the single point of failure during this time, you are taking a certain risk that the spare could be lost as well, which may or may not be acceptable.

Once you have identified where you need redundancy, you have to choose between two fundamental alternatives: you can either keep duplicates around for each component—ready to take over immediately if the original component should fail—or you can ensure you have extra capacity in the system so that if a component fails, you can still handle the load. This choice does not have to be made in an all-or-nothing fashion: you can combine the two techniques so that you duplicate some components and use extra capacity for some other parts of the system.

On the surface, the easiest approach is to duplicate components, but duplication is expensive. You have to leave a standby around and keep it up-to-date with the main component all the time. The advantages of duplicating components are that you do not lose performance when switching and that switching to the standby is usually faster than restructuring the system, which you would have to do if you approached the problem by creating spare capacity.

Creating spare capacity lets you use all the components for running the business, possibly allowing you to handle higher peaks in your load. When a component breaks, you restructure the system so that all remaining components are in use. It is, however, important to have more capacity than you normally need.

To understand why, consider a simple case where you have a master that handles the writes—actually, you should have two, because you need to have redundancy—with a set of slaves connected to the master whose only purpose is to serve read requests.

Should one of the slaves fail, the system will still be responding, but the capacity of the system will be reduced. If you have 10 slaves, each running at 50% capacity, the failure of one slave will increase the load on each slave to 55%, which is easy to handle. However, if the slaves are running at 95% capacity and one of the slaves fails, each server would have to handle 105% of the original load to handle the same load, which is clearly not possible. In this case, the read capacity of the system will be reduced and the response time will be longer.

And planning for the loss of one server is not sufficient: you have to consider the probability of losing more than one server and prepare for that situation as well. Continuing with our previous example, even if each server is running at 80% capacity, the system will be able to handle the loss of one server. However, the loss of two servers means that the load on each remaining server will increase to 100%, leaving you with no room for unexpected bursts in traffic. If this occurs once a year, it might be manageable, but you have to know how often it is likely to happen.

Table 5-1 gives example probabilities for losing 1, 2, or 3 servers in a setup of 100 servers, given different probabilities of losing a single server. As you can see, with a 1% probability of losing a server, you have a 16% risk of losing three or more servers. If you are not prepared to handle that, you're in for some problems if it actually happens.

For a stochastic variable X representing the number of servers lost, the probabilities are calculated using the binomial tail distribution:

$$P(X \geq k) = \binom{n}{k} p^k$$

Table 5-1. Probabilities of losing servers

Probability of losing a single server	1	2	3
1.00%	100.00%	49.50%	16.17%
0.50%	50.00%	12.38%	2.02%
0.10%	10.00%	0.50%	0.02%

To avoid such a situation, you have to monitor the deployment closely to know what the load is, figure out the capacity of your system through measurements, and do your math to see where the response times will start to suffer.

Planning

Having redundancy is not sufficient; you also need to have plans for what to do when the components fail. In the previous example, it is easy to handle a failing slave, because new connections will be redirected to the working slaves, but consider the following:

- What happens with the existing connections? Just aborting and returning an error message to the user is probably not a good idea. Typically, there is an application layer between the user and the database, so in this case the application layer has to retry the query with another server.

- What happens if the master fails? In the previous example, only the slaves failed, but the master can also fail. Assuming you have added redundancy by keeping an extra master around (we will cover how to do that later in the chapter), you must also have plans for moving all the slaves over to the new master.

This chapter will cover some of the techniques and topologies that you can use to handle various situations for failing MySQL servers. There are basically three server roles to consider: master failures, slave failures, and relay failures. Slave failures are just failures of slaves that are used for read scale-out. The slaves that also act as masters are relay slaves and need special care. Master failures are the most important ones to handle quickly, because the deployment will be unavailable until the master is restored.

Slave Failures

By far, the easiest failures to handle are slave failures. Because the slaves are used only for read queries, it is sufficient to inform the load balancer that the slave is missing, and the load balancer will direct new queries to the functioning slaves. There have to be enough slaves to handle the reduced capacity of the system, but apart from that, a failing slave does not normally affect the replication topology and there are no specific topologies that you need to consider to make slave failure easier to manage.

When a slave has failed, there are inevitably some queries that have been sent to the slave that are waiting for a reply. Once these connections report an error resulting from a lost server, the queries have to be repeated with a functioning slave.

Master Failures

If the master fails, it has to be replaced to keep the deployment up, and it has to be replaced quickly. The moment the master fails, all write queries will be aborted, so the first thing to do is to get a new master available and direct all clients to it.

Because the main master failed, all the slaves are now without a master as well, meaning that all the slaves have stale data, but they are still up and can reply to read queries.

However, some queries may block if they are waiting for changes to arrive at the slave. Some queries may make it into the relay log of the slave and therefore will eventually be executed by the slave. No special consideration has to be taken on the behalf of these queries.

For queries that are waiting for events that did not leave the master before it crashed, the situation is bleaker. In this case, it is necessary to ensure they are handled. This usually means they are reported as failures, so the user will have to reissue the query.

Relay Failures

For servers acting as relay servers, the situation has to be handled specially. If they fail, the remaining slaves have to be redirected to use some other relay or the master itself. Because the relay has been added to relieve the master of some load, it is likely that the master will not be able to handle the load of a batch of slaves connected to one of its relays.

Disaster Recovery

In the world of high availability, "disaster" does not have to mean earthquakes or floods; it just means that something went very bad for the computer and it is not local to the machine that failed.

Typical examples are lost power in the data center—not necessarily because the power was lost in the city; just losing power in the building is sufficient.

The nature of a disaster is that many things fail at once, making it impossible to handle redundancy by duplicating servers at a single data center. Instead, it is necessary to ensure data is kept safe at another geographic location, and it is quite common for companies to ensure high availability by having different components at different offices, even when the company is relatively small.

Procedures

After you have eliminated all single points of failure, ensured you have sufficient redundancy for the system, and made plans for every contingency, you should be ready for the last step.

All your resources and careful planning are of no use unless you can wield them properly. You can usually manage a small site with a few servers manually with very little planning, but as the number of servers increases, automation becomes a necessity—and if you run a successful business, the number of servers might have to increase quickly.

You're likely better off if you plan from day one to have automation—if you have to grow, you will be busy handling other matters and will probably not have time to create the necessary automation support.

Some of the basic procedures have already been discussed, but you need to consider having ready-made procedures for at least the following tasks:

Adding new slaves

Creating new slaves when you need to scale is the basis for running a big site. There are several options for creating new slaves. They all circle around methods for taking a snapshot of an existing server, usually a slave, restoring the snapshot on a new server, and then starting replication from the correct position.

The time for taking a snapshot will, of course, affect how quickly you can bring the new slave up; if the backup time is too long, the master may have issued a lot of changes, which means that the new slave will take longer to catch up. For this reason, the snapshot time is important. Figure 5-1 shows the snapshot time when the slave has caught up. You can see that when the slave is stopped to take a snapshot, the changes will start to accumulate, which will cause the outstanding changes to increase. Once the slave is restarted, it will start to apply the outstanding changes and the number of outstanding changes will decrease.

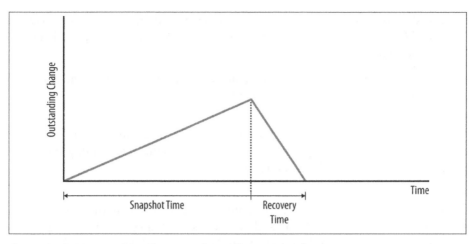

Figure 5-1. Outstanding changes when taking a snapshot

Some different methods of taking a snapshot include the following:

Using mysqldump

Using *mysqldump* is safe but slow. If you use InnoDB tables, *mysqldump* has options to allow you to take a consistent snapshot, meaning you do not have to bring the server offline. There are also options that allow you to get the master and slave positions for the snapshot so that replication will start at the right position.

Copying the database files

This is relatively fast, but requires you to bring the server offline before copying the files. It also require you to manage the positions for starting replication at the right place, something that *mysqldump* does for you.

Using an online backup method

There are different methods available, such as the MySQL Enterprise Backup and XtraBackup.

Using LVM to get a snapshot

On Linux, it is possible to take a snapshot of a volume using Logical Volume Manager (LVM). It does require that you prepare beforehand, because a special LVM volume has to be created. Just like copying the database files, this method requires you to manage the replication positions yourself.

Using filesystem snapshot methods

The Solaris ZFS, for example, has built-in support for taking snapshots. This is a very fast technique for creating backups, but it is similar to the other techniques (except for *mysqldump*). It also requires you to manage the replication positions yourself.

If it should be necessary to use a different engine when restoring, you have to use *mysqldump*: all the other methods have to restore to the same engine that was used for taking the backup.

Techniques for creating new slaves are covered in Chapter 3, and the different backup methods are covered in Chapter 15.

Removing slaves from the topology

Removing slaves from the setup only requires notifying the load balancer that the slave is absent. An example load balancer—with methods for adding and removing servers—can be found in Chapter 6.

Switching the master

For routine maintenance, it is common to have to switch all the slaves of a master over to a secondary master as well as notify load balancers of the master's absence. This procedure can and should be handled with no downtime at all, so it should not affect normal operations.

Using slave promotion (described later in this chapter) is one way to handle this, but it might be easier to use a hot standby instead (also covered later in this chapter).

Handling slave failures

Your slaves will fail—it is just a matter of how often. Handling slave failures must be a routine event in any deployment. It is only necessary to detect that the slave is absent and remove it from the load balancer's pool, as described in Chapter 6.

Handling master failures

When the master goes down suddenly, you have to detect the failure and move all the slaves over to a standby, or promote one of the slaves to be the new master. Techniques for this are described later in this chapter.

Upgrading slaves

Upgrading slaves to new versions of the server should usually not be a problem. However, bringing the slave out of the system for the upgrade requires removing it from the load balancer and maybe notifying other systems of the slave's absence.

Upgrading masters

To upgrade the master, you first need to upgrade all the slaves to ensure that they can read all the replication events of the master. To upgrade the master, it is usually necessary to either use a standby as a master while you are performing the upgrade or promote one of the slaves to be the master for the duration of the upgrade.

Hot Standby

The easiest topology for duplicating servers is *hot standby*, shown in Figure 5-2. The hot standby is a dedicated server that just duplicates the main master. The hot standby server is connected to the master as a slave, so that it reads and applies all changes. This setup is often called *primary-backup configuration*, where the primary is the master and the "backup" is the secondary. There can be multiple hot standbys.

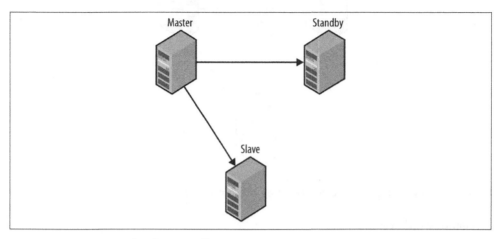

Figure 5-2. Master with a hot standby

Failure is inevitable, at least when you run a large deployment. It is not a question of *if* servers fail, but *when* and *how often* they fail. The idea in this topology is that when the main master fails, the hot standby provides a faithful replica of the master, and all the clients and slaves can therefore be switched over to the hot standby and continue operating. Operations can proceed with hardly a lapse, and the hot standby gives you a chance to fix or replace the main master. After you have repaired the master, you have to bring it back on track and either set it to be the hot standby, or redirect the slaves to the original master again. As with many ideas, the reality is not always that rosy.

All these are relevant issues, but for starters, let's just consider the first case: that of switching over to a hot standby when the primary is still running, as illustrated in Figure 5-3.

MySQL 5.6 introduced the concept of *global transaction identifiers*, which significantly simplifies this problem of handling failover. However, because MySQL 5.6 is relatively new, this section demonstrates how to perform failover before MySQL 5.6. For a description of how to handle failover using global transaction identifiers, have a look in "Global Transaction Identifiers" on page 260, where you will also see how to set the server up for using global transaction identifiers. If you are using a pre-MySQL 5.6 server and want to use global transaction identifiers, you have to roll them yourself. An example of how to do this can be found in Appendix B.

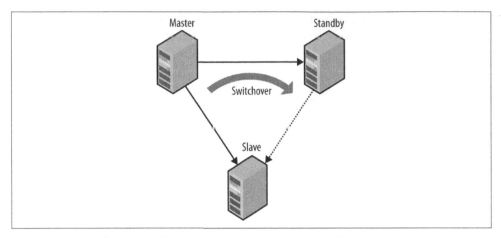

Figure 5-3. Switching over from a running master to a standby

Handling a switchover

The main challenge with switching over to a standby before MySQL 5.6 is to perform the switchover in such a way that the slave starts replicating from the standby at precisely the position where it stopped replicating from the original master. If the positions were easy to translate—for example, if the positions were the same on both the master and the standby—we would not have a problem. Unfortunately, the positions may be different on the master and the standby for a number of reasons. The most common cause is when a standby was not attached to the master when the master was started. But even if they were attached from the start, events cannot be guaranteed to be written the same way to the binary log on the standby as they were written to the binary log on the master.

The basic idea for performing the switchover is to stop the slave and the standby at exactly the same position and then just redirect the slave to the standby. Because the standby hasn't made any changes after the position where you stopped it, you can just check the binlog position on the standby and direct the slave to start at that position. This task has to be performed manually, because just stopping the slave and the standby will not guarantee that they are synchronized.

To do this, stop both the slave and the standby and compare the binlog positions. Because both positions refer to positions on the same master—the slave and standby are both connected to the same master—you can check the positions just by comparing the filename and the byte position lexicographically (in that order):

```
standby> SHOW SLAVE STATUS\G
      ...
  Relay_Master_Log_File: master-bin.000096
      ...
    Exec_Master_Log_Pos: 756648
1 row in set (0.00 sec)
```

```
slave> SHOW SLAVE STATUS\G
      ...
  Relay_Master_Log_File: master-bin.000096
      ...
    Exec_Master_Log_Pos: 743456
1 row in set (0.00 sec)
```

In this case, the standby is ahead of the slave: they are in the same file, but the standby is at position 756648 whereas the slave is at 743456. So just write down the slave position of the standby (756648) and stop the slave from running until it has caught up with the standby. To have the slave catch up with the standby and stop at the right position, use the START SLAVE UNTIL command, as we did when stopping the reporting slave earlier in this chapter:

```
slave> START SLAVE UNTIL
    ->    MASTER_LOG_FILE = 'master-bin.000096',
    ->    MASTER_LOG_POS = 756648;
Query OK, 0 rows affected (0.18 sec)

slave> SELECT MASTER_POS_WAIT('master-bin.000096', 756648);
Query OK, 0 rows affected (1.12 sec)
```

The slave and standby have now stopped at exactly the same position, and everything is ready to do the switchover to the standby using CHANGE MASTER to direct the slave to the standby and start it. But what position should you specify? Because the file and position that the master recorded for its stopping point are different from the file and position recorded by the standby for the same point, it is necessary to fetch the position that the standby recorded while recording the changes as a master. To do this, execute SHOW MASTER STATUS on the standby:

```
standby> SHOW MASTER STATUS\G
*************************** 1. row ***************************
            File: standby-bin.000019
        Position: 56447
    Binlog_Do_DB:
Binlog_Ignore_DB:
1 row in set (0.00 sec)
```

Now you can redirect the slave to the standby using the correct position:

```
slave> CHANGE MASTER TO
    ->    MASTER_HOST = 'standby.example.com',
    ->    MASTER_PORT = 3306,
    ->    MASTER_USER = 'repl_user',
    ->    MASTER_PASSWORD = 'xyzzy',
    ->    MASTER_LOG_FILE = '
standby-bin.000019',
    ->    MASTER_LOG_POS = 56447;
  Query OK, 0 rows affected (0.18 sec)
```

```
slave> START SLAVE;
Query OK, 0 rows affected (0.25 sec)
```

If the opposite is true—if the slave is ahead of the standby—you can just switch the roles of the standby and the slave in the previous steps. This is possible because the master is running and can provide either the slave or the standby with the missing changes. In the next section, we will consider how to handle the situation in which the master has stopped unexpectedly and hence cannot provide either the slave or the standby with the missing changes.

Handling a switchover in Python

Example 5-1 shows the Python code for switching a slave over to another master. The `replicate_to_position` function instructs a server to read from the master only to the given position. When the procedure returns, the slave will have stopped at exactly this position. The `switch_to_master` directs a slave to a new master. The procedure assumes that both the server on which it executes and the new master are connected to the same original master. If they are not, the positions are not comparable and the procedure will raise an exception. The procedure allows the position on the master to be given explicitly instead of computed, which we will use later in the chapter when implementing failover.

Example 5-1. Procedure for switching to a new master

```
from mysql.replicant.commands import (
    fetch_slave_position,
    fetch_master_position,
    change_master,
)

def replicate_to_position(server, pos):
    server.sql("START SLAVE UNTIL MASTER_LOG_FILE=%s, MASTER_LOG_POS=%s",
               (pos.file, pos.pos))
    server.sql("SELECT MASTER_POS_WAIT(%s,%s)", (pos.file, pos.pos))


def switch_to_master(server, standby, master_pos=None):
    server.sql("STOP SLAVE")
    server.sql("STOP SLAVE")
    if master_pos is None:
        server_pos = fetch_slave_position(server)
        standby_pos = fetch_slave_position(standby)
        if server_pos < standby_pos:
            replicate_to_position(server, standby_pos)
        elif server_pos > standby_pos:
            replicate_to_position(standby, server_pos)
        master_pos = fetch_master_position(standby)
    change_master(server, standby, master_pos)
    standby.sql("START SLAVE")
    server.sql("START SLAVE")
```

Dual Masters

One frequently mentioned setup for high availability is the *dual masters* topology. In this setup, two masters replicate each other to keep both current. This setup is very simple to use because it is symmetric. Failing over to the standby master does not require any reconfiguration of the main master, and failing back to the main master again when the standby master fails in turn is very easy.

Servers can be either active or passive. If a server is active it means that the server accepts writes, which are likely to be propagated elsewhere using replication. If a server is passive, it does not accept writes and is just following the active master, usually to be ready to take over when it fails.

When using dual masters, there are two different setups, each serving a different purpose:

Active-active

In an active-active setup, writes go to both servers, which then transfer changes to the other master.

Active-passive

In this setup, one of the masters, called the active master, handles writes while the other server, called the passive master, just keeps current with the active master.

This is almost identical to the hot standby setup, but because it is symmetric, it is easy to switch back and forth between the masters, each taking turns being the active master.

Note that this setup does not necessarily let the passive master answer queries. For some of the solutions that you'll see in this section, the passive master is a cold standby.

These setups do not necessarily mean that replication is used to keep the servers synchronized—there are other techniques that can serve that purpose. Some techniques can support active-active masters, while other techniques can only support active-passive masters.

The most common use of an active-active dual masters setup is to have the servers geographically close to different sets of users—for example, in branch offices at different places in the world. The users can then work with the local server, and the changes will be replicated over to the other master so that both masters are kept in sync. Because the transactions are committed locally, the system will be perceived as more responsive. It is important to understand that the transactions are committed locally, meaning that the two masters are not consistent (i.e., they might not have the same information). The changes committed to one master will be propagated to the other master eventually, but until that has been done, the masters have inconsistent data.

This has two main consequences that you need to be aware of:

- If the same information is updated on the two masters—for example, a user is accidentally added to both masters—there will be a conflict between the two updates and it is likely that replication will stop.

- If a crash occurs while the two masters are inconsistent, some transactions will be lost.

To some extent, you can avoid the problem with conflicting changes by allowing writes to only one of the servers, thereby making the other master a passive master. This is called an active-passive setup. The active server is called the *primary* and the passive server is called the *secondary*.

Losing transactions when the server crashes is an inevitable result of using asynchronous replication, but depending on the application, it does not necessarily have to be a serious problem. You can limit the number of transactions that are lost when the server crashes by using a new feature in MySQL 5.5 called *semisynchronous replication*. The idea behind semisynchronous replication is that the thread committing a transaction blocks until at least one slave acknowledges that it has received the transaction. Because the events for the transaction are sent to the slave after the transaction has been committed to the storage engine, the number of lost transactions can be kept down to at most one per thread.

Similar to the active-active approach, the active-passive setup is symmetrical and therefore allows you to switch easily from the main master to the standby and back. Depending on the way you handle the mirroring, it may also be possible to use the passive master for administrative tasks such as upgrading the server and use the upgrade server as the active master once the upgrade is finished without any downtime at all.

One fundamental problem that has to be resolved when using an active-passive setup is the risk of both servers deciding that they are the primary master. This is called the *split-brain syndrome*. This can occur if network connectivity is lost for a brief period, long enough to have the secondary promote itself to primary, but then the primary is brought online again. If changes have been made to both servers while they are both in the role of primary, there may be a conflict. In the case of using a shared disk, simultaneous writes to the disks by two servers are likely to cause "interesting" problems with the database (i.e., problems that are probably disastrous and difficult to pinpoint). In other words, two running MySQL servers are not allowed to shard the same data directory, so it is necessary to ensure that at most one MySQL server using the data directory is active at any time (you can find a more elaborate discussion on this in "Shared disks" on page 137).

The easiest and most common way to prevent such a situation is to ensure that the server that was deemed "dead" is really not active. This is done using a technique called, somewhat morbidly, STONITH (*Shoot The Other Node In The Head*). This can be accomplished in several different ways, such as connecting to the server and executing a `kill -9` (if the server can be reached), turning of the network card to isolate the server, or turning the power switch on the machine. If the server is truly unreachable (e.g., it ended up on a different partition), you have to use a "poison pill" so that when the server is accessible again, it will "commit suicide."

Shared disks

A straightforward dual masters approach is shown in Figure 5-4, where a pair of masters is connected using a shared disk architecture such as a storage area network (SAN). In this approach, both servers are connected to the same SAN and are configured to use the same files. Because one of the masters is passive, it will not write anything to the files while the active master is running as usual. If the main server fails, the standby will be ready to take over.

The advantage of this approach is that, because the binlog files are on a shared disk, there is no need for translating binlog positions. The two servers are truly mirror images of each other, but they are running on two different machines. This means that switching over from the main master to the standby is very fast. There is no need for the slaves to translate positions to the new master; all that is necessary is to note the position where the slave stopped, issue a CHANGE MASTER command, and start replication again.

When you failover using this technique, you have to perform recovery on the tables, because it is very likely that updates were stopped midstream. Each storage engine behaves differently in this situation. For example, InnoDB has to perform a normal recovery from the transaction log, as it would in the event of a crash, whereas if you use MyISAM you probably have to repair the tables before being able to continue operation. Of these two choices, InnoDB is preferred because recovery is significantly faster than repairing a MyISAM table.

You should also consider the time it takes to warm up the caches, which can be lengthy.

Notice that the position uses the server ID of the main server, but it represents the same position on the standby because it uses the same files and is a mirror image of the main server. Because the position contains the server ID as well, this will also catch any mistakes made by the user, such as passing a master that is not a mirror image of the main master.

Setting up dual masters using shared disks is dependent on the shared storage solution used, a discussion that is beyond the scope of this book.

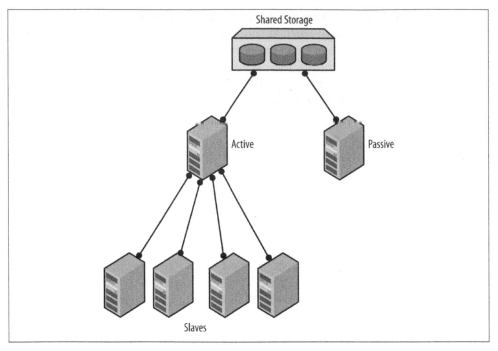

Figure 5-4. Dual masters using a shared disk

The problem with using shared storage is that the two masters are using the same files for storing data, so you have to be very careful when doing any administrative tasks on the passive master. Overwriting the configuration files, even by mistake, can be fatal. It is not sufficient to enforce one server to be read-only because there are files written (e.g., by InnoDB) even when the server is in read-only mode.

The handling of split-brain syndrome depends on which shared disk solution is used and is beyond the scope of this book. One example, however, occurs when using SCSI, which has support for reserving disks by servers. This allows a server to detect that it is really not the primary anymore by noticing that the disks are reserved by another server, and bringing itself offline.

Replicated disks using DRBD

The Linux High Availability project (*http://www.linux-ha.org/*) contains a lot of useful tools for maintaining high availability systems. Most of these tools are beyond the scope of this book, but there is one tool that is interesting for our purposes: Distributed Replicated Block Device (DRBD), which is software for replicating block devices over the network.

Figure 5-5 shows a typical setup of two nodes where DRBD is used to replicate a disk to a secondary server. The setup creates two DRBD block devices, one on each node, which in turn write the data to the real disks. The two DRBD processes communicate over the network to ensure any changes made to the primary are replicated over to the secondary. To the MySQL server, the device replication is transparent. The DRBD devices look and behave like normal disks, so no special configuration is needed for the servers.

You can only use DRBD in an active-passive setup, meaning that the passive disk cannot be accessed at all. In contrast with the shared disk solution outlined earlier and the bidirectional replication implementation described later in this chapter, the passive master cannot be accessed at all.

Similar to the shared disk solution, DRBD has the advantage of not needing to translate positions between the two masters because they share the same files. However, failing over to the standby master takes longer than in the shared disk setup described earlier.

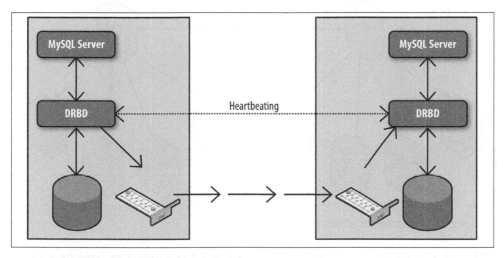

Figure 5-5. Using DRBD to replicate disks

For both the shared disk and the DRBD setup, it is necessary to perform recovery of the database files before bringing the servers online. Because recovery of MyISAM tables is quite expensive, it is recommended that you use a transactional engine with good recovery performance for the database tables. InnoDB is the proven solution in this case, but investigating alternative transactional engines might prove to be well-invested time.

The *mysql* database contains strictly MyISAM tables so you should, as a general principle, avoid unnecessary changes to these tables during normal operations. It is, of course, impossible to avoid when you need to perform administrative tasks.

One advantage of DRBD over shared disks is that for the shared disk solution, the disks actually provide a single point of failure. Should the network to the shared disk array go down, it is possible that the server will not work at all. In contrast, replicating the disks means that the data is available on both servers, which reduces the risk of a total failure.

DRBD also has support built in to handle split-brain syndrome and can be configured to automatically recover from it.

Bidirectional replication

When using dual masters in an active-passive setup, there are no significant differences compared to the hot standby solution outlined earlier. However, in contrast to the other dual-masters solutions outlined earlier, it is possible to have an active-active setup (shown in Figure 5-6).

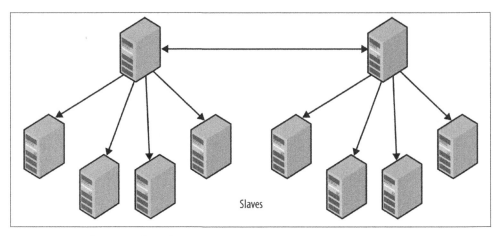

Figure 5-6. Bidirectional replication

Although controversial in some circles, an active-active setup does have its uses. A typical case is when there are two (or more) offices working with local information in the same database (e.g., sales data or employee data) and each office wants low response times when working with the database, while ensuring the data is available in both places. In this case, the data is naturally local to each office—each salesperson is normally working with his own sales and rarely, if ever, makes changes to another salesperson's data.

Use the following steps to set up bidirectional replication:

1. Ensure both servers have different server IDs.
2. Ensure both servers have the same data (and that no changes are made to either system until replication has been activated).

3. Create a replication user and prepare replication (using the information in Chapter 1) on both servers.

4. Start replication on both servers.

 When using bidirectional replication, be forewarned that replication includes no concept of conflict resolution. If both servers update the same piece of data, you will have a conflict that may or may not be noticed. If you are lucky, replication will stop at the offending statement, but you shouldn't count on it. If you intend to have a high availability system, you should ensure, at the application level, that two servers do not try to update the same data.

Even if data is naturally partitioned—as in the example given previously with two offices in separate locations—it is critical to put provisions in place to ensure data is not accidentally updated at the wrong server.

In this case, the application has to connect to the server responsible for the employee and update the information there, not just update the information locally and hope for the best.

If you want to connect slaves to either of the servers, you have to ensure the `log-slave-updates` option is enabled. The other master is also connected as a slave, so an obvious question is this: what happens to events that the server sends out when they return to the server?

When replication is running, the server ID of the server that created the event is attached to each event. This server ID is then propagated further when the slave writes the event to its binary log. When a server sees an event with the same server ID as its own server ID, that event is simply skipped and replication proceeds with the next event.

Sometimes, you want to process the event anyway. This might be the case if you have removed the old server and created a new one with the same server ID and you are in the process of performing a PITR. In those cases, it is possible to disable this checking using the `replicate-same-server-id` configuration variable. However, to prevent you from shooting yourself in the foot, you cannot set this option at the same time that `log-slave-updates` is set. Otherwise, it would be possible to send events in a circle and quickly thrash all the servers. To prevent that from happening, MySQL prevents events from being forwarded if `replicate-same-server-id` is set.

When using an active-active setup, there is a need to handle conflicts in a safe way, and by far the easiest way—and indeed the only recommended way to handle an active-active setup—is to ensure the different active servers write to different areas.

One possible solution is to assign different databases—or different tables—to different masters. Example 5-2 shows a setup that uses two different tables, each updated by different masters. To make it easy to view the split data, a view is created that combines the two tables.

Example 5-2. Different tables for different offices

```
CREATE TABLE Employee_Sweden (
    uid INT AUTO_INCREMENT PRIMARY KEY,
    name VARCHAR(20)
);

CREATE TABLE Employee_USA (
    uid INT AUTO_INCREMENT PRIMARY KEY,
    name VARCHAR(20)
);


-- This view is used when reading from the two tables simultaneously.
CREATE VIEW Employee AS
    SELECT 'SWE', uid, name FROM Employee_Sweden
  UNION
    SELECT 'USA', uid, name FROM Employee_USA;
```

This approach is best to use if the split is natural in that, for example, different offices have different tables for their local data and the data only needs to be combined for reporting purposes. This might seem easy enough, but the following issues can complicate usage and administration of the tables:

Reads and writes to different tables

Because of the way the view is defined, you cannot update it. Writes have to be directed at the real tables, while reads can either use the view or read directly from the tables.

It might therefore be necessary to introduce application logic to handle the split into reads and writes that go to different tables.

Accurate and current data

Because the two tables are managed by different sites, simultaneous updates to the two tables will cause the system to temporarily enter a state where both servers have information that is not available on the other server. If a snapshot of the information is taken at this time, it will not be accurate.

If accurate information is required, generate methods for ensuring the information is accurate. Because such methods are highly application-dependent, they will not be covered here.

Optimization of views

When using views, two techniques are available to construct a result set. In the first method—called MERGE—the view is expanded in place, optimized, and executed as if it were a SELECT query. In the second method—called TEMPTABLE—a temporary table is constructed and populated with the data.

If the server uses a TEMPTABLE view, it performs very poorly, whereas the MERGE view is close to the corresponding SELECT. MySQL uses TEMPTABLE whenever the view definition does not have a simple one-to-one mapping between the rows of the view and the rows of the underlying table—for example, if the view definition contains UNION, GROUP BY, subqueries, or aggregate functions—so careful design of the views is paramount for getting good performance.

In either case, you have to consider the implications of using a view for reporting, as it might affect performance.

If each server is assigned separate tables, there will be no risk of conflict at all, given that updates are completely separated. However, if all the sites have to update the same tables, you will have to use some other scheme.

The MySQL server has special support for handling this situation in the form of two server variables:

auto_increment_offset

This variable controls the starting value for any AUTO_INCREMENT column in a table (i.e., the value that the first row inserted into the table gets for the AUTO_INCRE MENT column). For subsequent rows, the value is calculated using auto_incre ment_increment.

auto_increment_increment

This is the increment used to compute the next value of an AUTO_INCREMENT column.

> There are session and global versions of these two variables and they affect all tables on the server, not just the tables created. Whenever a new row is inserted into a table with an AUTO_INCREMENT column, the next value available in this sequence is used:
>
> $value_N$ = auto_increment_offset + N*auto_increment_increment
>
> You should notice that the next value is *not* computed by adding the auto_increment_increment to the last value in the table.

Building on the previous example, auto_increment_increment to ensure new rows added to a table are assigned numbers from different sequences of numbers depending on which server is used. The idea is that the first server uses the sequence 1, 3, 5… (odd numbers), while the second server uses the sequence 2, 4, 6… (even numbers).

Continuing with Example 5-2, Example 5-3 uses these two variables to ensure the two servers use different IDs when inserting new employees into the Employee table.

Example 5-3. Two servers writing to the same table

```
-- The common table can be created on either server
CREATE TABLE Employee (
   uid INT AUTO_INCREMENT PRIMARY KEY,
   name VARCHAR(20),
   office VARCHAR(20)
);

-- Setting for first master
SET GLOBAL AUTO_INCREMENT_INCREMENT = 2;
SET GLOBAL AUTO_INCREMENT_OFFSET = 1;

-- Setting for second master
SET GLOBAL AUTO_INCREMENT_INCREMENT = 2;
SET GLOBAL AUTO_INCREMENT_OFFSET = 2;
```

This scheme handles the insertion of new items in the tables, but when entries are being updated, it is still critical to ensure the update statements are sent to the correct server (i.e., the server responsible for the employee). Otherwise, data is likely to be inconsistent. If updates are not done correctly, the slaves will normally not stop—they will just replicate the information, which leads to inconsistent values on the two servers.

For example, if the first master executes the statement:

```
master-1> UPDATE Employee SET office = 'Vancouver' WHERE uid = 3;
Query OK, 1 rows affected (0.00 sec)
```

and at the same time, the same row is updated at the second server using the statement:

```
master-2> UPDATE Employee SET office = 'Paris' WHERE uid = 3;
Query OK, 1 rows affected (0.00 sec)
```

the result will be that the first master will place the employee in Paris while the second master will place the employee in Vancouver (note that the order will be swapped because each server will update the other server's statement after its own).

Detecting and preventing such inconsistencies is important because they will cascade and create more inconsistency over time. Statement-based replication executes statements based on the data in the two servers, so one inconsistency can lead to others.

If you take care to separate the changes made by the two servers as outlined previously, the row changes will be replicated and the two masters will therefore be consistent.

If users use different tables on the different servers, the easiest way to prevent such mistakes is to assign privileges so that a user cannot accidentally change tables on the wrong server. This is, however, not always possible and cannot prevent the case just shown.

Slave Promotion

The procedures described so far work well when you have a master running that you can use to synchronize the standby and the slave before the switchover, but what happens when the master dies all of a sudden? Because replication has stopped in its tracks with all slaves (including the standby), there is no way to know what is on each slave. If the standby is ahead of all the slaves that need to be reassigned, there is no problem, because you can run replication on each slave to the place where the standby stopped. You will lose any changes that were made on the master but not yet sent to the standby. We will cover how to handle the recovery of the master in this case separately.

If the standby is behind one of the slaves, you shouldn't use the standby as the new master, because the slave knows more than the standby. As a matter of fact, it would be better if the slave that has replicated most events from the common master (which is now "more knowledgeable") were the master instead!

This is exactly the approach taken to handle master failures using slave promotion: instead of trying to keep a dedicated standby around (which then might not be the best candidate), ensure that any one of the slaves connected to the master can be promoted to master and take over at the point where the master was lost. By selecting the "most knowledgeable" slave as the new master, you guarantee that none of the other slaves will be more knowledgeable than the new master, so they can connect to the new master and read events from it.

There is, however, a critical issue that needs to be resolved: osynchronizing all slaves with the new master so that no events are lost or repeated. The problem in this situation is that all of the slaves need to read events from the new master.

The traditional method for promoting a slave

Before delving into the final solution, let us first take a look at the traditionally recommended way for handling slave promotion. This will work as a good introduction to the problem.

Figure 5-7 shows a typical setup with a master and several slaves.

For the traditional method of slave promotion, the following are required:

- Each promotable slave must have a user account for the replication user.
- Each promotable slave should run with `log-bin` with the binary log enabled.
- Each promotable slave should run *without* the `log-slave-updates` option (the reason will become obvious shortly).

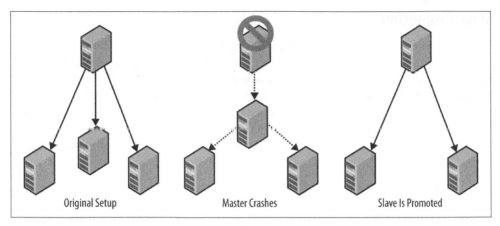

| Original Setup | Master Crashes | Slave Is Promoted |

Figure 5-7. Promoting a slave to replace a failed master

Assume you are starting with the original setup shown in Figure 5-7 and that the master fails. You can promote a slave to be the new master by doing the following:

1. Stop the slave using `STOP SLAVE`.

2. Reset the slave that is going to be the new master using `RESET MASTER`. This will ensure the slave starts as the new master and that any connecting slave will start reading events from the time the slave was promoted.

3. Connect the other slaves to the new master using `CHANGE MASTER`. Because you reset the new master, you can start replication from the beginning of the binary log, so it is not necessary to provide any position to `CHANGE MASTER`.

Unfortunately, this approach is based on an assumption that is not generally true—that the slaves have received all changes that the master has made. In a typical setup, the slaves will lag behind the master to various degrees. It might be just a few transactions, but nevertheless, they lag behind. This means that each slave needs to fetch the missing transactions somehow, and if none of the other slaves have a binary log enabled, there is no way to provide these changes to the slaves. The situation can be handled by figuring out what slave has seen most of the master's changes (the *most knowlegeable* slave) and then synchronize all the other slaves with the most knowledgeable slave by either copying the entire database, or using something like the *mysqldbcompare* to get the changes to the slaves.

Regardless of that, this approach is so simple that it is useful if you can handle lost transactions or if you are operating under a low load.

A revised method for promoting a slave

The traditional approach to promoting a slave is inadequate in most cases because slaves usually lag behind the master. Figure 5-8 illustrates the typical situation when the master disappears unexpectedly. The box labeled "binary log" in the center is the master's binary log and each arrow represents how much of the binary log the slave has executed.

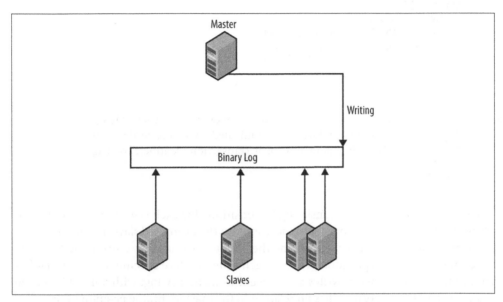

Figure 5-8. Binary log positions of the master and the connected slaves

In the figure, each slave has stopped at a different binlog position, and even the most knowledgeable slave has not got all the transactions from the now defunct master. The transactions that have not been replicated to the new master are lost forever (it will become clear why in "Consistency in a Hierarchical Deployment" on page 180), and the transactions missing from the lagging slaves have to be transferred from the most knowledgeable slave. The situation is resolved by promoting one slave (the most knowledgeable one) to be the new master and then synchronizing the other slaves to it. In Example 5-4, you can find code to order the slaves based on their master positions. This works if the slaves are connected to the same master, which means that the coordinates are comparable.

Example 5-4. Python code to find the best slave

```python
from mysql.replicant.commands import (
    fetch_slave_position,
)

def fetch_gtid_executed(server):
    server.connect()
```

```
    result = server.sql(
        "SELECT server_id, trans_id FROM Last_Exec_Trans"
        )
    server.disconnect()
    return result

def order_slaves_on_position(slaves):
    entries = []
    for slave in slaves:
        pos = fetch_slave_position(slave)
        gtid = fetch_gtid_executed(slave)
        entries.append((pos, gtid, slave))
    entries.sort(key=lambda x: x[0])
    return [ entry[1:2] for entry in entries ]
```

 With the introduction of native support for GTIDs in MySQL version 5.6, this problem was eliminated. A complete description of GTIDs can be found in "Global Transaction Identifiers" on page 260.

The critical problem lies in translating the positions for each slave (which are the positions in the now-defunct master) to positions on the promoted slave. In versions prior to 5.6, the history of events executed and the binlog positions they correspond to on the slaves are lost in the replication process. Each time the slave executes an event that has arrived from the master, it writes a *new* event to its binary log, with a *new* binary log position. The slave's position has no relation to the master's binlog position of the same event. The only option that remains is to implement an alternative version of GTIDs and scan the binary log of the promoted slave. The alternative implementation of GTIDs is described in Appendix B. You can see a Python implementation of slave promotion in Example 5-5.

Example 5-5. Slave promotion in Python

```
def promote_best_slave(slaves):
    entries = order_slaves_on_position(slaves) ❶
    _, master = entries.pop() ❷
    for gtid, slave in entries:
        pos_on_master = find_position_from_gtid(master, gtid) ❸
        switch_to_master(master, slave, pos_on_master) ❹
```

❶ Here the positions of each slave are fetched using the function introduced in Appendix B, which uses SHOW SLAVE STATUS to fetch the position of the last executed event.

❷ Pick the slave with the highest position to promote to master. If there are several that have the highest position, pick either one.

❸ This will connect to the promoted slave and scan the binary log to find the GTID of the last executed transaction for each slave. This step will give you a binlog position on the promoted slave for each GTID that you collected.

❹ Reconnect each slave to the promoted slave, starting at the position retrieved from the new master's binary log.

Circular Replication

After reading about dual masters, you might wonder whether it is possible to set up a multimaster with more than two masters replicating to each other. Because each slave can only have a single master, it is possible to get this configuration only by setting up replication in a circular fashion.

Before MySQL 5.6, this this was not a recommended setup, but it is certainly possible. With the introduction of global transaction IDs in MySQL 5.6, many of the reasons for rejecting circular replication are no longer valid, because the main problem is to get it to work correctly in the presence of failure.

Using a circular replication setup with three or more servers can be quite practical for reasons of locality. As a real-life example, consider the case of a mobile phone operator with subscribers all over Europe. Because mobile phone users travel around quite a lot, it is convenient to have the registry for the customers close to the actual phone, so by placing the data centers at some strategic places in Europe, it is possible to quickly verify call data and also register new calls locally. The changes can then be replicated to all the servers in the ring, and eventually all servers will have accurate billing information. In this case, circular replication is a perfect setup: all subscriber data is replicated to all sites, and updates of data are allowed in all data centers.

Setting up circular replication (as shown in Figure 5-9) is quite easy. Example 5-6 provides a script that sets up circular replication automatically, so where are the complications? As in every setup, you should ask yourself, "What happens when something goes wrong?"

Example 5-6. Setting up circular replication

```
def circular_replication(server_list):
    from mysql.replicant.commands import change_master
    for source, target in zip(server_list, server_list[1:] + [server_list[0]]):
        change_master(target, source)
```

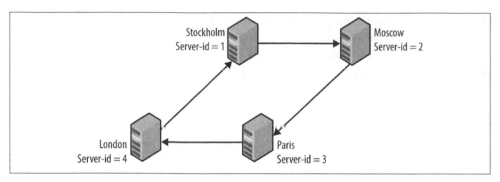

Figure 5-9. Circular replication setup

In Figure 5-9, there are four servers named for the cities in which they are located (the names are arbitrarily picked and do not reflect a real setup). Replication goes in a circle: Stockholm to Moscow to Paris to London and back to Stockholm. This means that Moscow is upstream of Paris, but downstream of Stockholm. Suppose that Moscow goes down suddenly and unexpectedly. To allow replication to continue, it is necessary to reconnect the "downstream" server Paris to the "upstream" server Stockholm to ensure the continuing operation of the system.

Figure 5-10 shows a scenario in which a single server fails and the servers reconnect to allow replication to continue. Sounds simple enough, doesn't it? Well, it's not really as simple as it looks. There are basically three potential problems:

- The downstream server—the server that was slave to the failed master—needs to connect to the upstream server and start replication from what it last saw. How is that position decided?

- Suppose that the crashed server has managed to send out some events before crashing. What happens with those events?

- We need to consider how we should bring the failed server into the topology again. What if the server applied some transactions of its own that were written to the binary log but not yet sent out? It is clear that these transactions are lost, so we need to handle this.

As you will see, all of these issues are easy to solve with the global transaction identifiers introduced in MySQL 5.6. When detecting that one of the servers failed, just use the CHANGE MASTER command to connect the downstream server to the upstream server using the MASTER_AUTO_POSITION=1 option:

```
paris> CHANGE MASTER TO
    ->    MASTER_HOST='stockholm.example.com',
    ->    MASTER_AUTO_POSITION = 1;
```

Because each server remembers what transactions were seen, any transactions that was sent out by the failing server will be applied to each remaining server in the ring exactly *once*. This means that it automatically handles the second and third issues from our list.

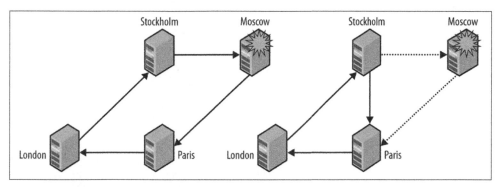

Figure 5-10. Changing topology in response to a failing server

Because the failed server can be in an alternative future (see Figure 6-8) compared to the other servers, bringing the server back in the ring will cause the missing transaction to "suddenly appear" (from the perspective of the application using the database), and this might not be what you want. The safest way to bring it into the circle again is to restore the server from one of the servers in the ring and reconnect the circle so that the new server is in the ring again.

Conclusion

High availability is a nontrivial concept to implement in practice. In this chapter, we presented a look into high availability and how you can achieve it with MySQL. In the next chapter, we will look more at high availability as we examine a companion topic: scaling out.

Joel's email notification chime sounded. He clicked on his email and opened the latest message. It was from Mr. Summerson, who made comments about his report. He read it through and at the bottom found what he expected. It read, "I like the redundancy ideas and especially the hot standby strategy. Make this happen."

Joel sighed as he realized his plans for getting to know some of his coworkers were going to have to wait. He had a lot of work to do.

## CHAPTER 6

MySQL Replication for Scale-Out

Joel stood and stretched and figured it was time for a soda. As he walked around his desk, headed to the break room, his boss met him at his door. "Good afternoon, sir."

"Hey, Joel. We just sold a bunch of licenses for our new applications. The marketing people tell me we can expect to see an increase in load of at least tenfold on the database server."

Joel raised his eyebrows. He had added a single slave just last week and that had improved the load problem, but not entirely.

"We need to scale out, Joel."

"Yes, sir. I'll get right on it."

Mr. Summerson tapped Joel on the shoulder and smiled, then walked down the hall to his office.

Joel stood still for a few moments as he pondered what "scale out" meant and formed a plan. "I've got to do a little more reading," he mumbled as he headed to the break room.

When the load starts to increase—and if you are running a successful deployment, it is just a matter of *when* it will start to increase—you can handle it in two ways. The first is to buy larger and more powerful servers to handle the increased load, which is called *scaling up*, whereas the second is to add more servers to handle the increased load, which is called *scaling out*. Of these two, scaling out is by far the more popular solution because it usually involves buying a batch of low-cost standard servers and is much more cost-effective.

In addition to handling an increased load, additional servers can support high availability and other business requirements. When used effectively, scaling out puts the combined resources—such as computing power—of all the servers to best use.

This chapter doesn't go into all the hardware, network, and other considerations involved in scaling out—those are beyond the scope of this book and are covered to some degree in *High Performance MySQL*, but we will talk about how to set up replication in MySQL to make the best use of scale-out. After some basic instructions for replication, we'll start to develop a Python library that makes it easy to administer replication over large sets of servers, and we'll examine how replication fits into your organization's business needs.

All the code in this chapter (as well as the other chapters of the book) can be found in the MySQL Replicant source code repository at Launchpad (*http://bit.ly/mysqllaunch*).

The most common uses for scaling out and replication are:

Load balancing for reads
> The master is occupied with updating data, so it can be wise to have separate servers to answer queries. Because queries only need to read data, you can use replication to send changes on the master to slaves—as many as you feel you need—so that they have current data and can process queries.

Load balancing for writes
> High-traffic deployments distribute processing over many computers, sometimes several thousand. Here, replication plays a critical role in distributing the information to be processed. The information can be distributed in many different ways based on the business use of your data and the nature of the use:
>
> - Distributed based on the information's role. Rarely updated tables can be kept on a single server, while frequently updated tables are partitioned over several servers.
>
> - Partitioned by geographic region so that traffic can be directed to the closest server.

Disaster avoidance through hot standby
> If the master goes down, everything will stop—it will not be possible to execute (perhaps critical) transactions, get information about customers, or retrieve other critical data. This is something that you want to avoid at (almost) any cost as it can severely disrupt your business. The easiest solution is to configure a slave with the sole purpose of acting as a hot standby, ready to take over the job of the master if it fails.

Disaster avoidance through remote replication
> Every deployment runs the risk of having a data center go down due to a disaster, be it a power failure, an earthquake, or a flood. To mitigate this, use replication to transport information between geographically remote sites.

Making backups

> Keeping an extra server around for making backups is very common. This allows you to make your backups without having to disturb the master at all, because you can take the backup server offline and do whatever you like with it.

Report generation

> Creating reports from data on a server will degrade the server's performance, in some cases significantly. If you're running lots of background jobs to generate reports, it's worth creating a slave just for this purpose. You can get a snapshot of the database at a certain time by stopping replication on the slave and then running large queries on it without disturbing the main business server. For example, if you stop replication after the last transaction of the day, you can extract your daily reports while the rest of the business is humming along at its normal pace.

Filtering or partitioning data

> If the network connection is slow, or if some data should not be available to certain clients, you can add a server to handle data filtering. This is also useful when the data needs to be partitioned and reside on separate servers.

Scaling Out Reads, Not Writes

It is important to understand that scaling out in this manner scales out reads, not writes. Each new slave has to handle the same write load as the master. The average load of the system can be described as follows:

$$AverageLoad = \frac{\Sigma\, ReadLoad + \Sigma\, WriteLoad}{\Sigma\, Capacity}$$

So if you have a single server with a total capacity of 10,000 transactions per second, and there is a write load of 4,000 transactions per second on the master, while there is a read load of 6,000 transactions per second, the result will be:

$$AverageLoad = \frac{\Sigma\, ReadLoad + \Sigma\, WriteLoad}{\Sigma\, Capacity} = \frac{6000 + 4000}{10000} = 100\ \%$$

Now, if you add three slaves to the master, the total capacity increases to 40,000 transactions per second. Because the write queries are replicated as well, each query is executed a total of four times—once on the master and once on each of the three slaves—which means that each slave has to handle 4,000 transactions per second in write load. The total read load does not increase because it is distributed over the slaves. This means that the average load now is:

$$AverageLoad = \frac{\sum ReadLoad + \sum WriteLoad}{\sum Capacity} = \frac{6000 + 4 * 4000}{4 * 10000} = 55\%$$

Notice that in the formula, the capacity is increased by a factor of 4, as we now have a total of four servers, and replication causes the write load to increase by a factor of 4 as well.

It is quite common to forget that replication forwards to each slave all the write queries that the master handles. So you cannot use this simple approach to scale writes, only reads. In the next chapter, you will see how to scale writes using a technique called *sharding*.

The Value of Asynchronous Replication

MySQL replication is *asynchronous*, a type of replication particularly suitable for modern applications such as websites.

To handle a large number of reads, sites use replication to create copies of the master and then let the slaves handle all read requests while the master handles the write requests. This replication is considered asynchronous because the master does not wait for the slaves to apply the changes, but instead just dispatches each change request to the slaves and assumes they will catch up eventually and replicate all the changes. This technique for improving performance is usually a good idea when you are scaling out.

In contrast, synchronous replication keeps the master and slaves in sync and does not allow a transaction to be committed on the master unless the slave agrees to commit it as well (i.e., synchronous replication makes the master wait for all the slaves to keep up with the writes).

Asynchronous replication is a lot faster than synchronous replication, for reasons our description should make obvious. Compared to asynchronous replication, synchronous replication requires extra synchronizations to guarantee consistency. It is usually implemented through a protocol called *two-phase commit*, which guarantees consistency between the master and slaves, but requires extra messages to ping-pong between them. Typically, it works like this:

1. When a commit statement is executed, the transaction is sent to the slaves and the slave is asked to prepare for a commit.

2. Each slave prepares the transaction so that it can be committed, and then sends an OK (or ABORT) message to the master, indicating that the transaction is prepared (or that it could not be prepared).

3. The master waits for all slaves to send either an OK or an ABORT message:

a. If the master receives an OK message from all slaves, it sends a commit message to all slaves asking them to commit the transaction.

b. If the master receives an ABORT message from any of the slaves, it sends an ABORT message to all slaves asking them to abort the transaction.

4. Each slave is then waiting for either an OK or an ABORT message from the master.

a. If the slaves receive the commit request, they commit the transaction and send an acknowledgment to the master that the transaction is committed.

b. If the slaves receive an abort request, they abort the transaction by undoing any changes and releasing any resources they held, then send an acknowledgment to the master that the transaction was aborted.

5. When the master has received acknowledgments from all slaves, it reports the transaction as committed (or aborted) and continues with processing the next transaction.

What makes this protocol slow is that it requires a total of four messages, including the messages with the transaction and the prepare request. The major problem is not the amount of network traffic required to handle the synchronization, but the latency introduced by the network and by processing the commit on the slave, together with the fact that the commit is blocked on the master until all the slaves have acknowledged the transaction. In contrast, asynchronous replication requires only a single message to be sent with the transaction. As a bonus, the master does not have to wait for the slave, but can report the transaction as committed immediately, which improves performance significantly.

So why is it a problem that synchronous replication blocks each commit while the slaves process it? If the slaves are close to the master on the network, the extra messages needed by synchronous replication make little difference, but if the slaves are not nearby— maybe in another town or even on another continent—it makes a big difference.

Table 6-1 shows some examples for a server that can commit 10,000 transactions per second. This translates to a commit time of 0.1 ms (but note that some implementations, such as MySQL Cluster, are able to process several commits in parallel if they are independent). If the network latency is 0.01 ms (a number we've chosen as a baseline by pinging one of our own computers), the transaction commit time increases to 0.14 ms, which translates to approximately 7,000 transactions per second. If the network latency is 10 ms (which we found by pinging a server in a nearby city), the transaction commit time increases to 40.1 ms, which translates to about 25 transactions per second! In contrast, asynchronous replication introduces no delay at all, because the transactions are reported as committed immediately, so the transaction commit time stays at the original 10,000 per second, just as if there were no slaves.

Table 6-1. Typical slowdowns caused by synchronous replication

Latency (ms)	Transaction commit time (ms)	Equivalent transactions per second	Example case
0.01	0.14	~7,100	Same computer
0.1	0.5	~2,000	Small LAN
1	4.1	~240	Bigger LAN
10	40.1	~25	Metropolitan network
100	400.1	~2	Satellite

The performance of asynchronous replication comes at the price of consistency. Recall that in asynchronous replication the transaction is reported as committed immediately, *without* waiting for any acknowledgment from the slave. This means the master may consider the transaction committed when the slave does not. As a matter of fact, it might not even have left the master, but is still waiting to be sent to the slave.

There are two problems with this that you need to be aware of:

- In the event of crashes on the master, transactions can "disappear."
- A query executed on the slaves might return old data.

Later in this chapter, we will talk about how to ensure you are reading current data, but for now, just remember that asynchronous replication comes with its own set of caveats that you have to handle.

Managing the Replication Topology

A deployment is scaled by creating new slaves and adding them to the collection of computers you have. The term *replication topology* refers to the ways you connect servers using replication. Figure 6-1 shows some examples of replication topologies: a simple topology, a tree topology, a dual-master topology, and a circular topology.

These topologies are used for different purposes: the dual-master topology handles failovers elegantly, for example, and circular replication and dual masters allow different sites to work locally while still replicating changes over to the other sites.

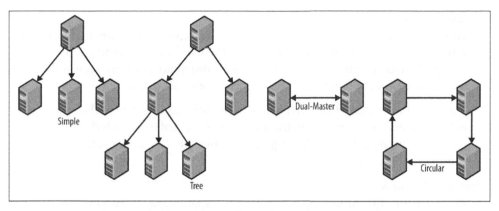

Figure 6-1. Simple, tree, dual-master, and circular replication topologies

The simple and tree topologies are used for scale-out. The use of replication causes the number of reads to greatly exceed the number of writes. This places special demands on the deployment in two ways:

It requires load balancing

We're using the term *load balancing* here to describe any way of dividing queries among servers. Replication creates both reasons for load balancing and methods for doing so. First, replication imposes a basic division of the load by specifying writes to be directed to the masters while reads go to the slaves. Furthermore, you sometimes have to send a particular query to a particular slave.

It requires you to manage the topology

Servers crash sooner or later, which makes it necessary to replace them. Replacing a crashed slave might not be urgent, but you'll have to replace a crashed master quickly.

In addition to this, if a master crashes, clients have to be redirected to the new master. If a slave crashes, it has to be taken out of the pool of load balancers so no queries are directed to it.

To handle load balancing and management, you should put tools in place to manage the replication topology, specifically tools that monitor the status and performance of servers and tools to handle the distribution of queries.

For load balancing to be effective, it is necessary to have spare capacity on the servers. There are a few reasons for ensuring you have spare capacity:

Peak load handling

You need to have margins to be able to handle peak loads. The load on a system is never even, but fluctuates up and down. The spare capacity necessary to handle a large deployment depends a lot on the application, so you need to monitor it closely to know when the response times start to suffer.

Distribution cost

You need to have spare capacity for running the replication setup. Replication always causes a "waste" of some capacity on the overhead of running a distributed system. It involves extra queries to manage the distributed system, such as the extra queries necessary to figure out where to execute a read query.

One item that is easily forgotten is that each slave has to perform the same writes as the master. The queries from the master are executed in an orderly manner (i.e., serially), with no risk of conflicting updates, but the slave needs extra capacity for running replication.

Administrative tasks

Restructuring the replication setup requires spare capacity so you can support temporary dual use, like when moving data between servers.

Load balancing works in two basic ways: either the application asks for a server based on the type of query, or an intermediate layer—usually referred to as a *proxy*—analyzes the query and sends it to the correct server.

Using an intermediate layer to analyze and distribute the queries (as shown in Figure 6-2) is by far the most flexible approach, but it has two disadvantages:

- There is a performance degradation when using a proxy because of two reasons: processing resources have to be spent on analyzing queries and there is an extra hop introduced for the queries that now have to go through the proxy. Processing the query may delay it—because it has to be parsed and analyzed twice (once by the proxy and again by the MySQL server)—but the latency introduced by the extra hop is likely to exceed the time for analyzing the query. Depending on the application, this may or may not be a problem.

- Correct query analysis can be hard to implement, sometimes even impossible. A proxy will often hide the internal structure of the deployment from the application programmer so that it should not be necessary to make the hard choices. For this reason, the client may send a query that can be very hard to analyze properly and might require a significant rewrite before being sent to the servers.

One of the tools that you can use for proxy load balancing is MySQL Proxy. It contains a full implementation of the MySQL client protocol, and therefore can act as a server for the real client connecting to it and as a client when connecting to the MySQL server. This means that it can be fully transparent: a client can't distinguish between the proxy and a real server.

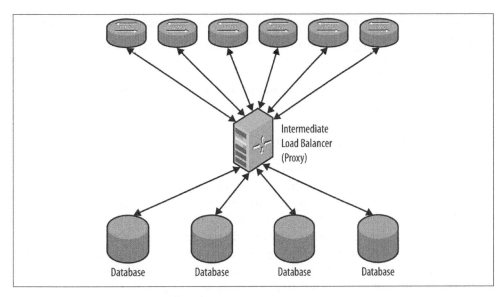

Figure 6-2. Using a proxy to distribute queries

The MySQL Proxy is controlled using the Lua programming language. It has a built-in Lua engine that executes small—and sometimes not so small—programs to intercept and manipulate both the queries and the result sets. Because the proxy is controlled using a real programming language, it can carry out a variety of sophisticated tasks, including query analysis, query filtering, query manipulation, and query distribution.

Configuration and programming of the MySQL Proxy are beyond the scope of this book, but there are extensive publications about it online. Some of the ones we find useful are:

Jan Kneschke (http://jan.kneschke.de)
> Jan Kneschke is the original author of the MySQL Proxy and has several good presentations and posts about the Proxy.

The MySQL Reference Manual (http://bit.ly/mysql-56-ref)
> The MySQL Proxy section of the MySQL Reference Manual contain the details of the implementation as well as an introduction to writing scripts for the MySQL Proxy.

The precise methods for using a proxy depend entirely on the type of proxy you use, so we will not cover that information here. Instead, we'll focus on using a load balancer in the application layer. There are a number of load balancers available, including:

- Hardware
- Simple software load balancers, such as Balance (*http://www.inlab.de/balance.html*)

- Peer-based systems, such as Wackamole (*http://www.backhand.org/wackamole/*)
- Full-blown clustering solutions, such as the Linux Virtual Server (*http://www.linux virtualserver.org/*)

It is also possible to distribute the load on the DNS level and to handle the distribution directly in the application.

Application-Level Load Balancing

The most straightforward approach to load balancing at the application level is to have the application ask the load balancer for a connection based on the type of query it is going to send. In most cases, the application already knows whether the query is going to be a read or write query, and which tables will be affected. In fact, forcing the application developer to consider these issues when designing the queries may produce other benefits for the application, usually in the form of improved overall performance of the system. Based on this information, a load balancer can provide a connection to the right server, which the application can then use to execute the query.

A load balancer on the application layer needs to have a store with information about the servers and what queries they should handle. Functions in the application layer send queries to this store, which returns the name or IP address of the MySQL server to query. The lookup procedure can either be placed in the application, or inside the connector if it supports it. Many connectors support ways for providing information about servers without a central store, but then you need to have means for seeding the connectors with this information, or provide it through the application.

Example of an application-level load balancer

Let's develop a simple load balancer like the one shown in Figure 6-3 for use by the application layer. PHP is being used for the presentation logic because it's so popular on web servers. It is necessary to write functions for updating the server pool information and functions to fetch servers from the pool.

The pool is implemented by creating a table with all the servers in the deployment in a common database that is shared by all nodes. In this case, we just use the host and port as primary key for the table (instead of creating a host ID) and create a *common* database to contain the tables of the shared data.

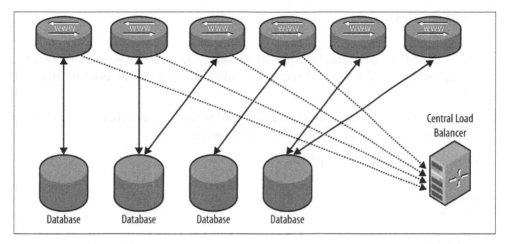

Figure 6-3. Load balancing on the application level

You should duplicate the central store so that it doesn't create a single point of failure. In addition, because the list of available servers does not often change, load balancing information is a perfect candidate for caching.

For the sake of simplicity—and to avoid introducing dependencies on other systems— we demonstrate the application-level load balancer using a pure MySQL implementation. There are many other techniques that you can use that do not involve MySQL. The most common technique is to use round-robin DNS; another alternative is using Memcached, which is a distributed in-memory key/value store.

Also note that the addition of an extra query (to query the common database) is a significant overhead for high-performing systems and should be avoided. This is traditionally done using a cache for the information, but we start with an implementation without caches. You will see how to add caches in Example 6-5.

The load balancer lists servers in the load balancer pool, separated into categories based on what kind of queries they can handle. Information about the servers in the pool is stored in a central repository. The implementation consists of a table in the common database given in Example 6-1, the load balancer in Example 6-2 for querying the load balancer from the application, and the Python functions in Example 6-3 for updating information about the servers.

Example 6-1. Database tables for the load balancer

```
CREATE TABLE nodes (
  host VARCHAR(28) NOT NULL,
  port INT UNSIGNED NOT NULL,
  sock VARCHAR(80)
  type ENUM('OL','RO','RW') NOT NULL DEFAULT '',
```

```
  PRIMARY KEY (host, port)
);
```

The store contains the host and the port of the server, as well as if it is an offline (OL), read-only (RO), or read-write (RW) server. The offline setting can be used for maintenance.

Example 6-2 shows code for implementing a load balancer. It consists of a dictionary class responsible for dealing out connections to servers.

Example 6-2. Load balancer in PHP

```
define('DB_OFFLINE', 'OL')
define('DB_RW', 'RW');
define('DB_RO', 'RO');

$FETCH_QUERY = <<<END_OF_QUERY
SELECT host, port FROM nodes ❶
 WHERE FIND_IN_SET(?, type)
ORDER BY RAND() LIMIT 1
END_OF_QUERY;

class Dictionary { ❷
  private $server;

  public function __construct($host, $user, $pass, $port = 3306) {
    $this->server = new mysqli($host, $user, $pass, 'metainfo', $port);
  }

  public function get_connection($user, $pass, $db, $hint) { ❸
    global $FETCH_QUERY;
    $type = $hint['type'];
    if ($stmt = $this->server->prepare($FETCH_QUERY)){
      $stmt->bind_param('s', $type);
      $stmt->execute();
      $stmt->bind_result($host, $port);
      if ($stmt->fetch())
        return new mysqli($host, $user, $pass, $db, $port);
    }
    return null;
  }
}
```

❶   A simple SELECT will suffice to find all the servers that can accept the query. Because we want just a single server, we limit the output to a single line using the LIMIT modifier to the SELECT query, and to distribute queries evenly among available servers, we use the ORDER BY RAND() modifier.

❷ A dictionary class is introduced (and will be used in the remainder of the book) whose responsibility is to deal out connections to MySQL instances. When a dictionary class instance is constructed, information about the MySQL server that stores the information needs to be provided. This server stores information about each server in the deployment, in order to manage the connections to them.

❸ The `get_connection` function is used to request a connection to a server in the deployment. What server to connect to is decided based on a *hint* passed to `get_connection`. The hint is an associative array with information about what sort of connection is requested, and the function will deliver a connection to a server matching the criteria. In this case, the hint conveys only whether a read-only or read-write server is requested.

The final task is to provide utility functions for adding and removing servers and for updating the capabilities of a server. Because these are mainly to be used from the administration logic, we've implemented this function in Python using the Replicant library. The utility consists of three functions, demonstrated in Example 6-3:

`pool_add(common, server, type)`
Adds a *server* to the pool. The pool is stored at the server denoted by *common*, and the *type* to use is a list—or other iterable—of values to set.

`pool_del(common, server)`
Deletes a server from the pool.

`pool_set(common, server, type)`
Changes the type of the *server*.

Example 6-3. Administrative functions for the load balancer

```
from mysql.replicant.errors import (
    Error,
)

from MySQLdb import IntegrityError

class AlreadyInPoolError(Error):
    pass

_INSERT_SERVER = ("INSERT INTO nodes(host, port, sock, type)"
                  "VALUES (%s, %s, %s, %s)")

_DELETE_SERVER = ("DELETE FROM nodes"
                  " WHERE host = %s AND port = %s")

_UPDATE_SERVER = ("UPDATE nodes SET type = %s"
                  " WHERE host = %s AND port = %s")
```

```python
def pool_add(common, server, types=None):
    if types is None:
        types = []
    common.use("common")
    try:
        common.sql(_INSERT_SERVER,
                   (server.host, server.port, server.socket, ','.join(types)))
    except IntegrityError:
        raise AlreadyInPoolError

def pool_del(common, server):
    common.use("common")
    common.sql(_DELETE_SERVER,
               (server.host, server.port))

def pool_set(common, server, types=None):
    if types is None:
        types = []
    common.use("common")
    common.sql(_UPDATE_SERVER,
               (','.join(types), server.host, server.port))
```

These functions can be used as shown in the following examples:

```python
pool_add(common, master, ['READ', 'WRITE'])

for slave in slaves:
    pool_add(common, slave, ['READ'])
```

With everything in place, the load balancer can be used as in Example 6-4, where the dictionary is set up to use central.example.com for the central repository. After that, get_connection can be used to get connections to the server based on the hint provided.

Example 6-4. PHP code using the load balancer

```php
$DICT = new Dictionary("central.example.com", "mats", "");

$QUERY = <<<END_OF_QUERY
SELECT first_name, last_name, dept_name
FROM employees JOIN dept_emp USING (emp_no)
               JOIN departments USING (dept_no)
WHERE emp_no = ?
END_OF_QUERY;

$mysql = $DICT->get_connection('mats', 'xyzzy', 'employees',
                               array('type' => DB_RO));
$stmt = $mysql->prepare($QUERY);
if ($stmt) {
  $stmt->bind_param("d", $emp_no);
  $stmt->execute();
  $stmt->bind_result($first_name, $last_name, $dept_name);
  while ($stmt->fetch())
    print "$first_name $last_name $dept_name\n";
```

```
  $stmt->close();
}
else {
  echo "Error: " . $mysql->error;
}
```

In Example 6-2, a query is sent to the central repository for each query dispatched. This doubles the number of queries sent out by the application, and can lead to performance degradation. To solve this, you should cache the data from the central repository and fetch the information from the cache instead, as shown in Example 6-5.

Caches require a strategy for when to invalidate the cache. In this case, a simple *time to live* caching strategy is employed, where the cache is reloaded if it is too old. This is a very simple implementation, but it means that any changes to the topology are not recognized immediately. If any changes are made to the topology and you change the information in the centralized store, you have to keep the old servers available until the timer expires; the information is guaranteed to be reloaded from the centralized store.

Example 6-5. Caching a load balancer in PHP

```
define('DB_RW', 'RW');
define('DB_RO', 'RO');
define('TTL', 60); ❶

$FETCH_QUERY = <<<END_OF_QUERY
SELECT host, port, type FROM nodes ❷
END_OF_QUERY;

class Dictionary {
  private $server;
  private $last_update;
  private $cache;

  public function __construct($host, $user, $pass, $port = 3306)
  {
    $this->server = new mysqli($host, $user, $pass,
                                    'metainfo', $port);
  }

  public function get_connection($user, $pass, $db, $hint)
  {
    if (time() > $this->last_update + TTL) ❸
      $this->update_cache();
    $type = $hint['type'];
    if (array_key_exists($type, $this->cache)) {
      $servers = $this->cache[$type];
      $no = rand(0, count($servers) - 1);
      list($host, $port) = $servers[$no]; ❹
      return new mysqli($host, $user, $pass, $db, $port);
    }
    else
```

```
      return null;
    }

  private function update_cache() {
    global $FETCH_QUERY;
    if ($stmt = $this->server->prepare($FETCH_QUERY)){ ❺
      $cache = array();
      $stmt->execute();
      $stmt->bind_result($host, $port, $type);
      while ($stmt->fetch()) ❻
        $cache[$type][] = array($host, $port);
      $this->cache = $cache;
      $this->last_update = time();
    }
  }
o }
}
```

❶ This constant is used for the "time to live" for the cache. A long time means that the centralized store is not queried as often, but it also means that changes in the topology are not recognized as fast.

❷ In contrast to Example 6-2, the entire contents of the centralized store are loaded with the query. In this case, it is assumed that the entire contents can be loaded, but for really large data sets, it might be more sensible to create a query that does not load parts of the dictionary table that are not going to be used.

❸ Check the last time the cache was updated. If it was more than TTL seconds ago, the cache will be updated. After this if statement has executed, it is guaranteed that the cache is up-to-date (or at least as up-to-date as it can be).

❹ Fetch the host and the port from the cache instead of from the server, as done in Example 6-2. Here, a random server is picked, but other policies are possible.

❺ Here we only update the cache if it is possible to prepare the query on the server. If the server cannot be contacted for some reason, you still have to be able to execute queries. In this code, it is assumed that the current contents of the cache can be used, at least for a while longer, while the database with the information restarts.

❻ Here the cache is filled based on the type of the server. Each entry in the cache contains a list of candidate servers for that type.

MySQL native driver replication and load balancing plug-in

The PHP team at MySQL has created several plug-ins to the MySQL Native Driver (*mysqlnd*). One of these plug-ins can be used for handling read-write splitting, load-balancing using a few different strategies, and failover handling. You can find more information on PHP.net (*http://bit.ly/mysqlnd*).

In contrast to the example implementation used earlier, *mysqlnd_ms* uses a configuration file containing information about where to failover. This means that it is very efficient (all the info is in memory), but also that it is static.

The information about the masters and the slaves is stored in a configuration file in JSON format similar to the file in Example 6-6. Here, the `master` is assumed to be read-write and the `slaves` are all read-only servers.

Example 6-6. Example of mysqlnd_ms configuration file

```
{
    "myapp": {
        "master": [
            { "host": "master1.example.com" }
            ],
        "slave": [
            { "host": "slave1.example.com", "port": "3306" },
            { "host": "slave2.example.com", "port": "3307" },
            { "host": "slave3.example.com", "port": "3308" }
            ]
        }
    }
}
```

When a connection is established, the hostname is used as a key into the structure in Example 6-6, and if a match is found, the connection information in one of the entries under the key is used instead. Which connection information is used depends on the policy set for the load balancer. The load balancer investigates the statement to decide where to send it. Any statement starting with SELECT is considered a read-only statement and will be sent to the slave, while any other statement is sent to the master. You can see example code for using *mysqlnd_ms* in Example 6-7.

Example 6-7. PHP code for using mysqlnd_ms

```
$QUERY = <<<END_OF_QUERY
SELECT first_name, last_name, dept_name ❶
FROM employees JOIN dept_emp USING (emp_no)
                JOIN departments USING (dept_no)
WHERE emp_no = ?
END_OF_QUERY;

$mysqli = new mysqli("myapp", "mats", "xyzzy", "employees"); ❷
$stmt = $mysql->prepare($QUERY);
if ($stmt) {
  $stmt->bind_param("d", $emp_no);
  $stmt->execute();
  $stmt->bind_result($first_name, $last_name, $dept_name);
  while ($stmt->fetch())
    print "$first_name $last_name $dept_name\n";
  $stmt->close();
}
```

```
else {
  echo "Error: " . $mysql->error;
}
```

❶   The query contains SELECT first, so the plug-in will assume that this is a read query and should be sent to a read slave.

❷   Note that the hostname given is not a real hostname, but rather a reference to the myapp key in the configuration file. The plug-in will use this information to dispatch the query to the correct server.

Hierarchical Replication

Although the master is quite good at handling a large number of slaves, there is a limit to how many slaves it can handle before the load becomes too high for comfort (roughly 70 slaves for each master seems to be a practical limit, but as you probably realize, this depends a lot on the application), and an unresponsive master is always a problem. In those cases, you can add an extra slave (or several) as a *relay slave* (or simply *relay*), whose only purpose is to lighten the load of replication on the master by taking care of a bunch of slaves. Using a relay in this manner is called *hierarchical replication*. Figure 6-4 illustrates a typical setup with a master, a relay, and several slaves connected to the relay.

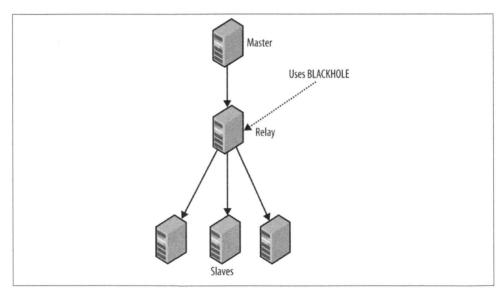

Figure 6-4. Hierarchical topology with master, relay, and slaves

By default, the changes the slave receives from its master are not written to the binary log of the slave, so if SHOW BINLOG EVENTS is executed on the slave in the previous setup,

---

you will not see any events in the binlog. The reason for this is that there is no point in wasting disk space by recording the changes; if there is a problem and, say, the slave crashes, you can always recover by cloning the master or another slave.

On the other hand, the relay server needs to keep a binary log to record all the changes, because the relay passes them on to other slaves. Unlike typical slaves, however, the relay doesn't need to actually apply changes to a database of its own, because it doesn't answer queries.

In short, a typical slave needs to apply changes to a database, but not to a binary log. A relay server needs to keep a binary log, but does not apply changes to a database.

To avoid writing changes to the database, it is necessary to keep tables around (so the statements can be executed), but the changes should just be thrown away. A storage engine named Blackhole was created for purposes just like this one. The Blackhole engine accepts all statements and always reports success in executing them, but any changes are just thrown away. A relay introduces an extra delay that can cause its slaves to lag further behind the master than slaves that are directly connected to the master. This lag should be balanced against the benefits of removing some load from the master, because managing a hierarchical setup is significantly more difficult than managing a simple setup.

Setting Up a Relay Server

Setting up a relay server is quite easy, but we have to consider what to do with tables that are being created on the relay as well as what to do with tables that already exist on the relay when we change its role. Not keeping data in the databases will make processing events faster and reduce the lag for the slaves at the end of the replication process, because there is no data to be updated. To set up a relay server, we thus have to:

1. Configure the slave to forward any events executed by the slave thread by writing them to the binlog of the relay slave.

2. Change the storage engine for all tables on the relay server to use the BLACKHOLE storage engine to preserve space and improve performance.

3. Ensure that any new tables added to the relay also use the BLACKHOLE engine.

Configuring the relay server to forward events executed by the slave thread is done by adding the log-slave-updates option to *my.cnf*, as demonstrated earlier.

In addition to setting log-slave-updates, it is necessary to change the default storage engine using the default-storage-engine in the *my.cnf* file. You can temporarily change the storage engine on the relay by issuing the command **SET STORAGE_ENGINE = 'BLACKHOLE'**, but that setting will not persist if the server is restarted.

The final task is to change the storage engine for all tables *already* on the relay server to use BLACKHOLE. Do this using the ALTER TABLE statement to change the storage engine for each table on the server. Because the ALTER TABLE statements shouldn't be written to the binary log (the last thing we want is for slaves to discard the changes they receive!), turn off the binary log temporarily while executing the ALTER TABLE statements. This is shown in Example 6-8.

Example 6-8. Changing the engine for all tables in database windy

```
relay> SHOW TABLES FROM windy;
+-----------------+
| Tables_in_windy |
+-----------------+
| user_data       |
     .
     .
     .
| profile         |
+-----------------+
45 row in set (0.15 sec)
relay> SET SQL_LOG_BIN = 0;
relay> ALTER TABLE user_data ENGINE = 'BLACKHOLE';
     .
     .
     .
relay> ALTER TABLE profile ENGINE = 'BLACKHOLE';
relay> SET SQL_BIN_LOG = 1;
```

This is all you need to turn a server into a relay server. The usual way you come to employ a relay is to start with a setup in which all slaves attach directly to a master and discover after some time that it is necessary to introduce a relay server. The reason is usually that the master has become too loaded, but there could be architectural reasons for making the change as well. So how do you handle that?

You can use what you learned in the previous sections and modify the existing deployment to introduce the new relay server by:

1. Connecting the relay server to the master and configuring it to act as a relay server.

2. Switching over the slaves one by one to the relay server.

Adding a Relay in Python

Let's turn to the task of developing support for administering relays by extending our library. Because we have a system for creating new roles and imbuing servers with those roles, let's use that by defining a special role for the relay server. This is shown in Example 6-9.

Example 6-9. Role definition for relay

```
from mysql.replicant import roles

class Relay(roles.Role):
    def __init__(self, master):
        super(Relay, self).__init__()
        self.__master = master

    def imbue(self, server):
        config = server.get_config()
        self._set_server_id(server, config)
        self._enable_binlog(server)
        config.set('mysqld', 'log-slave-updates' '1')
        server.put_config(config)
        server.sql("SET SQL_LOG_BIN = 0")
        for db in list of databases:
            for table in server.sql("SHOW TABLES FROM %s", (db)):
                server.sql("ALTER TABLE %s.%s ENGINE=BLACKHOLE",
                           (db,table))
        server.sql("SET SQL_LOG_BIN = 1")
```

Specialized Slaves

In the simple scale-out deployment—like the one described thus far—all slaves receive all data and can therefore handle any kind of query. It is, however, not very common to distribute requests evenly over the different parts of the data. Instead, there is usually some data that needs to be accessed very frequently and some that is rarely accessed. For example, consider the needs of an ecommerce site:

- The product catalog is browsed almost all the time.
- Data about items in stock may not be requested very often.
- User data is not requested very often, because most of the critical information is recorded using session-specific information stored in the browser as cookies.
- On the other hand, if cookies are disabled, the session data will be requested from the server with almost every page request.
- Newly added items are usually accessed more frequently than old items (e.g., "special offers" might be accessed more frequently than other items).

It would clearly be a waste of resources to keep the rarely accessed data on each and every slave just in case it is requested. It would be much better to use the deployment shown in Figure 6-5, where a few servers are dedicated to keeping rarely accessed data, while a different set of servers are dedicated to keeping data that is accessed frequently.

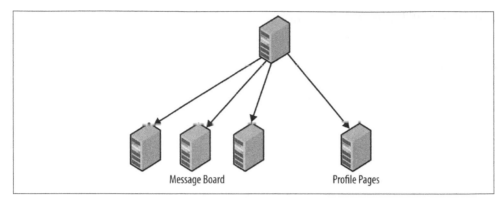

Figure 6-5. Replication topology with master and specialized slaves

To do this, it is necessary to separate tables when replicating. MySQL can do this by filtering the events that leave the master or, alternatively, filtering the events when they come to the slave.

Filtering Replication Events

The two different ways of filtering events are called *master filters* when the events are filtered on the master and *slave filters* when the events are filtered on the slave. The master filters control what goes into the binary log and therefore what is sent to the slaves, while slave filters control what is executed on the slave. For the master filters, events for filtered-out tables are not stored in the binary log at all, while for slave filters, the events are stored in the binary log and also sent to the slave and not filtered out until just before they are going to be executed.

This means that it is not possible to use PITR to recover these databases properly—if the databases are stored in the backup image, they will still be restored when restoring the backup, but any changes made to tables in the database since that moment will not be recovered, because the changes are not in the binary log.

If slave filters are used, all changes are sent over the network.

This clearly wastes network bandwidth, especially over long-haul network connections.

Later in this chapter, you will see a detailed discussion of the relative merits of master and slave filtering and an approach that allows the binary log to remain intact while still saving network bandwidth.

Master filters

There are two configuration options for creating master filters:

`binlog-do-db=`*db*

> If the current database of the statement is *db*, the statement will be written to the binary log; otherwise, the statement will be discarded.

`binlog-ignore-db=`*db*

> If the current database of the statement is *db*, the statement will be discarded; otherwise, the statement will be written to the binary log.

If you want to replicate everything except a few databases, use `binlog-ignore-db`. If you want to replicate just a few databases, use `binlog-do-db`. Combining them is *not* recommended, because the logic for deciding whether a database should be replicated or not is complicated (see Figure 4-3). The options do not accept lists of databases, so if you want to list several databases, you have to repeat an option multiple times.

As an example, to replicate everything except the `top` and `secret` databases, add the following options to the configuration file:

```
[mysqld]
...
binlog-ignore-db = top
binlog-ignore-db = secret
```

> Using `binlog-*-db` options to filter events means that the two databases will not be stored in the binary log at all, and hence cannot be recovered using PITR in the event of a crash. For that reason, it is strongly recommended that you use slave filters, not master filters, when you want to filter the replication stream. You should use master filters only for data that can be considered volatile and that you can afford to lose.

Slave filters

Slave filtering offers a longer list of options. In addition to being able to filter the events based on the database, slave filters can filter individual tables and even groups of table names by using wildcards.

In the following list of rules, the `replicate-wild` rules look at the full name of the table, including both the database and table name. The pattern supplied to the option uses the same patterns as the LIKE string comparison function—that is, an underscore (_) matches a single character, whereas a percent sign (%) matches a string of any length. Note, however, that the pattern must contain a period to be legitimate. This means that the database name and table name are matched individually, so each wildcard applies only to the database name or table name.

`replicate-do-db=`*db*

> If the current database of the statement is *db*, execute the statement.

`replicate-ignore-db=`*db*

> If the current database of the statement is *db*, discard the statement.

`replicate-do-table=`*db_name*`.`*tbl_name*
`replicate-wild-do-table=`*db_pattern*`.`*tbl_pattern*

> If the name of the table being updated is *table* or matches the pattern, execute updates to the table.

`replicate-ignore-table=`*db_name*`.`*tbl_name*
`replicate-wild-ignore-table=`*db_pattern*`.`*tbl_pattern*

> If the name of the table being updated is *table* or matches the pattern, discard updates to the table.

These filtering rules are evaluated just before the server decides whether to execute them, so all events are sent to the slave before being filtered.

Using Filtering to Partition Events to Slaves

So what are the benefits and drawbacks of filtering on the master versus filtering on the slave? At a brief glance, it might seem like a good idea to structure the databases so that it is possible to filter events on the master using the `binlog-*-db` options instead of using the `replicate-*-db` options. That way, the network is not laden with a lot of useless events that will be removed by the slave anyway. However, as mentioned earlier in the chapter, there are problems associated with filtering on the master:

- Because the events are filtered from the binary log and there is only a single binary log, it is not possible to "split" the changes and send different parts of the database to different servers.

- The binary log is also used for PITR, so if there are any problems with the server, it will not be possible to restore everything.

- If, for some reason, it becomes necessary to split the data differently, it will no longer be possible, because the binary log has already been filtered and cannot be "unfiltered."

It would be ideal if the filtering could be on the events sent from the master and not on the events written to the binary log. It would also be good if the filtering could be controlled by the slave so that the slave could decide which data to replicate. For MySQL version 5.1 and later, this is not possible, and instead, it is necessary to filter events using the `replicate-*` options—that is, to filter the events on the slave.

As an example, to dedicate a slave to the user data stored in the two tables `users` and `profiles` in the *app* database, shut down the server and add the following filtering options to the *my.cnf* file:

```
[mysqld]
...
replicate-wild-do-table=app.users
replicate-wild-do-table=app.profiles
```

If you are concerned about network traffic—which could be significant if you replicate over long-haul networks—you can set up a relay server on the same machine as the master, as shown in Figure 6-6 (or on the same network segment as the master), whose only purpose is to produce a filtered version of the master's binary log.

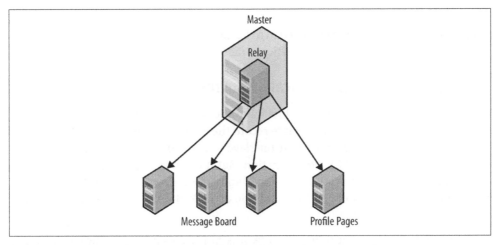

Figure 6-6. Filtering by putting master and relay on the same machine

Managing Consistency of Data

As discussed earlier in the chapter, one of the problems with asynchronous replication is managing consistency. To illustrate the problem, let's imagine you have an ecommerce site where customers can browse products and put items they want to purchase in a cart. You've set up your servers so that when a user adds an item to the cart, the change request goes to the master, but when the web server requests information about the contents of the cart, the query goes to one of the slaves tasked with answering such queries. Because the master is ahead of the slave, it is possible that the change has not reached the slave yet, so a query to the slave will then find the cart empty. This will, of course, come as a big surprise to the customer, who will then promptly add the item to the cart again only to discover that the cart now contains *two* items, because this time, the slave managed to catch up and replicate both changes to the cart. This situation clearly needs to be avoided or you will risk a bunch of irritated customers.

To avoid getting data that is too old, it is necessary to somehow ensure that the data provided by the slave is recent enough to be useful. As you will see, the problem becomes even trickier when a relay server is added to the mix. The basic idea of handling this is to somehow mark each transaction committed on the master, and then wait for the slave to reach that transaction (or later) before trying to execute a query on the slave.

With the introduction of *global transaction identifiers* (GTID) in MySQL 5.6, failing over slaves and clients has become significantly simpler because most of the techniques described here are handled automatically. The global transaction IDs are described in detail in "Global Transaction Identifiers" on page 260, but this chapter will to a large extent focus on the old solution for the benefit of users that have not transitioned to MySQL 5.6 yet. The differences between pre-5.6 and 5.6-based solution are highlighted in the reminder of the chapter.

Prior to MySQL 5.6, the problem needed to be handled in different ways depending on whether there are any relay servers between the master and the slave.

Consistency in a Nonhierarchical Deployment

When all the slaves are connected directly to the master, it is very easy to check for consistency. In this case, it is sufficient to record the binlog position after the transaction has been committed and then wait for the slave to reach this position using the previously introduced MASTER_POS_WAIT function. But it is not possible to get the exact position where a transaction was written in the binlog. Why? Because in the time between the commit of a transaction and the execution of SHOW MASTER STATUS, several events can be written to the binlog.

This does not matter, because in this case, it is not necessary to get the exact binlog position where the transaction was written; it is sufficient to get a position that is *at or later than* the position of the transaction. Because the SHOW MASTER STATUS command will show the position where replication is currently writing events, executing this after the transaction has committed will be sufficient for getting a binlog position that can be used for checking consistency.

Example 6-10 shows the PHP code for processing an update to guarantee that the data presented is not stale.

Example 6-10. PHP code for avoiding read of stale data

```
function fetch_master_pos($server) {
  $result = $server->query('SHOW MASTER STATUS');
  if ($result == NULL)
    return NULL;                          // Execution failed
  $row = $result->fetch_assoc();
  if ($row == NULL)
    return NULL;                          // No binlog enabled
  $pos = array($row['File'], $row['Position']);
  $result->close();
  return $pos;
}
```

```
function sync_with_master($master, $slave) {
  $pos = fetch_master_pos($master);
  if ($pos == NULL)
    return FALSE;
  if (!wait_for_pos($slave, $pos[0], $pos[1]))
    return FALSE;
  return TRUE;
}

function wait_for_pos($server, $file, $pos) {
  $result = $server->query(
    "SELECT MASTER_POS_WAIT('$file', $pos)");
  if ($result == NULL)
    return FALSE;                           // Execution failed
  $row = $result->fetch_row();
  if ($row == NULL)
    return FALSE;                           // Empty result set ?!
  if ($row[0] == NULL || $row[0] < 0)
    return FALSE;                           // Sync failed
  $result->close();
  return TRUE;
}

function commit_and_sync($master, $slave) {
  if ($master->commit()) {
    if (!sync_with_master($master, $slave))
      return NULL;                          // Synchronization failed
    return TRUE;                            // Commit and sync succeeded
  }
  return FALSE;                             // Commit failed (no sync done)
}

function start_trans($server) {
  $server->autocommit(FALSE);
}
```

Example 6-10 contains the functions commit_and_sync and start_trans together with three support functions, fetch_master_pos, wait_for_pos, and sync_with_master. The commit_and_sync function commits a transaction and waits for it to reach a designated slave. It accepts two arguments, a connection object to a master and a connection object to the slave. The function will return TRUE if the commit and the sync succeeded, FALSE if the commit failed, and NULL if the commit succeeded but the synchronization failed (either because there was an error in the slave or because the slave lost the master).

The function works by committing the current transaction and then, if that succeeds, fetching the current master binlog position through SHOW MASTER STATUS. Because other threads may have executed updates to the database between the commit and the call to SHOW MASTER STATUS, it is possible (even likely) that the position returned is not at the end of the transaction, but rather somewhere after where the transaction was written in the binlog. As mentioned earlier, this does not matter from an accuracy perspective, because the transaction will have been executed anyway when we reach this later position.

After fetching the binlog position from the master, the function proceeds by connecting to the slave and executing a wait for the master position using the MASTER_POS_WAIT function. If the slave is running, a call to this function will block and wait for the position to be reached, but if the slave is *not* running, NULL will be returned immediately. This is also what will happen if the slave stops while the function is waiting (like if an error occurs when the slave thread executes a statement). In either case, NULL indicates the transaction has not reached the slave, so it's important to check the result from the call. If MASTER_POS_WAIT returns 0, it means that the slave had already seen the transaction and therefore synchronization succeeds trivially.

To use these functions, it is sufficient to connect to the server as usual, but then use the functions to start, commit, and abort transactions. Example 6-11 shows examples of their use in context, but the error checking has been omitted because it is dependent on how errors are handled.

Example 6-11. Using the start_trans and commit_and_sync functions

```
require_once './database.inc';

start_trans($master);
$master->query('INSERT INTO t1 SELECT 2*a FROM t1');
commit_and_sync($master, $slave);
```

 PHP scripts have a maximum execution time, which defaults to 30 seconds. If the script exceeds this time, execution will be terminated. You need to keep that in mind when using the code in Example 6-10 by either running in safe mode, or changing the maximum execution time.

Consistency in a Hierarchical Deployment

Thanks to the global transaction identifiers introduced in MySQL 5.6, managing consistency in a MySQL 5.6 server is just as easy as in "Consistency in a Nonhierarchical Deployment" on page 178. Because the transaction identifier does not change between machines, it does not matter how many relay servers there are between the origin of the transaction and the server you connect to.

Managing consistency in a hierarchical deployment *before* MySQL 5.6 is significantly different from managing consistency in a simple replication topology where each slave is connected directly to the master. Because the positions are changed by every intermediate relay server, it is not possible to wait for a master position at the ultimate slave (the slave at the bottom at the hierarchy). Instead, it is necessary to figure out another way to wait for the transactions to reach the ultimate slave. There are basically two alternatives that you can use to ensure you are not reading stale data.

The first solution is to use the global transaction identifiers shown in Appendix B to handle slave promotions and to poll the slave repeatedly until it has processed the transaction. In contrast with the global transaction identifiers in MySQL 5.6, there is no wait function that we can use for these, so it is necessary to poll repeatedly.

The MASTER_POS_WAIT function is quite handy when it comes to handling the wait, so if it were possible to use that function, it would solve a lot of problems. The second solution, illustrated in Figure 6-7, uses this function to connect to each of the relay servers in the path from the master to the final slave to ensure the change propagates to the slave. It is necessary to connect to each relay slave between the master and the slave, because it is not possible to know which binlog position will be used on each of the relay servers.

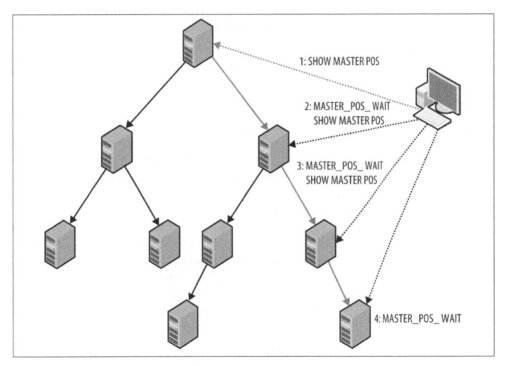

Figure 6-7. Synchronizing with all servers in a relay chain

Both solutions have their merits, so let's consider the advantages and disadvantages of each of them.

If the slaves are normally up-to-date with respect to the master, the first solution will perform a simple check of the final slave only and will usually show that the transaction has been replicated to the slave and that processing can proceed. If the transaction has not been processed yet, it is likely that it will be processed before the next check, so the second time the final slave is checked, it will show that the transaction has reached the slave. If the checking period is small enough, the delay will not be noticeable for the user, so a typical consistency check will require one or two extra messages when polling the final slave. This approach requires only the final slave to be polled, not any of the intermediate slaves. This can be an advantage from an administrative point as well, because it does not require keeping track of the intermediate slaves and how they are connected.

On the other hand, if the slaves normally lag behind, or if the replication lag varies a lot, the second approach is probably better. The first solution will repeatedly poll the slave, and most of the time will report that the transaction has *not* been committed on the slave. You can handle this by increasing the polling period, but if the polling period has to be so large that the response time is unacceptable, the first solution will not work well. In this case, it is better to use the second solution and wait for the changes to ripple down the replication tree and then execute the query.

For a tree of size N, the number of extra requests will then be proportional to $\log N$. For instance, if you have 50 relay servers and each relay server handles 50 final slaves, you can handle all 2,500 slaves with exactly two extra requests: one to the relay server and then one to the final slave.

The disadvantages of the second approach are:

- It requires the application code to have access to the relay slaves so that they can connect to each relay server in turn and wait for the position to be reached.
- It requires the application code to keep track of the architecture of your replication so that the relay servers can be queried.

Querying the relay servers will slow them down, because they have to handle more work, but in practice, this might turn out not to be a problem. By introducing a caching database connection layer, you can avoid some of the traffic. The caching layer will remember the binlog position each time a request is made and query the relay only if the binlog position is greater than the cached one. The following is a rough stub for the caching function:

```
function wait_for_pos($server, $wait_for_pos) {
  if (cached position for $server > $wait_for_pos)
    return TRUE;
  else {
    code to wait for position and update cache
  }
}
```

Because the binlog positions are always increasing—once a binlog position is passed it remains passed—there is no risk of returning an incorrect result. The only way to know for sure which technique is more efficient is to monitor and profile the deployment to make sure queries are executed fast enough for the application.

Example 6-12 shows sample code to handle the first solution; it queries the slave repeatedly to see whether the transaction has been executed. This code uses the Last_Ex ec_Trans table introduced in Chapter 5 by checking it on the master, and then repeatedly reading the table on the slave until it finds the correct transaction.

Example 6-12. PHP code for avoiding read of stale data using polling

```php
function fetch_trans_id($server) {
  $result = $server->query(
    "SELECT server_id, trans_id FROM Last_Exec_Trans");
  if ($result == NULL)
    return NULL;                          // Execution failed
  $row = $result->fetch_assoc();
  if ($row == NULL)
    return NULL;                          // Empty table !?
  $gid = array($row['server_id'], $row['trans_id']);
  $result->close();
  return $gid;
}

function wait_for_trans_id($server, $server_id, $trans_id) {
  if ($server_id == NULL || $trans_id == NULL)
    return TRUE;         // No transactions executed, in sync

  $server->autocommit(TRUE); ❶
  $gid = fetch_trans_id($server); ❷
  if ($gid == NULL)
    return FALSE;
  list($current_server_id, $current_trans_id) = $gid;
  while ($current_server_id != $server_id || $current_trans_id < $trans_id) {
    usleep(500000);                          // Wait half a second
    $gid = fetch_trans_id($server);
    if ($gid == NULL)
      return FALSE;
    list($current_server_id, $current_trans_id) = $gid;
  }
  return TRUE;
}

function commit_and_sync($master, $slave) {
  if ($master->commit()) {
    $gid = fetch_trans_id($master);
    if ($gid == NULL)
      return NULL;
    if (!wait_for_trans_id($slave, $gid[0], $gid[1]))
      return NULL;
```

```
    return TRUE;
  }
  return FALSE;
}

function start_trans($server) {
  $server->autocommit(FALSE);
}
```

The two functions commit_and_sync and start_trans behave the same way as in
Example 6-10, and can therefore be used in the same way as in Example 6-11. The
difference is that the functions in Example 6-12 internally call fetch_trans_id and
wait_for_trans_id instead of fetch_master_pos and wait_for_pos. Some points
worth noting in the code:

❶   Autocommit is turned on in wait_for_trans_id before starting to query the
    slave. This is necessary because if the isolation level is REPEATABLE READ or
    stricter, the select will find the same global transaction identifier every time. To
    prevent this, each SELECT is committed as a separate transaction by turning on
    autocommit. An alternative is to use the READ COMMITTED isolation level.

❷   To avoid unnecessary sleeps in wait_for_trans_id, the global transaction
    identifier is fetched and checked once before entering the loop.

This code requires access only to the master and slave, not to the intermediate relay
servers.

Example 6-13 includes code for ensuring you do not read stale data. It uses the technique
of querying all servers between the master and the final slave. This method proceeds by
first finding the entire chain of servers between the final slave and the master, and then
synchronizing each in turn all the way down the chain until the transaction reaches the
final slave. The code reuses the fetch_master_pos and wait_for_pos from
Example 7-8, so they are not repeated here. The code does not implement any caching
layer.

Example 6-13. PHP code for avoiding reading stale data using waiting

```
function fetch_relay_chain($master, $final) {
  $servers = array();
  $server = $final;
  while ($server !== $master) {
    $server = get_master_for($server);
    $servers[] = $server;
  }
  $servers[] = $master;
  return $servers;
}

function commit_and_sync($master, $slave) {
```

```
  if ($master->commit()) {
    $server = fetch_relay_chain($master, $slave);
    for ($i = sizeof($server) - 1; $i > 1 ; --$i) {
      if (!sync_with_master($server[$i], $server[$i-1]))
        return NULL;                      // Synchronization failed
    }
  }
}

function start_trans($server) {
  $server->autocommit(FALSE);
}
```

To find all the servers between the master and the slave, we use the function `fetch_re` `lay_chain`. It starts from the slave and uses the function `get_master_for` to get the master for a slave. We have deliberately not included the code for this function, as it does not add anything to our current discussion. However, this function has to be defined for the code to work.

After the relay chain is fetched, the code synchronizes the master with its slave all the way down the chain. This is done with the `sync_with_master` function, which was introduced in Example 6-10.

One way to fetch the master for a server is to use `SHOW SLAVE STATUS` and read the `Master_Host` and `Master_Port` fields. If you do this for each transaction you are about to commit, however, the system will be very slow.

Because the topology rarely changes, it is better to cache the information on the application servers, or somewhere else, to avoid excessive traffic to the database servers.

In Chapter 5, you saw how to handle the failure of a master by, for example, failing over to another master or promoting a slave to be a master. We also mentioned that once the master is repaired, you need to bring it back to the deployment. The master is a critical component of a deployment and is likely to be a more powerful machine than the slaves, so you should restore it to the master position when bringing it back. Because the master stopped unexpectedly, it is very likely to be out of sync with the rest of the deployment. This can happen in two ways:

- If the master has been offline for more than just a short time, the rest of the system will have committed many transactions that the master is not aware of. In a sense, the master is in an *alternative future* compared to the rest of the system. An illustration of this situation is shown in Figure 6-8.

- If the master committed a transaction and wrote it to the binary log, then crashed just after it acknowledged the transaction, the transaction may not have made it to the slaves. This means the master has one or more transactions that have not been seen by the slaves, nor by any other part of the system.

If the original master is not too far behind the current master, the easiest solution to the first problem is to connect the original master as a slave to the current master, and then switch over all slaves to the master once it has caught up. If, however, the original master has been offline for a significant period, it is likely to be faster to clone one of the slaves and then switch over all the slaves to the master.

If the master is in an alternative future, it is not likely that its extra transactions should be brought into the deployment. Why? Because the sudden appearance of a new transaction is likely to conflict with existing transactions in subtle ways. For example, if the transaction is a message in a message board, it is likely that a user has already recommitted the message. If a message written earlier but reported as missing—because the master crashed before the message was sent to a slave—suddenly reappears, it will befuddle the users and definitely be considered an annoyance. In a similar manner, users will not look kindly on shopping carts suddenly having items added because the master was brought back into the system.

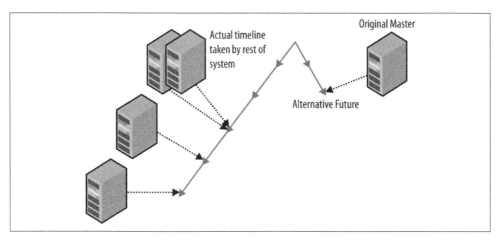

Figure 6-8. Original master in an alternative future

In short, you can solve both of the out-of-sync problems—the master in an alternative future and the master that needs to catch up—by simply cloning a slave to the original master and then switching over each of the current slaves in turn to the original master.

These problems, however, highlight how important it is to ensure consistency by checking that changes to a master are available on some other system before reporting the transaction as complete, in the event that the master should crash. The code that we have discussed in this chapter assumes that a user will try to read the data immediately, and therefore checks that it has reached the slave before a read query is carried out on the server. From a recovery perspective, this is excessive; it is sufficient to ensure the transaction is available on at least one other machine (e.g., on one of the slaves or relay servers connected to the master). In general, you can tolerate $n-1$ failures if you have the change available on n servers.

As of MySQL 5.6, you can use global transaction identifiers to handle this. Simply use the WAIT_UNTIL_SQL_THREAD_AFTER_GTIDS function instead of the MASTER_POS_WAIT in Example 6-10, leading to the definition of wait_for_pos:

```
function wait_for_pos($server, $gtids) {
  $result = $server->query(
    "SELECT WAIT_UNTIL_SQL_THREAD_AFTER_GTIDS($gtids)");
  if ($result == NULL)
    return FALSE;      // Execution failed
  $row = $result->fetch_row();
  if ($row == NULL)
    return FALSE;      // Empty result set ?!
  if ($row[0] == NULL || $row[0] < 0)
    return FALSE;      // Sync failed
  $result->close();
  return TRUE;
}
```

You can find a full description of global transaction identifiers in "Global Transaction Identifiers" on page 260.

Conclusion

In this chapter, we looked at techniques to increase the throughput of your applications by scaling out, whereby we introduced more servers to handle more requests for data. We presented ways to set up MySQL for scaling out using replication and gave practical examples of some of the concepts. In the next chapter, we will look at some more advanced replication concepts.

A rap on Joel's door drew his attention to Mr. Summerson standing in the doorway. "I like your report on scaling out our servers, Joel. I want you to get started on that right away. Use some of those surplus servers we have down in the computer room."

Joel was happy he had decided to send his boss a proposal first. "Yes, sir. When do we need these online?"

Mr. Summerson smiled and glanced at his watch. "It's not quitting time yet," he said and walked away.

Joel wasn't sure whether he was joking or not, so he decided to get started right away. He picked up his now-well-thumbed copy of *MySQL High Availability* and his notes and headed to the computer room. "I hope I set the TiVo," he muttered, knowing this was going to be a late night.

## CHAPTER 7

Data Sharding

Joel finished reviewing his server logs and noted a few issues with a couple of queries. He made notes in his engineering notebook to watch these queries so he could learn whether they are simply long running or queries that need to be refactored to be more efficient. He was just noting the username for each query when his boss pinged him on the company's Jabber channel.

"I wish I'd never suggested we adopt instant messaging," he thought. Joel typed the normal response, "pong," and waited for his boss to fire off another microtask. While it was nice not to get ambushed in his own office, Joel knew his boss well enough that sooner or later Mr. Summerson would give up using Jabber and return to his usual drive-by tasking routine.

"J, I need u to wrt a WP on shrdin. Do we need? Hlp new acct?"

Joel took a moment to decipher his boss's propensity to think instant messaging was the same as texting, where typing is more difficult and some services charge by the letter. "OK, so he's discovered sharding. Now, what is a WP?" Joel typed his response, "Sure, I'll get right on it. Do you mean white paper?"

"Ack" appeared a moment later.

Joel minimized his Jabber window, opened his browser, entered "sharding mysql white paper pdf" in the search box, and pressed Enter. "If it's out there, I'll find it."

In the previous chapter, you learned how to scale reads by attaching slaves to a master and directing reads to the slaves while writes go to the master. As the load increases, it is easy to add more slaves to the master and serve more read queries. This allows you to easily scale when the read load increases, but what about the write load? All writes still go to the master, so if the number of writes increases enough, the master will become the bottleneck preventing the system from scaling. At this point, you will probably ask whether there is some way to scale writes as well as reads. We'll present sharding as a solution in this chapter, but let's start with a look at some background.

In previous chapters, the data in the database is fully stored in a single server, but in this chapter, you will see the data in the database distributed over several servers. To avoid confusion, we'll use the term *schema* to denote the name that you use with the statement USE *schema* or CREATE DATABASE *schema*.[1] We'll reserve the term *database* for the collection of all the data that you have stored, regardless of how many machines it is distributed over.

For example, you can choose to break up a database by placing some tables on different machines (also known as *functional partitioning*), and splitting some tables placing some of the rows on different machines (called *horizontal partitioning*, which is what we are talking about in this chapter).

What Is Sharding?

Most attempts to scale writes start with using the setup in Figure 7-1, consisting of two masters using bidirectional replication and a set of clients that update different masters depending on which data they need to change. Although the architecture appears to double the capacity for handling writes (because there are two masters), it actually doesn't. Writes are just as expensive as before because each statement has to be executed twice: once when it is received from the client and once when it is received from the other master. All the writes done by the A clients, as well as the B clients, are replicated and get executed twice, which leaves you in no better position than before. In short, a dual-master setup doesn't help you scale writes, so it is necessary to find some other means to scale the system. The only way forward is to remove replication between the servers so that they are completely separate.

With this architecture, it is possible to scale writes by partitioning the data into two completely independent sets and directing the clients to the partition that is responsible for each item of data the clients attempt to update. This way, no resources need to be devoted to processing updates for other partitions. Partitioning the data in this manner is usually referred to as *sharding* (other common names are *splintering* or *horizontal partitioning*) and each partition in this setup is referred to as a *shard*.

---

1. The MySQL Reference Manual refers to a schema as a *database*, making that term ambiguous. The SQL standard actually uses the name *schema* and the syntax for the create statement is CREATE SCHEMA schema in the SQL standard.

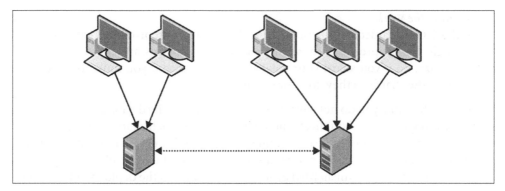

Figure 7-1. Pair of masters with bidirectional replication

Why Should You Shard?

Depending on where your application is experiencing strain, you have different reasons to shard. The biggest advantages of sharding, and the most common reasons to shard, are:

Placing data geographically close to the user
By placing bulky data such as pictures or videos close to the user, it is possible to reduce latency. This will improve the perceived performance of the system.

Reducing the size of the working set
If the table is smaller, it is possible that a larger part of the table, maybe even the entire table, can fit into main memory. Searching through a table that is entirely in main memory is very efficient, so splitting a large table into many small tables may improve performance drastically. This means that performance can be improved by sharding tables, even if multiple shards are stored on a single server.

Another aspect that affects performance is that the algorithms that search the tables are more efficient if the table is smaller. This can give a performance boost even when multiple shards are stored on the same machine. There are, however, technical limitations and overheads associated with storing multiple shards on a machine, so it is necessary to strike a balance between the number of shards and the size of the shards.

Deciding the optimal size of the tables requires monitoring the performance of the MySQL server and also monitoring InnoDB (or any other storage engine you use) to learn the average number of I/O operations required on average for each row scanned and to see if you need to make the shards even smaller. You will learn more about monitoring the server using the performance schema in Chapter 11 and monitoring InnoDB in Chapter 12 (especially getting statistics on the buffer pool, as it is important to optimize the size of the shards).

Distributing the work

If the data is sharded, it is possible to parallelize the work, provided that it is simple enough. This approach is most efficient when the shards are approximately the same size. So if you shard your database for this reason, you must find a way to balance the shards as they grow or shrink over time.

It's worth noting that you do not have to shard all the data in the database. You can shard some of the big tables, and duplicate the smaller tables on each shard (these are usually called *global tables*). You can also combine sharding and functional partitioning and shard bulky data such as posts, comments, pictures, and videos, while keeping directories and user data in an unsharded central store, similar to the deployment shown in Figure 7-2.

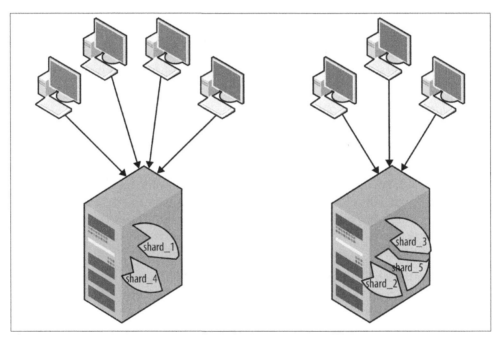

Figure 7-2. Shards with a centralized database

Limitations of Sharding

Sharding can improve performance, but it is not a panacea and comes with its own set of limitations that may or may not affect you. Many of these can be handled, and you will in this section learn about the limitations and how to handle them.

The challenge is to ensure that all queries give the same result when executed toward the unsharded database and the sharded database. If your queries access multiple tables (which is usually the case) you have to be careful to ensure that you get the same result for the unsharded database and the sharded database. This means that you have to pick a sharding index that ensures that the queries get the same result on a sharded or unsharded database.

In some cases, it is not practical or possible to solve the problem using sharding indexes, and it is necessary to rewrite the query (or eliminate it entirely, if possible). Two common problems you need to handle are cross-shard joins and AUTO_INCREMENT columns. We'll briefly cover them in the following sections.

Cross-shard joins

One of the most critical limitations that might affect you are *cross-shard joins*. Because the tables are partitioned, it is not possible to join two tables that belong to different shards and get the same result as if you executed the query in an unsharded database.

The most common reason for using cross-shard joins is to create reports. This usually requires collecting information from the entire database, so two approaches are generally used:

- Execute the query in a map-reduce fashion (i.e., send the query to all shards and collect the result into a single result set).
- Replicate all the shards to a separate reporting server and run the query there.

The advantage of executing the query in a map-reduce fashion is that you can get a snapshot of the live database, but it means that you take resources from the business application that is using the database. If your query is short and you really need to have a result reflecting the current state of the application database, this might be a useful approach. It is probably wise to monitor these queries, though, to make sure that they are not taking up too many resources and impacting application performance.

The second approach, replication, is easier. It's usually feasible, as well, because most reporting is done at specific times, is long-running, and does not depend on the current state of the database.

Later, in "Mapping the Sharding Key" on page 206, you will see a technique to automatically detect cross-shard joins and raise an error when attempts are made to execute such queries.

Using AUTO_INCREMENT

It is quite common to use AUTO_INCREMENT to create a unique identifier for a column. However, this fails in a sharded environment because the shards do not synchronize their AUTO_INCREMENT identifiers. This means that if you insert a row in one shard, it might well happen that the same identifier is used on another shard. If you truly want to generate a unique identifier, there are basically two approaches:

- Generate a unique UUID (*http://bit.ly/rfc-4122*). The drawback is that the identifier takes 128 bits (16 bytes). There is also a slight possibility that the same UUID is picked independently, but it is so small that you can ignore it.

- Use a *composite identifier*, as in Figure 7-3, where the first part is the shard identifier (see "Mapping the Sharding Key" on page 206) and the second part is a locally generated identifier (which can be generated using AUTO_INCREMENT). Note that the shard identifier is used when generating the key, so if a row with this identifier is moved, the original shard identifier has to move with it. You can solve this by maintaining, in addition to the column with the AUTO_INCREMENT, an extra column containing the shard identifier for the shard where the row was created.

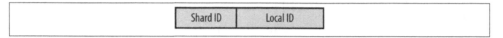

Figure 7-3. A composite key

 In case you are interested, the probability of a collision can be computed using the equation that solves the Birthday Problem (*http://mathworld.wolfram.com/BirthdayProblem.html*), where d is the number of "days" and n is the number of "people":

$$P_2(n, d) = 1 - \frac{d!}{(d - n)!\, d^n}$$

Elements of a Sharding Solution

The way you shard your database is ultimately determined by the queries that users intend to execute. For instance, it may make sense to shard sales data by year (2012 in one shard, 2013 in another, etc.), but if users run a lot of queries comparing sales in one December to another December, you will force the queries to cross shards. As we noted before, cross-shard joins are notoriously difficult to handle, so this would hamper performance and even force users to rewrite their queries.

In this section, we will cover the issues you need to handle in order to build a good sharding solution. These decide how you can distribute the data, as well as how you can reshard the data in an efficient manner:

- You have to decide how to *partition* the application data. What tables should be split? What tables should be available on all shards? What columns are the tables going to be sharded on?

- You have to decide what *sharding metadata* (information *about* the shards) you need and how to manage it. This covers such issues as how to allocate shards to MySQL servers, how to map sharding keys to shards, and what you need to store in the "sharding database."

- You have to decide how to handle the *query dispatch*. This covers such issues as how to get the sharding key necessary to direct queries and transactions to the right shard.

- You have to create a scheme for *shard management*. This covers issues such as how to monitor the load on the shards, how to move shards, and how to rebalance the system by splitting and merging shards.

In this chapter, you will become familiar with each of these areas and understand what decisions you have to make to develop a working sharding solution.

Applications are usually not designed originally to handle shards. After, such an extensive redesign does not emerge as a requirement until the database is starting to grow enough to impact performance. So normally you start off with an unsharded database and discover that you need to start sharding it. To describe the elements of sharding, we use the example employee schema in Figure 7-4. The entities in that figure represent a schema of employees, one of the standard example schema available on the MySQL site (*http://bit.ly/ex-schema*). To get an idea of how big the database is, you can see a row count in Table 7-1.

Table 7-1. Row count of the tables in the employees schema

Table	Rows
departments	9
dept_emp	331603
dept_manager	24
employees	300024
salaries	2844047
titles	443308

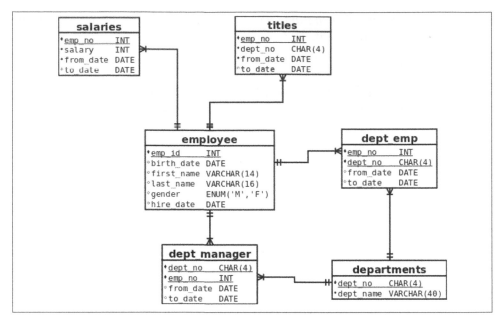

Figure 7-4. Employee schema

High-Level Sharding Architecture

Figure 7-5 shows the high-level architecture of a sharding solution. Queries come from an application and are received by a broker. The broker decides where to send the query, possibly with the help of a *sharding database* that keeps track of sharding information. The query is then sent to one or more shards of the application database and executed. The result set from the executions are collected by the broker, possibly post-processed, and then sent back to the application.

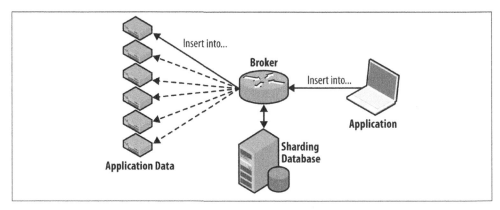

Figure 7-5. High-level sharding architecture

Partitioning the Data

Writing each item of data to a particular server allows you to scale writes efficiently. But that's not sufficient for scalability: efficient data retrieval is also important, and to achieve that, it is necessary to keep associated data together. For this reason, the biggest challenge in efficient sharding is to have a good *sharding index* so that data commonly requested together is on the same shard. As you will see, a sharding index is defined over columns in multiple tables; typically you use only a single column from each table, but multiple columns are also possible. The sharding index will decide what tables will be sharded and how they will be sharded.

After having picked a sharding index, you will end up with something similar to Figure 7-6.

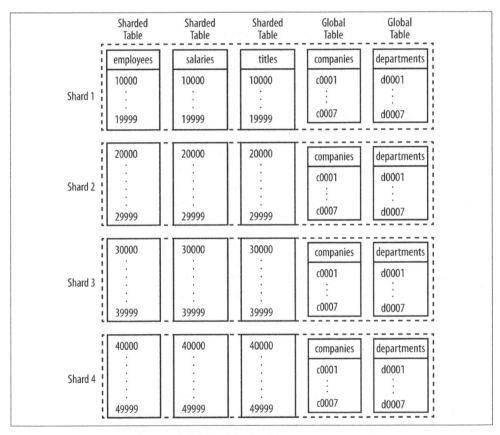

Figure 7-6. Schema with sharded and global tables

Here you can see several tables that have been sharded and where the rows are distributed over the shards (`employees`, `salaries`, and `titles`). Identical copies of the global tables (`companies` and `departments`) are present on each shard. We'll cover how to select columns for the sharding index and show how we came up with this particular solution for our sample schema.

To split the database over shards, you need to pick one or more of the columns for the sharding index and use them to distribute the rows over the shards. Using multiple sharding columns from a single table for the index can be hard to maintain unless they are used correctly. For this reason, it is usually best to pick a single column in a table and use that for the sharding index.

Sharding on a column that is a primary key offers significant advantages. The reason for this is that the column should have a unique index, so that each value in the column uniquely identifies the row.

To illustrate the problem of picking a sharding column that does not contain unique values, suppose that you picked the country of an employee as the sharding key. In this case, all rows that belong to Sweden (for example) will go to one shard, and all that belong to China (for example) will go to another shard. This can be an appealing choice for sharding the database if reports or updates are often done on a per-country basis. But even though this might work as long as the size of each shard is relatively small, it will break down once the shards start to grow and need to be split further. At this point, because all rows in a shard will have the same sharding key, it won't be possible to split the shards further when they have grown to the point where they need to be split again. In the end, the shard for Sweden can contain a maximum of 9 million entries, while the shard for China can contain a maximum of 1.3 billion entries, and these shards cannot be split further. This is a quite unfair distribution, and the server managing China has to perform more than 100 times better than the server managing Sweden to achieve the same performance.

If you instead pick the primary key of the table (in this case, the column with the employee number), you can group the employees any way you like and create partitions of arbitrary sizes. This will allow you to distribute the rows into shards of roughly the same size, hence distributing the workload evenly over the servers.

So how should you pick columns for the sharding index for the schema in Figure 7-4? Well, the first question is what tables need to be sharded. A good starting point for deciding that is to look at the number of rows in the tables as well as the dependencies between the tables.

Table 7-1 shows the number of rows in each table in the employees schema. Now, the numbers are nothing like what you would see in a real database in need of sharding—the contents of this database easily fit onto a single server—but it serves as a good example to demonstrate how to construct a sharded database from an unsharded one. A good candidate table for sharding is `employees`. Not only is it a big table, but several other tables are dependent on it, and as you will see later, if there are dependencies between tables, there are opportunities for sharding them as well.

The primary key of the employees table is the emp_no column. Because this is the primary key, sharding on this column will allow you to distribute the rows of the employees table on the shards evenly and split the tables as you need.

So if we shard on the emp_no column in the employees table, how does that affect the tables that are dependent on employees? Because there is a foreign key reference to the employees table, this suggests that the intention is to support joining the tables on that column. Take a look at this query, which could be a typical query for fetching the title and salary of an employee:

```
SELECT first_name, last_name, title
  FROM titles JOIN employees USING (emp_no)
WHERE emp_no = employee number
   AND CURRENT_DATE BETWEEN from_date AND to_date
```

As previously mentioned, the goal is to make sure the query returns the same result in both the sharded and unsharded databases. Because employees is sharded on column emp_no, this query can never reference rows in titles and employees that are on different shards. So after sharding employees, all rows in titles that have an emp_no that is not in the employees shard you use will never be referenced. To fix this, titles should be sharded on column emp_no as well. The same reasoning holds for all tables that have a foreign key reference into the employees table, so employees, titles, salaries, emp_dep, and dept_manager need to be sharded. In short, even though you picked a single column to start with, you will shard several tables, each on a column that is related to your original sharding of the employees table.

Now that we have sharded almost all the tables in the schema, only the departments table remains. Can this also be sharded? The table is so small that it is not necessary to shard it, but what would be the consequence if it was sharded? As noted before, it depends on the queries used to retrieve information from the database, but because dept_manager and dept_emp are used to connect departments and employees, it is a strong hint that the schema is designed to execute queries joining these tables. For example, consider this query to get the name and department for an employee:

```
SELECT first_name, last_name, dept_name
FROM employees JOIN dept_emp USING (emp_no)
               JOIN departments USING (dept_no)
WHERE emp_no = employee number
```

This query puts more stress on your sharding choices than the previous SELECT, because it is not dealing with a single column shared by two tables (the primary key of the employees table) but with two columns that can range anywhere throughout the three tables involved. So how can you ensure that this query returns all the results from a sharded database as it would in the unsharded one? Because the employees table is sharded on the `emp_no` column, every row where `dept_emp.emp_no = employ ees.emp_no` and `dept_emp.dept_no = departments.dept_no` has to be in the same shard. If they are in different shards, no rows will match, and the query will return an empty result.

Because employees in the same department can reside on different shards, it is better *not* to shard the `departments` table, but instead to keep it available on all shards as a global table. Duplicating a table on multiple shards makes updating the tables a little more complicated (this will be covered later) but because the `departments` table is not expected to change frequently, this is likely to be a good trade-off.

Automatically Computing Possible Sharding Indexes

As this section has shown, even when you pick a single sharding key, you need to shard all tables that depend on the table that you picked for sharding. Sharding a single table on one of its columns can force you to shard other tables on the related column. For example, because the `emp_no` column in the `employees` table is related to the `emp_no` column in the `salaries` table, sharding the `employees` table will allow the `salaries` table to also be sharded on the same column.

For small schemas, it is easy to follow the foreign key relations, but if you have a schema with many tables and many relations, it is not as easy to find all the dependencies. If you are careful about using foreign keys to define all your dependencies, you can compute all the possible sharding indexes of dependent columns by using the information schema available in MySQL. The query to find all sets of dependent columns is:

```
USE information_schema;
SELECT
  GROUP_CONCAT(
    CONCAT_WS('.', table_schema, table_name, column_name)
  ) AS indexes
FROM
  key_column_usage JOIN table_constraints
    USING (table_schema, table_name, constraint_name)
WHERE
  constraint_type = 'FOREIGN KEY'
GROUP BY
  referenced_table_schema,
  referenced_table_name,
  referenced_column_name
ORDER BY
  table_schema, table_name, column_name;
```

If you run this query on the employees schema, the result is two possible sharding indexes:

Candidate #1	Candidate #2
salaries.emp_no	dept_manager.dept_no
dept_manager.emp_no	dept_emp.dept_no
dept_emp.emp_no	
titles.emp_no	

A single query can compute this because each foreign key has to reference a primary key in the target table. This means that there will be no further references that have to be followed, as would be the case if a foreign key could refer to another foreign key.

By counting the number of rows in the tables, you can get an idea of what index would give the best sharding. You can also see that dept_manager and dept_emp are in both alternatives, so these are conflicting and you can use only one of them.

Usually, you have only one big set of tables that need to be sharded, as in the example schema in Figure 7-4. In other cases, however, you have several "sets" of tables that you want to shard *independently*. For example, assume that, in addition to the employees of the company, you want to keep track of all the publications of each department. The relation between employees and publications is a many-to-many relationship, which in classic database schema design is created by a junction table with foreign keys pointing to the employees and publications tables. So tracking publications requires, in addition to the schema shown earlier, a publications table and a dept_pub table to be added to the schema, as in Figure 7-7.

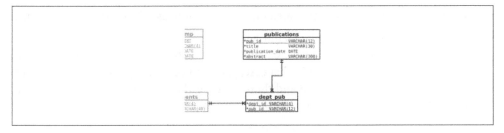

Figure 7-7. Publication schema added to employees schema

If the publications table is so large that it needs to be sharded as well, you can do so. If you look carefully in Figure 7-7, you'll see that the departments table is still available on all nodes, and there are foreign key references from dept_pub to publications and departments. This means that you can shard the publications and dept_pub tables, leading to a system where you have *multiple independent sharding indexes*.

What are the consequences of multiple independent sharding indexes? A single query can contain references to tables in one of the sets in Table 7-2 plus global tables, but it must never reference tables from different sets at the same time. In other words, you can query employees together with their titles, or query employees together with their publications, but you must not write a query that asks for information on titles and publications.

An example of a query that *cannot* be executed with this sharding in place is a query that joins a table in the "employee" part of the schema with the "publications" part of the schema:

```
SELECT first_name, last_name, dept_name, COUNT(pub_id)
    FROM employee JOIN dept_manager ON (emp_no)
                  JOIN departments ON (dept_no)
                  JOIN dept_pub ON (dept_no)
                  JOIN publications ON (pub_id)
    WHERE emp_no = 110386;
```

Table 7-2. Sharding index with columns

Index name	Sharding column set
si_emps	employees.emp_no, dept_emp.emp_no, salaries.emp_no, dept_manager.emp_no, titles.emp_no
si_pubs	publications.pub_no, dept_pub.pub_no

Shard Allocation

To work efficiently with shards, you need to store them in a way that speeds up physical access. The most straightforward approach is to keep one shard per server, but it is also possible to keep multiple *virtual shards* per server.

To decide how shards should be allocated for your solution, ask the following questions:

Do your applications use cross-schema queries?
> If each of your queries always uses a single schema (e.g., the employees schema), sharding becomes a lot easier. In that case, you can keep multiple shards on a server by using one schema per shard and there is no need to rewrite the queries because they will always go to a single schema.

Can queries be tailored to the sharding solution?
> If your queries are cross-schema but you can request the application developers to write queries with the sharding solution in mind, you can still keep multiple shards per server.
>
> This will allow you to rewrite queries in a controlled manner, which means that you can have, for example, the shard number as a suffix on the names of all databases.

Do you need to re-shard frequently?
> If you cannot rewrite the queries easily, or if you require the application programmer to write queries a specific way, you have to use a single shard per server because they can potentially be cross-schema queries. If, however, you are required to re-

shard frequently (to reflect changes in the application or other reasons), a single shard per server can be a performance bottleneck, so there is always a trade-off between having to adapt the application and getting the performance you need.

If you need to re-shard frequently, having multiple shards on each server can be part of a solution. This allow you to move shards between servers to balance the load. However, you might still have to split shards if a single shard grows too hot.

How can you back up a shard?

Apart from being able to easily back up a single shard at a time, you also need to be able to easily create backups to move shards between servers. Most backup methods can create a backup of an entire server, or one or more schemas. For that reason, it is prudent to ensure that a schema is entirely in a shard (but there can be multiple schemas in each shard).

Single shard per server

The most straightforward approach is to keep a single shard on each server. This allows cross-schema queries, so it is not necessary to rewrite queries. There are two drawbacks to this approach: multiple tables may exceed the size of main memory on the server, which affects performance, and balancing the load between servers becomes more expensive in case you need to re-shard the tables.

As mentioned earlier, one of the goals of sharding a database is to reduce the size of the tables so that it can fit into memory. Smaller tables take less time to search, both because they contain fewer rows and because more of each table can fit in memory.

If the server becomes overloaded and it is necessary to reduce the load, this principle suggests the solution: split the shard and either create a new shard using a spare server, or move the now extraneous rows to another shard and merge them with the rows there. If the rows are moved to an existing shard, and there is just one shard per server, the rows have to be merged with the rows already on that shard. Because merging is very difficult to do as an online operation, splitting and remerging is expensive when only one shard is allowed per server. In the next section, we will consider how to avoid having to merge shards when moving them.

Multiple shards per server (virtual shards)

As we've explained, if you can keep multiple shards on a single machine, the data can be moved between machines in a more efficient manner because the data is already sharded. This offers some flexibility to move shards around to balance the load on the machines, but if you do that, you need to be able to distinguish between the shards that coexist on the same server. For example, you need to be able to distinguish table employees.dept_emp in shard 123 from employees.dept_emp in shard 234 even if they are on the same machine.

A common approach is to attach the shard identifier to the name of the schema. For example, the schema employees in shard 123 would then be named employees_123 and a partition of each table is placed in each schema (e.g., the dept_emp table consists of employees_1.dept_emp, employees_2.dept_emp, ... employees_N.dept_emp).

Because the MySQL server stores each schema in its own directory, most backup methods can make backups of schemas but have problems backing up individual tables.[2] The approach just shown separates the tables for different shards into different directories, making it easy to take backups of shards (something that you will need later). Because you can limit replicate-do-db to specific schemas on a server, you can replicate changes to the individual shards as well, which will prove useful when you move shards between servers.

Keeping multiple shards on each server makes it comparably easy to move one of the shards to another server to reduce the load on the server. Because you can have multiple shards on each server, you can even move the shard to a server that already has other shards, without having to merge the rows of the shards. Note that this approach is not a replacement for re-sharding, because you need to have techniques in place to split a shard anyway.

In addition to adding the schema names with the shard identifier, you can add the shard identifier to the name of the table. So, with this approach, the names would be employ ees_123.dept_emp_123, employees_124.dept_emp_124, and so on. Although the shard number on the table seems redundant, it can be useful for catching problems where the application code mistakenly queries the wrong shard.

The drawback of adding the shard number to the schema names and/or the tables is that users need to rewrite their queries. If all your queries always go to a single schema, never executing cross-schema queries, it is easy to issue USE employee_identifier before sending the query to the server and keep the old table names. But if cross-schema queries are allowed, it is necessary to rewrite the query to locate all the schema names and append the shard identifier to each.

Inserting specific table numbers into queries can be quite error-prone, so if you can, generalize the query and automate the insertion of the right table number. For example, you can use braces to wrap the number in the schema name, and then use a regular expression to match and replace the schema and table name with the schema and table name for the shard in question. Example PHP code is shown in Example 7-1.

---

2. Many backup techniques can handle individual tables as well, but it is more complicated to manage backup and restore of individual tables. Using databases to structure the database makes the job of managing backups easier.

Example 7-1. Replacing table references in queries

```php
class my_mysqli extends mysqli {
  public $shard_id;

  private function do_replace($query) {
    return preg_replace(array('/\{(\w+)\.(\w+)\}/', '/\{(\w+)\}/'),
                        array("$1_{$this->shard_id}.$2", "$1"),
                        $query);
  }

  public function __construct($shard_id, $host, $user, $pass,
                             $db, $port)
  {
    parent::__construct($host, $user, $pass,
                        "{$db}_{$shard_id}", $port);
    $this->shard_id = $shard_id;
  }

  public function prepare($query) {
    return parent::prepare($this->do_replace($query));
  }

  public function query($query, $resultmode = MYSQLI_STORE_RESULT) {
    return parent::query($this->do_replace($query), $resultmode);
  }
}
```

The code creates a subclass of `mysqli`, overriding the `prepare` and `query` functions with specialized versions that rewrite the names of the databases. Then the original function is called, passing the correct database name to connect to. Because there are no changes to the `mysqli` interface, no changes are normally necessary in the application code. An example using the class is:

```php
if ($result = $mysqli->query("SELECT * FROM {test.t1}")) {
  while ($row = $result->fetch_object())
    print_r($row);
  $result->close();
}
else {
  echo "Error: " . $mysql->error;
}
```

However, this works only if the application writers are willing (and able) to add this markup to the queries. It is also error-prone because application writers can forget to add the markup.

Mapping the Sharding Key

In the previous section, you saw how the choice of sharding column decides what tables need to be sharded. You also saw how to partition a table by range. In this section, partition functions will be discussed in more depth: you will see what sharding metadata is needed to compute the right shards as well as how to map the rows of a sharded table to actual shards.

As explained earlier in the chapter, the goal of mapping the sharding key is to create a *partition function* that accepts a sharding key value and outputs a shard identifier for the shard where the row exists. As also noted earlier, there can be several sharding keys, but in that case, we create a separate partition function for each sharding key. For the discussions in this section, we assume that each shard has a unique *shard identifier*, which is just an integer and can be used to identify each database or table as shown in the previous section.

You saw in "Partitioning the Data" on page 197 that each partition function is associated with several columns if there are foreign keys relationships between the tables. So when you have a sharding key value you want to map (e.g., "20156") it does not matter whether it was the `employees.emp_no` column or the `dept_emp.emp_no` column: both tables are sharded the same way. This means that when talking about mapping a sharding key value to a shard, the columns are implicitly given by the partition function and it is sufficient to provide the key.

Sharding Scheme

The partition function can be implemented using either a *static sharding scheme* or a *dynamic sharding scheme* (as the names suggest, the schemes just tell whether the sharding can change or is fixed):

Static sharding
> In a static sharding scheme, the sharding key is mapped to a shard identifier using a fixed assignment that never changes. The computation of the shard identifier is usually done in the connector or in the application, which means that it can be done very efficiently.
>
> For example, you could use range-based assignment, such as making the first shard responsible for users 0 through 9,999, the second shard responsible for users 10,000 through 19,999, and so on. Or you could scatter users semirandomly through a hash based on the value of the last four digits of the identifier.

Dynamic sharding schemes
> In a dynamic sharding scheme, the sharding key is looked up in a dictionary that indicates which shard contains the data. This scheme is more flexible than a static scheme, but requires a centralized store called the *sharding database* in this chapter.

Static sharding schemes

As you might have realized, static sharding schemes run into problems when the distribution of the queries is not even. For example, if you distribute the rows to different shards based on country, you can expect the load on the China shard to be about 140 times that of the Sweden shard. Swedes would love this, because assuming that the servers have the same capacity, they will experience very short response times. Chinese visitors may suffer, however, because their shard has to take 140 times that load. The skewed distribution can also occur if the hash function does not offer a good distribution. For this reason, picking a good partition key and a good partition function is of paramount importance.

An example partition function for a static schema appears in Example 7-2.

Example 7-2. Example PHP implementation of a dictionary for static sharding

```php
class Dictionary { ❶
  public $shards;                          /* Our shards */

  public function __construct() {
    $this->shards = array(array('127.0.0.1', 3307),
                          array('127.0.0.1', 3308),
                          array('127.0.0.1', 3309),
                          array('127.0.0.1', 3310));
  }

  public function get_connection($key, $user, $pass, $db) { ❷
    $no = $key % count($this->shards); ❸
    list($host, $port) = $this->shards[$no];
    $link = new my_mysqli($host, $user, $pass, $db, $port); ❹
    $link->shard_id = $no;
    $link->select_db("{$db}_{$no}");
    return $link;
  }
}

$DICT = new Dictionary('localhost', 'mats', 'xyzzy', 'sharding');
```

❶ We define a `Dictionary` class to be responsible for managing the connections to the sharded system. All logic for deciding what host to use is made inside this class.

❷ This is a factory method that provides a new connection when given a sharding key. Because each sharding key potentially can go to a different server, a new connection is established each time this function is called.

❹ This creates a new connection using the `my_mysqli` function that we defined in Example 7-1. It is also possible to fetch a connection from a connection pool here, if you decide to implement one. However, for the sake of simplicity, no such pooling mechanism was implemented here.

❸ The partition function that we use here computes a shard based on the modulo of the employee number (which is the sharding key).

In Example 7-2, you can see an example of how to create a dictionary for static sharding using PHP. The `Dictionary` class is used to manage connections to the sharded system and will return a connection to the correct shard given the sharding key. In this case, assume that the sharding key is the employee number, but the same technique can be generalized to handle any sharding key. In Example 7-3, you can see an example usage where a connection is fetched and a query executed on the shard.

Example 7-3. Example of using the dictionary

```
$mysql = $DICT->get_connection($key, 'mats', 'xyzzy', 'employees');
$stmt = $mysql->prepare(
    "SELECT last_name FROM {employees} WHERE emp_no = ?");
if ($stmt)
{
  $stmt->bind_param("d", $key);
  $stmt->execute();
  $stmt->bind_result($first_name, $last_name);
  while ($stmt->fetch())
    print "$first_name $last_name\n";
  $stmt->close();
}
else {
  echo "Error: " . $mysql->error;
}
```

Dynamic sharding schemes

Dynamic sharding schemes are distinguished from static ones by their flexibility. Not only do they allow you to change the location of the shards, but it is also easy to move data between shards if you have to. As always, the flexibility comes at the price of a more complex implementation, and potentially also impacts performance. Dynamic schemes require extra queries to find the correct shard to retrieve data from, which adds to complexity as well as to performance. A caching policy will allow information to be cached instead of sending a query each time, helping you reduce the performance impact. Ultimately, good performance requires a careful design that matches the patterns of user queries. Because the dynamic sharding scheme is the most flexible, we will concentrate on that for the rest of the chapter.

The simplest and most natural way to preserve the data you need for dynamic sharding is to store the sharding database as a set of tables in a MySQL database on a sharding server, which you query to retrieve the information. Example 7-4 shows a sample `loca tions` table containing information for each shard, and a `partition_function` table containing one row for each partition function. Given a sharding identifier, you can figure out what service instance to contact by joining with the `locations` table. We'll look at the sharding types later.

Example 7-4. Tables used for dynamic sharding

```
CREATE TABLE locations (
        shard_id INT AUTO_INCREMENT,
        host VARCHAR(64),
        port INT UNSIGNED DEFAULT 3306,
        PRIMARY KEY (shard_id)
);

CREATE TABLE partition_functions (
        func_id INT AUTO_INCREMENT,
        sharding_type ENUM('RANGE','HASH','LIST'),
        PRIMARY KEY (func_id)
);
```

Now we'll change the static implementation of the `Dictionary` class from Example 7-2 to use the tables in Example 7-4. In Example 7-5, the class now fetches the shard information from a sharding database instead of looking it up statically. It uses the information returned to create a connection as before. As you can see, the query for fetching the shard information is not filled in. This is dependent on how the mapping is designed and is what we'll discuss next.

Example 7-5. Implementation of dictionary for dynamic sharding

```
$FETCH_SHARD = <<<END_OF_QUERY
query to fetch sharding key
END_OF_QUERY;

class Dictionary {
  private $server;

  public function __construct($host, $user, $pass, $port = 3306) {
    $mysqli = new mysqli($host, $user, $pass, 'sharding', $port);
    $this->server = $mysqli;
  }

  public function get_connection($key, $user, $pass, $db, $tables) {
    global $FETCH_SHARD;
    if ($stmt = $this->server->prepare($FETCH_SHARD)){
      $stmt->bind_param('i', $key);
      $stmt->execute();
      $stmt->bind_result($no, $host, $port);
      if ($stmt->fetch()) {
        $link = new my_mysqli($no, $host, $user, $pass, $db, $port);
        $link->shard_id = $no;
        return $link;
      }
    }
    return null;
```

```
    }
}
```

Shard Mapping Functions

Our sharding database in Example 7-4 showed three different sharding types in the `partition_function` table. Each partition type, described in the online MySQL documentation (*http://bit.ly/part-types*), uses a different kind of mapping between the data in the sharded column and the shards themselves. Our table includes the three most interesting ones:

List mapping
> Rows are distributed over the shards based on a set of distinct values in the sharding column. For example, the list could be a list of countries.

Range mapping
> Rows are distributed over the shards based on where the sharding column falls within a range. This can be convenient when you shard on an ID column, dates, or other information that falls conveniently into ranges.

Hash mapping
> Rows are distributed over the shards based on a hash value of the sharding key value. This theoretically provides the most even distribution of data over shards.

Of these mappings, the list mapping is the easiest to implement, but is the most difficult to use when you want to distribute the load efficiently. It can be useful when you shard for locality, because it can ensure that each shard is located close to its users. The range partitioning is easy to implement and eliminates some of the problems with distributing the load, but it can still be difficult to distribute the load evenly over the shards. The hash mapping is the one that distributes the load best over the shards of all three, but it is also the most complicated to implement in an efficient manner, as you will see in the following sections. The most important mappings are the range mapping and the hash mapping, so let's concentrate on those.

For each shard mapping, we will consider both how to add a new shard and how to select the correct shard based on the sharding key chosen.

Range mapping

The most straightforward approach to range mapping is to separate the rows of a table into ranges based on the sharding column and to assign one shard for each range. Even though ranges are easy to implement, they have the problem of potentially becoming very fragmented. This solution also calls for a data type that supports ranges efficiently, which you are not always lucky to have. For example, if you are using URIs as keys, "hot" sites will be clustered together when you actually want the opposite, to spread them out.

To get a good distribution in that case, you should use a hash mapping, which we cover in "Hash mapping and consistent hashing" on page 212.

Creating the index table. To implement a range mapping, create a table containing the ranges and map them to the shard identifiers:

```
CREATE TABLE ranges (
        shard_id INT,
        func_id INT,
        lower_bound INT,
        UNIQUE INDEX (lower_bound),
        FOREIGN KEY (shard_id)
            REFERENCES locations(shard_id),
        FOREIGN KEY (func_id)
            REFERENCES partition_functions(func_id)
)
```

Table 7-3 shows the typical types of information contained in such a table, which also includes the function identifier from the `partition_functions` table (you will see what the function identifier is used for momentarily). Only the lower bound is kept for each shard, because the upper bound is implicitly given by the lower bound of the next shard in the range. Also, the shards do not have to be the same size, and having to maintain both an upper and lower bound when splitting the shards is an unnecessary complication. Table 7-3 shows the definition of the table.

Table 7-3. Range mapping table ranges

Lower bound	Key ID	Shard ID
0	0	1
1000	0	2
5500	0	4
7000	0	3

Adding new shards. To add new shards when using range-based sharding, you insert a row in the `ranges` table as well as a row in the `locations` table. So, assuming that you want to add a shard `shard-1.example.com` with the range 1000–2000 for the partition function given by `@func_id`, you would first insert a row into the `locations` table, to get a new shard identifier, and then use the new shard identifier to add a row in the `ranges` table:

```
INSERT INTO locations(host) VALUES ('shard-1.example.com');
SET @shard_id = LAST_INSERT_ID();
INSERT INTO ranges VALUES (@shard_id, @func_id, 1000);
```

Note that the upper bound is implicit and given by the next row in the `ranges` table. This means that you do not need to provide the upper bound when adding a new shard.

Fetching the shard. After defining and populating this table, you can fetch the shard number, hostname, and port for the shard using the following query, to be used in Example 7-5:

```
SELECT shard_id, hostname, port
  FROM ranges JOIN locations USING (shard_id)
 WHERE func_id = 0 AND ? >= ranges.lower_bound
ORDER BY ranges.lower_bound DESC
 LIMIT 1;
```

The query fetches all rows that have a lower bound below the key provided, orders them by lower bound, and then takes the first one. Note that the code in Example 7-5 prepares the query before executing it, so the question mark in the query will be replaced with the sharding key in use. Another option would be to store both the lower and upper bound, but that makes it more complicated to update the sharding database if the number of shards or the ranges for the shards should change.

Hash mapping and consistent hashing

One of the issues you might run into when using a range mapping is that you do not get a good distribution of the "hot" clusters of data, which means that one shard can become overloaded and you have to split it a lot to be able to cope with the increase in load. If you instead use a function that distributes the data points evenly over the range, the load will also be distributed evenly over the shards. A hash function takes some input and computes a number from it called the *hash*. A good hash function distributes the input as evenly as possible, so that a small change in the input string still generates a very different output number. You saw one very common hash function in Example 7-2, where modulo arithmetic was used to get the number of the shard.

The naïve hash function in common use computes a hash of the input in some manner (e.g., using MD5 or SHA-1 or even some simpler functions) and then uses modulo arithmetic to get a number between 1 and the number of shards. This approach does not work well when you need to re-shard to, for example, add a new shard. In this case, you can potentially move a lot of rows between the shards, because computing the modulo of the hashed string can potentially move all the elements to a new shard. To avoid this problem, you can instead use *consistent hashing*, which is guaranteed to move rows from just one old shard to the new shard.

To understand how this is possible, look at Figure 7-8. The entire hash range (the output of the hash function) is shown as a ring. On the hash ring, the shards are assigned to points on the ring using the hash function (we'll show you how to do this later). In a similar manner, the rows (here represented as the red dots) are distributed over the ring using the same hash function. Each shard is now responsible for the region of the ring that starts at the shard's point on the ring and continues to the next shard point. Because a region may start at the end of the hash range and wrap around to the beginning of the hash range, a ring is used here instead of a flat line. But this cannot happen when using the regular hash function shown earlier, as each shard has a slot on the line and there is no slot that wraps around from the end to the beginning of the range.

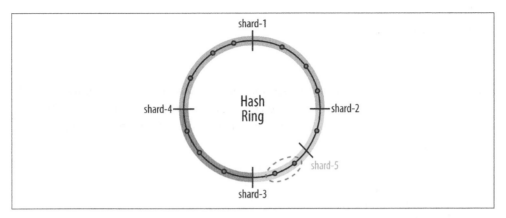

Figure 7-8. Hash ring used for consistent hashing

Now suppose that a new shard is added to the ring, say shard-5 in the figure. It will be assigned to a position on the ring. Here it happens to split shard-2, but it could have been either of the existing shards. Because it splits shard-2, only the circled rows from the old shard-2 will have to be moved to shard-5. This means that the new shard will just take over the rows that are in one shard and move them to the new shard, which improves performance significantly.

So, how do you implement this consistent hashing? Well, the first thing that you need is a good hash function, which will generate values on the hash ring. It must have a *very* big range, hence a lot of "points" on the hash ring where rows can be assigned. A good set of hash functions having the needed properties comes from cryptography.

Cryptography uses hash functions to create "signatures" of messages to detect tampering. These functions take as input an arbitrary string, and produce a number as output. Cryptography requires a number of complex mathematical properties from its hash functions, but for our purpose, the two most important properties are to provide a hash value containing a large number of bits and to distribute the input strings evenly over the output range. Cryptographic hash functions have these properties, so they are a good choice for us.

The most commonly used functions are MD5 and the SHA family of hash functions (i.e., SHA-1, SHA-256/224, and SHA-512/384). Table 7-4 shows the most common hash functions and the number of bits in the numbers they produce. These functions are designed to be fast and accept any string as input, which makes them perfect for computing a hash of arbitrary values.

Table 7-4. Common cryptographic hash functions

Hash function	Output size (bits)
MD5	128
SHA-1	160
SHA-256	256
SHA-512	512

Creating the index table. To define a hash mapping, define a table containing the hash values of the servers containing the shards (as usual, we store the location of the shards in a separate table, so only the shard identifier needs to be stored in the table):

```
CREATE TABLE hashes (
    shard_id INT,
    func_id INT,
    hash BINARY(32),
    UNIQUE INDEX (hash)
    FOREIGN KEY (shard_id)
        REFERENCES locations(shard_id),
    FOREIGN KEY (func_id)
        REFERENCES partition_functions(func_id)
)
```

An index is added to allow fast searching on the hash value. Table 7-5 shows typical contents of such a table.

Table 7-5. Hash mapping table hashes

Key ID	Shard ID	Hash
1	0	dfd59508d347f5e4ba41defcb973d9de
2	0	2e7d453c8d2f9d2b75a421569f758da0
3	0	468934ac4c69302a77cbe5e7fa7dcb13
4	0	47a9ae8f8b8d5127fc6cc46b730f4f22

Adding new shards. To add new shards, you need to insert an entry both in the `loca tions` table and in the `hashes` table. To compute the row for the `hashes` table, you build a string for the server and compute the hash value for the strings. The string representing the server could, for example, be the fully qualified domain name, but any representation will do. For example, you might need to add the port to the string if you want to distinguish the servers. The hash values are stored in the `hashes` table, and assuming that the function identifier is in `@func_id`, the following statements will do the job:

```
INSERT INTO locations(host) VALUES ('shard-1.example.com');
SET @shard_id = LAST_INSERT_ID();
INSERT INTO hashes VALUES (@shard_id, @func_id, MD5('shard-1.example.com'));
```

Fetching the shard. You have now prepared the table containing information about the shards. When you need to look up the location of a shard using the sharding key, you compute the hash value of the sharding key and locate the shard identifier with the largest hash value that is smaller than the hash value of the sharding key. If no hash value is smaller than the hash key, pick the largest hash value.

```
(
   SELECT shard_id FROM hashes ❶
   WHERE MD5(sharding key) > hash
   ORDER BY hash DESC
) UNION ALL (
   SELECT shard_id FROM shard_hashes ❷
   WHERE hash = (SELECT MAX(hash) from hashes)
) LIMIT 1 ❸
```

❶   This SELECT picks all shards that have a hash value smaller than the hash of the sharding key. Note that this select might be empty.

❷   This SELECT provides a default value in case the previous one does not match anything.

❸   Because you need only one row, and the union of SELECT statements can potentially match multiple shards, just pick the first shard. This will either be the a shard from ❶ or, if that select did not match any shards, the shard from ❷.

Processing Queries and Dispatching Transactions

By now you have decided how to partition your data by selecting an appropriate sharding column, how to handle the sharding data (the data about the sharding setup, such as where the shards are located), and how to map your sharding keys to shards. The next steps are to work out:

- How to dispatch transactions to the right shard
- How to get the sharding key for the transaction
- How to use caching to improve performance

If you recall the high-level architecture in "High-Level Sharding Architecture" on page 196, it includes a broker that has the responsibility of dispatching the queries to the right shards. This broker can either be implemented as an intermediate proxy or be part of the connector.

To implement the broker as a proxy, you usually send all queries to a dedicated host that implements the MySQL protocol. The proxy extracts the sharding key from each query somehow and dispatches the query to the correct shard. The advantage of using a proxy as broker is that the connectors can be unaware that they are connecting to a proxy: it behaves just as if they connected to a server. This looks like a very transparent solution, but in reality, it is not. For simple applications, a proxy works well, but as you will see in "Handling Transactions" on page 216, using a proxy requires you to extend the protocol and/or limit what the application can do.

Handling Transactions

To dispatch transactions correctly through a broker, you need to know the parameters of transactions that it needs to handle.

From the application's side, each transaction consists of a sequence of queries or statements, where the last statement is a commit or an abort. To get an understanding for how transaction processing needs to be handled, take a look at the following transaction and consider what problems you need to solve for each line of the transaction:

```
START TRANSACTION; ❶
SELECT salary INTO @s FROM salaries WHERE emp_no = 20101; ❷
SET @s = 1.1 * @s; ❸
INSERT INTO salaries(emp_no, salary) VALUES (20101, @s); ❹
COMMIT; ❺
START TRANSACTION; ❻
INSERT INTO …;
COMMIT;
```

❶ ❻ At the start of a transaction, there is no way to know the sharding key of the tables or databases it will affect. It is not possible to deduce it from the query, because it is not present at all. However, the `START TRANSACTION` can be deferred until a real statement is seen, which then hopefully would contain the sharding key.

However, a broker needs to know when a new transaction starts, because it may cause a switch to a different server, and it's important to know this for load balancing.

❷ The first statement of this transaction makes it look like a read transaction. If it is a read transaction, it means it can be sent to a slave to balance the load. Here you can also find the sharding key, so at this point, you can figure out what shard the transaction should go to.

❸ Setting a user-defined variable creates a session-specific state. The user variable is not global, so all following transactions can refer to (and hence be dependent on) the user-defined variable.

❹ It is now clear that this is a read-write transaction, so if you assumed at ❷ that the transaction was a read-only transaction and sent it to a slave, you will now start updating the slave instead of the master.

If you can generate an error here, it is possible to abort the transaction to indicate that there was a user error, but in that case, you still have to be able to indicate that this is a read-write transaction and that it should go to the master despite the initial SELECT.

❺ This is guaranteed to end the transaction, but what do you do with the session state? In this example, a few user-defined variables were set: do they persist to the next transaction?

From this example, you can see that your proxy needs to handle several issues:

- To be able to send the transaction to the right shard, the sharding key has to be available to the broker when it sees the first statement in the transaction.
- You have to know whether the transaction is a read-only or read-write transaction before sending the first statement to a server.
- You need to be able to deduce that you are inside a transaction and that the next statement should go to the same connection.
- You need to be able to see whether the previous statement committed a transaction, so that you can switch to another connection.
- You need to decide how to handle session-specific state information such as user-defined variables, temporary tables, and session-specific settings of server variables.

It is theoretically possible to solve the first issue by holding back the START TRANSAC TION and then extracting the sharding key from the first statement of the transaction by parsing the query. This is, however, very error-prone and still requires the application writer to know that it has to make the sharding key clearly visible in the first statement. A better solution is for the application to provide the sharding key explicitly with the first statement of the transaction, either through special comments or by allowing the broker to accept the sharding key out of band (i.e., not as part of the query).

To solve the second issue, you can use the same technique just described and mark a transaction as read-write or read-only. This can be done either through a special comment in the query or by providing the broker with this information out-of-band. A transaction marked as read-only will then be sent to the slave and executed there.

For the first and second issues, you need to be able to detect when the user makes an error by either issuing update statements in a read-only transaction or sending a transaction to the wrong shard. Fortunately, MySQL 5.6 has added START TRANSACTION READ ONLY so you can easily make sure that the application does not succeed in issuing an update statement. Detecting whether the statement is sent to the right shard can be more tricky. If you rewrite your queries as shown in Example 7-2, you will automatically get an error when you access the wrong shard because the schema name will be wrong. If you do not rewrite the queries, you have to tailor some assert-like functionality to ensure that the query is executed on the correct shard.

To detect whether a transaction is in progress, the response packet of the MySQL Protocol contains two flags: SERVER_STATUS_IN_TRANS and SERVER_STATUS_AUTOCOMMIT. The first flag is true if a transaction has been started *explicitly* using START TRANSACTION, but will not be set when AUTOCOMMIT=0. The flag SERVER_STATUS_AUTOCOMMIT is set if autocommit is on, and is clear otherwise. By combining these two flags, it is possible to see whether a statement is part of a transaction and the next statement should be sent to the same connection. There is currently no support in the MySQL connectors to check these flags, so currently you have to track transaction-starting statements and the autocommit flag in the broker.

Handling the fourth issue (detecting whether a new transaction has started) would be easy if there were a server flag in the response packet that told you if a new transaction had started. Unfortunately, this is currently not available in the server, so you just have to monitor queries as they come in and recognize those that start a new transaction. Remember that some statements cause an implicit commit, so make sure to include them if you want a generic solution.

Dispatching Queries

As explained in the discussion in "Handling Transactions" on page 216, handling transactions in a sharded environment is far from transparent, and applications have to take into account that they are working with a sharded database. For this reason, the goal for the sample implementation demonstrated in this chapter is not to make query dispatch transparent, but rather to make it easy to use for the application developer.

Most of the discussion in this section applies both when using a proxy as a broker and when placing the broker close to the application, such as if you implement the broker in a PHP program on the application server. For the purposes of illustration, we'll assume a PHP implementation in this section. Let's continue with the model introduced in Example 7-2 through Example 7-5, and implement a dynamic sharding scheme for range sharding.

So what kind of information can you reasonably ask the application developer to provide? As you saw previously, it is necessary to provide the sharding key one way or the other. A typical range mapping, such as shown in Table 7-3, allows you to fetch the shard identifier only if you also provide the function identifier of the function used to shard the tables used in the query. It's unreasonable to expect the application developer to know the function identifier that is needed for the query, and doing so would not be very robust either because the partition functions might change. However, because each *table* in a query is sharded based on the function identifier, it is possible to deduce the function identifier if all the tables accessed in the query are provided. It will also be possible to check that the query truly accesses only the tables sharded using one partition function, along with optional global tables.

To figure out the partition function from the tables, we need to add an additional table that maps tables to partition functions. Such a table is shown in Example 7-6, where each fully qualified table name is mapped to the partition function used for that table. If a table is not present here, it is a global table and exists on all shards.

Example 7-6. Table for tracking the partition function used for tables

```
CREATE TABLE columns (
      schema_name VARCHAR(64),
      table_name VARCHAR(64),
      func_id INT,
      PRIMARY KEY (schema_name, table_name),
      FOREIGN KEY (func_id) REFERENCES partition_functions(func_id)
)
```

Given a set of tables, we can both compute the partition function identifier and the shard identifier at the same time (as in Example 7-7).

Example 7-7. Full PHP code to fetch shard information from a sharding database

```
$FETCH_SHARD = <<<END_OF_QUERY
SELECT shard_id, host, port ❶
FROM ranges JOIN locations USING (shard_id)
WHERE ranges.func_id = (
      SELECT DISTINCT func_id
        FROM columns JOIN partition_functions USING (func_id)
        WHERE CONCAT(schema_name, '.', table_name) IN (%s) ❷
  ) AND %s >= ranges.lower_bound
ORDER BY ranges.lower_bound DESC LIMIT 1; ❸
END_OF_QUERY;

class Dictionary {
  private $server;

  public function __construct($host, $user, $pass, $port = 3306) {
    $mysqli = new mysqli($host, $user, $pass, 'sharding', $port); ❹
    $this->server = $mysqli;
  }

  public function get_connection($key, $user, $pass, $db, $tables) {
    global $FETCH_SHARD;
    $quoted_tables = array_map(function($table) { return "'$table'"; },
                              $tables); ❺
    $fetch_query = sprintf($FETCH_SHARD,
                          implode(', ', $quoted_tables),
                          $this->server->escape_string($key));
    if ($res = $this->server->query($fetch_query)) {
```

```
        list($shard_id, $host, $port) = $res->fetch_row();
        $link = new my_mysqli($shard_id, $host, $user, $pass, $db, $port); ❻
        return $link;
      }
      return null;
    }
}
```

❶   This query fetches the shard identifier, the host, and the port of the shard using the tables accessed in a query and the sharding key.

❷   This query returns one row for each partition function being used by the tables. This means that if the tables belong to more than one partition function, this subselect will return more than one row. Because this subselect is not allowed to return more than one row, an error will be raised and the entire query will fail with a "subselect returned more than one row."

❸   The where condition can match more than one row (i.e., all rows that have a lower bound smaller than the key). Because only the row with the highest lower bound is needed, the result sets are ordered in descending order (placing the highest lower bound first in the result set) and only the first row is picked using a LIMIT clause.

❹   Establish a connection to the sharding database so that we can fetch information about the shards. For this we use a "plain" connector.

❺   Construct the list of tables to look up and insert them into the statement.

❻   Establish a connection to the shard by passing the necessary information. Here we use the specialized connector that can handle schema name replacement in the queries.

Shard Management

To keep the system responsive even as the load on the system changes, or just for administrative reasons, you will sometimes have to move data around, either by moving entire shards to different nodes or moving data between shards. Each of these two procedures presents its own challenges in rebalancing the load with a minimum of downtime—preferably no downtime at all. Automated solutions should be preferred.

Moving a Shard to a Different Node

The easiest solution is to move an entire shard to a different node. If you have followed our earlier advice and placed each shard in a separate schema, moving the schema is as easy as moving the directory. However, doing this while continuing to allow writes to the node is a different story.

Moving a shard from one node (the source node) to another node (the target node) without any downtime at all is not possible, but it is possible to keep the downtime to a minimum. The technique is similar to the description in Chapter 3 of creating a slave. The idea is to make a backup of the shard, restore it on the target node, and use replication to re-execute any changes that happened in between. This is what you'll need to do:

1. Create a backup of the schemas on the source node that you want to move. Both online and offline backup methods can be used.

2. Each backup, as you could see in earlier chapters, backs up data to a particular point in the binary log. Write this log position down.

3. Bring the target node down by stopping the server.

4. While the server is down:

    a. Set the option `replicate-do-db` in the configuration file to replicate only the shard that you want to move:

    ```
    [mysqld]
    replicate-do-db=shard_123
    ```

    b. If you have to restore the backup from the source node while the server is down, do that at this time.

5. Bring the server up again.

6. Configure replication to start reading from the position that you noted in step 2 and start replication on the target server. This will read events from the source server and apply any changes to the shard that you are moving.

    Plan to have excess capacity on the target node so that you can temporarily handle an increase in the number of writes on it.

7. When the target node is sufficiently close to the source node, lock the shard's schema on the source node in order to stop changes. It is not necessary to stop changes to the shard on the target node, because no writes will go there yet.

    The easiest way to handle that is to issue LOCK TABLES and lock all the tables in the shard, but other schemes are possible, including just removing the tables (e.g., if the application can handle a table that disappears, as outlined next, this is a possible alternative).

8. Check the log position on the source server. Because the shard is not being updated anymore, this will be the highest log position you need to restore.

9. Wait for the target server to catch up to this position, such as by using START SLAVE UNTIL and MASTER_POS_WAIT.

10. Turn off replication on the target server by issuing RESET SLAVE. This will remove all replication information, including *master.info*, *relay-log.info*, and all relay log-

files. If you added any replication options to the *my.cnf* file to configure replication, you have to remove them, preferably in the next step.

11. Optionally bring the target server down, remove the `replicate-do-db` from the *my.cnf* file for the target server, and bring the server up again.

    This step is not strictly necessary, because the `replicate-do-db` option is used only to move shards and does not affect the functioning of the shard after the shard has been moved. When the time comes to move a shard here again, you have to change the option at that time anyway.

12. Update the shard information so that update requests are directed to the new location of the shard.

13. Unlock the schema to restart writes to the shard.

14. Drop the shard schema from the source server. Depending on how the shard is locked, there might still be readers of the shard at this point, so you have to take that into consideration.

Whew! That took quite a few steps. Fortunately, they can be automated using the MySQL Replicant library. The details for each individual step vary depending on how the application is implemented.

Various backup techniques are covered in Chapter 15, so we won't list them here. Note that when designing a solution, you don't want to tie the procedure to any specific backup method, because it might later turn out that other ways of creating the backup are more suitable.

To implement the backup procedure just described, it is necessary to bring the shard offline, which means that it is necessary to prevent updates to the shard. You can do this either by locking the shard in the application or by locking tables in the schema.

Implementing locking in the application requires coordination of all requests so that there are no known conflicts, and because web applications are inherently distributed, lock management can become quite complicated very quickly.

In our case, we simplify the situation by locking a single table—the `locations` table— instead of spreading out the locks among the various tables accessed by many clients. Basically, all lookups for shard locations go through the `locations` table, so a single lock on this table ensures that no new updates to any shard will be *started* while we perform the move and remap the shards. It is possible that there are updates *in progress* that either have started to update the shard or are just about to start updating the shard. So you should also lock the entire server using READ_ONLY. Any updates about to start will be locked out and be given an error message. Updates in progress will be allowed to finish (or might be killed after a timeout). When the lock on the shard is released, the shard will be gone, so the statements doing the update will fail and will have to be redone on the new shard.

Example 7-8 automates the procedures just described. You can also use the Replicant library to do it.

Example 7-8. Procedure for moving a shard between nodes

```
_UPDATE_SHARD_MAP = """
UPDATE locations
   SET host = %s, port = %d
 WHERE shard_id = %d
"""

def lock_shard(server, shard):
    server.use("common")
    server.sql("BEGIN")
    server.sql(("SELECT host, port, sock"
                "  FROM locations"
                " WHERE shard_id = %d FOR UPDATE"), (shard,))

def unlock_shard(server):
    server.sql("COMMIT")

def move_shard(common, shard, source, target, backup_method):
    backup_pos = backup_method.backup_to()
    config = target.fetch_config()
    config.set('replicate-do-db', shard)
    target.stop().replace_config(config).start()
    replicant.change_master(target, source, backup_pos)
    replicant.slave_start(target)

    # Wait until slave is at most 10 seconds behind master
    replicant.slave_status_wait_until(target,
                                      'Seconds_Behind_Master',
                                      lambda x: x < 10)
    lock_shard(common, shard)
    pos = replicant.fetch_master_pos(source)
    replicant.slave_wait_for_pos(target, pos)
    source.sql("SET GLOBAL READ_ONLY = 1")
    kill_connections(source)
    common.sql(_UPDATE_SHARD_MAP,
               (target.host, target.port, target.socket, shard))
    unlock_shard(common, shard)
    source.sql("DROP DATABASE shard_%s", (shard))
    source.sql("SET GLOBAL READ_ONLY = 1")
```

As described earlier, you have to keep in mind that even though the table is locked, some client sessions may be using the table because they have retrieved the node location but are not yet connected to it, or alternatively may have started updating the shard.

The application code has to take this into account. The easiest solution is to have the application recompute the node if the query to the shard fails. Example 7-9 shows the changes that are necessary to fix Example 7-3 to re-execute the lookup if certain errors occurred.

Example 7-9. Changes to application code to handle shard moving

```
do {
  $error = 0;
  $mysql = $DICT->get_connection($key, 'mats', 'xyzzy', 'employees',
                                 array('employees.employees', 'employees.dept_emp',
                                       'employees.departments'));
  if ($stmt = $mysql->prepare($QUERY))
  {
    $stmt->bind_param("d", $key);
    if ($stmt->execute()) {
      $stmt->bind_result($first_name, $last_name, $dept_name);
      while ($stmt->fetch())
        print "$first_name $last_name $dept_name @{$mysql->shard_id}\n";
    }
    else
      $error = $stmt->errno;
    $stmt->close();
  }
  else
    $error = $mysql->errno;

  /* Handle the error */
  switch ($error) {
  case 1290: ❶
  case 1146: ❷
  case 2006: ❸
    continue;
  }
} while (0);
```

❶   In this case, execution failed because the server was set in read-only mode. The application looked up the shard, but the move procedure started before it had a chance to start executing the query.

❷   In this case, execution failed because the schema disappeared. The connection looked up the shard location before it was moved, and tried to execute the query after it was moved.

Recall from "Multiple shards per server (virtual shards)" on page 203 that the shard identifier is part of each schema name. This is how you can detect that the shard is gone. If you did not have a unique name for each schema, you would not be able to distinguish the shards.

❸   In this case, execution failed because the connection was killed. The connection looked up the shard location before it was moved and started to execute the query, but the server decided that it took too long to execute.

Splitting Shards

When a host becomes too loaded, you can move one of the shards on the host to another server, but what do you do when the *shard* becomes too hot? The answer is: you split it.

Splitting a shard into multiple smaller shards can be very expensive, but the downtime can be kept to a minimum if done carefully. Assume that you need to split a shard and move half of the contents of the shard to a new node. Here's a step-by-step explanation:

1. Take a backup of all the schemas in the shard. If you use an online backup method, such as MEB, XtraDB, or filesystem snapshots, the shard can be kept online while the backup is taken.

2. Write down the binary log position that this backup corresponds to.

3. Restore the backup from step 1 on the destination node.

4. Start replication from the source node to the destination node. If you want to avoid copying more changes than necessary, you can use `binlog-do-db` or `replication-do-db` to just replicate changes for the schemas that you moved. At this point, all requests still go to the original shard and the new shard is "dark" and not visible.

5. Wait until replication has caught up and the destination is close enough to the source. Then lock the source shard so that neither reads nor writes are possible.

6. Wait until the destination host is fully up to date with the source. During this step, all data in the shard will be unavailable.

7. Update the sharding database so that all requests for data in the new shard go to the new shard.

8. Unlock the source shard. At this point, all data is available, but there is too much data on both the source and destination shards. This data is, however, not part of the new shard data and queries sent to the server will not access this data.

9. Start two jobs in parallel that remove the superfluous rows on each shard using a normal `DELETE`. To avoid a large impact on performance, you can remove just a few rows at a time by adding a `LIMIT`.

Conclusion

This chapter presented techniques for increasing the throughput of your applications by scaling out, whereby we introduced more servers to handle more requests for data. We presented ways to set up MySQL for scaling out using replication and gave practical examples of some of the concepts. In the next chapter, we will look at some more advanced replication concepts.

Joel felt pretty good. He had delivered his first company white paper to Mr. Summerson earlier in the day. He knew the response would come soon. While his boss was a bit on the "hyper alpha boss" high end, he could count on his work being reviewed promptly. A little while later, on his way to the break room, Joel met his boss in the hall. "I liked your paper on scaling, Joel. You can get started on that right away; we've got some extra servers lying around downstairs." "Right away," Joel said with a smile as his boss moved on to deliver another drive-by tasking.

## CHAPTER 8

Replication Deep Dive

A knock on his door drew Joel's attention away from reading his email. He wasn't surprised to see Mr. Summerson standing in his doorway.

"Yes, sir?"

"I am getting a little concerned about all this replication stuff we've got now. I'd like you to do some research into what we need to do to improve our knowledge of how it all works. I want you to put together a document explaining not only the current configuration, but also troubleshooting ideas with specific details on what to do when things go wrong and what makes it tick."

Joel was expecting such a task. He, too, was starting to be concerned that he needed to know more about replication. "I'll get right on it, sir."

"Great. Take your time on this one. I want to get it right."

Joel nodded as his boss walked away. He sighed and gathered his favorite MySQL books together. He needed to do some reading on the finer points of replication.

Previous chapters introduced the basics of configuring and deploying replication to keep your site up and available, but to understand replication's potential pitfalls and how to use it effectively, you should know something about its operation and the kinds of information it uses to accomplish its tasks. This is the goal of this chapter. We will cover a lot of ground, including:

- How to promote slaves to masters more robustly
- Tips for avoiding corrupted databases after a crash
- Multisource replication
- Row-based replication

- Global transaction identifiers
- Multithreaded replication

Replication Architecture Basics

Chapter 4 discussed the binary log along with some of the tools that are available to investigate the events it records. But we didn't describe how events make it over to the slave and get re-executed there. Once you understand these details, you can exert more control over replication, prevent it from causing corruption after a crash, and investigate problems by examining the logs.

Figure 8-1 shows a schematic illustration of the internal replication architecture, consisting of the clients connected to the master, the master itself, and several slaves. For each client that connects to the master, the server runs a *session* that is responsible for executing all SQL statements and sending results back to the client.

The events flow through the replication system from the master to the slaves in the following manner:

1. The session accepts a statement from the client, executes the statement, and synchronizes with other sessions to ensure each transaction is executed without conflicting with other changes made by other sessions.

2. Just before the statement finishes execution, an entry consisting of one or more events is written to the binary log. This process is covered in Chapter 3 and will not be described again in this chapter.

3. After the events have been written to the binary log, a *dump thread* in the master takes over, reads the events from the binary log, and sends them over to the slave's I/O thread.

4. When the slave I/O thread receives the event, it writes it to the end of the relay log.

5. Once in the relay log, a *slave SQL thread* reads the event from the relay log and executes the event to apply the changes to the database on the slave.

If the connection to the master is lost, the slave I/O thread will try to reconnect to the server in the same way that any MySQL client thread does. Some of the options that we'll see in this chapter deal with reconnection attempts.

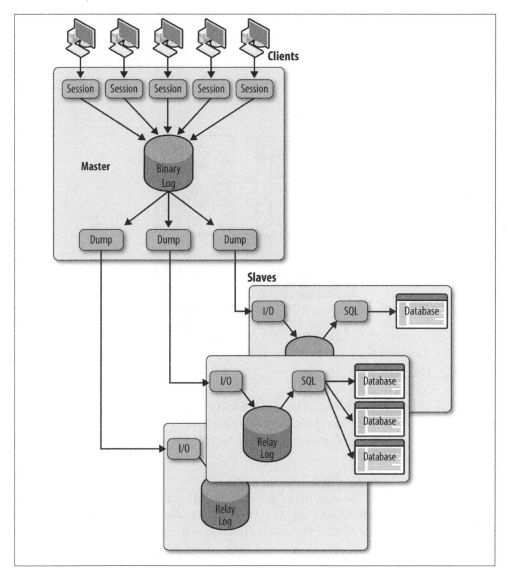

Figure 8-1. Master and several slaves with internal architecture

The Structure of the Relay Log

As the previous section showed, the relay log is the information that ties the master and slave together—the heart of replication. It's important to be aware of how it is used and how the slave threads coordinate through it. Therefore, we'll go through the details here of how the relay log is structured and how the slave threads use the relay log to handle replication.

As described in the previous section, the events sent from the master are stored in the relay log by the I/O thread. The relay log serves as a buffer so that the master does not have to wait for the slave execution to finish before sending the next event.

Figure 8-2 shows a schematic view of the relay log. It's similar in structure to the binlog on the master but has some extra files.

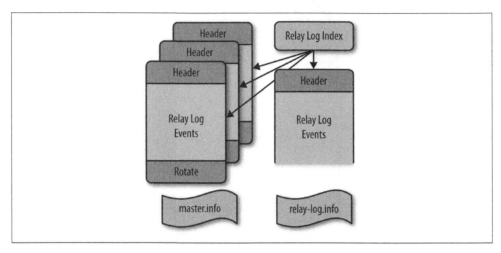

Figure 8-2. Structure of the relay log

In addition to the content files and the index files in the binary log, the relay log maintains two files to keep track of replication progress: the *relay log information file* and the *master log information file*. The names of these two files are controlled by two options in the *my.cnf* file:

`relay-log-info-file=`*filename*
> This option sets the name of the relay log information file. It is also available as the read-only server variable `relay_log_info_file`. Unless an absolute filename is given, the filename is relative to the data directory of the server. The default filename is *relay-log.info*.

`master-info-file=`*filename*
> This option sets the name of the master log information file. The default filename is *master.info*.

The information in the *master.info* file takes precedence over information in the *my.cnf* file. This means that if you change information in the *my.cnf* file and restart the server, the information will still be read from the *master.info* file instead of from the *my.cnf* file.

For this reason, we recommend *not* to put any of the options that can be specified with the CHANGE MASTER TO command in the *my.cnf* file, but instead to use the CHANGE MASTER TO command to configure replication. If, for some reason, you want to put any of the replication options in the *my.cnf* file and you want to make sure that the options are read from it when starting the slave, you have to issue RESET SLAVE before editing the *my.cnf* file.

Beware when executing RESET SLAVE! It will delete the *master.info* file, the *relay-log.info* file, and all the relay logfiles!

For convenience, we will use the default names of the information files in the discussion that follows.

The *master.info* file contains the master read position as well as all the information necessary to connect to the master and start replication. When the slave I/O thread starts up, it reads information from this file, if it is available.

Example 8-1 shows a short example of a *master.info* file. We've added a line number before each line and an annotation in italics at the end of each line (the file itself cannot contain comments). If the server is not compiled with SSL support, lines 9 through 15—which contain all the SSL options—will be missing. Example 8-1 shows what these options look like when SSL is compiled. The SSL fields are covered later in the chapter.

The password is written unencrypted in the *master.info* file. For that reason, it is critical to protect the file so it can be read only by the MySQL server. The standard way to ensure this is to define a dedicated user on the server to run the server, assign all the files responsible for replication and database maintenance to this user, and remove all permissions from the files except read and write by this user.

Example 8-1. Contents of the master.info file (MySQL version 5.6.12)

1	23	*Number of lines in the file*
2	master-bin.000001	*Current binlog file being read (Master_Log_File)*
3	151	*Last binlog position read (Read_Master_Log_Pos)*
4	localhost	*Master host connected to (Master_Host)*
5	root	*Replication user (Master_User)*
6		*Replication password*
7	13000	*Master port used (Master_Port)*

8	60	*Number of times slave will try to reconnect (Connect_Retry)*
9	0	*1 if SSL is enabled, otherwise 0*
10		*SSL Certification Authority (CA)*
11		*SSL CA Path*
12		*SSL Certificate*
13		*SSL Cipher*
14		*SSL Key*
15	0	*SSL Verify Server Certificate*
16	60.000	*Heartbeat*
17		*Bind Address*
18	0	*Ignore Server IDs*
19	*Master UUID*	
		8c6d027e-cf38-11e2-84c7-0021cc6850ca
20	10	*Retry Count*
21		*SSL CRL*
22		*SSL CRL Path*
23	0	*Auto Position*

If you have an old server, the format can be slightly different.

In MySQL versions earlier than 4.1, the first line did not appear. Developers added a line count to the file in version 4.1.1 so they could extend the file with new fields and detect which fields are supported by just checking the line count.

Version 5.1.16 introduced line 15, *SSL Verify Server Certificate*, and the lines after that were introduced in different versions of 5.6.

The *relay-log.info* file tracks the progress of replication and is updated by the SQL thread. Example 8-2 shows a sample excerpt of a *relay-log.info* file. These lines correspond to the beginning of the next event to execute.

Example 8-2. Contents of the relay-log.info file

./slave-relay-bin.000003	*Relay log file (Relay_Log_File)*
380	*Relay log position (Relay_Log_Pos)*
master1-bin.000001	*Master log file (Relay_Master_Log_File)*
234	*Master log position (Exec_Master_Log_Pos)*

If any of the files are not available, they will be created from information in the *my.cnf* file and the options given to the CHANGE MASTER TO command *when the slave is started.*

 It is *not* enough to just configure a slave using *my.cnf* and execute a CHANGE MASTER TO statement. The relay logfiles, the *master.info* file, and the *relay-log.info* file are *not* created until you issue START SLAVE.

The Replication Threads

As you saw earlier in the chapter, replication requires several specialized threads on both the master and the slave. The dump thread on the master handles the master's end of replication. Two slave threads—the I/O thread and the SQL thread—handle replication on the slave.

Master dump thread

This thread is created on the master when a slave I/O thread connects. The dump thread is responsible for reading entries from the binlog on the master and sending them to the slave.

There is one dump thread per connected slave.

Slave I/O thread

This thread connects to the master to request a dump of all the changes that occur and writes them to the relay log for further processing by the SQL thread.

There is one I/O thread on each slave. Once the connection is established, it is kept open so that any changes on the master are immediately received by the slave.

Slave SQL thread

This thread reads changes from the relay log and applies them to the slave database. The thread is responsible for coordinating with other MySQL threads to ensure changes do not interfere with the other activities going on in the MySQL server.

From the perspective of the master, the I/O thread is just another client thread and can execute both dump requests and SQL statements on the master. This means a client can connect to a server and pretend to be a slave to get the master to dump changes from the binary log. This is how the *mysqlbinlog* program (covered in detail in Chapter 4) operates.

The SQL thread acts as a session when working with the database. This means it maintains state information similar to that of a session, but with some differences. Because the SQL thread has to process changes from several different threads on the master— the events from *all* threads on the master are written in commit order to the binary log —the SQL thread keeps some extra information to distinguish events properly. For example, temporary tables are session-specific, so to keep temporary tables from different sessions separated, the session ID is added to the events. The SQL thread then refers to the session ID to keep actions for different sessions on the master separate.

The details of how the SQL thread executes events are covered later in the chapter.

The I/O thread is significantly faster than the SQL thread because the I/O thread merely writes events to a log, whereas the SQL thread has to figure out how to execute changes against the databases. Therefore, during replication, several events are usually buffered in the relay log. If the master crashes, you have to handle these before connecting to a new master.

To avoid losing these events, wait for the SQL thread to catch up before trying to reconnect the slave to another master.

Later in the chapter, you will see several ways of detecting whether the relay log is empty or has events left to execute.

Starting and Stopping the Slave Threads

In Chapter 3, you saw how to start the slave using the START SLAVE command, but a lot of details were glossed over. We're now ready for a more thorough description of starting and stopping the slave threads.

When the server starts, it will also start the slave threads if there is a *master.info* file. As mentioned earlier in this chapter, the *master.info* file is created if the server was configured for replication and if START SLAVE commands were issued on the slaves to start their I/O and SQL threads. So if the previous session had been used for replication, replication will be resumed from the last position stored in the *master.info* and *relay-log.info* files, with slightly different behavior for the two slave threads:

Slave I/O thread
> The slave I/O thread will resume by reading from the last read position according to the *master.info* file.
>
> For writing the events, the I/O thread will rotate the relay logfile and start writing to a new file, updating the positions accordingly.

Slave SQL thread
> The slave SQL thread will resume reading from the relay log position given in *relay-log.info*.

You can start the slave threads explicitly using the START SLAVE command and stop them explicitly with the STOP SLAVE command. These commands control the slave threads and can be used to stop and start the I/O thread or SQL thread separately:

START SLAVE *and* STOP SLAVE
> These will start or stop both the I/O and the slave thread.

START SLAVE IO_THREAD *and* STOP SLAVE IO_THREAD
> These will start or stop only the I/O thread.

`START SLAVE SQL_THREAD` *and* `STOP SLAVE SQL_THREAD`
These will start or stop only the SQL thread.

When you stop the slave threads, the current state of replication is saved to the *master.info* and *relay-log.info* files. This information is then picked up when the slave threads are started again.

 If you specify a master host using the `master-host` option (which can be either in the *my.cnf* file or passed as an option when starting *mysqld*), the slave will also start.

Because the recommendation is not to use this option, but instead to use the `MASTER_HOST` option to the `CHANGE MASTER` command, the `master-host` option will not be covered here.

Running Replication over the Internet

There are many reasons to replicate between two geographically separated data centers. One reason is to ensure you can recover from a disaster such as an earthquake or a power outage. You can also locate a site strategically close to some of your users, such as content delivery networks, to offer them faster response times. Although organizations with enough resources can lease dedicated fiber, we will assume you use the open Internet to connect.

The events sent from the master to the slave should never be considered secure in any way: as a matter of fact, it is easy to decode them to see the information that is replicated. As long as you are behind a firewall and do not replicate over the Internet—for example, replicating between two data centers—this is probably secure enough, but as soon you need to replicate to another data center in another town or on another continent, it is important to protect the information from prying eyes by encrypting it.

The standard method for encrypting data for transfer over the Internet is to use SSL. There are several options for protecting your data, all of which involve SSL in some way:

- Use the support that is built into the server to encrypt the replication from master to slave.
- Use Stunnel, a program that establishes an SSL tunnel (essentially a virtual private network) to a program that lacks SSL support.
- Use SSH in tunnel mode.

This last alternative does not appear to really offer any significant advantages over using Stunnel, but can be useful if you are not allowed to install any new programs on a machine and can enable SSH on your servers. In that case, you can use SSH to set up a tunnel. We will not cover this option further.

When using either the built-in SSL support or `stunnel` for creating a secure connection, you need:

- A certificate from a certification authority (CA)
- A (public) certificate for the server
- A (private) key for the server

The details of generating, managing, and using SSL certificates is beyond the scope of this book, but for demonstration purposes, Example 8-3 shows how to generate a self-signed public certificate and associated private key. This example assumes you use the configuration file for OpenSSL in */etc/ssl/openssl.cnf.*

Example 8-3. Generating a self-signed public certificate with a private key

```
$ sudo openssl req -new -x509 -days 365 -nodes \
      -config /etc/ssl/openssl.cnf \
>     -out /etc/ssl/certs/master.pem -keyout /etc/ssl/private/master.key
Generating a 1024 bit RSA private key
.....++++++
.++++++
writing new private key to '/etc/ssl/private/master.key'
-----
You are about to be asked to enter information that will be incorporated
into your certificate request.
What you are about to enter is what is called a Distinguished Name or a DN.
There are quite a few fields but you can leave some blank
For some fields there will be a default value,
If you enter '.', the field will be left blank.
-----
Country Name (2 letter code) [AU]:SE
State or Province Name (full name) [Some-State]:Uppland
Locality Name (eg, city) []:Storvreta
Organization Name (eg, company) [Internet Widgits Pty Ltd]:Big Inc.
Organizational Unit Name (eg, section) []:Database Management
Common Name (eg, YOUR name) []:master-1.example.com
Email Address []:mats@example.com
```

The certificate signing procedure puts a self-signed public certificate in */etc/ssl/certs/ master.pem* and the private key in */etc/ssl/private/master.key* (which is also used to sign the public certificate).

On the slave, you have to create a server key and a server certificate in a similar manner. For the sake of discussion, we'll use */etc/ssl/certs/slave.pem* as the name of the slave server's public certificate and */etc/ssl/private/slave.key* as the name of the slave server's private key.

Setting Up Secure Replication Using Built-in Support

The simplest way to encrypt the connection between the master and slave is to use a server with SSL support. Methods for compiling a server with SSL support are beyond the scope of this book; if you are interested, consult the online reference manual.

To use the built-in SSL support, it is necessary to do the following:

- Configure the master by making the master keys available.
- Configure the slave to encrypt the replication channel.

To configure the master to use SSL support, add the following options to the *my.cnf* file:

```
[mysqld]
ssl-capath=/etc/ssl/certs
ssl-cert=/etc/ssl/certs/master.pem
ssl-key=/etc/ssl/private/master.key
```

The `ssl-capath` option contains the name of a directory that holds the certificates of trusted CAs, the `ssl-cert` option contains the name of the file that holds the server certificate, and the `ssl-key` option contains the name of the file that holds the private key for the server. As always, you need to restart the server after you have updated the *my.cnf* file.

The master is now configured to provide SSL support to any client, and because a slave uses the normal client protocol, it will allow a slave to use SSL as well.

To configure the slave to use an SSL connection, issue `CHANGE MASTER TO` with the `MASTER_SSL` option to turn on SSL for the connection, then issue `MASTER_SSL_CAPATH`, `MASTER_SSL_CERT`, and `MASTER_SSL_KEY`, which function like the `ssl-capath`, `ssl-cert`, and `ssl-key` configuration options just mentioned, but specify the slave's side of the connection to the master:

```
slave> CHANGE MASTER TO
    ->      MASTER_HOST = 'master-1',
    ->      MASTER_USER = 'repl_user',
    ->      MASTER_PASSWORD = 'xyzzy',
    ->      MASTER_SSL_CAPATH = '/etc/ssl/certs',
    ->      MASTER_SSL_CERT = '/etc/ssl/certs/slave.pem',
    ->      MASTER_SSL_KEY = '/etc/ssl/private/slave.key';
Query OK, 0 rows affected (0.00 sec)

slave> START SLAVE;
Query OK, 0 rows affected (0.15 sec)
```

Now you have a slave running with a secure channel to the master.

Setting Up Secure Replication Using Stunnel

Stunnel is an easy-to-use SSL tunneling application that you can set up either as an SSL server or as an SSL client.

Using Stunnel to set up a secure connection is almost as easy as setting up an SSL connection using the built-in support, but requires some additional configuration. This approach can be useful if the server is not compiled with SSL support or if for some reason you want to offload the extra processing required to encrypt and decrypt data from the MySQL server (which makes sense only if you have a multicore CPU).

As with the built-in support, you need to have a certificate from a CA as well as a public certificate and a private key for each server. These are then used for the `stunnel` command instead of for the server.

Figure 8-3 shows a master, a slave, and two Stunnel instances that communicate over an insecure network. One Stunnel instance on the slave server accepts data over a standard MySQL client connection from the slave server, encrypts it, and sends it over to the Stunnel instance on the master server. The Stunnel instance on the master server, in turn, listens on a dedicated SSL port to receive the encrypted data, decrypts it, and sends it over a client connection to the non-SSL port on the master server.

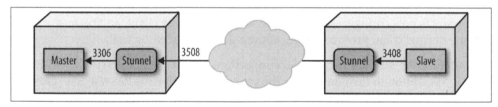

Figure 8-3. Replication over an insecure channel using Stunnel

Example 8-4 shows a configuration file that sets up Stunnel to listen on socket 3508 for an SSL connection, where the master server is listening on the default MySQL socket 3306. The example refers to the certificate and key files by the names we used earlier.

Example 8-4. Master server configuration file /etc/stunnel/master.conf

```
cert=/etc/ssl/certs/master.pem
key=/etc/ssl/private/master.key
CApath=/etc/ssl/certs
[mysqlrepl]
accept = 3508
connect = 3306
```

Example 8-5 shows the configuration file that sets up Stunnel on the client side. The example assigns port 3408 as the intermediate port—the non-SSL port that the slave will connect to locally—and Stunnel connects to the SSL port 3508 on the master server, as shown in Example 8-4.

Example 8-5. Slave server configuration file /etc/stunnel/slave.conf

```
cert=/etc/ssl/certs/slave.pem
key=/etc/ssl/private/slave.key
CApath=/etc/ssl/certs
[mysqlrepl]
accept = 3408
connect = master-1:3508
```

You can now start the Stunnel program on each server and configure the slave to connect to the Stunnel instance on the slave server. Because the Stunnel instance is on the same server as the slave, you should give localhost as the master host to connect to and the port that the Stunnel instance accepts connections on (3408). Stunnel will then take care of tunneling the connection over to the master server:

```
slave> CHANGE MASTER TO
    ->     MASTER_HOST = 'localhost',
    ->     MASTER_PORT = 3408,
    ->     MASTER_USER = 'repl_user',
    ->     MASTER_PASSWORD = 'xyzzy';
Query OK, 0 rows affected (0.00 sec)

slave> START SLAVE;
Query OK, 0 rows affected (0.15 sec)
```

You now have a secure connection set up over an insecure network.

 If you are using Debian-based Linux (e.g., Debian or Ubuntu), you can start one Stunnel instance for each configuration file in the */etc/ stunnel* directory by setting ENABLED=1 in */etc/default/stunnel4*.

So if you create the Stunnel configuration files as given in this section, one slave Stunnel and one master Stunnel instance will be started automatically whenever you start the machine.

Finer-Grained Control Over Replication

With an understanding of replication internals and the information replication uses, you can control it more expertly and learn how to avoid some problems that can occur. We'll give you some useful background in this section.

Information About Replication Status

You can find most of the information about replication status on the slave, but there is some information available on the master as well. Most of the information on the master relates to the binlog (covered in Chapter 4), but information relating to the connected slaves is also available.

The SHOW SLAVE HOSTS command only shows information about slaves that use the report-host option, which the slave uses to give information to the master about the server that is connected. The master cannot trust the information about the connected slaves, because there are routers with NAT between the master and the slave. In addition to the hostname, there are some other options that you can use to provide information about the connecting slave:

report-host
> The name of the connecting slave. This is typically the domain name of the slave, or some other similar identifier, but can in reality be any string. In Example 8-6, we use the name "Magic Slave."

report-port
> The port on which the slave listens for connections. This default is 3306.

report-user
> This is the user for connecting to the master. The value given does not have to match the value used in CHANGE MASTER TO. This option is only shown when the show-slave-auth-info option is given to the server.

report-password
> This is the password used when connecting to the master. The password given does not have to match the password given to CHANGE MASTER TO.

show-slave-auth-info
> If this option is enabled, the master will show the additional information about the reported user and password in the output from SHOW SLAVE HOSTS.

Example 8-6 shows sample output from SHOW SLAVE HOSTS where three slaves are connected to the master.

Example 8-6. Sample output from SHOW SLAVE HOSTS

```
master> SHOW SLAVE HOSTS;
+-----------+-------------+------+-------------------+-----------+
| Server_id | Host        | Port | Rpl_recovery_rank | Master_id |
+-----------+-------------+------+-------------------+-----------+
|         2 | slave-1     | 3306 |                 0 |         1 |
|         3 | slave-2     | 3306 |                 0 |         1 |
|         4 | Magic Slave | 3306 |                 0 |         1 |
+-----------+-------------+------+-------------------+-----------+
1 row in set (0.00 sec)
```

The output shows slaves that are connected to the master and some information about the slaves. Notice that this display also shows slaves that are indirectly connected to the master via relays. There are two additional fields shown when `show-slave-auth-info` is enabled (which we do not show here).

The following fields are purely informational and do not necessarily show the real slave host or port, nor the user and password used when configuring the slave in `CHANGE MASTER TO`:

`Server_id`
> This is the server ID of the connected slave.

`Host`
> This is the name of the host as given by `report-host`.

`User`
> This is the username reported by the slave by using `report-user`.

`Password`
> This column shows the password reported by the slave using `report-password`.

`Port`
> This shows the port.

`Master_id`
> This shows the server ID that the slave is replicating from.

`Rpl_recovery_rank`
> This field has never been used and is removed in MySQL version 5.5.

 The information about indirectly connected slaves cannot be entirely trusted, because it is possible for the information to be inaccurate in certain situations where slaves are being added.

For this reason, there is an effort underway to remove this information and show only directly connected slaves, as this information can be trusted.

You can use the `SHOW MASTER LOGS` command to see which logs the master is keeping track of in the binary log. A typical output from this command can be seen in Example 8-7.

The `SHOW MASTER STATUS` command (shown in Example 8-8) shows where the next event will be written in the binary log. Because a master has only a single binlog file, the table will always contain only a single line. And because of that, the last line of the output of `SHOW MASTER LOGS` will match the output of this command, only with different headers. This means that if you need to execute a `SHOW MASTER LOGS` to implement some

feature, you do not need to execute a SHOW MASTER STATUS as well but can instead use
the last line of SHOW MASTER LOGS.

Example 8-7. Typical output from SHOW MASTER LOGS

```
master> SHOW MASTER LOGS;
+--------------------+-----------+
| Log_name           | File_size |
+--------------------+-----------+
| master-bin.000011  |    469768 |
| master-bin.000012  |   1254768 |
| master-bin.000013  |    474768 |
| master-bin.000014  |      4768 |
+--------------------+-----------+
1 row in set (0.00 sec)
```

Example 8-8. Typical output from SHOW MASTER STATUS

```
master> SHOW MASTER STATUS;
+-------------------+----------+--------------+------------------+
| File              | Position | Binlog_Do_DB | Binlog_Ignore_DB |
+-------------------+----------+--------------+------------------+
| master-bin.000014 |     4768 |              |                  |
+-------------------+----------+--------------+------------------+
1 row in set (0.00 sec)
```

To determine the status for the slave threads, use the SHOW SLAVE STATUS command.
This command contains almost everything you need to know about the replication
status. Let's go through the output in more detail. A typical output from SHOW SLAVE
STATUS is given in Example 8-9.

Example 8-9. Sample output from SHOW SLAVE STATUS

```
               Slave_IO_State: Waiting for master to send event
                  Master_Host: master1.example.com
                  Master_User: repl_user
                  Master_Port: 3306
                Connect_Retry: 1
              Master_Log_File: master-bin.000001
          Read_Master_Log_Pos: 192
               Relay_Log_File: slave-relay-bin.000006
                Relay_Log_Pos: 252
        Relay_Master_Log_File: master-bin.000001
             Slave_IO_Running: Yes
            Slave_SQL_Running: Yes
              Replicate_Do_DB:
          Replicate_Ignore_DB:
           Replicate_Do_Table:
       Replicate_Ignore_Table:
      Replicate_Wild_Do_Table:
  Replicate_Wild_Ignore_Table:
                   Last_Errno: 0
```

```
                Last_Error:
              Skip_Counter: 0
       Exec_Master_Log_Pos: 192
           Relay_Log_Space: 553
           Until_Condition: None
            Until_Log_File:
             Until_Log_Pos: 0
         Master_SSL_Allowed: No
         Master_SSL_CA_File:
         Master_SSL_CA_Path:
            Master_SSL_Cert:
          Master_SSL_Cipher:
             Master_SSL_Key:
      Seconds_Behind_Master: 0
Master_SSL_Verify_Server_Cert: No
             Last_IO_Errno: 0
             Last_IO_Error:
            Last_SQL_Errno: 0
            Last_SQL_Error:
```

The state of the I/O and SQL threads

The two fields Slave_IO_Running and Slave_SQL_Running indicate whether the slave I/O thread or the SQL thread, respectively, is running. If the slave threads are not running, it could be either because they have been stopped or because of an error in the replication.

If the I/O thread is not running, the fields Last_IO_Errno and Last_IO_Error will show the reason it stopped. Similarly, Last_SQL_Errno and Last_SQL_Error will show the reason why the SQL thread stopped. If either of the threads stopped without error—for example, because they were explicitly stopped or reached the until condition—there will be no error message and the errno field will be 0, similar to the output in Example 8-9. The fields Last_Errno and Last_Error are synonyms for Last_SQL_Err no and Last_SQL_Error, respectively.

The Slave_IO_State shows a description of what the I/O thread is currently doing. Figure 8-4 shows a state diagram of how the message can change depending on the state of the I/O thread.

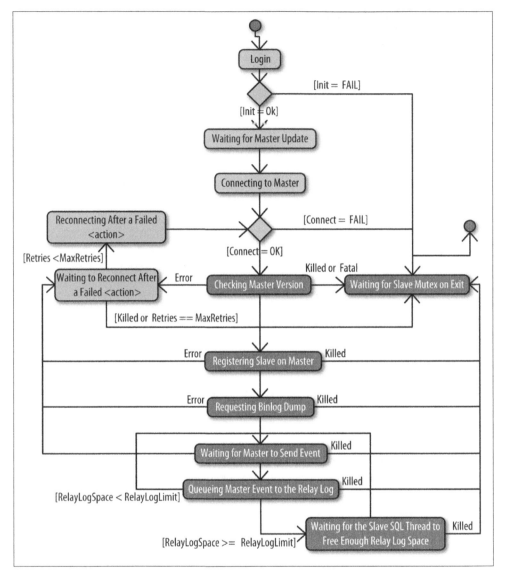

Figure 8-4. Slave I/O thread states

The messages have the following meanings:

Waiting for master update
> This message is shown briefly when the I/O thread is initialized and before it tries to establish a connection with the master.

Connecting to master

> This message is shown while the slave is trying to establish a connection with the master, but has not yet made the connection.

Checking master version

> This message is shown when the slave has managed to connect to the master and is performing a handshake with the master.

Registering slave on master

> This message is shown while the slave is trying to register itself with the master. When registering, it sends the value of the `report-host` option described earlier to the master. This usually contains the hostname or the IP number of the slave, but can contain any string. The master cannot depend simply on checking the IP address of the TCP connection, because there might be routers running inetwork address translation (NAT) between the master and slave.

Requesting binlog dump

> This message is shown when the slave starts to request a binlog dump by sending the binlog file, binlog position, and server ID to the master.

Waiting for master to send event

> This message is printed when the slave has established a connection with the master and is waiting for the master to send an event.

Queueing master event to the relay log

> This message is shown when the master has sent an event and the slave I/O thread is about to write it to the relay log. This message is displayed regardless of whether the event is actually written to the relay log or skipped because of the rules outlined in "Filtering Replication Events" on page 174.

> Note the spelling in the previous message ("Queueing" instead of "Queuing").
>
> When checking for messages using scripts or other tools, it is very important to check what the message really says and not just what you think it should read.

Waiting to reconnect after `action`

> This message is shown when a previous `action` failed with a transient error and the slave will try to reconnect. Possible values for `action` are:

`registration on master`

> When attempting to register with the master

`binlog dump request`

> When requesting a binlog dump from the master

`master event read`
> When waiting for or reading an event from the master

Reconnecting after failed `action`
> This message is shown when the slave is trying to reconnect to the master after trying `action` but has not yet managed to establish a connection. The possible values for `action` are the same as for the "Waiting to reconnect after `action`" message.

Waiting for slave mutex on exit
> This message is shown while the I/O thread is shutting down.

Waiting for the slave SQL thread to free enough relay log space
> This message is shown if the relay log space limit (as set by the `relay-log-space-limit` option) has been reached and the SQL thread needs to process some of the relay log to write the new events.

The binary log and relay log positions

As replication processes events on the slave, it maintains three positions in parallel.

These positions are shown in the output from SHOW SLAVE STATUS in Example 8-9, as the following pairs of fields:

`Master_Log_File, Read_Master_Log_Pos`
> The *master read position*: the position in the master's binary log of the next event to be read by the I/O thread.
>
> The values of these fields are taken from lines 2 and 3 of *master.info*, as shown in Example 8-1.

`Relay_Master_Log_File, Exec_Master_Log_Pos`
> The *master execute position*: the position in the master's binlog of the next event to be executed by the SQL thread.
>
> The values of these fields are taken from lines 3 and 4 of *relay-log.info*, as shown in Example 8-2.

`Relay_Log_File, Relay_Log_Pos`
> The *relay log execute position*: the position in the slave's relay log of the next event to be executed by the SQL thread.
>
> The values of these fields are taken from lines 1 and 2 of *relay-log.info*, as shown in Example 8-2.

You can use the positions to gain information about replication progress or to optimize some of the algorithms developed in Chapter 5.

For example, by comparing the master read position and the master execute position, it is possible to determine whether there are any events waiting to be executed. This is particularly interesting if the I/O thread has stopped, because it allows an easy way to wait for the relay log to become empty: once the positions are equal, there is nothing waiting in the relay log, and the slave can be safely stopped and redirected to another master.

Example 8-10 shows sample code that waits for an empty relay log on a slave. MySQL provides the convenient MASTER_POS_WAIT function to wait until a slave's relay log has processed all waiting events. In the event that the slave thread is not running, then MASTER_POS_WAIT will return NULL, which is caught and generates an exception.

Example 8-10. Python script to wait for an empty relay log

```
from mysql.replicant.errors import Error

class SlaveNotRunning(Error):
    pass

def slave_wait_for_empty_relay_log(server):
    result = server.sql("SHOW SLAVE STATUS")
    log_file = result["Master_Log_File"]
    log_pos = result["Read_Master_Log_Pos"]
    running = server.sql(
        "SELECT MASTER_POS_WAIT(%s,%s)", (log_file, log_pos))
    if running is None:
        raise SlaveNotRunning
```

Using these positions, you can also optimize the scenarios in Chapter 5. For instance, after running Example 8-21, which promotes a slave to master, you will probably have to process a lot of events in each of the other slaves' relay logs before switching the slave to the new master. In addition, ensuring that the promoted slave has executed all events before allowing any slaves to connect will allow you to lose a minimum of data.

By modifying the function order_slaves_on_position in Example 5-5 to create Example 8-11, you can make the former slaves execute all events they have in their relay logs before performing the switch. The code uses the slave_wait_for_empty_re lay_log function in Example 8-10 to wait for the relay log to become empty before reading the slave position.

Example 8-11. Minimizing the number of lost events when promoting a slave

```
from mysql.replicant.commands import (
    fetch_slave_position,
    slave_wait_for_empty_relay_log,
    )

def order_slaves_on_position(slaves):
    entries = []
    for slave in slaves:
```

```
    slave_wait_for_empty_relay_log(slave)
    pos = fetch_slave_position(slave)
    gtid = fetch_gtid_executed(slave)
    entries.append((pos, gtid, slave))
entries.sort(key=lambda x: x[0])
return [ entry[1:2] for entry in entries ]
```

In addition to the technique demonstrated here, another technique mentioned in some of the literature is to check the status of the SQL thread in the `SHOW PROCESSLIST` output. If the `State` field is "Has read all relay log; waiting for the slave I/O thread to update it," the SQL thread has read the entire relay log. This `State` message is generated only by the SQL thread, so you can safely search for it in all threads.

Options for Handling Broken Connections

The I/O thread has the responsibility for maintaining the connection with the master and, as you have seen in Figure 8-4, includes quite a complicated bit of logic to do so.

If the I/O thread loses the connection with the master, it will attempt to reconnect to the master a limited number of times. The period of inactivity after which the I/O thread reacts, the retry period, and the number of retries attempted are controlled by three options:

`--slave-net-timeout`

The number of seconds of inactivity accepted before the slave decides that the connection with the master is lost and tries to reconnect. This does not apply to a situation in which a broken connection can be detected explicitly. In these cases, the slave reacts immediately, moves the I/O thread into the reconnection phase, and attempts a reconnect (possibly waiting according to the value of `master-connect-retry` and only if the number of retries done so far does not exceed `master-retry-count`).

The default is 3,600 seconds.

`--master-connect-retry`

The number of seconds between retries. You can specify this option as the `CONNECT_RETRY` parameter for the `CHANGE MASTER TO` command. Use of the option in *my.cnf* is deprecated.

The default is 60 seconds.

`--master-retry-count`

The number of retries before finally giving up.

The default is 86,400.

These defaults are probably not what you want, so you're better off supplying your own values.

How the Slave Processes Events

Central to replication are the log events: they are the information carriers of the replication system and contain all the metadata necessary to ensure replication can execute the changes made on the master to produce a replica of the master. Because the binary log on the master is in commit order for all the transactions executed on the master, each transaction can be executed in the same order in which it appears in the binary log to produce the same result on the slave as on the master.

The slave SQL thread executes events from *all* the sessions on the master *in sequence*. This has some consequences for how the slave executes the events:

The slave reply is single-threaded, whereas the master is multithreaded
> The log events are executed in a single thread on the slave, but on multiple threads on the master. This can make it difficult for the slave to keep up with the master if the master is committing a lot of transactions.

Some statements are session-specific
> Some statements on the master are session-specific and will cause different results when executed from the single session on the slave:
>
> - Every user variable is session-specific.
> - Temporary tables are session-specific.
> - Some functions are session-specific (e.g., CONNECTION_ID).

The binary log decides execution order
> Even though two transactions in the binary log appear to be independent—and in theory could be executed in parallel—they may in reality not be independent. This means that the slave is forced to execute the transactions in sequence to guarantee the master and the slave are consistent.

Housekeeping in the I/O Thread

Although the SQL thread does most of the event processing, the I/O does some housekeeping before the events even come into the SQL thread's view. So we'll look at I/O thread processing before discussing the "real execution" in the SQL thread. To keep up processing speed, the I/O thread inspects only certain bytes to determine the type of the event, then takes the necessary action to the relay log:

Stop events
> These events indicate that a slave further up in the chain has been stopped in an orderly manner. This event is ignored by the I/O thread and is not even written to the relay log.

Rotate event

> If the master binary log is rotated, so is the relay log. The relay log might be rotated more times than the master, but the relay log is rotated at least each time the master's binary log is rotated.

Format description events

> These events are saved to be written when the relay log is rotated. Recall that the format between two consecutive binlog files might change, so the I/O thread needs to remember this event to process the files correctly.

If replication is set up to replicate in a circle or through a dual-master setup (which is circular replication with only two servers), events will be forwarded in the circle until they arrive at the server that originally sent them. To avoid having events continue to replicate around in the circle indefinitely, it is necessary to remove events that have been executed before.

To implement this check, each server determines whether the event has the server's own server ID. If it does, this event was sent from this server previously, and replication on the slave has come full circle. To avoid an event that circulates infinitely (and hence is applied infinitely) this event is not written to the relay log, but just ignored. You can turn this behavior off using the `replicate-same-server-id` option on the server. If you set this option, the server will not carry out the check for an identical server ID and the event will be written to the relay log regardless of which server ID it has.

SQL Thread Processing

The slave SQL thread reads the relay log and re-executes the master's database statements on the slave. Some of these events require special information that is not part of the SQL statement. The special handling includes:

Passing master context to the slave server

> Sometimes state information needs to be passed to the slave for the statement to execute correctly. As mentioned in Chapter 4, the master writes one or more *context events* to pass this extra information. Some of the information is thread-specific but different from the information in the next item.

Handling events from different threads

> The master executes transactions from several sessions, so the slave SQL thread has to decide which thread generated some events. Because the master has the best knowledge about the statement, it marks any event that it considers thread-specific. For instance, the master will usually mark events that operate on temporary tables as thread-specific.

Filtering events and tables

> The SQL thread is responsible for doing filtering on the slave. MySQL provides both database filters, which are set up by `replicate-do-db` and `replicate-`

ignore-db, and table filters, which are set up by `replicate-do-table`, `replicate-ignore-table`, `replicate-wild-do-table`, and `replicate-wild-ignore-table`.

Skipping events
> To recover replication after it has stopped, there are features available to skip events when restarting replication. The SQL thread handles this skipping.

Context events

On the master, some events require a context to execute correctly. The context is usually thread-specific features such as user-defined variables, but can also include state information required to execute correctly, such as autoincrement values for tables with autoincrement columns. To pass this context from the master to the slave, the master has a set of context events that it can write to the binary log.

The master writes each context event before the event that contains the actual change. Currently, context events are associated only with `Query` events and are added to the binary log before the `Query` events.

Context events fall into the following categories:

User variable event
> This event holds the name and value of a user-defined variable.
>
> This event is generated whenever the statement contains a reference to a user-defined variable.
>
> ```
> SET @foo = 'SmoothNoodleMaps';
> INSERT INTO my_albums(artist, album) VALUES ('Devo', @foo);
> ```

Integer variable event
> This event holds an integer value for either the `INSERT_ID` session variable or the `LAST_INSERT_ID` session variable.
>
> The `INSERT_ID` integer variable event is used for statements that insert into tables with an `AUTO_INCREMENT` column to transfer the next value to use for the autoincrement column. This information, for example, is required by this table definition and statement:
>
> ```
> CREATE TABLE Artist (id INT AUTO_INCREMENT PRIMARY KEY, artist TEXT);
> INSERT INTO Artist VALUES (DEFAULT, 'The The');
> ```
>
> The `LAST_INSERT_ID` integer variable event is generated when a statement uses the `LAST_INSERT_ID` function, as in this statement:
>
> ```
> INSERT INTO Album VALUES (LAST_INSERT_ID(), 'Mind Bomb');
> ```

Rand event

> If the statement contains a call to the RAND function, this event will contain the random seeds, which will allow the slave to reproduce the "random" value generated on the master:

```
INSERT INTO my_table VALUES (RAND());
```

These context events are necessary to produce correct behavior in the situations just described, but there are other situations that cannot be handled using context events. For example, the replication system cannot handle a user-defined function (UDF) unless the UDF is deterministic and also exists on the slave. In these cases, the user variable event can solve the problem.

User variable events can be very useful for avoiding problems with replicating nondeterministic functions, for improving performance, and for integrity checks.

As an example, suppose that you enter documents into a database table. Each document is automatically assigned a number using the AUTO_INCREMENT feature. To maintain the integrity of the documents, you also add an MD5 checksum of the documents in the same table. A definition of such a table is shown in Example 8-12.

Example 8-12. Definition of document table with MD5 checksum

```
CREATE TABLE document(
    id INT UNSIGNED AUTO_INCREMENT PRIMARY KEY,
    doc BLOB,
    checksum CHAR(32)
);
```

Using this table, you can now add documents to the table together with the checksum and also verify the integrity of the document, as shown in Example 8-13, to ensure it has not been corrupted. Although the MD5 checksum is currently not considered cryptographically secure, it still offers some protection against random errors such as disk and memory problems.

Example 8-13. Inserting into the table and checking document integrity

```
master> INSERT INTO document(doc) VALUES (document);
Query OK, 1 row affected (0.02 sec)

master> UPDATE document SET checksum = MD5(doc) WHERE id = LAST_INSERT_ID();
Query OK, 1 row affected (0.04 sec)

master> SELECT id,
    ->        IF(MD5(doc) = checksum, 'OK', 'CORRUPT!') AS Status
    ->   FROM document;
+-----+----------+
| id  |  Status  |
+-----+----------+
|   1 | OK       |
```

```
|    2 | OK       |
|    3 | OK       |
|    4 | OK       |
|    5 | OK       |
|    6 | OK       |
|    7 | CORRUPT! |
|    8 | OK       |
|    9 | OK       |
|   10 | OK       |
|   11 | OK       |
+------+----------+
11 row in set (5.75 sec)
```

But how well does this idea play with replication? Well, it depends on how you use it. When the INSERT statement in Example 8-13 is executed, it is written to the binary log as is, which means the MD5 checksum is recalculated on the slave. So what happens if the document is corrupted on the way to the slave? In that case, the MD5 checksum will be recalculated using the corrupt document, and the corruption will not be detected. So the statement given in Example 8-13 is not replication-safe. We can, however, do better than this.

Instead of following Example 8-13, write your code to look like Example 8-14, which stores the checksum in a user-defined variable and uses it in the INSERT statement. The user-defined variable contains the actual value computed by the MD5 function, so it will be identical on the master and the slave even if the document is corrupted in the transfer (but, of course, not if the checksum is corrupted in the transfer). Either way, a corruption occurring when the document is replicated will be noticed.

Example 8-14. Replication-safe method of inserting a document in the table

```
master> INSERT INTO document(doc) VALUES (document);
Query OK, 1 row affected (0.02 sec)

master> SELECT MD5(doc) INTO @checksum FROM document WHERE id = LAST_INSERT_ID();
Query OK, 0 rows affected (0.00 sec)

master> UPDATE document SET checksum = @checksum WHERE id = LAST_INSERT_ID();
Query OK, 1 row affected (0.04 sec)
```

Thread-specific events

As mentioned earlier, some statements are thread-specific and will yield a different result when executed in another thread. There are several reasons for this:

Reading and writing thread-local objects
A thread-local object can potentially clash with an identically named object in another thread. Typical examples of such objects are temporary tables or user-defined variables.

We have already examined how replication handles user-defined variables, so this section will just concentrate on how replication handles the temporary tables.

Using variables or functions that have thread-specific results
Some variables and functions have different values depending on which thread they are running in. A typical example of this is the server variable `connection_id`.

The server handles these two cases slightly differently. In addition, there are a few cases in which replication does not try to account for differences between the server and client, so results can differ in subtle ways.

To handle thread-local objects, some form of thread-local store (TLS) is required, but because the slave is executing from a single thread, it has to manage this storage and keep the TLSes separate. To handle temporary tables, the slave creates a unique (mangled) filename for the table based on the server process ID, the thread ID, and a thread-specific sequence number. This means that the two statements in Example 8-15—each runs from a different client on the master—create two different filenames on the slave to represent the temporary tables.

Example 8-15. Two threads, each creating a temporary table

```
master-1> CREATE TEMPORARY TABLE cache (a INT, b INT);
Query OK, 0 rows affected (0.01 sec)

master-2> CREATE TEMPORARY TABLE cache (a INT, b INT);
Query OK, 0 rows affected (0.01 sec)
```

All the statements from all threads on the master are stored in sequence in the binary log, so it is necessary to distinguish the two statements. Otherwise, they will cause an error when executed on the slave.

To distinguish the statements in the binary log so that they do not conflict, the server tags the `Query` events containing the statement as thread-specific and also adds the thread ID to the event. (Actually, the thread ID is added to all `Query` events, but is not really necessary except for thread-specific statements.)

When the slave receives a thread-specific event, it sets a variable special to the replication slave thread, called the *pseudothread ID*, to the thread ID passed with the event. The pseudothread ID will then be used when constructing the temporary tables. The process ID of the slave server—which is the same for all master threads—will be used when constructing the filename, but that does not matter as long as there is a distinction among tables from different threads.

We also mentioned that thread-specific functions and variables require special treatment to work correctly when replicated. This is not, however, handled by the server. When a server variable is referenced in a statement, the value of the server variable will be retrieved on the slave. If, for some reason, you want to replicate exactly the same value, you have to store the value in a user-defined variable as shown in Example 8-14, or use row-based replication, which we will cover later in the chapter.

Filtering and skipping events

In some cases, events may be skipped either because they are filtered out using replication filters or because the slave has been specifically instructed to skip a number of events.

The `SQL_SLAVE_SKIP_COUNTER` variable instructs the slave server to skip a specified number of events. The SQL thread should not be running when you set the variable. This condition is typically easy to satisfy, because the variable is usually used to skip some events that caused replication to stop already.

An error that stops replication should, of course, be investigated and handled, but if you fix the problem manually, it is necessary to ignore the event that stopped replication and force replication to continue after the offending event. This variable is provided as a convenience, to keep you from having to use `CHANGE MASTER TO`. Example 8-16 shows the feature in use after a bad statement has caused replication to stop.

Example 8-16. Using the SQL_SLAVE_SKIP_COUNTER

```
slave> SET GLOBAL SQL_SLAVE_SKIP_COUNTER = 3;
Query OK, 0 rows affected (0.02 sec)

slave> START SLAVE;
Query OK, 0 rows affected (0.02 sec)
```

When you start the slave, three events will be skipped before resuming replication. If skipping three events causes the slave to end up in the middle of a transaction, the slave will continue skipping events until it finds the end of the transaction.

Events can also be filtered by the slave if replication filters are set up. As we discussed in Chapter 4, the master can handle filtering, but if there are slave filters, the events are filtered in the SQL thread, which means that the events are still sent from the master and stored in the relay log.

Filtering is done differently depending on whether database filters or table filters are set up. The logic for deciding whether a statement for a certain database should be filtered out from the binary log was detailed in Chapter 4, and the same logic applies to slave filters, with the addition that here a set of table filters have to be handled as well.

One important aspect of filtering is that a filter applying to a single table causes the entire statement referring to that filter to be left out of replication. The logic for filtering statements on the slave is shown in Figure 8-5.

Filtering that involves tables can easily become difficult to understand, so we advise the following rules to avoid unwanted results:

- Do not qualify table names with the database they're a part of. Precede the statement with a USE statement instead to set a new default database.

- Do not update tables in different databases using a single statement.

- Avoid updating multiple tables in a statement, unless you know that all tables are filtered or none of the tables are filtered. Notice that from the logic in Figure 8-5, the whole statement will be filtered if even one of the tables is filtered.

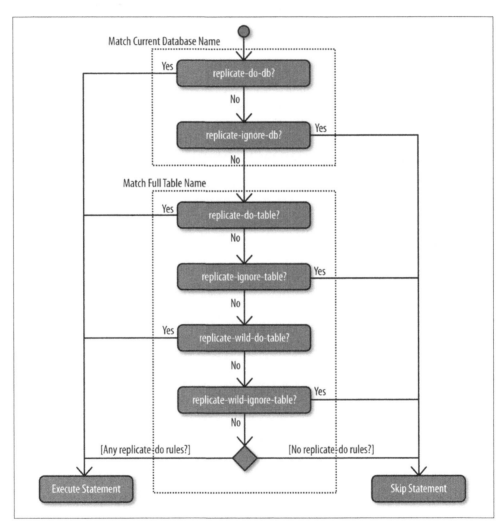

Figure 8-5. Replication filtering rules

Semisynchronous Replication

Google has an extensive set of patches for MySQL and InnoDB to tailor the server and the storage engine. One of the patches that is available for MySQL version 5.0 is the semisynchronous replication patch. MySQL has since reworked the patch and released it with MySQL 5.5.

The idea behind semisynchronous replication is to ensure the changes are written to disk on at least one slave before allowing execution to continue. This means that for each connection, at most one transaction can be lost due to a master crash.

It is important to understand that the semisynchronous replication patch does not hold off commits of the transaction; it just avoids sending a reply back to the client until the transaction has been written to the relay log of at least one slave. Figure 8-6 shows the order of the calls when committing a transaction. As you can see, the transaction is committed to the storage engine before the transaction is sent to the slave, but the return from the client's commit call occurs after the slave has acknowledged that the transaction is in durable storage.

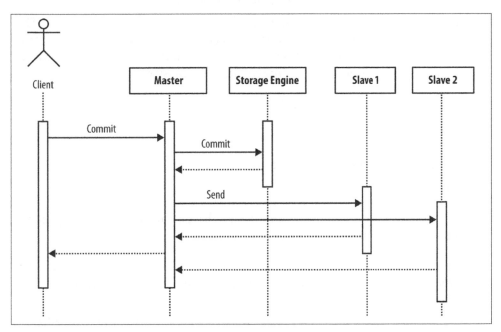

Figure 8-6. Transaction commit with semisynchronous replication

For each connection, one transaction can be lost if a crash occurs after the transaction has been committed to the storage engine but before the transaction has been sent to the slave. However, because the acknowledgment of the transaction goes to the client after the slave has acknowledged that it has the transaction, at most one transaction can be lost. This usually means that one transaction can be lost per client.

Configuring Semisynchronous Replication

To use semisynchronous replication, both the master and the slave need to support it, so both the master and the slave have to be running MySQL version 5.5 or later and have semisynchronous replication enabled. If either the master or the slave does not support semisynchronous replication, it will not be used, but replication works as usual, meaning that more than one transaction can be lost unless special precautions are taken to ensure each transaction reaches the slave before a new transaction is started.

Use the following steps to enable semisynchronous replication:

1. Install the master plug-in on the master:

   ```
   master> INSTALL PLUGIN rpl_semi_sync_master SONAME 'semisync_master.so';
   ```

2. Install the slave plug-in on each slave:

   ```
   slave> INSTALL PLUGIN rpl_semi_sync_slave SONAME 'semisync_slave.so';
   ```

3. Once you have installed the plug-ins, enable them on the master and the slave. This is controlled through two server variables that are also available as options, so to ensure that the settings take effect even after restart, it is best to bring down the server and add the options to the *my.cnf* file of the master:

   ```
   [mysqld]
   rpl-semi-sync-master-enabled = 1
   ```

   and to the slave:

   ```
   [mysqld]
   rpl-semi-sync-slave-enabled = 1
   ```

4. Restart the servers.

If you followed the instructions just given, you now have a semisynchronous replication setup and can test it, but consider these cases:

- What happens if all slaves crash and therefore no slave acknowledges that it has stored the transaction to the relay log? This is not unlikely if you have only a single server attached to the master.

- What happens if all slaves disconnect gracefully? In this case, the master has no slave to which the transaction can be sent for safekeeping.

In addition to `rpl-semi-sync-master-enabled` and `rpl-semi-sync-slave-enabled`, there are two options that you can use to handle the situations we just laid out:

`rpl-semi-sync-master-timeout=milliseconds`

To prevent semisynchronous replication from blocking if it does not receive an acknowledgment, it is possible to set a timeout using the `rpl-semi-sync-master-timeout=milliseconds` option.

If the master does not receive any acknowledgment before the timeout expires, it will revert to normal asynchronous replication and continue operating without semisynchronous replication.

This option is also available as a server variable and can be set without bringing the server down. Note, however, that as with every server variable, the value will not be saved between restarts.

`rpl-semi-sync-master-wait-no-slave={ON|OFF}`

If a transaction is committed but the master does not have any slaves connected, it is not possible for the master to send the transaction anywhere for safekeeping. By default, the master will then wait for a slave to connect—as long as it is within the timeout limit—and acknowledge that the transaction has been properly written to disk.

You can use the `rpl-semi-sync-master-wait-no-slave={ON|OFF}` option to turn off this behavior, in which case the master reverts to asynchronous replication if there are no connected slaves.

 Note that if the master does not receive any acknowledgment before the timeout given by `rpl-semi-sync-master-timeout` expires, or if `rpl-semi-sync-master-wait-no-slave=ON`, semisynchronous replication will silently revert to normal asynchronous replication and continue operating without semisynchronous replication.

Monitoring Semisynchronous Replication

Both plug-ins install a number of status variables that allow you to monitor semisynchronous replication. We will cover the most interesting ones here (for a complete list, consult the online reference manual for semisynchronous replication (*http://bit.ly/semi sync*)):

`rpl_semi_sync_master_clients`

This status variable reports the number of connected slaves that support and have been registered for semisynchronous replication.

`rpl_semi_sync_master_status`

The status of semisynchronous replication on the master is 1 if it is active, and 0 if it is inactive—either because it has not been enabled or because it was enabled but has reverted to asynchronous replication.

```
rpl_semi_sync_slave_status
```
The status of semisynchronous replication on the slave is 1 if active (i.e., if it has been enabled and the I/O thread is running) and 0 if it is inactive.

You can read the values of these variables either using the SHOW STATUS command or through the information schema table GLOBAL_STATUS. If you want to use the values for other purposes, the SHOW STATUS command is hard to use and a query as shown in Example 8-17 uses SELECT on the information schema to extract the value and store it in a user-defined variable.

Example 8-17. Retrieving values using the information schema

```
master> SELECT Variable_value INTO @value
    ->    FROM INFORMATION_SCHEMA.GLOBAL_STATUS
    -> WHERE Variable_name = 'Rpl_semi_sync_master_status';
Query OK, 1 row affected (0.00 sec)
```

Global Transaction Identifiers

Starting with MySQL 5.6, the concept of *global transaction identifiers* (GTIDs) was added, which means that each transaction is assigned a unique identifier. This section introduces GTIDs and demonstrates how they can be used. For a detailed description of GTIDs, look in "Replication with Global Transaction Identifiers" in the MySQL 5.6 Reference Manual (*http://bit.ly/global-ti*).

In MySQL 5.6, each transaction on a server is assigned a *transaction identifier*, which is a nonzero 64-bit value assigned to a transaction based on the order in which they *committed*. This number is local to the server (i.e., some other server might assign the same number to some other transaction). To make this transaction identifier global, the server UUID is added to form a pair. For example, if the server has a server UUID (as given by the server variable @@server_uuid) 2298677f-c24b-11e2-a68b-0021cc6850ca, the 1477th transaction committed on the server will have GTID 2298677f-c24b-11e2-a68b-0021cc6850ca:1477.

When a transaction is replicated from a master to a slave, the binary log position of the transaction changes because the slave has to write it to the binary logfile on the slave. Because a slave might be configured differently, the positions can be vastly different from the position on the master—but the global transaction identifier will be the same.

When transactions are replicated and global transaction identifiers are enabled, the GTID of the transaction is retained regardless of the number of times that the transaction is propagated. This simple idea makes GTIDs a very powerful concept, as you will soon see.

While the notation just shown indicates an *individual* transaction, it is also necessary to have a notation for a *global transaction identifier set* (or *GTID set*). This helps, for example, when talking about transactions that have been logged on a server. A GTID set is written by giving a range, or list of ranges, of transaction identifiers. So the set of transactions 911-1066 and 1477-1593 is written as `2298677f-c24b-11e2-a68b-0021cc6850ca:911-1066:1477-1593`.

 GTIDs are written to the binary log and assigned only to transactions that are written to the binary log. This means that if you turn off the binary log, transactions will not get assigned GTIDs. This applies to the slave as well as the master. The consequence is that if you want to use a slave for failover, you need to have the binary log enabled on it. If you do not have a binary log enabled, the slave will not remember the GTIDs of the transactions it has executed.

Setting Up Replication Using GTIDs

To set up replication using global transaction identifiers, you must enable global transaction identifiers when configuring the servers. We'll go through what you need to do to enable global transaction identifers here. To configure a standby for using global transaction identifiers, you need to update *my.cnf* as follows:

```
[mysqld]
user              = mysql
pid-file          = /var/run/mysqld/mysqld.pid
socket            = /var/run/mysqld/mysqld.sock
port              = 3306
basedir           = /usr
datadir           = /var/lib/mysql
tmpdir            = /tmp
log-bin           = master-bin ❶
log-bin-index     = master-bin.index
server-id         = 1
gtid-mode         = ON ❷
log-slave-updates ❸
enforce-gtid-consistency ❹
```

❶ It is necessary to have the binary log enabled on the standby. This ensures that all changes are logged to the binary log when the master becomes the primary, but it is also a requirement for `log-slave-updates`.

❷ This option is used to enable the generation of global transaction identifiers.

❸ This option ensures that events received from the master and executed are also written to the standby's binary log. If this is not enabled, it will not be possible for the standby to send out changes done indirectly to slaves connected to it. Note that by default, this option is *not* enabled.

❹ This option ensures that statements throw an error if they cannot be logged consistently with global transaction identifiers enabled. This is recommended to ensure that failover happens correctly.

After updating the options file, you need to restart the server for the changes to take effect. Once you've done this for all servers that are going to be used in the setup, you're set for doing a failover. Using the GTID support in MySQL 5.6, switching masters just requires you to issue the command:

```
CHANGE MASTER TO
MASTER_HOST = host_of_new_master,
MASTER_PORT = port_of_new_master,
MASTER_USER = replication_user_name,
MASTER_PASSWORD = replication_user_password,
MASTER_AUTO_POSITION = 1
```

The MASTER_AUTO_POSITION causes the slave to automatically negotiate what transactions should be sent over when connecting to the master.

To see status of replication in GTID positions, SHOW SLAVE STATUS has been extended with a few new columns. You can see an example of those in Example 8-18.

Example 8-18. Output of SHOW SLAVE STATUS with GTID enabled

```
    Slave_IO_State: Waiting for master to send event
          .
          .
          .
 Slave_IO_Running: Yes
Slave_SQL_Running: Yes
          .
          .
          .
      Master_UUID: 4e2018fc-c691-11e2-8c5a-0021cc6850ca
          .
          .
          .
Retrieved_Gtid_Set: 4e2018fc-c691-11e2-8c5a-0021cc6850ca:1-1477
 Executed_Gtid_Set: 4e2018fc-c691-11e2-8c5a-0021cc6850ca:1-1593
     Auto_Position: 1
```

Master_UUID

> This is the server UUID of the master. The field is not strictly tied to the GTID implementation (it was added before the GTIDs were introduced), but it is useful when debugging problems.

Retrieved_Gtid_Set

> This is the set of GTIDs that have been fetched from the master and stored in the relay log.

Executed_Gtid_Set

> This is the set of GTIDs that have been executed on the slave *and written to the slave's binary log*.

Failover Using GTIDs

"Hot Standby" on page 130 described how to switch to a hot standby without using global transaction identifiers. That process used binary log positions, but with global transaction identifiers, there is no longer a need to check the positions.

Switching over to a hot standby with global transaction identifiers is very easy (it is sufficient to just redirect the slave to the new master using CHANGE MASTER):

```
CHANGE MASTER TO MASTER_HOST = 'standby.example.com';
```

As usual, if no other parameters change, it is not necessary to repeat them.

When you enable MASTER_AUTO_POSITION, the master will figure out what transactions need to be sent over. The failover procedure is therefore easily defined using the Replicant ilibrary:

```
_CHANGE_MASTER = (
    "CHANGE MASTER TO "
    "MASTER_HOST = %s, MASTER_PORT = %d, "
    "MASTER_USER = %s, MASTER_PASSWORD = %s, "
    "MASTER_AUTO_POSITION = 1"
    )

def change_master(server, master):
    server.sql(_CHANGE_MASTER,
               master.host, master.port,
               master.user, master.password)

def switch_to_master(server, standby):
    change_master(server, standby)
    server.sql("START SLAVE")
```

By comparing this procedure with the one in Example 5-1, you can see that there are a few things that have been improved by using GTIDs:

- Because you do not need to check the position of the master, it is not necessary to stop it to ensure that it is not changing.
- Because the GTIDs are global (i.e., they never change when replicated), there is no need for the slave to "align" with the master or the standby to get a good switchover position.
- It is not necessary to fetch the position on the standby (which is a slave to the current primary) because everything is replicated to the slave.
- It is not necessary to provide a position when changing the master because the servers automatically negotiate positions.

Because the GTIDs are global (i.e., it is not necessary to do any sort of translation of the positions), the preceding procedure works just as well for switchover and failover, even when a hierarchical replication is used. This was not the case in "Hot Standby" on page 130, where different procedures had to be employed for switchover, non-hierarchical failover, and failover in a hierarchy.

In order to avoid losing transactions when the master fails, it is a good habit to empty the relay log before actually executing the failover. This avoids re-fetching transactions that have already been transferred from the master to the slave. The best approach would be to redirect only the I/O thread to the new master, but unfortunately, this is (not yet) possible. To wait for the relay log to become empty, the handy `WAIT_UN TIL_SQL_THREAD_AFTER_GTIDS` function will block until all the GTIDs in a GTID set have been processed by the SQL thread. To use this function, we change the function in Example 8-19 .

Example 8-19. Python code for failover to a standby using GTID

```
def change_master(server, standby):
    fields = server.sql("SHOW SLAVE STATUS")
    server.sql("SELECT WAIT_UNTIL_SQL_THREAD_AFTER_GTIDS(%s)",
               fields['Retrieved_Gtid_Set'])
    server.sql("STOP SLAVE")
    change_master(server, standby)
    server.sql("START SLAVE")
```

Slave Promotion Using GTIDs

The procedure shown in the previous section for failover works fine when the slave is actually behind the standby. But, as mentioned in "Slave Promotion" on page 145, if the slave knows more transactions than the standby, failing over to the standby does not put you in a better situation. It would actually be better if the slave were the new master. So how can this be implemented using global transaction identifiers?

The actual failover using the procedure in Example 8-19 can still be used, but if there are multiple slaves to a master, and the master fails, it is necessary to compare the slaves to see what slave is more knowledgable. To help with this, MySQL 5.6 introduced the variable `GTID_EXECUTED`. This global variable contains a GTID set consisting of all transactions that have been written to the binary log on the server. Note that no GTID is generated unless the transaction is written to the binary log, so only transactions that were written to the binary log are represented in this set.

There is also a global variable `GTID_PURGED` that contains the set of all transactions that have been purged (i.e., removed) from the binary log and are no longer available to replicate. This set is *always* a subset of (or equal to) `GTID_EXECUTED`.

This variable can be used to check that a candidate master has enough events in the binary log to act as master to some slave. If there are any events in `GTID_PURGED` on the master that are not in `GTID_EXECUTED` on the slave, the master will not be able to replicate some events that the slave needs because they are not in the binary log. The relation between these two variables can be seen in Figure 8-7, where each variable represents a "wavefront" through the space of all GTIDs.

Using `GTID_EXECUTED`, it is easy to compare the slaves and decide which one knows the most transactions. The code in Example 8-20 orders the slaves based on `GTID_EXECUT ED` and picks the "best" one as the new master. Note that GTID sets are not normally totally ordered (i.e., two GTID sets can differ but have the same size). In this particular case, however, the GTID sets *will* be totally ordered, because they were ordered in the binary log of the master.

Example 8-20. Python code to find the best slave

```python
from mysql.replicant.server import GTIDSet

def fetch_gtid_executed(server):
    return GTIDSet(server.sql("SELECT @@GLOBAL.GTID_EXECUTED"))

def fetch_gtid_purged(server):
    return GTIDSet(server.sql("SELECT @@GLOBAL.GTID_PURGED"))

def order_slaves_on_gtid(slaves):
    entries = []
    for slave in slaves:
        pos = fetch_gtid_executed(slave)
        entries.append((pos, slave))
    entries.sort(key=lambda x: x[0])
    return entries
```

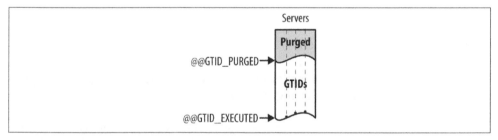

Figure 8-7. GTID_EXECUTED and GTID_PURGED

Combining the examples in Example 8-19 and Example 8-20 allows the function to promote the best slave to be written as simply as what is shown in Example 8-21.

Example 8-21. Slave promotion with MySQL 5.6 GTIDs

```python
def promote_best_slave_gtid(slaves):
    entries = order_slaves_on_gtid(slaves)
    _, master = entries.pop(0)   # "Best" slave will be new master
    for _, slave in entries:
        switch_to_master(master, slave)
```

Replication of GTIDs

The previous sections showed how to set up the MySQL server to use global transaction identifiers and how to handle failover and slave promotion, but one piece of the puzzle is still missing: how are GTIDs propagated between the servers?

A GTID is assigned to every group in the binary log—that is, to each transaction, single-statement DML (whether transactional or nontransactional), and DDL statement. A special GTID event is written before the group and contains the full GTID for the transaction, as illustrated in Figure 8-8.

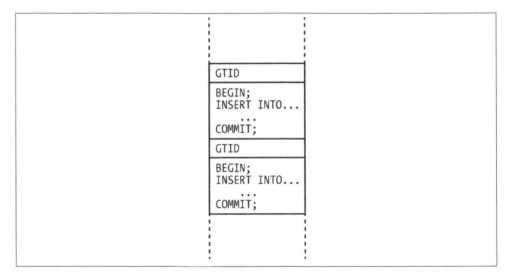

Figure 8-8. A binary logfile with GTIDs

To handle the replication of transactions with a GTID assigned, the SQL thread processes the GTID event in the following manner:

1. If the GTID is already present in the GTID_EXECUTED, the transaction will be skipped entirely, not even written to the binary log. (Recall that GTID_EXECUTED contains all transactions already in the binary log, so there is no need to write it again.)

2. Otherwise, the GTID will be assigned to the transaction that follows, and the next transaction is executed as normal.

3. When the transaction commits, the GTID assigned to the transaction is used to generate a new GTID event, which is then written to the binary log before the transaction.

4. The contents of the transaction cache are then written to the binary log after the GTID event.

Note that with GTIDs assigned to every transaction, it is possible to filter out transactions that have already been executed in the first step, which was not possible before MySQL 5.6.

You can control what GTID is assigned to a transaction through a new variable named GTID_NEXT. This variable can either contain a GTID or have the value AUTOMATIC. (It can also take the value ANONYMOUS, but this can be used only when GTID_MODE = ON, so we disregard this case.) When committing a transaction, different actions are taken depending on the value of GTID_NEXT:

- If GTID_NEXT has the value AUTOMATIC, a new GTID is created and assigned to the transaction.
- If GTID_NEXT has a GTID as a value, that GTID will be used when the transaction is written to the binary log.

The GTID assigned to GTID_NEXT is *not* changed after the transaction commits. This means you have to set it either to a new GTID or to AUTOMATIC after you have committed the transaction. If you do not change the value of GTID_NEXT, you will get an error when you try to start a new transaction, regardless of whether it is done explicitly or implicitly.

Observe that GTID_NEXT has to be set *before* the transaction starts. If you try to set the variable after starting a transaction, you will just get an error.

Once you set GTID_NEXT and start a transaction, the GTID is *owned* by the transaction. This will be reflected in the variable GTID_OWNED:

```
mysql> SELECT @@GLOBAL.GTID_OWNED;
+------------------------------------------+
| @@GLOBAL.GTID_OWNED                      |
+------------------------------------------+
| 02020202-0202-0202-0202-020202020202:4#42 |
+------------------------------------------+
1 row in set (0.00 sec)
```

In this case, the only owned GTID, which is owned by the session with ID 42, is 02020202-0202-0202-0202-020202020202:4.

GTID_OWNED should be considered internal and is intended for testing and debugging.

Replicating from a master to a slave directly is not the only way changes can be replicated. MySQL replication is also designed to work with *mysqlbinlog* so that SQL statements can be generated, saved to a file, and applied to a server. To handle propagation of GTIDs even when it is done indirectly through *mysqlbinlog*, GTID_NEXT is used. Whenever *mysqlbinlog* encounters a GTID event, it will generate a statement to set GTID_NEXT. In Example 8-22, you can see an example of the output.

Example 8-22. Example output from mysqlbinlog with GTID events

```
# at 410
#130603 20:57:54 server id 1  end_log_pos 458 CRC32 0xc6f8a5eb
#        GTID [commit=yes]
SET @@SESSION.GTID_NEXT= '01010101-0101-0101-0101-010101010101:3'/*!*/;
# at 458
#130603 20:57:54 server id 1  end_log_pos 537 CRC32 0x1e2e40d0
# Position  Timestamp  Type  Master ID       Size      Master Pos    Flags
#        Query   thread_id=4    exec_time=0    error_code=0
SET TIMESTAMP=1370285874/*!*/;
BEGIN
/*!*/;
# at 537
#130603 20:57:54 server id 1  end_log_pos 638 CRC32 0xc16f211d
#        Query   thread_id=4    exec_time=0    error_code=0
SET TIMESTAMP=1370285874/*!*/;
INSERT INTO t VALUES (1004)
/*!*/;
# at 638
#130603 20:57:54 server id 1  end_log_pos 669 CRC32 0x91980f0b
COMMIT/*!*/;
```

Slave Safety and Recovery

Slave servers can crash too, and when they do, you need to recover them. The first step in handling a crashed slave is always to investigate why it crashed. This cannot be automated, because there are so many hard-to-anticipate reasons for crashes. A slave might be out of disk space, it may have read a corrupt event, or it might have re-executed a statement that resulted in a duplicate key error for some reason. However, it is possible to automate some recovery procedures and use this automation to help diagnose a problem.

Syncing, Transactions, and Problems with Database Crashes

To ensure slaves pick up replication safely after a crash on the master or slave, you need to consider two different aspects:

- Ensuring the slave stores all the necessary data needed for recovery in the event of a crash
- Executing the recovery of a slave

Slaves do their best to meet the first condition by syncing to disk. To provide acceptable performance, operating systems keep files in memory while working with them, and write them to disk only periodically or when forced to. This means data written to a file is not necessarily in safe storage. If there is a crash, data left only in memory will be lost.

To force a slave to write files to disk, the database server issues an `fsync` call, which writes all data stored in memory to disk. To protect replication data, the MySQL server normally executes `fsync` calls for the relay log, the *master.info* file, and the *relay-log.info* file at regular intervals.

I/O thread syncing

For the I/O thread, two `fsync` calls are made whenever an event has been processed: one to flush the relay log to disk and one to flush the *master.info* file to disk. Doing the flushes in this order ensures that no events will be lost if the slave crashes between flushing the relay log and flushing the *master.info* file. This, however, means that an event can be duplicated if a crash occurs in any of the following cases:

- The server flushes the relay log and is about to update the master read position in *master.info*.
- The server crashes, which means that the master read position now refers to the position before the event that was flushed to the relay log.
- The server restarts and gets the master read position from *master.info*, meaning the position before the last event written to the relay log.
- Replication resumes from this position, and the event is duplicated.

If the files were flushed in the opposite order—the *master.info* file first and the relay log second—there would be potential for losing an event in the same scenario, because the slave would pick up replication after the event that it was about to write to the relay log. Losing an event is deemed to be worse than duplicating one, hence the relay log is flushed first.

SQL thread syncing

The SQL thread processes the groups in the relay log by processing each event in turn. When all the events in the group are processed, the SQL thread commits the transaction using the following process:

1. It commits the transaction to the storage engine (assuming the storage engine supports commit).
2. It updates the *relay-log.info* file with the position of the next event to process, which is also the beginning of the next group to process.
3. It writes *relay-log.info* to disk by issuing an `fsync` call.

While executing inside a group, the thread increments the event position to keep track of where the SQL thread is reading in the relay log, but if there is a crash, execution will resume from the last recorded position in the *relay-log.info* file.

This behavior leaves the SQL thread with its own version of the atomic update problem mentioned for the I/O thread, so the slave database and the *relay-log.info* file can get out of sync in the following scenario:

1. The event is applied to the database and the transaction is committed. The next step is to update the *relay-log.info* file.

2. The slave crashes, which means *relay-log.info* now points to the beginning of the just-completed transaction.

3. On recovery, the SQL thread reads the information from the *relay-log.info* file and starts replication from the saved position.

4. The last executed transaction is repeated.

What all this boils down to is that committing a transaction on the slave and updating the replication information is not atomic: it is possible that *relay-log.info* does not accurately reflect what has been committed to the database. The next section describes how transactional replication is implemented in MySQL 5.6 to solve this problem.

Transactional Replication

As noted in the previous section, replication is not crash-safe, because the information about the progress of replication is not always in sync with what has actually been applied to the database. Although transactions are not lost if the server crashes, it can require some tweaking to bring the slaves up again.

MySQL 5.6 has increased crash safety for the slave by committing the replication information together with the transaction as shown in Figure 8-9. This means that replication information will always be consistent with what has been applied to the database, even in the event of a server crash. Also, some fixes were done on the master to ensure that it recovers correctly.

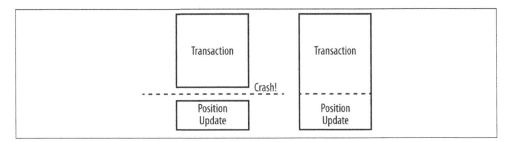

Figure 8-9. Position information updated after the transaction and inside the transaction

Recall that the replication information is stored in two files: *master.info* and *relay-log.info*. The files are arranged so that they are updated after the transaction has been applied. This means that if you have a crash between the transaction commit and the update of the files, as on the left in Figure 8-9, the position information will be wrong. In other words, a *transaction* cannot be lost this way, but there is a risk that a transaction could be applied again when the slave recovers.

The usual way to avoid this is to have a primary key on all your tables. In that case, a repeated update of the table would cause the slave to stop, and you would have to use `SQL_SLAVE_SKIP_COUNTER` to skip the transaction and get the slave up and running again (or `GTID_NEXT` to commit a dummy transaction). This is better than losing a transaction, but it is nevertheless a nuisance. Removing the primary key to prevent the slave from stopping will only solve the problem partially: it means that the transaction would be applied twice, which would both place a burden on the application to handle dual entries and also require that the tables be cleaned regularly. Both of these approaches require either manual intervention or scripting support. This does not affect reliability, but crashes are much easier to handle if the replication information is committed in the same transaction as the data being updated.

To implement transactional replication in MySQL 5.6, the replication information can be stored either in files (as before) or in tables. Even when storing the replication information in tables, it is necessary either to store the data and the replication information in the same storage engine (which must be transactional) or to support XA on both storage engines. If neither of these steps are taken, the replication information and the data cannot be committed as a single transaction.

Setting up transactional replication

The default in MySQL 5.6 is to use files for the replication information, so to use transactional replication, it is necessary to reconfigure the server to use tables for the replication information. To control where the replication information is placed, two new options have been added: `master_info_repository` and `relay_log_info_reposito ry`. These options take the value `FILE` or `TABLE` to use either the file or the table for the respective piece of information.

Thus, to use transactional replication, edit your configuration file, add the options as shown in Example 8-23, and restart the server.

Example 8-23. Adding options to turn on transactional replication

```
[mysqld]
...
master_info_repository = TABLE
relay_log_info_repository = TABLE
...
```

Before MySQL 5.6.6, the default engine for `slave_master_info` and `slave_relay_log_info` was MyISAM. For replication to be transactional, you need to change the engine to use a transactional engine, typically InnoDB, using ALTER TABLE:

```
slave> ALTER TABLE mysql.slave_master_info ENGINE = InnoDB;
slave> ALTER TABLE mysql.slave_relay_log_info ENGINE = InnoDB;
```

Details of transactional replication

Two tables in the *mysql* database preserve information needed for transactional replication: `slave_master_info`, corresponding to the file *master.info*, and `slave_relay_log_info`, corresponding to the file *relay_log.info*.

Just like the *master.info* file, the `slave_master_info` table stores information about the connection to the master. Table 8-1 shows each field of the table, and which row in the *master.info* file and SHOW SLAVE STATUS output it corresponds to.

Table 8-1. Fields for slave_master_info

Field	Line in file	Slave status column
Number_of_lines	1	
Master_log_name	2	Master_Log_File
Master_log_pos	3	Read_Master_Log_Pos
Host	3	Master_Host
User_name	4	Master_User
User_password	5	
Port	6	Master_Port
Connect_retry	7	Connect_Retry
Enabled_ssl	8	Master_SSL_Allowed
Ssl_ca	9	Master_SSL_CA_File
Ssl_capath	10	Master_SSL_CA_Path
Ssl_cert	11	Master_SSL_Cert
Ssl_cipher	12	Master_SSL_Cipher
Ssl_key	13	Master_SSL_Key
Ssl_verify_servert_cert	14	Master_SSL_Verify_Server_Cert
Heartbeat	15	
Bind	16	Master_Bind
Ignored_server_ids	17	Replicate_Ignore_Server_Ids
Uuid	18	Master_UUID
Retry_count	19	Master_Retry_Count
Ssl_crl	20	Master_SSL_Crl

Field	Line in file	Slave status column
Ssl_crlpath	21	Master_SSL Crlpath
Enabled_auto_position	22	Auto_Position

Similarly, Table 8-2 shows the definition of the slave_relay_log_info table corresponding to the *relaylog.info* file.

Table 8-2. Fields of slave_relay_log_info

Field	Line in file	Slave status column
Number_of_lines	1	
Relay_log_name	2	Relay_Log_File
Relay_log_pos	3	Relay_Log_Pos
Master_log_name	4	Relay_Master_Log_File
Master_log_pos	5	Exec_Master_Log_Pos
Sql_delay	6	SQL_Delay
Number_of_workers	7	
Id	8	

Now, suppose that the following transaction was executed on the master:

```
START TRANSACTION;
UPDATE titles, employees SET titles.title = 'Dictator-for-Life'
 WHERE first_name = 'Calvin' AND last_name IS NULL;
UPDATE salaries SET salaries.salary = 1000000
 WHERE first_name = 'Calvin' AND last_name IS NULL;
COMMIT;
```

When the transaction reaches the slave and is executed there, it behaves as if it was executed the following way (where *Exec_Master_Log_Pos*, *Relay_Master_Log_File*, *Relay_Log_File*, and *Relay_Log_Pos* are taken from the SHOW SLAVE STATUS output):

```
START TRANSACTION;
UPDATE titles, employees SET titles.title = 'Dictator-for-Life'
 WHERE first_name = 'Calvin' AND last_name IS NULL;
UPDATE salaries SET salaries.salary = 1000000
 WHERE first_name = 'Calvin' AND last_name IS NULL;
SET @@SESSION.LOG_BIN = 0;
UPDATE mysql.slave_relay_log_info
   SET Master_log_pos = Exec_Master_Log_Pos,
       Master_log_name = Relay_Master_Log_File,
       Relay_log_name = Relay_Log_File,
       Relay_log_pos = Relay_Log_Pos;
SET @@SESSION.LOG_BIN = 1;
COMMIT;
```

Note that the added "statement" is not logged to the binary log on the master, because the binary log is temporarily disabled when the "statement" is executed. If both `slave_relay_log_info` and the tables are placed in the same engine, this will be committed as a unit.

The result is to update `slave_relay_log_info` with each transaction executed on the slave, but note that `slave_master_info` does not contain information that is critical for ensuring that transactional replication works. The only fields that are updated are the positions of events fetched from the master. On a crash, the slave will pick up from the last *executed* position, and not from the last *fetched* position, so this information is interesting to have only in the event that the *master* crashes. In this case, the events in the relay log can be executed to avoid losing more events than necessary.

Similar to flushing the disk, committing to tables is expensive. Because the `slave_master_info` table does not contain any information that is critical for ensuring transactional replication, avoiding unnecessary commits to this table improves performance.

For this reason, the `sync_master_info` option was introduced. The option contains an integer telling how often the replication information should be committed to the `slave_master_info` (or flushed to disk, in the event that the information is stored in the traditional files). If it is nonzero, replication information is flushed each time the master fetches the number of events indicated by the variable's value. If it is zero, no explicit flushing is done at all, but the operating system will flush the information to disk. Note, however, that the information is flushed to disk or committed to the table when the binary log is rotated or the slave starts or stops.

If you are using tables for storing the replication information, this means that if:

```
sync_master_info = 0
```

the `slave_master_info` table is updated only when the slave starts or stops, or the binary log is rotated, so changes to the fetched position are not visible to other threads. If it is critical for your application that you can view this information, you need to set `sync_master_info` to a nonzero value.

Rules for Protecting Nontransactional Statements

Statements executed outside of transactions cannot be tracked and protected from re-execution after a crash. The problem is comparable on masters and slaves. If a statement against a MyISAM table is interrupted by a crash on the master, the statement is not logged at all, because logging is done after the statement has completed. Upon restart (and successful repair) the MyISAM table will contain a partial update, but the binary log will not have logged the statement at all.

The situation is similar on the slave: if a crash occurs in the middle of execution of a statement (or a transaction that modifies a nontransactional table), the changes might remain in the table, but the group position will not be changed. The nontransactional statement will be re-executed when the slave starts up replication again.

It is not possible to automatically catch problems with crashes in the middle of updating a nontransactional table, but by obeying a few rules, it is possible to ensure you at least receive an error when this situation occurs.

INSERT *statements*

> To handle these statements, you need to have a primary key on the tables that you replicate. In this way, an INSERT that is re-executed will generate a duplicate key error and stop the slave so that you can check why the master and the slave are not consistent.

DELETE *statements*

> To handle these, you need to stay away from LIMIT clauses. If you do this, the statement will just delete the same rows again (i.e., the rows that match the WHERE clause), which is fine since it will either pick up where the previous statement left off or do nothing if all specified rows are already deleted. However, if the statement has a LIMIT clause, only a subset of the rows matching the WHERE condition will be executed, so when the statement is executed again, another set of rows will be deleted.

UPDATE *statements*

> These are the most problematic statements. To be safe, either the statement has to be *idempotent*—executing it twice should lead to the same result—or the occasional double execution of the statement should be acceptable, which could be the case if the UPDATE statement is just for maintaining statistics over, say, page accesses.

Multisource Replication

As you may have noticed, it is not possible to have a slave connect to multiple masters and receive changes from all of them. This topology is called *multisource* and should not be confused with the multimaster topology introduced in Chapter 6. In a multisource topology, changes are received from several masters, but in a multimaster topology, the servers form a group that acts as a single master by replicating changes from each master to all the other masters.

There have been plans for introducing multisource replication into MySQL for a long time, but one issue stands in the way of the design: what to do with conflicting updates. These can occur either because different sources make truly conflicting changes, or because two intermediate relays are forwarding a change made at a common master. Figure 8-10 illustrates both types of conflicts. In the first, two masters (sources) make changes to the same data and the slave cannot tell which is the final change. In the second, only a single change is made, but it looks to the slave like two changes from two different sources. In both cases, the slave will not be able to distinguish between events coming from the two relays, so an event sent from the master will be seen as two different events when arriving at the slave.

The diamond configuration does not have to be explicitly set up: it can occur inadvertently as a result of switching from one relay to another if the replication stream is overlapping during a switchover. For this reason, it is important to ensure all events in queue—on the slave and on all the relays between the master and the slave—have been replicated to the slave before switching over to another master.

You can avoid conflicts by making sure you handle switchovers correctly and—in the case of multiple data sources—ensuring updates are done so that they never have a chance of conflicting. The typical way to accomplish this is to update different databases, but it is also possible to assign updates of different rows in the same table to different servers.

Although MySQL does not currently let you replicate from several sources simultaneously, you can come close by switching a slave among several masters, replicating periodically from each of them in turn. This is called *round-robin multisource replication*. It can be useful for certain types of applications, such as when you're aggregating data from different sources for reporting purposes. In these cases, you can separate data naturally by storing the writes from each master in its own database, table, or partition. There is no risk of conflict, so it should be possible to use multisource replication.

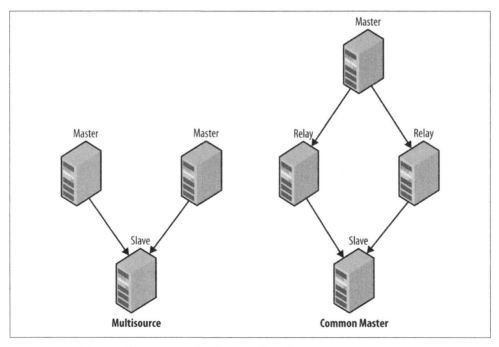

Figure 8-10. True multisource and a diamond configuration

Figure 8-11 shows a slave that replicates from three masters in a round-robin fashion, running a client dedicated to handling the switches between the masters. The process for round-robin multisource replication is as follows:

1. Set the slave up to replicate from one master. We'll call this the *current master*.

2. Let the slave replicate for a fixed period of time. The slave will then read changes from the current master and apply them while the client responsible for handling the switching just sleeps.

3. Stop the I/O thread of the slave using STOP SLAVE IO_THREAD.

4. Wait until the relay log is empty.

5. Stop the SQL thread using STOP SLAVE SQL_THREAD. CHANGE MASTER requires that you stop both threads.

6. Save the slave position for the current master by saving the values of the Ex ec_Master_Log_Pos and Relay_Master_Log_File columns from the SHOW SLAVE STATUS output.

7. Change the slave to replicate from the next master in sequence by taking the previously saved positions and using CHANGE MASTER to set up replication.

8. Restart the slave threads using START SLAVE.

9. Repeat the sequence starting from step 2.

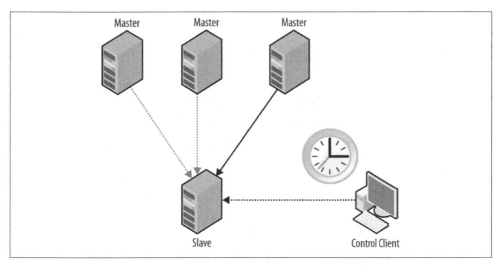

Figure 8-11. Round-robin multisource replication using a client to switch

Note that in steps 3 through 5, we stop first the I/O thread and then the SQL thread. The reason for doing this and not just stopping replication on the slave is that the SQL thread can be lagging behind (and usually is), so if we just stop both threads, there will be a bunch of outstanding events in the relay log that will just be thrown away. If you are more concerned about executing only, say, one minute's worth of transactions from each master and don't care about throwing away those additional events, you can simply stop replication instead of performing steps 3 through 5. The procedure will still work correctly, because the events that were thrown away will be refetched from the master in the next round.

This can, of course, be automated using a separate client connection and the MySQL Replicant library, as shown in Example 8-24. By using the `cycle` function from the `itertools` module, you can repeatedly read from a list of masters in turn.

Example 8-24. Round-robin multisource replication in Python

```python
import itertools

position = {}
def round_robin_multi_master(slave, masters):
    current = masters[0]
    for master in itertools.cycle(masters):
        slave.sql("STOP SLAVE IO_THREAD");
        slave_wait_for_empty_relay_log(slave)
        slave.sql("STOP SLAVE SQL_THREAD");
        position[current.name] = fetch_slave_position(slave)
        slave.change_master(position[current.name])
        master.sql("START SLAVE")
        current = master
        sleep(60)                  # Sleep 1 minute
```

Details of Row-Based Replication

"Row-Based Replication" on page 97 left out one major subject concerning row-based replication: how the rows are executed on the slave. In this section, you will see the details of how row-based replication is implemented on the slave side.

In statement-based replication, statements are handled by writing the statement in a single `Query` event. However, because a significant number of rows can be changed in each statement, row-based replication handles this differently and therefore requires multiple events for each statement.

To handle row-based replication, four new events have been introduced:

Table_map
> This maps a table ID to a table name (including the database name) and some basic information about the columns of the table on the master.

> The table information does not include the names of the columns, just the types. This is because row-based replication is positional: each column on the master goes into the same position in the table on the slave.

Write_rows, Delete_rows, *and* Update_rows

> These events are generated whenever rows are inserted, deleted, or updated, respectively. This means that a single statement can generate multiple events.
>
> In addition to the rows, each event contains a table ID that refers to a table ID introduced by a preceding Table_map event and one or two *column bitmaps* specifying the columns of the table affected by the event. This allows the log to save space by including only those columns that have changed or that are necessary to locate the correct row to insert, delete, or update.

Whenever a statement is executed, it is written into the binary log as a sequence of Table_map events, followed by a sequence of row events. The last row event of the statement is marked with a special flag indicating it is the last event of the statement.

Example 8-25 shows the execution of a statement and the resulting events. We have skipped the format description event here, because you have already seen it.

Example 8-25. Execution of an INSERT statement and the resulting events

```
master> START TRANSACTION;
Query OK, 0 rows affected (0.00 sec)

master> INSERT INTO t1 VALUES (1),(2),(3),(4);
Query OK, 4 rows affected (0.01 sec)
Records: 4  Duplicates: 0  Warnings: 0

master> INSERT INTO t1 VALUES (5),(6),(7),(8);
Query OK, 4 rows affected (0.01 sec)
Records: 4  Duplicates: 0  Warnings: 0

master> COMMIT;
Query OK, 0 rows affected (0.00 sec)

master> SHOW BINLOG EVENTS IN 'master-bin.000053' FROM 106\G
*************************** 1. row ***************************
   Log_name: master-bin.000054
        Pos: 106
 Event_type: Query
  Server_id: 1
End_log_pos: 174
       Info: BEGIN
*************************** 2. row ***************************
   Log_name: master-bin.000054
        Pos: 174
 Event_type: Table_map
  Server_id: 1
End_log_pos: 215
       Info: table_id: 18 (test.t1)
*************************** 3. row ***************************
   Log_name: master-bin.000054
        Pos: 215
```

```
  Event_type: Write_rows
    Server_id: 1
  End_log_pos: 264
         Info: table id: 18 flags: STMT_END_F
*************************** 4. row ***************************
    Log_name: master-bin.000054
         Pos: 264
  Event_type: Table_map
    Server_id: 1
  End_log_pos: 305
         Info: table_id: 18 (test.t1)
*************************** 5. row ***************************
    Log_name: master-bin.000054
         Pos: 305
  Event_type: Write_rows
    Server_id: 1
  End_log_pos: 354
         Info: table_id: 18 flags: STMT_END_F
*************************** 6. row ***************************
    Log_name: master-bin.000054
         Pos: 354
  Event_type: Xid
    Server_id: 1
  End_log_pos: 381
         Info: COMMIT /* xid=23 */
6 rows in set (0.00 sec)
```

This example adds two statements to the binary log. Each statement starts with a Table_map event followed by a single Write_rows event holding the four rows of each statement.

You can see that each statement is terminated by setting the statement-end flag of the row event. Because the statements are inside a transaction, they are also wrapped with Query events containing BEGIN and COMMIT statements.

The size of the row events is controlled by the option binlog-row-event-max-size, which gives a threshold for the number of bytes in the binary log. The option does *not* give a maximum size for a row event: it is possible to have a binlog row event that has a larger size if a row contains more bytes than binlog-row-event-max-size.

Table_map Events

As already mentioned, the Table_map event maps a table name to an identifier so that it can be used in the row events, but that is not its only role. In addition, it contains some basic information about the fields of the table on the master. This allows the slave to check the basic structure of the table on the slave and compare it to the structure on the master to make sure they match well enough for replication to proceed.

The basic structure of the table map event is shown in Figure 8-12. The common header—the header that all replication events have—contains the basic information about the event. After the common header, the post header gives information that is special for the table map event. Most of the fields in Figure 8-12 are self-explanatory, but the representation of the field types deserves a closer look.

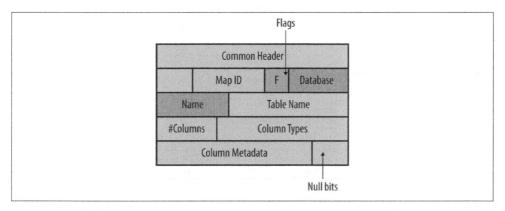

Figure 8-12. Table map event structure

The following fields together represent the column type:

Column type array

An array listing the base types for all the columns. It indicates whether this is an integer, a string type, a decimal type, or any of the other available types, but it does not give the parameters for the column type. For example, if the type of a column is CHAR(5), this array will contain 254 (the constant representing a string), but the length of the string (in this case, 5) is stored in the column metadata mentioned later.

Null bit array

An array of bits that indicate whether each field can be NULL.

Column metadata

An array of metadata for the fields, fleshing out details left out of the column type array. The piece of metadata available to each field depends on the type of the field. For example, the DECIMAL field stores the precision and decimals in the metadata, whereas the VARCHAR type stores the maximum length of the field.

By combining the data in these three arrays, it is possible to deduce the type of the field.

Not all type information is stored in the arrays, so in two particular cases, it is not possible for the master and the slave to distinguish between two types:

- When there is no information about whether an integer field is signed or unsigned. This means the slave will be unable to distinguish between a signed and unsigned field when checking the tables.

- When the character sets of string types are not part of the information. This means that replicating between different character sets is not supported and may lead to strange results, because the bytes will just be inserted into the column with no checking or conversion.

The Structure of Row Events

Figure 8-13 shows the structure of a row event. This structure can vary a little depending on the type of event (write, delete, or update).

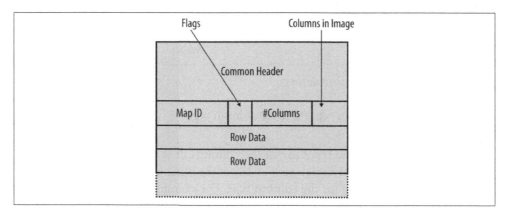

Figure 8-13. Row event header

In addition to the table identifier, which refers to the table ID of a previous table map event, the event contains the following fields:

Table width

The width of the table on the master. This width is length-encoded in the same way as for the client protocol, which is why it can be either one or two bytes. Most of the time, it will be one byte.

Columns bitmap

The columns that are sent as part of the payload of the event. This information allows the master to send a selected set of fields with each row. There are two types of column bitmaps: one for the *before image* and one for the *after image*. The before image is needed for deletions and updates, whereas the after image is needed for writes (inserts) and updates. See Table 8-3 for more information.

Table 8-3. Row events and their images

Before image	After image	Event
None	Row to insert	Write rows
Row to delete	None	Delete rows
Column values before update	Column values after update	Update rows

Execution of Row Event

Because multiple events can represent a single statement executed by the master, the slave has to keep state information to execute the row events correctly in the presence of concurrent threads that update the same tables. Recall that each statement in the binary log starts with one or more table map events followed by one or more row events, each of the same type. Use the following procedure to process a statement from the binary log:

1. Each event is read from the relay log.

2. If the event is a table map event, the SQL thread extracts the information about the table and saves a representation of how the master defines the table.

3. When the first row event is seen, all tables in the list are locked.

4. For each table in the list, the thread checks that the definition on the master is compatible with the definition on the slave.

5. If the tables are not compatible, the thread reports an error and stops replication on the slave.

6. Row events are processed according to the procedure shown later in this section, until the thread reads the last event of the statement (i.e., an event with the statement end flag set).

This procedure is required to lock tables the correct way on the slave and is similar to how the statement was executed on the master. All tables are locked in step 3 and then checked in step 4. If the tables are not locked before checking the definitions, a thread on the slave can come between the steps and change the definition, causing the application of the row events to fail later.

Each row event consists of a set of rows that are used differently depending on the event type. For `Delete_rows` and `Write_rows` events, each row represents a change. For the `Update_rows` event, it is necessary to have two rows—one to locate the correct row to update and one with values to use for the update—so the event consists of an even number of rows, where each pair represents an update.

Events that have a before image require a search to locate the correct row to operate on: for a `Delete_rows` event, the row will be removed, whereas for the `Update_rows` event, it will be changed. In descending order of preference, the searches are:

Primary key lookup

If the table on the slave has a primary key, it is used to perform a primary key lookup. This is the fastest of all the methods.

Index scan

If there is no primary key defined for the table but an index is defined, this will be used to locate the correct row to change. All rows in the index will be scanned and the columns compared with the row received from the master.

If the rows match, this row will be used for the `Delete_rows` or `Update_rows` operation. If no rows match, the slave will stop replication with an error indicating that it could not locate the correct row.

Table scan

If there is no primary key or index on the table, a full table scan is used to locate the correct row to delete or update.

In the same way as for the index scan, each row in the scan will be compared with the row received from the master, and if they match, that row will be used for the delete or update operation.

Because the index or primary key on the *slave* rather than the master is used to locate the correct row to delete or update, you should keep a couple of things in mind:

- If the table has a primary key on the slave, the lookup will be fast. If the table does not have a primary key, the slave has to do either a full table scan or an index scan to find the correct row to update, which is slower.
- You can have different indexes on the master and slave.

When replicating a table, it is always wise to have a primary key on the table regardless of whether row-based or statement-based replication is used.

Because statement-based replication actually executes each statement, a primary key on updates and deletes speeds up replication significantly for statement-based replication as well.

Events and Triggers

The execution of events and triggers differs in statement-based replication and row-based replication. The only difference for events is that row-based replication generates row events instead of query events.

Triggers, on the other hand, reveal a different and more interesting story.

As discussed in Chapter 4, for statement-based replication, trigger definitions are replicated to the slave so that when a statement is executed that affects a table with a trigger, the trigger will be executed on the slave as well.

For row-based replication, it doesn't matter how the rows change—whether changes come from a trigger, a stored procedure, an event, or directly from the statement. Because the rows updated by the trigger are replicated to the slave, the trigger does not need to be executed on the slave. As a matter of fact, executing it on the slave would lead to incorrect results.

Consider Example 8-26, which defines a table with a trigger.

Example 8-26. Definition of a table and triggers

```
CREATE TABLE log (
    number INT AUTO_INCREMENT PRIMARY KEY,
    user CHAR(64),
    brief TEXT
);


CREATE TABLE user (
    id INT AUTO_INCREMENT PRIMARY KEY,
    email CHAR(64),
    password CHAR(64)
);


CREATE TRIGGER tr_update_user AFTER UPDATE ON user FOR EACH ROW
    INSERT INTO log SET
        user = NEW.email,
        brief = CONCAT("Changed password from '",
                       OLD.password, "' to '",
                       NEW.password, "'");

CREATE TRIGGER tr_insert_user AFTER INSERT ON user FOR EACH ROW
    INSERT INTO log SET
        user = NEW.email,
        brief = CONCAT("User '", NEW.email, "' added");
```

Given these table and trigger definitions, this sequence of statements can be executed:

```
master> INSERT INTO user(email,password) VALUES ('mats@example.com', 'xyzzy');
Query OK, 1 row affected (0.05 sec)

master> UPDATE user SET password = 'secret' WHERE email = 'mats@example.com';
Query OK, 1 row affected (0.01 sec)
Rows matched: 1  Changed: 1  Warnings: 0

master> SELECT * FROM log;
+--------+--------------+-------------------------------------------+
| number | user         | brief                                     |
+--------+--------------+-------------------------------------------+
|      1 | mats@sun.com | User 'mats@example.com' added             |
|      2 | mats@sun.com | Changed password from 'xyzzy' to 'secret' |
```

```
+---------+-------------+----------------------------------------------+
2 rows in set (0.00 sec)
```

This is, of course, not very secure, but at least it illustrates the situation. So, how do these changes appear in the binary log when using row-based replication?

```
master> SHOW BINLOG EVENTS IN 'mysqld1-bin.000054' FROM 2180;
+--------------+----+-----------+---------+-----------+------------------------+
|Log_name      |Pos |Event_type |Server_id|End_log_pos|Info                    |
+--------------+----+-----------+---------+-----------+------------------------+
|master-bin…54|2180|Query      |       1|      2248|BEGIN                   |
|master-bin…54|2248|Table_map  |       1|      2297|table_id: 24 (test.user)|
|master-bin…54|2297|Table_map  |       1|      2344|table_id: 26 (test.log) |
|master-bin…54|2344|Write_rows |       1|      2397|table_id: 24            |
|master-bin…54|2397|Write_rows |       1|      2471|table_id: 26 flags:     |
|             |    |           |        |          |   STMT_END_F           |
|master-bin…54|2471|Query      |       1|      2540|COMMIT                  |
|master-bin…54|2540|Query      |       1|      2608|BEGIN                   |
|master-bin…54|2608|Table_map  |       1|      2657|table_id: 24 (test.user)|
|master-bin…54|2657|Table_map  |       1|      2704|table_id: 26 (test.log) |
|master-bin…54|2704|Update_rows|       1|      2783|table_id: 24            |
|master-bin…54|2783|Write_rows |       1|      2873|table_id: 26 flags:     |
|             |    |           |        |          |   STMT_END_F           |
|master-bin…54|2873|Query      |       1|      2942|COMMIT                  |
+--------------+----+-----------+---------+-----------+------------------------+
12 rows in set (0.00 sec)
```

As you can see, each statement is treated as a separate transaction containing only a single statement. The statement changes two tables—the test.user and test.log tables—and therefore there are two table maps at the beginning of the statement in the binary log. When replicated to the slave, these events are executed directly and the execution goes "below the trigger radar," thereby avoiding execution of the triggers for the tables on the slave.

Filtering in Row-Based Replication

Filtering also works differently in statement-based and row-based replication. Recall from Chapter 4 that statement-based replication filtering is done on the entire statement (i.e., either all of the statement is executed or the statement is not executed at all) because it is not possible to execute just part of a statement. For the database filtering options, the current database is used and not the database of the table that is being changed.

Row-based replication offers more choice. Because each row for a specific table is caught and replicated, it is possible to filter on the actual table being updated and even filter out some rows based on arbitrary conditions. For this reason, row-based replication also filters changes based on the actual table updated and is not based on the current database for the statement.

Consider what will happen with filtering on a slave set up to ignore the ignore_me database. What will be the result of executing the following statement under statement-based and row-based replication?

```
USE test; INSERT INTO ignore_me.t1 VALUES (1),(2);
```

For statement-based replication, the statement will be executed, but for row-based replication, the changes to table t1 will be ignored, because the *ignore_me* database is on the ignore list.

Continuing on this path, what will happen with the following multitable update statement?

```
USE test; UPDATE ignore_me.t1, test.t2 SET t1.a = 3, t2.a = 4 WHERE t1.a = t2.a;
```

With statement-based replication, the statement will be executed, expecting the table ignore_me.t1 to exist—which it might not, because the database is ignored—and will update both the ignore_me.t1 and test.t2 tables. Row-based replication, on the other hand, will update only the test.t2 table.

Partial Execution of Statements

As already noted, statement-based replication works pretty well unless you have to account for failures, crashes, and nondeterministic behavior. Because you can count on the failure or crash to occur at the worst possible moment, this will almost always lead to partially executed statements.

The same situation occurs when the number of rows affected by an UPDATE, DELETE, or INSERT statement is artificially limited. This may happen explicitly through a LIMIT clause or because the table is nontransactional and, say, a duplicate key error aborts execution and causes the statement to be only partially applied to the table.

In such cases, the changes that the statement describes are applied to only an initial set of rows. The master and the slave can have different opinions of how the rows are ordered, which can therefore result in the statement being applied to different sets of rows on the master and the slave.

MyISAM maintains all the rows in the order in which they were inserted. That may give you confidence that the same rows will be affected in case of partial changes. Unfortunately, however, that is not the case. If the slave has been cloned from the master using a logical backup or restored from a backup, it is possible that the insertion order changed.

Normally, you can solve this problem by adding an ORDER BY clause, but even that does not leave you entirely safe, because you are still in danger of having the statement partially executed because of a crash.

Partial Row Replication

As mentioned earlier, the events `Write_rows`, `Delete_rows`, and `Update_rows` each contain a column bitmap that tells what columns are present in the rows in the body of the event. Note that there is one bitmap for the before image and one for the after image.

Prior to MySQL 5.6.2, only the MySQL Cluster engine uses the option of limiting the columns written to the log, but starting with MySQL 5.6.2, it is possible to control what colums are written to the log using the option `binlog-row-image`. The option accepts three different values: `full`, `noblob`, and `minimal`.

`full`
> This is the default for `binlog-row-image` and will replicate all columns. Prior to MySQL 5.6.2, this is how the rows were always logged.

`noblob`
> With this setting, blobs will be omitted from the row unless they change as part of the update.

`minimal`
> With this setting, only the primary key (in the before image) and the columns that change values (in the after image) are written to the binary log.

The reason for having `full` as default is because there might be different indexes on the master, and the slave and columns that are not part of the primary key on the *master* might be needed to find the correct row on the slave.

If you look at Example 8-27, there are different definitions of the tables on the master and slave, but the only difference is that there are different indexes. The rationale for this difference could be that on the master it is necessary for the `id` column to be a primary key for autoincrement to work, but on the slave all selects are done using the `email` column.

In this case, setting `binlog-row-image` to `minimal` will store the values of the `id` column in the binary log, but this column cannot be used to find the correct row on the slave. This will cause replication to fail. Because it is expected that replication should work even if this mistake is made, the default for `binlog-row-image` is `full`.

If you are using identical indexes on the master and slave (or at least have indexes on the slave on the columns that are indexed on the master), you can set `binlog-row-image` to `minimal` and save space by reducing the size of the binary log.

So what's the role of the `noblob` value then? Well... it acts as a middle ground. Even though it is possible to have different indexes on the master and slave, it is very rare for blobs to be part of an index. Because blobs usually take a lot of space, using `noblob` will be almost as safe as `full`, under the assumption that blobs are never indexed.

Example 8-27. Table with different indexes on master and slave

```
/* Table definition on the master */
CREATE TABLE user (
    id INT AUTO_INCREMENT PRIMARY KEY,
    email CHAR(64),
    password CHAR(64)
);

/* Table definition on the slave */
CREATE TABLE user (
    id INT,
    email CHAR(64) PRIMARY KEY,
    password CHAR(64)
);
```

Conclusion

This chapter concludes a series of chapters about MySQL replication. We discussed advanced replication topics such as how to promote slaves to masters more robustly, looked at tips and techniques for avoiding corrupted databases after a crash, examined multisource replication configurations and considerations, and finally looked at row-based replication in detail.

In the next chapters, we examine another set of topics for building robust data centers, including monitoring, performance tuning of storage engines, and replication.

Joel met his boss in the hallway on his way back from lunch. "Hello, Mr. Summerson."

"Hello, Joel."

"Have you read my report?"

"Yes, I have, Joel. Good work. I've passed it around to some of the other departments for comment. I want to add it to our SOP manual."

Joel imagined SOP meant standard operating procedures.

"I've asked the reviewers to send you their comments. It might need some wordsmithing to fit into an SOP, but I know you're up to the task."

"Thank you, sir."

Mr. Summerson nodded, patted Joel on the shoulder, and continued on his way down the hall.

## CHAPTER 9

MySQL Cluster

A subdued knock on his door alerted Joel to his visitor. He looked up to see a worried-looking Mr. Summerson.

"I've got to dump on you this time, Joel. We're in a real bind here."

Joel remained silent, wondering what his definition of "dump on you" meant. So far, he had tasked Joel with some pretty intense work.

"We've just learned of a new customer who wants to use our latest database application in a real-time, five-nines environment."

"Always up and no downtime?"

"That's right. Now, I know MySQL is very reliable, but there's no time to change the application to use a fault-tolerant database server."

Joel remembered skimming a chapter on a special version of MySQL and wondered if that would work. He decided to take a chance: "We could use the cluster technology."

"Cluster?"

"Yes, MySQL has a cluster version that is a fault-tolerant database system. It has worked in some pretty demanding environments, like telecom, as I recall...."

Mr. Summerson's eyes brightened and he appeared to stand a little straighter as he delivered his coup de grâce. "Perfect. Give me a report by tomorrow morning. I want cost, hardware requirements, limitations—the works. Don't pull any punches. If we can get this to work, I want to do it, but I don't want to risk our reputation on a hunch."

"I'll get right on it," Joel said, wondering what he had gotten himself into this time. After Mr. Summerson left, he sighed and opened his favorite MySQL book. "This may be my greatest challenge yet," he said.

When high performance, high availability, redundancy, and scalability are paramount concerns for database planners, they often seek to improve their replication topologies with commodity high-availability hardware and load-balancing solutions. Although this approach often meets the needs of most organizations, if you need a solution with no single points of failure and extremely high throughput with 99.999% uptime, chances are the MySQL Cluster technology will meet your needs.

In this chapter, you will be introduced to the concepts of the MySQL Cluster technology. It provides you an example of starting and stopping a simple cluster, and discusses the key points of using MySQL Cluster, including high availability, distributed data, and data replication. We begin by describing what MySQL Cluster is and how it differs from a normal MySQL server.

What Is MySQL Cluster?

MySQL Cluster is a shared-nothing storage solution with a distributed node architecture designed for fault tolerance and high performance. Data is stored and replicated on individual *data nodes*, where each data node runs on a separate server and maintains a copy of the data. Each cluster also contains management nodes. Updates use read-committed isolation to ensure all nodes have consistent data and a two-phased commit to ensure the nodes have the same data (if any one write fails, the update fails).

The original implementation of MySQL Cluster stored all information in main memory with no persistent storage. Later releases of MySQL Cluster permit storage of the data on disk. Perhaps the best quality of MySQL Cluster is that it uses the MySQL server as the query engine via the storage engine layer. Thus, you can migrate applications designed to interact with MySQL to MySQL Cluster transparently.

The shared-nothing, peer node concept permits an update executed on one server to become visible immediately on the other servers. The transmission of the updates uses a sophisticated communication mechanism designed for very high throughput across networks. The goal is to have the highest performance possible by using multiple MySQL servers to distribute the load, and high availability and redundancy by storing data in different locations.

Terminology and Components

Typical installations of the MySQL Cluster involve installing the components of the cluster on different machines on a network. Hence, MySQL Cluster is also known as a network database (NDB). When we use the term "MySQL Cluster," we refer to the MySQL server plus the NDB components. However, when we use "NDB" or "NDB Cluster" we refer specifically to the cluster components.

MySQL Cluster is a database system that uses the MySQL server as the frontend to support standard SQL queries. A storage engine named NDBCluster is the interface that links the MySQL server with the cluster technology. This relationship is often confused. You cannot use the NDBCluster storage engine without the NDBCluster components. However is it is possible to use the NDB Cluster technologies without the MySQL server, but this requires lower-level programming with the NDB API.

The NDB API is object-oriented and implements indexes, scans, transactions, and event handling. This allows you to write applications that retrieve, store, and manipulate data in the cluster. The NDB API also provides object-oriented error-handling facilities to allow orderly shutdown or recovery during failures. If you are a developer and want to learn more about the NDB API, see the MySQL NDB API online documentation (*http://bit.ly/ndb-api*).

How Does MySQL Cluster Differ from MySQL?

You may be wondering, "What is the difference between a cluster and replication?" There are several definitions of clustering, but it can generally be viewed as something that has membership, messaging, redundancy, and automatic failover capabilities. Replication, in contrast, is simply a way to send messages (data) from one server to another. We discuss replication within a cluster (also called *local replication*) and MySQL replication in more detail later in this chapter.

Typical Configuration

You can view the MySQL Cluster as having three layers:

- Applications that communicate with the MySQL server
- The MySQL server that processes the SQL commands and communicates to the NDB storage engine
- The NDB Cluster components (i.e., the *data nodes*) that process the queries and return the results to the MySQL server

 You can scale up each layer independently with more server processes to increase performance.

Figure 9-1 shows a conceptual drawing of a typical cluster installation.

The applications connect to the MySQL server, which accesses the NDB Cluster components via the storage engine layer (specifically, the NDB storage engine). We will discuss the NDB Cluster components in more detail momentarily.

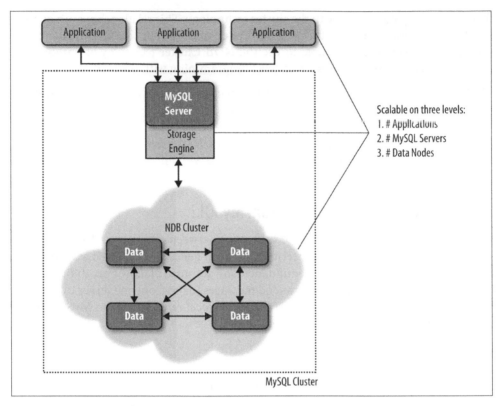

Figure 9-1. MySQL Cluster

There are many possible configurations. You can use multiple MySQL servers to connect to a single NDB Cluster and even connect multiple NDB Clusters via MySQL replication. We will discuss more of these configurations in later sections.

Features of MySQL Cluster

To satisfy the goals of having the highest achievable performance, high availability, and redundancy, data is replicated inside the cluster among the peer data nodes. The data is stored on multiple data nodes and is replicated synchronously, each data node connecting to every other data node.

It is also possible to replicate data between clusters, but in this case, you use MySQL replication, which is *asynchronous* rather than *synchronous*. As we've discussed in previous chapters, asynchronous replication means you must expect a delay in updating the slaves; slaves do not report back the progress in committing changes, and you cannot expect a consistent view across all servers in the replicated architecture like you can expect within a single MySQL cluster.

MySQL Cluster has several specialized features for creating a highly available system. The most significant ones are:

Node recovery

Data node failures can be detected via either communication loss or heartbeat failure, and you can configure the nodes to restart automatically using copies of the data from the remaining nodes. Failure and recovery can comprise single or multiple storage nodes. This is also called *local recovery*.

Logging

During normal data updates, copies of the data change events are written to a log stored on each data node. You can use the logs to restore the data to a point in time.

Checkpointing

The cluster supports two forms of checkpoints, local and global. Local checkpoints remove the tail of the log. Global checkpoints are created when the logs of all data nodes are flushed to disk, creating a transaction-consistent snapshot of all node data to disk. In this way, checkpointing permits a complete system restore of all nodes from a known good synchronization point.

System recovery

In the event the whole system is shut down unexpectedly, you can restore it using checkpoints and change logs. Typically, the data is copied from disk into memory from known good synchronization points.

Hot backup and restore

You can create simultaneous backups of each data node without disturbing executing transactions. The backup includes the metadata about the objects in the database, the data itself, and the current transaction log.

No single point of failure

The architecture is designed so that any node can fail without bringing down the database system.

Failover

To ensure node recovery is possible, all transactions arc committed using read commit isolation and two-phase commits. Transactions are then doubly safe (i.e., they are stored in two separate locations before the user gets acceptance of the transaction).

Partitioning

Data is automatically partitioned across the data nodes. Starting with MySQL version 5.1, MySQL Cluster supports user-defined partitioning.

Online operations

You can perform many of the maintenance operations online without the normal interruptions. These are operations that normally require stopping a server or placing locks on data. For example, it is possible to add new data nodes online, alter table structures, and even reorganize the data in the cluster.

For more information about MySQL Cluster, see the MySQL Cluster Documentation (*http://bit.ly/sql-cluster*) containing reference guides for the different versions of cluster.

Local and Global Redundancy

You can create local redundancy (inside a particular cluster) using a two-phase commit protocol. In principle, each node goes through a round in which it agrees to make a change, then undergoes a round in which it commits the transaction. During the agreement phase, each node ensures that there are enough resources to commit the change in the second round. In NDB Cluster, the MySQL server commit protocol changes to allow updates to multiple nodes. NDB Cluster also has an optimized version of two-phase commit that reduces the number of messages sent using synchronous replication. The two-phase protocol ensures the data is redundantly stored on multiple data nodes, a state known as *local redundancy*.

Global redundancy uses MySQL replication between clusters. This establishes two nodes in a replication topology. As discussed previously, MySQL replication is asynchronous because it does not include an acknowledgment or receipt for arrival or execution of the events replicated. Figure 9-2 illustrates the differences.

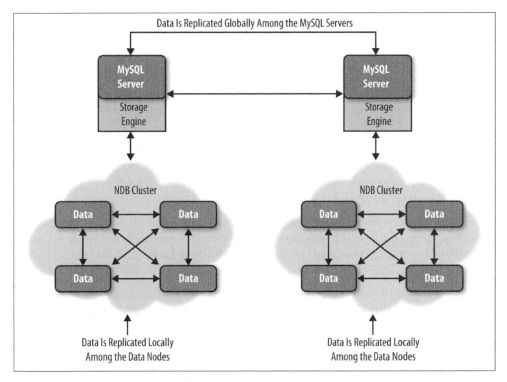

Figure 9-2. Local and global redundancy

Log Handling

MySQL Cluster implements two types of checkpoints: local checkpoints to purge part of the redo log, and a global checkpoint that is mainly for synchronizing between the different data nodes. The global checkpoint becomes important for replication because it forms the boundary between sets of transactions known as *epochs*. Each epoch is replicated between clusters as a single unit. In fact, MySQL replication treats the set of transactions between two consecutive global checkpoints as a single transaction.

Redundancy and Distributed Data

Data redundancy is based on replicas, where each replica has a copy of the data. This allows a cluster to be fault tolerant. If any data node fails, you can still access the data. Naturally, the more replicas you allow in a cluster, the more fault tolerant the cluster will be.

Split-Brain Syndrome

If one or more data nodes fail, it is possible that the remaining data nodes will be unable to communicate. When this happens, the two sets of data nodes are in a split-brain scenario. This type of situation is undesirable, because each set of data nodes could theoretically perform as a separate cluster.

To overcome this, you need a network partitioning algorithm to decide between the competing sets of data nodes. The decision is made in each set independently. The set with the minority of nodes will be restarted and each node of that set will need to join the majority set individually.

If the two sets of nodes are exactly the same size, a theoretical problem still exists. If you split four nodes into two sets with two nodes in each, how do you know which set is a minority? For this purpose, you can define an arbitrator. In the case that the sets are exactly the same size, the set that first succeeds in contacting the arbitrator wins.

You can designate the arbitrator as either a MySQL server (SQL node) or a management node. For best availability, you should locate the arbitrator on a system that does not host a data node.

The network partitioning algorithm with arbitration is fully automatic in MySQL Cluster, and the minority is defined with respect to node groups to make the system even more available than it would be compared to just counting the nodes.

You can specify how many copies of the data (NoOfReplicas) exist in the cluster. You need to set up as many data nodes as you want replicas. You can also distribute the data across the data nodes using partitioning. In this case, each data node has only a portion of the data, making queries faster. But because you have multiple copies of the data, you can still query the data in the event that a node fails, and the recovery of the missing node is assured (because the data exists in the other replicas). To achieve this, you need multiple data nodes for each replica. For example, if you want two replicas and partitioning, you need to have at least four data nodes (two data nodes for each replica).

Architecture of MySQL Cluster

MySQL Cluster is composed of one or more MySQL servers communicating via the NDB storage engine to an NDB cluster. An NDB cluster itself is composed of several components: data or storage nodes that store and retrieve the data and one or more management nodes that coordinate startup, shutdown, and recovery of data nodes. Most of the NDB components are implemented as daemon processes, while MySQL Cluster also offers client utilities to manipulate the daemons' features. Here is a list of the daemons and utilities (Figure 9-3 depicts how each of these components communicates):

mysqld
> The MySQL server

ndbd
> A data node

ndbmtd
> A multithreaded data node

ndb_mgmd
> The cluster's management server

ndb_mgm
> The cluster's management client

Each MySQL server with the executable name *mysqld* typically supports one or more applications that issue SQL queries and receive results from the data nodes. When discussing MySQL Cluster, the MySQL servers are sometimes called *SQL nodes*.

The data nodes are NDB daemon processes that store and retrieve the data either in memory or on disk depending on their configuration. Data nodes are installed on each server participating in the cluster. There is also a multithreaded data node daemon named *ndbmtd* that works on platforms that support multiple CPU cores. You can see improved data node performance if you use the multithreaded data node on dedicated servers with modern multiple-core CPUs.

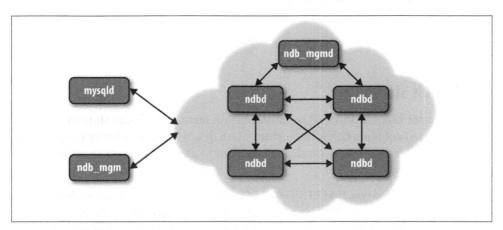

Figure 9-3. The MySQL Cluster components

The management daemon, *ndb_mgmd*, runs on a server and is responsible for reading a configuration file and distributing the information to all of the nodes in the cluster. *ndb_mgm*, the NDB management client utility, can check the cluster's status, start backups, and perform other administrative functions. This client runs on a host convenient to the administrator and communicates with the daemon.

There are also a number of utilities that make maintenance easier. Here are a few of the more popular ones (consult the NDB Cluster documentation (*http://bit.ly/cluster-ndb*) for a complete list):

ndb_config
Extracts configuration information from existing nodes.

ndb_delete_all
Deletes all rows from an NDB table.

ndb_desc
Describes NDB tables (like SHOW CREATE TABLE).

ndb_drop_index
Drops an index from an NDB table.

ndb_drop_table
Drops an NDB table.

ndb_error_reporter
Diagnoses errors and problems in a cluster.

ndb_redo_log_reader
Checks and prints out a cluster redo log.

ndb_restore
Performs a restore of a cluster. Backups are made using the NDB management client.

How Data Is Stored

MySQL Cluster keeps all indexed columns in main memory. You can store the remaining nonindexed columns either in memory or on disk with an in-memory page cache. Storing nonindexed columns on disk allows you to store more data than the size of available memory.

When data is changed (via INSERT, UPDATE, DELETE, etc.), MySQL Cluster writes a record of the change to a redo log, checkpointing data to disk regularly. As described previously, the log and the checkpoints permit recovery from disk after a failure. However, because the redo logs are written asynchronously with the commit, it is possible that a limited number of transactions can be lost during a failure. To mitigate against this risk, MySQL Cluster implements a write delay (with a default of two seconds, but this is configurable). This allows the checkpoint write to complete so that if a failure occurs, the last checkpoint is not lost as a result of the failure. Normal failures of individual data nodes do not result in any data loss due to the synchronous data replication within the cluster.

When a MySQL Cluster table is maintained in memory, the cluster accesses disk storage only to write records of the changes to the redo log and to execute the requisite checkpoints. Because writing the logs and checkpoints is sequential and few random access patterns are involved, MySQL Cluster can achieve higher write throughput rates with limited disk hardware than the traditional disk caching used in relational database systems.

You can calculate the size of memory you need for a data node using the following formula. The size of the database is the sum of the size of the rows times the number of rows for each table. Keep in mind that if you use disk storage for nonindexed columns, you should count only the indexed columns in calculating the necessary memory.

$$(SizeofDatabase \times NumberOfReplicas \times 1.1) / NumberOfDataNodes$$

This is a simplified formula for rough calculation. When planning the memory of your cluster, you should consult the online MySQL Cluster Reference Manual for additional details to consider.

You can also use the Perl script *ndb_size.pl* found in most distributions. This script connects to a running MySQL server, traverses all the existing tables in a set of databases, and calculates the memory they would require in a MySQL cluster. This is convenient, because it permits you to create and populate the tables on a normal MySQL server first, then check your memory configuration before you set up, configure, and load data into your cluster. It is also useful to run periodically to keep ahead of schema changes that can result in memory issues and to give you an idea of your memory usage. Example 9-1 depicts a sample report for a simple database with a single table. To find the total size of the database, multiply the size of the data row from the summary by the number of rows. In Example 9-1, we have (for MySQL version 5.1) 84 bytes per row for data and index. If we had 64,000 rows, we would need to have 5,376,000 bytes of memory to store the table.

 If the script generates an error about a missing *Class/MethodMaker.pm* module, you need to install this class on your system. For example, on Ubuntu you can install it with the following command:

```
sudo apt-get install libclass-methodmaker-perl
```

Example 9-1. Checking the size of a database with ndb_size.pl

```
$ ./ndb_size.pl \
> --database=cluster_test --user=root
ndb_size.pl report for database: 'cluster_test' (1 tables)
--------------------------------------------------------
Connected to: DBI:mysql:host=localhost
```

```
Including information for versions: 4.1, 5.0, 5.1

cluster_test.City
----------------

DataMemory for Columns (* means varsized DataMemory):
        Column Name   Type   Varsized   Key   4.1   5.0   5.1
           district          char(20)           20    20    20
         population          int(11)             4     4     4
              ccode          char(3)             4     4     4
               name          char(35)           36    36    36
                 id          int(11)    PRI      4     4     4
                                                --    --    --
Fixed Size Columns DM/Row                       68    68    68
 Varsize Columns DM/Row                          0     0     0

DataMemory for Indexes:
        Index Name       Type       4.1     5.0     5.1
           PRIMARY       BTREE       N/A     N/A     N/A
                                     --      --      --
          Total Index DM/Row          0       0       0

IndexMemory for Indexes:
                Index Name     4.1         5.0         5.1
                   PRIMARY      29          16          16
                                --          --          --
             Indexes IM/Row     29          16          16

Summary (for THIS table):
                               4.1         5.0         5.1
        Fixed Overhead DM/Row   12          12          16
            NULL Bytes/Row       0           0           0
            DataMemory/Row      80          80          84
(Includes overhead, bitmap and indexes)

   Varsize Overhead DM/Row       0           0           8
   Varsize NULL Bytes/Row        0           0           0
     Avg Varside DM/Row          0           0           0

                No. Rows         3           3           3

        Rows/32kb DM Page      408         408         388
Fixedsize DataMemory (KB)       32          32          32

Rows/32kb Varsize DM Page        0           0           0
   Varsize DataMemory (KB)       0           0           0

        Rows/8kb IM Page       282         512         512
          IndexMemory (KB)       8           8           8

Parameter Minimum Requirements
------------------------------
```

```
* indicates greater than default

           Parameter    Default     4.1     5.0     5.1
      DataMemory (KB)      81920      32      32      32
   NoOfOrderedIndexes        128       1       1       1
          NoOfTables        128       1       1       1
     IndexMemory (KB)      18432       8       8       8
 NoOfUniqueHashIndexes        64       0       0       0
        NoOfAttributes     1000       5       5       5
          NoOfTriggers      768       5       5       5
```

Although Example 9-1 uses a very simple table, the output shows not only the row size, but also a host of statistics for the tables in the database. The report also shows the indexing statistics, which are the key mechanism the cluster uses for high performance.

The script displays the different memory requirements across MySQL versions. This allows you to see any differences if you are working with older versions of MySQL Cluster.

Partitioning

One of the most important aspects of MySQL Cluster is data partitioning. MySQL Cluster partitions data horizontally (i.e., the rows are automatically divided among the data nodes using a function to distribute the rows). This is based on a hashing algorithm that uses the primary key for the table. In early versions of MySQL, the software uses an internal mechanism for partitioning, but MySQL versions 5.1 and later allow you to provide your own function for partitioning data. If you use your own function for partitioning, you should create a function that ensures the data is distributed evenly among the data nodes.

 If a table does not have a primary key, MySQL Cluster adds a surrogate primary key.

Partitioning allows the MySQL Cluster to achieve higher performance for queries because it supports distribution of queries among the data nodes. Thus, a query will return results much faster when gathering data across several nodes than from a single node. For example, you can execute the following query on each data node, getting the sum of the column on each one and summing those results:

```
SELECT SUM(population) FROM cluster_db.city;
```

Data distributed across the data nodes is protected from failure if you have more than one replica (copy) of the data. If you want to use partitioning to distribute your data across multiple data nodes to achieve parallel queries, you should also ensure you have at least two replicas of each row so that your cluster is fault tolerant.

Transaction Management

Another aspect of MySQL Cluster's behavior that differs from MySQL server concerns transactional data operations. As mentioned previously, MySQL Cluster coordinates transactional changes across the data nodes. This uses two subprocesses called the *transaction coordinator* and the *local query handler*.

The transaction coordinator handles distributed transactions and other data operations on a global level. The local query handler manages data and transactions local to the cluster's data nodes and acts as a coordinator of two-phase commits at the data node.

Each data node can be a transaction coordinator (you can tune this behavior). When an application executes a transaction, the cluster connects to a transaction coordinator on one of the data nodes. The default behavior is to select the closest data node as defined by the networking layer of the cluster. If there are several connections available within the same distance, a round-robin algorithm selects the transaction coordinator.

The selected transaction coordinator then sends the query to each data node, and the local query handler executes the query, coordinating the two-phased commit with the transaction coordinator. Once all data nodes verify the transaction, the transaction coordinator validates (commits) the transaction.

MySQL Cluster supports the read-committed transaction isolation level. This means that when there are changes during the execution of the transaction, only committed changes can be read while the transaction is underway. In this way, MySQL Cluster ensures data consistency while transactions are running.

For more information about how transactions work in MySQL Cluster and a list of important limitations on transactions, see the MySQL Cluster chapter in the online MySQL Reference Manual.

Online Operations

In MySQL versions 5.1 and later, you can perform certain operations while a cluster is online, meaning that you do not have to either take the server down or lock portions of the system or database. The following list briefly discusses a few of the online operations available in MySQL Cluster and lists the versions that include each feature:

Backup (versions 5.0 and later)
> You can use the NDB management console to perform a snapshot backup (a non-blocking operation) to create a backup of your data in the cluster. This operation includes a copy of the metadata (names and definitions of all tables), the table data, and the transaction log (a historical record of changes). It differs from a *mysql-*

dump backup in that it does not use a table scan to read the records. You can restore the data using the special *ndb_restore* utility.

Adding and dropping indexes (MySQL Cluster version 5.1 and later)

You can use the `ONLINE` keyword to perform the `CREATE INDEX` or `DROP INDEX` command online. When online operation is requested, the operation is noncopying —it does not make a copy of the data in order to index it—so indexes do not have to be recreated afterward. One advantage of this is that transactions can continue during alter table operations, and tables being altered are not locked against access by other SQL nodes. However, the table is locked against other queries on the SQL node performing the alter operation.

 In MySQL Cluster version 5.1.7 and later, add and drop index operations are performed online when the indexes are on variable-width columns only.

Alter table (MySQL Cluster version 6.2 and later)

You can use the `ONLINE` keyword to execute an `ALTER TABLE` statement online. It is also noncopying and has the same advantages as adding indexes online. Additionally, in MySQL Cluster version 7.0 and later, you can reorganize the data across partitions online using the `REORGANIZE PARTITION` command as long as you don't use the `INTO (partition_definitions)` option.

 Changing default column values or data types online is currently not supported.

Add data nodes and node groups (MySQL Cluster version 7.0 and later)

You can manage the expansion of your data nodes online, either for scale-out or for node replacement after a failure. The process is described in great detail in the reference manual. Briefly, it involves changing the configuration file, performing a rolling restart of the NDB management daemon, performing a rolling restart of the existing data nodes, starting the new data nodes, and then reorganizing the partitions.

For more information about MySQL Cluster, its architecture and features, you can find white papers (*http://bit.ly/mysql-wps*) covering MySQL Cluster, but also many other MySQL-related topics.

Example Configuration

In this section, we present a sample configuration of a MySQL Cluster running two data nodes on two systems, with the MySQL server and NDB management node on a third system. We present examples of simplified data node setup. Our example system is shown in Figure 9-4.

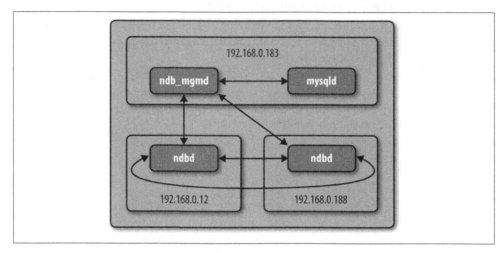

Figure 9-4. Sample cluster configuration

You can see one node that contains both the NDB management daemon and the SQL node (the MySQL server). There are also two data nodes, each on its own system. You need a minimum of three computers to form a basic MySQL Cluster configuration with either increased availability or performance.

This is a minimal configuration for MySQL Cluster and, if the number of replicas is set to two, the minimal configuration for fault tolerance. If the number of replicas is set to one, the configuration will support partitioning for better performance but will not be fault tolerant.

It is generally permissible to run the NDB management daemon on the same node as a MySQL server, but you may want to move this daemon to another system if you are likely to have a high number of data nodes or want to ensure the greatest level of fault tolerance.

Getting Started

You can obtain MySQL Cluster from the MySQL downloads page (*http://bit.ly/dl-mysqlc*). It is open source, like the MySQL server. You can download either a binary distribution or an installation file for some of the top platforms. You can also download the source code and build the cluster on your own platform. Be sure to check the platform notes for specific issues for your host operating system.

You should follow the normal installation procedures outlined in the MySQL Reference Manual. Aside from one special directory, the NDB tools are installed in the same location as the MySQL server binaries.

Before we dive into our example, let us first review some general concepts concerning configuring a MySQL cluster. The cluster configuration is maintained by the NDB management daemon and is read (initially) from a configuration file. There are many parameters that you can use to tune the various parts of the cluster, but we will concentrate on a minimal configuration for now.

There are several sections in the configuration file. At a minimum, you need to include each of the following sections:

[mysqld]

> The familiar section of the configuration file that applies to the MySQL server, the SQL node.

[ndb default]

> A default section for global settings. Use this section to specify all of the settings you want applied to every node, both data and management. Note that the name of the section contains a space, not an underscore.

[ndb_mgmd]

> A section for the NDB management daemon.

[ndbd]

> You must add one section with this name for each data node.

Example 9-2 shows a minimal configuration file that matches the configuration in Figure 9-4.

Example 9-2. Minimal configuration file

```
[ndbd default]
NoOfReplicas= 2
DataDir= /var/lib/mysql-cluster

[ndb_mgmd]
hostname=192.168.0.183
datadir= /var/lib/mysql-cluster

[ndbd]
hostname=192.168.0.12

[ndbd]
hostname=192.168.0.188
```

```
[mysqld]
hostname=192.168.0.183
```

This example includes the minimal variables for a simple two data-node cluster with replication. Thus, the `NoOfReplicas` option is set to 2. Notice we have set the `datadir` variable to *var/lib/mysql-cluster*. You can set it to whatever you want, but most installations of MySQL Cluster use this directory.

Finally, notice we have specified the hostname of each node. This is important, because the NDB management daemon needs to know the location of all of the nodes in the cluster. If you have downloaded and installed MySQL Cluster and want to follow along, make the necessary changes to the hostnames so they match our example.

The MySQL Cluster configuration file is by default placed in *var/lib/mysql-cluster* and is named *config.ini*.

 It is not necessary to install the complete MySQL Cluster binary package on the data nodes. As you will see later, you need only the *ndbd* daemon on the data nodes.

Starting a MySQL Cluster

Starting MySQL Cluster requires a specific order of commands. We will step through the procedures for this example, but it is good to briefly examine the general process:

1. Start the management node(s).
2. Start the data nodes.
3. Start the MySQL servers (SQL nodes).

For our example, we first start the NDB management node on 192.168.0.183. Then we start each of the data nodes (192.168.0.12 and 192.168.0.188, in either order). Once the data nodes are running, we can start the MySQL server on 192.168.0.183 and, after a brief startup delay, the cluster is ready to use.

Starting the management node

The first node to start is the NDB management daemon named *ndb_mgmd*. This is located in the *libexec* folder of the MySQL installation. For example, on Ubuntu it is located in */usr/local/mysql/libexec*.

Start the NDB management daemon by issuing a superuser launch and specify the `--initial` and `--config-file` options. The `--initial` option tells the cluster that this is our first time starting and we want to erase any configurations stored from previous launches. The --config-file option tells the daemon where to find the configuration file. Example 9-3 shows how to start the NDB management daemon for our example.

Example 9-3. Starting the NDB management daemon

```
$ sudo ../libexec/ndb_mgmd --initial \
--config-file /var/lib/mysql-cluster/config.ini
MySQL Cluster Management Server mysql-5.6.11 ndb-7.3.2
```

It is always a good idea to provide the --config-file option when you start, because some installations have different default locations for the configuration file search pattern. You can discover this pattern by issuing the command ndb_mgmd --help and searching for the phrase "Default options are read from." It is not necessary to specify the --config-file option on subsequent starts of the daemon.

Starting the management console

While not absolutely necessary at this point, it is a good idea to now launch the NDB management console and check that the NDB management daemon has correctly read the configuration. The name of the NDB management console is *ndb_mgm* and it is located in the *bin* directory of the MySQL installation. We can view the configuration by issuing the SHOW command, as shown in Example 9-4.

Example 9-4. Initial start of the NDB management console

```
$ ./ndb_mgm
-- NDB Cluster -- Management Client --
ndb_mgm> SHOW
Connected to Management Server at: 192.168.0.183:1186
Cluster Configuration
---------------------
[NDBd(NDB)]     2 node(s)
id=2 (not connected, accepting connect from 192.168.0.188)
id=3 (not connected, accepting connect from 192.168.0.12)

[NDB_mgmd(MGM)]    1 node(s)
id=1    @192.168.0.183  (mysql-5.5.31 ndb-7.2.13)

[mysqld(API)]    1 node(s)
id=4 (not connected, accepting connect from 192.168.0.183)

ndb_mgm>
```

This command displays the data nodes and their IP addresses as well as the NDB management daemon and the SQL node. This is a good time to check that all of our nodes are configured with the right IP addresses and that all of the appropriate data nodes are loaded. If you have changed your cluster configuration but see the old values here, it is likely the NDB management daemon has not read the new configuration file.

This output tells us that the NDB management daemon is loaded and ready. If it were not, the SHOW command would fail with a communication error. If you see that error, be sure to check that you are running the NDB management client on the same server as the NDB management daemon. If you are not, use the --ndb-connectstring option and provide the IP address or hostname of the machine hosting the NDB management daemon.

Finally, notice the node IDs of your nodes. You will need this information to issue commands to a specific node in the cluster from the NDB management console. Issue the HELP command at any time to see the other commands available. You will also need to know the node ID for your SQL nodes so that they start up correctly.

 You can specify the node IDs for each node in your cluster using the --ndb-nodeid parameter in the *config.ini* file.

You can also use the STATUS command to see the status of your nodes. Issue ALL STA TUS to see the status of all nodes or *node-id* STATUS to see the status of a specific node. This command is handy for watching the cluster start up, because the output reports which startup phase the data node is in. If you want to see the details, look in a version of the online MySQL Reference Manuals containing MySQL Cluster for more details about the phases of data node startup.

Starting data nodes

Now that we have started our NDB management daemon, it is time to start the data nodes. However, before we do that, let's examine the minimal setup needed for an NDB data node.

To set up an NDB data node, all you need is the NDB data node daemon (*ndbd*) compiled for the targeted host operating system. First, create the folder */var/lib/mysql-cluster*, then copy in the *ndbd* executable, and you're done! Clearly, this makes it very easy to script the creation of data nodes (and many have).

You can start the data nodes (*ndbd*) using the --initial-start option, which signals that this is the first time the cluster has been started. You also must provide the --ndb-connectstring option, providing the IP address of the NDB management daemon. Example 9-5 shows starting a data node for the first time. Do this on each data node.

Example 9-5. Starting the data node

```
$ sudo ./ndbd --initial-start --ndb-connectstring=192.168.0.183
2013-02-11 06:22:52 [ndbd] INFO     -- Angel connected to '192.168.0.183:1186'
2013-02-11 06:22:52 [ndbd] INFO     -- Angel allocated nodeid: 2
```

If you are starting a new data node, have reset a data node, or are recovering from a failure, you can specify the --initial option to force the data node to erase any existing configuration and cached data and request a new copy from the NDB management daemon.

 Be careful when using the --initial options. They really do delete your data!

Return to the management console and check the status (Example 9-6).

Example 9-6. Status of data nodes

```
ndb_mgm> SHOW
Cluster Configuration
---------------------
[ndbd(NDB)]     2 node(s)
id=2    @192.168.0.188  (mysql-5.5.31 ndb-7.2.13, Nodegroup: 0, Master)
id=3    @192.168.0.12  (mysql-5.5.31 ndb-7.2.13, Nodegroup: 0, Master)

[ndb_mgmd(MGM)] 1 node(s)
id=1    @192.168.0.183  (mysql-5.5.31 ndb-7.2.13)

[mysqld(API)]   1 node(s)
id=4 (not connected, accepting connect from 192.168.0.183)
```

You can see that the data nodes started successfully, because information about their daemons is shown. You can also see that one of the nodes has been selected as the master for cluster replication. Because we set the number of replicas to 2 in our configuration file, we have two copies of the data. Don't confuse this notion of master with a master in MySQL replication. We discuss the differences in more detail later in the chapter.

Starting the SQL nodes

Once the data nodes are running, we can connect our SQL node. There are several options we must specify that enable a MySQL server to connect to an NDB cluster. Most people specify these in the *my.cnf* file, but you can also specify them on the startup command line if you start the server in that manner:

ndbcluster
    Tells the server that you want to include the NDB Cluster storage engine.

ndb_connectstring
    Tells the server the location of the NDB management daemon.

ndb_nodeid *and* `server_id`

Normally set to the node ID. You can find the node ID in the output from the SHOW command in the NDB management console.

Example 9-7 shows a correct startup sequence for the SQL node in our cluster example.

Example 9-7. Starting the SQL node

```
$ sudo ../libexec/mysqld --ndbcluster \
--console -umysql
130211  9:14:21 [Note] Plugin 'FEDERATED' is disabled.
130211  9:14:21  InnoDB: Started; log sequence number 0 1112278176
130211  9:14:21 [Note] NDB: NodeID is 4, management server '192.168.0.183:1186'
130211  9:14:22 [Note] NDB[0]: NodeID: 4, all storage nodes connected
130211  9:14:22 [Note] Starting Cluster Binlog Thread
130211  9:14:22 [Note] Event Scheduler: Loaded 0 events
130211  9:14:23 [Note] NDB: Creating mysql.NDB_schema
130211  9:14:23 [Note] NDB: Flushing mysql.NDB_schema
130211  9:14:23 [Note] NDB Binlog: CREATE TABLE Event: REPL$mysql/NDB_schema
130211  9:14:23 [Note] NDB Binlog: logging ./mysql/NDB_schema (UPDATED,USE_WRITE)
130211  9:14:23 [Note] NDB: Creating mysql.NDB_apply_status
130211  9:14:23 [Note] NDB: Flushing mysql.NDB_apply_status
130211  9:14:23 [Note] NDB Binlog: CREATE TABLE Event: REPL$mysql/NDB_apply_status
130211  9:14:23 [Note] NDB Binlog: logging ./mysql/NDB_apply_status
(UPDATED,USE_WRITE)
2013-02-11 09:14:23 [NdbApi] INFO     -- Flushing incomplete GCI:s < 65/17
2013-02-11 09:14:23 [NdbApi] INFO     -- Flushing incomplete GCI:s < 65/17
130211  9:14:23 [Note] NDB Binlog: starting log at epoch 65/17
130211  9:14:23 [Note] NDB Binlog: NDB tables writable
130211  9:14:23 [Note] ../libexec/mysqld: ready for connections.
Version: '5.5.31-ndb-7.2.13-cluster-gpl-log'  socket: '/var/lib/mysql/mysqld.sock'
port: 3306  Source distribution
```

The output includes extra comments about the NDB Cluster connection, logs, and status. If you do not see these or if you see errors, be sure that you started your SQL node with the proper options. Of particular importance is the message stating the node ID and the management server. If you have multiple management servers running, be sure your SQL node is communicating with the correct one.

Once the SQL node starts correctly, return to the management console and check the status of all of your nodes (Example 9-8).

Example 9-8. Example status of a running cluster

```
ndb_mgm> SHOW
Cluster Configuration
---------------------
[NDBd(NDB)]     2 node(s)
id=2    @192.168.0.188  (mysql-5.5.31 ndb-7.2.13, Nodegroup: 0, Master)
id=3    @192.168.0.12   (mysql-5.5.31 ndb-7.2.13, Nodegroup: 0)
```

```
[NDB_mgmd(MGM)]   1 node(s)
id=1    @192.168.0.183  (mysql-5.5.31 ndb-7.2.13)

[mysqld(API)]   1 node(s)
id=4    @192.168.0.183  (mysql-5.5.31 ndb-7.2.13)
```

As you can see, all of our nodes are now connected and running. If you see any details other than what is shown here, you have a failure in the startup sequence of your nodes. Be sure to check the logs for each node to determine what went wrong. The most common cause is network connectivity (e.g., firewall issues). The NDB nodes use port 1186 by default.

The logfiles for the data nodes and the NDB management daemon are located in the data directory. The SQL node logs are located in the usual location for a MySQL server.

Testing the Cluster

Now that our example cluster is running, let's perform a simple test (shown in Example 9-9) to ensure we can create a database and tables using the NDB Cluster storage engine.

Example 9-9. Testing the cluster

```
mysql> create database cluster_db;
Query OK, 1 row affected (0.06 sec)

mysql> create table cluster_db.t1 (a int) engine=NDBCLUSTER;
Query OK, 0 rows affected (0.31 sec)

mysql> show create table cluster_db.t1 \G
*************************** 1. row ***************************
       Table: t1
Create Table: CREATE TABLE `t1` (
  `a` int(11) DEFAULT NULL
) ENGINE=NDBcluster DEFAULT CHARSET=latin1
1 row in set (0.00 sec)

mysql> insert into cluster_db.t1 VALUES (1), (100), (1000);
Query OK, 3 rows affected (0.00 sec)
Records: 3  Duplicates: 0  Warnings: 0

mysql> select * from cluster_db.t1 \G
*************************** 1. row ***************************
a: 1
*************************** 2. row ***************************
a: 1000
*************************** 3. row ***************************
a: 100
3 rows in set (0.00 sec)
```

Now that you have a running cluster, you can experiment by loading data and running sample queries. We invite you to "fail" one of the data nodes during data updates and restart it to see that the loss of a single data node does not affect accessibility.

Shutting Down the Cluster

Just as there is a specific order for startup, there is a specific order to shutting down your cluster:

1. If you have replication running between clusters, allow the slaves to catch up, then stop replication.
2. Shut down your SQL nodes (*mysqld*).
3. Issue SHUTDOWN in the NDB management console.
4. Exit the NDB management console.

If you have MySQL replication running among two or more clusters, the first step will ensure the replication slaves catch up (synchronize) with the master before you shut the SQL nodes down.

When you issue the SHUTDOWN command in the NDB management console, it will shut down all of your data nodes and the NDB management daemon.

Achieving High Availability

The main motivation for using high availability is to keep a service accessible. For database systems, this means we must always be able to access the data. MySQL Cluster is designed to meet this need. MySQL Cluster supports high availability through distribution of data across data nodes (which reduces the risk of data loss from a single node), replication among replicas in the cluster, automatic recovery (failover) of lost data nodes, detection of data node failures using heartbeats, and data consistency using local and global checkpointing.

Let's examine some of the qualities of a high-availability database system. To be considered highly available, a database system (or any system) must meet the following requirements:

- 99.999% uptime
- No single point of failure
- Failover
- Fault tolerance

A 99.999% uptime means the data is, for practical purposes, always available. In other words, the database server is considered a nonstop, continuous service. The assumption is that the server is never offline due to a component failure or maintenance. All operations such as maintenance and recovery are expected to work online, where access is not interrupted, to complete the procedure.

This ideal situation is rarely required, and only the most critical industries have a real need for this quality. Additionally, a small period of routine, preventive maintenance is expected (hence the asymptotic percentage rating). Interestingly, there is an accepted granularity of uptime related to the number of nines in the rating. Table 9-1 shows the acceptable downtime (offline time) per calendar year for each level of the rating.

Table 9-1. Acceptable downtime chart

Uptime	Acceptable downtime
99.000%	3.65 days
99.900%	8.76 hours
99.990%	52.56 minutes
99.999%	5.26 minutes

Notice in this chart that the more nines there are in the rating, the lower the acceptable downtime. For a 99.999% uptime rating, it must be possible to perform all maintenance online without interruption except for a very short period of time in a single year. MySQL Cluster meets this need in a variety of ways, including the capability to perform rolling restarts of data nodes, several online database maintenance operations, and multiple access channels (SQL nodes and applications connecting via NDB API) to the data.

Having no single point of failure means that no single component of the system should determine the accessibility of the service. You can accomplish this with MySQL Cluster by configuring every type of node in the cluster with redundancy. In the small example in the previous section, we had two data nodes. Thus, the data was protected against one data node failing. However, we had only one management node and one SQL node. Ideally, you would also add extra nodes for these functions. MySQL Cluster supports multiple SQL nodes so that if the management node fails, the cluster can still operate.

Failover means that if a component fails, another can replace its functionality. In the case of a MySQL data node, failover occurs automatically if the cluster is configured to contain multiple replicas of the data. If a MySQL data node fails for one replica, access to the data is not interrupted. When you restart the missing data node, it will copy back its data from the other replica. In the case of SQL nodes, because the data is actually stored in the data nodes, any SQL node can substitute for another.

In the case of a failed NDB management node, the cluster can continue to operate without it and you can start a new management node at any time (provided the configuration has not changed).

And you can employ the normal high availability solutions discussed in previous chapters, including replication and automated failover between whole clusters. We discuss cluster replication in more detail later in this chapter.

Fault tolerance is normally associated with hardware such as backup power supplies and redundant network channels. For software systems, fault tolerance is a by-product of how well failover is handled. For MySQL Cluster, this means it can tolerate a certain number of failures and continue to provide access to the data. Much like a hardware RAID system that loses two drives on the same RAID array, loss of multiple data nodes across replicas can result in an unrecoverable failure. However, with careful planning, you can configure MySQL Cluster to reduce this risk. A healthy dose of monitoring and active maintenance can also reduce risk.

MySQL Cluster achieves fault tolerance by actively managing the nodes in the cluster. MySQL Cluster uses a heartbeat to check that services are alive, and when it detects a failed node, it takes action to perform a recovery.

The logging mechanisms in MySQL Cluster also provide a level of recovery for failover and fault tolerance. Local and global checkpointing ensures data is consistent across the cluster. This information is critical for rapid recovery of data node failures. Not only does it allow you to recover the data, but the unique properties of the checkpointing also allow for rapid recovery of nodes. We discuss this feature in more detail later.

Figure 9-5 depicts a MySQL cluster configured for high availability in a web service scenario.

The dotted boxes in the figure denote system boundaries. These components should reside on separate hardware to ensure redundancy. Also, you should configure the four data nodes as two replicas. Not shown in this drawing are additional components that interact with the application, such as a load balancer to divide the load across the web and MySQL servers.

When configuring a MySQL cluster for high availability, you should consider employing all of the following best practices (we discuss these in more detail later in this chapter when we examine high performance MySQL Cluster techniques):

- Use multiple replicas with data nodes on different hardware.
- Use redundant network links to guard against network failures.
- Use multiple SQL nodes.
- Use multiple data nodes to improve performance and decentralize the data.

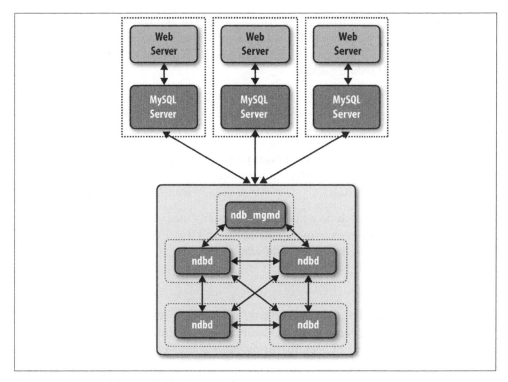

Figure 9-5. A highly available MySQL cluster

System Recovery

There are two types of system recovery. In one type, you shut down the server for maintenance or similar planned events. The other is an unanticipated loss of system capability. Fortunately, MySQL Cluster provides a mechanism to recover functionality even if the worst should occur.

When MySQL Cluster is shut down properly, it restarts from the checkpoints in the logs. This is largely automatic and a normal phase of the startup sequence. The system loads the most recent data from the local checkpoints for each data node, thereby recovering the data to the latest snapshot on restart. Once the data nodes have loaded the data from their local checkpoints, the system executes the redo log up to the most recent global checkpoint, thereby synchronizing the data to the last change made prior to the shutdown. The process is the same for either a restart following an intentional shutdown or a full system restart after a failure.

You may not think a startup is something that would "recover," but remember that MySQL Cluster is an in-memory database and, as such, the data must be reloaded from disk on startup. Loading the data up to the most recent checkpoint accomplishes this.

When recovering a system from a catastrophic failure or as a corrective measure, you can also recover from a backup of the data. As mentioned previously, you can restore data by invoking the *ndb_restore* utility from the NDB management console and using the output of a recent online backup.

To perform a complete system restore from backup, you should first place the cluster in single-user mode using the following command in the NDB management console:

    ENTER SINGLE USER MODE *node-id*

The *node-id* is the node ID of the data node you want to use for the *ndb_restore* utility. See the online MySQL Reference Manual for more details about single-user mode and connecting API-based utilities.

You then run restore on each data node in the cluster. Once you have restored the data on each data node, you can exit single-user mode and the cluster will be ready for use. To exit single-user mode, issue the following command in the NDB management console:

    EXIT SINGLE USER MODE

For more information about MySQL Cluster backup and restore, see the "Using the MySQL Cluster Management Client to Create a Backup" (*http://bit.ly/create-backup*) and "Restore a MySQL Cluster Backup" (*http://bit.ly/cluster-bkup*) sections of the online MySQL Reference Manual.

 Do not use the `--initial` option when restarting your server after a failure or scheduled takedown.

Node Recovery

There can be several reasons for a node failure, including network, hardware, memory, or operating system issues or failures. Here, we discuss the most common causes of these failures and how MySQL Cluster handles node recovery. In this section, we concentrate on data nodes, as they are the most important nodes with respect to data accessibility:

Hardware
> In the event the host computer hardware fails, clearly the data node running on that system will fail. In this case, MySQL Cluster will fail over to the other replicas. To recover from this failure, replace the failed hardware and restart the data node.

Network
> If the data node becomes isolated from the network due to some form of network hardware or software failure, the node may continue to execute, but because it

cannot contact the other nodes (via heartbeating), MySQL Cluster will mark the node as "down" and fail over to another replica until the node returns and can be recovered. To recover from this failure, replace the failed network hardware and restart the data node.

Memory

If there is insufficient memory on the host system, the cluster can essentially run out of space for data. This will result in that data node failing. To solve the problem, add more memory or increase the values of the configuration parameters for memory allocation and perform a rolling restart of the data node.

Operating system

If the operating system configuration interferes with the execution of the data node, resolve the problems and restart the data node.

For more information about database high availability and MySQL high availability using MySQL Cluster, see the white papers on the MySQL website (*http://bit.ly/mysql-wps*).

Replication

We have already briefly discussed how MySQL replication and replication inside the cluster differ. MySQL Cluster replication is sometimes called *internal cluster replication* or simply *internal replication* to clarify that it is not MySQL replication. MySQL replication is sometimes called *external replication*.

In this section, we discuss MySQL Cluster internal replication. We will also look at how MySQL replication (external replication) replicates data between MySQL clusters instead of between individual MySQL servers.

Replication inside the cluster versus MySQL replication

We mentioned earlier that MySQL Cluster uses synchronous replication inside the cluster. This is done to support the two-phase commit protocol for data integrity. Conversely, MySQL replication uses asynchronous replication, which is a one-way transfer of data that relies on the stable delivery and execution of events without verification that the data has been received before the commit.

Replicating inside the cluster

Internal MySQL Cluster replication provides redundancy by storing multiple copies of the data (which are called *replicas*). The process ensures data is written to multiple nodes before the query is acknowledged as complete (committed). This is done using a two-phase commit.

This form of replication is synchronous in that the data is guaranteed to be consistent at the point at which the query is acknowledged or that the commit has completed.

Data is replicated as *fragments*, where a fragment is defined as a subset of rows in a table. Fragments are distributed across the data nodes as a result of partitioning, and a copy of the fragment exists on another data node in each replica. One of the fragments is designated as the primary and is used for query execution. All other copies of the same data are considered secondary fragments. During an update, the primary fragment is updated first.

MySQL replication between clusters

Replication between clusters is very easy to do. If you can set up replication between two MySQL servers, you can set up replication between two MySQL clusters. This is because there are no special configuration steps or extra commands or parameters needed to start replication between clusters. MySQL replication works just as it does between individual servers. It just so happens that in this case, the data is stored in NDB clusters. However, there are some limitations to external replication. We list a few here for your consideration when planning external replication (consult the "MySQL Cluster Replication" section of the online MySQL Reference Manual for the latest details concerning external replication):

- External replication must be row-based.
- External replication cannot be circular.
- External replication does not support the auto_increment_* options.
- The size of the binary log may be larger than for normal MySQL replication.

MySQL replication to replicate data from one cluster to another permits you to leverage the advantages of MySQL Cluster at each site and still replicate the data to other sites.

Can MySQL Replication Be Used with MySQL Cluster?

You can replicate from a MySQL Cluster server to a non-MySQL Cluster server (or vice versa). No special configuration is necessary other than to accommodate some potential storage engine conflicts, which is similar to replicating among MySQL servers with different storage engines. In this case, use default storage engine assignment and forgo specifying the storage engine in your CREATE statements.

Replicating from a MySQL cluster to a non-MySQL cluster requires creating the special table called ndb_apply_status to replicate the epochs committed. If this table is missing on the slave, replication will stop with an error reporting that ndb_apply_status does not exist. You can create the table with the following command:

```
CREATE TABLE `mysql`.`ndb_apply_status` (
  `server_id` INT(10) UNSIGNED NOT NULL,
  `epoch` BIGINT(20) UNSIGNED NOT NULL,
  `log_name` VARCHAR(255) CHARACTER SET latin1
```

```
        COLLATE latin1_bin NOT NULL,
    `start_pos` BIGINT(20) UNSIGNED NOT NULL,
    `end_pos` BIGINT(20) UNSIGNED NOT NULL,
    PRIMARY KEY (`server_id`) USING HASH
) ENGINE=NDBCLUSTER DEFAULT CHARSET=latin1;
```

Replication of the MySQL cluster using external replication requires row-based MySQL replication, and the master SQL node must be started with `--binlog-format=ROW` or `--binlog-format=MIXED`. All other requirements for MySQL replication also apply (e.g., unique server IDs for all SQL nodes). `

External replication also requires some special additions to the replication process, including use of the cluster binary log, the binlog injector thread, and special system tables to support updates between clusters. External replication also handles transactional changes a bit differently. We discuss these concepts in more detail in the next section.

Architecture of MySQL Cluster (external) replication

You can consider the basic concepts of the operations of external replication to be the same as MySQL replication. Specifically, we define the roles of master and slave for certain cluster installations. As such, the master contains the original copy of the data, and the slaves receive copies of the data in increments based on the incoming flow of changes to the data.

Replication in MySQL Cluster makes use of a number of dedicated tables in the *mysql* database on each SQL node on the master and the slave (whether the slave is a single server or a cluster). These tables are created during the MySQL installation process. The two tables are `ndb_binlog_index`, which stores index data for the binary log (local to the SQL node), and `ndb_apply_status`, which stores a record of the operations that have been replicated to the slave. The `ndb_apply_status` table is maintained on all SQL nodes and kept in sync so that is the same throughout the cluster. You can use it to execute PITR of a failed replicated slave that is part of a MySQL cluster.

These tables are updated by a new thread called the *binlog injector thread*. This thread keeps the master updated with any changes performed in the NDB Cluster storage engine by recording the changes made in the cluster. The binlog injector thread is responsible for capturing all the data events within the cluster as recorded in the binary log and ensures all events that change, insert, or delete data are recorded in the `ndb_bin log_index` table. The master's dump thread sends the events to the slave I/O thread using MySQL replication.

One important difference in external replication involving MySQL Cluster is that each epoch is treated as a transaction. Because an epoch is a span of time between checkpoints, and MySQL Cluster ensures consistency at each checkpoint, epochs are considered atomic and are replicated using the same mechanism as a transaction in MySQL replication. The information about the last applied epoch is stored in the NDB system tables that support external replication between MySQL clusters.

Single-channel and multichannel replication

The MySQL replication connection between a master and slave is called a *channel*. A channel is, in effect, the networking protocol and medium used to connect the master to its slaves. Normally, there is only a single channel, but to ensure maximum availability, you can set up a secondary channel for fault tolerance. This is called *multichannel replication*. Figure 9-6 shows multichannel external replication.

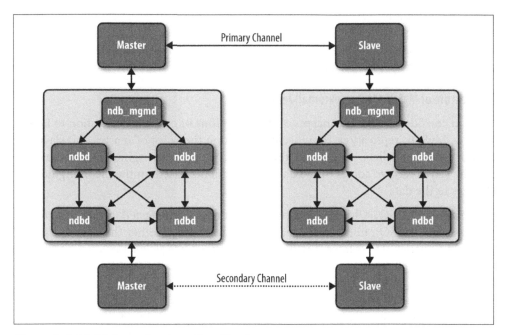

Figure 9-6. Multichannel external replication

Multichannel replication enhances recovery of a network link failure dramatically. Ideally, you would use active monitoring to trigger a potential failure of the network link to signal when the link is down. This can be accomplished in a variety of ways, from scripts that use simple heartbeat mechanisms to alerts and advisors such as those available in the MySQL Enterprise Monitor.

Notice that the setup in Figure 9-6 has a total of four SQL nodes (i.e., MySQL servers). The cluster acting as the master cluster has two SQL nodes acting as masters, one primary and one secondary. Likewise, the cluster acting as a slave cluster has two SQL nodes acting as primary and secondary slaves. The primary master/slave pair communicates over one network connection, and the secondary master/slave pair communicates over a different network connection.

 Don't take your networking components for granted. Even a switch can fail. Using different cabling on the same switched network gains very little. It is best to use a completely separate set of redundant connections and intermediary networking components to achieve true network redundancy.

Setup of multichannel replication does not differ much from single-channel (normal) MySQL replication. However, the replication failover is a little different. The idea is that you do not start the slave on the secondary channel. Failover to the secondary channel requires some special steps.

Use the following procedure to start multichannel external replication with the primary channel active and the second channel in standby mode (we assume the redundant networking communication and hardware is in place and working properly):

1. Start the primary master.
2. Start the secondary master.
3. Connect the primary slave to the primary master.
4. Connect the secondary slave to the secondary master.
5. Start the primary slave.

 Do not start the secondary slave (using START SLAVE). If you do, you risk primary key conflicts and duplicate data issues. You should, however, configure the secondary slave with information about the secondary master (using CHANGE MASTER) so the secondary channel can be started quickly if the primary channel fails.

Failover to the secondary channel requires a different procedure. It is not enough to just start the secondary slave. To avoid having the same data replicated twice, you must first establish the last replicated epoch and use it to start replication. The procedure is as follows (notice that we use variables to store intermediate results):

1. Find the time of the most recent global checkpoint the slave received. This requires finding the most recent epoch from the ndb_apply_status table on the primary slave:

    ```
    SELECT @latest := MAX(epoch) FROM mysql.ndb_apply_status;
    ```

2. Get the rows that appear in the `ndb_binlog_index` table on the primary master following the failure. You can find these rows from the primary master with the following query:

```
SELECT @file := SUBSTRING_INDEX(File, '/', -1), @pos := Position
FROM mysql.ndb_binlog_index
WHERE epoch > @latest ORDER BY ASC LIMIT 1;
```

3. Synchronize the secondary channel. Run this command on the secondary slave, where *file* is the actual filename and *pos* is the position:

```
CHANGE MASTER TO MASTER_LOG_FILE = 'file', MASTER_LOG_POS = pos;
```

4. Start replication on the secondary channel by running this command on the secondary slave:

```
START SLAVE;
```

This failover procedure will switch the replication channel. If you have failures of any of the SQL nodes, you must deal with those issues and repair them before executing this procedure.

 It is a good idea to ensure the primary channel is indeed offline. You may want to consider stopping the primary slave just in case.

Achieving High Performance

MySQL Cluster is designed not only for high availability, but also for high performance. We have already reviewed many of these features, as they are often beneficial for high availability. In this section, we examine a few features that provide high performance. We conclude with a list of best practices for tuning your system for high performance.

The following features support high performance in MySQL Cluster; we have examined many of these in previous sections:

Replication between clusters (global redundancy)
    All data is replicated to a remote site that can be used to offload the primary site.

Replication inside a cluster (local redundancy)
    Multiple data nodes can be used to read data in parallel.

Main memory storage
    Not needing to wait for disk writes ensures quick processing of updates to data.

Considerations for High Performance

There are three main considerations when tuning your system to support high performance.

- Ensure your applications are as efficient as they can be. Sometimes this requires modification of your database servers (e.g., optimizing the configuration of the servers or modifying the database schema), but often the application itself can be designed or refactored for higher performance.

- Maximize access to your databases. This includes having enough MySQL servers for the number of connections (scale-out) and distributing the data for availability, such as through replication.

- Consider making performance enhancements to your MySQL Cluster, for instance, by adding more data nodes.

Queries with joins can often be very time-consuming. The main source is the distributed nature of MySQL Cluster and that the MySQL server did not have good support for handling MySQL Cluster joins. Before MySQL Cluster 7.2, a JOIN operation was executed by fetching data from the data nodes and performing the join inside the SQL node, requiring the data to be transferred several times over the network. With MySQL Cluster 7.2, MySQL Server 5.5 has added support to allowing the join to be "pushed down" into the engine, which then performs the actual join. This reduces the amount of data that needs to be sent over the network and also allows increased parallelism by executing the join on multiple data nodes.

You may need to make certain trade offs between the level of high availability you desire and high performance. For example, adding more replicas increases availability. However, while more replicas protect against loss of data nodes, they require more processing power and you may see lower performance during updates. The reads are still quick, because multiple replicas do not need to be read for the same data. Having a greater number of data nodes (scale out) while keeping the number of replicas low leads to higher write performance.

Another primary consideration is the distributed nature of MySQL Cluster. Because each node performs best when run on a separate server, the performance of each server is critical, but so are the networking components. Coordination commands and data are being transported from node to node, so the performance of the networking interconnect must be tuned for high performance. You should also consider parameters such as selection of transport (e.g., TCP/IP, SHM, and SCI), latency, bandwidth, and geographic proximity.

You can set up and run MySQL Cluster in a cloud environment. One advantage of doing so is that the network interconnections are very fast and optimized. Because the data nodes require mainly a fast processor, adequate memory, and a fast network, virtual server technology is more than adequate for using MySQL Cluster in the cloud. Note, however, that MySQL Cluster is not officially supported in virtual server environments.

You can find a complete list of all of the considerations for high performance in the "MySQL Cluster" section of the online MySQL Reference Manual. For general MySQL performance improvements, see *High Performance MySQL*.

High Performance Best Practices

There are a number of things you can do to ensure your MySQL Cluster is running at peak performance. We list a few of the top performance enhancement practices here, along with a brief discussion of each. Some of these are more general in nature, but we do not want to overlook these in our quest for the highest performance possible.

Tune for access patterns
> Consider the methods your applications use to access data. Because MySQL Cluster stores indexed columns in memory, accesses referencing these columns show an even greater speed-up over nonindexed columns than you get on single MySQL servers. MySQL Cluster requires a primary key in every table, so applications that retrieve data by primary key are almost guaranteed to be fast.

Make your applications distribution-aware
> The best-case scenario for accessing data on a partitioned data store is to isolate a query to a single node in the cluster. By default, MySQL Cluster uses the primary key for hashing the rows across the partitions. Unfortunately, this isn't always optimal if you consider the behavior of master/detail queries (common applications that consult a master table followed by details in other tables that refer back to the master table). In this case, you should alter the hashing function to ensure the master row and the detail rows are on the same node. One way to accomplish this is *partition pruning*, whereby you drop the secondary field used in the detail table partition hash and partition the detail rows with only the master's primary key (which is the foreign key in the detail table). This allows both the master and detail rows to be allocated to the same node in the partition tree.

Use batch operations
> Each round trip of a query has significant overhead. For certain operations like inserts, you can save some of that overhead by using a multiple insert query (an INSERT statement that inserts multiple rows). You can also batch operations by turning on the transaction_allow_batching parameter and including multiple operations within a transaction (within the BEGIN and END blocks). This lets you list multiple data manipulation queries (INSERT, UPDATE, etc.) and reduce overhead.

The `transaction_allow_batching` option does not work with SELECT statements or UPDATE statements that include variables.

Optimize schemas

Optimizing your database schemas has the same effect for MySQL Cluster as it does for normal database systems. For MySQL Cluster, consider using efficient data types (e.g., the minimum size needed to save memory; 30 bytes per row in a million-row table can save you a significant amount of memory). You should also consider denormalization for certain schemas to take advantage of MySQL Cluster's parallel data access methods (partitioning).

Optimize queries

Clearly, the more optimized the query, the faster the query performance. This is a practice common to all databases and should be one of the first things you do to improve the performance of your application. For MySQL Cluster, consider query optimization from the standpoint of how the data is retrieved. Specifically, joins are particularly sensitive to performance in MySQL Cluster. Poorly performing queries can sometimes cause anomalies that are easily mistaken for inefficiencies in other parts of your system.

Optimize server parameters

Optimize your cluster configuration to ensure it is running as efficiently as possible. This may mean spending some time to understand the many configuration options as well as securing the correct hardware to exploit. There is no magic potion for this task—each installation becomes more and more unique as you change more parameters. Use this practice with care, tune one parameter at a time, and always compare the results to known baselines before instituting a change.

Use connection pools

By default, SQL nodes use only a single thread to connect to the NDB cluster. With more threads to connect, the SQL nodes can execute several queries at once. To use connection pooling for your SQL nodes, add the `ndb-cluster-connection-pool` option in your configuration file. Set the value to be greater than 1 (say, 4) and place it in the [`mysqld`] section. You should experiment with this setting because it is frequently too high for the application or hardware.

Use multithreaded data nodes

If your data node has multiple CPU cores or multiple CPUs, you will gain additional performance by running the multithreaded data node daemon named *ndbmtd*. This daemon can make use of up to eight CPU cores or threads. Using multiple threads allows the data node to run many operations in parallel, such as the local query handler (LQH) and communication processes, to achieve even higher throughput.

Use the NDB API for custom applications

While the MySQL server (the SQL node) offers a fast query processor frontend, MySQL has built a direct-access C++ mechanism called the NDB API. For some operations, such as interfacing MySQL Cluster with LDAP, this may be the only way to connect the MySQL cluster (in this case just the NDB cluster) to your application. If performance is critical to your application and you have the necessary development resources to devote to a custom NDB API solution, you can see significant improvements in performance.

Use the right hardware

Naturally, faster hardware results in faster performance (generally speaking). However, you should consider every aspect of the cluster configuration. Consider not only faster CPUs and more and faster memory, but also high-speed interconnect solutions such as SCI and high-speed, hardware-redundant network connections. In many cases, these hardware solutions are built as turnkey commodities and do not require reconfiguring the cluster.

Do not use swap space

Make sure your data nodes are using real memory and not swap space. You will notice a dramatic performance drop when the data nodes start using swap space. This affects not only performance, but also possibly the stability of the cluster.

Use processor affinity for data nodes

In multiple-CPU machines, lock your data node processes to CPUs that are not involved in network communications. You can do this on some platforms (e.g., Sun CMT processor systems) using the `LockExecuteThreadToCPU` and `LockMaint ThreadsToCPU` parameters in the `[ndbd]` section of the configuration file.

If you follow these best practices, you will be well on your way to making MySQL Cluster the best high-performance, high-availability solution for your organization. For more information about optimizing MySQL Cluster, see the white paper "Optimizing Performance of the MySQL Cluster Database." (*http://bit.ly/opt-cluster*)

Conclusion

In this chapter, we discussed the unique high availability solution for MySQL using MySQL Cluster. The strengths of MySQL Cluster include partitioning tables and distributing them across separate nodes and the parallel architecture of MySQL Cluster as a multimaster database. This allows the system to execute high volumes of both read and write operations concurrently. All updates are instantly available to all application nodes (via SQL commands or the NDB API) accessing data stored in the data nodes.

Because write loads are distributed across all of the data nodes, you can achieve very high levels of write throughput and scalability for transactional workloads. Finally, with the implementation of multiple MySQL server nodes (SQL nodes) running in parallel, where each server shares the load with multiple connections, and the use of MySQL replication to ensure data shipping among geographic sites, you can build highly efficient, high-concurrency transactional applications.

Although few applications may have such stringent needs, MySQL Cluster is a great solution for those applications that demand the ultimate form of MySQL high availability.

"Joel!"

Joel smiled as his boss backtracked to stand in his doorway.

"Yes, Bob?" Joel asked.

Mr. Summerson stepped into the office and closed the door, then pulled up a chair and sat down directly across from Joel.

Momentarily taken off-guard, Joel merely smiled and said, "What can I do for you, Bob?"

"It's what you have done for me, Joel. You've come up to speed on this MySQL stuff very quickly. You have kept pace with our ramp-up and recent acquisitions. And now you've helped make us a lot of money on this last deal. I know I've thrown a lot at you and you deserve something in return." After an uncomfortable pause, he asked, "Do you play golf, Joel?"

Joel shrugged. "I haven't played since college, and I was never very good at it."

"That won't be a problem. I love the game, but the feeling isn't mutual. I lose half a box of balls every time I play. Are you free Saturday for a game of nine holes?"

Joel wasn't sure where this was going, but something told him he should accept. "Sure, I'm free."

"Good. Meet me at the Fair Oaks course at 1000 hours. We'll play nine holes, then discuss your future over lunch."

"OK. See you there, Bob."

Mr. Summerson stood, opened the door, and paused. "I've told the accounting office to create a budget for you to manage, including enough to cover the cost of the MySQL Enterprise subscription and funding for two full-time assistants."

"Thanks," Joel said, stunned. He wasn't prepared for outright acceptance of his proposal, much less more responsibility.

As Mr. Summerson disappeared down the hall, Joel's friend Amy came in and stood next to him. "Are you OK?" she asked with concern.

"Yeah, why?"

"I've never seen him close the door to talk to someone. If you don't mind me asking, what was that all about?"

With a wave of his hand over the documentation on his desk, Joel said, "He asked me to play golf and then said I had my own budget and could buy the MySQL Enterprise subscription."

Amy smiled and touched his arm. "That's good, Joel—really good."

Joel was confused. He didn't think the responsibility of managing money or the approval for a purchase order was worthy of such a reaction. "What?"

"The last person who played golf with Mr. Summerson got a promotion and a raise. Mr. Summerson may be tough on the outside, but he rewards loyalty and determination."

"Really?" Joel stared at the papers on his desk. He told himself not to get his hopes up.

"Are you free for lunch?" Amy asked with a light squeeze of his arm.

Joel looked at her hand on his arm and smiled. "Sure. Let's go somewhere nice." But in accepting her offer, Joel knew he would be up late working on a plan for their next date.

## PART II

Monitoring and Managing

Now that you have a sophisticated, multiserver system that hopefully meets your site's needs, you must keep on top of it. This part of the book explains monitoring, with some topics in performance, and covers backups and other aspects of handling the inevitable failures that sometimes occur.

## CHAPTER 10

Getting Started with Monitoring

Joel placed his nonfat half-caf latte, fruit cup, and cheese pastry on his desk and smiled at the parody of nutrition awaiting him. Ever since he found the upscale shopping center on his walk to work, his breakfasts had gotten rather creative.

He turned on his monitor and waited for his email application to retrieve his messages while he opened the top of his latte. Scanning the message subjects and hoping there wasn't yet another message from his boss, he noticed several messages from users with subjects that hinted at performance issues.

Joel clicked through them, scanning the text. "Well, I guess something must be wrong," he mumbled, as he read complaints about how applications that queried the database system were taking too long to respond.

He unwrapped his pastry and pondered what could be causing the problems. "Things were just fine yesterday," he reasoned. After a few sips of his latte he remembered something he read about performance monitoring while working on the lab machines at college.

Joel finished his pastry and reached for his *MySQL High Availability* book. "There has got to be something in here," he said.

How do you know when your servers are performing poorly? If you wait for your users to tell you something is wrong, chances are there has been something wrong for some time. Leaving problems unaddressed for an extended period complicates the diagnosis and repair process.

In this chapter, we will begin our examination of monitoring MySQL at the operating system level, using the basic tools available on various systems. We look here first because a system service or application always relies on the performance of the operating system and its hardware. If the operating system is performing poorly, so will the database system or application.

We will first examine the reasons for monitoring systems, then we'll look at basic monitoring tasks for popular operating systems and discuss how monitoring can make your preventive maintenance tasks easier. Once you've mastered these skills, you can begin to look more closely at your database system. In the next chapter, we will look in greater detail at monitoring a MySQL server, along with some practical guides to solving common performance problems.

Ways of Monitoring

When we think of monitoring, we normally think about some form of early warning system that detects problems. However, the definition of monitor (as a verb) is "to observe, record, or detect an operation or condition with instruments that do not affect the operation or condition." This early warning system uses a combination of automated sampling and an alert system.

The Linux and Unix operating systems are very complex and have many parameters that affect all manner of minor and major system activities. Tuning these systems for performance can be more art than science. Unlike some desktop operating systems, Linux and Unix (and their variants) do not hide the tuning tools nor do they restrict what you can tune. Some systems, such as Mac OS X and Windows, hide many of the underlying mechanics of the system behind a very user-friendly visual interface.

The Mac OS X operating system, for example, is a very elegant and smoothly running operating system that needs little or no attention from the user under normal conditions. However, as you will see in the following sections, the Mac OS X system provides a plethora of advanced monitoring tools that can help you tune your system if you know where to look for them.

The Windows operating system has many variants, the newest at the time of this writing being Windows 8. Fortunately, most of these variants include the same set of monitoring tools, which allow the user to tune the system to meet specific needs. While not considered as suave as Mac OS X, Windows offers a greater range of user-accessible tuning options.

There are three primary categories of system monitoring: system performance, application performance, and security. You may commence monitoring for more specific reasons, but in general, the task falls into one of these categories.

Each category uses a different set of tools (with some overlap) and has a different objective. For instance, you should monitor system performance to ensure the system is operating at peak efficiency. Application performance monitoring ensures a single application is performing at peak efficiency, and security monitoring helps you ensure the systems are protected in the most secure manner.

Monitoring a MySQL server is akin to monitoring an application. This is because MySQL, like most database systems, lets you measure a number of variables and status indicators that have little or nothing to do with the operating system. However, a database system is very susceptible to the performance of the host operating system, so it is important to ensure your operating system is performing well before trying to diagnose problems with the database system.

Because the goal is to monitor a MySQL system to ensure the database system is performing at peak efficiency, the following sections discuss monitoring the operating system for performance. We leave monitoring for security to other texts that specialize in the details and nuances of security monitoring.

Benefits of Monitoring

There are two approaches to monitoring. You may want to ensure nothing has changed (no degradation of performance and no security breaches) or to investigate what has changed or gone wrong. Monitoring the system to ensure nothing has changed is called *proactive monitoring*, whereas monitoring to see what went wrong is called *reactive monitoring*. Sadly, most monitoring occurs in a reactive manner. Very few IT professionals have the time or resources to conduct proactive monitoring. Reactive monitoring is therefore the only form of monitoring some professionals understand.

However, if you take the time to monitor your system proactively, you can eliminate a lot of reactive work. For example, if your users complain about poor performance (the number one trigger for reactive monitoring), you have no way of knowing how much the system has degraded unless you have previous monitoring results with which to compare. Recording such results is called *forming a baseline* of your system (i.e., you monitor the performance of your system under low, normal, and high loads over a period of time). If you do the sampling frequently and consistently, you can determine the typical performance of the system under various loads. Thus, when users report performance problems, you can sample the system and compare the results to your baseline. If you include enough detail in your historical data, you can normally see, at a glance, which part of the system has changed.

System Components to Monitor

You should examine four basic parts of the system when monitoring performance:

Processor
    Check to see how much of it is utilized and what peaks are reached by utilization.

Memory
> Check to see how much is being used and how much is still available to run programs.

Disk
> Check to see how much disk space is available, how disk space is used, and what demand there is for it and how fast it delivers content (response time).

Network
> Check for hroughput, latency, and error rates when communicating with other systems on the network.

Processor

Monitor the system's CPU to ensure there are no runaway processes and that the CPU cycles are being shared equally among the running programs. One way to do this is to call up a list of the programs running and determine what percentage of the CPU each is using. Another method is to examine the load average of the system processes. Most operating systems provide several views of the performance of the CPU.

 A process is a unit of work in a Linux or Unix system. A program may have one or more processes running at a time. Multithreaded applications, such as MySQL, generally appear on the system as multiple processes.

When a CPU is under a performance load and contention is high, the system can exhibit very slow performance and even periods of seeming inactivity. When this occurs, you must either reduce the number of processes or reduce the CPU usage of processes that seem to be consuming more CPU time. You can find which processes are consuming more CPU by using the *top* utility for Linux and Unix systems, Activity Monitor on Mac OS X, or the Task Manager Performance tab on Windows. But be sure to monitor the CPUs to make sure that high CPU utilization is really the cause of the problem—slowness is even more likely to occur because of memory contention, discussed in the next section.

Some of the common solutions to CPU overloading include:

Provision a new server to run some processes
> This is, of course, the best method, but requires money for new systems. Experienced system administrators can often find other ways to reduce CPU usage, especially when the organization is more willing to spend your time than to spend money.

Remove unnecessary processes
> An enormous number of systems run background processes that may be useful for certain occasions but just bog down the system most of the time. However, an administrator must know the system very well to identify which processes are non-essential.

Kill runaway processes
> These probably stem from buggy applications, and they are often the culprit when performance problems are intermittent or rare. In the event that you cannot stop a runaway process using a controlled or orderly method, you may need to terminate the process abruptly using a *force quit* dialog or the command line.

Optimize applications
> Some applications routinely take up more CPU time or other resources than they really need. Poorly designed SQL statements are often a drag on the database system.

Lower process priorities
> Some processes run as background jobs, such as report generators, and can be run more slowly to make room for interactive processes.

Reschedule processes
> Maybe some of those report generators can run at night when system load is lower.

Processes that consume too much CPU time are called *CPU-bound* or *processor-bound*, meaning they do not suspend themselves for I/O and cannot be swapped out of memory.

If you find the CPU is not under contention and there are either few processes running or no processes consuming large amounts of CPU time, the problem with performance is likely to be elsewhere (waiting on disk I/O, insufficient memory, excessive page swapping, etc.).

Memory

Monitor memory to ensure your applications are not requesting so much memory that they waste system time on memory management. From the very first days of limited random access memory (RAM, or main memory), operating systems have evolved to employ a sophisticated method of using disk memory to store unused portions or pages of main memory. This technique, called *paging* or *swapping*, allows a system to run more processes than main memory can load at one time, by storing the memory for suspended processes and later retrieving the memory when the process is reactivated. While the cost of moving a page of memory from memory to disk and back again is relatively high (it is time-consuming compared to accessing main memory directly), modern operating systems can do it so quickly that the penalty isn't normally an issue unless it reaches such a high level that the processor and disk cannot keep up with the demands.

However, the operating system may perform some swapping at a high level periodically to reclaim memory. Be sure to measure memory usage over a period of time to ensure you are not observing a normal cleanup operation.

When periods of high paging occur, it is likely that low memory availability may be the result of a runaway process consuming too much memory or too many processes requesting too much memory. This kind of high paging, called *thrashing*, can be treated the same way as a CPU under contention. Processes that consume too much memory are called *memory-bound*.

When treating memory performance problems, the natural tendency is to add more memory. While that may indeed solve the problem, it is also possible that the memory is not allocated correctly among the various subsystems.

There are several things you can do in this situation. You can allocate different amounts of memory to parts of the system—such as the kernel or filesystem—or to various applications that permit such tweaking, including MySQL. You can also change the priority of the paging subsystem so the operating system begins paging earlier.

 Be very careful when tweaking memory subsystems on your server. Be sure to consult your documentation or a book dedicated to improving performance for your specific operating system.

If you monitor memory and find that the system is not paging too frequently, but performance is still an issue, the problem is likely related to one of the other subsystems.

Disk

Monitor disk usage to ensure there is enough free disk space available, as well as sufficient I/O bandwidth to allow processes to execute without significant delay. You can measure this using either a *per-process* or *overall transfer* rate to and from disk. The per-process rate is the amount of data a single process can read or write. The overall transfer rate is the maximum bandwidth available for reading and writing data on disk. Some systems have multiple disk controllers; in these cases, overall transfer rate may be measured per disk controller.

Performance issues can arise if one or more processes are consuming too much of the maximum disk transfer rate. This can have very detrimental effects on the rest of the system in much the same way as a process that consumes too many CPU cycles: it "starves" other processes, forcing them to wait longer for disk access.

Processes that consume too much of the disk transfer rate are called *disk-bound*, meaning they are trying to access the disk at a frequency greater than the available share of the disk transfer rate. If you can reduce the pressure placed on your I/O system by a disk-bound process, you'll free up more bandwidth for other processes.

 You may hear the terms *I/O-bound* or *I/O-starved* when referring to processes. This normally means the process is consuming too much disk.

One way to meet the needs of a process performing a lot of I/O to disk is to increase the block size of the filesystem, thus making large transfers more efficient and reducing the overhead imposed by a disk-bound process. However, this may cause other processes to run more slowly.

 Be careful when tuning filesystems on servers that have only a single controller or disk. Be sure to consult your documentation or a book dedicated to improving performance for your specific operating system.

If you have the resources, one strategy for dealing with disk contention is to add another disk controller and disk array and move the data for one of the disk-bound processes to the new disk controller. Another strategy is to move a disk-bound process to another, less utilized server. Finally, in some cases it may be possible to increase the bandwidth of the disk by upgrading the disk system to a faster technology.

There are differing opinions as to where to optimize first or even which is the best choice. We believe:

- If you need to run a lot of processes, maximize the disk transfer rate or split the processes among different disk arrays or systems.
- If you need to run a few processes that access large amounts of data, maximize the per-process transfer rate by increasing the block size of the filesystem.

You may also need to strike a balance between the two solutions to meet your unique mix of processes by moving some of the processes to other systems.

Network Subsystem

Monitor network interfaces to ensure there is enough bandwidth and that the data being sent or received is of sufficient quality.

Processes that consume too much network bandwidth, because they are attempting to read or write more data than the network configuration or hardware make possible, are called *network-bound*. These processes keep other processes from accessing sufficient network bandwidth to avoid delays.

Network bandwidth issues are normally indicated by utilization of a percentage of the maximum bandwidth of the network interface. You can solve these issues with processes by assigning the processes to specific ports on a network interface.

Network data quality issues are normally indicated by a high number of errors encountered on the network interface. Luckily, the operating system and data transfer applications usually employ *checksumming* or some other algorithm to detect errors, but retransmissions place a heavy load on the network and operating system. Solving the problem may require moving some applications to other systems on the network or installing additional network cards, which normally requires a diagnosis followed by changing the network hardware, reconfiguring the network protocols, or moving the system to a different subnet on the network.

 When referring to a process that is taking too much time accessing networking subsystems, we say it is *network-bound*.

Monitoring Solutions

For each of the four subsystems just discussed, a modern operating system offers its own specific tools that you can use to get information about the subsystem's status. These tools are largely standalone applications that do not correlate (at least directly) with the other tools. As you will see in the next sections, the tools are powerful in their own right, but it requires a fair amount of effort to record and analyze all of the data they produce.

Fortunately, a number of third-party monitoring solutions are available for most operating and database systems. It is often best to contact your systems providers for recommendations on the best solution to meet your needs and maintain compatibility with your infrastructure. Most vendors offer system monitoring tools as an option. The following are a few of the more notable offerings:

up.time (http://www.uptimesoftware.com)
> An integrated system for monitoring and reporting performance for servers. It supports multiple platforms.

Cacti (http://www.cacti.net)
> A graphical reporting solution for graphing data from the RRDtool (*http://oss.oetik er.ch/rrdtool*). RRDtool is an open source data logging system and can be tailored using Perl, Python, Ruby, LUA, or TCL.

KDE System Guard (KSysGuard) (http://userbase.kde.org/KSysGuard)
   Permits users to track and control processes on their system. Designed to be easy to set up.

Gnome System Monitor (http://bit.ly/gnome-lib)
   A graphical tool to monitor CPU, network, memory, and processes on a system.

Nagios (http://www.nagios.org/)
   A complete solution for monitoring all of your servers, network switches, applications, and services.

MySQL Enterprise Monitor (http://bit.ly/ent-monitor)
   Provides real-time visibility into the performance and availability of all your MySQL databases.

 We will discuss the MySQL Enterprise Monitor and automated monitoring and report in greater detail in Chapter 16.

The following sections describe the built-in monitoring tools for some of the major operating systems. We will study the Linux and Unix commands in a little more detail, as they are particularly suited to investigating the performance issues and strategies we've discussed. However, we will also include an examination of the monitoring tools for Mac OS X and Microsoft Windows.

Linux and Unix Monitoring

Database monitoring on Linux or Unix can involve tools for monitoring the CPU, memory, disk, network, and even security and users. In classic Unix fashion, all of the core tools run from the command line and most are located in the *bin* or *sbin* folders. Table 10-1 includes the list of tools we've found useful, with a brief description of each.

Table 10-1. System monitoring tools for Linux and Unix

Utility	Description
ps	Shows the list of processes running on the system.
top	Displays process activity sorted by CPU utilization.
vmstat	Displays information about memory, paging, block transfers, and CPU activity.
uptime	Displays how long the system has been running. It also tells you how many users are logged on and the system load average over 1, 5, and 15 minutes.
free	Displays memory usage.
iostat	Displays average disk activity and processor load.

Utility	Description
sar	System activity report. Allows you to collect and report a wide variety of system activity.
pmap	Displays a map of how a process is using memory.
mpstat	Displays CPU usage for multiprocessor systems.
netstat	Displays information about network activity.
cron	A subsystem that allows you to schedule the execution of a process. You can schedule execution of these utilities so you can collect regular statistics over time or check statistics at specific times, such as during peak or minimal loads.

> Some operating systems provide additional or alternative tools. Consult your operating system documentation for additional tools for monitoring your system performance.

As you can see from Table 10-1, a rich variety of tools is available with a host of potentially useful information. The following sections discuss some of the more popular tools and explain briefly how you can use them to identify the problems described in the previous sections.

Process Activity

Several commands provide information about processes running on your system—notably top, iostat, mpstat, and ps.

The top command

The top command provides a summary of system information and a dynamic view of the processes on your system ranked by the most CPU-intensive tasks. The display typically contains information about the process, including the process ID, the user who started the process, its priority, the percentage of CPU it is using, how much time it has consumed, and of course, the command used to start the process. However, some operating systems have slightly different reports. This is probably the most popular utility in the set because it presents a snapshot of your system every few seconds. Figure 10-1 shows the output when running top on a Linux (Ubuntu) system under moderate load.

The system summary is located at the top of the listing and has some interesting data. It shows the percentages of CPU time for user (%us); system (%sy); nice (%ni), which is the time spent running users' processes that have had their priorities changed; I/O wait (%wa); and even the percentage of time spent handling hardware and software interrupts. Also included are the amount of memory and swap space available, how much is being used, how much is free, and the size of the buffers.

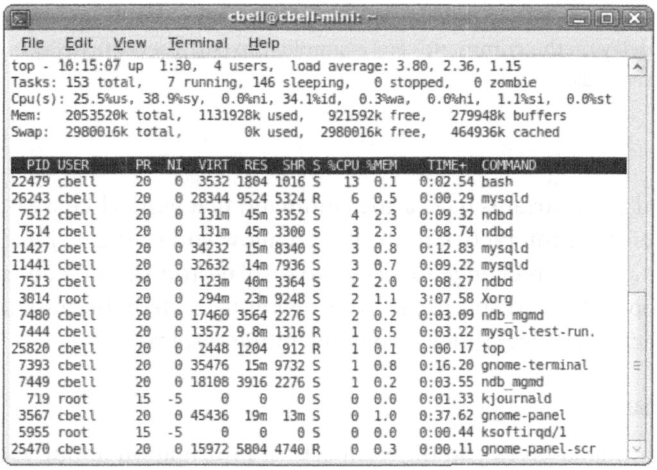

Figure 10-1. The top command

Below the summary comes the list of processes, in descending order (which is from where the name of the command derives) based on how much CPU time is being used. In this example, a Bash shell is currently the task leader followed by one or several installations of MySQL.

Niceness

You can change the priority of a process on a Linux or Unix system. You may want to do this to lower the priorities of processes that require too much CPU power, are of lower urgency, or could run for an extended period but that you do not want to cancel or reschedule. You can use the commands `nice`, `ionice`, and `renice` to alter the priority of a process.

Most distributions of Linux and Unix now group processes that have had their priorities changed into a group called `nice`. This allows you to get statistics about these modified processes without having to remember or collate the information yourself. Having commands that report the CPU time for nice processes gives you the opportunity to see how much CPU these processes are consuming with respect to the rest of the system. For example, a high value on this parameter may indicate there is at least one process with too high of a priority.

Perhaps the best use of the `top` command is to allow it to run and refresh every three seconds. If you check the display at intervals over time, you will begin to see which processes are consuming the most CPU time. This can help you determine at a glance whether there is a runaway process.

You can change the refresh rate of the command by specifying the delay on the command. For example, top -d 3 sets the delay to three seconds.

Most Linux and Unix variants have a top command that works like we have described. Some have interesting interactive hot keys that allow you to toggle information on or off, sort the list, and even change to a colored display. You should consult the manual page for the top command specific to your operating system, because the special hot keys and interactive features differ among operating systems.

The iostat command

The iostat command gives you different sets of information about your system, including statistics about CPU time, device I/O, and even partitions and network filesystems (NFS). The command is useful for monitoring processes because it gives you a picture of how the system is doing overall related to processes and the amount of time the system is waiting for I/O. Figure 10-2 shows an example of running the iostat command on a system with moderate load.

```
cbell@cbell-mini: ~
File  Edit  View  Terminal  Help
cbell@cbell-mini:~$ iostat
Linux 2.6.28-15-generic (cbell-mini)    10/13/2009    _i686_    (2 CPU)

avg-cpu:  %user   %nice %system %iowait  %steal   %idle
          10.65    1.09    3.18    2.40    0.00   82.86

Device:            tps   Blk_read/s   Blk_wrtn/s   Blk_read   Blk_wrtn
sda              16.69       222.49       366.84    1260455    2078184
sda1             16.68       222.14       366.84    1258473    2078184
sda2              0.00         0.00         0.00          6          0
sda5              0.01         0.29         0.00       1656          0

cbell@cbell-mini:~$
```

Figure 10-2. The iostat command

The iostat, mpstat, and sar commands might not be installed on your system by default, but they can be installed as an option. For example, they are part of the *sysstat* package in Ubuntu distributions. Consult your operating system documentation for information about installation and setup.

Figure 10-2 shows the percentages for CPU usage from the time the system was started. These are calculated as averages among all processors. As you can see, the system is running on a dual-core CPU, but only one row of values is given. This data includes the percentage of CPU utilization:

- Executing at the user level (running applications)
- Executing at the user level with nice priority
- Executing at the system level (kernel processes)
- Waiting on I/O
- Waiting for virtual processes
- Idle time

A report like this can give you an idea of how your system has been performing since it was started. While this means that you might not notice periods of poor performance (because they are averaged over time), it does offer a unique perspective on how the processes have been consuming available processing time or waiting on I/O. For example, if %idle is very low, you can determine that the system was kept very busy. Similarly, a high value for %iowait can indicate a problem with the disk. If %system or %nice is much higher than %user, it can indicate an imbalance of system and prioritized processes that are keeping normal processes from running.

The mpstat command

The mpstat command presents much of the same information as iostat for processor time, but splits the information out by processor. If you run this command on a multi-processor system, you will see the percentage of data per processor as well as the totals for all processors. Figure 10-3 shows an example of the mpstat command.

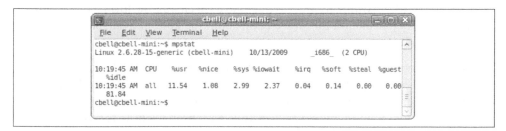

Figure 10-3. The mpstat command

There is an option to tell the mpstat command to refresh the information based on an interval passed. This can be helpful if you want to watch how your processors are performing with respect to the processes over a period of time. For instance, you can see whether your processor affinity is unbalanced (too many processes are assigned to one specific processor).

Some implementations of mpstat provide an option to see a more comprehensive display including show statistics for all processors. This may be -A or -P ALL depending on your operating system.

To find out more about the mpstat command, consult the manual page for your operating system.

The ps command

The ps command is one of those commands we use on a daily basis but never take the time to consider its power and utility. This command gives you a snapshot of the processes running on your system. It displays the process ID, the terminal the process is running from, the amount of time it has been running, and the command used to start the process. It can be used to find out how much memory a process uses, how much CPU a process uses, and more. You can also pipe the output to grep to more easily find processes. For example, the command ps -A | grep mysqld is a popular command to find information about all of the MySQL processes running on your system. This will send the list of all processes to the grep command, which will in turn only show those rows with "mysqld" in them. You can use this technique to find a process ID so you can get detailed information about that process using other commands.

What makes the ps command so versatile is the number of options available for displaying data. You can display the processes for a specific user, get related processes for a specific process by showing its process tree, and even change the format of the output. Consult your documentation for information about the options available on your operating system.

One of the ways you can use this output to diagnose problems is to look for processes that have been running for a long time or check process status (e.g., check those that are stuck in a suspicious state or sleeping). Unless they are known applications like MySQL, you might want to investigate why they have been running for so long.

Figure 10-4 shows an abbreviated example of the ps command run on a system under moderate load.

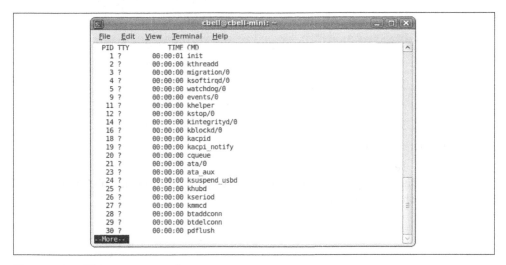

Figure 10-4. The ps command

Another use for the output is to see whether there are processes that you do not recognize or a lot of processes run by a single user. Many times this indicates a script that is spawning processes, perhaps because it has been set up improperly, and can even indicate a dangerous security practice.

There are many other utilities built into operating systems to display information about processes. As always, a good reference on performance tuning for your specific operating system will be the best source for more in-depth information about monitoring processes.

Memory Usage

Several commands provide information about memory usage on your system. The most popular ones include free and pmap.

The free command

The free command shows you the amount of physical memory available. It displays the total amount of memory, the amount used, and the amount free for physical memory, and it displays the same statistics for your swap space. It also shows the memory buffers used by the kernel and the size of the cache. Figure 10-5 shows an example of free run on a system with a moderate load.

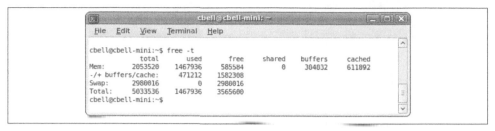

Figure 10-5. The free command

In the output from an Ubuntu system, shown in Figure 10-5, the shared column is obsolete.

There is a switch that puts the command into a polling mode where the statistics are updated for the number of seconds provided. For example, to poll memory every five seconds, issue `free -t -s 5`.

The pmap command

The `pmap` command gives you a detailed map of the memory used for a process. To use this command, you must first find the process ID for the process you want to explore. You can get this information using the `ps` command, or even the `top` command if you are looking at a process that is consuming lots of CPU time.

You can also get the memory map of multiple processes by listing the process IDs on the command line. For example, `pmap 12578 12579` will show the memory map for process IDs 12578 and 12579.

The output shows a detailed map of all of the memory addresses and the sizes of the portions of memory used by the process at the instant the report was created. It displays the command used to launch the process, including the full path and parameters, which can be very useful for determining where the process was started and what options it is using. You'd be amazed how handy that is when trying to figure out why a process is behaving abnormally. The display also shows the mode (access rights) for the memory block. This can be useful in diagnosing interprocess issues. Figures 10-6 and 10-7 show an example of a *mysqld* process map when running on a system with moderate load.

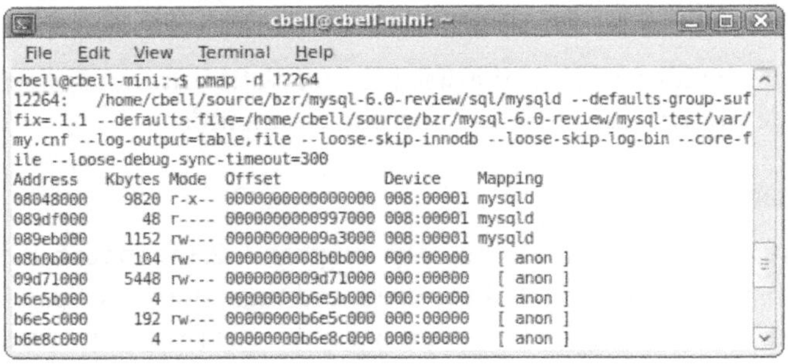

Figure 10-6. The pmap command—part 1

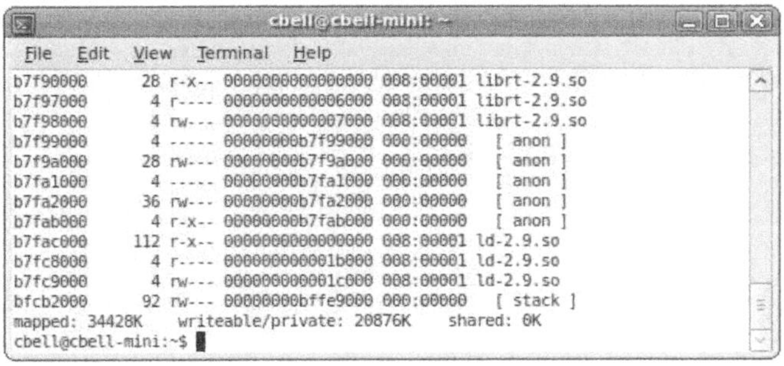

Figure 10-7. The pmap command—part 2

Notice that the listing chosen is the device output format (selected by issuing the -d parameter on startup) as well as where the memory is being mapped or used. This can be handy in diagnosing why a particular process is consuming lots of memory and which part (e.g., a library) is consuming the most.

Figure 10-7 shows the final line of the pmap output, which displays some useful summary information.

The final line shows how much memory is mapped to files, the amount of private memory space, and the amount shared with other processes. This information may be a key piece of data needed to solve memory allocation and sharing issues.

There are several other commands and utilities that display information about memory usage (e.g., dmesg, which can display messages from bootup); consult a good reference on performance tuning for your operating system.

Disk Usage

A number of commands can reveal the disk usage statistics on your system. This section describes and demonstrates the `iostat` and `sar` commands.

The iostat command

As you have already seen in "Process Activity" on page 342, the `iostat` command shows the CPU time used and a list of all of the disks and their statistics. Specifically, `iostat` lists each device, its transfer speed, the number of blocks read and written per second, and the total number of blocks read and written. For easy consultation, Figure 10-8 repeats Figure 10-2, which is an example of the `iostat` command run on a system with a moderate load.

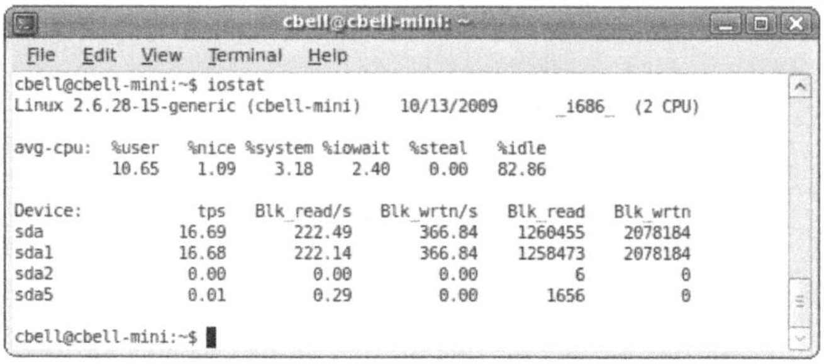

Figure 10-8. The iostat command

This report can be very important when diagnosing disk problems. At a glance, it can tell you whether some devices are being used more than others. If this is the case, you can move some processes to other devices to reduce demand for a single disk. The output can also tell you which disk is experiencing the most reads or writes—this can help you determine whether a particular device needs to be upgraded to a faster one. Conversely, you can learn which devices are underutilized. For example, if you see that your shiny new super-fast disk is not being accessed much, it is likely that you have not configured the high-volume processes to use the new disk. On the other hand, it could be that your program is using memory caches that I/O is seldom performed on.

The sar command

The `sar` command is a very powerful utility that displays all sorts of information about your system. It records data over time and can be configured in a variety of ways, so it can be a little tricky to set up. Consult your operating system's documentation to ensure you have it set up correctly. Like most of the system utilization commands we show, you can also configure `sar` to generate reports at regular intervals.

The sar command can also display CPU usage, memory, cache, and a host of other data similar to that shown by the other commands. Some administrators set up sar to run periodically to cull the data and form a benchmark for their system. A complete tutorial on sar is beyond the scope of this book. For a more detailed examination, see System Performance Tuning by Gian-Paolo D. Musumeci and Mike Loukides (O'Reilly).

In this section, we will look at how to use the sar command to display information about disk usage. We do this by combining displays of the I/O transfer rates, swap space and paging statistics, and block device usage. Figure 10-9 shows an example of the sar command used to display disk usage statistics.

```
                                    cbell@cbell-mini: ~                              _ □ x
 File   Edit   View   Terminal   Help
cbell@cbell-mini:~$ sar -bBdS 1 1
Linux 2.6.28-15-generic (cbell-mini)     10/13/2009     _i686_    (2 CPU)

03:20:30 PM   pgpgin/s  pgpgout/s    fault/s  majflt/s  pgfree/s  pgscank/s  pgscand/s  pgsteal/s     %vmeff
03:20:31 PM       0.00       0.00      32.00      0.00     72.00       0.00       0.00       0.00       0.00

03:20:30 PM        tps       rtps       wtps    bread/s   bwrtn/s
03:20:31 PM       0.00       0.00       0.00       0.00      0.00

03:20:30 PM  kbswpfree kbswpused   %swpused   kbswpcad   %swpcad
03:20:31 PM    2978124      1892       0.06       1892    100.00

03:20:30 PM        DEV        tps   rd_sec/s   wr_sec/s  avgrq-sz   avgqu-sz      await      svctm      %util
03:20:31 PM     dev8-0       0.00       0.00       0.00      0.00       0.00       0.00       0.00       0.00

Average:      pgpgin/s  pgpgout/s    fault/s  majflt/s  pgfree/s  pgscank/s  pgscand/s  pgsteal/s     %vmeff
Average:          0.00       0.00      32.00      0.00     72.00       0.00       0.00       0.00       0.00

Average:           tps       rtps       wtps    bread/s   bwrtn/s
Average:          0.00       0.00       0.00       0.00      0.00

Average:     kbswpfree kbswpused   %swpused   kbswpcad   %swpcad
Average:       2978124      1892       0.06       1892    100.00

Average:           DEV        tps   rd_sec/s   wr_sec/s  avgrq-sz   avgqu-sz      await      svctm      %util
Average:        dev8-0       0.00       0.00       0.00      0.00       0.00       0.00       0.00       0.00
cbell@cbell-mini:~$ ▊
```

Figure 10-9. The sar command for disk usage

The report displays so much information that it seems overwhelming at first glance. Notice the first section after the header. This is the paging information that displays the performance of the paging subsystem. Below that is a report of the I/O transfer rates, followed by the swap space report and then a list of the devices with their statistics. The last portion of the report displays averages calculated for all parameters sampled.

The paging report shows the rate of pages paged in or out of memory, the number of page faults per second that did not require disk access, the number of major faults requiring disk access, and additional statistics about the performance of the paging system. This information can be helpful if you are seeing a high number of page faults (major page faults are more costly), which could indicate too many processes running.

Large numbers of major page faults can cause disk usage problems (i.e., if this value is very high and disk usage is high, poor performance may not be located in the disk subsystems). It is possible the observation is just a symptom of something going wrong in the application or operating system.

The I/O transfer report shows the number of transactions per second (tps), the read and write requests, and the totals for blocks read and written. In this example, the system is not using I/O but is under heavy CPU load. This is a sign of a healthy system. If the I/O values were very high, we would suspect one or more processes of being stuck in an I/O-bound state. For MySQL, a query generating a lot of random disk accesses or tables that reside across a fragmented disk could cause such a problem.

The swap space report shows the amount of swap space available, how much is used, the percentage used, and how much cache memory is used. This can be helpful in indicating a problem with swapping out too many processes and, like the other reports, can help you determine whether the problem lies in your disks and other devices or with memory or too many processes.

The block device (any area of the system that moves data in blocks like disk, memory, etc.) report shows the transfer rate (tps), the reads and writes per second, and average wait times. This information can be helpful in diagnosing problems with your block devices. If these values are all very high (unlike this example, which shows almost no device activity), it could mean you have reached the maximum bandwidth of your devices. However, this information should be weighed against the other reports on this page to rule out a thrashing system, a system with too many processes, or a system without enough memory (or a combination of such problems).

This composite report can be helpful in determining where your disk usage problems lie. If the paging report shows an unusually high rate of faults, it's an indication you may have too many applications running or not enough memory. However, if these values are low or average, you need to look to the swap space; if that is normal, you can examine the device usage report for anomalies.

Disk usage analyzer

In addition to operating system utilities, the GNOME desktop project has created a graphical application called the Disk Usage Analyzer. This tool gives you an in-depth look at how your storage devices are being used. It also gives you a graphic that depicts disk usage. The utility is available in most distributions of Linux.

Figure 10-10 shows a sample report from the Disk Usage Analyzer.

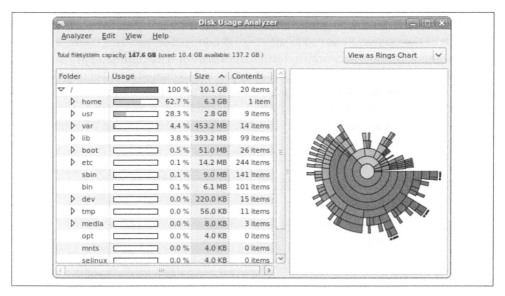

Figure 10-10. Disk Usage Analyzer

Basically, this report gives you a look at how the devices are performing alongside the paging and swap systems. Naturally, if a system is swapping a lot of processes in and out of memory, the disk usage will be unusual. This is why it is valuable to look at these items together on the same report.

Diagnosing disk problems can be challenging, and only a few commands give you the kind of detailed statistics about disk usage we've described. However, some operating systems provide more detailed and specific tools for examining disk usage. Don't forget that you can also determine available space, what is mounted, which filesystems each disk has, and much more from more general commands such as `ls`, `df`, and `fdisk`. Consult your operating system documentation for a list and description of all disk-related commands, as well as for disk usage and monitoring commands.

> The `vmstat` command, shown later in this chapter, can also show this data. Use the `vmstat -d` command to get a text-based representation of the data.

Network Activity

Diagnosing network activity problems may require specialized knowledge of hardware and networking protocols. Detailed diagnostics are normally left to the networking specialists, but there are two commands you, as a MySQL administrator, can use to get an initial picture of the problem.

The netstat command

The `netstat` command allows you to see network connections, routing tables, interface statistics, and additional networking-related information. The command provides a lot of the information that a network specialist would use to diagnose and configure complex networking problems. However, it can be helpful to see how much traffic is passing through your network interfaces and which interfaces are being accessed the most. Figure 10-11 shows a sample report of all of the network interfaces and how much data has been transmitted over each one.

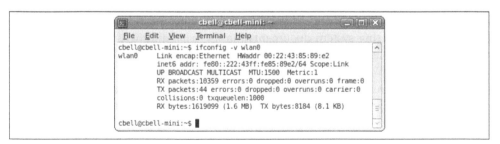

```
cbell@cbell-mini: ~

File   Edit   View   Terminal   Help

cbell@cbell-mini:~$ netstat -i
Kernel Interface table
Iface    MTU Met    RX-OK RX-ERR RX-DRP RX-OVR    TX-OK TX-ERR TX-DRP TX-OVR Flg
eth0     1500 0      6584      0    0 0     5071      0      0      0 BMRU
lo       16436 0  3473256      0    0 0  3473256      0      0      0 LRU
wlan0    1500 0     10359      0    0 0       44      0      0      0 BMU
wmaster0 1500 0         0      0    0 0        0      0      0      0 BMRU
cbell@cbell-mini:~$
```

Figure 10-11. The netstat command

In systems that have multiple network interfaces, it may be helpful to determine whether any interface is being overutilized or if the wrong interfaces are active.

The ifconfig command

The `ifconfig` command, an essential tool for any network diagnostics, displays a list of the network interfaces on your system, including the status and settings for each. Figure 10-12 shows an example of the `ifconfig` command.

```
cbell@cbell-mini: ~

File   Edit   View   Terminal   Help

cbell@cbell-mini:~$ ifconfig -v wlan0
wlan0     Link encap:Ethernet  HWaddr 00:22:43:85:89:e2
          inet6 addr: fe80::222:43ff:fe85:89e2/64 Scope:Link
          UP BROADCAST MULTICAST  MTU:1500  Metric:1
          RX packets:10359 errors:0 dropped:0 overruns:0 frame:0
          TX packets:44 errors:0 dropped:0 overruns:0 carrier:0
          collisions:0 txqueuelen:1000
          RX bytes:1619099 (1.6 MB)  TX bytes:8184 (8.1 KB)

cbell@cbell-mini:~$
```

Figure 10-12. The ifconfig command

The output lists each interface, whether it is up or down, along with its configuration information. This can be very helpful in determining how an interface is configured and can tell you, for example, that instead of communicating over your super-fast Ethernet adapter, your network has failed over to a much slower interface. The root of networking problems is often not the traffic on the network, but rather the network interface choice or setup.

If you produce the reports shown here for your system and still need help diagnosing the problem, having this data ahead of time can help your networking specialist zero in on the problem more quickly. Once you have eliminated any processes consuming too much network bandwidth and determined where you have a viable network interface, the networking specialist can then configure the interface for optimal performance.

General System Statistics

Along with the subsystem-specific commands we've discussed, and grouped statistical reporting commands, Linux and Unix offer additional commands that give you more general information about your system. These include commands such as uptime and vmstat.

The uptime command

The uptime command displays how long a system has been running. It displays the current time; how long the system has been running; how many users have been using the system (logged on); and load averages for the past 1, 5, and 15 minutes. Figure 10-13 shows an example of the command.

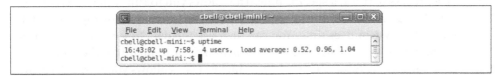

Figure 10-13. The uptime command

This information can be helpful if you want to see how the system has been performing on average in the recent past. The load averages given are for processes in an active state (not waiting on I/O or the CPU). Therefore, this information has limited use for determining performance issues, but can give you a general sense of the health of the system.

The vmstat command

The vmstat command is a general reporting tool that gives you information about processes, memory, the paging system, block I/O, disk, and CPU activity. It is sometimes used as a first stop on a quest for locating performance issues. High values in some fields may lead you to examine those areas more closely using other commands discussed in this chapter.

Figure 10-14 shows an example of the vmstat command run on a system with low load.

The data shown here includes the number of processes, where r indicates those waiting to run and b indicates those in an uninterruptible state. The next set of columns shows the swap space totals including amount of memory swapped in (si) or out (so). The next area shows the I/O reports for blocks received (bi) or sent (bo). The next area shows the number of interrupts per second (in), number of context switches per second (cs), time spent running processes in user space (us), time spent running processes in kernel space (sy), idle time (id), and time waiting for I/O (wa). These times are all in seconds.

There are more parameters and options for the vmstat command. Check your operating system manual for more details on the options available for your operating system.

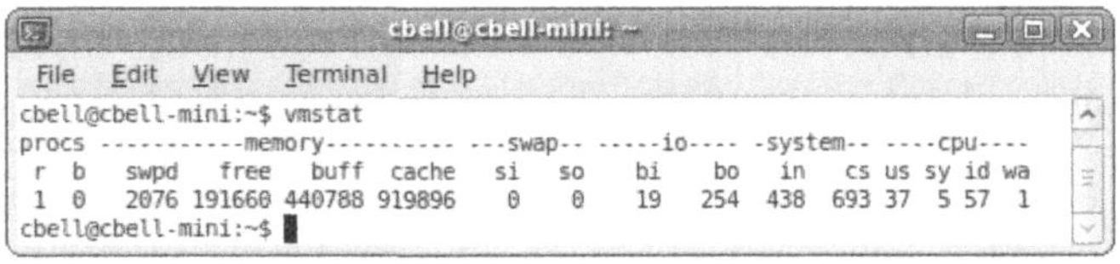

Figure 10-14. The vmstat command

Automated Monitoring with cron

Perhaps the most important tool to consider is the cron facility. You can use cron to schedule a process to run at a specific time. This allows you to run commands and save the output for later analysis. It can be a very powerful strategy, allowing you to take snapshots of the system over time. You can then use the data to form averages of the system parameters, which you can use as a benchmark to compare to when the system performs poorly in the future. This is important because it allows you to see at a glance what has changed, saving you considerable time when diagnosing performance problems.

If you run your performance monitoring tools daily, and then examine the results and compare them to your benchmark, you may be able to detect problems before your users start complaining. Indeed, this is the basic premise behind the active monitoring tools we've described.

Mac OS X Monitoring

Because the Mac OS X operating system is built on the Unix Mac kernel, you can use most of the tools described earlier to monitor your operating system. However, there are other tools specific to the Mac. These include the following graphical administration tools:

- System Profiler
- Console
- Activity Monitor

This section will present an overview of each of these tools for the purposes of monitoring a Mac OS X system. These tools form the core monitoring and reporting facilities for Mac OS X. In good Mac fashion, they are all well-written and well-behaved graphical user interfaces (GUIs). The GUIs even show the portions of the tools that report information from files. As you will see, each has a very important use and can be very helpful in diagnosing performance issues on a Mac.

System Profiler

The System Profiler gives you a snapshot of the status of your system. It provides an incredible amount of detail about just about everything in your system, including all of the hardware, the network, and the software installed. Figure 10-15 shows an example of the System Profiler.

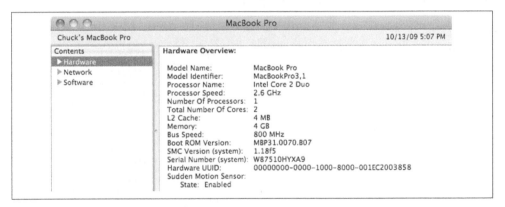

Figure 10-15. The System Profiler

You can find the System Profiler in the *Applications/Utilities* folder on your hard drive. You can also launch the System Profiler via Spotlight. As Figure 10-15 shows, the tool offers a tree pane on the left and a detail pane on the right. You can use the tree pane to dive into the various components of your system.

 If you would prefer a console-based report, the System Profiler has a command-line-equivalent application in */usr/sbin/system_profiler*. There are many parameters and options that allow you to restrict the view to certain reports. To find out more, open a terminal and type **man system_profiler**.

If you open the Hardware tree, you will see a listing of all of the hardware on your system. For example, if you want to see what type of memory is installed on your system, you can click the Memory item in the Hardware tree.

System Profiler provides a network report, which we have seen in another form on Linux. Click the Network tree to get a basic report of all of the network interfaces on your system. Select one of the network interfaces in the tree or in the detail pane to see all of the same (and more) information that the network information commands in Linux and Unix generate. You can also find out information about firewalls, locations you've defined, and even which volumes are shared on the network.

Another very useful report displays the applications installed on your system. Click Software→Applications report to see a list of all of the software on your system, including the name, version, when it was updated, whether it is a 64-bit application, and what kind of application it is—for instance, whether it's a universal or a native Intel binary. This last detail can be very important. For example, you can expect a universal binary to run slower than an Intel binary. It is good to know these things in advance, as they can set certain expectations for performance.

Figure 10-16 shows an example of this report.

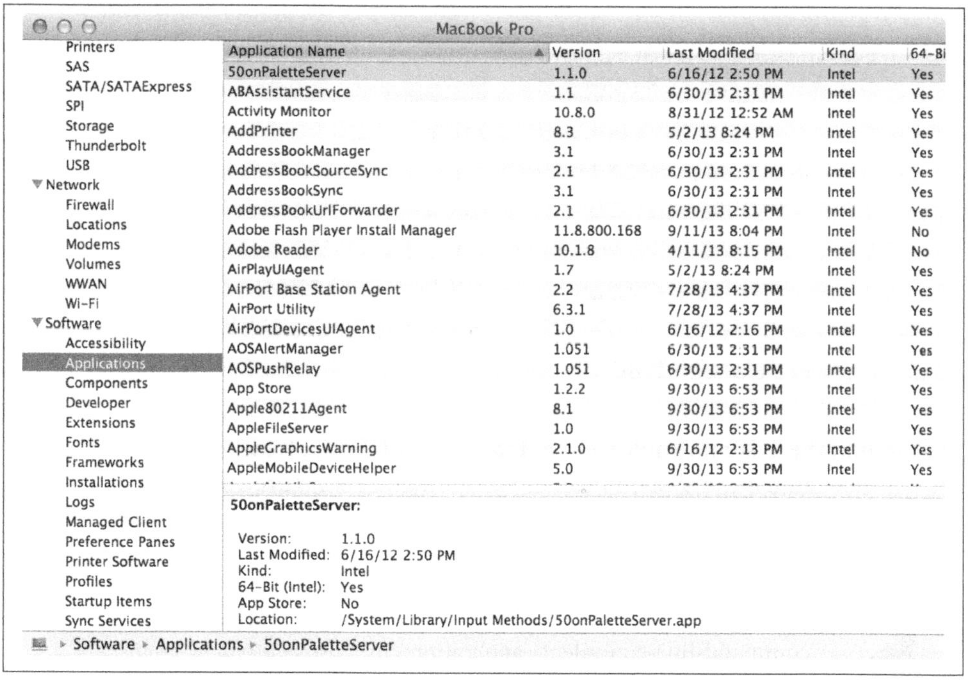

Figure 10-16. Memory report from System Profiler

As you can see, this is a lot of detail. You can see how many memory cards are installed, their speed, and even the manufacturer code and part number. Wow!

 We call each detail pane a *report* because it's essentially a detailed report for a given category. Some people may refer to all of the data as a report, which is not incorrect, but we think it's better to consider the whole thing a collection of reports.

If you are intrigued with the power of this tool, feel free to experiment and dig around in the tree for more information about your system. You will find just about any fact about it here.

The System Profiler can be very valuable during diagnostics of system problems. Many times AppleCare representatives and Apple-trained technicians will ask for a report of your system. Generate the report from the System Profiler by using the File→Save command. This saves an XML file that Apple professionals can use. You can also export the report to RTF using the File→Export command. Finally, you can print the report after saving it as a PDF file.

You can also change the level of detail reported using the View menu. It has options for *Mini*, *Basic*, and *Full*, which change the level of detail from very minimal to a complete report. Apple professionals usually ask for the full report.

A System Profiler report is the best way to determine what is on your system without opening the box. It should be your first source to determine your system configuration.

Console

The Console application displays the logfiles on your system, and is located in the */Applications/Utilities* folder or via Spotlight. Unlike the System Profiler, this tool provides you not only a data dump, but also the ability to search the logs for vital information. When diagnosing problems, it is sometimes helpful to see whether there are any messages in the logs that give more information about an event. Figure 10-17 shows an example of the Console application.

When you launch the Console application, it reads all of the system logs and categorizes them into console diagnostic messages. As you can see in Figure 10-17, the display features a log search pane on the left and a log view on the right. You can also click the individual logfiles in the Files tree to see the contents of each log. The logfiles include the following:

~/Library/Logs
> Stores all messages related to user applications. Check here for messages about applications that crash while logged in, information about iDisk activity, and other user-related tasks.

/Library/Logs

Stores all system messages. Check here for information generated at the system level for crashes and other unusual events.

/private/var/log

Stores all Unix BSD process-related messages. Check here for information about the system daemon or BSD utility.

 Logs are sequential text files where data is always appended, never updated in the middle, and rarely deleted.

The most powerful feature of Console is its search capability. You can create reports containing messages for a given phrase or keyword and view them later. To create a new search, select File→New Database Search in the menu. You will be presented with a generalized search builder that you can use to create your query. When you are finished, you can name and save the report for later processing. This can be a very handy way to keep an eye on troublesome applications.

Another really cool feature is the capability to mark a spot in a log that indicates the current date and time—you can use this to determine the last time you looked at the log. If your experience is like ours, you often find interesting messages in several places in the logs and need to review them later, but don't know where you found them or where you left off reviewing the log. Having the ability to mark a log is a real help in this case. To mark a log, highlight a location in the file and click the Mark button on the toolbar.

Although the data reported is a static snapshot of the logs upon launch and any reports you run are limited to this snapshot, you can also set up alerts for new messages in the logs. Use Console→Preferences to turn on notifications, which are delivered to you either via a bouncing icon on the Dock or by bringing the Console application to the forefront after a delay.

The Console application can be very helpful for seeing how various aspects of your system work by monitoring the events that occur and for finding errors from applications or hardware. When you are faced with a performance issue or another troublesome event, be sure to search the logs for information about the application or event. Sometimes the cure for the problem is presented to you in the form of a message generated by the application itself.

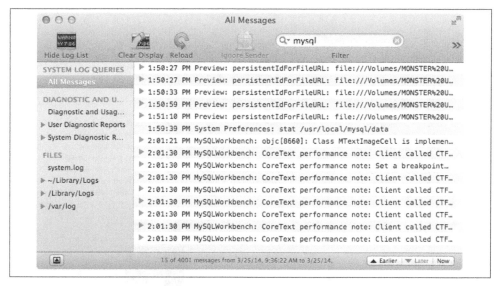

Figure 10-17. The Console application

Activity Monitor

Unlike the static nature of the previously described tools, the Activity Monitor is a dynamic tool that gives you information about the system as it is running. The bulk of the data you will need to treat performance issues can be found in the Activity Monitor. Indeed, you will see information comparable to every tool presented in the Linux and Unix section as you explore the Activity Monitor: information about the CPU, system memory, disk activity, disk usage, and network interfaces.

With the Activity Monitor, for example, you can find out which processes are running and how much memory they are using as well as the percentage of CPU time each is consuming. In this case, the use is analogous to the top command from Linux.

The CPU display shows useful data such as the percentage of time spent executing in user space (user time), the percentage spent in system space (system time), and the percentage of time spent idle. This screen also displays the number of threads and processes running, along with a color-coded graph displaying an aggregate of the user and system time. Combined with the top-like display, this can be an excellent tool if you are investigating problems related to CPU-bound processes.

Figure 10-18 shows the Activity Monitor displaying a CPU report.

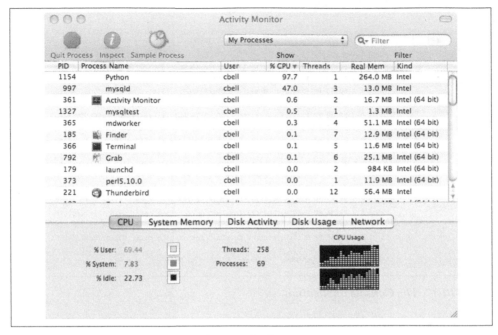

Figure 10-18. The Activity Monitor's CPU display

Notice that there is a Python script that, at the time of the sampling, was consuming a considerable portion of the CPU time. In this case, the system was running a Bazaar branch in a terminal window. The Activity Monitor shows why my system gets sluggish when branching a code tree.

You can double-click a process to get more information about it. You can also cancel a process either in a controlled manner or by forcing it to quit. Figure 10-19 shows an example of the process inspection dialog.

 You can export the list of processes by selecting File→Save. You can save the list of processes either as a text file or as an XML file. Some Apple professionals may ask for the process list in addition to the System Profiler report when diagnosing problems.

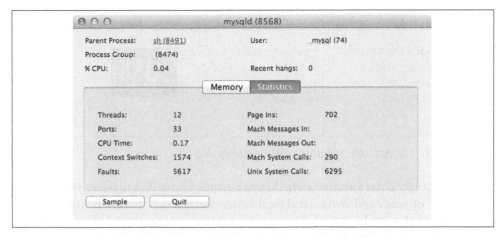

Figure 10-19. The Activity Monitor's process inspection dialog

The System Memory display (Figure 10-20) shows information about the distribution of memory. It shows how much memory is free, how much memory cannot be cached and must stay in RAM (in other words, the wired memory), how much is being used, and how much is inactive. With this report, you can see at a glance whether you have a memory issue.

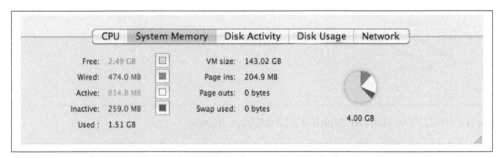

Figure 10-20. The Activity Monitor's System Memory display

The Disk Activity display (Figure 10-21) shows the disk activity for all of your disks. Shown in the first column are the total number of data transfers from (reads in) and to (writes out) disk along with disk performance for reads and writes per second. The next column shows the total size of the data read from and written to disk along with the throughput for each. Included is a graph that displays reads and writes over time in a color-coded graph.

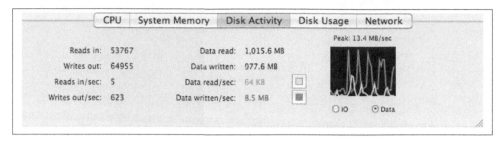

Figure 10-21. The Activity Monitor's Disk Activity display

The Disk Activity data can tell you whether you invoke a lot of disk accesses and whether the number of reads and writes (and total amount of data) is unusually high. An unusually high value could indicate you may have to run processes at different times so they do not compete for the disk or you may have to add another disk to balance the load.

The Disk Usage display (Figure 10-22) shows the used and free space for each of your drives. It also shows a color-coded pie chart to give you a quick view of the disk utilization. You can view another disk by selecting the disk in the drop-down list.

Figure 10-22. The Activity Monitor's Disk Usage display

This display allows you to monitor the free space on your disk so you know when to add more disks and/or extend partitions to add more space when you run low.

The Network display (Figure 10-23) shows a lot of information about how your system is communicating with the network. Shown in the first column is how many packets were read or received (packets in) and written or sent (packets out) over the network. There are also performance statistics measured in packets per second for reads and writes. The next column shows the size of the data read and written on the network along with the transfer rate for each direction. A color-coded chart shows the relative performance of the network. Note the peak value over the chart. You can use the data on this display to determine whether a process is consuming the maximum bandwidth of your system's network interfaces.

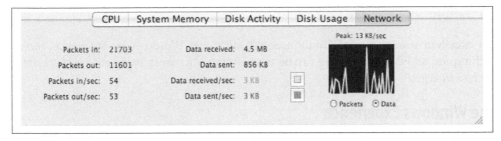

Figure 10-23. The Activity Monitor's Network display

This section has given you a window into the powerful monitoring tools available on Mac OS X. It's not a complete tutorial, but it will get you started with monitoring a Mac OS X system. For complete details about each of the applications shown, be sure to consult the documentation provided by Apple on the Help menu of each application.

Microsoft Windows Monitoring

Windows is saddled with the reputation of lacking tools; some have called its monitoring counterintuitive. The good news is the barriers to monitoring a Windows system are a myth. In fact, Windows comes with some very powerful tools, including a scheduler for running tasks. You can take performance snapshots, examine errors in the Event Viewer (the Windows equivalent of logs), and monitor performance in real time.

 The images shown in this section were taken from several Windows machines. The tools do not differ much in Windows XP or newer versions, including Windows Server 2008 and Windows 8. However, there are differences in accessing the tools in Windows 7 and later, and these differences are noted for each tool.

Indeed, there are a great many tools available to the Windows administrator. We won't try to cover them all here, but instead we'll focus on tools that let you monitor a Windows system in real time. Let's examine some of the basic reporting tools first.

The following are the most popular tools you can use to diagnose and monitor performance issues in Windows:

- Windows Experience Index
- System Health Report
- Event Viewer
- Task Manager
- Reliability Monitor

- Performance Monitor

An excellent source for information about Microsoft Windows performance, tools, techniques, and documentation can be found at the Microsoft Technet website (*http:// bit.ly/win-client*).

The Windows Experience

If you want a quick glance at how your system is performing compared to the expectations of Microsoft's hardware performance indexes, you can run the Windows Experience report.

To launch the report, click Start, then select Control Panel→System and Maintenance→Performance Information and Tools. You will have to acknowledge the User Account Control (UAC) to continue.

You can also access the System Health Report using the search feature on the Start menu. Click Start and enter "performance" in the search box, then click Performance Information and Tools. Click Advanced Tools and then click the link "Generate a system health report" at the bottom of the dialog. You will have to acknowledge the UAC to continue.

 Microsoft has changed the Windows Experience in Windows 7. The report is very similar to that of earlier Windows versions, but it supplies more information that you can use to judge the performance of your system.

The report is run once after installation, but you can regenerate the report by clicking Update My Score.

This report rates five areas of your system's performance: processor (CPU), memory, video controller (graphics), video graphics accelerator (gaming graphics), and the primary hard drive. Figure 10-24 shows an example of the Windows Experience report.

There is a little-known feature of this report you may find valuable—click on the link "Learn how you can improve your computer's performance" to get a list of best practices for improving each of these scores.

 You should run this report and regenerate the metrics every time you change the configuration of your system. This will help you identify situations where configuration changes affect the performance of your server.

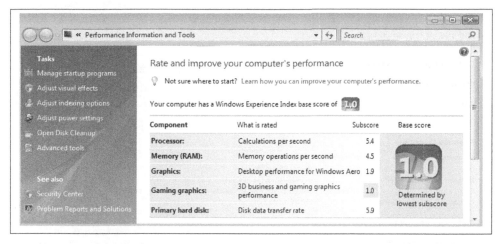

Figure 10-24. The Windows Experience report

The best use for this tool is to get a general impression of how your system is performing without analyzing a ton of metrics. A low score in any of the categories can indicate a performance issue. If you examine the report in Figure 10-24, for instance, you will see that the system has a very low graphics and gaming graphics score. This is not unexpected for a Windows system running as a virtual machine or a headless server, but it might be alarming to someone who just shelled out several thousand dollars for a high-end gaming system.

The System Health Report

One of the unique features and diagnostic improvements in Windows Vista and later is the ability to generate a report that takes a snapshot of all of the software, hardware, and performance metrics for your system. It is analogous to the System Profiler of Mac OS X, but also contains performance counters.

To launch the System Health Report, click Start, then select Control Panel→System and Maintenance→Performance Information and Tools. Next, select Advanced Tools, then click the link "Generate a system health report" at the bottom of the dialog. You will have to acknowledge the UAC to continue.

You can also access the System Health Report using the search feature on the Start menu. Click Start and enter "performance" in the search box, then click Performance Information and Tools. Click Advanced Tools and select the link "Generate a system health report" at the bottom of the dialog. Another way to access the System Health Report is to use the search feature on the Start menu. Click Start and enter "system health report" in the search box, then click the link in the Start menu. You will have to acknowledge the UAC to continue. Figure 10-25 shows an example of the System Health Report.

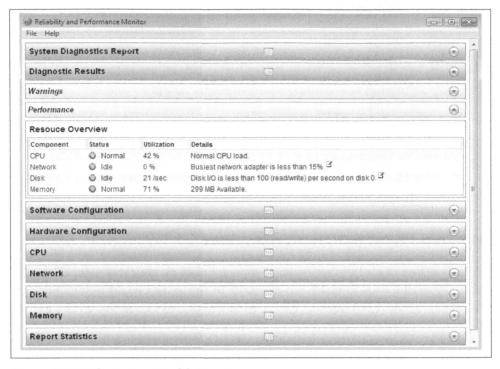

Figure 10-25. The System Health Report

This report has everything—all of the hardware, software, and many other aspects of your system are documented here. Notice the report is divided into sections that you can expand or collapse for easier viewing. The following list briefly describes the information displayed by each section:

System Diagnostics Report
> The system name and the date the report was generated.

Diagnostic Results
> Warning messages generated while the report was being run, identifying potential problem areas on your computer. Also included is a brief overview of the performance of your system at the time the report was run.

Software Configuration
> A list of all of the software installed on your system, including system security settings, system services, and startup programs.

Hardware Configuration
> A list of the important metadata for disk, CPU performance counters, BIOS information, and devices.

CPU
> A list of the processes running at report time and metadata about system components and services.

Network
> Metadata about the network interfaces and protocols on your system.

Disk
> Performance counters and metadata about all of the disk devices.

Memory
> Performance counters for memory, including the process list and memory usage.

Report Statistics
> General information about the system when the report was run, such as processor speed and the amount of memory installed.

The System Health Report is your key to understanding how your system is configured and is performing at a glance. It is a static report, representing a snapshot of the system.

There is a lot of detailed information in the Hardware Configuration, CPU, Network, Disk, and Memory sections. Feel free to explore those areas for greater details about your system.

The best use of this tool, beyond examining the performance counters, is to save the report for later comparison to other reports when your system is performing poorly. You can save an HTML version of the report by selecting File→Save As.

You can use the saved report as a baseline for performance of your system. If you generate the report several times over the course of low, medium, and high usage, you should be able to put together a general expectation for performance. These expectations are important because you can use them to determine whether your performance issues are within the bounds of expectations. When a system enters a period of unusually high load during a time when it is expected to have a low load, the users' experience may generate complaints. If you have these reports to compare to, you can save yourself a lot of time investigating the exact source of the slowdown.

The Event Viewer

The Windows Event Viewer shows all the messages logged for application, security, and system events. It is a great source of information about events that have occurred (or continue to occur) and should be one of the primary tools you use to diagnose and monitor your system.

You can accomplish a great deal with the Event Viewer. For example, you can generate custom views of any of the logs, save the logs for later diagnosis, and set up alerts for specific events in the future. We will concentrate on viewing the logs. For more information about the Event Viewer and how you can set up custom reports and subscribe to events, consult your Windows help files.

To launch the Event Viewer, click the Start button, then right-click Computer and choose Manage. You will have to acknowledge the UAC to continue. You can then click the Event Viewer link in the left panel. You can also launch the Event Viewer by clicking Start, typing "event viewer," and pressing Enter.

The dialog has three panes by default. The left pane is a tree view of the custom views, logfiles, and applications and services logs. The logs are displayed in the center pane, and the right pane contains the Action menu items. The log entries are sorted, by default, in descending order by date and time. This allows you to see the most recent messages first.

 You can customize the Event Viewer views however you like. You can even group and sort events by clicking on the columns in the log header.

Open the tree for the Windows logs to see the base logfiles for the applications, security, and system (among others). Figure 10-26 shows the Event Viewer open and the log tree expanded.

The logs available to view and search include:

Application
> All messages generated from user applications as well as operating system services. This is a good place to look when diagnosing problems with applications.

Security
> Messages related to access and privileges exercised, as well as failed attempts to access any secure object. This can be a good place to look for application failures related to username and password issues.

Setup
> Messages related to application installation. This is the best place to look for infor-mation about failures to install or remove software.

System
> Messages about device drivers and Windows components. This can be the most useful set of logs for diagnosing problems with devices or the system as a whole. It contains information about all manner of devices running at the system level.

Forwarded Events
> Messages forwarded from other computers. Consult the Windows documentation about working with remote event logging.

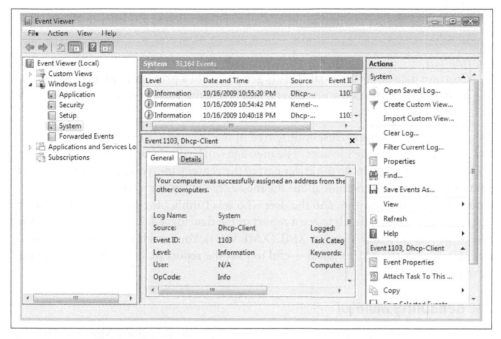

Figure 10-26. The Windows Event Viewer

Digging through these logs can be challenging, because many of them display information that is interesting to developers and not readable by mere mortals. To make things easier, you can search any of the logs by clicking the Find operation in the Actions pane and entering a text string. For example, if you are concerned about memory issues, you can enter "memory" to filter all of the log entries for ones containing the string "memory," which will then be shown in the center pane.

 You can also click the Details tab to make things easier to read.

Each log message falls into one of the following three categories (these apply to user processes, system components, and applications alike):

Error
> Indicates a failure of some magnitude, such as a failed process, out-of-memory problem, or system fault.

Warning
> Indicates a less serious condition or event of note, such as low memory or low disk space.

Information
> Conveys data about an event. This is generally not a problem, but it could provide additional information when diagnosing problems, such as when a USB drive was removed.

To view a log, open the corresponding tree in the left pane. To view the details about any message, click on the message. The message will be displayed below the log entries, as shown in Figure 10-26. In the lower part of the center pane, you can click the General tab to see general information about the message, such as the statement logged, when it occurred, what log it is in, and the user who was running the process or application. You can click the Details tab to see a report of the data logged. You can view the information as text (Friendly View) or XML (XML View). You can also save the information for later review; the XML View is useful to pass the report to tools that recognize the format.

The Reliability Monitor

The most interesting monitoring tool in Windows is the Reliability Monitor. This is a specialized tool that plots the significant performance and error events that have occurred over time in a graph.

A vertical bar represents each day over a period of time. The horizontal bar is an aggregate of the performance index for that day. If there are errors or other significant events, you will see a red X on the graph. Below the bar is a set of drop-down lists that contain the software installations and removals, any application failures, hardware failures, Windows failures, and any additional failures.

This tool is great for checking the performance of the system over a period of time. It can help diagnose situations when an application or system service has performed correctly in the past but has started performing poorly, or when a system starts generating error messages. The tool can help locate the day the event first turned up, as well as give you an idea of how the system was performing when it was running well.

Another advantage of this tool is that it gives you a set of daily baselines of your system over time. This can help you diagnose problems related to changing device drivers (one of the banes of Windows administration), which could go unnoticed until the system degrades significantly.

In short, the Reliability Monitor gives you the opportunity to go back in time and see how your system was performing. The best part of all? You don't have to turn it on—it runs automatically, gleaning much of its data from the logs, and therefore automatically knowing your system's history.

One big source of problems on Windows is connecting and configuring hardware. We will not discuss this subject here, as it can easily fill a book in its own right. The good news is there is a plethora of information about Windows on the Internet. Try googling for your specific driver or hardware to see the most popular hits. You can also check out the Microsoft support forums (*http://support.micro soft.com/*). Another excellent resource and host of some popular Windows tools is Sysinternals (*http://bit.ly/winternals*).

You can access the Reliability Monitor by clicking Start, typing "reliability," and pressing Enter or clicking on Reliability and Performance Monitor. You will have to acknowledge the UAC. Click Reliability Monitor in the tree pane on the left. Figure 10-27 shows an example of the Reliability Monitor.

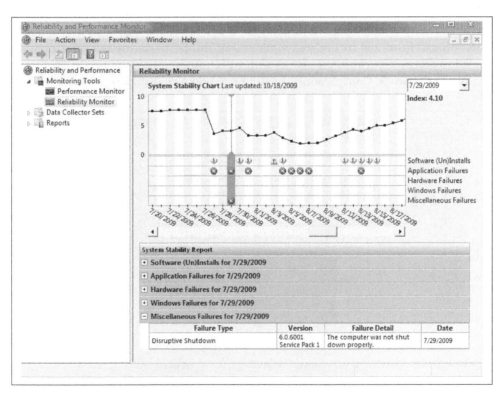

Figure 10-27. The Reliability Monitor

In Windows 7, you can launch the Reliability Monitor by clicking Start, typing "action center" in the search box, and pressing Enter. You can then select Maintenance → View reliability report. The report differs from previous versions of Windows, but offers the same information in a tidier package. For example, instead of the drop-down lists, the new Reliability Monitor report lists known incidents in a single list.

The Task Manager

The Windows Task Manager (shown in Figure 10-28) displays a dynamic list of running processes. It has been around for a long time and has been improved over various versions of Windows.

The Task Manager offers a tabbed dialog with displays for running applications, processes (this is most similar to the Linux top command), services active on the system, a CPU performance meter, a network performance meter, and a list of users. Unlike some other reports, this tool generates its data dynamically, refreshing periodically. This makes the tool a bit more useful in observing the system during periods of low performance.

The reports display the same information as the System Health Report, but in a much more compact form, and are updated continuously. You can find all of the critical metrics needed to diagnose performance issues with CPU, resource-hogging processes, memory, and the network. Conspicuously missing is a report on disk performance.

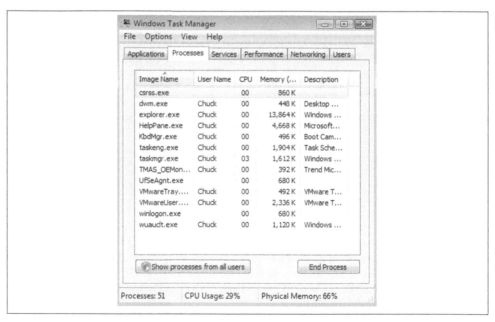

Figure 10-28. The Task Manager

One of the interesting features of the Task Manager is that it shows a miniature performance meter in the notification area on the Start bar that gives you a chance to watch for peaks in usage. You can launch the Task Manager any time by pressing Ctrl+Alt+Del and choosing Task Manager from the menu.

 Running a dynamic performance monitoring tool consumes resources and can affect a system that already suffers poor performance.

The Performance Monitor

The Performance Monitor is the premier tool for tracking performance in a Windows system. It allows you to select key metrics and plot their values over time. It can also store the session so you can later review it and create a baseline for your system.

The Performance Monitor has metrics for just about everything in your system. There are counters for many of the smaller details having to do with the basic areas of performance: CPU, memory, disk, and network. There are a great many other categories as well.

To launch the Performance Monitor, click Start, then select Control Panel→System and Maintenance→Performance Information and Tools. Click Advanced Tools and then click the link Open Reliability and Performance Monitor near the middle of the dialog. You will have to acknowledge the UAC to continue. Click Reliability Monitor in the tree pane on the left to access the Performance Monitor feature.

You can also launch the Performance Monitor by clicking Start, typing "reliability," and pressing Enter or clicking on Reliability and Performance Monitor. You will have to acknowledge the UAC. Click Reliability Monitor in the tree pane on the left to access the Performance Monitor feature. Figure 10-29 shows an example of the Performance Monitor.

Microsoft has two levels of metrics: objects that offer a high-level view of an area such as the processor or memory, and counters that represent a specific detail of the system. Thus, you can monitor the CPU's performance as a whole or watch the finer details, such as percentage of time idle or the number of user processes running. Add these objects or counters to the main chart by clicking the green plus sign on the toolbar. This opens a dialog that allows you to choose from a long list of items to add to the chart. Adding the items is a simple matter of selecting the object and expanding the dropdown list on the left, then dragging the desired object to the list on the right.

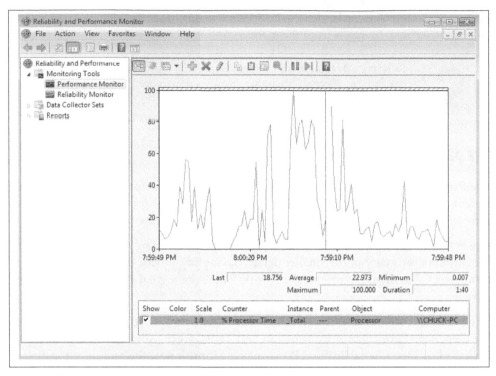

Figure 10-29. The Performance Monitor

You can add as many items as you want; the chart will change its axis accordingly. If you add too many items to track or the values are too diverse, however, the chart may become unreliable. It is best to stick to a few related items at a time (such as only memory counters) to give you the best and most meaningful chart.

A full description of the features of the Performance Monitor is well beyond the scope of this chapter. We encourage you to investigate additional features such as Data Collector Sets and changing the chart's display characteristics. There are many excellent texts that describe these features and more in great detail.

The versatility of the Performance Monitor makes it the best choice for forming baselines and recording the behavior of the system over time. You can use it as a real-time diagnostic tool.

If you have used the Reliability or Performance Monitor, you may have noticed a seldom-commented-on feature called the Resource Overview. This is the default view of the Reliability and Performance Monitor. It provides four dynamic performance graphs for CPU, disk, network, and memory. Below the graphs are drop-down detail panes containing information about these areas. This report is an expanded form of the Task Manager performance graphs and provides yet another point of reference for performance monitoring and diagnosis on Microsoft Windows.

This brief introduction to monitoring performance on Microsoft Windows should persuade you that the belief that Microsoft's Windows platform is difficult to monitor and lacks sophisticated tools is a myth. The tools are very extensive (some could argue too much so) and provide a variety of views of your system's data.

Monitoring as Preventive Maintenance

The techniques discussed so far give you a snapshot of the status of the system. However, most would agree that monitoring is normally an automated task that samples the available statistics for anomalies. When an anomaly is found, an alert is sent to an administrator (or group of administrators) to let someone know there may be a problem. This turns the reactive task of checking the system status into a proactive task.

A number of third-party utilities combine monitoring, reporting, and alerts into easy-to-use interfaces. There are even monitoring and alert systems for an entire infrastructure. For example, Nagios can monitor an entire IT infrastructure and set up alerts for anomalies.

There are also monitoring and alert systems available either as part of or an add-on for operating systems and database systems. We will examine the Enterprise Monitor for MySQL in Chapter 16.

Conclusion

There are a great many references on both performance tuning and security monitoring. This chapter provides a general introduction to system monitoring. While it is not comprehensive, the material presented is an introduction to the tools, techniques, and concepts of monitoring your operating system and server performance. In the next chapter, we will take on the task of monitoring a MySQL system and discuss some common practices to help keep your MySQL system running at peak performance.

"Joel!"

He knew that voice and that tone. Joel's boss was headed his way and about to conduct another drive-by tasking. He turned to face his office door as his boss stepped through it. "Did you read Sally's email about the slowdown?"

Joel recalled that Sally was one of the employees who sent him a message asking why her application was running slowly. He had just finished checking the low-hanging fruit—there was plenty of memory and disk space wasn't an issue.

"Yes, I was just looking into the problem now."

"Make it your top priority. Marketing has a deadline to produce their quarterly sales projections. Let me know what you find." His boss nodded once and stepped away.

Joel sighed and returned to examining the reports on CPU usage while wondering how to describe technology to the nontechnical.

## CHAPTER 11

Monitoring MySQL

Joel had a feeling today was going to be a better day. Everything was going well: the performance measurements for the servers were looking good and the user complaints were down. He had successfully reconfigured the server and improved performance greatly. There was only one application still performing poorly, but he was sure it wasn't a hardware- or operating-system-related problem; more likely, it was an issue with a poorly written query. Nevertheless, he had sent his boss an email message explaining his findings and that he was working on the remaining problems.

Joel heard quickened footsteps approaching his office. He instinctively looked toward his door, awaiting the now-routine appearance of his boss. He was shocked as Mr. Summerson zipped by without so much as a nod in his direction.

He shrugged his shoulders and returned to reading his email messages. Just then a new message appeared with "HIGH PRIORITY" in the subject line in capital letters. It was from his boss. Chiding himself for holding his breath, Joel relaxed and opened the message. He could hear his boss's voice in his mind as he read through the message.

"Joel, good work on those reports. I especially like the details you included about memory and disk performance. I'd like you to generate a similar report about the database server. I'd also like you to look into a problem one of the developers is having with a query. Susan will send you the details."

With a deep sigh, Joel once again opened his favorite MySQL book to learn more about monitoring the database system. "I hope it has something about drilling down into individual components," he mumbled, knowing he needed to get up to speed quickly on an advanced feature of MySQL.

Now that you understand how monitoring works and how to keep your host's operating systems at peak efficiency, how do you know whether your MySQL servers are performing at their peak efficiency? Better still, how do you know when they aren't?

In this chapter, we begin with a look at monitoring MySQL, a brief discussion of monitoring techniques for MySQL, and the taxonomy of monitoring MySQL, and then move on to monitoring and improving performance in your databases. We conclude with a look into best practices for improving database performance.

What Is Performance?

Before we begin discussions about database performance and general best practices for monitoring and tuning a MySQL server, it is important to define what we mean by performance. For the purposes of this chapter, good performance is defined as meeting the needs of the user such that the system performs as expediently as the user expects, whereas poor performance is defined as anything less. Typically, good performance means that response time and throughput meet the users' expectations. While this may not seem very scientific, savvy administrators know the best gauge of how well things are going is the happiness of the users.

That doesn't mean we don't measure performance. On the contrary, we can and must measure performance in order to know what to fix, when, and how. Furthermore, if you measure performance regularly, you can even predict when your users will begin to be unhappy. Your users won't care if you reduce your cache hit rate by 3%, beating your best score to date. You may take pride in such things, but metrics and numbers are meaningless when compared to the user's experience at the keyboard.

There is a very important philosophy that you should adopt when dealing with performance. Essentially, you should never adjust the parameters of your server, database, or storage engine unless you have a deliberate plan and a full understanding of the expectations of the change as well as the consequences. More important, never adjust without measuring the effects of the change over time. It is entirely possible that you can improve the performance of the server in the short run but negatively impact performance in the long run. Finally, you should always consult references from several sources, including the reference manuals.

Now that we've issued that stern warning, let's turn our attention to monitoring and improving performance of the MySQL server and databases.

 Administrators monitoring MySQL almost always focus on improving performance. Certainly performance is important, in terms of how long the user must wait for a query to execute. But monitoring can also check for the exhaustion of resources, or a high demand for those resources which can cause timeouts or other failures to get access to your server.

MySQL Server Monitoring

Managing the MySQL server falls in the category of application monitoring. This is because most of the performance parameters are generated by the MySQL software and are not part of the host operating system. As mentioned previously, you should always monitor your base operating system in tandem with monitoring MySQL because MySQL is very sensitive to performance issues in the host operating system.

There is an entire chapter in the online MySQL Reference Manual that covers all aspects of monitoring and performance improvement, intriguingly titled "Optimization." (*http://bit.ly/mysql-opt*) Rather than repeat the facts and rhetoric of that excellent reference, we will discuss a general approach to monitoring the MySQL server and examine the various tools available.

This section is an introduction to the finer details of monitoring the MySQL server. We'll start with a short discussion of how to change and monitor the behavior of the system, then discuss monitoring primarily for the purposes of diagnosing performance issues and forming a performance benchmark. We will also discuss best practices for diagnosing performance issues and take a look at monitoring the storage engine sublayer in MySQL—an area not well understood or covered by other reference sources.

How MySQL Communicates Performance

There are two mechanisms you can use to govern and monitor behavior in the MySQL server. You use server variables to control behavior and status variables to read behavior configuration and statistical information regarding features and performance.

There are many variables you can use to configure the server. Some can be set only at startup (called startup options, which can also be set in option files). Others can be set at the global level (across all connections), the session level (for a single connection), or both the global and session levels.

You can read server variables using the following commands:

```
SHOW [GLOBAL | SESSION] VARIABLES;
```

You can change those variables that are not static (read-only) using the following commands (you can include multiple settings on a single line using a comma separator):

```
SET [GLOBAL | SESSION] variable_name = value;
SET [@@global. | @@session. | @@]variable_name = value;
```

 Session variable settings are not persistent beyond the current connection and are reset when the connection is closed.

You can read status variables using the following commands—the first two commands display the value of all local or session scope variables (the default is session) and the third command displays those variables that are global in scope:

```
SHOW STATUS;
SHOW SESSION STATUS;
SHOW GLOBAL STATUS;
```

We discuss how and when to use these commands in the next section.

Two of the most important commands for discovering information about the server and how it is performing are SHOW VARIABLES and SHOW STATUS. There are a great many variables (over 290 status variables alone). The variable lists are generally in alphabetical order and are often grouped by feature. However, sometimes the variables are not neatly arranged. Filtering the command by a keyword through the LIKE clause can produce information about the specific aspects of the system you want to monitor. For example, SHOW STATUS LIKE '%thread%' shows all of the status variables related to thread execution.

Performance Monitoring

Performance monitoring in MySQL is the application of the previous commands—specifically, setting and reading system variables and reading status variables. The SHOW and SET commands are only two of the possible tools you can use to accomplish the task of monitoring the MySQL server.

Indeed, there are several tools you can use to monitor your MySQL server. The tools available in the standard distributions are somewhat limited in that they are console tools and include special commands you can execute from a MySQL client (e.g., SHOW STATUS) and utilities you can run from a command line (e.g., *mysqladmin*).

> The MySQL client tool is sometimes called the MySQL monitor, but should not be confused with a monitoring tool.

There are also GUI tools available that make things a little easier if you prefer or require such options. In particular, you can download the MySQL GUI tools, which include advanced tools that you can use to monitor your system, manage queries, and migrate your data from other database systems.

We begin by examining how to use the SQL commands and then discuss the MySQL Workbench tool. We also take a look at one of the most overlooked tools available to the administrator: the server logs.

Some savvy administrators may consider the server logs the first and primary tool for administering the server. Although they are not nearly as vital for performance monitoring, they can be an important asset in diagnosing performance issues.

SQL Commands

All of the SQL monitoring commands could be considered variants of the SHOW command, which displays internal information about the system and its subsystems. For example, one pair of commands that can be very useful in monitoring replication is SHOW MASTER STATUS and SHOW SLAVE STATUS. We will examine these in more detail later in this chapter.

 Many of these commands can be achieved by querying the INFORMA TION_SCHEMA tables directly. See the online MySQL Reference Manual for more details about the INFORMATION_SCHEMA database and its features.

While there are many forms of the SHOW command, the following are the most common SQL commands you can use to monitor the MySQL server:

SHOW INDEX FROM *table*
> Describes the indexes in the table. This can let you know whether you have the right indexes for the way your data is used.

SHOW PLUGINS
> Displays the list of all known plug-ins. It shows the name of the plug-in and its current status. The storage engines in newer releases of MySQL are implemented as plug-ins. Use this command to get a snapshot of the currently available plug-ins and their status. While not directly related to monitoring peformance, some plug-ins supply system variables. Knowing which plug-ins are installed can help determine whether you can access plug-in–specific variables.

SHOW [FULL] PROCESSLIST
> Displays data for all threads (including those handling connections to clients) running on the system. This command resembles the process commands of the host operating system. The information displayed includes connection data along with the command executing, how long it has been executing, and its current state. Like the operating system command it resembles, it can diagnose poor response (too many threads), a zombie process (long running or nonresponding), or even connection issues. When dealing with poor performance or unresponsive threads, use the KILL command to terminate them. The default behavior is to show the processes for the current user. The FULL keyword displays all processes.

You must have the SUPER privilege to see all processes running on the system.

SHOW [GLOBAL | SESSION] STATUS

Displays the values of all of the system variables. You will probably use this command more frequently than any other. Use this command to read all of the statistical information available on the server. Combined with the GLOBAL or SESSION keyword, you can limit the display to those statistics that are global- or session-only.

SHOW TABLE [FROM *db*] STATUS

Displays detailed information about the tables in a given database. This includes the storage engine, collation, creation data, index data, and row statistics. You can use this command along with the SHOW INDEX command to examine tables when diagnosing poorly performing queries.

SHOW [GLOBAL | SESSION] VARIABLES

Displays the system variables. These are typically configuration options for the server. Although they do not display statistical information, viewing the variables can be very important when determining whether the current configuration has changed or if certain options are set. Some variables are read-only and can be changed only via the configuration file or the command line on startup, while others can be changed globally or set locally. You can combine this command with the GLOBAL or SESSION keyword to limit the display to those variables that are global- or session-only.

Limiting the Output of SHOW Commands

The SHOW commands in MySQL are very powerful. However, they often display too much information. This is especially true for the SHOW STATUS and SHOW VARIABLES commands.

To see less information, you can use the LIKE *pattern* clause, which limits the output to rows matching the pattern specified. The most common example is using the LIKE clause to see only variables for a certain subset, such as replication or logging. You can use the standard MySQL pattern symbols and controls in the LIKE clause in the same manner as a SELECT query.

For example, the following displays the status variables that include the name "log":

```
mysql> SHOW SESSION STATUS LIKE '%log%';
+----------------------------+-------+
| Variable_name              | Value |
+----------------------------+-------+
```

```
|  Binlog_cache_disk_use    |  0    |
|  Binlog_cache_use         |  0    |
|  Com_binlog               |  0    |
|  Com_purge_bup_log        |  0    |
|  Com_show_binlog_events   |  0    |
|  Com_show_binlogs         |  0    |
|  Com_show_engine_logs     |  0    |
|  Com_show_relaylog_events |  0    |
|  Tc_log_max_pages_used    |  0    |
|  Tc_log_page_size         |  0    |
|  Tc_log_page_waits        |  0    |
+---------------------------+-------+
11 rows in set (0.11 sec)
```

The commands specifically related to storage engines include the following:

SHOW ENGINE *engine_name* LOGS
> Displays the log information for the specified storage engine. The information displayed is dependent on the storage engine. This can be very helpful in tuning storage engines. Some storage engines do not provide this information.

SHOW ENGINE *engine_name* STATUS
> Displays the status information for the specified storage engine. The information displayed depends on the storage engine. Some storage engines display more information than others. For example, the InnoDB storage engine displays dozens of status variables, while the NDB storage engine shows a few, and the MyISAM storage engine displays no information. This command is the primary mechanism for viewing statistical information about a given storage engine and can be vital for tuning certain storage engines (e.g., InnoDB).

> Older synonyms for the SHOW ENGINE commands (SHOW *en gine* LOGS and SHOW *engine* STATUS) have been deprecated. Also, these commands can display information only on certain engines, including InnoDB and Performance_Schema.

SHOW ENGINES
> Displays a list of all known storage engines for the MySQL release and their status (i.e., whether the storage engine is enabled). This can be helpful when deciding which storage engine to use for a given database or in replication to determine if the same storage engines exist on both the master and the slave.

The commands specifically related to MySQL replication include:

SHOW BINLOG EVENTS [IN *log_file*] [FROM *pos*] [LIMIT *offset row_count*]
> Displays the events as they were recorded to the binary log. You can specify a logfile to examine (omitting the IN clause tells the system to use the current logfile), and

limit output to the last events from a particular position or to the first number of rows after an offset into the file. This command is the primary command used in diagnosing replication problems. It comes in very handy when an event occurs that disrupts replication or causes an error during replication.

 If you do not use a LIMIT clause and your server has been running and logging events for some time, you could get a very lengthy output. If you need to examine a large number of events, you should consider using the *mysqlbinlog* utility instead.

SHOW BINARY LOGS
: Displays the list of the binary logs on the server. Use this command to get information about past and current binlog filenames. The size of each file is also displayed. This is another useful command for diagnosing replication problems because it will permit you to specify the binlog file for the SHOW BINLOG EVENTS command, thereby reducing the amount of data you must explore to determine the problem. The SHOW MASTER LOGS command is a synonym.

SHOW RELAYLOG EVENTS [IN *log_file*] [FROM *pos*] [LIMIT *offset row_count*]
: Available in MySQL version 5.5.0, this command does the same thing as SHOW BIN LOG EVENTS, only with relay logs on the slave. If you do not supply a filename for the log, events from the first relay log are shown. This command has no effect when run on the master.

SHOW MASTER STATUS
: Displays the current configuration of the master. It shows the current binlog file, the current position in the file, and all inclusive or exclusive replication settings. Use this command when connecting or reconnecting slaves.

SHOW SLAVE HOSTS
: Displays the list of slaves connected to the master that used the --report-host option. Use this information to determine which slaves are connected to your master.

SHOW SLAVE STATUS
: Displays the status information for the system acting as a slave in replication. This is the primary command for tracking the performance and status of your slaves. A considerable amount of information is displayed that is vital to maintaining a healthy slave. See Chapter 3 for more information about this command.

Example 11-1 shows the SHOW VARIABLES command and its output from a recent beta release of MySQL.

Example 11-1. Showing thread status variables

```
mysql> SHOW VARIABLES LIKE '%thread%';
+---------------------------+---------------------------+
| Variable_name             | Value                     |
+---------------------------+---------------------------+
| innodb_file_io_threads    | 4                         |
| innodb_read_io_threads    | 4                         |
| innodb_thread_concurrency | 0                         |
| innodb_thread_sleep_delay | 10000                     |
| innodb_write_io_threads   | 4                         |
| max_delayed_threads       | 20                        |
| max_insert_delayed_threads| 20                        |
| myisam_repair_threads     | 1                         |
| pseudo_thread_id          | 1                         |
| thread_cache_size         | 0                         |
| thread_handling           | one-thread-per-connection |
| thread_stack              | 262144                    |
+---------------------------+---------------------------+
12 rows in set (0.00 sec)
```

This example shows not only those status variables for thread management, but also the thread control for the InnoDB storage engine. Although you sometimes get more information than you expected, a keyword-based LIKE clause is sure to help you find the specific variable you need.

Knowing which variables to change and which variables to monitor can be the most challenging part of monitoring a MySQL server. As mentioned, a great deal of valuable information on this topic is included in the online MySQL Reference Manual.

To illustrate the kinds of features you can monitor in a MySQL server, let us examine the variables that control the query cache. The query cache is one of the most important performance features in MySQL if you use the MyISAM storage engine for your application data. It allows the server to buffer frequently used queries and their results in memory. Thus, the more often a query is run, the more likely it is that the results can be read from the cache rather than reexamining the index structures and tables to retrieve the data. Clearly, reading the results from memory is much faster than reading them from disk every time. This can be a performance improvement if your data is read much more frequently than it is written (updated).

Each time you run a query, it is entered into the cache and has a lifetime governed by how recently it was used (old queries are dumped first) and how much memory there is available for the query cache. Additionally, there are a number of events that can invalidate (remove) queries from the cache.

We include a partial list of these events here:

- Changes to data or indexes.

- Subtle differences of the same query that have a different result set, which can cause missed cache hits. Thus, it is important to use standardized queries for commonly accessed data. You will see later in this chapter how views can help in this area.

- When a query derives data from temporary tables (not cached).

- Transaction events that can invalidate queries in the cache (e.g., COMMIT).

You can determine whether the query cache is configured and available in your MySQL installation by examining the have_query_cache variable. This is a system variable with global scope, but it is read-only. You control the query cache using one of several variables. Example 11-2 shows the server variables for the query cache.

Example 11-2. Query cache server variables

```
mysql> SHOW VARIABLES LIKE '%query_cache%';
+------------------------------+----------+
| Variable_name                | Value    |
+------------------------------+----------+
| have_query_cache             | YES      |
| query_cache_limit            | 1048576  |
| query_cache_min_res_unit     | 4096     |
| query_cache_size             | 33554432 |
| query_cache_type             | ON       |
| query_cache_wlock_invalidate | OFF      |
+------------------------------+----------+
6 rows in set (0.00 sec)
```

As you can see, there are several things you can change to affect the query cache. Most notable is the ability to temporarily turn off the query cache by setting the query_cache_size variable, which sets the amount of memory available for the query cache. If you set this variable to 0, it effectively turns off the query cache and removes all queries from the cache. This is not related to the have_query_cache variable, which merely indicates that the feature is available. Furthermore, it is not sufficient to set query_cache_type = OFF because it does not deallocate the query cache buffer. You must also set the size to completely turn off the query cache. For more information about configuring the query cache, see the section titled "Query Cache Configuration" in the online MySQL Reference Manual.

You can observe the performance of the query cache by examining several status variables, as shown in Example 11-3.

Example 11-3. Query cache status variables

```
mysql> SHOW STATUS LIKE '%Qcache%';
+-------------------------+-------+
| Variable_name           | Value |
+-------------------------+-------+
| Qcache_free_blocks      | 0     |
| Qcache_free_memory      | 0     |
```

```
| Qcache_hits              | 0    |
| Qcache_inserts           | 0    |
| Qcache_lowmem_prunes     | 0    |
| Qcache_not_cached        | 0    |
| Qcache_queries_in_cache  | 0    |
| Qcache_total_blocks      | 0    |
+--------------------------+------+
8 rows in set (0.00 sec)
```

Here we see one of the more subtle inconsistencies in the MySQL server. You can control the query cache using variables that start with query_cache, but the status variables start with Qcache. While the inconsistency was intentional (to help distinguish a server variable from a status variable), oddities like this can make searching for the right items a challenge.

There are many nuances to the query cache that allow you to manage and configure it and monitor its performance. This makes the query cache an excellent example to demonstrate the complexity of monitoring the MySQL server.

For example, you can and should periodically defragment the query cache with the FLUSH QUERY CACHE command. This does not remove results from the cache, but instead allows for internal reorganization to better utilize memory.

While no single volume (or chapter in a broader work) can cover all such topics and nuances of the query cache, the practices described in this chapter therefore are general and are designed to be used with any feature in the MySQL server. However, the specific details may require additional research and a good read through the online MySQL Reference Manual.

The mysqladmin Utility

The *mysqladmin* command-line utility is the workhorse of the suite of command-line tools. There are many options and tools (called "commands") this utility can perform. The online MySQL Reference Manual discusses the *mysqladmin* utility briefly. In this section, we examine the options and tools for monitoring a MySQL server.

The utility runs from the command line, so it allows administrators to script sets of operations much more easily than they can process SQL commands. Indeed, some of the third-party monitoring tools use a combination of the *mysqladmin* and SQL commands to gather information for display in other forms.

You must specify connection information (user, password, host, etc.) to connect to a running server. The following is a list of commonly used commands (as you will see, most of these have equivalent SQL commands that produce the same information):

status

Displays a concise description of the status of the server, including uptime, number of threads (connections), number of queries, and general statistical data. This command provides a quick snapshot of the server's health.

extended-status

Displays the entire list of system statistics and is similar to the SQL SHOW STATUS command.

processlist

Displays the list of current processes and works the same way as the SQL SHOW PROCESSLIST command.

kill *thread id*

Allows you to kill a specified thread. Use this in conjunction with processlist to help manage runaway or hung processes.

variables

Displays the system server variables and values. This is equivalent to the SQL SHOW VARIABLES command.

There are many options and other commands not listed here, including commands to start and stop a slave during replication and manage the various system logs.

One of the best features of the *mysqladmin* utility is its comparison of information over time. The --sleep *n* option tells the utility to execute the specified command once every *n* seconds. For example, to see the process list refreshed every three seconds on the local host, use the following command:

```
mysqladmin -uroot --password processlist --sleep 3
```

This command will execute until you cancel the utility using Ctrl-C.

Perhaps the most powerful option is the comparative results for the extended status command. Use the --relative option to compare the previous execution values with the current values. For example, to see the previous and current values for the system status variables, use this command:

```
mysqladmin -uroot --password extended-status --relative --sleep 3
```

You can also combine commands to get several reports at the same time. For example, to see the process list and status information together, issue the following command:

```
mysqladmin --root … processlist status
```

mysqladmin has many other uses. You can use it to shut down the server, flush the logs, ping a server, start and stop slaves in replication, and refresh the privilege tables. For more information about the mysqladmin tool, see the section titled "mysqladmin— Client for Administering a MySQL Server" in the online MySQL Reference Manual. Figure 11-1 shows the sample output of a system with no load.

```
+-----+------+------------------+----+---------+------+-------+------------------+
| Id  | User | Host             | db | Command | Time | State | Info             |
+-----+------+------------------+----+---------+------+-------+------------------+
| 51  | root | localhost:52264  |    | Sleep   | 423  |       |                  |
| 52  | root | localhost:52265  |    | Sleep   | 426  |       |                  |
| 204 | root | localhost        |    | Query   | 0    |       | show processlist |
+-----+------+------------------+----+---------+------+-------+------------------+
Uptime: 533  Threads: 3  Questions: 50  Slow queries: 0  Opens: 17  Flush tables: 1
 Open tables: 10  Queries per second avg: 0.93
```

Figure 11-1. Sample mysqladmin process and status report

MySQL Workbench

The MySQL Workbench application is a GUI tool designed as a workstation-based administration tool. MySQL Workbench, which we'll just call Workbench henceforth, is available for download on the MySQL website and is offered as a community edition (GPL) and a commercial version called the Standard Edition. The Standard Edition is bundled with the MySQL Enterprise offerings.

The major features of Workbench include:

- Server administration
- SQL development
- Data modeling
- Database Migration Wizard

We will discuss server administration in more detail and briefly introduce SQL development in the following sections. Data modeling is beyond the scope of this chapter, but if you want to implement configuration management for your database schemas, we encourage you to explore the feature presented in the Workbench documentation. The database migration wizard is designed to automate the migration of database schema and data from other database systems. These include Microsoft SQL Server 2000, 2005, 2008, and 2012, PostgreSQL 8.0 and later, and Sybase Adaptive Server Enterprise 15.x and greater. It can be a really handy tool to make adoption of MySQL easier and faster.

 MySQL Workbench replaces the older MySQL GUI Tools, including MySQL Administrator, MySQL Query Browser, and MySQL Migration Toolkit.

When you launch Workbench, the main screen displays three distinct sections representing SQL development, data modeling, and server administration (Figure 11-2). The links below each section permit you to start working with each of these features. The database migration feature is accessed via the "Database Migrate…" menu option.

Figure 11-2. MySQL Workbench home window

You can use Workbench on any platform and can access one or more servers connected to the client. This makes the tool much more convenient when monitoring several servers on the network.

For more information and details about installation and setup, refer to the online MySQL Workbench documentation (*http://bit.ly/mysql-workb*).

MySQL server administration

The server administration feature provides facilities for viewing and changing system variables, managing configuration files, examining the server logs, monitoring status variables, and even viewing graphical representations of performance for some of the more important features. It also has a full set of administration options that allow you to manage users and view database configurations. While it was originally intended to replace the *mysqladmin* tool, popular demand ensures we will have both for the foreseeable future.

To use the server administration feature, you must first define an instance of a MySQL server to administer. Click the New Server Instance link and follow the steps to create a new instance (connection) to your server. The process will connect to and validate the parameters you entered to ensure it has a valid instance. Once the instance is created, it will be displayed in the box under the Server Administration section of the home window.

To administer your server, choose the server instance from the list then click Server Administration. You will see a new window like Figure 11-3.

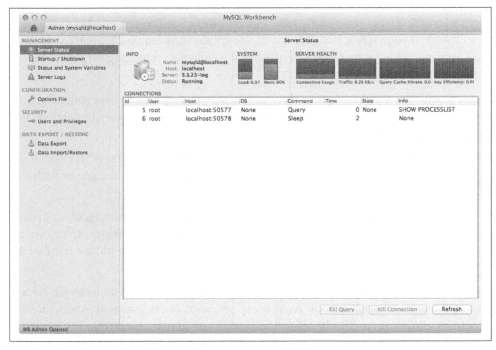

Figure 11-3. Server Administration window

Notice on the left side of the window there are four sections: management, configuration, security, and data export/restore. We discuss each of these briefly.

Management. The management group of tools permits you to see an overview of the server status, start and stop the server, view system and status variables, and view the server logs.

In the first edition of this book, we presented the MySQL Administrator application that contained a feature to produce detailed graphs of memory usage, connections, and more. This feature is not present in MySQL Workbench but is included in the MySQL Enterprise Monitor application that contains advanced monitoring tools for enterprises. The graphing feature is vastly superior to the features in the deprecated MySQL Administrator tool.

We see an example of the server status in Figure 11-3. Notice we see a small graph of the server load and its memory usage. To the right of that, we see graphs for connection usage, network traffic, query cache hits, and key efficiency. You can use these graphs as a quick look at your server status. If any of the graphs show unusually high (or, in rare cases, unusually low) values, you can use that as a clue to start looking for performance problems before they become critical.

If you would like a tool that offers finer granularity in graphing system status, health, and so on, you may want to explore the MySQL Enterprise Monitor application. We discuss the MySQL Enterprise Monitor in Chapter 16.

The startup and shutdown tool lets you start or stop the server instance. It also shows the most recent messages from the server, should you start or stop the server with the tool.

The status and system variable tool is one of the handiest of the management group. Figure 11-4 shows an example screenshot of this tool. You can choose to explore status variables by category or search for any status variable matching a phrase (similar to LIKE '%test%').

The system variable tab has the same search feature. Figure 11-5 is an example screen shot of the system variables tool. As you can see, a lot of categories are defined. The categories allow you to quickly zoom to the area you are most interested in viewing. Any variable prefixed by [rw] is read/write and therefore can be changed by the administrator at runtime.

The administrator account must have the SUPER privilege.

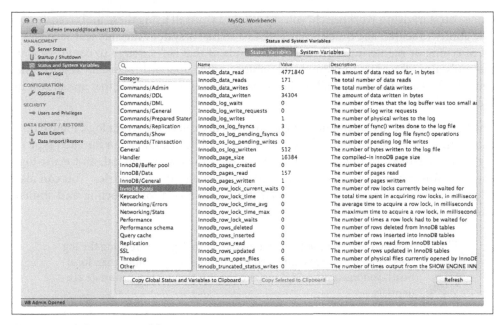

Figure 11-4. Status variables

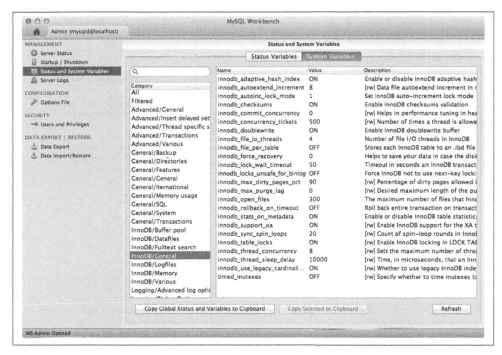

Figure 11-5. System variables

Once you start using Workbench, you should find yourself using these tools frequently. The ability to search and quickly navigate to a status or system variable will save you a lot of typing or reentering SQL SHOW commands. If that isn't enough to convince you, the tools also allow you to copy the variables to the clipboard for use in reports and similar efforts. You can copy all of the global variables or just those that are shown in the result list.

The last tool in the management group allows you to explore the server logs. Figure 11-6 shows an example screenshot of the server logs tool. It displays a tab for each type of log that is enabled. In the example, we have the slow query, general, and error logs enabled. You can view each log in turn, paging through the log entries. You can also select portions of the logs and copy them to the clipboard for reporting and similar efforts.

You may be prompted to enter elevated privileges for reading the log files. Also, if you are connected to a remote server (other than localhost), you must use a SSH instance connection with appropriate credentials.

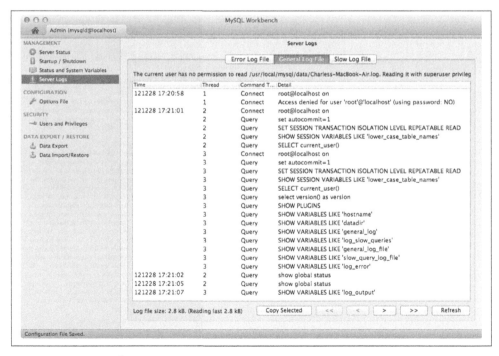

Figure 11-6. Server logs

As you can see, the graphical tools for managing MySQL servers are designed to make rudimentary and repetitive tasks easier.

Configuration. The next group includes a powerful tool for managing your configuration file. Figure 11-7 shows a sample screenshot of the options file tool. Not only can you view what options are set in your configuration file, but you can change their values and save the new values. More on that in a moment.

The user account used must have write privileges at the OS-level for this file.

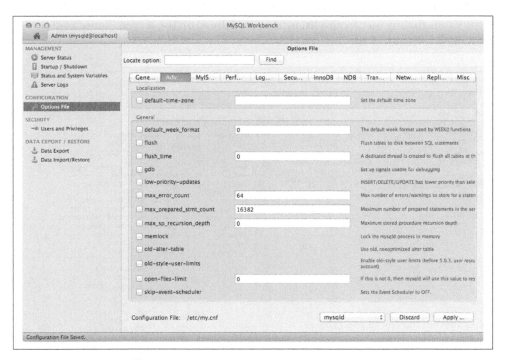

Figure 11-7. Options file

There are several categories listed in tabs across the top. These include general, advanced, MyISAM, performance, logfiles, security, InnoDB, NDB, transactions, networking, replication, and miscellaneous. The tool includes all of the server options known for the version of your server. The use of categories makes finding and setting configuration file entries easier. A short help text is provided to the right of each option.

Setting options requires first checking the tick box to indicate the option should appear in the file. In addition, if the option takes a value, enter or change the value in the provided text box. Once you have all of the options set the way you want, you can make them take effect by clicking Apply. When you click Apply, a dialog opens that displays a summary of the changes to the file. You can cancel or apply the changes or you can see the complete contents of the file from this dialog. When you click Apply, the tool saves the changes to the file, which will take effect on the next start of the server.

There is one other powerful feature to this tool. Notice the drop-down box labeled "mysqld" near the bottom. This allows you to set the section of the configuration file you are editing, and thereby use the tool to modify options for certain applications. Combined with the ability to restart the server, you can use this tool to help tune your server. You may find this easier and faster to use than traditional command-line tools.

Security. The next group contains a permissions tool that allows you to quickly see the permissions for any user from a list of all users defined on the server. Figure 11-8 shows a sample screenshot of the tool.

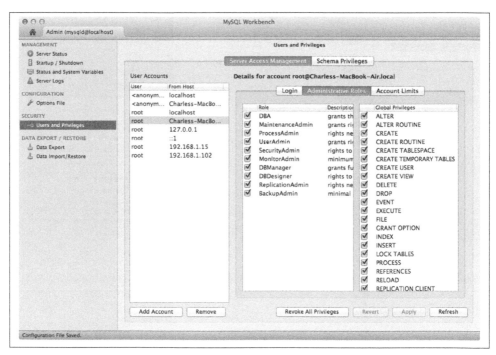

Figure 11-8. Privileges

You can use this tool to help diagnose access issues and to help prune your permission sets to minimal access for your users. The tool also permits you to change permissions for a given user by clicking the tick box to toggle access (no checkmark means the user does not have the permission). Once you've made changes to one or more users, you can click Apply to issue the appropriate changes on the server.

Data export/restore. The last group of tools encapsulate the basic data export and import features of *mysqldump*. While not strictly devoted to monitoring, you would do well to include such features in your collection of tools. For example, it may be necessary to make copies or export data from one server to another for further analysis of a performance-related query issue.

You can select entire databases or any combination of objects to export. Figure 11-9 shows a sample screenshot of the export feature.

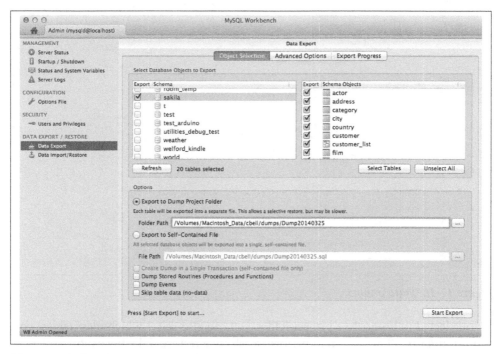

Figure 11-9. Data export

You can dump all the objects and data to a single file, or specify a project folder where each table is saved as a separate *.sql* file that contains the table creation and data insert SQL statements. After you select either option, along with the databases and tables you want to export, and then click Start Export, the associated *mysqldump* commands will run. A summary dialog is opened to display progress of the operation and the exact commands used to issue the export. You can save these commands for use in scripts.

You can also choose to export procedures and functions, events, or not export any data at all (exporting only the table structure). If your database uses InnoDB, you can also tell the tool to use a single transaction to avoid prolonged locking of the tables. In this case, the tool tells *mysqldump* to use the consistent snapshot feature of InnoDB to lock the tables.

Importing data is done via the data import/restore tool (Figure 11-10). It allows you to select an export folder or file to import, a target default database (schema).

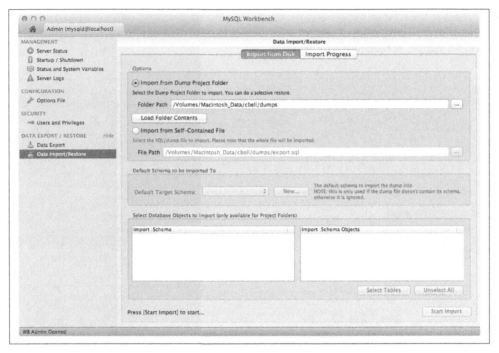

Figure 11-10. Data import

If you elected to export to a project folder, you can also select which files (tables) you want to import, allowing you to perform a selective restore. Like the export tool, executing the import will open a dialog that shows you the progress of the import as well as the *mysqldump* commands.

SQL development

The SQL Editor is another of the GUI tools available in Workbench. It also is not a monitoring tool in and of itself, but, as you shall see, provides a robust environment for constructing complex SQL statements.

You can access the tool from the home window. Here you select an instance, then click Open Connection to Start Querying. Figure 11-11 shows a sample screenshot.

You can use the SQL Editor to build queries and execute them in a graphical form. Result sets are returned and displayed in a spreadsheet-like display. The SQL Editor allows for vertical scrolling through all of the results as well as changing the size of the columns and horizontally scrolling to better view the data. Many users find this tool more convenient and easier to use than the traditional *mysql* command-line client.

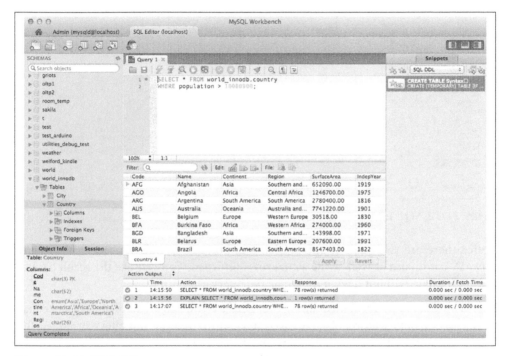

Figure 11-11. SQL Editor

The performance-related functionality and the value added for administrators is the graphical display of the results of the EXPLAIN command for any given query. Figure 11-12 shows a sample explanation of a query from the *world (InnoDB)* database. We will discuss this in greater detail later in the chapter.

The SQL Editor example shown here should give you an indication of the utilitarian value of the GUI. You can enter any query and see the explanation of the query execution by first executing the query, then selecting Explain Query from the Query menu.

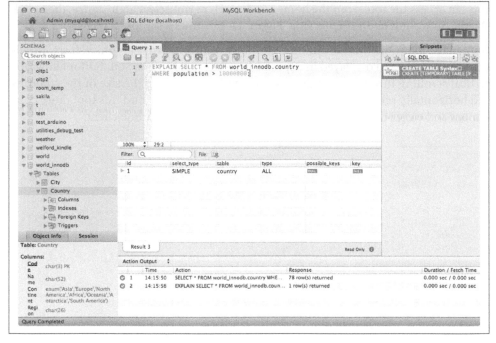

Figure 11-12. SQL Editor: Results view

Notice there are two parts to the results. The bottom part shows the results of the EXPLAIN command as well as the actual rows returned. You can use the scroll bars to view more data without having to reissue the query.

This is a valuable performance tuning tool because you can write the query once, use the Explain Query feature, observe the results, either rewrite the query or adjust the indexes, then reissue the query and observe the changes in the GUI. And you thought query tools were for users only—not so with this tool.

But wait, there's more. The SQL Editor has enhanced editing tools, such as color-coding. To see all of the advanced features and uses for the SQL Editor, check the online MySQL Workbench documentation (*http://bit.ly/mysql-workb*).

Third-Party Tools

Some third-party tools are also useful. Some of the more popular are MySAR, *mytop*, InnoTop, and MONyog. Except for MONyog, they are all text-based (command-line) tools that you can run in any console window and connect to any MySQL server reachable across the network. We discuss each of these briefly in the following sections.

MySAR

MySAR is a system activity report that resembles the output of the Linux `sar` command. MySAR accumulates the output of the `SHOW STATUS`, `SHOW VARIABLES`, and `SHOW FULL PROCESSLIST` commands and stores them in a database on the server named *mysar*. You can configure the data collection in a variety of ways, including limiting the data collected. You can delete older data in order to continue to run MySAR indefinitely and not worry about filling up your disk with status dumps.

MySAR (*http://bit.ly/mysar*) is open source and licensed under the GNU Public License version 2 (GPL v2).

 If you use `sar` to gather a lot of data, you may want to check out the `ksar` (*http://sourceforge.net/projects/ksar/*) tool. The ksar tool is a graphical presentation tool that operates on the output of `sar`.

mytop

The *mytop* utility monitors the thread statistics and general performance statistics of MySQL. It lists common statistics like hostname, version of the server, how many queries have run, the average times of queries, total threads, and other key statistics. It runs the `SHOW PROCESSLIST` and `SHOW STATUS` commands periodically and displays the information in a listing like the `top` command found on Linux. Figure 11-13 shows an example.

```
mytop
MySQL on localhost (5.6.13-log)                         up 0+01:59:56 [16:45:00]
Queries: 129.0   qps:     0 Slow:     0.0      Se/In/Up/De(%):    00/00/00/00
            qps now:     0 Slow qps: 0.0  Threads:    4 (   1/   1) 00/00/00/00
Key Efficiency: 84.0%  Bps in/out:  0.4/ 88.3   Now in/out:   8.4/ 1.9k

      Id      User         Host/IP           DB     Time   Cmd Query or State
      --      ----         -------           --     ----   --- --------------
    6850      root         localhost                   0   Query show full processlist
    6917      root localhost:38019                    251   Sleep
    6918      root localhost:38020                    251   Sleep
       5  ltd_user localhost:57628         mysql    7177   Sleep
       1 system us                                  7195   Connec Slave has read all rela
       2 system us                                  7196   Connec Connecting to master
```

Figure 11-13. The mytop utility

Jeremy D. Zawodny wrote *mytop* (*http://bit.ly/mytop-clone*), and it is still maintained by him along with the MySQL community. It is open source and licensed under the GNU Public License version 2 (GPL v2).

InnoTop

InnoTop is another system activity report that resembles the top command. Inspired by the *mytop* utility, InnoTop has many of the same tools as *mytop*, but is specifically designed to monitor InnoDB performance as well as the MySQL server. You can monitor critical statistics concerning transactions, deadlocks, foreign keys, query activity, replication activity, system variables, and a host of other details.

InnoTop is widely used and considered by some to be a general performance monitoring tool. It has many features that allow you to monitor the system dynamically. If you are using InnoDB primarily as your default (or standard) storage engine and want a well-rounded monitoring tool you can run in text mode, look no further than InnoTop. Figure 11-14 shows an example of the InnoTop utility.

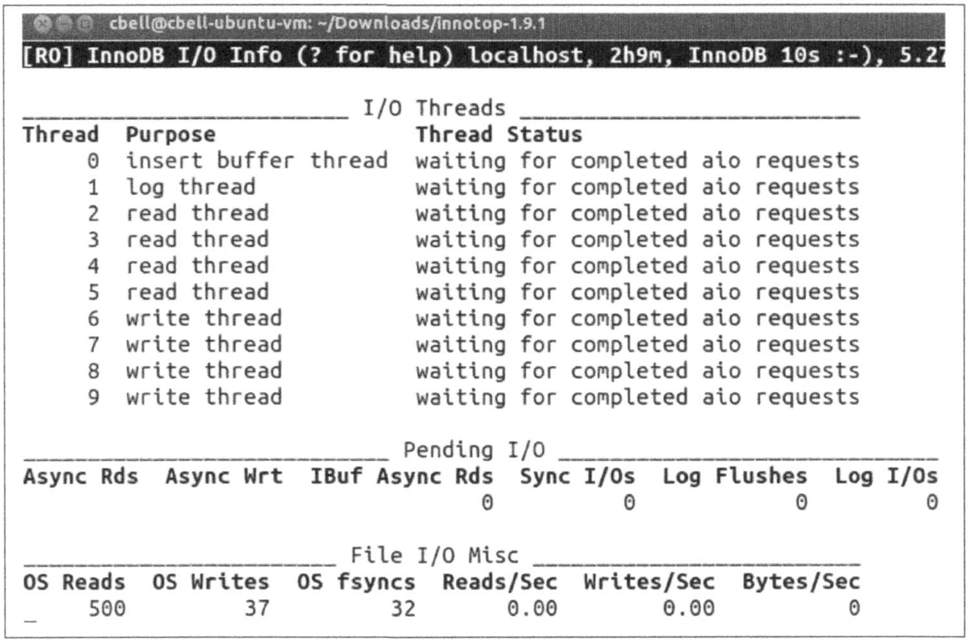

Figure 11-14. The InnoTop utility

The InnoTop utility (*http://bit.ly/innotop-util*) is licensed under the GNU Public License version 2 (GPL v2).

MONyog

MySQL Monitor and Advisor (MONyog) (*http://www.webyog.comf/en*) is another good MySQL monitoring tool. It allows you to set parameters for key components for security and performance, and includes tools to help tune your servers for maximum performance. You can set events to monitor specific parameters and get alerts when the system reaches the specified thresholds. The major features of MONyog are:

- Server resource monitoring
- Identification of poorly executing SQL statements
- Server log monitoring (e.g., the error log)
- Real-time query performance monitoring and identification of long-running queries
- Alerting for significant events

MONyog also provides a GUI component if you prefer to graph the output.

The MySQL Benchmark Suite

Benchmarking is the process of determining how a system performs under certain loads. The act of benchmarking varies greatly and is somewhat of an art form. The goal is to measure and record statistics about the system while running a well-defined set of tests whereby the statistics are recorded under light, medium, and heavy load on the server. In effect, benchmarking sets the expectations for the performance of the system.

This is important because it gives you a hint if your server isn't performing as well as expected. For example, if you encounter a period during which users are reporting slower performance on the server, how do you know the server is performing poorly? Let's say you've checked all of the usual things—memory, disk, etc.—and all are performing within tolerance and without error or other anomalies. How, then, do you know if things are running more slowly?

Enter the benchmarks. You can rerun the benchmark test and if the values produced are much larger (or smaller, depending on what you are measuring), you know the system is performing below expectations.

You can use the MySQL benchmark suite to establish your own benchmarks. The benchmark tool is located in the *sql-bench* folder and is normally included in the source code distribution. The benchmarks are written in Perl and use the Perl DBI module for access to the server. If you do not have Perl or the Perl DBI module, see the section titled "Installing Perl on Unix" in the online MySQL Reference Manual.

Use the following command to run the benchmark suite:

```
./run-all-tests --server=mysql --cmp=mysql --user=root
```

This command will run the entire set of standard benchmark tests, recording the current results and comparing them with known results of running the tests on a MySQL server. Example 11-4 shows an excerpt of the results of running this command on a system with limited resources.

Example 11-4. The MySQL benchmark suite results

```
cbell@cbell-mini:~/source/bzr/mysql-6.0-review/sql-bench$
Benchmark DBD suite: 2.15
Date of test:        2009-12-01 19:54:19
Running tests on:    Linux 2.6.28-16-generic i686
Comments:
Limits from:         mysql
Server version:      MySQL 6.0.14 alpha debug log
Optimization:        None
Hardware:

alter-table: Total time: 77 wallclock secs
 ( 0.12 usr  0.05 sys +  0.00 cusr  0.00 csys =  0.17 CPU)
ATIS: Total time: 150 wallclock secs
 (20.22 usr  0.56 sys +  0.00 cusr  0.00 csys = 20.78 CPU)
big-tables: Total time: 135 wallclock secs
 (45.73 usr  1.16 sys +  0.00 cusr  0.00 csys = 46.89 CPU)
connect: Total time: 1359 wallclock secs
 (200.70 usr 30.51 sys +  0.00 cusr  0.00 csys = 231.21 CPU)
...
```

Although the output of this command isn't immediately valuable, recall that benchmarking is used to track changes in performance over time. Whenever you run the benchmark suite, you should compare it to your known baseline and your last several benchmark checks. Because load can influence the benchmarks, taking the benchmark data over several increments can help mitigate the influence of load for systems that run 24-7.

For example, if you see the wallclock times jump considerably from one run to another, this may not be an indication of a performance slowdown. You should also compare the detailed values, such as user and system time. Of course, an increase in the majority of these values can be an indication that the system is experiencing a heavy load. In this case, you should check the process list to see whether there are indeed a lot of users and queries running. If that is the case, run the benchmark suite again when the load is less and compare the values. If they decrease, you can deduce it was due to sporadic load. On the other hand, if the values remain larger (hence, the system is slower), you should begin investigation as to why the system is taking longer to execute the benchmark tests.

The Benchmark Function

MySQL contains a built-in function called benchmark() that you can use to execute a simple expression and obtain a benchmark result. It is best used when testing other functions or expressions to determine if they are causing delays. The function takes two parameters: a counter for looping and the expression you want to test. The following example shows the results of running 10,000,000 iterations of the CONCAT function:

```
mysql> SELECT BENCHMARK(10000000, "SELECT CONCAT('te','s',' t')");
+----------------------------------------------------+
| BENCHMARK(10000000, "SELECT CONCAT('te','s',' t')") |
+----------------------------------------------------+
|                                                  0 |
+----------------------------------------------------+
1 row in set (0.06 sec)
```

The diagnostic output of this function is the time it takes to run the benchmark function. In this example, it took 0.06 seconds to run the iterations. If you are exploring a complex query, consider testing portions of it using this command. You may find the problem is related to only one part of the query. For more information about the benchmark suite, see the online MySQL Reference Manual.

Now that we have discussed the various tools available for monitoring MySQL and have looked at some best practices, we turn our attention to capturing and preserving operational and diagnostic information using logfiles.

Server Logs

If you are a seasoned Linux or Unix administrator, you are familiar with the concepts and importance of logging. The MySQL server was born of this same environment. Consequently, MySQL creates several logs that contain vital information about errors, events, and data changes.

This section examines the various logs in a MySQL server, including the role each log plays in monitoring and performance improvement. Logfiles can provide a lot of information about past events.

There are several types of logs in the MySQL server:

- General query log
- Slow query log
- Error log
- Binary log

You can turn any of the logs on or off using startup options. Most installations have at least the error log enabled.

The general query log, as its name implies, contains information about what the server is doing, such as connections from clients, as well as a copy of the commands sent to the server. As you can imagine, this log grows very quickly. Examine the general query log whenever you are trying to diagnose client-related errors or to determine which clients are issuing certain types of commands.

Commands in the general query log appear in the same order in which they were *received* from the clients and may not reflect the actual order of execution.

Turn on the general query log by specifying the --general-log startup option. You can also specify the name of the logfile using the --log-output startup option. These options have dynamic variable equivalents. For example, SET GLOBAL log_output = FILE; sets the log output for a running server to write to a file. Finally, you can read the values of either of these variables using the SHOW VARIABLES command.

The slow query log stores a copy of long-running queries. It is in the same format as the general log, and you can control it in the same manner with the --log-slow-queries startup option. The server variable that controls which queries go into the slow query log is log_query_time (in seconds). You should tune this variable to meet the expectations for your server and applications to help track times when queries perform slower than desired. You can send log entries to a file, a table, or both using the FILE, TABLE, or BOTH option, respectively.

The slow query log can be a very effective tool for tracking problems with queries before the users complain. The goal, of course, is to keep this log small or, better still, empty at all times. That is not to say you should set the variable very high; on the contrary, you should set it to your expectations and adjust the value as your expectations or circumstances change.

The slave does not log slow queries by default. However, if you use the --log-slow-slave-statements option, it will write slow-running events to its slow log.

The error log contains information gathered when the MySQL server starts or stops. It also contains the errors generated while the server is running. The error log is your first stop when analyzing a failed or impaired MySQL server. On some operating systems, the error log can also contain a stack trace (or core dump).

You can turn the error log on or off using the --log-error startup option. The default name for the error log is the hostname appended by the extension *.err*. It is saved in the base directory (the same location as the host of the data directory) by default but can be overridden by setting the path with the general_log_file option.

If you start your server with --console, errors are written to standard error output as well as to the error log.

The binary log stores all of the changes made to the data on the server as well as statistical information about the execution of the original command on the server.

The online MySQL Reference Manual states that the binary logs are used for backup; however, practice shows that replication is a more popular use of the binary log.

The unique format of the binary log allows you to use the log for incremental backups, where you store the binlog file created between each backup. You do this by flushing and rotating the binary logs (closing the log and opening a new log); this allows you to save a set of changes since your last backup. This same technique lets you perform PITR, where you restore data from a backup and apply the binary log up to a specific point or date. For more information about the binary log, see Chapter 4. For more information about PITR, see Chapter 15.

Because the binary log makes copies of every data change, it does add a small amount of overhead to the server, but the performance penalty is well worth the benefits. However, system configuration such as disk setup and storage engine choice can greatly affect the overhead of the binary log. For example, there is no concurrent commit when using the InnoDB storage engine. This may be a concern in high-write scenarios with binary logging and InnoDB.

Turn on the binary log using the --log-bin startup option, specifying the root filename of the binary log. The server appends a numeric sequence to the end of the filename, allowing for automatic and manual rotations of the log. While not normally necessary, you can also change the name of the index for the binary logs by specifying the --log-bin-index startup option. Perform log rotations using the FLUSH LOGS command.

You can also control what is logged (inclusive logging) or what is excluded (exclusive logging) using --binlog-do-db and --binlog-ignore-db, respectively.

Performance Schema

In this section, we present the Performance Schema feature as a technique for measuring the internal execution of the server, which can help you diagnose performance problems. While this section introduces the feature and contains a brief startup guide, it does not contain all of the possible configuration and setup parameters and options nor does it contain a complete guide to using the Performance Schema views. For a complete detailed explanation of how to set up and use the Performance Schema tables, see the online reference manual under the heading "MySQL Performance Schema."

A recent addition to the MySQL Server, the Performance Schema feature is presented as a database named performance_schema (sometimes shown in all capitals). It contains a set of dynamic tables (stored in memory) that enable you to see very low-level metrics of server execution. This feature was added to the server in version 5.5.3. The Performance Schema feature provides metadata on the execution of the server, right down to the line of code being executed. Indeed, it is possible to monitor precisely a mechanism in a particular source file.

For this reason, the Performance Schema is often considered a developer tool for diagnosing execution of the server code itself. This is because it is most often used to diagnose deadlocks, mutex, and thread problems. However, it is much more than that! You can get metrics for stages of query optimization, file I/O, connections, and much more. Yes, it is very low level and will indeed show you references to source code. But although most metrics target specific code components, the tool also provides historical data as well as current values for a metric. This can be particularly useful if you are diagnosing a difficult performance problem that you can isolate to a specific use case.

You may be thinking that this would create a tremendous load on the server and incur a severe penalty on performance. For some external monitoring solutions, this is true, but the Performance Schema is designed to have little or no measurable impact on server performance. This is possible because of the way the feature is intertwined with the server: it takes advantage of many of the optimizations in the server that external tools simply cannot.

The following section presents a terse introduction to the terms and concepts used in Performance Schema. Later sections will show you how to use the feature to diagnose performance problems.

Concepts

This section presents the basic concepts of the Performance Schema in an effort to make it easier for you to get started using it to gather metrics.

The Performance Schema appears in your list of databases (SHOW DATABASES) as per formance_schema and contains a number of dynamic tables that you can see with SHOW TABLES. Example 11-5 lists the available tables in an early release candidate for the MySQL 5.6 server.

The number of tables is likely to expand with future releases of the server.

Example 11-5. performance_schema tables

```
mysql> SHOW TABLES;;
+--------------------------------------------------+
| Tables_in_Performance Schema                     |
+--------------------------------------------------+
| accounts                                         |
| cond_instances                                   |
| events_stages_current                            |
| events_stages_history                            |
| events_stages_history_long                       |
| events_stages_summary_by_account_by_event_name   |
| events_stages_summary_by_host_by_event_name      |
| events_stages_summary_by_thread_by_event_name    |
```

```
| events_stages_summary_by_user_by_event_name         |
| events_stages_summary_global_by_event_name          |
| events_statements_current                           |
| events_statements_history                           |
| events_statements_history_long                      |
| events_statements_summary_by_account_by_event_name  |
| events_statements_summary_by_digest                 |
| events_statements_summary_by_host_by_event_name     |
| events_statements_summary_by_thread_by_event_name   |
| events_statements_summary_by_user_by_event_name     |
| events_statements_summary_global_by_event_name      |
| events_waits_current                                |
| events_waits_history                                |
| events_waits_history_long                           |
| events_waits_summary_by_account_by_event_name       |
| events_waits_summary_by_host_by_event_name          |
| events_waits_summary_by_instance                    |
| events_waits_summary_by_thread_by_event_name        |
| events_waits_summary_by_user_by_event_name          |
| events_waits_summary_global_by_event_name           |
| file_instances                                      |
| file_summary_by_event_name                          |
| file_summary_by_instance                            |
| host_cache                                          |
| hosts                                               |
| mutex_instances                                     |
| objects_summary_global_by_type                      |
| performance_timers                                  |
| rwlock_instances                                    |
| session_account_connect_attrs                       |
| session_connect_attrs                               |
| setup_actors                                        |
| setup_consumers                                     |
| setup_instruments                                   |
| setup_objects                                       |
| setup_timers                                        |
| socket_instances                                    |
| socket_summary_by_event_name                        |
| socket_summary_by_instance                          |
| table_io_waits_summary_by_index_usage               |
| table_io_waits_summary_by_table                     |
| table_lock_waits_summary_by_table                   |
| threads                                             |
| users                                               |
+-----------------------------------------------------+
52 rows in set (0.01 sec)
```

Performance Schema monitors *events*, where an event is any discrete execution that has been instrumented (enabled in code and called "instrument points") and has a measurable duration. For example, the event could be a method call, a mutex lock/unlock, or a file I/O. Events are stored as a current event (the most recent value), historical values, and summaries (aggregates).

 Performance Schema events are not the same as binary log events.

An instrument, therefore, consists of the instrument points in the server (source) that produce events when they execute. An instrument must be enabled in order to fire an event.

You can monitor specific users (threads) using the setup_actors table. You can monitor specific tables or all tables in certain databases using the setup_objects table. Currently, only table objects are supported.

A *timer* is a type of execution that is measured by a time duration. Timers include idle, wait, stage, and statement. You can change the duration of timers to change the frequency of the measurement. Values include CYCLE, NANOSECOND, MICROSECOND, MILLI SECOND, and TICK. You can see the available timers by examining the rows in the per formance_timers table.

Setup tables are used to enable or disable actors, instruments, objects (tables), and timers.

Getting Started

Performance Schema can be enabled at startup or at runtime. You can check to see whether your server supports Performance Schema and whether it is turned on by examining the performance_schema variable. A value of ON indicates the feature is enabled. To enable Performance Schema at startup, use the --performance-schema startup option:

```
[mysqld]
…
performance_schema=ON
…
```

Enabling Performance Schema and configuring events to monitor at startup requires the use of several startup options. Depending on the level of detail you want to collect, enabling Performance Schema at startup can become complicated. Fortunately, all of the required and voluntary options and their values can be stored in your configuration file. If you want to collect all available events for a specific server under controlled conditions, it may be easier to enable Performance Schema at startup.

However, most administrators will want to enable Performance Schema at runtime. You must enable Performance Schema either via the --performance-schema startup variable or via your configuration file. Once enabled, you must configure the events you want to record. This involves modifying the rows in the setup and configuration tables. This section will demonstrate the process you use to enable events and instruments for preparing to collect data for diagnosing performance problems.

To enable monitoring with Performance Schema, begin by setting the timers you want to use, setting the events you want to enable, and enabling the instruments you want to monitor.

For example, if you want to monitor all SHOW GRANTS events, begin by setting the timer for the statement object. In this case, we will use the standard NANOSECOND timing. You can check the current setting by examining the setup_timers table:

```
mysql> select * from setup_timers;
+-----------+-------------+
| NAME      | TIMER_NAME  |
+-----------+-------------+
| idle      | MICROSECOND |
| wait      | CYCLE       |
| stage     | NANOSECOND  |
| statement | NANOSECOND  |
+-----------+-------------+
4 rows in set (0.01 sec)
```

Next, enable the instrument for the SQL statement as follows. In this case, we set some columns in the setup_instruments table to YES for the specific command (SHOW GRANTS). More specifically, we enable the instrumentation of the metric and enable the timer property for the metric:

```
mysql> UPDATE setup_instruments SET enabled='YES', timed='YES'
WHERE name = 'statement/sql/show_grants';
Query OK, 1 row affected (0.00 sec)
Rows matched: 1  Changed: 1  Warnings: 0
```

Next, enable the consumers for the events_statements_current and events_statements_history statements:

```
mysql> UPDATE setup_consumers SET enabled='YES'
WHERE name = 'events_statements_current';
Query OK, 0 rows affected (0.00 sec)
Rows matched: 1  Changed: 1  Warnings: 0

mysql> UPDATE setup_consumers SET enabled='YES'
WHERE name = 'events_statements_history';
Query OK, 1 row affected (0.00 sec)
Rows matched: 1  Changed: 1  Warnings: 0
```

Now execute the SHOW GRANTS command and examine the events_statements_current and events_statements_history tables:

```
mysql> show grants \G
*************************** 1. row ***************************
Grants for root@localhost: GRANT ALL PRIVILEGES ON *.* TO 'root'@'localhost'
IDENTIFIED BY PASSWORD '*81F5E21E35407D884A6CD4A731AEBFB6AF209E1B'
WITH GRANT OPTION
*************************** 2. row ***************************
Grants for root@localhost: GRANT PROXY ON ''@'' TO 'root'@'localhost' WITH
GRANT OPTION
2 rows in set (0.01 sec)

mysql> select * from events_statements_current \G
*************************** 1. row ***************************
              THREAD_ID: 22
               EVENT_ID: 80
           END_EVENT_ID: NULL
             EVENT_NAME: statement/sql/select
                 SOURCE: mysqld.cc:903
            TIMER_START: 13104624563678000
              TIMER_END: NULL
             TIMER_WAIT: NULL
              LOCK_TIME: 136000000
               SQL_TEXT: select * from events_statements_current
                 DIGEST: NULL
            DIGEST_TEXT: NULL
         CURRENT_SCHEMA: performance_schema
            OBJECT_TYPE: NULL
          OBJECT_SCHEMA: NULL
            OBJECT_NAME: NULL
   OBJECT_INSTANCE_BEGIN: NULL
            MYSQL_ERRNO: 0
      RETURNED_SQLSTATE: NULL
           MESSAGE_TEXT: NULL
                 ERRORS: 0
               WARNINGS: 0
          ROWS_AFFECTED: 0
              ROWS_SENT: 0
          ROWS_EXAMINED: 0
CREATED_TMP_DISK_TABLES: 0
     CREATED_TMP_TABLES: 0
       SELECT_FULL_JOIN: 0
 SELECT_FULL_RANGE_JOIN: 0
           SELECT_RANGE: 0
     SELECT_RANGE_CHECK: 0
            SELECT_SCAN: 1
      SORT_MERGE_PASSES: 0
             SORT_RANGE: 0
              SORT_ROWS: 0
              SORT_SCAN: 0
          NO_INDEX_USED: 1
     NO_GOOD_INDEX_USED: 0
       NESTING_EVENT_ID: NULL
     NESTING_EVENT_TYPE: NULL
```

```
1 row in set (0.00 sec)

mysql> select * from events_statements_history \G
*************************** 1. row ***************************
              THREAD_ID: 22
               EVENT_ID: 77
           END_EVENT_ID: 77
             EVENT_NAME: statement/sql/select
                 SOURCE: mysqld.cc:903
            TIMER_START: 12919040536455000
              TIMER_END: 12919040870255000
             TIMER_WAIT: 333800000
              LOCK_TIME: 143000000
               SQL_TEXT: select * from events_statements_history
                 DIGEST: 77d3399ea8360ffc7b8d584c0fac948a
            DIGEST_TEXT: SELECT * FROM `events_statements_history`
         CURRENT_SCHEMA: performance_schema
            OBJECT_TYPE: NULL
          OBJECT_SCHEMA: NULL
            OBJECT_NAME: NULL
  OBJECT_INSTANCE_BEGIN: NULL
            MYSQL_ERRNO: 0
      RETURNED_SQLSTATE: NULL
           MESSAGE_TEXT: NULL
                 ERRORS: 0
               WARNINGS: 0
          ROWS_AFFECTED: 0
              ROWS_SENT: 1
          ROWS_EXAMINED: 1
CREATED_TMP_DISK_TABLES: 0
     CREATED_TMP_TABLES: 0
       SELECT_FULL_JOIN: 0
 SELECT_FULL_RANGE_JOIN: 0
           SELECT_RANGE: 0
     SELECT_RANGE_CHECK: 0
            SELECT_SCAN: 1
      SORT_MERGE_PASSES: 0
             SORT_RANGE: 0
              SORT_ROWS: 0
              SORT_SCAN: 0
          NO_INDEX_USED: 1
     NO_GOOD_INDEX_USED: 0
       NESTING_EVENT_ID: NULL
     NESTING_EVENT_TYPE: NULL
*************************** 2. row ***************************
              THREAD_ID: 22
               EVENT_ID: 78
           END_EVENT_ID: 78
             EVENT_NAME: statement/sql/show_grants
                 SOURCE: mysqld.cc:903
            TIMER_START: 12922392541028000
              TIMER_END: 12922392657515000
```

```
              TIMER_WAIT: 116487000
               LOCK_TIME: 0
                SQL_TEXT: show grants
                  DIGEST: 63ca75101f4bfc9925082c9a8b06503b
             DIGEST_TEXT: SHOW GRANTS
          CURRENT_SCHEMA: performance_schema
             OBJECT_TYPE: NULL
           OBJECT_SCHEMA: NULL
             OBJECT_NAME: NULL
    OBJECT_INSTANCE_BEGIN: NULL
             MYSQL_ERRNO: 0
        RETURNED_SQLSTATE: NULL
            MESSAGE_TEXT: NULL
                  ERRORS: 0
                WARNINGS: 0
           ROWS_AFFECTED: 0
               ROWS_SENT: 0
           ROWS_EXAMINED: 0
  CREATED_TMP_DISK_TABLES: 0
       CREATED_TMP_TABLES: 0
         SELECT_FULL_JOIN: 0
   SELECT_FULL_RANGE_JOIN: 0
             SELECT_RANGE: 0
       SELECT_RANGE_CHECK: 0
              SELECT_SCAN: 0
        SORT_MERGE_PASSES: 0
               SORT_RANGE: 0
                SORT_ROWS: 0
                SORT_SCAN: 0
            NO_INDEX_USED: 0
       NO_GOOD_INDEX_USED: 0
         NESTING_EVENT_ID: NULL
       NESTING_EVENT_TYPE: NULL
*************************** 3. row ***************************
               THREAD_ID: 22
                EVENT_ID: 74
            END_EVENT_ID: 74
              EVENT_NAME: statement/sql/show_grants
                  SOURCE: mysqld.cc:903
             TIMER_START: 12887992696398000
               TIMER_END: 12887992796352000
              TIMER_WAIT: 99954000
               LOCK_TIME: 0
                SQL_TEXT: show grants
                  DIGEST: 63ca75101f4bfc9925082c9a8b06503b
             DIGEST_TEXT: SHOW GRANTS
          CURRENT_SCHEMA: performance_schema
             OBJECT_TYPE: NULL
           OBJECT_SCHEMA: NULL
             OBJECT_NAME: NULL
    OBJECT_INSTANCE_BEGIN: NULL
             MYSQL_ERRNO: 0
```

```
         RETURNED_SQLSTATE: NULL
            MESSAGE_TEXT: NULL
                  ERRORS: 0
                WARNINGS: 0
           ROWS_AFFECTED: 0
               ROWS_SENT: 0
           ROWS_EXAMINED: 0
 CREATED_TMP_DISK_TABLES: 0
      CREATED_TMP_TABLES: 0
         SELECT_FULL_JOIN: 0
  SELECT_FULL_RANGE_JOIN: 0
            SELECT_RANGE: 0
      SELECT_RANGE_CHECK: 0
             SELECT_SCAN: 0
        SORT_MERGE_PASSES: 0
               SORT_RANGE: 0
                SORT_ROWS: 0
                SORT_SCAN: 0
            NO_INDEX_USED: 0
       NO_GOOD_INDEX_USED: 0
         NESTING_EVENT_ID: NULL
       NESTING_EVENT_TYPE: NULL
*************************** 4. row ***************************
                THREAD_ID: 22
                 EVENT_ID: 75
             END_EVENT_ID: 75
               EVENT_NAME: statement/sql/select
                   SOURCE: mysqld.cc:903
              TIMER_START: 12890520653158000
                TIMER_END: 12890521011318000
               TIMER_WAIT: 358160000
                LOCK_TIME: 148000000
                 SQL_TEXT: select * from events_statements_current
                   DIGEST: f06ce227c4519dd9d9604a3f1cfe3ad9
              DIGEST_TEXT: SELECT * FROM `events_statements_current`
           CURRENT_SCHEMA: performance_schema
              OBJECT_TYPE: NULL
            OBJECT_SCHEMA: NULL
              OBJECT_NAME: NULL
    OBJECT_INSTANCE_BEGIN: NULL
              MYSQL_ERRNO: 0
        RETURNED_SQLSTATE: NULL
             MESSAGE_TEXT: NULL
                   ERRORS: 0
                 WARNINGS: 0
            ROWS_AFFECTED: 0
                ROWS_SENT: 1
            ROWS_EXAMINED: 1
 CREATED_TMP_DISK_TABLES: 0
       CREATED_TMP_TABLES: 0
         SELECT_FULL_JOIN: 0
  SELECT_FULL_RANGE_JOIN: 0
```

```
                 SELECT_RANGE: 0
           SELECT_RANGE_CHECK: 0
                  SELECT_SCAN: 1
            SORT_MERGE_PASSES: 0
                   SORT_RANGE: 0
                    SORT_ROWS: 0
                    SORT_SCAN: 0
                NO_INDEX_USED: 1
           NO_GOOD_INDEX_USED: 0
            NESTING_EVENT_ID: NULL
          NESTING_EVENT_TYPE: NULL
*************************** 5. row ***************************
                    THREAD_ID: 22
                     EVENT_ID: 76
                 END_EVENT_ID: 76
                   EVENT_NAME: statement/sql/select
                       SOURCE: mysqld.cc:903
                  TIMER_START: 12895480384972000
                    TIMER_END: 12895480736605000
                   TIMER_WAIT: 351633000
                    LOCK_TIME: 144000000
                     SQL_TEXT: select * from events_statements_history
                       DIGEST: 77d3399ea8360ffc7b8d584c0fac948a
                  DIGEST_TEXT: SELECT * FROM `events_statements_history`
               CURRENT_SCHEMA: performance_schema
                  OBJECT_TYPE: NULL
                OBJECT_SCHEMA: NULL
                  OBJECT_NAME: NULL
         OBJECT_INSTANCE_BEGIN: NULL
                  MYSQL_ERRNO: 0
             RETURNED_SQLSTATE: NULL
                 MESSAGE_TEXT: NULL
                       ERRORS: 0
                     WARNINGS: 0
                ROWS_AFFECTED: 0
                    ROWS_SENT: 1
                ROWS_EXAMINED: 1
      CREATED_TMP_DISK_TABLES: 0
           CREATED_TMP_TABLES: 0
             SELECT_FULL_JOIN: 0
       SELECT_FULL_RANGE_JOIN: 0
                 SELECT_RANGE: 0
           SELECT_RANGE_CHECK: 0
                  SELECT_SCAN: 1
            SORT_MERGE_PASSES: 0
                   SORT_RANGE: 0
                    SORT_ROWS: 0
                    SORT_SCAN: 0
                NO_INDEX_USED: 1
           NO_GOOD_INDEX_USED: 0
             NESTING_EVENT_ID: NULL
```

```
          NESTING_EVENT_TYPE: NULL
  5 rows in set (0.00 sec)
```

Notice that the output for the `events_statements_table` shows only the last recorded statement executed, whereas the output for `events_statements_history` shows recent queries from those events enabled. We enabled both the `statement/sql/select` and `statement/sql/show_grants` instruments in this example, so events of both types are shown.

While the example is rather simplistic, there is a wealth of information we can gain from using this technique. For example, we see the output includes timing information, such as when the query started and ended as well as lock time. We also see warning and error counts, information about how the query was optimized, and indications of whether indexes were used.

The steps in this example are representative of the steps you would use to enable other instruments and events. In summary, you should do the following to enable monitoring using the Performance Schema:

1. Set the timer (applies to instruments with a timing element).
2. Enable the instrument.
3. Enable the consumer.

Filtering Events

There are two techniques for filtering events: *prefiltering* and *postfiltering*.

Prefiltering is accomplished by modifying the Performance Schema setup configuration to turn on only those events you want to collect from certain producers and collected by certain consumers. Prefiltering reduces overhead and avoids filling the history tables with metrics that you don't need, and avoid filling tables that are not needed (by not maintaining consumers). The drawback of prefiltering is that it requires you to predict which events you want to check before you run your test.

Postfiltering is typically done by enabling a host of producers and consumers to collect as much information as possible. Filtering is done after the data is collected by using WHERE clauses on the Performance Schema tables. Postfiltering is done on a per-user basis (in the WHERE clause). You would use postfiltering in cases where you are not certain which events you need to collect: for example, when there is no repeatable use case.

Which to use depends on your preference for the amount of data to collect. If you know what you are looking for (the metrics to measure) and you want only to record those events, prefiltering will be the technique to use. On the other hand, if you are unsure of what you are looking for or you need to generate data metrics over time, you may want to consider postfiltering and explore the Performance Schema tables using SELECT statements to narrow the scope of your search.

Using Performance Schema to Diagnose Performance Problems

This section presents an alternative to the methodology listed in the online reference manual for diagnosing problems using the Performance Schema. It includes a much improved process that ensures your server is returned to its original state.

Like the example in the reference manual, the methodology assumes you have a set of operations that exhibit a repeatable problem over several databases.

One word of caution: it is likely your use case will not be so cut and dry and you may need to be able to reproduce more than just the data and the queries. For example, if your diagnosis involves problems associated with load or certain other conditions (a number of connections, a certain application, etc.), you may need to be able to reproduce the load and similar conditions.

Another condition you should sort out before using Performance Schema is what parameters, variables, and options you will use to tune your server. It does little good to tinker with your server if you are not certain what you need to tune. You may not be able to know precisely what to tune, but you should have a good idea at this point. Also, be sure to record the current value before you change it. The normal course of tuning is to change one and only one thing at a time, and to compare the performance before and after the change. If no positive change occurs, you should restore the original value before moving on to another parameter or option.

The following lists the steps you can use to diagnose your performance problem with Performance Schema:

1. Query the setup_instruments table to identify all related instruments and enable them.

2. Set up the timers for the frequency that you need to record. Most times, the defaults are the correct timer values. If you change the timers, record their original values.

3. Identify the consumers (event tables) associated with the instruments and enable them. Be sure to enable the current, history, and history_long variants.

4. Truncate the *history and *history_long tables to ensure you start with a "clean" state.

5. Reproduce the problem.

6. Query the Performance Schema tables. If your server has multiple clients running, you can isolate the rows by thread ID.

7. Observe the values and record them.

8. Tune one option/parameter/variable set.

9. Return to step 5. Repeat until performance is improved.

10. Truncate the *history and history_long tables to ensure you end with a "clean" state.

11. Disable the events you enabled.

12. Disable the instruments you enabled.

13. Return the timers to their original state.

14. Truncate the *history and history_long tables once more to ensure you end with a "clean" state.

MySQL Monitoring Taxonomy

The previous sections have demonstrated a number of devices you can use to monitor MySQL. Some devices, such as system and status variables, have many metrics you can inspect for clues to uncover the cause of the performance, accessibility, or resource issue. Learning what can or should be used is crucial to solving the problem, and can save days of research.

What is needed is a map to the various devices, tools, and metrics for monitoring MySQL. The following table presents a classification of monitoring devices you can use to effectively monitor your MySQL servers. Table 11-1 organizes tasks by focus area, device, and metric. Examples are shown to give context for the metrics.

Table 11-1. MySQL monitoring taxonomy

Focus	Device	Metric	Example
Performance	System Variables	Query Cache	`SHOW VARIABLES LIKE '%query_cache%'`
Performance	Status Variables	Number of Inserts	`SHOW STATUS LIKE 'com_insert'`
Performance	Status Variables	Number of Deletes	`SHOW STATUS LIKE 'com_delete'`
Performance	Status Variables	Table Lock Collisions	`SHOW STATUS LIKE 'table_locks_wai ted'`
Performance	Logging	Slow Queries	`SELECT * FROM slow_log ORDER BY query_time DESC`
Performance	Logging	General	`SELECT * FROM general_log`
Performance	Logging	Errors	`--log-error=file name` (startup variable)
Performance	Performance Schema	Thread Information	`SELECT * FROM threads`
Performance	Performance Schema	Mutex Information	`SELECT * FROM events_wait_current`
Performance	Performance Schema	Mutex Information	`SELECT * FROM mutex_instances`
Performance	Performance Schema	File Use Summary	`SELECT * FROM file_summary_by_in stance`

Focus	Device	Metric	Example
Performance	Storage Engine Features	InnoDB Status	`SHOW ENGINE innodb STATUS`
Performance	Storage Engine Features	InnoDB Statistics	`SHOW STATUS LIKE '%Innodb%'`
Performance	External Tools	Processlist	`mysqladmin -uroot --password process list --sleep 3`
Performance	External Tools	Connection Health (graph)	MySQL Workbench
Performance	External Tools	Memory Health (graph)	MySQL Workbench
Performance	External Tools	InnoDB Rows Read	MySQL Workbench
Performance	External Tools	Logs	MySQL Workbench
Performance	External Tools	All Variables	MySQL Workbench
Performance	External Tools	Query Plan/Execution[a]	MySQL Workbench
Performance	External Tools	Benchmarking	MySQL Benchmark Suite
Availability	Status Variables	Connected Threads	`SHOW STATUS LIKE 'threads_connected'`
Availability	Operating System Tools	Accessibility	*ping*
Availability	External Tools	Accessibility	`mysqladmin -uroot --password extended-status --relative --sleep 3`
Resources	Status Variables	Storage Engines Supported	`SHOW ENGINES`
Resources	Operating System Tools	CPU Usage	`top -n 1 -pid mysqld_pid`
Resources	Operating System Tools	RAM Usage	`top -n 1 -pid mysqld_pid`
Resources	MySQL Utilities	Disk Usage	*mysqldiskusage*
Resources	MySQL Utilities	Server Information	*mysqlserverinfo*
Resources	MySQL Utilities	Replication Health	*mysqlrpladmin*

[a] You can also use the EXPLAIN SQL command.

As you can see, the bulk of monitoring techniques are geared toward performance monitoring. This is no surprise, given that the database server is often the focus of many applications and potentially thousands of users. You can also see from this table that there are several devices you can use to help investigate performance problems. Often, several of these devices and the metrics they expose will lead you to the solution to your performance issue. However, now that you have a road map of how to approach MySQL monitoring, you can use it to help focus your efforts on the appropriate devices.

It is often the case that you need to investigate performance problems for a particular database (or several databases) or must improve the performance of a set of queries that are causing performance bottlenecks in your applications. We study the techniques and best practices for improving database and query performance in the following sections.

Database Performance

Monitoring the performance of an individual database is one of the few areas in the MySQL feature set where community and third-party developers have improved the MySQL experience. MySQL includes some basic tools you can use to improve performance, but they do not have the sophistication of some other system-tuning tools. Due to this limitation, most MySQL DBAs earn their pay through experience in relational query optimization techniques. We recognize there are several excellent references that cover database performance in great detail and many readers are likely to be well versed in basic database optimization. Here are a few resources for you to turn to:

- Refactoring SQL Applications by Stephane Faroult and Pascal L'Hermite (O'Reilly)
- SQL and Relational Theory: How to Write Accurate SQL Code by C.J. Date (O'Reilly)
- SQL Cookbook by Anthony Mollinaro (O'Reilly)

Rather than reintroducing query optimization techniques, we will concentrate on how you can work with the tools available in MySQL to assist in optimizing databases. We will use a simple example and a known sample database to illustrate the use of the query performance command in MySQL. In the next section, we list best practices for improving database performance.

Measuring Database Performance

Traditionally, database management systems have provided profiling tools and indexing tools that report statistics you can use to fine-tune indexes. Although there are some basic elements that can help you improve database performance in MySQL, there is no advanced profiling tool available as open source.

Although the basic MySQL installation does not include formal tools for monitoring database improvement, the MySQL Enterprise Manager suite offers a host of performance monitoring features. We will discuss this tool in more detail in Chapter 16.

Fortunately, MySQL provides a few simple tools to help you determine whether your tables and queries are optimal. They are all SQL commands and include EXPLAIN, ANALYZE TABLE, and OPTIMIZE TABLE. The following sections describe each of these commands in greater detail.

Using EXPLAIN

The EXPLAIN command gives information about how a SELECT statement (EXPLAIN works only for SELECT statements) can be executed. Here is the syntax for EXPLAIN (note that EXPLAIN is a synonym for the DESCRIBE command found in other database systems):

```
[EXPLAIN | DESCRIBE] [EXTENDED] SELECT select options
```

You can also use the EXPLAIN and DESCRIBE commands to view details about the columns or partitions of a table. The syntax for this version of the command is:

```
[EXPLAIN | DESCRIBE] [PARTITIONS SELECT * FROM] table_name
```

 A synonym for EXPLAIN table_name is SHOW COLUMNS FROM table_name.

We will discuss the first use of the EXPLAIN command, examining a SELECT command to see how the MySQL optimizer executes the statement. The results of this contain a step-by-step list of join operations that the optimizer predicts it would require to execute the statement.

The best use of this command is to determine whether you have the best indexes on your tables to allow for more precise targeting of candidate rows. You can also use the results to test the various optimizer override options. While this is an advanced technique and generally discouraged, under the right circumstances you may encounter a query that runs faster with certain optimizer options. We will see an example of this later in this section.

Now let's look at some examples of the EXPLAIN command in action. The following examples are queries executed on the *sakila* sample database (*http://bit.ly/sakila-sd*) provided for MySQL development and experimentation.

Let's begin with a simple and seemingly harmless query. Let's say we want to see all of the films rated higher than a PG rating. The result set contains a single row with the following columns:

id
: Sequence number of the statement in order of execution

select_type
: The type of statement executed

table
: The table operated on for this step

type
: The type of join to be used

possible_keys
: A list of columns available if there are indexes that include the primary key

key
: The key selected by the optimizer

key_len
> The length of the key or portion of the key used

ref
> Constraints or columns to be compared

rows
> An estimate of the number of rows to process

extra
> Additional information from the optimizer

 If the type column shows ALL, you are doing a full table scan. You should strive to avoid that by adding indexes or rewriting your query. Similarly, if this column shows INDEX, you are doing a full index scan, which is very inefficient. See the online MySQL Reference Manual for more details on the types of joins and their consequences.

Example 11-6 shows how the MySQL optimizer executes this statement. We use the \G to request a vertical display format for clarity.

The table we are using in the example contains a field (column) that is defined as an enumerated type. Enumerated types permit you to provide a list of possible values. If you did not use the enumerated type and defined a lookup table, you would have to perform a join to select results with the value of the field. Thus, enumerated values can replace small lookup tables and therefore enumerated values can be used to improve performance.

This is because the text for the enumerated values is stored only once—in the table header structures. What is saved in the rows is a numeric reference value that forms an index (array index) of the enumerated value. Enumerated value lists can save space and can make traversing the data a bit more efficient. An enumerated field type allows one and only one value.

In the following example, the film table in the *sakila* database has an enumerated field named rating taking the values G, PG, PG-13, R, and NC-17. In the examples that follow, we will see how this enumerated value field can be used (and misused) in queries.

Example 11-6. A simple SELECT statement

```
mysql> EXPLAIN SELECT * FROM film WHERE rating > 'PG' \G
*************************** 1. row ***************************
           id: 1
  select_type: SIMPLE
        table: film
         type: ALL
possible_keys: NULL
          key: NULL
```

```
      key_len: NULL
          ref: NULL
         rows: 892
        Extra: Using where
1 row in set (0.01 sec)
```

You can see from this output that the optimizer has only one step to execute and that it is not using any indexes. This makes sense because we are not using any columns with indexes. Furthermore, even though there is a WHERE clause, the optimizer will still have to do a full table scan. This may be the right choice when you consider the columns used and the lack of indexes. However, if we ran this query hundreds of thousands of times, the full table scan would be a very poor use of time. In this case, we know from looking at the results that adding an index should improve execution (Example 11-7).

Example 11-7. Adding an index to improve query performance

```
mysql> ALTER TABLE film ADD INDEX film_rating (rating);
Query OK, 0 rows affected (0.42 sec)
Records: 0  Duplicates: 0  Warnings: 0
```

Let's add an index to the table and try again. Example 11-8 shows the improved query plan.

Example 11-8. Improved query plan

```
mysql> EXPLAIN SELECT * FROM film WHERE rating >  'PG' \G
*************************** 1. row ***************************
           id: 1
  select_type: SIMPLE
        table: film
         type: ALL
possible_keys: film_rating
          key: NULL
      key_len: NULL
          ref: NULL
         rows: 892
        Extra: Using where
1 row in set (0.00 sec)
```

 For those of you with sharp eyes who have already spotted the problem, bear with us as we work through it.

Here we see that the query has now identified an index (possible_keys) but is still not using the index, because the key field is NULL. So what can we do? For this simple example, you may note that only 892 rows are expected to be read. The actual row count is 1,000 rows and the result set would contain only 418 rows. Clearly, it would be a much faster query if it read only 42% of the rows!

Now let's see whether we can get any additional information from the optimizer by using the EXTENDED keyword. This keyword allows us to see extra information via the SHOW WARNINGS command. You should issue the command immediately after the EX PLAIN command. The warning text describes how the optimizer identifies table and column names in the statement, the internal rewrite of the query, any optimizer rules applied, and any additional notes about the execution. Example 11-9 shows the results of using the EXTENDED keyword.

Example 11-9. Using the EXTENDED keyword for more information

```
mysql> EXPLAIN EXTENDED SELECT * FROM film WHERE rating >  'PG' \G
*************************** 1. row ***************************
           id: 1
  select_type: SIMPLE
        table: film
         type: ALL
possible_keys: film_rating
          key: NULL
      key_len: NULL
          ref: NULL
         rows: 892
     filtered: 100.00
        Extra: Using where
1 row in set, 1 warning (0.00 sec)

mysql> SHOW WARNINGS \G
*************************** 1. row ***************************
  Level: Note
   Code: 1003
Message: select `sakila`.`film`.`film_id` AS `film_id`,
`sakila`.`film`.`title` AS `title`,`sakila`.`film`.`description` AS `description`,
`sakila`.`film`.`release_year` AS `release_year`,
`sakila`.`film`.`language_id` AS `language_id`,
`sakila`.`film`.`original_language_id` AS `original_language_id`,
`sakila`.`film`.`rental_duration` AS `rental_duration`,
`sakila`.`film`.`rental_rate` AS `rental_rate`,
`sakila`.`film`.`length` AS `length`,
`sakila`.`film`.`replacement_cost` AS `replacement_cost`,
`sakila`.`film`.`rating` AS `rating`,
`sakila`.`film`.`special_features` AS `special_features`,
`sakila`.`film`.`last_update` AS `last_update`
from `sakila`.`film` where (`sakila`.`film`.`rating` > 'PG')
1 row in set (0.00 sec)
```

This time, there is one warning that contains information from the optimizer, displaying a rewritten form of the query to include all columns and explicitly reference the column in the WHERE clause. While this has told us the query can be written a bit better, it doesn't suggest any performance improvements. Fortunately, we can make it more efficient.

Let's see what happens when we issue a query for a specific rating rather than using a range query. We will see the optimization with the index and without. Example 11-10 shows the results.

Example 11-10. Removing the range query

```
mysql> EXPLAIN SELECT * FROM film WHERE rating = 'R' \G
*************************** 1. row ***************************
           id: 1
  select_type: SIMPLE
        table: film
         type: ref
possible_keys: film_rating
          key: film_rating
      key_len: 2
          ref: const
         rows: 195
        Extra: Using where
1 row in set (0.00 sec)

mysql> ALTER TABLE film DROP INDEX film_rating;
Query OK, 0 rows affected (0.37 sec)
Records: 0  Duplicates: 0  Warnings: 0

mysql> EXPLAIN SELECT * FROM film WHERE rating = 'R' \G
*************************** 1. row ***************************
           id: 1
  select_type: SIMPLE
        table: film
         type: ALL
possible_keys: NULL
          key: NULL
      key_len: NULL
          ref: NULL
         rows: 892
        Extra: Using where
1 row in set (0.00 sec)
```

Now we see a little improvement. Notice that the first query plan does indeed use the index and results in a much improved plan. The question then remains, why doesn't the optimizer use the index? In this case, we've used a nonunique index on an enumerated field. What sounded like a really good idea is actually not much help at all for a range query of enumerated values. However, we could rewrite the query differently (in several ways, actually) to produce better performance. Let's look at the query again.

We know we want all films rated higher than PG. We assumed that the rating is ordered and that the enumerated field reflects the order. Thus, it appears the order is maintained if we accept the enumeration index for each value that corresponds to the order (e.g., G = 1, PG = 2, etc.). But what if the order is incorrect or if (like in this example) the list of values is incomplete?

In the example we've chosen, where we want all of the films that have a rating higher than PG, we know from our list of ratings that this includes films with a rating of R or NC-17. Rather than using a range query, let's examine what the optimizer would do if we listed these values.

Recall that we removed the index, so we will try the query first without the index, then add the index and see if we have an improvement. Example 11-11 shows the improved query.

Example 11-11. Improved query without range

```
mysql> EXPLAIN SELECT * FROM film WHERE rating = 'R' OR rating = 'NC-17' \G
*************************** 1. row ***************************
           id: 1
  select_type: SIMPLE
        table: film
         type: ALL
possible_keys: NULL
          key: NULL
      key_len: NULL
          ref: NULL
         rows: 892
        Extra: Using where
1 row in set (0.00 sec)

mysql> ALTER TABLE film ADD INDEX film_rating (rating);
Query OK, 0 rows affected (0.40 sec)
Records: 0  Duplicates: 0  Warnings: 0

mysql> EXPLAIN SELECT * FROM film WHERE rating = 'R' OR rating = 'NC-17' \G
*************************** 1. row ***************************
           id: 1
  select_type: SIMPLE
        table: film
         type: ALL
possible_keys: film_rating
          key: NULL
      key_len: NULL
          ref: NULL
         rows: 892
        Extra: Using where
1 row in set (0.00 sec)
```

Alas, that didn't work either. Again, we have chosen to query on a column that has an index but is not an index the optimizer can use. However, the optimizer can use the index for a simple equality comparison because the values being compared are stored in the index. We can exploit this by rewriting the query as the union of two queries. Example 11-12 shows the rewritten query.

Example 11-12. Query rewritten using UNION

```
mysql> EXPLAIN SELECT * FROM film WHERE rating = 'R' UNION
SELECT * FROM film WHERE rating = 'NC-17' \G
*************************** 1. row ***************************
           id: 1
  select_type: PRIMARY
        table: film
         type: ref
possible_keys: film_rating
          key: film_rating
      key_len: 2
          ref: const
         rows: 195
        Extra: Using where
*************************** 2. row ***************************
           id: 2
  select_type: UNION
        table: film
         type: ref
possible_keys: film_rating
          key: film_rating
      key_len: 2
          ref: const
         rows: 210
        Extra: Using where
*************************** 3. row ***************************
           id: NULL
  select_type: UNION RESULT
        table: <union1,2>
         type: ALL
possible_keys: NULL
          key: NULL
      key_len: NULL
          ref: NULL
         rows: NULL
        Extra:
3 rows in set (0.00 sec)
```

Success! Now we can see we have a query plan that is using the index and processing far fewer rows. We can see from the result of the EXPLAIN command that the optimizer is running each query individually (steps execute from row 1 down to row *n*) and combines the result in the last step.

MySQL has a session status variable named `last_query_cost` that stores the cost of the most recent query executed. Use this variable to compare two query plans for the same query. For example, after each `EXPLAIN`, check the value of the variable. The query with the lowest cost value is considered the more efficient (less time-consuming) query. A value of 0 indicates that no query has been submitted for compilation.

While this exercise may seem to be a lot of work for a little gain, consider that there are many such queries being executed in applications without anyone noticing the inefficiency. Normally we encounter these types of queries only when the row count gets large enough to notice. In the *sakila* database, there are only 1,000 rows, but what if there were a million or tens of millions of rows?

`EXPLAIN` is the only tool in a standard MySQL distribution that you can use by itself to profile a query in MySQL. The "Optimization" chapter in the online MySQL Reference Manual has a host of tips and tricks to help an experienced DBA improve the performance of various query forms.

Using ANALYZE TABLE

The MySQL optimizer, like most traditional optimizers, uses statistical information about tables to perform its analysis of the optimal query execution plan. These statistics include information about indexes, distribution of values, and table structure, among many items.

The `ANALYZE TABLE` command recalculates the key distribution for one or more tables. This information determines the table order for a join operation. The syntax for the `ANALYZE TABLE` command is:

```
ANALYZE [LOCAL | NO_WRITE_TO_BINLOG] TABLE table_list
```

You should run this command whenever there have been significant updates to the table (e.g., bulk-loaded data). The system must have a read lock on the table for the duration of the operation.

You can update the key distribution only for MyISAM and InnoDB tables. Other storage engines don't support this tool, but all storage engines must report index cardinality statistics to the optimizer if they support indexes. Some storage engines, particularly third-party engines, have their own specific built-in statistics. A typical execution of the command is shown in Example 11-13. Running the command on a table with no indexes has no effect, but will not result in an error.

Example 11-13. Analyzing a table to update key distribution

```
mysql> ANALYZE TABLE film;
+-------------+---------+----------+----------+
| Table       | Op      | Msg_type | Msg_text |
+-------------+---------+----------+----------+
| sakila.film | analyze | status   | OK       |
+-------------+---------+----------+----------+
1 row in set (0.00 sec)
```

 If you are using InnoDB, there are some cases when you should not use this command. See `innodb_stats_persistent` in the online reference manual for more details.

In this example, we see that the analysis is complete and there are no unusual conditions. Should there be any unusual events during the execution of the command, the `Msg_type` field can indicate `info`, `Error`, or `warning`. In these cases, the `Msg_text` field will give you additional information about the event. You should always investigate the situation if you get any result other than `status` and `OK`.

For example, if the *.frm* file for your table is corrupt or missing, you could see the following messages. In other cases, the output may indicate the table is unreadable (e.g., permission/access issues). Also, the command performs checks specific to the storage engine. In the case of InnoDB, the checks are more thorough and when there are errors, you are likely to see InnoDB-specific errors.

Example 11-14. Analyze table errors

```
mysql> ANALYZE TABLE test.t1;
+---------+---------+----------+-------------------------------+
| Table   | Op      | Msg_type | Msg_text                      |
+---------+---------+----------+-------------------------------+
| test.t1 | analyze | Error    | Table 'test.t1' doesn't exist |
| test.t1 | analyze | status   | Operation failed              |
+---------+---------+----------+-------------------------------+
2 rows in set (0.00 sec)
```

You can see the status of your indexes using the `SHOW INDEX` command. A sample of the output of the film table is shown in Example 11-15. In this case, we're interested in the cardinality of each index, which is an estimate of the number of unique values in it. We omit the other columns from the display for brevity. For more information about `SHOW INDEX`, see the online MySQL Reference Manual.

Example 11-15. The indexes for the film table

```
mysql> SHOW INDEX FROM film \G
*************************** 1. row ***************************
        Table: film
```

```
   Non_unique: 0
     Key_name: PRIMARY
 Seq_in_index: 1
  Column_name: film_id
    Collation: A
  Cardinality: 1028
…
*************************** 2. row ***************************
        Table: film
   Non_unique: 1
     Key_name: idx_title
 Seq_in_index: 1
  Column_name: title
    Collation: A
  Cardinality: 1028
…
*************************** 3. row ***************************
        Table: film
   Non_unique: 1
     Key_name: idx_fk_language_id
 Seq_in_index: 1
  Column_name: language_id
    Collation: A
  Cardinality: 2
…
*************************** 4. row ***************************
        Table: film
   Non_unique: 1
     Key_name: idx_fk_original_language_id
 Seq_in_index: 1
  Column_name: original_language_id
    Collation: A
  Cardinality: 2
…
*************************** 5. row ***************************
        Table: film
   Non_unique: 1
     Key_name: film_rating
 Seq_in_index: 1
  Column_name: rating
    Collation: A
  Cardinality: 11
     Sub_part: NULL
       Packed: NULL
         Null: YES
   Index_type: BTREE
      Comment:
5 rows in set (0.00 sec)
```

Using OPTIMIZE TABLE

Tables that are updated frequently with new data and deletions can become fragmented quickly and, depending on the storage engine, can have gaps of unused space or suboptimal storage structures. A badly fragmented table can result in slower performance, especially during table scans.

The OPTIMIZE TABLE command restructures the data structures for one or more tables. This is especially beneficial for row formats with variable length fields (rows). It can be used only for MyISAM and InnoDB tables. The syntax is:

```
OPTIMIZE [LOCAL | NO_WRITE_TO_BINLOG] TABLE table_list
```

 The LOCAL or NO_WRITE_TO_BINLOG keyword prevents the command from being written to the binary log (and thereby from being replicated in a replication topology). This can be very useful if you want to experiment or tune while replicating data or if you want to omit this step from your binary log and not replay it during PITR.

You should run this command whenever there have been significant updates to the table (e.g., a large number of deletes and inserts). This operation is designed to rearrange data elements into a more optimal structure and could run for quite a long time (holding write locks on the table). So this is one operation that is best run during times of low loads.

If the table cannot be reorganized (perhaps because there are no variable length records or there is no fragmentation), the command will recreate the table and update the statistics. A sample output from this operation is shown in Example 11-16.

Example 11-16. The optimize table command

```
mysql> OPTIMIZE TABLE film \G
*************************** 1. row ***************************
   Table: sakila.film
      Op: optimize
Msg_type: note
Msg_text: Table does not support optimize, doing recreate + analyze instead
*************************** 2. row ***************************
   Table: sakila.film
      Op: optimize
Msg_type: status
Msg_text: OK
2 rows in set (0.44 sec)
```

Here we see two rows in the result set. The first row tells us that the OPTIMIZE TABLE command could not be run and that the command will instead recreate the table and run the ANALYZE TABLE command. The second row is the result of the ANALYZE TABLE step.

Like the `ANALYZE TABLE` command, any unusual events during the execution of the command are indicated in the `Msg_type` field by `info`, `Error`, or `warning`. In these cases, the `Msg_text` field will give you additional information about the event. You should always investigate the situation if you get any result other than `status` and `OK`.

 When using InnoDB, especially when there are secondary indexes (which usually get fragmented), you may not see any improvement or may encounter long processing times for the operation unless you use the InnoDB "fast index create" option, but this depends on how the index was constructed. It may not apply to all indexes.

Best Practices for Database Optimization

As mentioned previously, there are many great examples, techniques, and practices concerning optimization that come highly recommended by the world's best database performance experts. Because monitoring is used to detect and diagnose performance issues, we include these best practices as a summary for the lessons learned about monitoring MySQL.

For brevity, and to avoid controversial techniques, we will discuss a few commonly agreed-upon best practices for improving database performance. We encourage you to examine some of the texts referenced earlier for more detail on each of these practices.

Use indexes sparingly but effectively

Most database professionals understand the importance of indexes and how they improve performance. Using the `EXPLAIN` command is often the best way to determine which indexes are needed. While the problem of not having enough indexes is understood, having too much of a good thing can also cause a performance issue.

As you saw when exploring the `EXPLAIN` command, it is possible to create too many indexes or indexes that are of little or no use. Each index adds overhead for every insertion and deletion against the table. In some cases, having too many indexes with wide (as in many values) distributions can slow insert and delete performance considerably. It can also lead to slower replication and restore operations.

You should periodically check your indexes to ensure they are all meaningful and utilized. Remove any indexes that are not used, have limited use, or have wide distributions. You can often use normalization to overcome some of the problems with wide distributions.

Use normalization, but don't overdo it

Many database experts who studied computer science or a related discipline may have fond memories (or nightmares) of learning the normal forms as described by C.J. Date and others. We won't revisit the material here; rather, we will discuss the impacts of taking those lessons too far.

Normalization (at least to third normal form) is a well-understood and standard practice. However, there are situations in which you may want to violate these rules.

The use of lookup tables is often a by-product of normalization (i.e., you create a special table that contains a list of related information that is used frequently in other tables). However, you can impede performance when you use lookup tables with limited distributions (only a few rows or a limited number of rows with small values) that are accessed frequently. In this case, every time your users query information, they must use a join to get the complete data. Joins are expensive, and frequently accessed data can add up over time. To mitigate this potential performance problem, you can use enumerated fields to store the data rather than a lookup table. For example, rather than creating a table for hair color (despite what some subcultures may insist upon, there really are only a limited number of hair color types), you can use an enumerated field and avoid the join altogether.

For example, if you created a child table to contain the possible values of hair color, the master table would contain a field whose value is an index into the hair color table. When you execute a query to get results from the master table, you would have to do a join to get the values for the hair color field. If you used an enumerated field, you can eliminate the need for the join and thus improve performance.

Another potential issue concerns calculated fields. Typically, we do not store data that is formed from other data (such as sales tax or the sum of several columns). Rather, the calculated data is performed either during data retrieval via a view or in the application. This may not be a problem if the calculations are simple or are seldom performed, but what if the calculations are complex and are performed many times? In this case, you are potentially wasting a lot of time performing these calculations. One way to mitigate this problem is to use a trigger to calculate the value and store it in the table. While this technically duplicates data (a big no-no for normalization theorists), it can improve performance when a lot of calculations are being performed.

Use the right storage engine for the task

One of the most powerful features of MySQL is its support for different storage engines. Storage engines govern how data is stored and retrieved. MySQL supports a number of them, each with unique features and uses. This allows database designers to tune their database performance by selecting the storage engine that best meets their application needs. For example, if you have an environment that requires transaction control for highly active databases, choose a storage engine best suited for this task. You may also have identified a view or table that is often queried but almost never updated (e.g., a lookup table). In this case, you may want to use a storage engine that keeps the data in memory for faster access.

Recent changes to MySQL have permitted some storage engines to become plug-ins, and some distributions of MySQL have only certain storage engines enabled by default. To find out which storage engines are enabled, issue the SHOW ENGINES command. Example 11-17 shows the storage engines on a typical installation.

Example 11-17. Storage engines

```
mysql> SHOW ENGINES \G
*************************** 1. row ***************************
      Engine: InnoDB
     Support: YES
     Comment: Supports transactions, row-level locking, and foreign keys
Transactions: YES
          XA: YES
  Savepoints: YES
*************************** 2. row ***************************
      Engine: MyISAM
     Support: DEFAULT
     Comment: Default engine as of MySQL 3.23 with great performance
Transactions: NO
          XA: NO
  Savepoints: NO
*************************** 3. row ***************************
      Engine: BLACKHOLE
     Support: YES
     Comment: /dev/null storage engine (anything you write to it disappears)
Transactions: NO
          XA: NO
  Savepoints: NO
*************************** 4. row ***************************
      Engine: CSV
     Support: YES
     Comment: CSV storage engine
Transactions: NO
          XA: NO
  Savepoints: NO
*************************** 5. row ***************************
      Engine: MEMORY
     Support: YES
     Comment: Hash based, stored in memory, useful for temporary tables
Transactions: NO
          XA: NO
  Savepoints: NO
*************************** 6. row ***************************
      Engine: FEDERATED
     Support: NO
     Comment: Federated MySQL storage engine
Transactions: NULL
          XA: NULL
  Savepoints: NULL
*************************** 7. row ***************************
      Engine: ARCHIVE
```

```
    Support: YES
    Comment: Archive storage engine
Transactions: NO
         XA: NO
 Savepoints: NO
*************************** 8. row ***************************
     Engine: MRG_MYISAM
    Support: YES
    Comment: Collection of identical MyISAM tables
Transactions: NO
         XA: NO
 Savepoints: NO
8 rows in set (0.00 sec)
```

The result set includes all of the known storage engines; whether they are installed and configured (where Support = YES); a note about the engine's features; and whether it supports transactions, distributed transactions (XA), or *savepoints*.

A savepoint is a named event that you can use like a transaction. You can establish a savepoint and either release (delete the savepoint) or roll back the changes since the savepoint. See the online MySQL Reference Manual for more details about savepoints.

With so many storage engines to choose from, it can be confusing when designing your database for performance. You can choose the storage engine for a table using the ENGINE parameter on the CREATE statement, and you can change the storage engine by issuing an ALTER TABLE command:

```
CREATE TABLE t1 (a int) ENGINE=InnoDB;
ALTER TABLE t1 ENGINE=MEMORY;
```

The following describes each of the storage engines briefly, including some of the uses for which they are best suited:

InnoDB

> The premier transactional support storage engine, InnoDB is also the default engine.[1] This engine will be used if you omit the ENGINE option on the CREATE statement. You should always choose this storage engine when requiring transactional support; InnoDB and NDB are currently the only transactional engines in MySQL. There are third-party storage engines in various states of production that can support transactions, but the only "out-of-the-box" option is InnoDB. InnoDB is the storage engine of choice for high reliability and transaction-processing environments.

MyISAM

> MyISAM is often used for data warehousing, ecommerce, and enterprise applications where most operations are reads (called read-mostly). MyISAM uses ad-

---

1. The InnoDB storage became the default storage engine in version 5.5

vanced caching and indexing mechanisms to improve data retrieval and indexing. MyISAM is an excellent choice when you need storage in a wide variety of applications requiring fast retrieval of data without the need for transactions.

Blackhole

This storage engine is very interesting. It doesn't store anything at all. In fact, it is what its name suggests—data goes in but never returns. All jocularity aside, the Blackhole storage engine fills a very special need. If binary logging is enabled, SQL statements are written to the logs, and Blackhole is used as a relay agent (or proxy) in a replication topology. In this case, the relay agent processes data from the master and passes it on to its slaves but does not actually store any data. The Blackhole storage engine can be handy in situations where you want to test an application to ensure it is writing data, but you don't want to store anything on disk.

CSV

This storage engine can create, read, and write comma-separated value (CSV) files as tables. The CSV storage engine is best used to rapidly export structured business data to spreadsheets. The CSV storage engine does not provide any indexing mechanisms and has certain issues in storing and converting date/time values (they do not obey locality during queries). The CSV storage engine is best used when you want to permit other applications to share or exchange data in a common format. Given that it is not as efficient for storing data, you should use the CSV storage engine sparingly.

 The CSV storage engine is used for writing logfiles. For example, the backup logs are CSV files and can be opened by other applications that use the CSV protocol (but not while the server is running).

Memory

This storage engine (sometimes called HEAP) is an in-memory storage that uses a hashing mechanism to retrieve frequently used data. This allows for much faster retrieval. Data is accessed in the same manner as with the other storage engines, but the data is stored in memory and is valid only during the MySQL session—the data is flushed and deleted on shutdown. Memory storage engines are typically good for situations in which static data is accessed frequently and rarely ever altered (e.g., lookup tables). Examples include zip code listings, state and county names, category listings, and other data that is accessed frequently and seldom updated. You can also use the Memory storage engine for databases that utilize snapshot techniques for distributed or historical data access.

Federated

Creates a single table reference from multiple database systems. The Federated storage engine allows you to link tables together across database servers. This mechanism is similar in purpose to the linked data tables available in other database systems. The Federated storage engine is best suited for distributed or data mart environments. The most interesting feature of the Federated storage engine is that it does not move data, nor does it require the remote tables to use the same storage engine.

The Federated storage engine is currently disabled in most distributions of MySQL. Consult the online MySQL Reference Manual for more details.

Archive

This storage engine can store large amounts of data in a compressed format. The Archive storage engine is best suited for storing and retrieving large amounts of seldom-accessed archival or historical data. Indexes are not supported and the only access method is via a table scan. Thus, you should not use the Archive storage engine for normal database storage and retrieval.

Merge

This storage engine (`MRG_MYISAM`) can encapsulate a set of MyISAM tables with the same structure (table layout or schema) referenced as a single table. Thus, the tables are partitioned by the location of the individual tables, but no additional partitioning mechanisms are used. All tables must reside on the same server (but not necessarily the same database).

When a `DROP` command is issued on a merged table, only the Merge specification is removed. The original tables are not altered.

The best attribute of the Merge storage engine is speed. It permits you to split a large table into several smaller tables on different disks, combine them using a merge table specification, and access them simultaneously. Searches and sorts will execute more quickly, because there is less data in each table to manipulate. Also, repairs on tables are more efficient because it is faster and easier to repair several smaller individual tables than a single large table. Unfortunately, this configuration has several disadvantages:

- You must use identical MyISAM tables to form a single merge table.

- The replace operation is not allowed.
- Indexes are less efficient than for a single table.

The Merge storage engine is best suited for very large database (VLDB) applications, like data warehousing, where data resides in more than one table in one or more databases. You can also use it to help solve some partitioning problems where you want to partition horizontally but do not want to add the complexity of setting up the partition table options.

Clearly, with so many choices of storage engines, it is possible to choose engines that can hamper performance or, in some cases, prohibit certain solutions. For example, if you never specify a storage engine when the table is created, MySQL uses the default storage engine. If not set manually, the default storage engine reverts to the platform-specific default, which may be MyISAM on some platforms. This may mean you are missing out on optimizing lookup tables or limiting features of your application by not having transactional support. It is well worth the extra time to include an analysis of storage engine choices when designing or tuning your databases.

Use views for faster results via the query cache

Views are a very handy way to encapsulate complex queries to make it easier to work with the data. You can use views to limit data both vertically (fewer columns) or horizontally (a WHERE clause on the underlying SELECT statement). Both uses are very handy, and of course, the more complex views use both practices to limit the result set returned to the user or to hide certain base tables or to ensure an efficient join is executed.

Using views to limit the columns returned can help you in ways you may not have considered. It not only reduces the amount of data processed, but can also help you avoid costly SELECT * operations that users tend to do without much thought. When many of these types of operations are run, your applications are processing far too much data and this can affect performance of not only the application, but also the server, and more important, can decrease available bandwidth on your network. It's always a good idea to use views to limit data in this manner and hide access to the base table(s) to remove any temptation users may have to access the base table directly.

Views that limit the number of rows returned also help reduce network bandwidth and can improve the performance of your applications. These types of views also protect against proliferation of SELECT * queries. Using views in this manner requires a bit more planning, because your goal is to create meaningful subsets of the data. You will have to examine the requirements for your database and understand the queries issued to form the correct WHERE clauses for these queries.

With a little effort, you may find you can create combinations of vertically and horizontally restrictive views, thereby ensuring your applications operate on only the data that is needed. The less data moving around, the more data your applications can process in the same amount of time.

Perhaps the best way to use views is to eliminate poorly formed joins. This is especially true when you have a complex normalized schema. It may not be obvious to users how to combine the tables to form a meaningful result set. Indeed, most of the work done by DBAs when striving for better performance is focused on correcting poorly formed joins. Sometimes this can be trivial—for example, fewer rows processed during the join operation—but most of the time the improved response time is significant.

Views can also be helpful when using the query cache in MySQL. The query cache stores the results of frequently used (accessed) queries. Using views that provide a standardized result set can improve the likelihood that the results will be cached and, therefore, retrieved more efficiently.

You can improve performance with a little design work and the judicious use of views in your databases. Take the time to examine how much data is being moved around (both the number of columns and rows) and examine your application for any query that uses joins. Spend some time forming views that limit the data and identify the most efficient joins and wrap them in a view as well. Imagine how much easier you'll rest knowing your users are executing efficient joins.

Use constraints

The use of constraints provides another tool in your arsenal for combating performance problems. Rather than proselytizing about limitations on using constraints, we encourage you to consider constraints a standard practice and not an afterthought.

There are several types of constraints available in MySQL, including the following:

- Unique indexes
- Primary keys
- Enumerated values
- Sets
- Default values
- NOT NULL option

We've discussed using indexes and overusing indexes. Indexes help improve data retrieval by allowing the system to store and find data more quickly.

Foreign keys are another form of constraint but are not directly related to performance. Rather, foreign keys can be used to protect referential integrity. However, it should be noted that updating tables with a lot of foreign keys or executing cascade operations can have some affect on performance. Currently, only InnoDB supports foreign keys. For more information about foreign keys, see the online MySQL Reference Manual.

Sets in MySQL are similar to enumerated values, allowing you to constrain the values in a field. You can use sets to store information that represents attributes of the data, instead of using a master/detail relationship. This not only saves space in the table (set values are bitwise combinations), but also eliminates the need to access another table for the values.

The use of the DEFAULT option to supply default values is an excellent way to prohibit problems associated with poorly constructed data. For example, if you have a numeric field that represents values used for calculations, you may want to ensure that when the field is unknown, a default value is stored for it. You can set defaults on most data types. You can also use defaults for date and time fields to avoid problems processing invalid date and time values. More important, default values can save your application from having to supply the values (or using the less reliable method of asking the user to provide them), thereby reducing the amount of data sent to the server during data entry.

You should also consider using the NOT NULL option when specifying fields that must have a value. If an entry is attempted where there are NOT NULL columns and no data values are provided, the INSERT statement will fail. This prevents data integrity issues by ensuring all important fields have values. Null values can also make certain queries on these fields take longer.

Use EXPLAIN, ANALYZE, and OPTIMIZE

We have already discussed the benefits of these commands. We list them here as a best practice to remind you that these tools are vital for diagnostic and tuning efforts. Use them often and with impunity, but follow their use carefully. Specifically, use ANALYZE and OPTIMIZE when it makes sense and not as a regular, scheduled event. We have encountered administrators who run these commands nightly, and in some cases that may be warranted, but in the general case it is not warranted and can lead to unnecessary table copies (like we saw in the earlier examples). Thus, forcing the system to copy data regularly can be a waste of time and could lead to limited access during the operation.

Now that we've discussed how to monitor and improve MySQL query performance, let us look at some best practices that you can use to help focus your investigation of performance.

Best Practices for Improving Performance

The details of diagnosing and improving performance of databases are covered by works devoted to the subject and indeed, the information fills many pages.

For completeness and as a general reference, we include in this section a set of best practices for combating performance anomalies; this is meant to be a checklist for you to use as a guide. We have grouped the practices by common problems.

Everything Is Slow

When the system as a whole is performing poorly, you must focus your efforts on how the system is running, starting with the operating system. You can use one or more of the following techniques to identify and improve the performance of your system:

- Check hardware for problems.
- Improve hardware (e.g., add memory).
- Consider moving data to isolated disks.
- Check the operating system for proper configuration.
- Consider moving some applications to other servers.
- Consider replication for scale-out.
- Tune the server for performance.

Slow Queries

Any query that appears in the slow query log or those identified as problematic by your users or developers can be improved using one or more of the following techniques:

- Normalize your database schema.
- Use EXPLAIN to identify missing or incorrect indexes.
- Use the benchmark() function to test parts of queries.
- Consider rewriting the query.
- Use views to standardize queries.
- Test using the query cache (this may not work for all queries or the frequency of your access patterns).

A replication slave does not write replicated queries to the slow query log, regardless of whether the query was written to the slow query log on the master.

Slow Applications

If an application is showing signs of performance issues, you should examine the application components to determine where the problem is located. Perhaps you will find only one module is causing the problem, but sometimes it may be more serious. The following techniques can help you identify and solve application performance problems:

- Turn on the query cache.
- In cases where the query cache is already enabled, turning it off may improve some queries. Consider using the query cache on demand using DEMAND mode and SELECT SQL_CACHE.
- Consider and optimize your storage engine choices.
- Verify the problem isn't in the server or operating system.
- Define benchmarks for your applications and compare to known baselines.
- Examine internalized (written in the application) queries and maximize their performance.
- Divide and conquer—examine one part at a time.
- Use partitioning to spread out the data.
- Examine your indexes for fragmentation.

Slow Replication

The performance problems related to replication, as discussed earlier, are normally isolated to problems with the database and server performance. Use the following techniques when diagnosing performance issues for replication:

- Ensure your network is operating at peak performance.
- Ensure your servers are configured correctly.
- Optimize your databases.
- Limit updates to the master.
- Divide reads across several slaves.
- Check the slaves for replication lag.

- Perform regular maintenance on your logs (binary and relay logs).
- Use compression over your network if bandwidth is limited.
- Use inclusive and exclusive logging options to minimize what is replicated.

Conclusion

There are a lot of things to monitor on a MySQL server. We've discussed the basic SQL commands available for monitoring the server, the *mysqladmin* command-line utility, the benchmark suite, and MySQL Workbench. We have also examined some best practices for improving database performance.

Now that you know the basics of operating system monitoring, database performance, MySQL monitoring, and benchmarking, you have the tools and knowledge to successfully tune your server for optimal performance.

Joel smiled as he compiled his report about Susan's nested query problem. It had taken a few hours of digging through logfiles to find the problem, but after he explained the overhead of the query to the developers, they agreed to change the query to use a lookup table stored in a memory table. Joel felt his boss was going to be excited to learn about his ingenuity. He clicked Send just as his boss appeared in his door frame.

"Joel!"

Joel jumped, despite knowing Mr. Summerson was there. "I've got the marketing application problem solved, sir," he said quickly.

"Great! I look forward to reading about your solution."

Joel wasn't sure his boss would understand the technical parts of his message, but he also knew his boss would keep asking if he didn't explain everything.

Mr. Summerson nodded once and went on his way. Joel opened an email message from Phil in Seattle complaining about replication problems and soon realized the problems extended much further than the server he had been working with.

## CHAPTER 12

Storage Engine Monitoring

> Joel was enjoying his morning latte when his office phone rang. It startled him because until now he had never heard it ring. He lifted the receiver and heard engine noises. Expecting the call was a wrong number, he said hesitantly, "Hello?"
>
> "Joel! Glad I caught you." It was Mr. Summerson, calling from his car.
>
> "Yes, sir."
>
> "I'm on my way to the airport to meet with the sales staff in the Seattle office. I wanted to ask you to look into the new application database. The developers in Seattle tell me they think we need to figure out a better configuration for performance."
>
> Joel had expected something like this. He knew a little about InnoDB and MyISAM, but he wasn't familiar with monitoring, much less tuning their performance. "I can look into it, sir."
>
> "Great. Thanks, Joel. I'll email you." The connection was severed before Joel could reply. Joel finished the last of his latte and started reading about storage engines in MySQL.

Now that you know when your servers are performing well (and when they aren't), how do you know how well your storage engines are performing? If you are hosting one or more transactional databases or need your storage engine to perform at its peak for fast queries, you will need to monitor your storage engines. In this chapter, we discuss advanced storage engine monitoring, focusing on improving storage engine performance, by examining the two most popular storage engines: InnoDB and MyISAM. We will discuss how to monitor each and offer some practical advice on how to improve performance.

InnoDB

The InnoDB storage engine is the default storage engine for MySQL (as of version 5.5). InnoDB provides high reliability and high performance transactional operations that support full ACID compliance. InnoDB has been proven to be very reliable and continues to be improved. The latest improvements include multicore processor support, improved memory allocation, and finer grain performance tuning capabilities. The online reference manual contains a detailed explanation of all of the features of the InnoDB storage engine.

There are many tuning options for the InnoDB storage engine, and a thorough examination of all of them and the techniques that go along with each can fill an entire volume. For example, there are 50 variables that control the behavior of InnoDB and over 40 status variables to communicate metadata about performance and status. In this section, we discuss how to monitor the InnoDB storage engine and focus on some key areas for improving performance.

Rather than discussing the broader aspects of these areas, we provide a strategy organized into the following areas of performance improvement:

- Using the `SHOW ENGINE` command
- Using InnoDB monitors
- Monitoring logfiles
- Monitoring the buffer pool
- Monitoring tablespaces
- Using `INFORMATION_SCHEMA` tables
- Using `PERFORMANCE_SCHEMA` tables
- Other parameters to consider
- Troubleshooting InnoDB

We will discuss each of these briefly in the sections that follow. However, before we get started, let's take a brief look at the InnoDB architectural features.

The InnoDB storage engine uses a very sophisticated architecture that is designed for high concurrency and heavy transactional activity. It has a number of advanced features that you should consider prior to attempting to improve performance. We focus on the features we can monitor and improve. These include indexes, the buffer pool, logfiles, and tablespaces.

The indexes in an InnoDB table use clustered indexes. Even if no index is specified, InnoDB assigns an internal value to each row so that it can use a clustered index. A clustered index is a data structure that stores not only the index, but also the data itself.

This means once you've located the value in the index, you can retrieve the data without additional disk seeks. Naturally, the primary key index or first unique index on a table is built as a clustered index.

When you create a secondary index, the key from the clustered index (primary key, unique key, or row ID) is stored along with the value for the secondary index. This allows very fast search by key and fast retrieval of the original data in the clustered index. It also means you can use the primary key columns when scanning the secondary index to allow the query to use only the secondary index to retrieve data.

The buffer pool is a caching mechanism for managing transactions and writing and reading data to or from disks and, properly configured, can reduce disk access. The buffer pool is also a vital component for crash recovery, as the buffer pool is written to disk periodically (e.g., during shutdown). By default, the buffer pool state is saved in a file named *ib_buffer_pool* in the same directory as the InnoDB datafiles. Because the state is an in-memory component, you must monitor the effectiveness of the buffer pool to ensure it is configured correctly.

InnoDB also uses the buffer pool to store data changes and transactions. InnoDB caches changes by saving them to a page (block) of data in the buffer pool. Each time a page is referenced, it is placed in the buffer pool and when changed, it is marked as "dirty." The changes are then written to disk to update the data and a copy is written into a redo log. These logfiles are stored as files named *ib_logfile0* or *ib_logfile1*. You can see these files in the data directory of the MySQL server.

> For more information about configuring and controlling the flushing of the buffer pool, see the section entitled "Improvements to Buffer Pool Flushing" in the online MySQL Reference Manual.

The InnoDB storage engine uses two disk-based mechanisms for storing data: logfiles and tablespaces. InnoDB also uses the logs to rebuild (or redo) data changes made prior to a shutdown or crash. On startup, InnoDB reads the logs and automatically writes the dirty pages to disk, thereby recovering buffered changes made before the crash.

Separate Tablespaces

One of the newest performance features permits the storage of undo logs as separate tablespaces. Because the undo logs can consume a lot of space during long-running transactions, placing the undo logs in separate or even multiple tablespaces reduces the size of the system tablespace. To place the undo logs in separate tablespaces, set the --innodb_undo_tablespaces configuration option to a value greater than zero. You can also specify the location of the undo log tablespaces by using the

`--innodb_undo_directory` option. MySQL assigns names to the undo log tablespaces using the form innodb*n*, where *n* is a sequential integer with leading zeros.

Tablespaces are an organizational tool InnoDB uses as machine-independent files that contain both data and indexes as well as a rollback mechanism (to roll back transactions). By default, all tables share one tablespace (called a *shared tablespace*). Shared tablespaces do not automatically extend across multiple files. By default, a tablespace takes up a single file that grows as the data grows. You can specify the `autoextend` option to allow the tablespace to create new files.

You can also store tables in their own tablespaces (called file-per-table). File-per-table tablespaces contain both the data and the indexes for your tables. While there is still a central InnoDB file that is maintained, file-per-table permits you to segregate the data to different files (tablespaces). These tablespaces automatically extend across multiple files, thereby allowing you to store more data in your tables than what the operating system can handle. You can divide your tablespace into multiple files to place on different disks.

 Use `innodb_file_per_table` to create a separate tablespace for each table. Any tables created prior to setting this option will remain in the shared tablespace. Using this command affects only new tables. It does not reduce or otherwise save space already allocated in the shared tablespace. To apply the change to existing tables, use the `ALTER TABLE ... ENGINE=INNODB` command. Do this after you have turned on the `innodb_file_per_table` feature.

Using the SHOW ENGINE Command

The `SHOW ENGINE INNODB STATUS` command (also known as the InnoDB monitor) displays statistical and configuration information concerning the state of the InnoDB storage engine. This is the standard way to see information about InnoDB. The list of statistical data displayed is long and very comprehensive. Example 12-1 shows an excerpt of the command run on a standard installation of MySQL.

Example 12-1. The SHOW ENGINE INNODB STATUS command

```
mysql> SHOW ENGINE INNODB STATUS \G
*************************** 1. row ***************************
  Type: InnoDB
  Name:
Status:
=====================================
2013-01-08 20:50:16 11abaa000 INNODB MONITOR OUTPUT
=====================================
Per second averages calculated from the last 3 seconds
----------------
```

```
BACKGROUND THREAD
-----------------
srv_master_thread loops: 1 srv_active, 0 srv_shutdown, 733 srv_idle
srv_master_thread log flush and writes: 734
----------
SEMAPHORES
----------
OS WAIT ARRAY INFO: reservation count 2
OS WAIT ARRAY INFO: signal count 2
Mutex spin waits 1, rounds 19, OS waits 0
RW-shared spins 2, rounds 60, OS waits 2
RW-excl spins 0, rounds 0, OS waits 0
Spin rounds per wait: 19.00 mutex, 30.00 RW-shared, 0.00 RW-excl
------------
TRANSACTIONS
------------
Trx id counter 1285
Purge done for trx's n:o < 0 undo n:o < 0 state: running but idle
History list length 0
LIST OF TRANSACTIONS FOR EACH SESSION:
---TRANSACTION 0, not started
MySQL thread id 3, OS thread handle 0x11abaa000, query id 32 localhost
127.0.0.1 root init
SHOW ENGINE INNODB STATUS
--------
FILE I/O
--------
I/O thread 0 state: waiting for i/o request (insert buffer thread)
I/O thread 1 state: waiting for i/o request (log thread)
I/O thread 2 state: waiting for i/o request (read thread)
I/O thread 3 state: waiting for i/o request (read thread)
I/O thread 4 state: waiting for i/o request (read thread)
I/O thread 5 state: waiting for i/o request (read thread)
I/O thread 6 state: waiting for i/o request (write thread)
I/O thread 7 state: waiting for i/o request (write thread)
I/O thread 8 state: waiting for i/o request (write thread)
I/O thread 9 state: waiting for i/o request (write thread)
Pending normal aio reads: 0 [0, 0, 0, 0] , aio writes: 0 [0, 0, 0, 0] ,
 ibuf aio reads: 0, log i/o's: 0, sync i/o's: 0
Pending flushes (fsync) log: 0; buffer pool: 0
171 OS file reads, 5 OS file writes, 5 OS fsyncs
0.00 reads/s, 0 avg bytes/read, 0.00 writes/s, 0.00 fsyncs/s
-------------------------------------
INSERT BUFFER AND ADAPTIVE HASH INDEX
-------------------------------------
Ibuf: size 1, free list len 0, seg size 2, 0 merges
merged operations:
 insert 0, delete mark 0, delete 0
discarded operations:
 insert 0, delete mark 0, delete 0
Hash table size 276671, node heap has 0 buffer(s)
0.00 hash searches/s, 0.00 non-hash searches/s
```

```
---
LOG
---
Log sequence number 1625987
Log flushed up to   1625987
Pages flushed up to 1625987
Last checkpoint at  1625987
0 pending log writes, 0 pending chkp writes
8 log i/o's done, 0.00 log i/o's/second
----------------------
BUFFER POOL AND MEMORY
----------------------
Total memory allocated 137363456; in additional pool allocated 0
Dictionary memory allocated 55491
Buffer pool size    8191
Free buffers        8034
Database pages      157
Old database pages 0
Modified db pages  0
Pending reads 0
Pending writes: LRU 0, flush list 0 single page 0
Pages made young 0, not young 0
0.00 youngs/s, 0.00 non-youngs/s
Pages read 157, created 0, written 1
0.00 reads/s, 0.00 creates/s, 0.00 writes/s
No buffer pool page gets since the last printout
Pages read ahead 0.00/s, evicted without access 0.00/s, Random read ahead 0.00/s
LRU len: 157, unzip_LRU len: 0
I/O sum[0]:cur[0], unzip sum[0]:cur[0]
--------------
ROW OPERATIONS
--------------
0 queries inside InnoDB, 0 queries in queue
0 read views open inside InnoDB
Main thread id 4718366720, state: sleeping
Number of rows inserted 0, updated 0, deleted 0, read 0
0.00 inserts/s, 0.00 updates/s, 0.00 deletes/s, 0.00 reads/s
----------------------------
END OF INNODB MONITOR OUTPUT
============================

1 row in set (0.00 sec)
```

The SHOW ENGINE INNODB MUTEX command displays mutex information about InnoDB and can be very helpful when tuning threading in the storage engine. Example 12-2 shows an excerpt of the command run on a standard installation of MySQL.

Example 12-2. The SHOW ENGINE INNODB MUTEX command

```
mysql> SHOW ENGINE INNODB MUTEX;
+--------+--------------------+---------------+
| Type   | Name               | Status        |
+--------+--------------------+---------------+
| InnoDB | trx/trx0rseg.c:167 | os_waits=1    |
| InnoDB | trx/trx0sys.c:181  | os_waits=7    |
| InnoDB | log/log0log.c:777  | os_waits=1003 |
| InnoDB | buf/buf0buf.c:936  | os_waits=8    |
| InnoDB | fil/fil0fil.c:1487 | os_waits=2    |
| InnoDB | srv/srv0srv.c:953  | os_waits=101  |
| InnoDB | log/log0log.c:833  | os_waits=323  |
+--------+--------------------+---------------+
7 rows in set (0.00 sec)
```

The Name column displays the source file and line number where the mutex was created. The Status column displays the number of times the mutex waited for the operating system (e.g., os_waits=5). If the source code was compiled with the UNIV_DEBUG directive, the column can display one of the following values:

count
> The number of times the mutex was requested

spin_waits
> The number of times a spinlock operation was run

os_waits
> The number of times the mutex waited on the operating system

os_yields
> The number of times a thread abandoned its time slice and returned to the operating system

os_wait_times
> The amount of time the mutex waited for the operating system

The SHOW ENGINE INNODB STATUS command displays a lot of information directly from the InnoDB storage engine. While it is unformatted (it isn't displayed in neat rows and columns), there are several tools that use this information and redisplay it. For example, the InnoTop (see "InnoTop" on page 404) command communicates data this way.

Using InnoDB Monitors

The InnoDB storage engine is the only native storage engine that supports monitoring directly. Under the hood of InnoDB is a special mechanism called a *monitor* that gathers and reports statistical information to the server and client utilities. All of the following (and most third-party tools) interact with the monitoring facility in InnoDB, hence InnoDB monitors the following items via the MySQL server:

- Table and record locks

- Lock waits

- Semaphore waits

- File I/O requests

- Buffer pool

- Purge and insert buffer merge activity

The InnoDB monitors are engaged automatically via the SHOW ENGINE INNODB STA
TUS command, and the information displayed is generated by the monitors. However,
you can also get this information directly from the InnoDB monitors by creating a
special set of tables in MySQL. The actual schema of the tables and where they reside
are not important (provided you use the ENGINE = INNODB clause). Once they are created, each of the tables tells InnoDB to dump the data to stderr. You can see this
information via the MySQL error log. For example, a default install of MySQL on Mac
OS X has an error log named *usr/local/mysql/data/localhost.err*. On Windows, you can
also display the output in a console by starting MySQL with the --console option. To
turn on the InnoDB monitors, create the following tables in a database of your choice:

```
mysql> SHOW TABLES LIKE 'innodb%';
+--------------------------+
| Tables_in_test (innodb%) |
+--------------------------+
| innodb_lock_monitor      |
| innodb_monitor           |
| innodb_table_monitor     |
| innodb_tablespace_monitor |
+--------------------------+
4 rows in set (0.00 sec)
```

To turn off the monitors, simply delete the table. The monitors automatically regenerate
data every 15 seconds.

> The tables are deleted on reboot. To continue monitoring after a
> reboot, you must recreate the tables.

Each monitor presents the following data:

innodb_monitor

> The standard monitor that prints the same information as the status SQL command.
> See Example 12-1 for an example of the output of this monitor. The only difference
> between the SQL command and the output of the innodb_monitor is that the output

to `stderr` is formatted the same way as if you used the vertical display option in the MySQL client.

`innodb_lock_monitor`

The lock monitor also displays the same information as the SQL command, but includes additional information about locks. Use this report to detect deadlocks and explore concurrency issues.

Example 12-3. The InnoDB lock monitor report

```
------------
TRANSACTIONS
------------
Trx id counter 2E07
Purge done for trx's n:o < 2C02 undo n:o < 0
History list length 36
LIST OF TRANSACTIONS FOR EACH SESSION:
---TRANSACTION 2E06, not started
mysql tables in use 1, locked 1
MySQL thread id 3, OS thread handle 0x10b2f3000, query id 30 localhost root
show engine innodb status
```

`innodb_table_monitor`

The table monitor produces a detailed report of the internal data dictionary. Example 12-4 shows an excerpt of the report generated (formatted for readability). Notice the extensive data provided about each table, including the column definitions, indexes, approximate number of rows, foreign keys, and more. Use this report when diagnosing problems with tables or if you want to know the details of indexes.

Example 12-4. The InnoDB table monitor report

```
===========================================
2013-01-08 21:11:00 11dc5f000 INNODB TABLE MONITOR OUTPUT
===========================================
----------------------------------------
TABLE: name SYS_DATAFILES, id 14, flags 0, columns 5, indexes 1, appr.rows 9
  COLUMNS: SPACE: DATA_INT len 4; PATH: DATA_VARCHAR prtype 524292 len 0;
   DB_ROW_ID: DATA_SYS prtype 256 len 6; DB_TRX_ID: DATA_SYS prtype 257 len 6;
   DB_ROLL_PTR: DATA_SYS prtype 258 len 7;
  INDEX: name SYS_DATAFILES_SPACE, id 16, fields 1/4, uniq 1, type 3
   root page 308, appr.key vals 9, leaf pages 1, size pages 1
   FIELDS:  SPACE DB_TRX_ID DB_ROLL_PTR PATH
----------------------------------------
...
----------------------------------------
END OF INNODB TABLE MONITOR OUTPUT
===================================
```

innodb_tablespace_monitor

Displays extended information about the shared tablespace, including a list of file segments. It also validates the tablespace allocation data structures. The report can be quite detailed and very long, as it lists all of the details about your tablespace. Example 12-5 shows an excerpt of this report.

Example 12-5. The InnoDB tablespace monitor report

```
================================================
2013-01-08 21:11:00 11dc5f000 INNODB TABLESPACE MONITOR OUTPUT
================================================
FILE SPACE INFO: id 0
size 768, free limit 576, free extents 3
not full frag extents 1: used pages 13, full frag extents 3
first seg id not used 180
SEGMENT id 1 space 0; page 2; res 2 used 2; full ext 0
fragm pages 2; free extents 0; not full extents 0: pages 0
SEGMENT id 2 space 0; page 2; res 1 used 1; full ext 0
fragm pages 1; free extents 0; not full extents 0: pages 0
SEGMENT id 3 space 0; page 2; res 1 used 1; full ext 0
fragm pages 1; free extents 0; not full extents 0: pages 0
SEGMENT id 4 space 0; page 2; res 1 used 1; full ext 0
fragm pages 1; free extents 0; not full extents 0: pages 0
SEGMENT id 5 space 0; page 2; res 1 used 1; full ext 0
fragm pages 1; free extents 0; not full extents 0: pages 0
SEGMENT id 6 space 0; page 2; res 0 used 0; full ext 0
fragm pages 0; free extents 0; not full extents 0: pages 0
SEGMENT id 7 space 0; page 2; res 1 used 1; full ext 0
fragm pages 1; free extents 0; not full extents 0: pages 0
SEGMENT id 8 space 0; page 2; res 0 used 0; full ext 0
fragm pages 0; free extents 0; not full extents 0: pages 0
SEGMENT id 9 space 0; page 2; res 1 used 1; full ext 0
fragm pages 1; free extents 0; not full extents 0: pages 0
SEGMENT id 10 space 0; page 2; res 0 used 0; full ext 0
fragm pages 0; free extents 0; not full extents 0: pages 0
SEGMENT id 11 space 0; page 2; res 1 used 1; full ext 0
fragm pages 1; free extents 0; not full extents 0: pages 0
SEGMENT id 12 space 0; page 2; res 0 used 0; full ext 0
fragm pages 0; free extents 0; not full extents 0: pages 0
SEGMENT id 13 space 0; page 2; res 1 used 1; full ext 0
fragm pages 1; free extents 0; not full extents 0: pages 0
SEGMENT id 14 space 0; page 2; res 0 used 0; full ext 0
fragm pages 0; free extents 0; not full extents 0: pages 0
SEGMENT id 15 space 0; page 2; res 160 used 160; full ext 2
fragm pages 32; free extents 0; not full extents 0: pages 0
SEGMENT id 16 space 0; page 2; res 1 used 1; full ext 0
fragm pages 1; free extents 0; not full extents 0: pages 0
SEGMENT id 17 space 0; page 2; res 1 used 1; full ext 0
fragm pages 1; free extents 0; not full extents 0: pages 0
SEGMENT id 18 space 0; page 2; res 1 used 1; full ext 0
fragm pages 1; free extents 0; not full extents 0: pages 0
SEGMENT id 19 space 0; page 2; res 1 used 1; full ext 0
```

```
fragm pages 1; free extents 0; not full extents 0: pages 0
SEGMENT id 20 space 0; page 2; res 1 used 1; full ext 0
fragm pages 1; free extents 0; not full extents 0: pages 0

...

NUMBER of file segments: 179
Validating tablespace
Validation ok
----------------------------------------
END OF INNODB TABLESPACE MONITOR OUTPUT
========================================
```

As you can see, the InnoDB monitor reports quite a lot of detail. Keeping these turned on for extended periods could add a substantial amount of data to your logfiles.

Monitoring Logfiles

Because the InnoDB logfiles buffer data between your data and the operating system, keeping these files running well will ensure good performance. You can monitor the logfiles directly by watching the following system status variables:

```
mysql> SHOW STATUS LIKE 'InnoDB%log%';
+-----------------------------+-------+
| Variable_name               | Value |
+-----------------------------+-------+
| InnoDB_log_waits            | 0     |
| InnoDB_log_write_requests   | 0     |
| InnoDB_log_writes           | 2     |
| InnoDB_os_log_fsyncs        | 5     |
| InnoDB_os_log_pending_fsyncs | 0    |
| InnoDB_os_log_pending_writes | 0    |
| InnoDB_os_log_written       | 1024  |
+-----------------------------+-------+
```

We saw some of this information presented by the InnoDB monitors, but you can also get detailed information about the logfiles using the following status variables:

InnoDB_log_waits
> A count of the number of times the log was too small (i.e., did not have enough room for all of the data) and the operation had to wait for the log to be flushed. If this value begins to increase and remains higher than zero for long periods (except perhaps during bulk operations), you may want to increase the size of the logfiles.

InnoDB_log_write_requests
> The number of log write requests.

InnoDB_log_writes
> The number of times data was written to the log.

InnoDB_os_log_fsyncs
> The number of operating system file syncs (i.e., fsync() method calls).

InnoDB_os_log_pending_fsyncs
> The number of pending file sync requests. If this value begins to increase and stays above zero for an extended period of time, you may want to investigate possible disk access issues.

InnoDB_os_log_pending_writes
> The number of pending log write requests. If this value begins to increase and stays higher than zero for an extended period of time, you may want to investigate possible disk access issues.

InnoDB_os_log_written
> The total number of bytes written to the log.

Because all of these options present numerical information, you can build your own custom graphs in MySQL Workbench to display the information in graphical form.

Monitoring the Buffer Pool

The buffer pool is where InnoDB caches frequently accessed data. Any changes you make to the data in the buffer pool are also cached. The buffer pool also stores information about current transactions. Thus, the buffer pool is a critical mechanism used for performance.

You can view information about the behavior of the buffer pool using the SHOW ENGINE INNODB STATUS command, as shown in Example 12-1. We repeat the buffer pool and memory section here for your convenience:

```
----------------------
BUFFER POOL AND MEMORY
----------------------
Total memory allocated 138805248; in additional pool allocated 0
Dictionary memory allocated 70560
Buffer pool size    8192
Free buffers        760
Database pages      6988
Modified db pages   113
Pending reads 0
Pending writes: LRU 0, flush list 0, single page 0
Pages read 21, created 6968, written 10043
0.00 reads/s, 89.91 creates/s, 125.87 writes/s
Buffer pool hit rate 1000 / 1000
LRU len: 6988, unzip_LRU len: 0
I/O sum[9786]:cur[259], unzip sum[0]:cur[0]
```

The critical items to watch for in this report are listed here (we discuss more specific status variables later):

Free buffers

The number of buffer segments that are empty and available for buffering data.

Modified pages

The number of pages that have changes (dirty).

Pending reads

The number of reads waiting. This value should remain low.

Pending writes

The number of writes waiting. This value should remain low.

Hit rate

A ratio of the number of successful buffer hits to the number of all requests. You want this value to remain as close as possible to 1:1.

There are a number of status variables you can use to see this information in greater detail. The following shows the InnoDB buffer pool status variables:

```
mysql> SHOW STATUS LIKE 'InnoDB%buf%';
+-----------------------------------+-------+
| Variable_name                     | Value |
+-----------------------------------+-------+
| InnoDB_buffer_pool_pages_data     | 21    |
| InnoDB_buffer_pool_pages_dirty    | 0     |
| InnoDB_buffer_pool_pages_flushed  | 1     |
| InnoDB_buffer_pool_pages_free     | 8171  |
| InnoDB_buffer_pool_pages_misc     | 0     |
| InnoDB_buffer_pool_pages_total    | 8192  |
| InnoDB_buffer_pool_read_ahead_rnd | 0     |
| InnoDB_buffer_pool_read_ahead_seq | 0     |
| InnoDB_buffer_pool_read_requests  | 558   |
| InnoDB_buffer_pool_reads          | 22    |
| InnoDB_buffer_pool_wait_free      | 0     |
| InnoDB_buffer_pool_write_requests | 1     |
+-----------------------------------+-------+
```

There are a number of status variables for the buffer pool that display key statistical information about the performance of the buffer pool. You can monitor such detailed information as the status of the pages in the buffer pool, the reads and writes from and to the buffer pool, and how often the buffer pool causes a wait for reads or writes. The following explains each status variable in more detail:

InnoDB_buffer_pool_pages_data

The number of pages containing data, including both unchanged and changed (dirty) pages.

InnoDB_buffer_pool_pages_dirty

The number of pages that have changes (dirty).

InnoDB_buffer_pool_pages_flushed
> The number of times the buffer pool pages have been flushed.

InnoDB_buffer_pool_pages_free
> The number of empty (free) pages.

InnoDB_buffer_pool_pages_misc
> The number of pages that are being used for administrative work by the InnoDB engine itself. This is calculated as:
>
> $X = $ InnoDB_buffer_pool_pages_total $-$ InnoDB_buffer_pool_pages_free $-$ InnoDB_buffer_pool_pages_data

InnoDB_buffer_pool_pages_total
> The total number of pages in the buffer pool.

InnoDB_buffer_pool_read_ahead_rnd
> The number of random read-aheads that have occurred by InnoDB scanning for a large block of data.

InnoDB_buffer_pool_read_ahead_seq
> The number of sequential read-aheads that have occurred as a result of a sequential full table scan.

InnoDB_buffer_pool_read_requests
> The number of logical read requests.

InnoDB_buffer_pool_reads
> The number of logical reads that were not found in the buffer pool and were read directly from the disk.

InnoDB_buffer_pool_wait_free
> If the buffer pool is busy or there are no free pages, InnoDB may need to wait for pages to be flushed. This value is the number of times the wait occurred. If this value grows and stays higher than zero, you may have either an issue with the size of the buffer pool or a disk access issue.

InnoDB_buffer_pool_write_requests
> The number of writes to the InnoDB buffer pool.

Because all of these options present numerical data, you can build your own custom graphs in MySQL Workbench to display the information in graphical form.

Monitoring Tablespaces

InnoDB tablespaces are basically self-sufficient, provided you have allowed InnoDB to extend them when they run low on space. You can configure tablespaces to automatically grow using the autoextend option for the innodb_data_file_path variable. For example, the default configuration of a MySQL installation sets the shared tablespace to 10 megabytes and can automatically extend to more files:

```
--innodb_data_file_path=ibdata1:10M:autoextend
```

See the "InnoDB Configuration" section in the online MySQL Reference Manual for more details.

You can see the current configuration of your tablespaces using the SHOW ENGINE INNODB STATUS command, and you can see the details of the tablespaces by turning on the InnoDB tablespace monitor (see the "Using Tablespace Monitors" section in the online MySQL Reference Manual for more details).

Using INFORMATION_SCHEMA Tables

The *INFORMATION_SCHEMA* database includes a number of tables devoted to InnoDB. These tables are technically views, in the sense that the data they present is not stored on disk; rather, the data is generated when the table is queried. The tables provide another way to monitor InnoDB and provide performance information to administrators. These tables are present by default in version 5.5 and later.

There are tables for monitoring compression, transactions, locks, and more. Here we'll describe some of the available tables briefly:

INNODB_CMP
  Displays details and statistics for compressed tables.

INNODB_CMP_RESET
  Displays the same information as *INNODB_CMP*, but has the side effect that querying the table resets the statistics. This allows you to track statistics periodically (e.g., hourly, daily, etc.).

INNODB_CMPMEM
  Displays details and statistics about compression use in the buffer pool.

INNODB_CMPMEM_RESET
  Displays the same information as *INNODB_CMPMEM*, but has the side effect that querying the table resets the statistics. This allows you to track statistics periodically (e.g., hourly, daily, etc.).

INNODB_TRX
  Displays details and statistics about all transactions, including the state and query currently being processed.

INNODB_LOCKS
  Displays details and statistics about all locks requested by transactions. It describes each lock, including the state, mode, type, and more.

INNODB_LOCK_WAITS

>   Displays details and statistics about all locks requested by transactions that are being blocked. It describes each lock, including the state, mode, type, and the blocking transaction.

> A complete description of each table, including the columns and examples of how to use each, is presented in the online reference manual.

You can use the compression tables to monitor the compression of your tables, including such details as the page size, pages used, time spent in compression and decompression, and much more. This can be important information to monitor if you are using compression and want to ensure the overhead is not affecting the performance of your database server.

You can use the transaction and locking tables to monitor your transactions. This is a very valuable tool in keeping your transactional databases running smoothly. Most important, you can determine precisely which state each transaction is in, as well as which transactions are blocked and which are in a locked state. This information can also be critical in diagnosing complex transaction problems such as deadlock or poor performance.

> Older versions of InnoDB, specifically during the MySQL version 5.1 era, were built as a plug-in storage engine. If you are using the older InnoDB storage engine plug-in, you also have access to seven special tables in the INFORMATION_SCHEMA database. You must install the INFORMATION_SCHEMA tables separately. For more details, see the InnoDB plug-in documentation.

Using PERFORMANCE_SCHEMA Tables

As of MySQL version 5.5, InnoDB now supports the PERFORMANCE_SCHEMA feature of the MySQL server. The PERFORMANCE_SCHEMA feature was introduced in Chapter 11. For InnoDB, this means you can monitor the internal behavior of the InnoDB subsystems. This enables you to tune InnoDB using a general knowledge of the source code. While it is not strictly necessary to read the InnoDB source code to use the PERFORMANCE_SCHE MA tables to tune InnoDB, expert users with this knowledge can obtain more precise performance tuning. But that comes at a price. It is possible to over tune such that the system performs well for certain complex queries at the expense of other queries that may not see the same performance improvements.

To use PERFORMANCE_SCHEMA with InnoDB, you must have MySQL version 5.5 or later, InnoDB 1.1 or later, and have PERFORMANCE_SCHEMA enabled in the server. All InnoDB-specific instances, objects, consumers, and so on are prefixed with "innodb" in the name. For example, the following shows a list of the active InnoDB threads (you can use this to help isolate and monitor how InnoDB threads are performing):

```
mysql> SELECT thread_id, name, type FROM threads WHERE NAME LIKE '%innodb%';
+-----------+------------------------------------------+------------+
| thread_id | name                                     | type       |
+-----------+------------------------------------------+------------+
|         2 | thread/innodb/io_handler_thread          | BACKGROUND |
|         3 | thread/innodb/io_handler_thread          | BACKGROUND |
|         4 | thread/innodb/io_handler_thread          | BACKGROUND |
|         5 | thread/innodb/io_handler_thread          | BACKGROUND |
|         6 | thread/innodb/io_handler_thread          | BACKGROUND |
|         7 | thread/innodb/io_handler_thread          | BACKGROUND |
|         8 | thread/innodb/io_handler_thread          | BACKGROUND |
|         9 | thread/innodb/io_handler_thread          | BACKGROUND |
|        10 | thread/innodb/io_handler_thread          | BACKGROUND |
|        11 | thread/innodb/io_handler_thread          | BACKGROUND |
|        13 | thread/innodb/srv_lock_timeout_thread    | BACKGROUND |
|        14 | thread/innodb/srv_error_monitor_thread   | BACKGROUND |
|        15 | thread/innodb/srv_monitor_thread         | BACKGROUND |
|        16 | thread/innodb/srv_purge_thread           | BACKGROUND |
|        17 | thread/innodb/srv_master_thread          | BACKGROUND |
|        18 | thread/innodb/page_cleaner_thread        | BACKGROUND |
+-----------+------------------------------------------+------------+
16 rows in set (0.00 sec)
```

You can find InnoDB-specific items in the rwlock_instances, mutex_instances, file_instances, file_summary_by_event_name, and file_summary_by_instances tables as well.

Other Parameters to Consider

There are many things to monitor and tune in the InnoDB storage engine. We have discussed only a portion of those and focused mainly on monitoring the various subsystems and improving performance. However, there are a few other items you may want to consider.

Thread performance can be improved under certain circumstances by adjusting the innodb_thread_concurrency option. The default value is zero in MySQL version 5.5 and later (8 in prior versions), meaning that there is infinite concurrency or many threads executing in the storage engine. This is usually sufficient, but if you are running MySQL on a server with many processors and many independent disks (and heavy use of InnoDB), you may see a performance increase by setting this value equal to the number of processors plus independent disks. This ensures InnoDB will use enough threads to allow maximum concurrent operations. Setting this value to a value greater than what your server can support has little or no effect—if there aren't any available threads, the limit will never be reached.

If your MySQL server is part of a system that is shut down frequently or even periodically (e.g., you run MySQL at startup on your Linux laptop), you may notice when using InnoDB that shutdown can take a long time to complete. Fortunately, InnoDB can be shut down quickly by setting the `innodb_fast_shutdown` option. This does not affect data integrity nor will it result in a loss of memory (buffer) management. It simply skips the potentially expensive operations of purging the internal caches and merging insert buffers. It still performs a controlled shutdown, storing the buffer pools on disk.

By setting the `innodb_lock_wait_timeout` variable, you can control how InnoDB deals with deadlocks. This variable exists at both the global and session level, and controls how long InnoDB will allow a transaction to wait for a row lock before aborting. The default value is 50 seconds. If you are seeing a lot of lock-wait timeouts, you can decrease the value to decrease the amount of time your locks wait. This may help diagnose some of your concurrency problems or at least allow your queries to time out sooner.

If you are importing lots of data, you can improve load time by making sure your incoming datafiles are sorted in primary key order. In addition, you can turn off the automatic commit by setting `AUTOCOMMIT` to 0. This ensures the entire load is committed only once. You can also improve bulk load by turning off foreign key and unique constraints.

 Remember, you should approach tuning InnoDB with great care. With so many things to tweak and adjust, it can be very easy for things to go wrong quickly. Be sure to follow the practice of changing one variable at a time (and only with a purpose) and measure, measure, measure.

Troubleshooting Tips for InnoDB

The best tools to use are those listed earlier, including the InnoDB monitors, the `SHOW ENGINE INNODB STATUS` command (another way to display the data from the InnoDB monitors), and the `PERFORMANCE_SCHEMA` features. However, there are additional strategies that you may find helpful in dealing with errors using InnoDB. This section provides some general best practices for troubleshooting InnoDB problems. Use these practices when faced with trying to solve errors, warnings, and data corruption issues.

Errors

When encountering errors related to InnoDB, find the error information in the error log. To turn on the error log, use the `--log-error` startup option.

Deadlocks

If you encounter multiple deadlock failures, you can use the option `--innodb_print_all_deadlocks` (available in version 5.5 and later) to write all deadlock messages to the error log. This allows you to see more than the last deadlock as shown in the SHOW ENGINE INNODB STATUS and may be informative if your application does not have its own error handlers to deal with deadlocks.

Data dictionary problems

Table definitions are stored in the *.frm* files having the same name as the table and stored under folders by database name. Definitions are also stored in the InnoDB data dictionary. If there is a storage corruption or file broken, you can encounter errors related to a mismatched data dictionary. Here are some of the more common symptoms and solutions:

Orphaned temporary table
> If an ALTER TABLE operation fails, the server may not clean up correctly, leaving a temporary table in the InnoDB tablespace. When this occurs, you can use the table monitor to identify the table name (temporary tables are named starting with #sql). You can then issue a DROP TABLE to drop this table to eliminate the orphaned table.

Cannot open a table
> If you see an error like Can't open file: 'somename.innodb' along with an error message in the error log like Cannot find table *somedb/somename*..., it means there is an orphaned file named *somename.frm* inside the database folder. In this case, deleting the orphaned *.frm* file will correct the problem.

Tablespace does not exist
> If you are using the --innodb_file_per_table option and encounter an error similar to InnoDB data dictionary has tablespace id *N*, but tablespace with the id or name does not exist..., you must drop the table and recreate it. However, it is not that simple. You must first recreate the table in another database, locate the *.frm* there and copy it to the original database, then drop the table. This may generate a warning about a missing *.ibd* file but it will correct the data dictionary. From there, you can recreate the table and restore the data from backup.

Cannot create a table
> If you encounter an error in the error log that tells you the table already exists in the data dictionary, you may have a case where there is no corresponding *.frm* file for the table in question. When this occurs, follow the directions in the error log.

Observe console messages

Some errors and warnings are only printed to the console (e.g., `stdout`, `stderr`). When troubleshooting errors or warnings, it is sometimes best to launch MySQL via the command line instead of using the *mysqld_safe* script. On Windows, you can use the `--console` option to prevent suppression of console messages.

I/O problems

I/O problems are generally encountered on startup or when new objects are created or dropped. These types of errors are associated with the InnoDB files and vary in severity. Unfortunately, these problems are normally very specific to the platform or OS and therefore may require specific steps to correct. As a general strategy, always check your error log or console for errors, checking particularly for OS-specific errors because these can indicate why I/O errors are occurring. Also check for missing or corrupt folders in the data directory along with properly named InnoDB files.

You can also experience I/O problems when there are problems with the data disks. These normally appear at startup but can occur anytime there are disk read or write errors. Hardware errors can sometimes be mistaken for performance problems. Be sure to check your operating system's disk diagnosis as part of your troubleshooting routine.

Sometimes the problem is a configuration issue. In this case, you should double-check your configuration file to ensure InnoDB is properly configured. For example, check to ensure the `innodb_data_*` options are set correctly.

Corrupted databases

If you encounter severe or critical errors in your databases that cause InnoDB to crash or keep the server from starting, you can launch the server with the `innodb_force_re covery` recovery option in your configuration file, assigning it an integer value ranging from 1 to 6 that causes InnoDB to skip certain operations during startup.

 This option is considered a last resort option and should be used only in the most extreme cases where all other attempts to start the server have failed. You should also export the data prior to attempting the procedure.

Here's a brief description of each option (more information can be found in the online reference manual):

1. Skip corrupt pages when select statements are issued. Allows partial data recovery.

2. Do not start the master or purge thread.

3. Do not execute rollbacks after crash recovery.

4. Do not execute insert buffer operations. Do not calculate table statistics.

5. Ignore undo logs on startup.

6. Do not execute the redo log when running recovery.

MyISAM

There are very few things to monitor on the MyISAM storage engine. This is because the MyISAM storage engine was built for web applications with a focus on fast queries and, as such, has only one feature in the server that you can tune—the key cache. That doesn't mean there is nothing else that you can do to improve performance. On the contrary, there are many things you can do, including using options like low priority and concurrent inserts. Most fall into one of three areas: optimizing storage on disk, using memory efficiently by monitoring and tuning the key cache, and tuning your tables for maximum performance.

Rather than discussing the broader aspects of these areas, we provide a strategy organized into the following areas of performance improvement:

- Optimizing disk storage
- Tuning your tables for performance
- Using the MyISAM utilities
- Storing a table in index order
- Compressing tables
- Defragmenting tables
- Monitoring the key cache
- Preloading key caches
- Using multiple key caches
- Other parameters to consider

We will discuss each of these briefly in the sections that follow.

Optimizing Disk Storage

Optimizing disk space for MyISAM is more of a system configuration option than a MyISAM-specific tuning parameter. MyISAM stores each table as its own *.myd* (data-file) and one or more *.myi* (index) files. They are stored with the *.frm* file in the folder under the name of the database in the data directory specified by the --datadir startup option. Thus, optimizing disk space for MyISAM is the same as optimizing disk space for the server (i.e., you can see performance improvements by moving the data directory to its own disk, and you can further improve performance of the disk with RAID or other high availability storage options).

 The latest release of MySQL Utilities includes a new utility named the *.frm* reader (*mysqlfrm*), which allows you to read *.frm* files and produce the CREATE statement for the table. You can use this utility whenever you need to diagnose problems with *.frm* files. See the MySQL Utilities documentation for more information about the *.frm* reader.

Repairing Your Tables

There are a couple of SQL commands that you can use to keep your tables in optimal condition. These include the ANALYZE TABLE, OPTIMIZE TABLE, and REPAIR TABLE commands.

The ANALYZE TABLE command examines and reorganizes the key distribution for a table. The MySQL server uses the key distribution to determine the join order when joining on a field other than a constant. Key distributions also determine which indexes to use for a query. We discuss this command in more detail in "Using ANALYZE TABLE" on page 431.

The REPAIR TABLE command is not really a performance tool—you can use it to fix a corrupted table for the MyISAM, Archive, and CSV storage engines. Use this command to try to recover tables that have become corrupt or are performing very poorly (which is usually a sign that a table has degraded and needs reorganizing or repair).

Use the OPTIMIZE TABLE command to recover deleted blocks and reorganize the table for better performance. You can use this command for MyISAM and InnoDB tables.

While these commands are useful, there are a number of more advanced tools you can use to further manage your MyISAM tables.

Using the MyISAM Utilities

There are a number of special utilities included in the MySQL distribution that are designed for use with the MyISAM storage engine (tables):

- *myisam_ftdump* allows you to display information about full-text indexes.
- *myisamchk* allows you to perform analysis on a MyISAM table.
- *myisamlog* allows you to view the change logs of a MyISAM table.
- *myisampack* allows you to compress a table to minimize storage.

myisamchk is the workhorse utility for MyISAM. It can display information about your MyISAM tables or analyze, repair, and optimize them. You can run the command for one or more tables, but you can only use it when the server is running if you flush the tables and lock them. Alternatively, you can shut down the server.

 Be sure to make a backup of your tables before running this utility in case the repair or optimization steps fail. In rare cases, this has been known to leave tables corrupted and irreparable.

The following list describes options related to performance improvement, recovery, and report status (see the online MySQL Reference Manual for a complete description of the available options):

analyze
: Analyzes the key distribution of indexes to improve query performance.

backup
: Makes a copy of the tables (the *.myd* file) prior to altering them.

check
: Checks the table for errors (report only).

extended-check
: Does a thorough check of the table for errors, including all indexes (report only).

force
: Performs a repair if any errors are found.

information
: Shows statistical information about the table. Use this command first to see the condition of your table before running recover.

medium-check
: Performs a more thorough check of the table (repair only). This does less checking than extended-check.

recover
: Performs a comprehensive repair of the table, repairing the data structures. Repairs everything except duplicate unique keys.

safe-recover
: Performs an older form of repair that reads through all rows in order and updates all of the indexes.

sort index

> Sorts the index tree in high-low order. This can reduce seek time to index structures and make accessing the index faster.

sort records

> Sorts the records in the order of a specified index. This can improve performance for certain index-based queries.

Example 12-6 shows the results of running the myisamchk command to display information about a MyISAM table.

Example 12-6. The myisamchk utility

```
MyISAM file:           /usr/local/mysql/data/employees/employees
Record format:         Packed
Character set:         latin1_swedish_ci (8)
File-version:          1
Creation time:         2012-12-03 08:13:03
Status:                changed
Data records:                297024  Deleted blocks:                3000
Datafile parts:              300024  Deleted data:                 95712
Datafile pointer (bytes):         6  Keyfile pointer (bytes):          6
Datafile length:            9561268  Keyfile length:             3086336
Max datafile length: 281474976710654
Max keyfile length: 288230376151710719
Recordlength:                    44

table description:
Key Start Len Index  Type          Rec/key       Root  Blocksize
1   1     4   unique long                1    2931712       1024
```

Storing a Table in Index Order

You can improve the efficiency of large data retrieval for range queries (e.g., WHERE a > 5 AND a < 15) by storing table data in the same order as it is stored in the index. This type of ordering allows the query to access data in order, without having to search the disk pages for the data. To sort a table in index order, use the *myisamchk* utility sort records option (-R) and specify which index you want to use, starting with number 1 for the first index. The following command sorts table1 from the test database in the order of the second index:

```
myisamchk -R 2 /usr/local/mysql/data/test/table1
```

You can accomplish the same effect using ALTER TABLE and ORDER BY.

Sorting the table like this does not ensure the order will remain by index when new rows are added. Deletions do not disturb the order, but as new rows are added the table can become less ordered and cause your performance advantages to dwindle. If you use this technique for tables that change frequently, you may want to consider running the command periodically to ensure optimal ordering.

Compressing Tables

Compressing data saves space. While there are methods to compress data in MySQL, the MyISAM storage engine allows you to compress (*pack*) read-only tables to save space. They must be read-only because MyISAM does not have the capability to decompress, reorder, or compress additions (or deletions). To compress a table, use the *myisampack* utility as follows:

```
myisampack -b /usr/local/mysql/data/test/table1
```

Always use the backup (-b) option to create a backup of your table prior to compressing it. This will allow you to make the table writable without having to rerun the `myisam pack` command.

There are two reasons for compressing a read-only table. First and foremost, it can save a lot of space for tables that include data that is easy to compress (e.g., text). Second, when a compressed table is read and the query uses the primary key or unique index to find a row, only the single-row data is decompressed prior to additional comparisons.

There are a great many options to the *myisampack* command. If you are interested in compressing your read-only tables for space, see the online MySQL Reference Manual for more details about how to control the compression features.

Defragmenting Tables

When MyISAM tables have had a lot of changes in the form of deletions and insertions, the physical storage can become fragmented. Often there are small gaps in the physical store representing deleted data, or there are records stored out of the original order, or both. To optimize the table and reorganize it back to the desired order and form, use either the `OPTIMIZE TABLE` command or the *myisamchk* utility.

You should run these commands periodically for tables where you have specified a sort order to ensure they are stored in the most optimal manner. You should also run one of these commands when data has undergone many changes over a period of time.

Monitoring the Key Cache

The key cache in MySQL is a very efficient structure designed to store frequently used index data. It is used exclusively for MyISAM and stores the keys using a fast lookup mechanism (usually a B-tree). The indexes are stored internally (in memory) as linked lists and can be searched very quickly. The key cache is created automatically when the first MyISAM table is opened for reading. Each time a query is issued for a MyISAM table, the key cache is examined first. If the index is found there, it performs the index search in memory rather than reading the index from disk first. The key cache is the secret weapon that makes MyISAM so much faster for rapid queries than some other storage engines.

A number of variables control the key cache, and you can monitor each using the SHOW VARIABLES and SHOW STATUS commands. The variables you can monitor with the SHOW commands are shown in Example 12-7.

Example 12-7. The key cache status and system variables

```
mysql> SHOW STATUS LIKE 'Key%';
+------------------------+-------+
| Variable_name          | Value |
+------------------------+-------+
| Key_blocks_not_flushed | 0     |
| Key_blocks_unused      | 6694  |
| Key_blocks_used        | 0     |
| Key_read_requests      | 0     |
| Key_reads              | 0     |
| Key_write_requests     | 0     |
| Key_writes             | 0     |
+------------------------+-------+
7 rows in set (0.00 sec)

mysql> SHOW VARIABLES LIKE 'key%';
+------------------------+---------+
| Variable_name          | Value   |
+------------------------+---------+
| key_buffer_size        | 8384512 |
| key_cache_age_threshold | 300    |
| key_cache_block_size   | 1024    |
| key_cache_division_limit | 100   |
+------------------------+---------+
4 rows in set (0.01 sec)
```

As you can imagine, the key cache can be a very complicated mechanism. Tuning the key cache can therefore be a challenge. We recommend monitoring usage and making changes to the size of the key cache rather than changing how it performs, as it performs very well in the default configuration.

If you want to improve cache hit behavior, use one of the two techniques discussed next: preloading the cache and using multiple key caches along with adding more memory to the default key cache.

Preloading Key Caches

You can preload your indexes into the key cache. This ensures your queries will be faster, because the index is already loaded in the key cache and the index is loaded sequentially (rather than randomly, as would occur when the key cache is loaded under concurrent operation, for example). However, you must ensure there is enough room in the cache to hold the index. Preloading can be a very effective way to speed up your queries for certain applications or modes of use. For example, if you know there will be a lot of queries against a particular table during the execution of an application (e.g., a typical payroll audit), you can preload the associated table indexes into the key cache, thereby improving performance during this activity. To preload the key cache for a table, use the LOAD INDEX command as shown in Example 12-8.

Example 12-8. Preloading indexes into the key cache

```
mysql> LOAD INDEX INTO CACHE salaries IGNORE LEAVES;
+--------------------+--------------+----------+----------+
| Table              | Op           | Msg_type | Msg_text |
+--------------------+--------------+----------+----------+
| employees.salaries | preload_keys | status   | OK       |
+--------------------+--------------+----------+----------+
1 row in set (1.49 sec)
```

This example loads the index for the salary table into the key cache. The IGNORE LEAVES clause preloads only the blocks for the nonleaf nodes of the index. While there is no special command to flush the key cache, you can forcibly remove an index from the key cache by modifying the table—for example, by reorganizing the index or simply dropping and recreating the index.

Using Multiple Key Caches

One of the little-known advanced features of MySQL is the creation of multiple key caches or custom key caches to reduce contention for the default key cache. This feature allows you to load the index of one or more tables into a special cache that you configure yourself. As you can imagine, this means allocating memory to the task and as such requires careful planning. However, the performance benefits may be substantial if there are periods in which you are executing many queries against a set of tables where the indexes are frequently referenced.

To create a secondary key cache, first define it with the SET command by allocating memory, then issue one or more CACHE INDEX commands to load the indexes for one or more tables. Unlike the default key cache, you can flush or remove a secondary key cache by setting its size to 0. Example 12-9 shows how to create a secondary key cache and add the index for a table to the cache.

Example 12-9. Using secondary key caches

```
mysql> SET GLOBAL emp_cache.key_buffer_size=128*1024;
Query OK, 0 rows affected (0.00 sec)

mysql> CACHE INDEX salaries IN emp_cache;
+--------------------+-------------------+----------+----------+
| Table              | Op                | Msg_type | Msg_text |
+--------------------+-------------------+----------+----------+
| employees.salaries | assign_to_keycache | status  | OK       |
+--------------------+-------------------+----------+----------+
1 row in set (0.00 sec)
```

```
mysql> SET GLOBAL emp_cache.key_buffer_size=0;
Query OK, 0 rows affected (0.00 sec)
```

Notice that the secondary cache involves defining a new variable named `emp_cache` and setting its size to 128 KB. This is a special syntax of the `SET` command and while it appears to create a new system variable, it is actually creating a new global user variable. You can discover the existence or size of a secondary key cache as follows:

```
mysql> select @@global.emp_cache.key_buffer_size;
+------------------------------------+
| @@global.emp_cache.key_buffer_size |
+------------------------------------+
|                             131072 |
+------------------------------------+
1 row in set (0.00 sec)
```

Secondary key caches are global and thus exist until you flush them by setting their size to 0 or when the server is restarted.

 You can save the configuration of multiple key caches by storing the statements in a file and using the `init-file=path_to_file` command in the `[mysqld]` section of the MySQL option file to execute the statements on startup.

Other Parameters to Consider

There are a number of other parameters to consider (remember that you should change only one thing at a time and only if you have a good reason to do so; you should never change the configuration of a complex feature like a storage engine without a good reason and reasonable expectations for the outcome):

`myisam_data_pointer_size`
> The default pointer size in bytes (2–7) used by `CREATE TABLE` if there is no value specified for `MAX_ROWS` (the maximum number of rows to store in the table). It has a default value of 6.

`myisam_max_sort_file_size`
> Maximum size of a temporary file used when sorting data. Increasing this value may make repairs and reorganization of index operations faster.

`myisam_recover_options`
> The recovery mode for MyISAM. You can use this for `OPTIMIZE TABLE` as well. The modes include default, backup, force, and quick, and can take any combination of these options. Default means recovery is performed without a backup, force, or quick checking. Backup means a backup will be created before recovery. Force means recovery continues even if data is lost (more than one row). Quick means

the rows in the table are not checked if there are no blocks marked as deleted. Consider the severity of the recovery when determining which options to use.

`myisam_repair_threads`
: If set to a value greater than 1, repair and sorting operations are done in parallel and can make the operations a bit faster. Otherwise, they are done sequentially.

`myisam_sort_buffer_size`
: The size of the buffer for sorting operations. Increasing this value can help with sorting indexes. However, values greater than 4 GB work only on 64-bit machines.

`myisam_stats_method`
: Controls how the server counts NULL values in index value distribution for statistical operations. This can also affect the optimizer, so use with care.

`myisam_use_mmap`
: Turns the memory map option on for reading and writing MyISAM tables. Can be helpful in situations where there are a lot of small writes that contend with read queries that return large data sets.

We have discussed a number of strategies for monitoring and improving MyISAM performance. While the discussion is brief, it covers the most important aspects of using MyISAM effectively. For more information about the key cache and the MyISAM storage engine, see the online MySQL Reference Manual.

MySQL, Replication, and High Availability

There is a higher probability of corruption of MyISAM data than InnoDB data and, as a result, MyISAM requires longer recovery times. Also, because MyISAM does not support transactions, events are executed one at a time, which could lead to partial statement execution and therefore an incomplete transaction. Add to this the fact that the slave executes as a single thread, which could allow the slave to fall behind when processing long-running queries. Thus, using MyISAM on a slave in a high-availability solution with transactions can be problematic.

Conclusion

This chapter examined how to monitor and improve the performance of storage engines in the MySQL server. We have discussed the specifics of two of the most popular storage engines, and in the next chapter, we turn our attention to the more advanced topic of monitoring and improving the performance of replication.

Joel paused with his mouse over the Send button. He had prepared a report on the InnoDB monitoring data he collected and had written some recommendations in an email message to his boss. But he wasn't sure he should send it without being asked. Shrugging, he figured it couldn't hurt, so he hit Send.

About two minutes later, his email application popped up a box from his system tray proclaiming a new email message. Joel clicked on the message. It was from his boss.

"Joel, nice work on the InnoDB stuff. I want you to call a meeting with the developers and the IT folks. Have a sit-down and get everyone on board with your recommendations. Make it happen. I'll be in the office on Monday."

"OK," Joel said, as he felt the burden of responsibility slip onto his shoulders. He realized this was his first meeting since being hired. He was a little nervous, so he decided to go for a walk before making an agenda and sending out an email message inviting people to attend. "Well, it can't be any worse than my thesis defense."

## CHAPTER 13

Replication Monitoring

Joel spent a few moments logging into the Seattle replication slave and determined that replication was still running.

A familiar voice spoke from his doorway. "What about that Seattle thing, Joel? Are you on it?"

"I'm still working on that one, sir. I need to figure out the replication configuration and monitor the problem." Joel thought to himself, "… and read more about replication monitoring."

"All right, Joel. I'll let you work. I'll check on you again after lunch."

As his boss left, Joel looked at his watch. "OK, so I've got about an hour to figure out how to monitor replication."

With a deep sigh, Joel once again opened his MySQL book to learn more about monitoring MySQL. "I didn't think replication could lead to so many problems of its own," he muttered.

Now that you know when your servers are performing well (and when they aren't), how do you know how well your replication is performing? Things may be going smoothly, but how do you know that?

In this chapter, we discuss advanced monitoring, focusing on monitoring and improving replication performance.

Getting Started

There are two areas that can affect the performance of your replication topology. You must ensure both are optimized to avoid affecting replication.

First, ensure your network has the bandwidth to handle the replicated data. As we've discussed, the master makes a copy of the changes and sends it to the slaves via a network connection. If the network connection is slow or is suffering from contention, so too will your replicated data. We discuss some ways to tune your network and ways you can tune replication to make the best of certain networking environments.

Second, and most important, ensure the databases you are replicating are optimized. This is vital because any inefficiency in the database on the master will be compounded by the same poor database performance on the slaves. This is especially true concerning indexing and normalization. However, a well-tuned database is only half of the equation. You must also ensure your queries are optimized. For example, a poorly tuned query run on the master will run just as poorly on your slaves.

Once you have your network performing well and your databases and queries optimized, you can focus on configuring your servers for optimal performance.

Server Setup

Another very important thing you can do to create the best platform for your replication topology is make sure your servers are configured for optimal performance. A poorly performing replication topology can often be traced back to poorly performing servers. Ensure your servers are operating with enough memory and that the storage devices and storage engine choices are optimal for your databases.

Some recommend using lower-performing machines for slaves, noting that the slave does not have as much running on it (typically, slaves only process SELECT queries, while the master handles updates to data). However, this is incorrect. In a typical single master and single slave where all databases are being replicated, both machines have about the same load, but because the slave is executing the events in a single thread versus many threads on the master, even though the workload is the same, the slave may take more time to process and execute the events.

Perhaps the best way to view this issue is to consider that one of the best uses of replication is failover. If your slaves are slower than your master and if you must fail over in the event that your master suffers a failure, the expectation is that your promoted slave should have the same performance as your demoted master.

Inclusive and Exclusive Replication

You can configure your replication to replicate all data (the default); log only some data or exclude certain data on the master, thereby limiting what is written to the binary log and what is replicated; or you can configure your slave to act on only certain data. Using inclusive or exclusive replication (or both) can help resolve complex load balancing or scale-out issues, making replication more powerful and more flexible. Another name for this process is *filtering data*, where the combination of the inclusive and exclusive lists form the filter criteria.

On the master, use the `--binlog-do-db` startup option to specify that you want only events for a certain database to be written to the binary log. You can specify one or more of these options, specifying one database per option, on the command line or in your configuration file.

You can also specify that you want to exclude (ignore) events for a certain database using the `--binlog-ignore-db` startup option. You can specify one or more of these options, specifying one database per option, on the command line or in your configuration file. This option tells the master to not log any events that act on the database(s) listed.

 You can use the `--binlog-do-db` and `--binlog-ignore-db` options together, provided the databases listed do not overlap. If a database name appears on both lists, the database in the `--binlog-ignore-db` list is ignored. Be sure to check the values of these variables when diagnosing data replication issues (e.g., missing data on the slave).

Additionally, when you use the `--binlog-do-db` or `--binlog-ignore-db` options, you are filtering what goes into the binary log. This severely limits the use of PITR, because you can only recover what was written to the binary log.

There are several options you can use to control which data is replicated on the slave. There are companion options for the binlog options on the master, options to restrict at the table level, and even a command to do a transformation (rename).

Performing inclusive or exclusive replication on the slave may not improve performance of replication across the topology. While the slaves may store less data, the same amount of data is transmitted by the master, and the overhead of doing the filter on the slave may not gain much if the inclusive and exclusive lists are complex. If you are worried about transmitting too much data over the network, it is best to perform the filtering on the master.

On the slave, you can specify that you want to include only those events for a certain database to be read and executed from the relay log with the `--replicate-do-db` startup option. You can specify one or more of these options, specifying one database per option, on the command line or in your configuration file. This option tells the slave to execute only those events that act on the database(s) listed.

You can also specify that you want to exclude (ignore) events for a certain database using the `--replicate-ignore-db` startup option. You can specify one or more of these options, specifying one database per option, on the command line or in your configuration file. This option tells the slave to not execute any events that act on the database(s) listed.

The replicate options on the slave behave differently depending on which format you use. This is especially important for statement-based replication and could lead to data loss. For example, if you are using statement-based replication and you use the `--replicate-do-db` option, the slave restricts events to only those statements following the `USE <db>` command. If you issue a statement for a different database without a change of database, the statement is ignored. See the online MySQL Reference Manual for additional details about these limitations.

You can perform inclusive and exclusive replication on the slave at the table level. Use the `--replicate-do-table` and `--replicate-ignore-table` options to execute or ignore only those events for a specific table. These commands are very handy if you have a table with sensitive data that isn't used by your application but is critical to administration or other special functions. For example, if you have an application that includes pricing information from your vendors (what you pay for something), you may want to hide that information if you employ or contract out sales services. Rather than building a special application for your contractors, you can deploy your existing application so that it uses a slave that replicates everything, excluding the tables that contain the sensitive information.

There are also forms of the last two options that permit the use of wildcard patterns. These options, `replicate-wild-do-table` and `replicate-wild-ignore-table`, perform the same functionality as their namesakes, but support the use of wildcards. For example, `--replicate-wild-do-table=db1.tbl%` executes events for any tables that start with "tbl" in *db1* (e.g., `tbl`, `tbl1`, `tbl_test`). Similarly, you can use `--replicate-wild-do-table=db1.%` to execute events for any object in the *db1* database. These wildcard versions of the slave-side filtering can be another asset when solving complex replication scenarios.

There is also a transformation option you can use on the slave to rename or change the name of a database for table operations on the slave. It applies only to tables. You can do this using the `--replicate-rewrite-db="<from>-><to>"` option (you must use the quotes). This option only changes the name of the database for table events; it does not change the names for commands like `CREATE DATABASE`, `ALTER DATABASE`, and so on. It only affects events for which a database is specified (or to redirect the default database for statement-based replication). You can use this option more than once for multiple database name transformations.

While not strictly an inclusive or exclusive replication option, `--replicate-same-server-id` prevents infinite loops in circular replication. If set to 0, it tells the slave to skip events that have the same `server_id`. If you set it to 1, the slave will process all events.

Replication Threads

Before we explore monitoring of the master and slave, we should reexamine the threads involved in replication. We present these again here from the perspective of monitoring and diagnosing problems.

There are three threads that control replication. Each performs a specific role. On the master, there is a single thread per connected slave called the Binlog Dump thread. It is responsible for sending the binlog events to the connected slaves. On the slave, there are two threads, the Slave IO thread and the Slave SQL thread. The I/O thread is responsible for reading the incoming binlog events from the master and writing them to the slave's relay log. The SQL thread is responsible for reading the events in the relay log and executing them.

You can monitor the current state of the Binlog Dump thread using the SHOW PROCESS LIST command:

```
mysql> SHOW PROCESSLIST \G
*************************** 1. row ***************************
     Id: 1
   User: rpl
   Host: localhost:54197
     db: NULL
Command: Binlog Dump
   Time: 25
  State: Master has sent all binlog to slave; waiting for binlog to be updated
   Info: NULL
```

Notice the State column. The data presented here is a description of what the master is doing with respect to the binary log and the slaves. This example is a typical result for a well-running replication topology. The display shows the following columns:

Id
> Displays the connection ID.

User
> Displays the user who ran the statement.

Host
> The host where the statement originated.

db
> The default database if specified; otherwise, NULL is displayed, indicating no default database was specified.

Command
> The type of command the thread is running. See the online MySQL Reference Manual for more information.

Time

> The time (in seconds) that the thread has been in the reported state.

State

> The description of the current action or state (e.g., waiting). This is normally a descriptive text message.

Info

> The statement the thread is executing. NULL indicates no statement is in progress. This is the case for the replication threads when they are in waiting states.

You can also see the thread status on the slave. You can monitor the I/O and SQL threads using the SHOW PROCESSLIST command:

```
mysql> SHOW PROCESSLIST \G
*************************** 1. row ***************************
     Id: 2
   User: system user
   Host:
     db: NULL
Command: Connect
   Time: 127
  State: Waiting for master to send event
   Info: NULL
*************************** 2. row ***************************
     Id: 3
   User: system user
   Host:
     db: NULL
Command: Connect
   Time: 10
  State: Slave has read all relay log; waiting for the slave I/O thread to
         update it
   Info: NULL
```

Again, the State column contains the most important information. If you are having problems with replication on your slave, be sure to issue the SHOW PROCESSLIST command on the slave and take note of the I/O and SQL thread states. In this example, we see the normal states of a slave waiting for information from the master (I/O thread) and having executed all events in the relay log (SQL thread).

 It is always a good idea to use the SHOW PROCESSLIST command to check the status of the replication when troubleshooting.

Monitoring the Master

There are several ways to monitor your master. You can issue SHOW commands to see status information and status variables or use MySQL Workbench. The primary SQL commands include SHOW MASTER STATUS, SHOW BINARY LOGS, and SHOW BINLOG EVENTS.

In this section, we will examine the SQL commands available for monitoring the master and provide a brief summary of the available status variables you can monitor either by using the SHOW STATUS command or by creating custom graphs.

Monitoring Commands for the Master

The SHOW MASTER STATUS command displays information about the master's binary log, including the name and offset position of the current binlog file. This information is vital in connecting slaves, as we have discussed in previous chapters. It also provides information about logging constraints. Example 13-1 shows the result of a typical SHOW MASTER STATUS command.

Example 13-1. The SHOW MASTER STATUS command

```
mysql> SHOW MASTER STATUS \G
*************************** 1. row ***************************
            File: mysql-bin.000002
        Position: 156058362
    Binlog_Do_DB: Inventory
 Binlog_Ignore_DB: Vendor_sales
Executed_Gtid_Set: 87e02a46-5363-11e2-9d4a-ed25ee3d6542
1 row in set (0.00 sec)
```

The data is displayed in the following columns:

File

    This column lists the name of the current binlog file.

Position

    This column lists the current position (next write) in the binary log.

Binlog_Do_DB

    This column lists any databases specified by the --binlog-do-db startup option discussed earlier.

Binlog_Ignore_DB

    This column lists any databases specified by the --binlog-ignore-db startup option discussed earlier.

Executed_Gtid_Set

This column lists the GTIDs that have been executed on the master. This column is valid on servers that have GTIDs enabled. It displays the same values as the gtid_executed server variable.

The SHOW BINARY LOGS command (also known by its alias, SHOW MASTER LOGS) displays the list of binlog files available on the master and their sizes in bytes. This command is useful for comparing the information on the slave concerning where the slave is with respect to the master (i.e., which binary log the slave is currently reading from on the master). Example 13-2 shows the results of a typical SHOW MASTER LOGS command.

 You can rotate the binary log on the master with the FLUSH LOGS command. This command closes and reopens all logs and opens a new log with an incremented file extension. You should periodically flush the log to help manage the growth of logs over time. It also helps with diagnosing replication problems.

Example 13-2. The SHOW MASTER LOGS command on the master

```
mysql> SHOW MASTER LOGS;
+-------------------+-----------+
| Log_name          | File_size |
+-------------------+-----------+
| master-bin.000001 | 103648205 |
| master-bin.000002 |   2045693 |
| master-bin.000003 |   1022910 |
| master-bin.000004 |   3068436 |
+-------------------+-----------+
4 rows in set (0.00 sec)
```

You can also use the SHOW BINLOG EVENTS command to show events in the binary log. The syntax of the command is as follows:

```
SHOW BINLOG EVENTS [IN <log>] [FROM <pos>] [LIMIT [<offset>,] <rows>]
```

Take care when using this command, as it can produce a lot of data. It is best used to compare events on the master with events on the slave read from its relay log. Example 13-3 shows the binlog events from a typical replication configuration.

Example 13-3. The SHOW BINLOG EVENTS command (statement-based)

```
mysql> SHOW BINLOG EVENTS IN 'master-bin.000001' FROM 2571 LIMIT 4 \G
*************************** 1. row ***************************
   Log_name: master-bin.000001
        Pos: 2571
  Event_type: Query
   Server_id: 1
End_log_pos: 2968
       Info: use `employees`; CREATE TABLE salaries (
```

```
     emp_no      INT              NOT NULL,
     salary      INT              NOT NULL,
     from_date   DATE             NOT NULL,
     to_date     DATE             NOT NULL,
     KEY         (emp_no),
     FOREIGN KEY (emp_no) REFERENCES employees (emp_no)
     ON DELETE CASCADE,
     PRIMARY KEY (emp_no, from_date)
)
*************************** 2. row ***************************
   Log_name: master-bin.000001
        Pos: 2968
 Event_type: Query
  Server_id: 1
End_log_pos: 3041
       Info: BEGIN
*************************** 3. row ***************************
   Log_name: master-bin.000001
        Pos: 3041
 Event_type: Query
  Server_id: 1
End_log_pos: 3348
       Info: use `employees`; INSERT INTO `departments` VALUES
       ('d001','Marketing'),('d002','Finance'),('d003','Human Resources'),
       ('d004','Production'),('d005','Development'),('d006','Quality
       Management'),('d007','Sales'),('d008','Research'),('d009',
       'Customer Service')
*************************** 4. row ***************************
   Log_name: master-bin.000001
        Pos: 3348
 Event_type: Xid
  Server_id: 1
End_log_pos: 3375
       Info: COMMIT /* xid=17 */
4 rows in set (0.01 sec)
```

In this example, we are using statement-based replication. Had we used row-based replication, the binlog events would have looked very different. You can see the difference in Example 13-4.

Example 13-4. The SHOW BINLOG EVENTS command (row-based)

```
mysql> SHOW BINLOG EVENTS IN 'master-bin.000001' FROM 2571 LIMIT 4 \G
*************************** 1. row ***************************
   Log_name: master-bin.000001
        Pos: 2571
 Event_type: Query
  Server_id: 1
End_log_pos: 2968
       Info: use `employees`; CREATE TABLE salaries (
     emp_no      INT              NOT NULL,
     salary      INT              NOT NULL,
```

```
   from_date   DATE          NOT NULL,
   to_date     DATE          NOT NULL,
   KEY         (emp_no),
   FOREIGN KEY (emp_no) REFERENCES employees (emp_no) ON DELETE CASCADE,
   PRIMARY KEY (emp_no, from_date)
)
*************************** 2. row ***************************
   Log_name: master-bin.000001
        Pos: 2968
 Event_type: Query
  Server_id: 1
End_log_pos: 3041
       Info: BEGIN
*************************** 3. row ***************************
   Log_name: master-bin.000001
        Pos: 3041
 Event_type: Table_map
  Server_id: 1
End_log_pos: 3101
       Info: table_id: 15 (employees.departments)
*************************** 4. row ***************************
   Log_name: master-bin.000001
        Pos: 3101
 Event_type: Write_rows
  Server_id: 1
End_log_pos: 3292
       Info: table_id: 15 flags: STMT_END_F
4 rows in set (0.01 sec)
```

Notice there is far less information to see in the binary log of a row-based format. It can sometimes be beneficial to switch to a statement-based row format when diagnosing complex problems with data corruption or intermittent failures. For example, it may be helpful to see exactly what is written to the binary log on the master and compare that to what is read from the relay log on the slave. If there are differences, they could be easier to find in a statement-based format than in a row-based format where the data is in a machine-readable format. See Chapter 3 for more details about the formats of the binary log and the advantages and trade-offs of using one versus the other.

 The *mysqlbinlog* tool includes the `--verbose` option, which constructs SQL commands from row events. Use this option when exploring row-based log events to discover more information about each event. Note that the reconstructed SQL statements are not complete in the sense that they are identical to the original query. Thus, the use of this option is not a complete reconstruction of the events from row format to SQL.

Master Status Variables

There are only a couple status variables for monitoring the master (these are limited to counters that indicate how many times a master-related command has been issued on the master):

Com_change_master

Shows the number of times the CHANGE MASTER command was issued. If this value changes frequently or is significantly higher than the number of your servers times the number of scheduled restarts on your slaves, you may have a situation where additional slaves are being restarted too frequently; this can be an indication of unstable connectivity.

Com_show_master_status

Shows the number of times the SHOW MASTER STATUS command was issued. As with Com_change_master, high values of this counter can indicate an unusual number of inquiries for reconnecting slaves.

Monitoring Slaves

There are several ways to monitor your slaves. You can issue SHOW commands to see status information and status variables or use MySQL Workbench. The primary SQL commands include SHOW SLAVE STATUS, SHOW BINARY LOGS, and SHOW BINLOG EVENTS.

In this section, we will examine the SQL commands available for monitoring a slave and give a brief summary of the available status variables that you can monitor with either the SHOW STATUS command or by creating custom graphs with the MySQL Workbench. We will look at the MySQL Workbench in "Replication Monitoring with MySQL Workbench" on page 493.

Monitoring Commands for the Slave

The SHOW SLAVE STATUS command displays information about the slave's binary log, its connection to the server, and replication activity, including the name and offset position of the current binlog file. This information is vital in diagnosing slave performance, as we have seen in previous chapters. Example 13-5 shows the result of a typical SHOW SLAVE STATUS command executed on a server running MySQL version 5.6.

Example 13-5. The SHOW SLAVE STATUS command

```
mysql> SHOW SLAVE STATUS \G
*************************** 1. row ***************************
               Slave_IO_State: Waiting for master to send event
                  Master_Host: localhost
                  Master_User: rpl
                  Master_Port: 3306
                Connect_Retry: 60
```

```
                Master_Log_File: mysql-bin.000002
            Read_Master_Log_Pos: 39016226
                 Relay_Log_File: relay-bin.000004
                  Relay_Log_Pos: 9353715
          Relay_Master_Log_File: mysql-bin.000002
               Slave_IO_Running: Yes
              Slave_SQL_Running: Yes
                Replicate_Do_DB:
            Replicate_Ignore_DB:
             Replicate_Do_Table:
         Replicate_Ignore_Table:
        Replicate_Wild_Do_Table:
    Replicate_Wild_Ignore_Table:
                     Last_Errno: 0
                     Last_Error:
                   Skip_Counter: 0
            Exec_Master_Log_Pos: 594
                Relay_Log_Space: 1008
                Until_Condition: None
                 Until_Log_File:
                  Until_Log_Pos: 0
             Master_SSL_Allowed: No
             Master_SSL_CA_File:
             Master_SSL_CA_Path:
                Master_SSL_Cert:
              Master_SSL_Cipher:
                 Master_SSL_Key:
          Seconds_Behind_Master: 0
Master_SSL_Verify_Server_Cert: No
                  Last_IO_Errno: 0
                  Last_IO_Error:
                 Last_SQL_Errno: 0
                 Last_SQL_Error:
     Replicate_Ignore_Server_Ids:
               Master_Server_Id: 2
                    Master_UUID: 87e02a46-5363-11e2-9d4a-ed25ee3d6542
               Master_Info_File: /Users/cbell/source/temp_13002/master.info
                      SQL_Delay: 0
            SQL_Remaining_Delay: NULL
        Slave_SQL_Running_State: Slave has read all relay log; waiting for the slave
                                 I/O thread to update it
             Master_Retry_Count: 86400
                    Master_Bind:
        Last_IO_Error_Timestamp:
       Last_SQL_Error_Timestamp:
                 Master_SSL_Crl:
             Master_SSL_Crlpath:
             Retrieved_Gtid_Set: 87e02a46-5363-11e2-9d4a-ed25ee3d6542:1-2
              Executed_Gtid_Set: 87e02a46-5363-11e2-9d4a-ed25ee3d6542:1-2,
                                 d28c2ea6-5362-11e2-9d45-c78c6761ae47:1
                  Auto_Position: 1
1 row in set (0.00 sec)
```

There is a lot of information here. This is the most important command for replication. It is a good idea to study the details of each item presented. Rather than listing the information item by item, we present the information from the perspective of an administrator (i.e., the information is normally inspected with a specific goal in mind). Thus, we group the information into categories for easier reference. These categories include master connection information, slave performance, log information, filtering, log performance, and error conditions.

The first row contains the most important information: the current status of the I/O thread. The status can be connecting to the master, waiting for events from the master, reconnecting to the master, and so on.

The information displayed about the master connection includes the current hostname of the master, the user account used to connect, and the port the slave is connected to on the master. Toward the bottom of the listing is the SSL connection information (if you are using an SSL connection).

The next category includes information about the binary log on the master and the relay log on the slave. The filename and position of each are displayed. It is important to note these values whenever you diagnose replication problems. Of particular note is Re lay_Master_Log_File, which shows the filename of the master binary log where the most recent event from the relay log has been executed.

Replication filtering configuration lists all of the slave-side replication filters. Check here if you are uncertain how your filters are set up.

Also included is the last error number and text for the slave and the I/O and SQL threads. Beyond the state values for the slave threads, this information is most often examined when there is an error. It can be helpful to check this information first when encountering errors on the slave, before examining the error log, as this information is the most current and normally gives you the reason for the failure.

There is also information about the configuration of the slave, including the settings for the skip counter and the until conditions. See the MySQL Reference Manual for more information about these fields.

Near the bottom of the list is the current error information. This includes errors for the slave's I/O and SQL threads. These values should always be 0 for a properly functioning slave.

Some of the more important performance columns are discussed in more detail here:

Connect_Retry
: The number of seconds that expire between retry connect attempts. This value should always be low, but you may want to set it higher if you have a case where the slave is having issues connecting to the master.

Exec_Master_Log_Pos

This shows the position of the last event executed from the master's binary log.

Relay_Log_Space

The total size of all of the relay logfiles. You can use this to determine if you need to purge the relay logs in the event you are running low on disk space.

Seconds_Behind_Master

The number of seconds between the time an event was executed and the time the event was written in the master's binary log. A high value here can indicate significant replication lag. We discuss replication lag in an upcoming section.

The value for Seconds_Behind_Master could become stale when replication stops due to network failures, loss of heartbeat from the master, and so on. It is most meaningful when replication is running.

Retrieved_Gtid_Set

The list of GTIDs (transactions) received by this slave. If the list of GTIDs received does not match the executed GTIDs on the master, the slave may be lagging behind reading events from the master. This value is empty when GTIDs are turned off.

Executed_Gtid_Set

The list of GTIDs (transactions) executed on the slave. If the list does not match Retrieved_Gtid_Set, it may indicate that the slave has not executed all of the transactions or there are transactions that originated on the slave. This value is empty when GTIDs are turned off.

If your replication topology is using GTIDs, Retrieved_Gtid and Execut ed_Gtid_Set can be very important when determining missing transactions or significant slave lag. See the online MySQL Reference Manual section titled "Replication with Global Transaction Identifiers" for more information about GTIDs and how to manage transactions among servers in the topology.

If your slave has binary logging enabled, the SHOW BINARY LOGS command displays the list of binlog files available on the slave and their sizes in bytes. Example 13-6 shows the results of a typical SHOW BINARY LOGS command.

You can rotate the relay log on the slave by using the FLUSH LOGS command.

Example 13-6. The SHOW BINARY LOGS command on the slave

```
mysql> SHOW BINARY LOGS;
+-------------------+-----------+
| Log_name          | File_size |
+-------------------+-----------+
| slave-bin.000001  |   5151604 |
| slave-bin.000002  |   1030108 |
| slave-bin.000003  |   1030044 |
+-------------------+-----------+
3 rows in set (0.00 sec)
```

You can also use the SHOW BINLOG EVENTS command to show events in the binary log on the slave, if the slave has binary logging enabled and the log_slave_updates option is specified. Example 13-7 shows the binlog events from a typical replication configuration.

In MySQL versions 5.5 and later, you can also inspect the slave's relay log with SHOW RELAYLOG EVENTS.

Example 13-7. The SHOW BINLOG EVENTS command (statement-based)

```
mysql> SHOW BINLOG EVENTS IN 'slave-bin.000001' FROM 2701 LIMIT 2 \G
*************************** 1. row ***************************
   Log_name: slave-bin.000001
        Pos: 2701
 Event_type: Query
  Server_id: 1
End_log_pos: 3098
       Info: use `employees`; CREATE TABLE salaries (
   emp_no      INT             NOT NULL,
   salary      INT             NOT NULL,
   from_date   DATE            NOT NULL,
   to_date     DATE            NOT NULL,
   KEY         (emp_no),
   FOREIGN KEY (emp_no) REFERENCES employees (emp_no) ON DELETE CASCADE,
   PRIMARY KEY (emp_no, from_date)
)
*************************** 2. row ***************************
   Log_name: slave-bin.000001
        Pos: 3098
 Event_type: Query
  Server_id: 1
End_log_pos: 3405
       Info: use `employees`; INSERT INTO `departments` VALUES
   ('d001','Marketing'),('d002','Finance'),
   ('d003','Human Resources'),('d004','Production'),
   ('d005','Development'),('d006','Quality Management'),
   ('d007','Sales'),('d008','Research'),
   ('d009','Customer Service')
2 rows in set (0.01 sec)
```

Slave Status Variables

There are only a few status variables for monitoring the slave. These include counters that indicate how many times a slave-related command was issued on the master and statistics for key slave operations. The first four listed here are simply counters of the various slave-related commands. The values should correspond with the frequency of the maintenance of your slaves. If they do not, you may want to investigate the possibility that there are more slaves in your topology than you expected or that a particular slave is being restarted too frequently. The variables include the following:

Com_show_slave_hosts
> The number of times the SHOW SLAVE HOSTS command was issued.

Com_show_slave_status
> The number of times the SHOW SLAVE STATUS command was issued.

Com_slave_start
> The number of times the SLAVE START command was issued.

Com_slave_stop
> The number of times the SLAVE STOP command was issued.

Slave_heartbeat_period
> The current configuration for the number of seconds that elapse between heartbeat checks of the master.

Slave_last_heartbeat
> The most recent heartbeat event received. It is displayed as a timestamp value. If the current value is less than the current value plus Slave_heartbeat_period, the heartbeat event may be delayed. Significant lag can indicate a possible connection problem with the master.

Slave_open_temp_tables
> The number of temporary tables the slave's SQL thread is using. A high value can indicate the slave is overburdened.

Slave_received_heartbeats
> The count of heartbeat replies from the master. This value should correspond roughly to the elapsed time since the slave was restarted divided by the heartbeat interval.

Slave_retried_transactions
> The number of times the SQL thread has retried transactions since the slave was started.

Slave_running
> Simply displays ON if the slave is connected to the master and the I/O and SQL threads are executing without error. Otherwise displays OFF.

Replication Monitoring with MySQL Workbench

You have seen how you can use MySQL Workbench to monitor network traffic and storage engines. MySQL Workbench can display the status variables and system variables using an easy to navigate set of lists. Figure 13-1 shows the MySQL Workbench system administration status and system variables page highlighting the replication status variables. You can use this page to quickly see how your replication is reporting status.

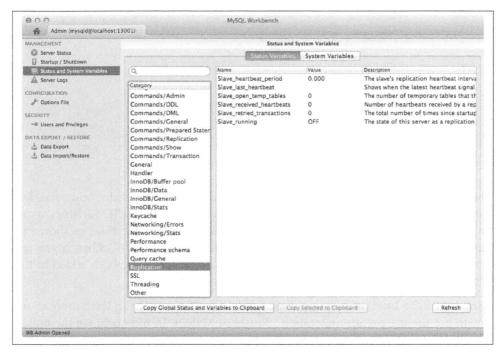

Figure 13-1. Replication status variables

MySQL Workbench also permits you to see the replication system variables and their values. If you click on the System Variables tab, you will see a long list of categories on the left. Choosing any of the replication categories will show the associated system variables. Figure 13-2 shows the replication slave system variables. Notice the [rw] prefix on some of the variables. This indicates the variables are read/write and therefore ones you can change at runtime.

Figure 13-2. Replication system variables

The system administration feature also allows you to search for status and variables. Currently, MySQL Workbench version 5.2.45 does not group the GTID variables under the replication categories. But you can search for the GTID variables as shown in Figure 13-3. In this way, regardless of which version of MySQL Workbench you are using, you can access any status or system variable that may have been added to the system or that Workbench does not group as you expect.

Chapter 11 has a brief tutorial on the use of MySQL Workbench. To learn more about how to use the system administration features of MySQL Workbench, see the online reference manual (*http://bit.ly/mysql-workb*).

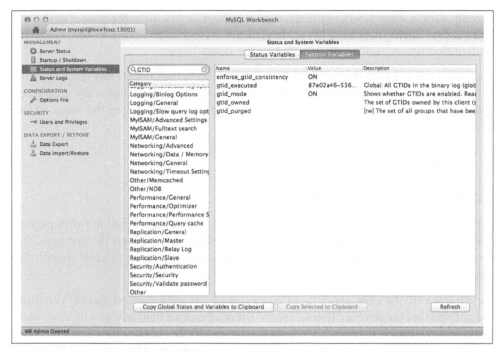

Figure 13-3. GTID system variables

Other Items to Consider

This section discusses some additional considerations for monitoring replication. It includes special networking considerations and monitoring lag (delays in replication).

Networking

If you have limited networking bandwidth, high contention for the bandwidth, or simply a very slow connection, you can improve replication performance by using compression. You can configure compression using the `slave_compressed_protocol` variable.

In cases where network bandwidth is not a problem but you have data that you want to protect while in transit from the master to the slaves, you can use an SSL connection. You can configure the SSL connection using the `CHANGE MASTER` command. See the section titled "Setting Up Replication Using SSL" in the online MySQL Reference Manual for details on using SSL connections in replication.

Another networking configuration you may want to consider is using master heartbeats. You have seen where this information is shown on the `SHOW SLAVE STATUS` command. A heartbeat is a mechanism to automatically check connection status between a master and a slave. It can detect levels of connectivity in milliseconds. Master heartbeat is used in replication scenarios where the slave must be kept in sync with the master with little or no delay. Having the capability to detect when a threshold expires ensures the delay is identified before replication is halted on the slave.

You can configure master heartbeat using a parameter in the CHANGE MASTER command with the `master_heartbeat_period=<value>` setting, where the value is the number of seconds at which you want the heartbeat to occur. You can monitor the status of the heartbeat with the following commands:

```
SHOW STATUS like 'slave_heartbeat period'
SHOW STATUS like 'slave_received_heartbeats'
```

Monitor and Manage Slave Lag

Periods of massive updates, overburdened slaves, or other significant network performance events can cause your slaves to lag behind the master. When this happens, the slaves are not processing the events in their relay logs fast enough to keep up with the changes sent from the master.

As you saw with the SHOW SLAVE STATUS command, Seconds_Behind_Master can show indications that the slave is running behind the master. This field tells you by how many seconds the slave's SQL thread is behind the slave's I/O thread (i.e., how far behind the slave is in processing the incoming events from the master). The slave uses the timestamps of the events to calculate this value. When the SQL thread on the slave reads an event from the master, it calculates the difference in the timestamp. The following excerpt shows a condition in which the slave is 146 seconds behind the master (in this case, the slave is more than two minutes behind, which can be a problem if your application is relying on the slaves to provide timely information):

```
mysql> SHOW SLAVE STATUS \G
...
        Seconds_Behind_Master: 146
...
```

The SHOW PROCESSLIST command (run on the slave) can also provide an indication of how far behind the slave is. Here, we see the number of seconds that the SQL thread is behind, measured using the difference between the timestamp of the last replicated event and the real time of the slave. For example, if your slaves have been offline for 30 minutes and have reconnected to the master, you would expect to see a value of approximately 1,800 seconds in the Time field of the SHOW PROCESSLIST results. The following excerpt shows this condition (large values in this field are indicative of significant delays that can result in stale data on the slaves):

```
mysql> SHOW PROCESSLIST \G
...
   Time: 1814
...
```

Depending on how your replication topology is designed, you may be replicating data for load balancing. In this case, you typically use multiple slaves, directing a portion of the application or users to the slaves for SELECT queries, thereby reducing the burden on the master.

Causes and Cures for Slave Lag

Slave lag can be a nuisance for some replication users. The main reason for lag is the single-threaded nature of the slave (actually, there are two threads, but only one executes events and this is the main culprit in slave lag). For example, a master with a multiple-core CPU can run multiple transactions in parallel and will be faster than a slave that is executing transactions (events from the binary log) in a single thread. We have already discussed some ways to detect slave lag. In this section, we discuss some common causes and solutions for reducing slave lag.

These issues can be mitigated by using the multithreaded slave feature.

There are several causes for slave lag (e.g., network latency). It is possible the slave I/O thread is delayed in reading events from the logs. The most common reason for slave lag is simply that the slave has a single thread to execute all events, whereas the master has potentially many threads executing in parallel. Some other causes include long-running queries with inefficient joins, I/O-bound reads from disk, lock contention, and InnoDB thread concurrency issues.

Now that you know more about what causes slave lag, let us examine some things you can do to minimize it:

Organize your data

> You can see performance improvements by normalizing your data and by using sharding to distribute your data. This helps eliminate duplication of data, but as you saw in Chapter 11, duplication of some data (such as lookup text) can actually improve performance. The idea here is to use just enough normalization and sharding to improve performance without going too far. This is something only you, the owner of the data, can determine either through experience or experimentation.

Divide and conquer

> We know that adding more slaves to handle the queries (scale-out) is a good way to improve performance, but not scaling out enough could still result in slave lag if the slaves are processing a much greater number of queries. In extreme cases, you can see slave lag on all of the slaves. To combat this, consider segregating your data

using replication filtering to replicate different databases among your slaves. You can still use scale-out, but in this case you use an intermediary slave for each group of databases you filter, then scale from there.

Identify long-running queries and refactor them
If long-running queries are the source of slave lag, consider refactoring the query or the operation or application to issue shorter queries or more compact transactions. However, if you use this technique combined with replication filtering, you must use care when issuing transactions that span the replication filter groups. Once you divide a long-running query that should be an atomic operation (a transaction) across slaves, you run the risk of causing data integrity problems.

Load balancing
You can also use load balancing to redirect your queries to different slaves. This may reduce the amount of time each slave spends on answering queries, thereby leaving more computational time to process replication events.

Ensure you are using the latest hardware
Clearly, having the best hardware for the job normally equates to better performance. At the very least, you should ensure your slave servers are configured to their optimal hardware capabilities and are at least as powerful as the master.

Reduce lock contention
Table locks for MyISAM and row-level locks for InnoDB can cause slave lag. If you have queries that result in a lot of locks on MyISAM or InnoDB tables, consider refactoring the queries to avoid as many locks as possible.

Working with GTIDs

If you are using GTIDs, you can use the GTID system variables on the master and slave to verify that transactions have been executed on the master, received by the slave, and executed on the slave. Let us review the system variables associated with GTIDs. The following lists the system variables, their uses, and notes on how to use them in monitoring and troubleshooting GTID enabled servers:

`enforce_gtid_consistency`
When enabled, the server prohibits unsafe transactions from executing including using the `CREATE TABLE ... SELECT` statements and `CREATE TEMPORARY TABLE` inside transactions. This variable is not a dynamic variable. It is disabled by default, read only, and global in scope.

`gtid_executed`
The variable can be read in either session or global scope. When used in session scope, it shows the set of transactions that are written to the cache in the current session. When used in global scope, it shows the set of all transactions that are logged in the binary log.

Issuing a RESET MASTER command clears this variable in the global scope. You may need to execute the reset command when copying or restoring data on a slave from the master.

`gtid_mode`
> Shows whether GTIDs are being used (value = ON). Note that future releases of the server may have additional values for this variable as new GTID features are introduced.

`gtid_next`
> Determines how GTIDs are created. A value of AUTOMATIC indicates GTIDs are created using the standard globally unique mechanism. A value of ANONYMOUS means the GTIDs are generated using file and position and therefore are not unique.

`gtid_owned`
> This variable also depends on its scope. When used in session scope, the list holds all GTIDs that are owned by this server. When used in global scope, it displays a list of all GTIDS along with the owner of each GTID.

`gtid_purged`
> This shows those transactions that have been purged from the binary log. You can use this variable to keep the slave from executing transactions that were executed on the master. For example, if you were copying or restoring data from the master, you would not want any transactions that have already been applied to the data to be executed on the slave when the GTIDs are received then executed. Thus, you can set this variable to include those GTIDs that been applied to the data.

It is not possible to isolate specific GTIDs for specific databases. Thus, when you do a backup on the master for restoring on the slave and you read the GTID set on the master, you will get the entire GTID set. When applied to the slave using this variable, you therefore tell the slave that *all* transactions in the GTID list have been executed. Thus, partial restore of data must be executed with care. The best solution is always do a full backup on the master and restore it on the slave, after populating `gtid_purged` with the GTID list from the master.

Conclusion

This chapter concludes our discussion of the many ways you can monitor MySQL, and provides a foundation for you to implement your own schedules for monitoring virtually every aspect of the MySQL server.

Now that you know the basics of operating system monitoring, database performance, and MySQL monitoring and benchmarking, you have the tools and knowledge to successfully tune your server for optimal performance.

Joel smiled as he compiled his report about the replication issue. He paused and glanced at his doorway. He could almost sense it coming.

"Joel!"

Joel jumped, unable to believe his prediction. "I've got the replication problem solved, sir," he said quickly.

"Great! Send me the details when you get a moment."

"I also discovered some interesting things about the order processing system." He noticed Mr. Summerson's eyebrow raise slightly in anticipation. Joel continued, "It seems we have sized the buffer pool incorrectly. I think I can make some improvements in that area as well."

Mr. Summerson said, "Monitoring again?"

"Yes, sir. I've got some reports on the InnoDB storage engine. I'll include that in my email, too."

"Good work. Good work, indeed."

Joel knew that look. His boss was thinking again, and that always led to more work. Joel was surprised when his boss simply walked away slowly. "Well, it seems I finally stumped him."

## CHAPTER 14

Replication Troubleshooting

The message subject was simply "Fix the Seattle server." Joel knew such cryptic subject lines came from only one person. A quick scan of the message header confirmed the email was from Mr. Summerson. Joel opened the message and read the contents.

"The Seattle server is acting up again. I think the replication thingy is hosed. Make this your top priority."

"OK," Joel muttered to himself. Because the monitoring reports he had produced last week showed no anomalies and he was sure the replication setup was correct the last time he checked, Joel wasn't sure how to attack the problem. But he knew where to find the answers. "It looks like I need to read that replication troubleshooting chapter after all."

A familiar head appeared in his doorway. Joel decided to perform a preemptive maneuver by saying, "I'm on it." This resulted in a nod and a casual salute as his boss continued down the hall.

MySQL replication is usually trouble-free and rarely needs tuning or tweaking once the topology is active and properly configured. However, there are times when things can go wrong. Sometimes an error is manifested, and you have clear evidence with which to start your investigations. Other times the condition or problem is easily understood, but the causes of the more difficult problems that can arise are not so obvious. Fortunately, you can resolve these problems if you follow some simple guidelines and practices for troubleshooting replication.

This chapter presents these ideas by focusing on techniques to resolve replication problems. We begin with a description of what can go wrong, then we discuss the basic tools available to help troubleshoot problems, and we conclude with some strategies for solving and preventing replication problems.

Troubleshooting replication problems involving the MySQL Cluster follows the same procedures presented in this chapter. If you are having problems with MySQL Cluster, see Chapter 9 for trouble-shooting cluster failures and startup issues.

Seasoned computer users understand that computing systems are prone to occasional failures. Information technology professionals make it part of their creed to prevent failures and ensure reliable access and data to users. However, even properly managed systems can have issues.

MySQL replication is no exception. In particular, the slave state is not crash-safe. This means that if the MySQL instance on the slave crashes, it is possible the slave will stop in an undefined state. In the worst case, the relay log or the *master.info* file could be corrupt.

Indeed, the more complex the topology (including load and database complexity) and the more diverse the roles are among the nodes in the topology, the more likely something will go wrong. That doesn't mean replication cannot scale—on the contrary, you have seen how replication can easily scale to massive replication topologies. What we are saying is that when replication problems occur, they are usually the result of an unexpected action or configuration change.

What Can Go Wrong

There are many things that can go wrong to disrupt replication. MySQL replication is most susceptible to problems with data, be it data corruption or unintended interruptions in the replication stream. System crashes that result in an unsafe and uncontrolled termination of MySQL can also cause replication restarting issues.

You should always prepare a backup of your data before changing anything to fix the problem. In some cases, the backup will contain data that is corrupt or missing, but the benefits are still valid—specifically, that no matter what you do, you can at least return the data to the state at the time of the error. You'd be surprised how easy it is to make a bad situation worse.

In the following sections, we begin exploring replication troubleshooting by describing the most common failures in MySQL replication. These are some of the more frequently encountered replication problems. While the list can't include all possible replication problems, it does give you an idea of the types of things that can go wrong. We include a brief statement of some likely causes for each.

Problems on the Master

While most errors will manifest on the slave, look to this section for potential solutions for problems originating on the master. Administrators sometimes automatically suspect the slave. You should take a look at both the master and the slave when diagnosing replication problems.

Master Crashed and Memory Tables Are in Use

When the master is restarted, any data for memory tables is purged, as is normal for the memory storage engine. However, if a table that uses the memory storage engine is being replicated and the slave was not restarted, the slave may have outdated data.

Fortunately, when the first access to the memory table occurs after a restart, a special delete event is sent to the slaves to signal the slaves to purge the data, thereby synchronizing the data. However, the interval between when the table is referenced and when the replication event is transmitted can result in the slave having outdated data. To avoid this problem, use a script to first purge the data, then repopulate it on the master at startup using the init_file option.

For example, if you have a memory table that stores frequently used data, create a file like the following and reference it with the init_file option:

```
# Force slaves to purge data
DELETE FROM db1.mem_zip;
# Repopulate the data
INSERT INTO ...
```

The first command is a delete query, which will be replicated to the slaves when replication is restarted. Following that are statements to repopulate the data. In this way, you can ensure there is no gap where the slave could have out-of-date information in a memory table.

Master Crashed and Binary Log Events Are Missing

It is possible for the master to fail and not write recent events to the binary log on disk. In other words, if the server crashes before MySQL flushes its binary events cache to disk (in the binary log), those cached events can be lost.

This is usually indicated by an error on the slave stating that the binary log offset event is missing or does not exist. In this case, the slave is attempting to reconnect on restart using the last known binlog file and position of the master, and while the binlog file may exist, the offset does not, because the events that incremented the offset were not written to disk.

Unfortunately, there is no way to retrieve the lost binlog events. To solve this problem, you must check the current binlog position on the master and use this information to tell the slave to start at the next known event on the master. Be sure to check the data on both your master and slave once the slave is synchronized. It should be noted that the next event may be the first event in the next binary logfile, so be sure to check to see whether the log spans multiple files.

It is also possible that some of the events that were lost on the master were applied to the data prior to the crash. You should always compare the tables in question on the master to determine if there are differences between the master and the slave. This situation is rare, but it can cause problems later on if an update for a row is executed on the master against one of these missing events, which then causes a failure when run on the slave. In this case, the slave is attempting to run an update on rows that do not exist.

For example, consider a scenario of a fictional, simplified database for an auto dealer where information about cars for sale is stored in tables corresponding to new and used cars. The tables are set up with autoincrement keys.

On the master, the following happens:

```
INSERT INTO auto.used_cars VALUES (2004, 'Porsche', 'Cayman', 23100, 'blue');
```

A crash occurs after the following statement is executed but before it is written to the binary log:

```
UPDATE auto.used_cars SET color = 'white' WHERE id = 17;
```

In this case, the update query was lost during the crash on the master. When the slave attempts to restart, an error is generated. You can resolve the problem using the suggestion just shown. A check on the number of rows on the master and slave shows the same row count. Notice the update that corrected the color of the 2004 Porsche to white instead of blue. Now consider what will happen when a salesperson tries to help a customer find the blue Porsche of her dreams by executing this query on the slave:

```
SELECT * FROM auto.used_cars
WHERE make = 'Porsche' AND  model = 'Cayman' AND color = 'blue';
```

Will the salesperson who runs the query discover he has a blue Porsche Cayman for sale? A good auto salesperson always ensures he has the car on the lot by visual inspection, but for argument's sake, let us assume he is too busy to do so and tells his customer he has the car of her dreams. Imagine his embarrassment (and loss of a sale) when his customer arrives to test-drive the car only to discover that it is white.

 To prevent loss of data should the master crash, turn on sync_bin log (set to 1) at startup or in your configuration file. This will tell the master to flush an event to the binary log immediately. While this may cause a noticeable performance drop for InnoDB, the protection afforded could be great if you cannot afford to lose any changes to the data (but you may lose the last event, depending on when the crash occurred).

While this academic example may not seem too bad, consider the possibilities of a missing update to a medical database or a database that contains scientific data. Clearly, a missing update, even a seemingly simple one, can cause problems for your users. Indeed, this scenario can be considered a form of data corruption. Always check the contents of your tables when encountering this problem. In this case, crash recovery ensures the binary log and InnoDB are consistent when `sync_binlog=1`, but it otherwise has no effect for MyISAM tables.

Query Runs Fine on the Master but Not on the Slave

While not strictly a problem on the master, it is sometimes possible that a query (e.g., an update or insert command) will run properly on the master but not on the slave. There are many causes of this type of error, but most point to a referential integrity issue or a configuration problem on the slave or the database.

The most common cause of this error is updating rows on the master that do not exist on the slave. It can also happen when a query refers to a table that does not exist on the slave or that has a different signature (different columns or column types). In this case, you must change the slave to match the server in order to properly execute the query. If you want to use tables that have different signatures, take care in designing the tables so that data that exists only on the master is not accessed by queries (reads) on the slaves.

In some cases, it is possible the query is referencing a table that is not replicated. For example, if you are using any of the replication filtering startup options (a quick check of the master and slave status will confirm this), it is possible that the database the query is referencing is not on the slave. In this situation, you must either adjust your filters accordingly or manually add the missing tables to the missing database on the slave.

In other cases, the cause of a failed query can be more complex, such as character set issues, corrupt tables, or even corrupt data. If you confirm your slave is configured the same as your master, you may need to diagnose the query manually. If you cannot correct the problem on the slave, you may need to perform the update manually and tell the slave to skip the event that contains the failed query.

 To skip an event on a slave, use the `sql_slave_skip_counter` variable and specify the number of events from the master you want to skip. Sometimes this is the fastest way to restart replication.

Table Corruption After a Crash

If your master or slave crashes and, after restarting them both, you find one or more tables are corrupt or find that they are marked as crashed by MyISAM, you will need to fix these problems before restarting replication.

You can detect which tables are corrupt by examining the server's logfiles, looking for errors like the following:

```
... [ERROR] /usr/bin/mysqld: Table 'db1.t1' is marked
as crashed and should be repaired ...
```

You can use the following command to perform optimization and repair in one step all of the tables for a given database (in this case, *db1*):

```
mysqlcheck -u <user> -p --check --optimize --auto-repair db1
```

For MyISAM tables, you can use the `myisam-recover` option to turn on automatic recovery. There are four modes of recovery. See the online MySQL Reference Manual for more details.

Once you have repaired the affected tables, you must also determine if the tables on the slave have been corrupted. This is necessary if the master and slave share the same data center and the failure was environmental (e.g., they were connected to the same power source).

Always perform a backup on a table before repairing it. In some cases, a repair operation can result in data loss or leave the table in an unknown state.

It is also possible that a repair can leave the master and slave out of sync, especially if there is data loss as a result of the repair. You may need to compare the data in the affected table to ensure the master and slave are synchronized. If they are not, you may need to reload the data for the affected table on the slave if the slave is missing data, or copy data from the slave if the master is missing data.

Binary Log Is Corrupt on the Master

If a server crash or disk problem results in a corrupt binary log on the master, you cannot restart replication. There are many causes and types of corruption that can occur in the binary log, but all result in the inability to execute one or more events on the slave, often resulting in errors such as "could not parse relay log event."

In this case, you must carefully examine the binary log for recoverable events and rotate the logs on the master with the `FLUSH LOGS` command. There may be data loss on the slave as a result, and the slave will most definitely fail in this scenario. The best recovery method is to resynchronize the slave with the master using a reliable backup and recovery tool. In addition to rotating the logs, you can ensure any data loss is minimized and get replication restarted without errors.

In some cases, if it is easy to determine how many events were corrupted or missing, it may be possible to skip the corrupted events by using the `sql_slave_skip_counter` option on the slave. You can determine this by comparing the master's binlog reference on the slave to the current binlog position on the master and computing the number of events to skip. One way to do this is to use the *mysqlbinlog* tool to read the binary log of the master and count the events.

Killing Long-Running Queries for Nontransactional Tables

If you are forced to terminate a query that is modifying a nontransactional table, it is possible the query has been replicated to and executed on the slave. When this occurs, it is likely that the changes on the master will be different than on the slave.

For example, if you terminate a query that would have updated 400 out of the 600 rows in a table, allowing only 200 of the 400 changes to complete on the master, it is possible that the slave completed all 400 updates.

Thus, whenever you terminate a query that updates data on the master, you need to confirm that the change has not executed on the slave. If it has (or even as a precaution), you should resynchronize the data on the slave once you've corrected the table on the master. Usually in this case, you will fix the master and then make a backup of the data on the master and restore it on the slave.

Unsafe Statements

If you have databases that use both transactional and nontransactional tables, you may not encounter any problems so long as changes to the databases or tables do not occur in the same transaction. However, combining transactional and nontransactional tables is likely to cause problems. This is especially true when using unsafe statements. Although some unsafe statements may execute without errors, it is best to avoid them.

The online reference manual lists a number of unsafe statements. Essentially, these include any statement or clause that can result in a different result on the master and slave. Unsafe statements and functions include `UUID()`, `FOUND_ROWS()`, `INSERT DELAYED`, and `LIMIT`. For example, using `LIMIT` without an `ORDER BY` clause can result in different results. If you use the `ORDER BY` clause and the tables are the same, the results will be predictable.

For a complete list of unsafe statements, see the section "Determination of Safe and Unsafe Statements in Binary Logging" in the online reference manual.

Although it is possible to detect when these statements are used by monitoring warnings closely, you could have a situation where you encounter these statements through user naïveté. For example, consider the following table:

```
CREATE TABLE test.t1 (a int, b char(20)) ENGINE=InnoDB;
```

Now suppose the following updates are occurring on different clients writing to the master and that statement-based binary logging is enabled. The clients are identified by different *mysql* prompts. Assume that the order the statements are executed represents the order in which the statements were executed:

```
client_1> BEGIN;
client_1> INSERT INTO test.t1
VALUES (1, 'client_1'), (2, 'client_1'), (3, 'client_1');
client_2> BEGIN;
client_2> INSERT INTO test.t1
VALUES (4, 'client_2'), (5, 'client_2'), (6, 'client_2');
client_2> COMMIT;
client_1> COMMIT;
```

Notice that although client 1 started its transaction first, client 2 completed (committed) its transaction first. Because InnoDB preserves the order of insert based on when the transacton started, the resulting table will look like the following (in this case, the rows are in the order in which they were inserted in the InnoDB caching mechanism; this is how it would appear in a SELECT without using indexes on the master):

```
mysql> SELECT * FROM test.t1;
+------+----------+
| a    | b        |
+------+----------+
|    1 | client_1 |
|    2 | client_1 |
|    3 | client_1 |
|    4 | client_2 |
|    5 | client_2 |
|    6 | client_2 |
+------+----------+
6 rows in set (0.00 sec)
```

However, because the transaction on client 2 actually executed first, that is the order reflected in the binary log and therefore the order read by a slave. Thus, on a connected slave, the same table will have a slightly different original, unindexed order (but the same data):

```
mysql> SELECT * FROM test.t1;
+------+----------+
| a    | b        |
+------+----------+
|    4 | client_2 |
|    5 | client_2 |
|    6 | client_2 |
```

```
|     1 | client_1 |
|     2 | client_1 |
|     3 | client_1 |
+------+----------+
6 rows in set (0.00 sec)
```

Now let's consider an unsafe statement executed on the master like the following:

```
UPDATE test.t1 SET b='this_client' LIMIT 3;
```

Here, the intention is to change only the first three rows correcting column b. On the master, this works as expected:

```
mysql> SELECT * FROM test.t1;
+------+-------------+
| a    | b           |
+------+-------------+
|    1 | this_client |
|    2 | this_client |
|    3 | this_client |
|    4 | client_2    |
|    5 | client_2    |
|    6 | client_2    |
+------+-------------+
6 rows in set (0.00 sec)
```

However, on the slave, we get an entirely different result when the statement is replicated. As you can see, this sort of unsafe statement can lead to some really interesting and frustrating data inconsistencies:

```
mysql> SELECT * FROM test.t1;
+------+-------------+
| a    | b           |
+------+-------------+
|    4 | this_client |
|    5 | this_client |
|    6 | this_client |
|    1 | client_1    |
|    2 | client_1    |
|    3 | client_1    |
+------+-------------+
6 rows in set (0.00 sec)
```

Clearly, unsafe statements should be avoided. One of the best ways to do so is to educate users as to which statements are unsafe, monitor your replication warnings, and consider using all transactional tables and row-based binary logging.

Problems on the Slave

Most problems you will encounter will be the result of some error on the slave. In some situations, like those described in the previous section, it may be a problem that originated on the master, but it almost always will be seen on the slave in one form or another. The following sections list some of the common problems on the slave.

Use Binary Logging on the Slave

One way to ensure a more robust slave is to turn on binary logging using the `log-slave-updates` option. This will cause the slave to log the events it executes from its relay log, thereby creating a binary log that you can use to replay events on the slave in the event that the relay log (or the data) becomes corrupt.

Slave Server Crashed and Replication Won't Start

When a slave server crashes, it is usually easy to reestablish replication with the master once you determine the last known good event executed on the slave. You can see this by examining the SHOW SLAVE STATUS output.

However, when you encounter errors regarding account access, it may become impossible to restart replication. This can be the result of authentication problems, such as if the slave had to be rebuilt and the replication account (the account used in the CHANGE MASTER command) was not created or the password is incorrect. Replication may also not be able to start due to corrupted tables on the master or slave(s). In these cases, you are likely to see connection errors in the console and logs for the slave MySQL server.

When this occurs, always check the permissions of the replication user on the master. Ensure the proper privileges are granted to the user defined in either your configuration file or on your CHANGE MASTER command. The privileges should be similar to the following:

```
GRANT REPLICATION SLAVE ON *.*
TO 'rpl_user'@'192.168.1.%' IDENTIFIED BY 'password_here';
```

You can change this command to suit your needs as a means to solve this problem.

Slave Connection Times Out and Reconnects Frequently

If you have multiple slaves in your topology and have either not set the `server_id` option or have the same value for `server_id` for two or more of your slaves, you may have conflicting server IDs. When this happens, one of the slaves may exhibit frequent timeouts or drop and reconnect sequences.

This problem is simply due to the nonunique IDs among your slaves. But it can be difficult to diagnose (or, we should say, it's easy to misdiagnose as a connection problem). You should always check the error log of the master and slave for error messages. In this case, it is likely the error will contain the nature of the timeout.

To prevent this type of problem, always ensure that all of your servers have a `serv er_id` option set either in the configuration file or in the startup command line.

Query Results Are Different on the Slave than on the Master

One of the more difficult problems to detect occurs when the results of a query performed on one or more slaves do not match that of the master. It is possible you may never notice the problem. The problem could be as simple or innocuous as sort order issues, or as severe as missing or extra rows in the result set.

The main causes of this type of error are the execution of unsafe statements, writes sent to the slave, mixing transactional and nontransactional storage engines, and different query options set on the master and slave (e.g., `SQL_MODE`).

A less common cause for this problem is differing character sets between the master and slave. For example, the master can be configured with one character set and collation defaults, while one or more slaves are configured with another. In most cases, this is fine so long as the character sets are compatible (same number of bytes for character storage). However, if your users start complaining of extra or missing rows or differing result orders, you should check the data carefully for rows that differ between the master and slaves.

Another possible cause of this problem is using different default storage engines on the master and slave (e.g., using the MyISAM storage engine on the master and the InnoDB storage engine on the slave). In this case, it is entirely likely that the query results will be in different orders if there are no primary key or any indexes to ensure correct order (and no `ORDER BY` clause).

Perhaps a more subtle cause of this type of problem is differing table definitions on the master and slave. For example, it is possible to leave some initial columns or ending columns missing on the slave. A solution to this problem is to ensure you always include the columns in each `SELECT` statement. For example, if the slave has more columns than the master, a `SELECT *` query executed on the slave will result in more data than what is on the master. This can be complicated if the slave has extra initial columns. In this case, the results of a `SELECT *` query will not align to the same query executed on the master.

Similar, and perhaps more serious, is the case where you execute an `INSERT INTO` query on the master without specifying the columns. Again, if the slave has more initial columns, the data may not align and the query may fail. It is best to write the query as `INSERT INTO <table>(a, b, c)` …, explicitly listing the columns.

Column order is important. Tables with different structures on the master and slave must have a common set of columns that appear at the beginning or end of the table.

There are many potential errors when you use this feature. For example, if the master has more columns than the slave, users could expect that the data for all columns is replicated but only those columns present on the slave are replicated. Sometimes you actually want fewer columns on the slave, and can make it work by careful querying. But a careless user can achieve this accidentally by dropping columns in such a way that replication can still proceed. In some cases, the SELECT queries executed on the slave will fail when referencing the missing columns, thereby giving you a clue to the problem. Other times, you can simply be missing data in your applications.

A common user error, which can result in different results from queries delivered to the master and to the slave, is making other types of changes to the tables or databases executed on the slave but not executed on the master (i.e., a user performs some non-replicated data manipulation on the slave that changes a table signature but does not execute the same statement on the master). When this occurs, queries can return wrong results, wrong columns, wrong order, or extra data, or simply fail due to referencing missing columns. It is always a good precaution to check the layout of a table involved in these types of problems to ensure it is the same on the master and slave. If it is not, resynchronize the table and retry the query.

Slave Issues Errors when Attempting to Restart with SSL

Problems related to SSL connections are typically the usual permission issues described previously. In this case, the privileges granted must also include the REQUIRE SSL option, as shown here (be sure to check that the replication user exists and has the correct privileges):

```
GRANT REPLICATION SLAVE ON *.*
TO 'rpl_user'@'%' IDENTIFIED BY 'password_here' REQUIRE SSL;
```

Other issues related to restarting replication when SSL connections are used are missing certificate files or incorrect values for the SSL-related options in the configuration file (e.g., ssl-ca, ssl-cert, and ssl-key) or the related options in the CHANGE MASTER command (e.g., MASTER_SSL_CA, MASTER_SSL_CAPATH, MASTER_SSL_CERT, and MAS TER_SSL_KEY). Be sure to check your settings and paths to ensure nothing has changed since the last time replication was started.

Memory Table Data Goes Missing

If one or more of your databases uses the memory storage engine, the data contained in these tables will be lost when a slave server is restarted (the server, not the slave threads). This is expected, as data in memory tables does not survive a restart. The table configuration still exists and the table can be accessed, but the data has been purged.

It is possible that when a slave server is restarted, queries directed to the memory table fail (e.g., UPDATE) or query results are inaccurate (e.g., SELECT). Thus, the error may not occur right away and could be as simple as missing rows in a query result.

To avoid this problem, you should carefully consider the use of memory tables in your databases. You should not create memory tables on the master to be updated on the slaves via replication without procedures in place to recover the data for the tables in the event of a crash or planned restart of the server. For example, you can execute a script before you start replication that copies the data for the table from the master. If the data is derived, use a script to repopulate the data on the slave.

Other things to consider are filtering out the table during replication or possibly not using the memory storage engine for any replicated table.

Temporary Tables Are Missing After a Slave Crash

If your replicated databases and queries make use of temporary tables, you should consider some important facts about temporary tables. When a slave is restarted, its temporary tables are lost. If any temporary tables were replicated from the master and you cannot restart the slave from that point, you may have to manually create the tables or skip the queries that reference the temporary tables.

This scenario often results in the case where a query will not execute on one or more slaves. The resolution to this problem is similar to missing memory tables. Specifically, in order to get the query to execute, you may have to manually recreate the temporary tables or resynchronize the data on the slave with the data on the master and skip the query when restarting the slave.

Slave Is Slow and Is Not Synced with the Master

In slave lag, also called *excessive lag*, the slave cannot process all of the events from the master fast enough to avoid delays in updates of the data. In the most extreme cases, the updates to the data on the slave become out of date and cause incorrect results. For example, if a slave server in a ticketing agency is many minutes behind the master, it is possible the ticketing agency can sell seats that are no longer available (i.e., they have been marked as "sold" on the master but the slave did not get the updates until too late).

We discussed this problem in previous chapters, but a summary of the resolution is still relevant here. To detect the problem, monitor the slave's SHOW SLAVE STATUS output and examine the `Seconds_Behind_Master` column to ensure the value is within tolerance for your application. To solve the problem, consider moving some of the databases to other slaves, reducing the number of databases being replicated to the slave, improving network delays (if any), and making data storage improvements.

For example, you can relieve the slave of processing extraneous events by using an additional slave for bulk or expensive data updates. You can relieve the replication load by making updates on a separate slave and applying the changes using a reliable backup and restore method on all of the other machines in the topology.

Data Loss After a Slave Crash

It is possible that a slave server may crash and not record the last known master binlog position. This information is saved in the *relay_log.info* file. When this occurs, the slave will attempt to restart at the wrong (older) position and therefore attempt to execute some queries that may have already been executed. This normally results in query errors; you can handle this by skipping the duplicate events.

However, it is also possible these duplicate events can cause the data to be changed (corrupted) so that the slave is no longer in sync with the master. Unfortunately, these types of problems are not that easy to detect. Careful examination of the logfiles may reveal that some events have been executed, but you may need to examine the binlog events and the master's binary log to determine which ones were duplicated.

There is a set of Python-based tools called MySQL Utilities for working with MySQL servers. They include a utility that can be used to identify differences in data and structure. MySQL Utilities are discussed in more detail in Chapter 17.

Table Corruption After a Crash

When you restart a master following a crash, you may find one or more tables are corrupt or marked as crashed by MyISAM. You need to resolve these issues before restarting replication. Once you have repaired the affected tables, ensure the tables on the slave have not suffered any data loss as a result of the repair. It is very unusual for this to occur, but it is something that you should check. When in doubt, always manually resynchronize these tables with the master using a backup and restore or similar procedure before restarting replication.

Data loss after a repair operation is a very real possibility for MyISAM when a partial page write occurs during a hardware or server crash. Unfortunately, it is not always easy to determine if the data has been lost.

Relay Log Is Corrupt on the Slave

If a server crash or disk problem results in a corrupt relay log on the slave, replication will stop with one of several errors related to the relay log. There are many causes and types of corruption that can occur in the relay log, but all result in the inability to execute one or more events on the slave.

When this occurs, your best choice for recovery is identifying where the last known good event was executed from the master's binary log and restarting replication using the CHANGE MASTER command, providing the master's binlog information. This will force the slave to recreate a new relay log. Unfortunately, this means any recovery from the old relay log can be compromised.

Multiple Errors During Slave Restart

One of the more difficult problems to detect and fix is multiple errors on the slave during initial start or a later restart. There are a variety of errors that occur and sometimes they occur at random or without a clearly identifiable cause.

When this occurs, check the error log and the output of SHOW SLAVE STATUS, looking for messages concerning errors reported during slave connection and replication start-up. You can also check the size of the max_allowed_packet on both the master and the slave. If the size is larger on the master than on the slave, it is possible the master has logged an event that exceeds the slave's size. This can cause random and seemingly illogical errors.

Consequences of a Failed Transaction on the Slave

Normally when there is a failed transaction, the changes are rolled back to avoid problems associated with partial updates. However, this is complicated when you mix transactional and nontransactional tables—the transactional changes are rolled back, but the nontransactional changes are not. This can lead to problems such as data loss or duplicated, redundant, or unwanted changes to the nontransactional tables.

The best way to avoid this problem is to avoid mixing transactional and nontransactional table relationships in your database and to always use transactional storage engines.

I/O Thread Problems

There are three common issues related to the I/O thread:

- Dropped connection to the master
- Intermittent connection to the master

- Slave lagging severely behind the master

You will find master connection errors in the slave status output in the `Last_IO_Err` `no` and `Last_IO_Error` fields. It is also likely that the state of the `Slave_IO_Running` will be `No`. The causes for these errors should be apparent in the error description. If the error is not easily understood, you should follow these steps to isolate the problem:

- Check the `CHANGE MASTER` command to ensure the correct user credentials are used.
- Check the replication user's credentials on the master.
- Check the network to ensure the master is reachable by using `ping` *hostname* on a client, where *hostname* is the hostname of the master.
- Check that the port used on the server is reachable using `telnet` *hostname n*, where *n* is the master's port.

If the connection to the master drops but the slave is able to reestablish the connection, you most likely are encountering problems with network bandwidth. In this case, use your network testing tools to ensure there is sufficient bandwidth and take appropriate steps to reduce excessive bandwidth use.

If the slave is very far behind the master, you should ensure there is no corruption in the relay log, there are no errors or warnings on the slave, and the slave is performing correctly (a common problem is that the system is burdened with another process). If all of these check out, you can consider using a multithreaded slave or replication filtering to isolate databases among groups of slaves.

SQL Thread Problems: Inconsistencies

The most common problem found with the SQL thread is a statement that has failed to execute on the slave. In this case, the slave's SQL thread will stop and the error will be presented in the slave status. You should look there for clues to why the statement failed and take corrective action.

Causes for statement errors on the slave but not the master were addressed earlier. They are often caused by key collisions, inadvertent writes to the slave, or by different data on the slave and master. Whenever you encounter these issues, you should trace the cause of the problem if possible to try and prevent it from happening in the future. One key step is to identify an application or user that issued data changes to a slave.

The cure for most of these problems is bringing the slave back into synchronization with the master. A nifty tool for checking consistency between the master and slave is the MySQL Utilities *mysqldbcompare* script. This utility is an offline tool that you can run on your slave during periods of low activity or when it is safe to lock the tables for a period of time. The utility will not only identify which objects differ in structure or are missing, it will also identify the data rows that differ and permit you to generate transformation statements that you can use to bring the slave into consistency with the master. This utility and several other replication utilities are discussed in more detail in Chapter 17.

Different Errors on the Slave

Although rare, it is possible you could encounter a situation where a statement results in a different error presented on the slave than the master. This is normally manifested as an error that reads, "Query X caused different errors on master and slave…" The message will present the error, but it might appear simply as something like "Error 0," which indicates that the statement succeeded on the slave but that there was an error on the master.

The most likely cause of this problem is an error during a trigger or event on the master. For example, if a trigger on the master failed but either the equivalent trigger succeeded on the slave or the trigger was missing on the slave (a common practice). In this case, the best way to solve the problem is to correct the error on the master, then tell the slave to skip the statement.

However, it is also possible the problem is related to a deadlock in the trigger brought on by data inconsistencies. If this occurs, you may need to correct the inconsistencies first and retry or skip the statement.

Advanced Replication Problems

There are some natural complications with some of the more advanced replication topologies. In this section, we examine some of the common problems you might encounter while using an advanced feature of replication.

A Change Is Not Replicated Among the Topology

In some cases, changes to a database object are not replicated. For example, ALTER TABLE may be replicated, while FLUSH, REPAIR TABLE, and similar maintenance commands are not. Whenever this happens, consult the limitations of data manipulation (DML) commands and maintenance commands.

This problem is typically the result of an inexperienced administrator or developer attempting database administration on the master, expecting the changes to replicate to the slaves.

Whenever there are profound changes to a database object that change its structure at a file level or you use a maintenance command, execute the command or procedure on all of the slaves to ensure the changes are propagated throughout your topology.

Savvy administrators often use scripts to accomplish this as routine scheduled maintenance. Typically, the scripts stop replication in an orderly manner, apply the changes, and restart replication automatically.

Circular Replication Issues

If you are using circular replication and you have recovered from a replication failure whereby one or more servers were taken out of the topology, you can encounter a problem in which an event is executed more than once on some of the servers. This can cause replication to fail if the query fails (e.g., a key violation). This occurs because the originating server was among those servers that were removed from the topology.

When this happens, the server designated as the originating server has failed to terminate the replication of the event. You can solve this problem by using the `IGNORE_SERV ER_IDS` option (available in MySQL versions 5.5.2 and later) with the `CHANGE MASTER` command, supplying a list of server IDs to ignore for an event. When the missing servers are restored, you must adjust this setting so that events from the replaced servers are not ignored.

Multimaster Issues

As with circular replication (which is a specific form of multimaster topology), if you are recovering from a replication failure, you may encounter events that are executed more than once. These events are typically events from a removed server. You can solve this problem the same way as you would with circular replication—by placing the server IDs of the removed servers in the list of the `IGNORE_SERVER_IDS` option with the `CHANGE MASTER` command.

Another possible problem with multimaster replication crops up when changes to the same table occur on both masters and the table has an autoincrement column for the primary key. In this case, you can encounter duplicate key errors. If you must insert new rows on more than one master, use the `auto_increment_increment` and `auto_incre ment_offset` options to stagger the increments. For example, you can allow one server to use only even numbers while the other uses only odd numbers. It can be even more complicated to get more than two masters to update the same table with an autoincrement primary key. Not only does it make it more difficult to stagger the increments, it becomes an administrative problem if you need to replace a server in the topology that is updating the table. If you make the increment too large (and you have massive amounts of data), you could exceed the maximum values of the data type for the key in a large table.

The HA_ERR_KEY_NOT_FOUND Error

This is a familiar error encountered in a row-based replication topology. The most likely cause of this error is a conflict whereby the row to be updated or deleted is not present or has changed, so the storage engine cannot find it. This can be the result of an error during circular replication or changes made directly to a slave on replicated data. When this occurs, you must determine the source of the conflict and repair the data or skip the offending event.

GTID Problems

The addition of Globally Unique Transaction Identifiers (GTID) is a recent feature for replication. As we discussed earlier in the book, GTIDs can solve the problem of failover for the loss of the master in a topology. Fortunately, there are few cases where replication encounters problems with GTIDs. Their very nature makes them stable. However, it is still possible to run into problems when working with slaves on topologies that have GTID enabled.

Most often you will not encounter errors but will find that the slave has an incomplete set of transactions. In this case, you will use the techniques discussed previously to identify which GTIDs have been executed on the slave. If it is not possible to wait for the slave to catch up to the master, you can use the new replication protocol to catch a slave up by making it a slave of another up-to-date slave. This will make the slave that is behind request those missing GTIDs from its new master. Once the slave is up-to-date, you can return it to its original master.

The one situation where you may encounter an error related to GTIDs is when you attempt to provision a slave. If you have a slave that is behind or does not have all of the data on the master, you would ordinarily perform a restore on the slave of a most recent backup of the master. You can still do this, but you also need to set the gtid_purged variable on the slave to include all of the GTIDs executed on the master (the value of the masters gtid_executed system variable).

If you use *mysqldump* or the *mysqldbcopy*, *mysqldbexport*, and *mysqldbimport* commands from MySQL Utilities, the correct GTID statements will be generated for you. However, if you attempt to set the gtid_purged variable on the slave, you may encounter an error similar to "GTID_PURGED can only be set when GTID_EXECUTED is empty." This occurs because the destination server is not in a clean replication state. To correct the error, you must first issue the RESET MASTER command on the slave to clear the gtid_purged variable, then set the gtid_purged variable.

Never issue RESET MASTER on your master for an active replication topology using GTIDs. Be very careful when using this command.

Tools for Troubleshooting Replication

If you have used or set up replication or performed maintenance, many of the tools you need to successfully diagnose and repair replication problems are familiar to you.

In this section, we discuss the tools required to diagnose replication problems along with a few suggestions about how and when to use each:

SHOW PROCESSLIST

> When encountering problems, it is always a good idea to see what else is running. This command tells you the current state of each of the threads involved in replication. Check here first when examining the problem.

SHOW MASTER STATUS *and* SHOW SLAVE STATUS

> These SQL commands are your primary tool for diagnosing replication problems. Along with the SHOW PROCESSLIST command, you should execute these commands on the master and then on the slave, then examine the output. The slave command has an extended set of parameters that are invaluable in diagnosing replication problems.

SHOW GRANTS FOR < *replication user* >

> Whenever you encounter slave user access problems, you should first examine the grants for the slave user to ensure they have not changed.

CHANGE MASTER

> Sometimes the configuration files have been changed, either knowingly or accidentally. Use this SQL command to override the last known connection parameters, which can correct slave connection problems.

STOP/START SLAVE

> Use these SQL commands to start and stop replication. It is sometimes a good idea to stop a slave if it is in an error state.

Examine the configuration files

> Sometimes the problem occurs as a result of an unsanctioned or forgotten configuration change. Check your configuration files routinely when diagnosing connection problems.

Examine the server logs

You should make this a habit whenever diagnosing problems. Checking the server logs can sometimes reveal errors that are not visible elsewhere. As cryptic as they can sometimes be, the error and warning messages can be helpful.

SHOW SLAVE HOSTS

Use this command to identify the connected slaves on the master if they use the `report-host` option.

SHOW BINLOG EVENTS

This SQL command displays the events in the binary log. If you use statement-based replication, this command will display the changes using SQL statements.

mysqlbinlog

This utility allows you to read events in the binary or relay logs, often indicating when there are corrupt events. Don't hesitate to use this tool frequently when diagnosing problems related to events and the binary log.

PURGE BINARY LOGS

This SQL command allows you to remove certain events from the binary log, such as those that occur after a specific time or after a given event ID. Your routine maintenance plan should include the use of this command for purging older binary logs that are no longer needed. You should use a specific time duration to prevent purging binary logs accidentally or too frequently.

Now that we have reviewed the problems you can encounter in replication and have seen a list of the tools available in a typical MySQL release, we turn our attention to strategies for attacking replication problems.

Best Practices

Reviewing the potential problems that can occur in replication and listing the tools available for fixing the problems is only part of the complete solution. There are some proven strategies and best practices for resolving replication problems quickly.

This section describes the strategies and best practices you should cultivate when diagnosing and repairing replication problems. We present these in no particular order—depending on the problem you are trying to solve, one or more may be helpful.

Know Your Topology

If you are using MySQL replication on a small number of servers, it may not be that difficult to commit the topology configuration to memory. It may be as simple as a single master and one or more slaves, or as complex as two servers in a multimaster topology. However, there is a point at which memorizing the topology and all of its configuration parameters becomes impossible.

The more complex the topology and the configuration, the harder it is to determine the cause of a problem and where to begin your repair operations. It would be very easy to forget a lone slave in a topology of hundreds of slave servers.

It is always a good idea to have a map of your topology and the current configuration settings. You should keep a record of your replication setup in a notebook or file and place it where you and your colleagues or subordinates can find it easily. This information will be invaluable to someone who understands replication administration but may have never worked with your installation.

You should include a textual or graphical drawing of your topology and indicate any filters (master and slave), as well as the role of each server in the topology. You should also consider including the CHANGE MASTER command, complete with options, and the contents of the configuration files for all of your servers.

A drawing of your topology need not be sophisticated or an artistic wonder. A simple line drawing will do nicely. Figure 14-1 shows a hybrid topology, complete with notations for filters and roles.

Note that the production relay slave (192.168.1.105) has two masters (192.168.1.100 and 192.168.1.101). This is strange, because no slave can have more than one master. To achieve this level of integration—consuming data from a third party—you would need a second instance of a MySQL server on the production relay slave to replicate the data from the strategic partner (192.168.1.101) and use a script to conduct periodic transfers of the data from the second MySQL instance to the primary MySQL instance on the production relay slave. This would achieve the integration depicted in Figure 14-1 with some manual labor and a time-delayed update of the strategic partner data.

There are certain problems inherent in certain topologies. We have already discussed many of these in this and previous chapters. What follows is a list of the types of topologies, including a short description and some common issues to be aware of concerning known vulnerabilities:

Star (also called single master)
>   This is the typical single master, many slaves topology. There are no special limitations or problems other than those that apply to replication as a whole. However, the process of promoting a slave to a master can be complicated in that you must use the slave that is most up-to-date with the master. This can be difficult to determine and may require examination of the state of every slave.

Chain
>   In this configuration, a server is a master to one slave, which is in turn a master to another slave, and so on, with the end point being a simple slave. Other than the server ID issue mentioned earlier, there is also the problem of determining which position an intermediate master/slave was at when it failed. Promoting a new master/slave node can require additional work to ensure consistency.

Circular (also called ring)

This is the same as the chain topology except there is no end point. This topology requires careful setup so that events are terminated at the originating server.

Multimaster

This is similar to a circular topology, but in this case, each master is a slave of every other master. This topology has all of the limitations and problems of circular replication as well as being one of the most complex topologies to manage due to the possibility of conflicting changes. To avoid this problem, you must ensure you make changes using only one of the masters. If a conflicting change occurs, say an UP DATE on one master and a DELETE statement on the other master, it is possible the DELETE statement will execute before the UPDATE, which will prevent the UPDATE from updating any rows.

Hybrid

A hybrid topology uses elements of some or all of the other topologies. You typically see this topology in a large organization that has compartmentalized functions or divisions that require similar but often isolated elements of the infrastructure. Isolation is accomplished using filtering whereby data is divided among several slaves from an original master (sometimes called the *prime* or *master master*) that contains all of the data sent to the slaves, which become masters to their own star topologies. This is by far the most complex topology and requires careful notation and diligence to keep your documentation updated.

Check the Status of All of Your Servers

One of the best preventive tasks you can perform is to regularly check the status of all of the servers in your topology. This need not be complicated. For instance, you can set up a scheduled task that launches the MySQL client and issues a SHOW MASTER STA TUS or SHOW SLAVE STATUS and prints out or emails the results.

Keeping a close eye on your server status is a good way to stay informed when there is a potential problem. It also gives you a chance to react more quickly when errors occur.

You should look for errors, monitor the slave lag, check your filters to see that they match your records, and ensure all of your slaves are running and not reporting warnings or connection errors.

Check Your Logs

Along with checking your server status regularly, you should also consider checking the logs of your servers periodically. You can accomplish this easily using the MySQL Workbench GUI to connect to each server in turn and look at the most recent entries in the logs.

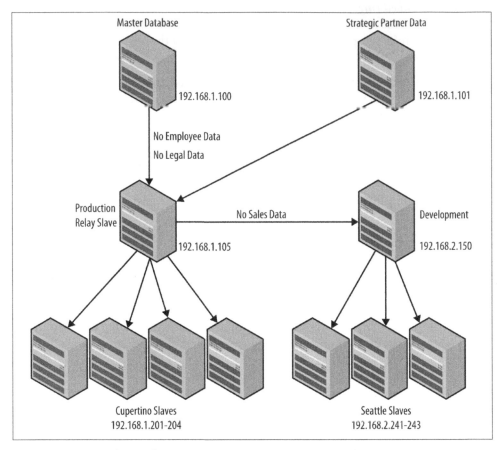

Figure 14-1. Sample topology map

If you are diligent in this effort, it will pay dividends in the form of early problem detection. Sometimes errors or warnings—which, at the time, do not manifest in anything detectable—are written to the log. Catching these telltale signs early can make your repair work much easier.

We recommend examining your logs at the same time you examine the status of your servers.

Check Your Configuration

Along with the servers and logfiles, you should also routinely examine your configuration files to ensure your documentation is up-to-date. This isn't as critical as checking the logs, but it is often overlooked. We recommend checking your configuration files and updating your documentation at least once a week if you have a lot of changes, and at least once a month if you have few changes to the topology or servers. If you have an environment in which there is more than one administrator, you may want to consider doing this more frequently.

Conduct Orderly Shutdowns

Sometimes it is necessary to stop replication while you diagnose and repair a problem. If replication has already stopped, you may not need to do anything, but if you have a complex topology and the error is related to data loss, it may be safer to stop replication across the topology. But you should do so in a controlled and safe manner.

There are several strategies for doing a controlled shutdown of your replication topology. If data loss is an issue and slave lag is not, you may want to lock the tables on your master and flush the binary logs, then wait for all of the (remaining) slaves to catch up and then shut the slaves down. This will ensure all events are replicated and executed on the slaves that are operational.

On the other hand, if the problem is severe, you may want to start with the slaves on the leaves of your topology and work your way up the topology, leaving the master running. However, if you leave the master running (i.e., you don't lock all of the tables) and you have a heavy load of updates running and your diagnostic and repair takes a long time, your slaves will be lagging behind your master when you restart replication. It is better to stop updates on the master if you think your repair will take a long time.

If you are faced with a difficult problem or (worse) a problem that appears randomly or without warning, you may want to consider shutting down replication completely. This is especially true if you have a problem with only one of your slaves. Shutting down replication will allow you to isolate the server while you diagnose the problem.

Conduct Orderly Restarts After a Failure

It is also important to restart replication in an orderly manner. It is often best to restart the replication topology under controlled conditions, such as on only one master and one slave. Even if your topology is more complex, having the most basic building blocks of replication started initially will allow you to test and ensure the problem is fixed before restarting all of your servers.

Isolation is essential when dealing with problems that are confined to a single slave or a set of events. It is also helpful to start with a single master and a single slave so that if you cannot fix the problem, you can get help from MySQL professionals more easily because you have isolated the problem to the smallest set of parameters as possible. See "Reporting Replication Bugs" on page 528 for more details.

Manually Execute Failed Queries

One of the most frequently overlooked strategies is examining the queries in the relay log or binary log for clues as to what has gone wrong. It is easy to get stuck on researching the error on the slave and diagnosing all of the many things that can go wrong, but sometimes (especially when there is a query involved) you can gain far more information about the problem by isolating the slave server in question and attempting the query manually.

If you are using statement-based replication, this is an easy task because the query is human-readable in the binary or relay log. If you use row-based replication, you can still execute the query, but you cannot read the query itself. In this case, a malformed query or a query that uses a missing, incorrect, or corrupt reference may not be obvious until you execute the query manually.

Remember, you should always make a backup of your data before attempting diagnostics that could result in changes to the data. Running a broken query is definitely one of those cases. We have seen queries that cause replication errors but sometimes succeed when run manually. When this occurs, it is usually indicative of a slave configuration error or binary or relay log issue rather than a problem with the query itself.

Don't Mix Transactional and Nontransactional Tables

This may be an obvious best practice to many, but it is good to remind ourselves nonetheless. Mixing transactional and nontransactional table updates in a transaction can lead to a host of problems, not the least of which is the inability to rollback changes to a nontransactional table. You should avoid this practice entirely.

That being said, it is possible that some mixing of nontransactional statements can be considered safe. For example, if your nontransactional tables are lookup tables that rarely get updated and, more important, are not updated in the course of the transaction, it may be safe to execute these statements.

The best way to avoid problems associated with mixing transactional and nontransactional tables is to convert all of your tables to InnoDB, thereby making them transactional. In most cases, this is perfectly reasonable and you will notice no ill effects. However, if your data requires a different storage engine (e.g., the Archive or CSV storage engines), it may not be convenient or even possible to convert them.

Common Procedures

There are also some common procedures you can use to execute the practices just discussed. These include troubleshooting replication and pausing replication on the master.

Troubleshooting replication failures

The following is a stepwise procedure you can use when attacking replication problems (most of these steps have been described elsewhere in this book or may already be familiar to you):

1. Check the status on the master. Record any anomalies.
2. Check the status on each slave. Record any anomalies.
3. Read the error logs on all of your servers.
4. Examine the process list on each server. Look for anomalies in status.
5. If no errors are reported, attempt to restart the slave. Record any errors presented.
6. Check the configuration of the server in question to ensure nothing has changed.
7. Examine your notes and form a plan to research and fix the problem.

This procedure is oversimplified, but it should help you diagnose the replication problem more quickly than chasing the errors presented will (if there are any errors to chase).

You should write down or electronically record all observations while you conduct this procedure. Seeing the information consolidated in one place can sometimes present a much clearer body of evidence.

Pausing replication

To pause replication, execute the following steps on each of your master servers, starting with the prime master (the first master):

On the master:

1. Run the `FLUSH TABLES WITH READ LOCK` command.
2. Run the `SHOW MASTER STATUS` command.
3. Record the master binary log and position.

On the slaves:

1. Run `SELECT MASTER_POS_WAIT (binary_log_name, position)`.

On each remaining active slave connected to this master, examine the results of `SHOW SLAVE STATUS` until the slave has synchronized with the master. Once the slave reaches this state, it is safe to shut down the slave.

When you restart your replication topology, all slaves will automatically start without any lag. This procedure is useful in cases where there has been a disruption and you want to get things going again to avoid a prolonged slave lag.

Reporting Replication Bugs

Once in a while you may encounter a replication problem that you cannot solve or there is no solution. In this case, you should report the problem to the MySQL developers, who may be better equipped to diagnose the problem (and correct it if it is a defect). Even if you do not have a support agreement in place, you can report a bug for the MySQL release you are using.

That is not to say that the bug database is a "free help" resource. It is reserved for reporting and tracking defects. The best advice for tricky problems is to check all MySQL database forums for ideas and solutions first. Only when it is clear that the problem is unique and unrelated to your environment or application should you report it as a defect.

The best bug reports are those that describe errors that can be demonstrated or repeated using an isolated test case (e.g., a replication problem that can be demonstrated on a test master and slave), and that have a minimal set of data needed for the problem. Often this is nothing more than a complete and accurate report of the configuration and event in question.

To report a bug, visit *http://bugs.mysql.com* and (if you have not done so already) register for an account. When you enter your bug report, be sure to describe the problem as completely as possible. For fastest results and a quick resolution, include as many of the following details as possible:

- Record all error messages verbatim.
- Include the binary log (in full or an excerpt).
- Include the relay log (in full or an excerpt).
- Record the configuration of the master and slave.
- Copy the results of the SHOW MASTER STATUS and SHOW SLAVE STATUS commands.
- Provide copies of all error logs.

 Be sure to exhaust all of these techniques and explore the problem using all of the available tools.

The MySQL bug tracking tool will keep you apprised of your bug submission by sending you email alerts whenever the bug report is updated.

Conclusion

This chapter includes suggestions for solving some of the common problems that can arise when using replication. We examined some of the ways replication can fail and discussed how to solve the problems and prevent them in the future. We also examined some tools and best practices for troubleshooting MySQL replication.

One resource that is often overlooked is the section titled "Replication Features and Issues" in the online reference manual. This section includes very important information about limitations with replication and how it interacts with certain server features, settings, and the design and implementation choices of your databases. You may want to read this section whenever a new version of the server is released to ensure you are informed about how new features may affect replication.

Joel smiled as he heard his boss coming toward his door. He was ready this time and started speaking as soon as he saw Mr. Summerson's polished wingtips. "I've got the Seattle server back online, sir. It was a problem with a couple of queries that failed because the tables were changed on the slave. I have advised the Seattle office to direct all schema changes and table maintenance to the master here. I will keep a watch on it from now on and let you know if the problem returns."

Mr. Summerson smiled. Joel could feel perspiration beading on his forehead. "Great! Good work."

Joel was relieved. "Thank you, sir."

His boss started to leave, but performed one of his now-routine pause, turn, and task maneuvers. "One more thing."

"Sir?" Joel said a little too quickly.

"It's Bob."

Joel was confused. Mr. Summerson's tasking usually involved a complete sentence. "Sir?" he said hesitantly.

"You can call me Bob. I think we're well past the 'sir' stuff."

Joel sat for a few moments until he realized he was staring into the middle distance of space. He blinked and realized his friend Amy from the development staff was standing in front of his desk.

"Are you OK, Joel?"

"What?"

"You were zoned out there. What were you thinking about?"

Joel smiled and reclined his chair. "I think I finally got to him."

"Who? Mr. Summerson?"

"Yeah, he just told me to call him Bob."

Amy smiled and crossed her arms, then jokingly said, "Well, I suppose we'll be calling you Mr. Joel from now on."

Joel laughed and said, "Have you had lunch yet?"

Protecting Your Investment

Joel pulled open the middle drawer of his desk and was rummaging for a working pen when he heard a familiar staccato rap on his door frame. "Joel, I need you to talk with the information assurance auditors and tell them what our recovery plans are. Oh, and be sure you order your tapes so they'll know we're prepared."

"Auditors? Tapes?" Joel asked as he made eye contact with Mr. Summerson.

"Be sure to start working on whatever disaster recovery planning document they're asking about. And tell the procurement office what kind of media you need to get started with your archives. They will show you what forms to fill out. Get some extras just in case," Joel's manager said as he disappeared from view.

Joel pushed his drawer closed and stood up. The boss must mean media for backups, he thought. But what was all that about auditors and planning? Joel pulled his chair over to his workstation and sat down. "Well, I guess I'll have to figure out what information assurance is and how to do a backup," he mumbled as he opened his browser.

Mr. Summerson popped his head back into the doorway and said, "Oh, and Joel, I'd like to see your recovery plan on my desk by tomorrow morning before the continuity of operations planning session at 1400."

Joel sighed as he realized his manager had asked for far more than he originally thought. Joel reached for his handy MySQL book. "Money well spent," he said as he opened the book to the chapter titled "Protecting Your Investment."

This chapter focuses on protecting data and providing data recovery. Practical topics in the chapter include backup planning, data recovery, and the procedures for backing up and restoring in MySQL. Any discussion of these topics would be incomplete without an introduction to the concepts of information assurance, information integrity, disaster recovery, and related terms. Indeed, once you have read through these sections you will see there is much more to protecting your investment than simply being able to back up and restore data.

What Is Information Assurance?

This section introduces the concept of information assurance, what it means to an organization, and how to get started practicing good information assurance. Although we do not intend to include a full description of all areas, we'll make sure to present the basics so you can begin your study of the subject well prepared. Oh, and so you can explain it to your boss too!

Information assurance (IA) is the management of technologies designed to administer, monitor, ensure the availability of, and control security in information systems. The goals of IA are to ensure the control and protection of the data and systems, the authenticity of access, and the confidentiality and availability of the information. While this book focuses on the database system, IA applies to all aspects of information technology. The following sites include useful background about IA:

- The NSA website's section on IA (*http://www.nsa.gov/ia/*)
- The Wikipedia page for IA (*http://bit.ly/wiki-ia*)

The Three Practices of Information Assurance

Some researchers break down the field of IA into three related practices:

Information security
> The protection of computing systems from damage by managing the risk of threats, both internal and external

Information integrity
> The assurance of continued availability and continuity of the system and its data (sometimes called *data protection*)

Information significance
> The assessment of the value of the system to the user

Information security is the most common and most well documented of the three practices. There are countless references on how best to maintain an expected level of protection for computing systems. There are also many references for physical security measures.

Information integrity is, however, the most important but also the most often overlooked practice. This chapter focuses on the importance of best practices for information integrity.

Information significance is the least commonly understood practice. Organizations that practice total quality management and related disciplines are familiar with assessing the value of the system, but generally consider only the financial aspects of the business instead of the value of information to employees in the course of doing their work. While one can argue that what is good for the company is good for the employees, we have encountered policies that seem well intended but may frustrate the employees.

When you consider information integrity and significance, IA comes to include disaster planning and disaster recovery, which otherwise are often left out of the calculations.

Well-planned IA includes both nonphysical (data, access codes, etc.) and physical (computers, access cards, keys, etc.) aspects. This chapter focuses on the physical aspect in some detail because database systems can be one of the most important resources to an organization.

Why Is Information Assurance Important?

With the increasing importance of computing systems to organizations and the rising costs of technology, conserving revenue and planning for the unexpected become priorities. As a result, the field of IA has grown beyond the scope of sequestered researchers and government agencies (two of the most interested groups). As these concepts become more popular, they are finding their way into many corporate auditors' toolboxes.

As an information technology leader, you need to be prepared to address the needs of your business to protect it from the unknown, including physical, nonphysical, and financial threats. One common place to turn is IA. If your organization has or is planning to initiate its own IA program, you owe it to yourself to learn how IA affects you.

Information Integrity, Disaster Recovery, and the Role of Backups

Information integrity is sometimes referred to as *business continuity*. The term underlines the importance of ensuring that an organization can continue its mission without interruption, and that you can carry out a controlled restore in the event of an unexpected catastrophic event. The effects of such an event can range from a minor problem to a devastating loss of operations or data that you cannot solve quickly (e.g., recovering from a power outage) or without considerable expense (e.g., replacing the information technology systems). It is important to acknowledge that there is no single solution that can help you prevent or recover from all events.

Remember, hardware can and will eventually fail; be prepared.

The areas of responsibility for information integrity include:

Data integrity
Ensures data will never be lost and that it is up to date and not corrupted

Communication integrity
Ensures that communication links are always available, are recoverable in the case of an outage, and can initiate a trusted connection

System integrity
Ensures you can restart the system in case of a malfunction, that you can recover the data and server state in case of loss or damage, and that the system maintains a level of continuity

As businesses grow more dependent on their information systems, the systems become more and more critical to business operations. Indeed, most modern businesses that utilize information technology have become so dependent on these systems that the business and its information technology become one (i.e., the business cannot exist without it).

When this becomes true, an organization must recognize that it cannot operate effectively (or perhaps at all) if its information technology becomes disabled. Businesses in this situation place a great deal of importance on being able to recover the system as quickly as possible. The ability to recover operational capability or data in the event of a sudden unplanned event is called *disaster recovery*.

Businesses that fall under the scrutiny of regulatory organizations are aware (or soon will be made so) that there are several legal decisions and standards that may require the company to adopt IA and disaster recovery. More importantly, there are efforts underway to ensure the protection of certain forms of data. In the United States, these include the , the Patriot Act, and the Health Insurance Portability and Accountability Act of 1996 (HIPAA), the Patriot Act, and the Sarbanes-Oxley Act of 2002 (SOX) (*http://soxlaw.com*).

High Availability Versus Disaster Recovery

Most businesses recognize they must invest in technologies that allow their systems to recover quickly from minor to moderate events. Technologies such as replication, redundant array of inexpensive disks (RAID) and redundant power supplies are all solutions to these needs. These are considered high availability options because they are

---

all intended to permit real-time or near real-time recovery without loss of any data (or to minimize the data loss to very small segments, such as the last changed record).

Unfortunately, few businesses take the extra step to ensure their investments are protected from devastating (and expensive) loss. Those that do are protecting their investments with the ultimate form of risk analysis: disaster recovery.

Certainly there is some overlap between the practices of high availability and disaster recovery. High availability solutions can address the minor disasters and even form one layer of defense for major disasters. However, each provides a different type of protection. High availability protects against the known or expected, while disaster recovery allows you to plan for the unexpected.

Disaster Recovery

Disaster recovery involves the process, policies, and planning for the continuation of information integrity after a catastrophic event. The most important aspect is creating and maintaining a document that contains this information: a *disaster recovery plan*.

Entire texts have been devoted to each aspect of disaster recovery. This section presents an overview of each so you can justify the importance of disaster recovery to your management team.

We have already discussed one form of disaster recovery in Chapter 3. These are sometimes the frontline tools that organizations use to recover from small disasters, but what happens if something really bad happens, like a RAID array fails beyond recovery or your server is destroyed by fire?

Before you can plan for the worst, you need to answer a series of questions that will form the premise or goals of the disaster recovery plan. These questions also form the criteria you can use to determine the effectiveness of the plan:

- What are the physical and nonphysical threats to your organization?
- What level of operational capability is needed or desired to maintain your business?
- How long can your business wait until operations are restored?
- What resources are available to plan and execute disaster recovery?

The first step of disaster recovery is acknowledging the worst-case scenario: the loss of the entire data center due to a catastrophic event. This includes not only the loss of the technology (servers, workstations, network equipment, etc.), but also the loss of the computing facility itself—and let's not forget the loss of personnel to operate the systems (this is seldom considered, but should be).

While that may seem like a doomsday story, real events have happened and may happen again that could result in just such a level of disruption. It could be as simple as a widespread power outage or as catastrophic as a hurricane, earthquake, or even war.

Imagine that the building that houses your information technology falls victim to a severe storm that damages the building beyond repair. The roof is torn away and 90% of the physical resources are damaged by water and falling debris. Let us also suppose your company is in the middle of a very lucrative and time-sensitive business transaction.

How will your company recover from this disaster? Were there any plans for such an event? How much will a prolonged loss of operations affect the revenue of the company? How quickly can you reestablish operations? This scenario may spur your management to invest in disaster recovery.

As another incentive, consider that if you plan for the worst and have procedures for recovering your systems, mundane outages become that much easier to endure. The planning aspect is the most important part of disaster recovery and offers the assurance of continuity of operations.

No One Is Exempt from Disaster

Disasters such as flood or fire can occur almost anywhere and to any organization. Some areas are more susceptible to natural disasters than others. However, no matter where your organization is located, there exists some element of risk. There is, however, one type of disaster that can strike anywhere and at any time: the man-made kind.

All organizations are responsible for preparing against malicious human activities, including those carried out by internal staff. And even if some parts of your operations are fully protected, some parts are likely to be distributed across less secure sites.

For example, suppose your company is located where natural disasters rarely happen. You are located far from earthquake fault lines and flooding is not a measurable risk. The building has an excellent fire suppression system, is protected physically, and is monitored 24-7 by trained responders. Overall, there is very low risk of physical loss due to natural disasters. Your predecessor had thought of everything, and management is not convinced of the need for a disaster recovery plan.

Now suppose an employee wants to damage the organization from within. When designing a disaster recovery plan, ask yourself, "What damage could an otherwise trusted employee do to the systems, data, or infrastructure?" While it may seem disconcerting and even paranoid to think like this, a glance through the reports of organizations victimized by sabotage from within should make you consider the unthinkable—that one of your employees could be a saboteur.

A good disaster recovery plan will include measures to reduce the risk of sabotage by identifying potential vulnerabilities, such as physical access to the building and equipment, as well as a review of all administrative rights to sensitive systems and data.

The goal of disaster recovery is to reestablish the operational capability of an organization as quickly as possible, which means its information technology must be restored. Best practices of disaster recovery include assessing the risk and planning recovery of all aspects of the information technology—both the physical and electronic. Good disaster planners include provisions for reestablishing a physical location for the organization as well as reconstructing the information technology from scratch. This should include the ability to acquire any equipment needed in an expedient manner by having a standby ready, by replacing a failed site with equipment taken from remaining sites, or by purchasing new equipment.

Rebuilding the network and the data from scratch includes acquiring a minimal set of computing and networking equipment to restore the data and applications to a state where the organization can operate at an acceptable level of reduced operations. Therefore, you need to determine the minimal set of technology that will allow the organization to continue its mission with little or no loss of revenue.

Personnel are also a key asset that your plan must consider. Thus, one recovery procedure is notifying all personnel in the case of an emergency. This may be as simple as a phone tree, where each employee is responsible for calling a set of her peers to pass on critical information. It may also be a sophisticated automated contact system that telephones all employees with a prerecorded message. Most automated systems provide a level of assessment by requiring each employee to acknowledge the message. The best notification systems include multiple point escalation. For example, the home phone numbers of employees are called first, followed by email, mobile, and text messages.

Disaster recovery also has a policy aspect, which includes the assessment of risks during emergencies (what assets are in danger, and how important is each one?) and who is to make decisions in the case of unavailability (or death) of members in the chain of command. For example, if the employee in charge of the networking systems is unavailable, his subordinate is designated to assume his responsibilities (and make any necessary decisions).

Disaster recovery planning

Planning is a much larger area and consists of making contingencies in the case of all known or expected scenarios. For example, a good disaster recovery plan has written procedures for establishing an alternative site and step-by-step instructions on how to build the information systems from scratch.

This is a good time to point out one fatal flaw in some disaster recovery plans. Little can be gained by expending countless hours and resources developing a disaster recovery plan if it is then stored on the hard drives of the systems it is designed to recover. Take the time to secure a copy of your disaster recovery plan in an offsite fireproof safe.

Disaster recovery workflow

You may have several questions by now. How do you get started with disaster recovery? How do you go from surveying your inventory of information technology to handing your boss a disaster recovery plan? It all begins with an examination of your goals. From there, you can proceed to planning and eventually evolve your own disaster recovery plan document.

If this sounds like a lot of work, it is. Most organizations form a team of experts from across the organization. The most successful teams are staffed by individuals who understand what is at stake (the organization could go bankrupt and everyone could lose their jobs), and who understand their areas of expertise well enough to identify critical systems.

It might seem obvious, but you must also plan for the possibility that those who create, test, and author a disaster recovery plan may not be the people who execute it. This consideration underscores the importance of comprehensive and unambiguous documentation, as well as clear assignment of responsibilities with some built-in redundancy.

The following describes the steps in typical disaster recovery planning. These steps provide an overview (later sections offer a more in-depth look):

1. Establish your disaster recovery team. Assuming your organization consists of more than a handful of employees, you should inform your manager now that you need to form a team to accomplish the goal of delivering a disaster recovery plan. Identify key roles you think will be needed to staff the team. Be sure to include personnel from all aspects of the organization and avoid the temptation to staff the group with only technology-savvy people. You need a complete perspective up and down the organization, and the only way to get that is to diversify.

2. Develop a mission statement. Conduct a study of your current state of operations, identify the acceptable minimal level of operations for your organization, and state the goals of your disaster recovery process.

3. Get management buy-in. Unless management initiated the task, it is your responsibility to persuade your management personnel that disaster recovery will require their support in order to succeed. It may be the only way you can get the needed resources (time, budget, personnel) to accomplish your goals.

4. Plan for the worst. This is the part that many people find the most fun. You should start recording scenarios that describe the types of catastrophic events that could

occur in your region. Include everything from theft, sabotage, weather events, and fire to disease and even worse. Be sure to start a file for these scenarios, as you will need them later when developing your recovery plans.

5. Assess your inventory and organizational resources. Make a list of all of the information technology in your organization. Be sure to include everything needed for operational success, including employee workstations and network connectivity. You should list things that exist now, not what you deem the minimal set. Reducing the assets to the minimum acceptable set will come later. You should also record the current organizational chart and the chain of command, complete with primary and secondary decision makers. Remember to write all of this down and save it for later.

6. Conduct risk assessment. Determine the effects that the loss of each of your resources could have on your organization. This will form your minimal level of operations. You should establish a priority for each resource and even establish more than one acceptable level of operations. Be sure to include a careful study of the applications and data needed. This will be used to help you decide which procedure to use when responding to events. You may be able to recover from partial losses, for instance, by redeploying your remaining systems instead of bringing up new systems, at a savings of critical time and money. It may be that you can operate for a short period of time with lower operational capability.

7. Develop contingency plans. Now that you have the disaster scenarios, your assessment of your inventory, and your risk assessment, you can begin writing the first draft of your disaster recovery plan. These contingency plans can take any form you find useful, but most planners start making procedures using lists and narration. Use whatever format makes sense to your team.

8. Create verification procedures. No plan is useful if it falls apart during execution. Now is the time to develop procedures to verify your disaster recovery plan. Start by having mock exercises in which you walk through your list of contingencies and make any adjustments needed. Go back to step 4 and cycle through the steps as you refine your disaster recovery plan.

9. Practice makes perfect. After refining your disaster recovery plan, start real-life exercises to ensure the plan works. The ultimate goal is to demonstrate to management that you can achieve each acceptable level of operations. If you can't, go back to step 6 and cycle through the remaining steps until you reach a complete and repeatable set of procedures.

Your disaster recovery plan should have at least one full operational test yearly or whenever a major element in the organization or information technology changes.

Tools for disaster recovery

Although disaster recovery involves more than just your data and computers, the focus of disaster recovery is always the data and the information technology capabilities. There are numerous tools and strategies that you can use in your disaster recovery plans. The following are a few of the more popular tools and strategies:

Backup power
> Always include some form of uninterruptible power supply. The durability and cost of such equipment are largely dependent on how much downtime your company can permit. If you must have continuous operational capability, you will need a system capable of powering your equipment for extended periods of time.

Network connectivity
> Depending on your need to reach customers and business partners electronically, you may need to consider redundant or alternative network access. This could be as simple as different media (say, an extra fiber trunk line to your access point) or as complex as alternative connection points (like satellite or cellular carriers).

Alternative site
> If your company must have full capability and as little downtime as possible, you may need to ensure rapid recovery with no data or operational loss. The ultimate strategy is to secure an alternative site to house your information technology or even your entire company. This can take the form of a mobile office (a temporary office trailer or similar platform) that contains a replica of your information technology.

Supplemental personnel
> Disaster recovery planners often overlook this component. One possible disaster you must consider is the loss of part or all of your staff in critical roles. This could take the form of infectious disease, a hostile takeover by a rival firm, or even mass loss of life. Whatever the possible cause, you should include an analysis of the critical roles in your organization and have contingencies for filling them in the event of a disaster. One obvious choice is to cross-train personnel. This will increase your talent pool, with the added benefit of making your employees more valuable.

Backup hardware
> Perhaps the most obvious aspect of continued operations is the need to have additional hardware. Your high availability technology can partially fulfill this need, but the ultimate strategy is to store replacement hardware off site (or at your alternative site) so that you can place it into service quickly. This hardware must not simply be left to gather dust, but should be up to date with your latest software and exercised regularly.

Secure vault

Another aspect that planners often overlook is a secure place to store backups of critical data. You should acquire a storage space at a secure facility (the level of security will depend on the value and sensitivity of your data) that matches your downtime needs. If you have a very low downtime threshold, a bank or similar repository may not be able to retrieve the data fast enough. In contrast, storing backups of critical data in your basement or in a public place may not be safe enough.

High availability

As mentioned earlier, high availability options form the first layer of defense in a disaster recovery plan. The ability to fail over to alternative data repositories can help you to overcome minor events.

 Always keep copies of your data and your disaster recovery plan in a secure offsite location.

One rule of thumb applies to all disaster recovery tools and strategies: the faster you need to recover from a disaster and the greater operational capability you need to restore, the higher the cost will be. This is why it is important to develop several levels of operational capability—so that you can adapt your plan and management will have options for different levels of loss and circumstances. It may be that your company is suffering from a recession or other financial limitation and may have to sacrifice operational capability. The more options you have, the stronger your disaster recovery plan will be.

The Importance of Data Recovery

Because most businesses consider their data their most valuable asset (outside of their personnel, the most difficult asset to replace), the primary focus of most disaster recovery plans is restoring the data and making it accessible. Yes, it *is* all about the data.

Data recovery is defined as the planning, policies, and procedures for restoring the organization's data to an acceptable operating state. The most important part of data recovery is the ability to back up and restore data. The success of a backup and recovery capability is sometimes called *resiliency* or *recoverability*.

The key aspects of data recovery are the ability to plan, execute, and audit data backup and to restore operations. The one aspect that is most often overlooked is auditing. A good backup and restore service should be one that you can rely on. Too often, backup systems fail without any indication that the data is absent, is corrupted in the archive, or has been destroyed. This is usually discovered the moment something goes wrong and a restore is attempted. Clearly, learning that data doesn't exist or has been corrupted during the moment of crisis can make data recovery very difficult.

Terminology

Two terms are found in almost all references to data recovery and backup solutions, so it's important to understand them:

Recovery Point Objective (RPO)
> The state of the system that is acceptable for use. Thus, RPO represents the maximum acceptable degradation of services (operational capability) or maximum acceptable data loss. Use these goals for measuring the success of a recovery action.

Recovery Time Objective (RTO)
> The maximum amount of time permitted to endure a loss of capability (also called downtime).

The RTO is affected a great deal by the RPO. If you need to recover all data (or almost all data, such as all transactions that were replicated), you will need work harder to recover it, so achieving a fast recovery—a low RTO—will be more costly. A higher RPO or lower RTO requires a bigger investment in hardware and software as well as training administrators to use systems that guarantee higher RTO and RPO, because they tend to be complex solutions. For example, if your RTO is less than three seconds and your RPO is full capability with no data loss, you must invest in an extensive high availability solution that can tolerate the complete loss of a server, data or repository without loss of data (or time).

Backup and Restore

This section describes the two most important tools in data recovery. It drills down into the concepts of backup and restore, the planning you need to do, and the backup and restore solutions available.

For database systems like MySQL, backup and restore capability means making copies of the data that you can store and later reload so that the state of the data returns to the point at which the backup was made.

The following sections are provided for those who may not be familiar with backup and recovery systems and the available solutions for MySQL. We'll explore the benefits of the various solutions and how to create an archival plan that you can use to recover your data with minimal loss.

Why back up?

Some might think that a backup is not necessary if you use replication or some form of hardware redundancy. While that may be true for recovering data quickly in the event of a mechanical or electronic failure, it will not help you recover from a loss due to a catastrophic event.

Table 15-1 describes some of the most likely ways data can be lost and corresponding ways of recovering. Many of these situations, as you can see, benefit from having backups. In addition to recovery from failures and errors, there are several excellent reasons to integrate backup into your daily data protection plans. These include generating a new slave for a replication topology, using it as a tool for failover, and even using it as a means to transport data from one network to another.

Table 15-1. Common causes of data loss

Type of failure	Description	Recovery method
User error	A user accidentally deletes data or updates it with incorrect values.	Recover deleted data with a restore from backup.
Power outage	One or more systems lose power.	Employ uninterruptible power supplies.
Hardware failures	One or more components or systems fail.	Use redundant systems or replicated data.
Software failure	Data is changed or lost due to transformation.	May be difficult to detect and may require restoring from backup (if there's no way to fix the transformation).
Facility issues	The facility that houses the equipment becomes uninhabitable and connectivity to the data is lost.	You may require a new facility in order to establish an acceptable level of operations.
Network failure	The servers that contain the data are not accessible.	This may require reestablishing connectivity or establishing a new data repository.
Sabotage	Data is stolen or damaged intentionally.	Close the security breach and inspect and sanitize the data.

If you have developed your own routine backup and utilize offsite storage, you may be more prepared for disaster recovery than you think. Consider, for example, what would happen if your database system, its redundant hardware, and even its replicant (the slave in MySQL replication) were to suddenly disappear either through theft or catastrophic failure. Having regular backups available off site will allow you to recover the data and the database system up to the last backup.

Now let's say your database system runs on commodity hardware (MySQL is famous for its hardware independence). Along with your last backup, you can order replacement hardware or repurpose existing hardware and restore your database server to operation quickly (depending, of course, on how much data you need to restore).

Hardware Horrors

Table 15-1 describes some generalized categories of data loss. However, hardware failures are seldom routine and can often be far more serious than the table indicates. Here are some real-world hardware failures that you may encounter, along with some tips for how to deal with the recovery:

Losing more than one disk of a hardware array
> If multiple disks of a single hardware RAID fail, it is likely that recovery will fail. If this happens (and it happens more often than you may think), you may have no choice but to restore the data in the array from backups.

Disk failure on both master and slave
> If both your master and slave systems fail (particularly if it's a disk failure), you may be without your hot standby. This can manifest in a variety of ways. For example, it is possible for a particular table (or shard) to become corrupt or for the disk it is stored on to fail on both the master and slave. Again, a restore of the data may be the only solution.

Backup power failure
> This is perhaps one of the most humiliating scenarios. Your high-value power backup system fails the moment you need it—during a power outage. If power outages are a possibility you need to prepare for, consider installing a backup plan in case your primary power backup fails.

The point is that having routine backups of your data is a basic and sound data recovery practice. High availability options such as replication or RAID hardware are clearly a better choice for up-to-the-second recovery, but none of these technologies can help you in the event of a catastrophic loss. You have seen that replication can help prevent data loss, but what happens, for example, if the disaster is such that both your masters and slaves are damaged beyond repair? In this case, only a good and recent backup can save you.

The following sections discuss backup in more detail and show you how you can begin making backups of your MySQL data right away.

Expectations for backups

A backup operation must have the capability to make copies of the data in a form that you can restore later. Furthermore, the backup copy must be consistent. For a transactional database, this means that the backup contains only transactions committed prior to the start of the copy, not partial or uncommitted data. Backups must also support monitoring so that you can validate the performance of the backup and the state of the data.

There are several forms of backup:

Full backup
> Makes a full backup of everything stored by the server. Nothing is omitted. This form requires the most time and storage space.

Differential backup
> Backs up just the data that changed since the last full backup. The backup contains the actual data (rows) at the time of backup. This typically requires less space than the full backup and is much faster.

Incremental backup
> Backs up just the data that changed since the last incremental or full backup. This normally takes the form of a change log (e.g., the binary log in MySQL). This backup typically takes much less time than a differential or full backup and, depending on the number of changes since the last backup, may require very little space.

Both differential and incremental backups record the differences between a previous backup and the current state of the data. But a differential backup includes the actual data, whereas the incremental backup refers to the log, from which it can reconstruct the data. Thus, when you restore a differential backup, the data is imported from the backup into the restored database. When you apply an incremental backup, it applies the changes to the data from the log.

When developing your data recovery plan, pick a naming convention for your backup archives (also called a backup image or simply backup file). For example, you might name each file with a date and any other pertinent information such as *full_back up_2013_09_09* or *incr_backup_week_3_september*. There is no right or wrong here, so feel free to use something that makes sense to you and meets your needs.

Expectations for the restore process

A restore operation must have the capability to replace the data on the system with data that is in an archive such that the data replaced is identical to that in the archive. Like backups, the restore process must support monitoring so that you can validate the performance of the restore and the state of the data.

Unfortunately, few backup systems meet all of these criteria for backup and restore. Those that do are often proprietary platforms (installations of customized hardware and software) that are expensive and difficult to maintain. This chapter includes economical options to back up and restore your MySQL data.

Logical versus physical backup

One misunderstood concept of backup is the difference between logical and physical modes; the choice you make can have significant effects on both the efficiency of your backups and options for restoring data.

A *logical backup* is simply a collection of normal SQL SELECT queries. The backup is usually built through a table scan, which is a record-by-record traversal of the data.

A *physical backup* is a copy of the original binary data (files) and it often makes a copy of the files at the operating-system level. Any backup method that involves copying the data, index, and buffer memory (files) that does not use record-by-record access is considered a physical backup.

As you might imagine, logical backups can be considerably slower than physical backups. This is because the system must use the normal SQL internal mechanisms to read one record at a time. Physical backups normally use operating system functions and do not have nearly as much overhead. Conversely, physical backups may require locking the tables associated with the binary files until the binary copy is complete, while some forms of logical backups do not lock or block access to the tables while the backup is running.

Deciding which method to use may be harder than you think. For example, if you want to make a copy of a MySQL database server that includes all of its data, you can simply take it offline, shut down the server, and copy the entire *mysql* directory to another computer. You must also include the data directories for the InnoDB files if you have changed their default locations. This will create a second instance of the server identical to the first. This may be a great way to build your replication topology, but it is very inconvenient for backing up a few important databases that cannot be taken offline. In this case, a logical backup may be your best (and only) choice. However, if your databases are all stored in InnoDB, MEB may be a possible solution instead of the logical backup, because you can backup InnoDB without blocking activity on the databases.

Forming an archival plan

Getting what you need from backup and restore tools requires discipline and some thought. The most overlooked step is developing what is called an *archival plan*. This is the analysis that determines how frequently you need to make copies of your data.

The first thing you must ask yourself is, "How much data can I afford to lose in the event that I need to recover from scratch?" In other words, how much data can you afford to skip or perhaps never recover in the event of a total loss of your data? This becomes your RPO, or the level of operational capability that your company must have in order to conduct business.

Clearly, any loss of data is bad. You must consider the value of the data itself when you plan your RPOs. You may find some data is more valuable than other data. Some data may be critical to the well-being and stability of your company while other data may be less valuable. Clearly, if you identify data that is critical to your organization, it must be recovered without loss. Thus, you may come up with a few different RPOs. It is always a good practice to define several levels, then determine which one fits the recovery needs at hand.

This is important because the archival plan determines how often you must perform a backup and at what capacity (how much is backed up). If you cannot tolerate any loss of data whatsoever, you are more than likely going to have to extend your high availability options to include replication of some sort to an offsite location. But even that is not 100% foolproof. For instance, corruption or sabotage in the master may propagate to the replicas and go undiscovered for some time.

You are more likely to measure your tolerance for data loss by the maximum amount of time you can allow for the recovery of lost data. In other words, how long can you afford to have the data unavailable while it is being recovered? This directly translates to how much money your organization can stand to lose during the downtime. For some organizations, every second that passes without access to the data is very costly. It may also be true that some data is more valuable to the company's income than other data and as such you can afford to spend more time recovering that data.

Again, you should determine several time frames, each of which is acceptable depending on the state of the business at the time. This forms your RTO options and you can match them with your RPO levels to get a picture of how much time each level of recovery requires. Determining your RTO levels can mean reentry of the data into the system or redoing some work to reacquire the data (e.g., performing another download of data or an update from a business partner).

Once you determine the amount of data loss you can tolerate (RPO) and how long you can tolerate for the recovery (RTO), you should examine the capabilities of your backup system and choose the frequency and method that meets your needs. But don't stop there. You should set up automated tasks that perform the backup during times when it is most beneficial (or least disruptive).

Finally, you should test the backups periodically by practicing data recovery (i.e., restoring the data). This will ensure you have good, viable backups free of defects, thereby ensuring safe data recovery with low risk.

Backup Tools and OS-Level Solutions

Oracle provides several solutions for backup and restore ranging from an advanced, commercial grade physical backup (MySQL Enterprise Backup) to GPL solutions for logical backups (MySQL Utilities and mysqldump). Additionally, there are several third-party solutions for performing backups on MySQL. You can also perform some unsophisticated but effective backups at the operating system level.

The final section of this chapter briefly discusses the most popular alternatives. There are other options for backups as well, but most are similar in purpose to the following methods:

- MySQL Enterprise Backup
- MySQL Utilities
- Physical file copy
- The `mysqldump` utility

- Logical Volume Manager snapshots
- XtraBackup

MySQL Enterprise Backup

If you are looking for a backup solution that permits you to make non-blocking, physical-level backups of your data and you have used the InnoDB storage engine as your primary data storage, you will want to examine the MySQL Enterprise Backup product from Oracle. MySQL Enterprise Backup is part of the MySQL Enterprise Edition product offering. More information about the MySQL Enterprise offerings can be found at MySQL Enterprise Documentation (*http://bit.ly/ent-prods*).

With MySQL Enterprise Backup, hence MEB, you can make full backups of your databases while MySQL is online without interrupting data access. MEB also supports incremental and partial backups. When restoring data, MEB supports point-in-time recovery (PITR), enabling restores to a specific point in time. When combined with the binary log features, MEB permits roll-forward recovery to a specific transaction, provided you have a backup capable of supporting a partial restoration. You can also use transportable tablespaces (supported in version 5.6 and later) to facilitate partial restores, but that requires the `--innodb_file_per_table=ON` option.

Two other valuable features of MEB including performing a partial restore for specific tables or tablespaces, and creating compressed backup files, which greatly reducing their sizes.

 MEB can also back up MyISAM, Merge, Partition, and Archive tables, but it blocks updates to these tables while the backup is running.

MEB supports MySQL version 4.0 and later and is supported on a wide variety of platforms including Linux, Mac OS X, and Windows. If you are interested in learning more about MySQL Enterprise Backup, visit the MySQL Enterprise Backup documentation website (*http://bit.ly/ent-backup*). The MEB utility has many additional features, many of which will be familiar to users of Oracle Backup tools. We list a few of the more interesting and important features here:

- Integration with external backup products (e.g., Oracle Secure backup, Netbackup, and Tivoli Storage Manager) using serial backup tape (SBT). This helps you integrate your MySQL Backup into your existing enterprise backup and recovery solution.

- Backup to a single file, which permits streaming across pipes and is also used with SBT.

- Parallel backup that permits splitting each of the files to be backed up into a separate buffer. The buffers are then processed in parallel for read, write, and compression operations. This feature can often improve backup duration times by a factor of 10. Note that the serial integrity of the backup is maintained via the use of multiple threads. In other words, you can still restore the file without using special options or procedures to put the streams back together. MEB does all that for you.

- In the latest release, MEB does full-instance backups. This means all datafiles, log files, and the state of global variables and plug-in configurations are stored in the backup image. Cool! If you examine the meta directory in your backup directory, you will see *backup_variables.txt*, which stores the settings of all global variables, *backup_content.xml*, which lists all files included, and *backup_create.xml*, which contains the manifest for the backup operation.

- Support for all of the features of the latest server release, including using different InnoDB page sizes, different InnoDB CRC calculation algorithms, and relocating InnoDB pages for optimization on solid state devices.

- Integration with MySQL Workbench. MEB can now be used from within the commercial version of MySQL Workbench.

 You can download a trial version of MySQL Enterprise Backup for evaluation purposes via Oracle's eDelivery system (*https://edeliv ery.oracle.com/*). You must have an Oracle Web account. If you do not have such an account, you can create one on the site.

Using *mysqlbackup* is very easy. You can initiate a number of commands by specifying the command name as one of the parameters. An overview of the available commands follows, broken out by the basic operations (see the online MEB documentation for more details on each command, along with examples on how to use them):

Backup commands
backup
> Make a backup to a specified backup directory. The resulting files contain a raw backup image and must have the log applied before it can be restored.

backup-and-apply-log
> Make a backup to a specified backup directory and apply the log operation on the snapshot. This makes the backup viable for a complete restore. Note that the resulting file cannot be compressed with the compression option and typically can consume more space than a backup without the log.

backup-dir-to-image

Make a backup to a single file (called an image) in a specific backup directory.

backup-to-image

Make a backup to a single file. The result file is a raw backup image and must have the log applied before it can be restored.

Restore/recovery commands

apply-incremental-backup

This operation uses an incremental backup and applies it to a full backup for preparing a backup image for restoring. Note that this works only for InnoDB tables.

apply-log

This operation uses an existing backup directory and applies the InnoDB logs so that the resulting InnoDB data and log files are the correct size for restoring data to the server. Note that in order to do apply-log on a backup image file, it must be extracted to a backup directory first.

copy-back

The restore command. In this case, the server is offline and the operation copies all files to the specific data directory. This is an offline restore. Note that you should never use this command on a server that is running. Also note that this does not apply the log.

copy-back-and-apply-log

The restore command. In this case, the server is offline and the operation copies all files to the specific data directory and applies the log. Effectively, this is a complete offline restore. Note that you should never use this command on a server that is running.

Utility commands (which manipulate the images)

extract

Extract the items in a backup image using relative paths. If you use the `--backup-dir` option, you can specify a directory to place the files being extracted. You can use the `--src-entry` to filter the extract to a specific file or directory.

image-to-backup-dir

Extract a backup image to a backup directory.

list-image

List the items in the image. The `--src-entry` option can be used to filter the output to list a specific file or directory.

validate

Compare the checksums in the file to detect corruption.

How MEB works

As we stated, MEB is a physical-level backup tool. As such, it makes binary copies of the actual disk files where the data is stored. It also makes direct copies of the InnoDB engine files, including the logs. Finally, MEB also makes copies of all other pertinent files (*.frm* files, MyISAM files, etc.). With the release of MEB 3.9.0, full instance backup is enabled, which also saves the global variable settings.

Because MEB copies the InnoDB files, it does so as a snapshot operation (thereby allowing hot backups). When this occurs, the state of the pointers inside the InnoDB storage engine may not match the data that is actually stored in the backup image. Thus, backups require two steps; first backup the data, and then apply the logs to the InnoDB files in the backup directory so that they are set to the correct pointers. In other words, you must make the backup files match the state of the InnoDB files by applying any changes to InnoDB tables that happened while the backup was in progress. Once you have done this, the backup image is in a state to be restored. Fortunately, you can do both of these in one pass by using the backup-and-apply-log command (described in the next section).

Restoring a full backup requires the server to be offline. This is because the backup performs a complete overwrite of all files and sets the global variables to their state recorded at the time of the backup (for MEB 3.9.0 and later).

The following sections demonstrate the three basic operations: full backup, incremental backup, and full restore. You can find examples of all commands in the MEB online reference manual (*http://bit.ly/ent-prods*).

Performing a full backup

To create a full backup, you simply specify the user, password, and port options (as appropriate—mysqlbackup follows the standard MySQL client practices for accessing servers by host, port, or socket). You also specify the backup command of your choice (here we will use backup-and-apply-log) and a backup directory to store the resulting file(s):

```
$ sudo ./mysqlbackup backup-and-apply-log --port=3306 \
  --backup-dir=./initial-backup --user=root --password --show-progress
Password:
MySQL Enterprise Backup version 3.9.0 [2013/08/23]
Copyright (c) 2003, 2013, Oracle and/or its affiliates. All Rights Reserved.

 mysqlbackup: INFO: Starting with following command line ...
 ./mysqlbackup backup --port=3306 --backup-dir=./initial-backup --user=root
        --password --show-progress

Enter password:
 mysqlbackup: INFO: MySQL server version is '5.5.23-log'.
 mysqlbackup: INFO: Got server configuration information from running server.
```

```
IMPORTANT: Please check that mysqlbackup run completes successfully.
          At the end of a successful 'backup' run mysqlbackup
          prints "mysqlbackup completed OK!".

130826 15:48:29 mysqlbackup: INFO: MEB logfile created at
/backups/initial-backup/meta/MEB_2013-08-26.15-48-29_backup.log


--------------------------------------------------------------------
                     Server Repository Options:
--------------------------------------------------------------------
  datadir = /usr/local/mysql/data/
  innodb_data_home_dir =
  innodb_data_file_path = ibdata1:10M:autoextend
  innodb_log_group_home_dir = /usr/local/mysql/data/
  innodb_log_files_in_group = 2
  innodb_log_file_size = 5242880
  innodb_page_size = Null
  innodb_checksum_algorithm = innodb


--------------------------------------------------------------------
                      Backup Config Options:
--------------------------------------------------------------------
  datadir = /backups/initial-backup/datadir
  innodb_data_home_dir = /backups/initial-backup/datadir
  innodb_data_file_path = ibdata1:10M:autoextend
  innodb_log_group_home_dir = /backups/initial-backup/datadir
  innodb_log_files_in_group = 2
  innodb_log_file_size = 5242880
  innodb_page_size = 16384
  innodb_checksum_algorithm = innodb

 mysqlbackup: INFO: Unique generated backup id for this is 13775524146819070

 mysqlbackup: INFO: Creating 14 buffers each of size 16777216.
130826 17:26:56 mysqlbackup: INFO: Full Backup operation starts with following
threads 1 read-threads    6 process-threads    1 write-threads
130826 17:26:56 mysqlbackup: INFO: System tablespace file format is Antelope.
130826 17:26:56 mysqlbackup: INFO: Starting to copy all innodb files...
130826 17:26:56 mysqlbackup: INFO: Progress: 0 of 27 MB; state: Copying system
tablespace
130826 17:26:56 mysqlbackup: INFO: Copying /usr/local/mysql/data/ibdata1
(Antelope file format).
130826 17:26:56 mysqlbackup: INFO: Found checkpoint at lsn 20121160.
130826 17:26:56 mysqlbackup: INFO: Starting log scan from lsn 20121088.
130826 17:26:56 mysqlbackup: INFO: Copying log...
130826 17:26:56 mysqlbackup: INFO: Log copied, lsn 20121160.
130826 17:26:56 mysqlbackup: INFO: Completing the copy of innodb files.
130826 17:26:57 mysqlbackup: INFO: Preparing to lock tables: Connected to mysqld
server.
130826 17:26:57 mysqlbackup: INFO: Starting to lock all the tables...
130826 17:26:57 mysqlbackup: INFO: All tables are locked and flushed to disk
```

```
130826 17:26:57 mysqlbackup: INFO: Opening backup source directory
'/usr/local/mysql/data/'
130826 17:26:57 mysqlbackup: INFO: Starting to backup all non-innodb files in
subdirectories of '/usr/local/mysql/data/'
130826 17:26:57 mysqlbackup: INFO: Copying the database directory 'menagerie'
130826 17:26:57 mysqlbackup: INFO: Copying the database directory
'my_sensor_network'
130826 17:26:57 mysqlbackup: INFO: Copying the database directory 'mysql'
130826 17:26:57 mysqlbackup: INFO: Copying the database directory 'newschema'
130826 17:26:57 mysqlbackup: INFO: Copying the database directory
'performance_schema'
130826 17:26:57 mysqlbackup: INFO: Copying the database directory 'test_arduino'
130826 17:26:57 mysqlbackup: INFO: Copying the database directory 'world'
130826 17:26:57 mysqlbackup: INFO: Copying the database directory 'world_innodb'
130826 17:26:57 mysqlbackup: INFO: Completing the copy of all non-innodb files.
130826 17:26:58 mysqlbackup: INFO: Progress: 27 of 27 MB; state:
Copying metadata to image
130826 17:26:58 mysqlbackup: INFO: A copied database page was modified
                              at 20121160.
        (This is the highest lsn found on page)
        Scanned log up to lsn 20123788.
        Was able to parse the log up to lsn 20123788.
        Maximum page number for a log record 776
130826 17:26:58 mysqlbackup: INFO: All tables unlocked
130826 17:26:58 mysqlbackup: INFO: All MySQL tables were locked for
0.913 seconds.
130826 17:26:58 mysqlbackup: INFO: Reading all global variables from the server.
130826 17:26:58 mysqlbackup: INFO: Completed reading of all global variables
from the server.
130826 17:26:58 mysqlbackup: INFO: Creating server config files server-my.cnf
and server-all.cnf in /Users/cbell/source/meb-3.9.0-osx10.6-universal/bin/
initial-backup
130826 17:26:58 mysqlbackup: INFO: Full Backup operation completed successfully.
130826 17:26:58 mysqlbackup: INFO: Backup created in directory
'/Users/cbell/source/meb-3.9.0-osx10.6-universal/bin/initial-backup'
130826 17:26:58 mysqlbackup: INFO: MySQL binlog position:
filename mysql-bin.000026, position 20734


-------------------------------------------------------------
   Parameters Summary
-------------------------------------------------------------
   Start LSN              : 20121088
   End LSN                : 20123788
-------------------------------------------------------------


 mysqlbackup: INFO: Creating 14 buffers each of size 65536.
130826 17:26:58 mysqlbackup: INFO: Apply-log operation starts with following
threads 1 read-threads    1 process-threads
130826 17:26:58 mysqlbackup: INFO: ibbackup_logfile's creation parameters:
        start lsn 20121088, end lsn 20123788,
        start checkpoint 20121160.
```

```
 mysqlbackup: INFO: InnoDB: Starting an apply batch of log records
to the database...
InnoDB: Progress in percent: 0 1 2 3 4 5 6 7 8 9 10 11 12 13 14 15 16 17
18 19 20 21 22 23 24 25 26 27 28 29 30 31 32 33 34 35 36 37 38 39 40 41
42 43 44 45 46 47 48 49 50 51 52 53 54 55 56 57 58 59 60 61 62 63 64 65
66 67 68 69 70 71 72 73 74 75 76 77 78 79 80 81 82 83 84 85 86 87 88 89
90 91 92 93 94 95 96 97 98 99
 mysqlbackup: INFO: InnoDB: Setting log file size to 5242880
 mysqlbackup: INFO: InnoDB: Setting log file size to 5242880
130826 17:26:58 mysqlbackup: INFO: We were able to parse ibbackup_logfile up to
          lsn 20123788.
 mysqlbackup: INFO: Last MySQL binlog file position 0 20653,
file name ./mysql-bin.000026
130826 17:26:58 mysqlbackup: INFO: The first datafile is
'/backups/initial-backup/datadir/ibdata1'
          and the new created log files are at '/backups/initial-backup/datadir'
130826 17:26:59 mysqlbackup: INFO: Progress: 27 of 27 MB; state: Completed
130826 17:26:59 mysqlbackup: INFO: Apply-log operation completed successfully.
130826 17:26:59 mysqlbackup: INFO: Full backup prepared for
recovery successfully.

mysqlbackup completed OK!
```

 You can use the --show-progress option to track progress by percent to stdout, a file, or a table. This option can also show the phase
of the operation. See the online MEB reference manual for more
details.

You can also make a compressed backup using the --compress option. But you cannot
do this with the backup-and-apply-log operation. To create a compressed full backup
that is viable for restore, you must do it in two steps, as follows (note that we must use
the --uncompress option with the apply-log command):

```
$ sudo ./mysqlbackup backup --compress  --port=3306 \
  --backup-dir=/backups/initial-backup --user=root \
  --password --show-progress
$ sudo ./mysqlbackup apply-log --port=3306 \
  --backup-dir=/backups/initial-backup --user=root \
  --password --show-progress --uncompress
```

Performing an incremental backup

An incremental backup is performed by specifying an existing backup image (full or
previous incremental backup image) to which you want to compare the current state of
the databases, using the --incremental-base option to specify the backup directory.
Use --backup-dir to specify the directory for the incremental backup image. Here we
demonstrate how to create the first incremental backup image from the most recent full
backup (see the online MEB reference manual for more details about performing in-

cremental backups including specifying the logical sequence number, or LSN, manually
to control the incremental backup):

```
$ sudo ./mysqlbackup backup --port=3306 \
  --backup-dir=/backups/incremental-backup-Monday \
  --incremental-base=dir:/backups/initial-backup-1 --user=root --password
MySQL Enterprise Backup version 3.9.0 [2013/08/23]
Copyright (c) 2003, 2013, Oracle and/or its affiliates. All Rights Reserved.

 mysqlbackup: INFO: Starting with following command line ...
 ./mysqlbackup backup --port=3306
        --backup-dir=/backups/incremental-backup-Monday
        --incremental-base=/backups/initial-backup-1 --user=root
        --password

Enter password:
 mysqlbackup: INFO: MySQL server version is '5.5.23-log'.
 mysqlbackup: INFO: Got some server configuration information from running
 server.

IMPORTANT: Please check that mysqlbackup run completes successfully.
           At the end of a successful 'backup' run mysqlbackup
           prints "mysqlbackup completed OK!".

130826 19:02:43 mysqlbackup: INFO: MEB logfile created at
/backups/incremental-backup-Monday/meta/MEB_2013-08-26.19-02-43_backup.log

--------------------------------------------------------------------
                     Server Repository Options:
--------------------------------------------------------------------
  datadir = /usr/local/mysql/data/
  innodb_data_home_dir =
  innodb_data_file_path = ibdata1:10M:autoextend
  innodb_log_group_home_dir = /usr/local/mysql/data/
  innodb_log_files_in_group = 2
  innodb_log_file_size = 5242880
  innodb_page_size = Null
  innodb_checksum_algorithm = innodb


--------------------------------------------------------------------
                      Backup Config Options:
--------------------------------------------------------------------
  datadir = /backups/incremental-backup-Monday/datadir
  innodb_data_home_dir = /backups/incremental-backup-Monday/datadir
  innodb_data_file_path = ibdata1:10M:autoextend
  innodb_log_group_home_dir = /backups/incremental-backup-Monday/datadir
  innodb_log_files_in_group = 2
  innodb_log_file_size = 5242880
  innodb_page_size = 16384
  innodb_checksum_algorithm = innodb

 mysqlbackup: INFO: Unique generated backup id for this is 13775581632965290
```

```
mysqlbackup: INFO: Creating 14 buffers each of size 16777216.
130826 19:02:45 mysqlbackup: INFO: Full Backup operation starts with following
threads
1 read-threads    6 process-threads    1 write-threads
130826 19:02:45 mysqlbackup: INFO: System tablespace file format is Antelope.
130826 19:02:45 mysqlbackup: INFO: Starting to copy all innodb files...
130826 19:02:45 mysqlbackup: INFO: Found checkpoint at lsn 20135490.
130826 19:02:45 mysqlbackup: INFO: Starting log scan from lsn 20135424.
130826 19:02:45 mysqlbackup: INFO: Copying /usr/local/mysql/data/ibdata1
(Antelope file format).
130826 19:02:45 mysqlbackup: INFO: Copying log...
130826 19:02:45 mysqlbackup: INFO: Log copied, lsn 20135490.
130826 19:02:45 mysqlbackup: INFO: Completing the copy of innodb files.
130826 19:02:46 mysqlbackup: INFO: Preparing to lock tables: Connected to
mysqld server.
130826 19:02:46 mysqlbackup: INFO: Starting to lock all the tables...
130826 19:02:46 mysqlbackup: INFO: All tables are locked and flushed to disk
130826 19:02:46 mysqlbackup: INFO: Opening backup source directory
'/usr/local/mysql/data/'
130826 19:02:46 mysqlbackup: INFO: Starting to backup all non-innodb files in
subdirectories of '/usr/local/mysql/data/'
130826 19:02:46 mysqlbackup: INFO: Copying the database directory 'menagerie'
130826 19:02:46 mysqlbackup: INFO: Copying the database directory
'my_sensor_network'
130826 19:02:46 mysqlbackup: INFO: Copying the database directory 'mysql'
130826 19:02:46 mysqlbackup: INFO: Copying the database directory 'newschema'
130826 19:02:46 mysqlbackup: INFO: Copying the database directory
'performance_schema'
130826 19:02:46 mysqlbackup: INFO: Copying the database directory 'test_arduino'
130826 19:02:46 mysqlbackup: INFO: Copying the database directory 'world'
130826 19:02:46 mysqlbackup: INFO: Copying the database directory 'world_innodb'
130826 19:02:46 mysqlbackup: INFO: Completing the copy of all non-innodb files.
130826 19:02:47 mysqlbackup: INFO: A copied database page was
modified at 20135490.
          (This is the highest lsn found on page)
          Scanned log up to lsn 20137372.
          Was able to parse the log up to lsn 20137372.
          Maximum page number for a log record 724
130826 19:02:47 mysqlbackup: INFO: All tables unlocked
130826 19:02:47 mysqlbackup: INFO: All MySQL tables were locked for
0.954 seconds.
130826 19:02:47 mysqlbackup: INFO: Reading all global variables from the server.
130826 19:02:47 mysqlbackup: INFO: Completed reading of all global variables
from the server.
130826 19:02:47 mysqlbackup: INFO: Creating server config files
server-my.cnf and server-all.cnf in /backups/incremental-backup-Monday
130826 19:02:47 mysqlbackup: INFO: Full Backup operation completed successfully.
130826 19:02:47 mysqlbackup: INFO: Backup created in directory
'/backups/incremental-backup-Monday'
130826 19:02:47 mysqlbackup: INFO: MySQL binlog position: filename
mysql-bin.000026, position 71731
```

```
-----------------------------------------------------------
   Parameters Summary
-----------------------------------------------------------
   Start LSN               : 20135424
   End LSN                 : 20137372
-----------------------------------------------------------

mysqlbackup completed OK!
```

 In MEB, incremental backups are performed by using the InnoDB redo log, thus capturing changes made since the last recorded position. The incremental backup feature targets InnoDB tables. For non-InnoDB tables, incremental backup includes the entire datafile rather than just the changes.

Restoring data

Data is restored by applying the log described in the previous section. This operation essentially points the MySQL instance to the backup copies of the database. It does not copy the files to the normal MySQL *datadir* location. If you want to do this, you must copy the files manually. The reason for this is that the *mysqlbackup* utility is designed to refuse to overwrite any data. To start a MySQL instance and use a backup of your data, execute a command like the following:

```
$ sudo ./mysqlbackup --defaults-file=/etc/my.cnf copy-back \
  --datadir=/usr/local/mysql/data --backup-dir=/backups/initial-backup
MySQL Enterprise Backup version 3.9.0 [2013/08/23]
Copyright (c) 2003, 2013, Oracle and/or its affiliates. All Rights Reserved.

 mysqlbackup: INFO: Starting with following command line ...
 ./mysqlbackup --defaults-file=/etc/my.cnf copy-back
        --datadir=/usr/local/mysql/data
        --backup-dir=/backups/initial-backup

IMPORTANT: Please check that mysqlbackup run completes successfully.
           At the end of a successful 'copy-back' run mysqlbackup
           prints "mysqlbackup completed OK!".

130826 19:52:46 mysqlbackup: INFO: MEB logfile created at
/backups/initial-backup/meta/MEB_2013-08-26.19-52-46_copy_back.log

-----------------------------------------------------------
                    Server Repository Options:
-----------------------------------------------------------
 datadir = /usr/local/mysql/data
 innodb_data_home_dir = /usr/local/mysql/data
 innodb_data_file_path = ibdata1:10M:autoextend
 innodb_log_group_home_dir = /usr/local/mysql/data
 innodb_log_files_in_group = 2
```

```
innodb_log_file_size = 5M
innodb_page_size = Null
innodb_checksum_algorithm = innodb


-----------------------------------------------------------------
                        Backup Config Options:
-----------------------------------------------------------------
datadir = /backups/initial-backup/datadir
innodb_data_home_dir = /backups/initial-backup/datadir
innodb_data_file_path = ibdata1:10M:autoextend
innodb_log_group_home_dir = /backups/initial-backup/datadir
innodb_log_files_in_group = 2
innodb_log_file_size = 5242880
innodb_page_size = 16384
innodb_checksum_algorithm = innodb


 mysqlbackup: INFO: Creating 14 buffers each of size 16777216.
130826 19:52:46 mysqlbackup: INFO: Copy-back operation starts with following
threads 1 read-threads    1 write-threads
130826 19:52:46 mysqlbackup: INFO: Copying
/backups/initial-backup/datadir/ibdata1.
130826 19:52:46 mysqlbackup: INFO: Copying the database directory 'menagerie'
130826 19:52:46 mysqlbackup: INFO: Copying the database directory
'my_sensor_network'
130826 19:52:46 mysqlbackup: INFO: Copying the database directory 'mysql'
130826 19:52:46 mysqlbackup: INFO: Copying the database directory 'newschema'
130826 19:52:46 mysqlbackup: INFO: Copying the database directory
'performance_schema'
130826 19:52:46 mysqlbackup: INFO: Copying the database directory 'test_arduino'
130826 19:52:46 mysqlbackup: INFO: Copying the database directory 'world'
130826 19:52:46 mysqlbackup: INFO: Copying the database directory 'world_innodb'
130826 19:52:46 mysqlbackup: INFO: Completing the copy of all non-innodb files.
130826 19:52:46 mysqlbackup: INFO: Copying the log file 'ib_logfile0'
130826 19:52:46 mysqlbackup: INFO: Copying the log file 'ib_logfile1'
130826 19:52:47 mysqlbackup: INFO: Creating server config files server-my.cnf
and server-all.cnf in /usr/local/mysql/data
130826 19:52:47 mysqlbackup: INFO: Copy-back operation completed successfully.
130826 19:52:47 mysqlbackup: INFO: Finished copying backup files to
'/usr/local/mysql/data'

mysqlbackup completed OK!
```

 You must specify the --defaults-file as the first option after the command. If you do not, an error message similar to *mysqlbackup: unknown variable 'defaults-file=/etc/my.cnf'* may be displayed.

Backing up a downed server

One of the tasks that is essential to good forensic recovery work is backing up the data of a downed server. Why would you do this? If the server is down due to hardware issues or some other non-database file (or MySQL) related problem, the data is most likely OK and you may not think a backup is necessary. But what if, during the course of restarting the server, something goes wrong? If you have a good backup and recovery plan in place you can always restore from the last backup, or from a backup plus the last incremental backups. However, having a full backup of the server—with all of its settings—is much more secure. Not only will you be able to restore the data should something go wrong during the repair, but you will also have a backup to which you can return if the problem is recurring or you want to attempt to re-create it.

This is one area where MEB shines. MEB can perform what it calls a "cold backup": a backup of a server that is not running. To accomplish this, execute a full backup specifying the --no-connection and the --defaults-file options. You also need to specify the --datadir. The following shows a sample command to run a cold backup (we omit the messages generated for brevity; they are the same sort of messages generated for a hot backup):

```
$ sudo ./mysqlbackup --defaults-file=/etc/my.cnf backup-and-apply-log \
  --no-connection --datadir=/usr/local/mysql/data \
  --backup-dir=/backups/emergency-cold-backup
MySQL Enterprise Backup version 3.9.0 [2013/08/23]
Copyright (c) 2003, 2013, Oracle and/or its affiliates. All Rights Reserved.

 mysqlbackup: INFO: Starting with following command line ...
 ./mysqlbackup --defaults-file=/etc/my.cnf backup-and-apply-log
       --no-connection --datadir=/usr/local/mysql/data
       --backup-dir=/Users/cbell/source/emergency-cold-backup

IMPORTANT: Please check that mysqlbackup run completes successfully.
          At the end of a successful 'backup-and-apply-log' run mysqlbackup
          prints "mysqlbackup completed OK!".
[...]

130826 20:09:09 mysqlbackup: INFO: Full backup prepared for recovery
successfully.

mysqlbackup completed OK!
```

MySQL Utilities Database Export and Import

MySQL Utilities is a subcomponent of the MySQL Workbench Tool. We cover the topic in more detail in Chapter 17, but this section introduces two utilities that you can use to help backup and restore your data. They may be helpful when you need to make a copy of your data either for transformation (bulk or targeted changes to your data) or to make a human-readable copy of the data.

The first utility is `mysqldbexport`. This utility permits you to read your databases (a selected list or all databases) and produces output in one of several forms, including SQL statements, comma- or tab-separated lists, and grid or vertical output, similar to how the *mysql* client displays data. You can redirect this to a file for later use.

The second utility is `mysqldbimport`. This utility reads the output produced by the `mysqldbexport` utility.

Both utilities allow you to import only the object definitions, only the data, or both. This may sound similar to *mysqldump*, and in many ways that it is true, but these utilities have simplified options (one criticism of *mysqldump* is the vast array of options available) and is written in Python, which permits database professionals to tailor the export and import to their own needs.

A more in-depth examination of *mysqldbexport* and *mysqldbimport* can be found in Chapter 17.

The mysqldump Utility

The most popular alternative to the physical file copy feature is the `mysqldump` client application. It has been part of the MySQL installation for some time and was originally donated to MySQL by Igor Romanenko. `mysqldump` creates a set of SQL statements that re-create the databases when you rerun them. For example, when you run a backup, the output contains all of the `CREATE` statements needed to create the databases and the tables they contain, as well as all the `INSERT` statements needed to re-create the data in those tables.

This can be very handy if you need to do a search-and-replace operation in the text of your data. Simply back up your database, edit the resulting file with a text editor, then restore the database to effect the changes. Many MySQL users use this technique to correct all sorts of errors caused by making batch edits to the data. You will find this much easier than writing, say, 1,000 `UPDATE` statements with complicated `WHERE` clauses.

There are two drawbacks to using `mysqldump`. It takes a lot more time than the binary copies made by file-level (physical) backups like MySQL Enterprise Backup, LVM, or a simple offline file copy, and it requires a lot more storage space. The cost in time can be significant if you make frequent backups, want to restore a database quickly after a system failure, or need to transfer the backup file across a network.

You can use `mysqldump` to back up all your databases, a specific subset of databases, or even particular tables within a given database. The following examples show each of these options:

```
mysqldump -uroot -all-databases
mysqldump -uroot db1, db2
mysqldump -uroot my_db t1
```

You can also use mysqldump to do a hot backup of InnoDB tables. The --single-transaction option issues a BEGIN statement at the start of the backup, which signals the InnoDB storage engine to read the tables as a consistent read. Thus, any changes you make are applied to the tables, but the data is frozen at the time of backup. However, no other connection should use data definition language (DDL) statements like ALTER TABLE, DROP TABLE, RENAME TABLE, TRUNCATE TABLE. This is because a consistent read is not isolated from DDL changes.

 The --single-transaction option and the --lock-tables option are mutually exclusive because LOCK TABLES issues an implicit commit.

The utility has several options that control the backup as well as what is included. Table 15-2 describes some of the more important options. See the online MySQL Reference Manual for a complete set of options.

Table 15-2. mysqlbackup options

Option	Function
--add-drop-database	Includes a DROP DATABASE statement before each database.
--add-drop-table	Includes a DROP TABLE statement before each table.
--add-locks	Surrounds each included table with LOCK TABLES and UNLOCK TABLES.
--all-databases	Includes all databases.
--create-options	Includes all MySQL-specific table options in the CREATE TABLE statements.
--databases	Includes a list of databases only.
--delete-master-logs	On a master, deletes the binary logs after performing the backup.
--events	Backs up events from the included databases.
--extended-insert	Uses the alternative INSERT syntax that includes each row as a VALUES clause.
--flush-logs	Flushes the logfiles before starting the backup.
--flush-privileges	Includes a FLUSH PRIVILEGES statement after backing up the *mysql* database.
--ignore-table=db.tbl	Does not back up the specified table.
--lock-all-tables	Locks all tables across all databases during the dump.
--lock-tables	Locks all tables before including them.
--log-error=filename	Appends warnings and errors to the specified file.
--master-data[=value]	Includes the binlog filename and position in the output.
--no-data	Does not write any table row information (only CREATE statements).
--password[=password]	The password to use when connecting to the server.
--port=port_num	The TCP/IP port number to use for the connection.
--result-file=filename	Outputs to a specific file.

Option	Function
--routines	Includes stored routines (procedures and functions).
--single-transaction	Issues a BEGIN SQL statement before dumping data from the server. This allows for a consistent snapshot of the InnoDB tables.
--tables	Overrides the --databases option.
--triggers	Includes triggers.
--where='condition'	Includes only rows selected by the condition.
--xml	Produces XML output.

 You can also include these options in a MySQL configuration file under the heading [mysqldump]. In most cases, you can specify the option simply by removing the initial dashes. For example, to always produce XML output, include xml in your configuration file.

One very handy feature of mysqldump is the ability to dump a database schema. You can normally do this using a set of the CREATE commands to re-create all of the objects without the INSERT statements that include the data. This usage can be very useful for keeping a historical record of the changes to your schema. If you use the --no-data option along with the options to include all of the objects (e.g., --routines, --triggers), you can use mysqldump to create a database schema.

Notice the option --master-data. This option can be very helpful for performing PITR because it saves the binary log information like MySQL Enterprise Backup does.

There are many more options that allow you to control how the utility works. If creating a backup in the form of SQL statements sounds like the best option for you, feel free to explore the rest of the options for making mysqldump work for you.

Physical File Copy

The easiest and most basic way to back up MySQL is to make a simple file copy. Unfortunately, this requires you to stop the server for best results. To perform a file copy, simply stop your server and copy the data directory and any setup files on the server. One common method for this is to use the Unix tar command to create an archive. You can then move this archive to another system and restore the data directory.

A typical sequence follows the pattern of tar commands that back up the data from one database server and restore it on another system. Execute the following command on the server you want to back up, where *backup_2013_09_09.tar.gz* is the file you want to create and */usr/loca/mysql/data* is the path for the data directory:

```
tar -czf backup_2013_09_09.tar.gz /usr/loca/mysql/data/*
```

The *backup_2013_09_09.tar.gz* file must reside on a directory shared by the two servers (or you must physically copy it to the new server). Now, on the server where you want to restore the data, change to the root installation of your new installation of MySQL. Delete the existing data directory, if it exists, then execute the following:

```
tar -xvf ../backup_2013_09_09.tar.gz
```

 As mentioned earlier, it is always a good idea to use meaningful file-names for your backup images.

As you can see from this example, it is very easy to back up your data at the operating system level. Not only can you get a single compressed archive file that you can move around easily, you also get the benefit of fast file copy. You can even do a selective backup by simply copying individual files or subdirectories from your data directory.

Unfortunately, the tar command is available only on Linux and Unix platforms. If you have Cygwin installed on a Windows system and have included its version of the command, you can also use tar there. You can also use 7zip to create tar archives on Windows.

Other than Cygwin or another Unix-on-Windows package, the closest equivalent to this command on Windows is the handy folder archive feature of the Explorer or an archive program such as WinZip. To create a WinZip file, open Windows Explorer and navigate to your data directory. But instead of opening the directory, right-click the data directory and choose an option that compresses the data, which will have a label such as Send To→Compressed (zipped) Folder, then provide a name for the *.zip* file.

Although a physical file copy is the quickest and easiest form of backup, it does require that you shut down the server. But that isn't necessary if you are careful to ensure no updates occur during the file copy, by locking all tables and performing a flush tables command. However, this practice is not recommended and you should always take your server offline (shutdown) before making the file copy.

 This is similar to the process for cloning a slave. See Chapter 3 for more details and an example of cloning a slave using file copy.

Additionally, depending on the size of the data, your server must be offline not only for the time to copy the files, but also for any additional data loads like cache entries or the use of memory tables for fast lookups. For this reason, physical copy backup may not be feasible for some installations.

Fortunately, there is a Perl script, created by Tim Bunce, to automate this process. The script is named *mysqlhotcopy.sh* and it is located in the *./scripts* folder of your MySQL installation. It allows you to make hot copies of databases. However, you can use it only to back up MyISAM or Archive storage engines and it works only on Unix and Netware operating systems.

The *mysqlhotcopy.sh* utility also includes customization features. You can find more information about it at the *mysqlhotcopy* documentation (*http://bit.ly/mysqlhotcopy*).

Logical Volume Manager Snapshots

Most Linux and some Unix systems provide another powerful method of backing up your MySQL database. It makes use of a technology called the *logical volume manager* (LVM).

Microsoft Windows has a similar technology called *Volume Shadow Copy*. Unfortunately, there are no generic utilities to make a snapshot of a random partition or folder structure as there are for LVM. You can, however, make snapshots of an entire drive, which can be useful if your database directory is the only thing on that drive. See the Microsoft online documentation for more information.

An LVM is a disk subsystem that gives you a lot of administrative power to create, remove, and resize volumes easily and quickly without using the older, often complicated and unforgiving disk tools.

The added benefit for backup is the concept of taking a *snapshot* (i.e., a copy of an active volume) without disrupting the applications that access the data on that volume. The idea is to take a snapshot, which is a relatively fast operation, and then back up the snapshot instead of the original volume. Deep inside LVM, a snapshot is managed using a mechanism that keeps track of the changes since you took the snapshot, so that it stores only the disk segments that have changed. Thus, a snapshot takes up less space than a complete copy of the volume and when the backup is made, the LVM copies the files as they existed at the time of the snapshot. Snapshots effectively freeze the data.

Another benefit of using LVM and snapshots for backing up database systems lies in how you use the volumes. The best practice is to use a separate volume for each of your MySQL installations so that all of the data is on the same volume, allowing you to create a backup quickly using a snapshot. Of course, it is also possible to use multiple logical volumes in some situations, such as using one logical volume for each tablespace or even different logical volumes for MyISAM and InnoDB tables.

Getting started with LVM

If your Linux installation does not have LVM installed, you can install it using your package manager. For example, on Ubuntu you can install LVM using the following command:

```
sudo apt-get install lvm2
```

Although not all LVM systems are the same, the following procedure is based on a typical Debian distribution and works well on systems like Ubuntu. We don't mean to write a complete tutorial on LVM but just to give you an idea of the complexity of using LVM for making database backups. Consult your operating system documentation for specifics about the type of LVM your system supports, or simply browse the many how-to documents available on the Web.

Before we get started with the details, let's take a moment to understand the basic concepts of LVM. There is a hierarchy of levels to the LVM implementation. At the lowest level is the disk itself. On top of that are *partitions,* which allow us to communicate with the disk. On top of the partition we create a *physical volume*, which is the control mechanism that the LVM provides. You can add a physical volume to a *volume group* (which can contain multiple physical volumes), and a volume group can contain one or more *logical volumes.* Figure 15-1 depicts the relationship among filesystems, volume groups, physical volumes, and block devices.

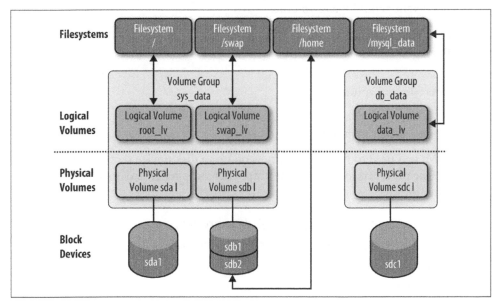

Figure 15-1. Anatomy of LVM

A logical volume can act as either a normal mounted filesystem or a snapshot. The creation of a snapshot logical volume is the key to using snapshots for backup. The following sections describe how you can get started experimenting with LVM and making backups of your data.

There are several useful commands that you should become familiar with. The following list contains the most frequently used commands and their uses. Be sure to consult the documentation for more information about these commands:

pvcreate
> Creates a physical volume

pvscan
> Shows details about the physical volumes

vgcreate
> Creates volume groups

vgscan
> Shows details about volume groups

lvcreate
> Creates a logical volume

lvscan
> Shows details about logical volumes

lvremove
> Removes a logical volume

mount
> Mounts a logical volume

umount
> Unmounts a logical volume

To use LVM, you need to have either a new disk or a disk device that you can logically unmount. The process is as follows (the output here was generated on a laptop running Ubuntu version 9.04):

1. Create a backup of an existing MySQL data directory:

    ```
    tar -czf ~/my_backups/backup.tar.gz /dev/mysql/datadir
    ```

2. Partition the drive:

    ```
    sudo parted
    select /dev/sdb
    mklabel msdos
    mkpart test
    quit
    ```

3. Create a physical volume for the drive:

```
sudo pvcreate /dev/sdb
```

4. Create a volume group:

```
sudo vgcreate /dev/sdb mysql
```

5. Create a logical volume for your data (here we create a 20 GB volume):

```
sudo lvcreate -L20G -ndatadir mysql
```

6. Create a filesystem on the logical volume:

```
mke2fs /dev/mysql/datadir
```

7. Mount the logical volume:

```
sudo mkdir /mnt
sudo mount /dev/mysql/datadir /mnt
```

8. Copy the archive and restore your data to the logical volume:

```
sudo cp ~/my_backups/backup.tar.gz
sudo tar -xvf backup.tar.gz
```

9. Create an instance of a MySQL server and use --datadir to point to the folder on the logical volume:

```
./mysqld --console -uroot --datadir=/mnt
```

 If you want to experiment with LVM, we recommend you use a disk whose data you can afford to lose. A good, cheap option is a small USB hard drive.

That's all you need to get started with a logical volume. Take some time to experiment with the LVM tools, until you are certain you can work with them effectively, before you start using them for your production systems.

LVM in a backup and restore

To do your backup, you need to flush and temporarily lock all of the tables, take the snapshot, and then unlock the tables. The lock is necessary to ensure all of your ongoing transactions are finished. The process is shown here along with the shell-level commands that perform the operations:

1. Issue a FLUSH TABLES WITH READ LOCK command in a MySQL client.

2. Create a snapshot of your logical volume (the -s option specifies a snapshot):

```
sudo lvcreate -L20M -s -n backup /dev/mysql/datadir
```

3. Issue an UNLOCK TABLES command in a MySQL client (your server can now resume its operations).

4. Mount the snapshot:

```
sudo mkdir /mnts
sudo mount /dev/mysql/backup /mnts
```

5. Perform a backup of the snapshot:

```
tar -[FIXTHIS]f snapshot.tar.gz /mnts
```

Of course, the best use of the snapshot is to initiate a copy periodically so that you can do another backup. There are scripts available from volunteers on the Web to automate this process, but the tried-and-true mechanism is to remove the snapshot and re-create it using the following procedure:

1. Unmount the snapshot:

```
sudo umount /mnts
```

2. Remove the snapshot (logical volume):

```
sudo lvremove /dev/mysql/backup
```

You can then re-create the snapshot and perform your backup. If you create your own script, we recommend adding the snapshot removal after you have verified the backup archive was created. This will ensure your script performs proper cleanup.

If you need to restore the snapshot, simply restore the data. The real benefit of LVM is that all of the operations for creating the snapshot and the backup using the tar utility allow you to create a customized script that you can run periodically (such as a cron job), which can help you automate your backups.

LVM in ZFS

The procedure for performing a backup using Sun Microsystems' ZFS filesystem (available in Solaris 10) is very similar to the Linux LVM procedure. We describe the differences here for those of you using Solaris.

In ZFS, you store your logical volumes (which Sun calls filesystems for read/write and snapshots for read-only copies) in a pool (similar to the volume group). To make a copy or backup, simply create a snapshot of a filesystem.

Issue the following commands to create a ZFS filesystem that you can manage:

```
zpool create -f mypool c0d0s5
zfs create mypool/mydata
```

Use the following command to make a backup (take a snapshot of the new filesystem):

```
zfs snapshot mypool/mydata@backup_12_Dec_2013
```

Use the following commands to restore the filesystem to a specific backup:

```
cd /mypool/mydata
zfs rollback mypool/mydata@backup_12_Dec_2013
```

ZFS provides not only full volume (filesystem) backups, but also supports selective file restore.

XtraBackup

Percona, an independent open source provider and consulting firm specializing in all things MySQL (LAMP, actually), has created a storage engine called XtraDB, which is an open source storage engine based on the InnoDB storage engine. XtraDB has several improvements for better scaling on modern hardware and is backward compatible with InnoDB.

In an effort to create a hot backup solution for XtraDB, Percona has created XtraBackup. This tool is optimized for InnoDB and XtraDB, but can also back up and restore MyISAM tables. It provides many of the features expected of backup solutions, including compression and incremental backup.

You can download and build XtraBackup by getting the source code from Launchpad (*http://bit.ly/perconaxtra*), as well as the online manual (*http://bit.ly/percona-doc*). You can compile and execute XtraBackup on most platforms. It is compatible with MySQL versions 5.0, 5.1, and 5.5.

Comparison of Backup Methods

MySQL Enterprise Backup, MySQL Utilities, `mysqldump`, and third-party backup options differ along a number of important dimensions, and there is almost no end to the nuances of how each method works. We provide a comparison of backup methods here based on whether they allow for hot backups, their cost, the speed of the backup, the speed of the restore, the type of backup (logical or physical), platform restrictions (operating system), and supported storage engines. Table 15-3 lists each of the backup methods mentioned in this chapter along with a column for each comparison item.

Table 15-3. Comparison of backup methods

	MySQL Enterprise Backup	MySQL Utilities	mysqldump	Physical copy	LVM/ZFS snapshot	XtraBackup
Hot backup?	Yes (InnoDB only)	Yes (InnoDB only)	Yes (InnoDB only requires `--single-transaction`)	No	Yes (requires table flush with lock)	Yes (InnoDB and XtraDB only)
Cost	Fee	Fee	Free	Free	Free	Free

	MySQL Enterprise Backup	MySQL Utilities	mysqldump	Physical copy	LVM/ZFS snapshot	XtraBackup
Backup speed	Medium	Slow	Slow	Fast	Fast	Medium
Restore speed	Fast	Slow	Slow	Fast	Fast	Fast
Type	Physical	Logical	Logical	Physical	Physical	Physical
OS	All	All	All	All	LVM supported only	All
Engines	All	All	All	All	All	InnoDB, XtraDB, MyISAM

Table 15-3 can help you plan your data recovery procedures by allowing you to find the best tool for the job given your needs. For example, if you need a hot backup for your InnoDB database and cost is not a factor, the MySQL Enterprise Backup application is the best choice. On the other hand, if speed is a factor, you need something that can back up all databases (all storage engines), and if you work on a Linux system, LVM is a good choice.

Backup and MySQL Replication

There are two ways to use backup with MySQL replication. In previous chapters, you learned about MySQL replication and its many uses for scale-out and high availability. In this chapter, we examine two more common uses for MySQL replication involving backup. These include using replication to create a backup copy of the data and using backups taken previously for PITR:

Backup and recovery
> Keeping an extra server around for creating backups is very common; it allows you to create your backups without disturbing the main server at all, because you can take the backup server offline and do whatever you like with it.

PITR
> Even if you create your backups regularly, you may have to restore the server to an exact point in time. By administering your backups properly, you can actually restore the server to the granularity of a specific second. This can be very useful in recovering from human error—such as mistyping commands or entering incorrect data—or reverting changes that are not needed anymore. The possibilities are endless, but they require the existence of proper backups.

Backup and Recovery with Replication

One shortcoming of backups in general is that they are created at a specific time (usually late at night to avoid disturbing other operations). If there is a problem that requires you to restore the master to some point after you created the backup, you will be out of luck, right? Nope! As it turns out, this is indeed not only possible, but quite easy if you combine the backups with the binary logs.

The binary log records all changes that are made to the database while the database is running, so by restoring the correct backup and playing back the binary log up to the appropriate second, you can actually restore a server to a precise moment in time.

The most important step in a recovery procedure is, of course, recovery. So let's focus on performing recovery before outlining the procedure for performing a backup.

PITR

The most frequent use for backup in replication is PITR, the ability to recover from an error (such as data loss or hardware failure) by restoring the system to a state as close as possible to the most recent correct state, thus minimizing the loss of data. For this to work, you must have performed at least one backup.

Once you repair the server, you can restore the latest backup image and apply the binary log using that binary log name and position as the starting point.

The following describes one procedure you can use to perform PITR using the backup system:

1. Return your server to an operational state after the event.
2. Find the latest backup for the databases you need to restore.
3. Restore the latest backup image.
4. Apply the binary log using the `mysqlbinlog` utility using the starting position (or starting date/time) from the last backup.

At this point, you may be wondering, "Which binary log do I use for PITR after a backup?" The answer depends on how you performed the backup. If you flushed the binary log prior to running the backup, you need to use the name and position of the current log (the newly opened logfile). If you did not flush the binary log prior to running the backup, use the name and position of the previous log.

 For easier PITR, always flush the logs prior to a backup. The starting point is then at the start of the file.

Restoring after an error is replicated

Now let's see how a backup can help you recover unintentional changes in a replication topology. Suppose one of your users has made a catastrophic (yet valid) change that is replicated to all of your slaves. Replication cannot help you here, but the backup system can come to the rescue.

Perform the following steps to recover from unintentional changes to data in a replication topology:

1. Drop the databases on the master.
2. Stop replication.
3. Restore the latest backup image before the event on the master.
4. Record the master's current binlog position.
5. Restore the latest backup image before the event on the slaves.
6. Perform a PITR on the master, as described in the previous section.
7. Restart replication from the recorded position and allow the slaves to sync.

In short, a good backup strategy is not only a necessary protection against data loss, but an important tool in your replication toolbox.

Recovery example

Now, let's look at a concrete example. Assume you're creating backups regularly every morning at 2:00 A.M. and save the backup images away somewhere for later usage. For this example, let's assume all binary logs are available and that none are removed. In reality, you will prune the binlog files regularly to keep the disk space down, but let's consider how to handle that later.

You have been tasked with recovering the database to its state at 2013-12-19 12:54:23, because that's when the manager's favorite pictures were accidentally deleted by his overzealous assistant, who took his "Could you please clean my desk?" request to include the computer desktop as well. Here are the steps you need to follow to recover the picture:

1. Locate the backup image that was taken before 2013-12-19 12:54:23.

   It does not actually make any difference which one you pick, but to save on the recovery time, you should probably pick the one closest, which would then be the backup image dated in the morning of the same day.

2. Restore the backup image on the machine to create an exact copy of the database at 2013-12-19 02:00:00.

3. Locate all the binlog files that include the entire range from 2013-12-19 02:00:00 to 2013-12-19 12:54:23. It does not matter if there are events from before the start time or after the end time, but it is critical that the binlog files cover the entire range you want.

4. Play the binlog files back using the mysqlbinlog utility and give a start time of 2013-12-19 02:00:00 and an end time of 2013-12-19 12:54:23.

You can now tell your manager that his favorite pictures are back.

To automate this, it is necessary to do some bookkeeping. This will give you an indication of what you need to save when doing the backup, so let's go through the information that you will require when doing a recovery.

- To use the backup images correctly, it is critical to label each with the start and end time it represents. This will help you determine which image to pick.

- You also need the binlog position of the backup. This is necessary because the time is not sufficiently precise in deciding where to start playing back the binlog files.

- You also need to keep information about what range each binlog file represents. Strictly speaking, this is not required, but it can be quite helpful because it helps you avoid processing all binlog files of a recovery image. This is not something that the MySQL server does automatically, so you have to handle it yourself.

- You cannot keep these files around forever, so it is important to sort all the information, backup images, and binlog files in such a way that you can easily archive them when you need to free up some disk space.

Recovery images

To help you administer all the information about your backups in manageable chunks, we introduce the concept of a *recovery image*. The recovery image is just a virtual container and is not a physical entity: it contains only information about where all the necessary pieces are to be able to perform recovery.

Figure 15-2 shows a sequence of recovery images and the contents of each. The final recovery image in the sequence is special and is called the *open recovery image*. This is the recovery image that you are still adding changes to, hence it does not have an end time yet. The other recovery images are called *closed recovery images* and these have an end time.

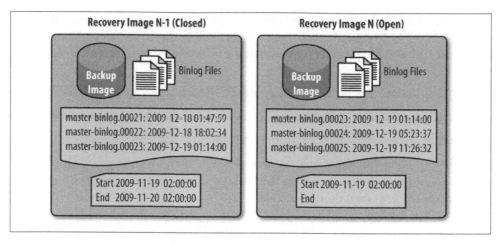

Figure 15-2. *A sequence of recovery images and contents*

Each recovery image has some pieces of information that are necessary to perform a recovery:

A backup image
> The backup image is required for restoring the database.

A set of binlog files
> Binlog files must cover the entire range for the recovery image.

Start time and an optional end time
> These are the start and end time that the recovery image represents. If this is the open recovery image, it does not have an end time. This recovery image is not practical to archive, so for our purposes, the end time of this recovery image is the current time.

 The binlog files usually contain events outside the range of start and end times, but all events in that range should be in the recovery image.

A list of the name and start time for each binlog file
> To extract the correct binlog files from, say, an archive, you need the names and the start and end times for each file. You can extract the start time for the binlog file using `mysqlbinlog`.

Backup procedure

The backup procedure gathers all the information required and structures it so that we can use it for both archiving and recovery (for this procedure, assume that we are going to create recovery image n and that we have a sequence of recovery images, $Image_1$ to $Image_{n-1}$):

1. Create a backup using your favorite method and note the name of the backup image and the binlog position it represents. The binlog position also contains the binlog filename.

   If you used an offline backup tool, the backup time is the time when you locked the tables, and the binlog position is the position given by SHOW MASTER STATUS after you locked the database.

2. Create a new open recovery $Image_n$ with the following parameters:

   - $Backup(Image_n)$ is now the backup image from step 1.
   - $Position(Image_n)$ is the position from step 1.
   - $BinlogFiles(Image_n)$ is unknown, but it starts with the filename from the position from step 1.
   - $StartTime(Image_n)$ is the start time of the image, which is taken from the event at the binlog position from step 1.

3. Close $Image_{n-1}$, noting the following:

   - $BinlogFiles(Image_{n-1})$ is now the binlog files from $Position(Image_{n-1})$ to $Position(Image_n)$.
   - $EndTime(Image_{n-1})$ is now the same as $StartTime(Image_n)$.

PITR in Python

To manage the various sorts of backup methods in a consistent manner, we've created the class `PhysicalBackup` in Example 15-1. The class holds three methods:

`class PhysicalBackup.PhysicalBackup(image_name)`
> The constructor for the class takes the name of an image that it will use when backing up or restoring a server.

`PhysicalBackup.backup_from(server)`
> This method will create a backup of the server and store it under the image name given to the constructor.

`PhysicalBackup.restore_on(server)`
> This method will use the backup image for the backup and restore it on server.

By using a class to represent a backup method in this manner, it is easy to replace the backup method with any other method as long as it has these methods.

Example 15-1. Class for representing the physical backup method

```python
class BackupImage(object):
    "Class for representing a backup image"

    def __init__(self, backup_url):
        self.url = urlparse.urlparse(backup_url)

    def backup_server(self, server, db):
        "Backup databases from a server and add them to the backup image."
        pass

    def restore_server(self, server):
        "Restore the databases in an image on the server"
        pass

class PhysicalBackup(BackupImage):
    "A physical backup of a database"

    def backup_server(self, server, db="*"):
        datadir = server.fetch_config().get('datadir')
        if db == "*":
            db = [d for d in os.listdir(datadir)
                    if os.path.isdir(os.path.join(datadir, d))]
        server.sql("FLUSH TABLES WITH READ LOCK")
        position = replicant.fetch_master_pos(server)
        if server.host != "localhost":
            path = basename(self.url.path)
        else:
            path = self.url.path
        server.ssh(["tar", "zpscf", path, "-C", datadir] + db)
        if server.host != "localhost":
            subprocess.call(["scp", server.host + ":" + path, self.url.path])
        server.sql("UNLOCK TABLES")
        return position

    def restore_server(self, server):
        if server.host == "localhost":
            path = self.url.path
        else:
            path = basename(self.url.path)

        datadir = server.fetch_config().get('datadir')

        try:
            server.stop()
            if server.host != "localhost":
                call(["scp", self.url.path, server.host + ":" + path])
            server.ssh(["tar", "zxf", path, "-C", datadir])
```

```
    finally:
        server.start()
```

The next step is to introduce a representation of the recovery image, as shown in Example 15-2. The recovery image stores the pieces of information as five fields:

`RecoveryImage.backup_image`
> The backup image to use.

`RecoveryImage.start_time`
> The start time of the recovery image.

`RecoveryImage.start_position`
> The binlog position that the backup image represents. Use this instead of the start time as the starting point for playing back the binlog files, because it will be accurate. There can be a lot of transactions executed during a second, and using the start time will fail because it will pick the first event with the start time, while the real start position may be somewhere else.

`RecoveryImage.binlog_files`
> A list of the binlog files that are part of this recovery image.

`RecoveryImage.binlog_datetime`
> A dictionary mapping binlog filenames to date/times, which are the date/time of the first event of the binlog file.

In addition, the recovery image must have the following utility methods:

`RecoveryImage.contains(datetime)`
> Decides whether `datetime` is contained in the recovery image. Because the binlog file may have been rotated mid-second, the `end_time` is inclusive.

`RecoveryImage.backup_from(server)`
> Creates a new open recovery image by creating a backup of `server` and collects information about the backup.

`RecoveryImage.restore_to(server, datetime)`
> Restores the recovery image on the server so that all changes up to and including `datetime` are applied. This assumes `datetime` is in the range for the recovery image. If `datetime` is before the recovery image's start time, nothing will be applied, and if it is after the recovery image's end time, all will be applied.

Example 15-2. A representation of a recovery image

```
class RecoveryImage(object):
    def __init__(self, backup_method):
        self.backup_method = backup_method
        self.backup_position = None
        self.start_time = None
        self.end_time = None
```

```
        self.binlog_files = []
        self.binlog_datetime = {}

    def backup_from(self, server, datetime):
        self.backup_position = backup_method.backup_from(server)

    def restore_to(self, server):
        backup_method.restore_on(server)

    def contains(self, datetime):
        if self.end_time:
            return self.start_time <= datetime < self.end_time
        else:
            return self.start_time <= datetime
```

Because managing the recovery images requires manipulating several images, we introduce the RecoveryImageManager class in Example 15-3. The class contains two methods in addition to the constructor:

RecoveryImageManager.point_in_time_recovery(server, datetime)
    A method to perform PITR of server to datetime

RecoveryImageManager.point_in_time_backup(server)
    A method to perform a backup of the server for PITR

The recovery image manager keeps track of all recovery images and the backup method used. Here we assume that the same backup method is used for all the recovery images, but that is not strictly required.

Example 15-3. RecoveryImageManager class

```
class RecoveryImageManager(object):
    def __init__(self, backup_method):
        self.__images = []
        self.__backup_method = backup_method

    def point_in_time_recovery(server, datetime):
        from itertools import takewhile
        from subprocess import Popen, PIPE

        for im in images:
            if im.contains(datetime):
                image = im
                break
        image.restore_on(server)

        def before(file):
            return image.binlog_datetime(file) < datetime

        files = takewhile(before, image.binlog_files)
        command = ["mysqlbinlog",
                   "--start-position=%s" % (image.backup_position.pos),
```

```
                          "--stop-datetime=%s" % (datetime)]
        mysqlbinlog_proc = Popen(mysqlbinlog_command + files, stdout=PIPE)

        mysql_command = ["mysql",
                         "--host=%s" % (server.host),
                         "--user=%s" % (server.sql_user.name),
                         "--password=%s" % (server.sql_user.password)]
        mysql_proc = Popen(mysql_command, stdin=mysqlbinlog_proc.stdout)
        output = mysql_proc.communicate()[0]

    def point_in_time_backup(self, server):
        new_image = RecoveryImage(self.__backup_method)
        new_image.backup_position = image.backup_from(server)
        new_image.start_time = event_datetime(new_image.backup_position)

        prev_image = self.__images[-1].binlog_files
        prev_image.binlog_files = binlog_range(prev_image.backup_position.file,
                                               new_image.backup_position.file)
        prev_image.end_time = new_image.start_time

        self.__images.append(new_image)
```

Automating Backups

It is fairly easy to automate backups. In the previous section, we demonstrated how to do a backup and recovery with replication. In this section, we generalize the procedure to make it easier to do nonreplication-related backup and restore.

The only issue you may encounter is providing a mechanism to automatically name the backup image file. There are many ways to do this, and Example 15-4 shows a method that names the file using the backup time. You can add this backup method to the Python library to complement your replication methods. This is the same library shown in previous chapters. Substitute the executable command for your backup solution for [*BACKUP COMMAND*].

Example 15-4. Backup script

```
#!/usr/bin/python

import MySQLdb, optparse

# --
# Parse arguments and read Configuration
# --
parser = optparse.OptionParser()
parser.add_option("-u", "--user", dest="user",
                  help="User to connect to server with")
parser.add_option("-p", "--password", dest="password",
                  help="Password to use when connecting to server")
parser.add_option("-d", "--database", dest="database",
```

```
                        help="Database to connect to")
(opts, args) = parser.parse_args()

if not opts.password or not opts.user or not opts.database:
   parser.error("You have to supply user, password, and database")

try:
   print "Connecting to server..."
   #
   # Connect to server
   #
   dbh = MySQLdb.connect(host="localhost", port=3306,
                         unix_socket="/tmp/mysql.sock",
                         user=opts.user, passwd=opts.password,
                         db=opts.database)

   #
   # Perform the restore
   #
   from datetime import datetime

   filename = datetime.time().strftime("backup_%Y-%m-%d_%H-%M-%S.bak")
   dbh.cursor().execute("[BACKUP COMMAND]%s'" % filename)
   print "\nBACKUP complete."

except MySQLdb.Error, (n, e):
   print 'CRITICAL: Connect failed with reason:', e
```

Automating restores is a bit easier if you consider that there is no need to create a backup image name. However, depending on your installation, usage, and configuration, you may need to add commands to ensure there is no destructive interaction with activities by other applications or users. Example 15-5 shows a typical restore method that you can add to the Python library to complement your replication methods. Substitute the executable command for your backup solution for [RESTORE COMMAND].

Example 15-5. Restore script

```
#!/usr/bin/python

import MySQLdb, optparse

# --
# Parse arguments and read Configuration
# --
parser = optparse.OptionParser()
parser.add_option("-u", "--user", dest="user",
                  help="User to connect to server with")
parser.add_option("-p", "--password", dest="password",
                  help="Password to use when connecting to server")
parser.add_option("-d", "--database", dest="database",
                  help="Database to connect to")
(opts, args) = parser.parse_args()
```

```
if not opts.password or not opts.user or not opts.database:
    parser.error("You have to supply user, password, and database")

try:
    print "Connecting to server..."
    #
    # Connect to server
    #
    dbh = MySQLdb.connect(host="localhost", port=3306,
                          unix_socket="/tmp/mysql.sock",
                          user=opts.user, passwd=opts.password,
                          db=opts.database)

    #
    # Perform the restore
    #
    from datetime import datetime

    filename = datetime.time().strftime("backup_%Y-%m-%d_%H-%M-%S.bak")
    dbh.cursor().execute("[RESTORE COMMAND]%S'",
                         (database, filename))
    print "\nRestore complete."
except MySQLdb.Error, (n, e):
    print 'CRITICAL: Connect failed with reason:', e
```

As you can see in Example 15-5, you can automate a restore. However, most people prefer to execute the restore manually. One scenario in which an automated restore might be helpful is in a testing environment where you want to start with a baseline and restore a database to a known state. Another use is in a development system where you want to preserve a certain environment for each project.

Conclusion

In this chapter, we studied IA and drilled down to the aspects that most affect you as an IT professional. We saw the importance of disaster recovery planning and how to make your own disaster recovery plan, and we saw how the database system is an integral part of disaster recovery. Finally, we examined several ways you can protect your MySQL data by making regular backups.

In the next few chapters, we will examine more advanced MySQL topics, including MySQL Enterprise and MySQL Cluster.

Joel glanced at his terminal window and issued another command to check on his database backups. He had set up a recurring backup script to back up all of his databases and felt confident this simple operation was working. He lamented that it was only a small start toward getting his disaster recovery plan written. He looked forward to experimenting with more scripts and scheduling his first disaster planning meeting. He already had several of his new colleagues in mind for the team. A sharp rap on his door startled him from his thoughts.

"Did you get that media order in yet, Joel? What about that plan thing?" Mr. Summerson asked.

Joel smiled and said, "Yes, and I've determined I can back up the entire database with just a…"

"Hey, that's great, Joel. I don't need the details; just keep us off of the auditor's radar. OK?"

Joel smiled and nodded as his boss disappeared on his way to execute a drive-by tasking on another employee. He wondered if his boss really understood the amount of work it would take to reach that goal. He opened his email application and started composing a message to request more personnel and resources.

MySQL Enterprise Monitor

Joel clicked open another terminal window and read the output. He rubbed his eyes until his vision cleared. The numbers were beginning to run together as he tried to keep tabs on all of his servers spread out over three sites. His report was overdue.

He had tried using a spreadsheet to tabulate the data, which had worked when he had only a few servers, but it was getting tedious now that he had more than 30 to monitor. His friends had tried to convince him to buy an enterprise monitoring suite, but his boss had a reputation of vetoing any purchases that didn't immediately contribute to the company's ability to produce revenue.

"Hey, Joel."

Joel looked up to see his friend Doug from customer support standing at his door with a stained coffee cup in hand. "Hey," Joel replied.

"You look like you could use a break."

"No time. I've got to get a report together that shows the status of all of the servers and I can't write it until I finish checking each server."

"Wow, that's a real hands-on approach."

"I know. I've read about these enterprise suites that make this all easier to do, but I don't know which one to buy or even if Mr. Summerson will sign off on it."

"Well, if you could show him how much time it takes you to do all this…" Doug said, with a dangerous wave of his mug.

Joel thought for a moment. "If only I could show him the difference between what I've had to slog through and what it would be like to use a good tool…"

"Good plan. Now how about a cup? My treat."

> Joel followed Doug to the break room and chatted with him about a recent Dave Matthews Band concert they'd attended.
>
> When Joel returned to his office, he started reading about the MySQL Enterprise Edition offering from Oracle.

Monitoring a group of servers can be a lot of work. The tools needed to properly monitor a server are numerous and while most are easy to use once you understand what they do, they still require a bit of work to get going. Scripting and even some creative web hosting can help manage the execution of the various tools and the collection of the data, but as the number of servers to monitor grows, the task of collecting and analyzing all of the data can become time consuming.

The monitoring techniques discussed so far in this book can become unmanageable for installations with more than a few servers. Indeed, manual monitoring and reporting can turn into a full-time job for one or more technicians in an organization with dozens of servers.

We focus on monitoring in this chapter, but the same can be said about administration. Specifically, administrators often see time savings when they use administration tools that permit automation of common tasks, such as running scripts to populate tables or performing table maintenance.

Fortunately, this problem isn't new, nor is it insurmountable. Indeed, there are several enterprise monitoring suites that can make life in a sea of servers much easier.

One of the most underestimated tools available for monitoring MySQL is the MySQL Enterprise Monitor (MEM), which comes with the MySQL Enterprise Edition license. The MEM tools can greatly enhance monitoring and preventive maintenance and can dramatically reduce diagnostic time and downtime. While it is a fee-based tool, the savings of having a well-maintained data center will more than cover the cost.

This chapter introduces the MySQL Enterprise Monitor version 3.0 and shows you how they will save you time while keeping your MySQL servers running at the highest levels of performance and availability. We also include an example of the monitoring tools running on a complex replication topology.

Getting Started with MySQL Enterprise Monitor

MEM is one component of the MySQL Enterprise Edition. When you purchase a commercial license for MySQL Enterprise Edition, you get all of the enterprise tools as well.

The MySQL Enterprise Edition was launched in 2006 and comprises the Enterprise MySQL server release, a set of monitoring tools, auditing, backup, and product support services. MySQL Enterprise Edition is intended for customers who use MySQL for data management. Early on, MySQL recognized the need organizations have for stability and reliability. MySQL Enterprise Edition was the answer to this need.

 If you are not ready to purchase a MySQL Enterprise Edition or you want to try it out for a while before deciding, you can get a trial license and download a copy of the software under a trial license on the Oracle Software Delivery Cloud (*https://edelivery.oracle.com*). If you are an Oracle customer, you can also find MySQL products for download on the Oracle support site.

The following sections describe the available options for purchasing commercial versions of MySQL. We also include an overview of the installation process. Later sections describe the features and benefits in more detail.

Commercial Offerings

MySQL is available for purchase in one of four editions. At the top of the heap is the full featured MySQL Enterprise Edition which includes a host of tools and products designed to help organizations manage large installations of MySQL. You can also purchase commercial licenses of the MySQL server, called the MySQL Standard Edition which provides the MySQL server as well as professional support. For specialized needs, Oracle offers two solutions. The MySQL Cluster Carrier Grade Edition for organizations that require large, redundant, high speed in memory database solutions. The MySQL Classic Edition is configured and licensed for use by ISVs/OEMs.

With so many options to choose from, you can add more support as your business grows. For more information about purchasing licenses for your MySQL servers or if you want to obtain professional support as well as advanced tools such as MEM, contact the Oracle MySQL Sales Team. Visit the MySQL Products and Services site (*http://www.mysql.com/buy-mysql*) for more information about contacting the sales team either by phone or electronically.

Anatomy of MySQL Enterprise Monitor

MySQL Enterprise Monitor includes a web-based MEM application hosted by its own web server (Tomcat), along with a separate MySQL server instance to be a repository for the metrics collected by other applications installed on your MySQL servers, called *agents*. MEM combines the metrics into reports that you can enhance with heuristics called *advisors* that help you enforce best practices based on MySQL research and expertise. The reports are displayed on a web page called a *dashboard*. We'll discuss later in this chapter how to install and use these components.

Thus, MEM is made up of two components. The web server and MySQL server instance is called the MEM Service Manager (sometimes referred to as the MySQL Enterprise

Monitor or simply monitor). The component you install on the MySQL server to monitor the MySQL instances and collect data is called the MEM Agent (or simply MySQL Agent). Although not part of MEM specifically (but is a prerequisite) is one or more MySQL server instances. A pictorial representation of these components and the flow of information is shown in Figure 16-1. We discuss each of these components in more detail in a later section.

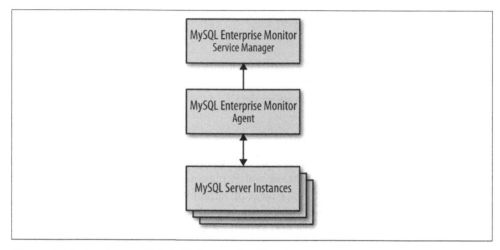

Figure 16-1. Anatomy of MySQL Enterprise Monitor

Now that we understand the components of MEM, let's see how we can install the components and get MEM running.

Installation Overview

While complete, detailed installation instructions are beyond the scope of this book, we briefly describe the steps necessary to install and configure the MySQL Enterprise Monitor. Fortunately, the install process is streamlined and very easy.

For example, if you're doing a new installation, the basic steps include the following:

1. Download, install and launch the Service Manager. To install the MySQL Enterprise Monitor Service Manager component, including the metrics repository (a separate installation of MySQL), which is operating system–specific. For example, you would install the file named *mysqlmonitor-3.0.0.2887-osx-installer.app* on a Mac OS X system.

2. Open the service manager using your browser (starts automatically for a new install) and configure your system using the first-time setup screen. You can also access the dashboard at *http://localhost:18443*.

3. Install the monitoring agent on your MySQL servers. This is also operating system–specific. For example, on Linux systems you would install an agent such as *mysqlmonitoragent-3.0.0.2887-linux-glibc2.3-x86-64bit-installer.bin*.

4. Configure the dashboard to reflect your environment. You can group servers and give each server a more descriptive name.

 You can find additional information about installing MEM in the online MEM reference manual (*http://bit.ly/ent-prods*).

Installing the MEM Service Manager

The installation of the MEM Service Manager component includes a self-contained web server and MySQL instance that you install on the system where you want to host the Dashboard and metrics collection. This system is the destination for the data from each of the monitoring agents. This process is very easy to perform and does not require any web administration expertise.

During the installation of the service manager component, you will have to make decisions about the names of certain accounts and the location (e.g., IP address) of your server. You will need this information when installing the monitoring agents. The Getting Started chapter in the online MEM reference manual discusses all of these items. It may be helpful to print out the guide and use it to write down the information you supply during the installation for later reference.

Installing the MEM Agent

Installation of the monitoring agents is also very easy. Once your monitoring server is up and running, you can install one agent on each of your servers where your MySQL server instances reside. Some systems may require manually starting the agent, which is explained in detail in the guide.

While it is possible to install the monitor agent on any server and monitor MySQL instances running on other servers, it is best to install the agent on the server with the MySQL instances you wish to monitor. This permits the agent to send operating system statistics, performance data, and configuration parameters to the Dashboard. If you install the agent on another system, the system section of the Dashboard report for the MySQL server will be blank.

You can use your existing MySQL server installations, but for the best return on your investment, you should be using the versions provided by your MySQL Enterprise Edition license purchase. Once your database servers are configured and running properly, you can begin the installation of the Enterprise Monitor and monitoring agents.

You should begin by installing the MEM service on a machine on your network that has connectivity to all of the servers you want to monitor (we recommend always using MEM to monitor your MySQL servers). During the installation process, be sure to write down the hostname or IP address of this server and the username and password you specified for the agent access. The installation process is very easy and is well documented on the MySQL Enterprise Edition documentation site (*http://bit.ly/ent-prods*).

 Several user accounts are involved in the installation of MEM: a MEM administrator account, an agent access account to your MEM server, and two agent access accounts for the monitoring agent running on each MySQL server. Getting these confused can lead to a failed installation.

Once the MEM service is up and running on your monitoring server, you can begin installing the monitoring agent on each of your MySQL servers. When you install the monitoring agent, you will need to provide a user account and password for a connection from the monitoring agent to your MySQL server. It is best to use the same username and password for all of your servers. Like the MEM services installation, installing the monitoring agent is very easy. Just be sure to record all of the user accounts and passwords used. Once again, you should use the same accounts and passwords for all of your monitoring agents. Once installation is complete, the server should show up in the MEM within a few moments depending on your refresh settings.

Repeat the installation on each of your servers and observe the results in the Dashboard. Figure 16-2 shows the Dashboard for the example information infrastructure with all monitoring agents reporting. You will see several graphs and sections in the interface. These include database availability, connection status to each server, aggregate database activity, query response times, and a list of critical issues identified among the servers.

Fixing monitoring agent problems

Although the installation process for the monitoring agent is very streamlined, there are times when things can go wrong. If you are careful to supply the correct information, everything should work correctly.

The following are some basic procedures for diagnosing and correcting problems in getting the monitoring agent to report to the MEM:

- Check the *mysql-monitor-agent.log* file if your monitoring agent starts but the server is not shown on the Dashboard, or if the agent or service status indicates an error (a red dot) in the heat chart. This file contains a wealth of information that can help you solve most problems. You can find the logfiles in the following locations:

Mac OS X
   /Applications/mysql/enterprise/agent/

Linux/Unix
   /opt/mysql/enterprise/agent

Windows
   C:\Program Files\MySQL\Enterprise\Agent

- Check the user account and permissions specified for the monitoring agent on the MySQL server.
- Verify the port and hostname of your local MySQL server. Be sure the information matches what is in the *\etc\bootstrap.profile* file.

If you feel you have used the wrong usernames and passwords, you can use the *\bin \agent.sh* script to change any of the parameters for the agent. The following shows the commands available (see the online MEM reference manual for more details):

```
$ ./agent.sh --help
Usage: java com.mysql.etools.agent.runtime.Main [options], where options are:

Option                          Description
------                          -----------
-D, --agent-instance-dir        Path to the directory that contains
                                per agent instance configuration and
                                runtime data. Only used for multiple
                                agent instances running from the
                                same base directory.
-G, --agent-group               MEM Group to use for all MySQL
                                connections from this agent
-I, --uuid                      MEM Agent UUID
-M, --migrate-agent             Migrate agent connections
-P, --port                      Port for the MySQL instance (Actions:
                                Create, Modify)
-S, --socket                    Socket for the MySQL instance
                                (Actions: Create, Modify)
-T, --test-credentials          Test MySQL connection credentials
-U, --url                       MEM Service Manager URL
-c, --create-connection         Create or Modify a MySQL connection
-d, --delete-connection         Close and Delete a MySQL connection
                                (must also specify --connection-id)
-f, --force-plain-stdin         Force the use of plain standard input
                                (clear password input)
-g, --connection-group          MEM Group to use for created/modified
                                connection (Actions: Create, Modify)
-h, --host                      Host for the MySQL instance (Actions:
                                Create, Modify)
--help                          Prints this usage message
-i, --connection-id             Connection ID (Actions: Modify, Delete)
-j, --admin-user                Admin level username (Actions: Create,
                                Modify)
```

```
-k, --general-user                 General level username (Actions:
                                   Create, Modify)
-l, --limited-user                 Limited level username (Actions:
                                   Create, Modify)
-m, --auto-manage-extra-users      Auto-create general / limited users
                                   (Actions: Create, Modify)
-s, --show                         Show information about all MySQL
                                   connections on this agent
-t, --run-collection-tests         Discover, and attempt to collect OS
                                   related assets and dump them to
                                   STDOUT (for debugging)
-u, --agent-user                   MEM Service Manager agent username
-v, --version                      Displays the version of the agent and
                                   components
```

Configuring the dashboard

After at least one agent is installed and started, you can return to the Dashboard and start configuring it to fit your needs. For example, you can create groups to organize your servers into logical units. For instance, you may want to define some servers as production servers and others as development servers.

You can rename the servers using the Manage Servers option on the Settings page. This allows you to use more meaningful names on the Dashboard while leaving the actual hostnames of the servers unaltered. You can also create groups to combine related servers. This can be very handy, because the group is displayed on the various controls, allowing you to collapse the group and alter the display as needed.

MySQL Enterprise Monitor Components

The MEM forms the core of the continuous server monitoring and alerts. The MySQL website states it best: "It's like having a 'Virtual DBA Assistant' at your side to recommend best practices to eliminate security vulnerabilities, improve replication, optimize performance and more." Despite the marketing angle, the MEM gives you professional-level tools to meet the growing needs of your business's data center.

The MEM includes the following key features:

- A single web-based display to monitor the health of all of your servers
- Over 600 metrics, including the MySQL server and its host operating system
- The ability to monitor performance, replication, schema, and security
- The ability to monitor operating system statistics of the servers where the agent is installed
- Immediate health status via an easy-to-read heat chart
- Notification of metric threshold violations

- Implementation of the best practices ruleset from the creators of MySQL

- Compliance with all of the latest features of the MySQL including UUIDs, GTIDs, and more

- Automatic adaptive measures to detect changes to servers such as replication roles, detecting new server instances, and more.

- Detection and ranking of the most critical issues on each server

- Trends, projections, and forecasting features added to all graphs and events to help identify potential problems

- The 3.0 version introduces many changes to the user interfaces for the Dashboard making it even easier to monitor your servers

Recall that MEM is composed of a distributed web-based application that you run on your internal network. A monitoring agent is installed on each MySQL server that sends metrics to the web server component, called the Dashboard. It is here that you can see all of the statistics and graphs that depict the status of your servers. There are also advisors that implement the best practices for ensuring your installations are properly configured and running at peak efficiency.

Dashboard

The face of the MySQL Enterprise Monitoring tools is the Dashboard, the web application running on your monitoring server. The Dashboard provides a single location where you can monitor all of your servers, either individually or in groups. You can see the availability, security, and performance data for all of your servers in one place. You can check the relative health of each, examine graphs of performance and memory use, and see vital operating system statistics for each server.

The Dashboard presents monitoring and alert information to you in an easy-to-read format. An example of a simple installation is shown in Figure 16-2. As you can see, the Dashboard provides all of the critical information on a single screen. There are tabs for various dashboard views (overview graphs, MySQL instances, and replication), events, the Query Analyzer, reports and graphs, and configuration settings. The "What's New?" tab contains links to news and events concerning the tools and your Enterprise licenses and products.

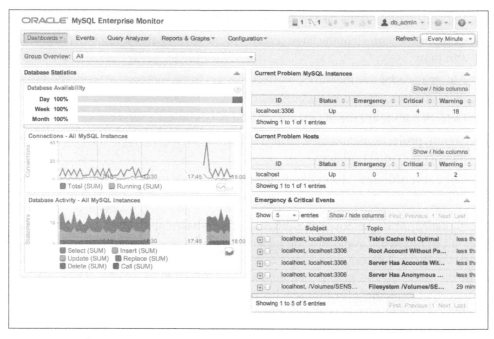

Figure 16-2. The MySQL Enterprise Monitor Dashboard

Notice the "Emergency & Critical Events" secton in the lower right of the page. This area shows you all of the critical issues detected for each server. In this case, we have purposely included servers with some issues to demonstrate the power of the automatic critical issue detection. However, it should be noted that these servers are development servers and not used for production. Had it been a production server, the issues identified would be most serious. Nevertheless, MEM treats all servers with the highest level of expectations and scrutiny. Here we see that MEM has detected several critical problems that need to be addressed.

Among these issues are a suboptimal setting for the table cache, several issues with user accounts, and a prediction about disk space. Let's look at one of the account issues. If you click on the alter, you will see a detailed explanation of the problem along with how to correct the problem, as shown in Figure 16-3.

Topic: Root Account Without Password

Categories: Security   Advisor: Root Account Without Password

Current State: Open   Current Status: Critical   Worst Status: Critical

Auto-Closes by Default: Yes Last Checked: Sep 7, 2013 6:36:15 PM   Worst Alarm Time: Sep 7, 2013 4:36:16

Notes:

No notes provided.

Details:

Problem Description

The root user account has unlimited privileges and is intended for administrative tasks. Privileged accounts should have strong passwords to prevent unauthorized users from accessing and changing the system.

Advice

Assign a strong password to the root user account. A strong password should be at least 8 characters long, contain lowercase and uppercase characters, numbers and symbols, and not contain words found in a dictionary. You should be sure to run the below SET PASSWORD statement for each and every root account that exists (for instance 'root@'127.0.0.1', 'root'@'localhost', 'root'@'::1', etc.).

Recommended Action

SET PASSWORD FOR 'root'@'localhost' = PASSWORD('strong_password');

Links and Further Reading

MySQL Knowledge Base: Checking Password Complexity

Expression

(%no_password% > THRESHOLD)

Evaluated Expression

(3 > 0)

Figure 16-3. The MySQL Enterprise Monitor Dashboard

As you can see from the explanation, there exists at least one account named "root" without a password. A quick query on the server reveals this to be true and the recommended actions most prudent. Clearly, this is something that must be fixed to ensure stronger security.

```
mysql> SELECT user, host, password FROM mysql.user WHERE user = 'root';
+------+--------------------------+------------------------------------------+
| user | host                     | password                                 |
+------+--------------------------+------------------------------------------+
| root | localhost                | *[...]                                    |
| root | 127.0.0.1                |                                          |
| root | ::1                      |                                          |
| root | 192.168.1.15             | *[...]                                    |
| root | 192.168.1.102            | *[...]                                    |
| root | %                        | *[...]                                    |
+------+--------------------------+------------------------------------------+
6 rows in set (0.00 sec)
```

We have masked out the passwords in the previous ouput. An actual query would show the digest value for the password column.

As each critical issue is corrected and the interface refreshed, the issue is removed from the list. You can also clear the issues if you feel they are not applicable. For example, you may have a development or test server that is configured intentionally to have issues for use in testing. You can also add your own notes about the conditions for future reference. In this way, you can quickly see those servers in your network that needs attention.

Monitoring Agent

The monitoring agent is a special lightweight application that gathers information about a MySQL server, including statistics about the host operating system. The monitoring agent is therefore the key component in the monitoring tools. Designed to be installed on each server you want to monitor, the agent is not only lightweight, but almost transparent, with no noticeable performance degradation.

Advisors

The MEM tools include one feature that departs from typical enterprise monitoring solutions: a mechanism that monitors specific areas of system performance and configuration and sends alerts when a server diverges from the best practices defined by the designers of MySQL. This means you can get immediate feedback on anything that can cause your system to become suboptimal in configuration, security, or performance. This mechanism is called an *advisor*, and there are many of them monitoring and reporting on a wide variety of areas. The advisors supplied are extensive:

Administration
    Monitors general database administration and performance.

Agent
    Checks the status of the agents installed on your network.

Availability
    Monitor MySQL connections and process health.

Backup
    Checks status of backup jobs, resources, and tasks for MySQL Enterprise Backup.

Cluster
    Advisors for the MySQL Cluster product.

Graphing
> Identifies issues for the graphing elements.

Memory Usage
> Identifies changes in memory usage and sends alerts when suboptimal conditions arise.

Monitoring and Support Services
> Advisors for the MEM services themselves. Yes, it even advises you on how to make it better!

Operating System
> Identifies potential problems about the operating system of the hosts for the MySQL servers.

Performance
> Identifies differences in performance based on MySQL performance best practice rules.

Query Analysis
> Identifies issues related to the Query Analyzer.

Replication
> Identifies replication-specific conditions related to configuration, health, synchronization (delays), and performance issues.

Schema
> Identifies changes to database and schema objects. Can monitor changes and provide alerts when unwanted or unexpected changes occur.

Security
> Identifies potential security vulnerabilities and sends alerts.

Each advisor provides comprehensive coverage of a specific area of the server using a set of rules based on best practices. The advisors help you identify where your servers need attention and give you advice on how to improve or correct the situation. If the set of advisors isn't broad enough, you can create your own advisors to meet your needs.

Query Analyzer

Complex databases and the complex applications that they tend to support can result in the execution of complex queries. Given the expressiveness of SQL, queries are often not written to execute as efficiently as possible. Furthermore, poorly written queries can often be the source of poor performance on other levels. Savvy DBAs acknowledge this and often look to the queries first for database performance diagnostics.

You can normally find a poorly performing query by watching the slow query log or the process list (i.e., issuing a SHOW PROCESSLIST command). Once you have identified a query that needs your attention, you can use the EXPLAIN command to see how MySQL will execute the query. Although this process is well known and has been used by DBAs for some time, it is a labor-intensive task that does not easily lend itself to scripting. As the complexity of the database grows, so too does the labor involved in diagnosing poorly performing queries.

You can examine user queries with this method, but what do you do when investigating application performance where the SQL statements are included in the application code itself? This situation is among the hardest to diagnose and repair, as it requires changing the application. Assuming that is possible, how do you advise the developers to improve their queries?

Unfortunately, the SQL statements in the application code are rarely suspected of being the source of performance problems. DBAs and developers are all too quick to blame the server or system instead of application code or embedded SQL queries. Worse still, the MySQL system does not support robust performance metric collection and there is little support for finding troublesome queries.

As a partial solution to these difficulties, you may find it useful to pull up a list of all of the long-running queries on your server and examine the slowest ones. The Query Analyzer component of the Enterprise Monitor tools provides this help.

You can enable the Query Analyzer via the Dashboard. Installation and configuration require a little work, so be sure to consult the Getting Started guide for details.

The Query Analyzer provides an aggregate display showing performance statistics for queries in real time. It shows all of your queries from all of your servers in one place so you don't need to go from server to server looking for poorly performing queries. This same list maintains a history of the queries so you don't have to worry about the additional space for logs.

You can get two different views for each query: a canonical view (no numeric data) to see a pictorial version of the query, and a version that shows specific timing and access data for the query. Best of all, the advisor can even alert you when a given query was executed and on which server.

The Query Analyzer allows you to see which queries are performing poorly and to identify a solution by examining the suspected query's execution plan. Clearly, this feature alone can provide huge time savings, especially for situations in which you are developing or tuning an application for deployment or need to optimize your queries for improved performance.

MySQL Production Support

The MySQL Enterprise Edition license includes access to support professionals who can help you with development, deployment, and management of your MySQL servers. Support includes problem resolution, consulting, access to an online knowledge base of common solutions, and a technical account manager who will be your point of contact, helping you with all of your support needs.

 Depending on how you purchased the MySQL Enterprise Edition, consultation and extended assistance may incur additional costs.

Using MySQL Enterprise Monitor

Now that we have described the features of MEM and its components, let's take a look at an example of how the tools can truly benefit an organization. In this example, we use a hypothetical—albeit not uncommon—information infrastructure for a web-based company. This example is representative of the types of replication models seen in industry. It includes a complex multiple-tier replication setup that replicates some databases but not others.

This scenario, shown in Figure 16-4, consists of two data centers connected via replication for high availability and load balancing. These data centers host the company's databases. The production data center in San Francisco is used for hosting their day-to-day operations. Connected to this master server is a slave for the development departments located in Seattle and responsible for building and enhancing the product lines.

Each of the slaves beneath the data centers can (and typically do) host additional databases that are not replicated. For example, the production server typically hosts a human resources database that is not replicated to most of its slaves (e.g., it is not replicated to the development center). Similarly, the development server has various incarnations of the product line databases in various states of development.

A topology such as this can be visualized easily with the MySQL Enterprise Monitor Dashboard. Figure 16-5 shows how the example topology would look in the dashboard.

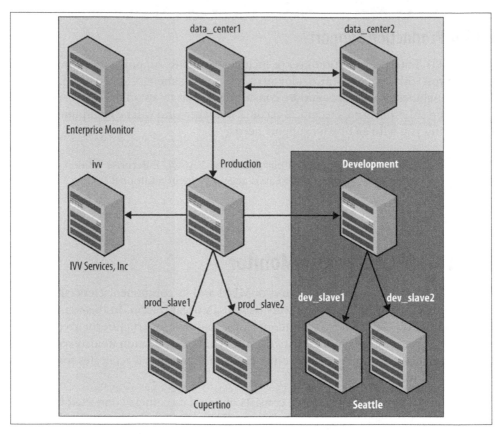

Figure 16-4. Sample information infrastructure

The topology of servers displayed in the following images is a basic replication setup with a single master and few slaves at each site. The master in the satellite office (Seattle) is connected as a slave to the master in the main office (San Francisco). The servers have not been configured in an optimal state to demonstrate the features and power of MEM to identify sub optimal configurations and critical issues.

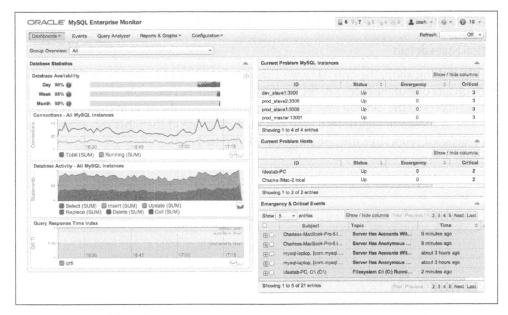

Figure 16-5. Dashboard

This is the default display mode for the dashboard. As we can see, each of the servers is reporting its availability, categorical database activity, query response times, and a long list of potential issues. There are additional views available in the dashboard that include a view of the servers participating in replication topologies and a detailed list of all MySQL servers monitored. We will see examples of these views in later sections.

As you can surmise, this page presents all of the pertinent information about your servers so that you can, at a glance, see the overall health of your information infra-structure, including all potential and critical issues identified by the monitoring agents. Clearly, monitoring can't get any easier than that!

Monitoring

There are several areas in which MEM makes monitoring much easier for the admin-istrators of a complex infrastructure. These areas include:

- Critical issues details
- Consolidated server graphs
- Server details
- Replication details
- Advisors

We will examine each of these in greater detail in the following sections.

Critical issues details

The best thing about the critical issues list, which may not be obvious, is that you can click on any one of the entries to get more information. For example, if you click on one of the servers in the *Current Problem Hosts*, you will see a list of all of the alerts for that system, as shown in Figure 16-6. You can then click one of the most recent alerts and get a detailed report like the one shown in Figure 16-7.

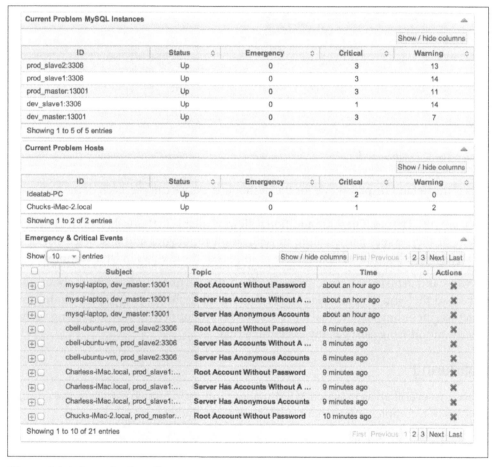

Figure 16-6. Sample alerts list

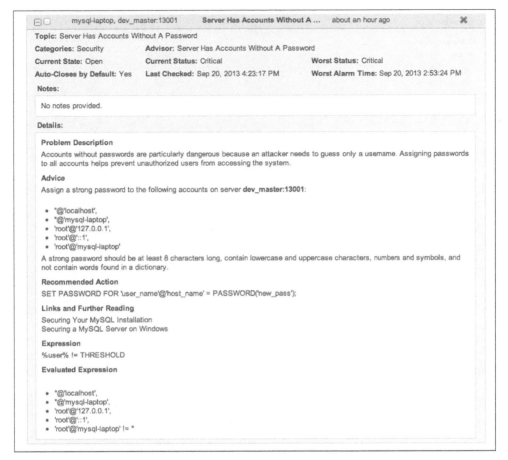

Figure 16-7. Sample alert report

This report indicates the server on which the alert occurred, the time it occurred, and advice following the established best practices including any pertinent links to documentation. The alert reports make the MEM stand alone among the monitoring options. This is what is meant by having a "virtual DBA assistant." The alerts will make your life much easier by trapping the problems from servers all over your organization and reporting them in a single place. This saves you the time and tedium of costly diagnostic efforts or active monitoring and gives you tips on how to solve problems quickly.

Consolidated server graphs

At the left of the Dashboard display is a consolidated set of graphs that show aggregate data from the servers being monitored (Figure 16-8), including database activity, connection status of all servers, and query response times.

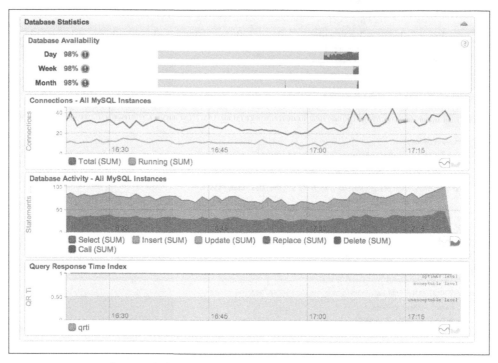

Figure 16-8. Sample consolidated server graphs

The database activity graph shows statistics concerning availability. Like all of the graphs, the data is aggregated from all servers monitored.

The connections graph shows the connection times for all of the servers monitored over time.

The database activity shows you a relative count of the most frequent queries based on category.

The query response time shows the average response time of queries executed.

 You can see many more reports including reports for specific metrics from the Reports and Graphs tab.

Server details

Another nice feature of the Dashboard is that it lets you click on a specific server in the list of servers to see more details about the system. The server details report shows the version of the MySQL server; when it was last started (uptime); where the data is located;

the host operating system; and CPU, memory size, disk space, and network information.

You can use this information for inventory purposes (determining what hardware is on your network) as well as for a quick look at what operating system is running to give you a clue about how to fix a problem. For example, you can remotely log into a server to fix something and know its hostname, IP address, MySQL version, and most importantly, the host operating system before you log in—all critical information that most administrators memorize or write down in a notebook. Figure 16-9 shows an excerpt of the server details portion of the Dashboard.

Figure 16-9. Server details

Replication details

The Replication tab of the Dashboard includes a list of all of your servers participating in replication. The information is presented in a list form and, like all lists in MEM, you can click on each item to get more information. Figure 16-10 shows a sample replication details report.

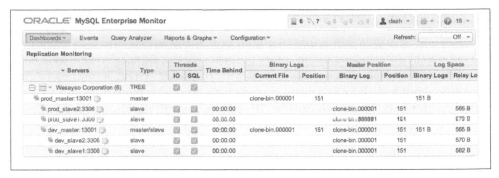

Figure 16-10. Replication details

Notice that items in the list are grouped by topology (e.g., "Wesayso Corporation," which you can rename), including the type of topology, what role(s) the server is performing, and critical statistics about replication, including status of the threads, time behind master, current binary log, log position, master log information, and the most recent errors.

This is an excellent example of how you can get a quick picture of your replication topology. The list shows the masters and slaves grouped hierarchically (i.e., a master is listed at a level directly under the group and its slaves under each master). In Figure 16-10, it is easy to see the *development* server has two slaves, *dev_slave1* and *dev_slave2*, and the *development* server is a slave to the *production* server. Having all the information about replication in one location makes the tedious task of monitoring replication on each server obsolete.

Advisors

What makes all of the alerts and pretty charts so informative are the best practices implemented in the advisors. You can see all of the active advisors (and create your own) on the Advisors tab in the Dashboard.

Figure 16-11 shows the advisors that are active for a specific server on your network. You can enable, disable, or unschedule any of the advisors (unscheduling removes the data collected).

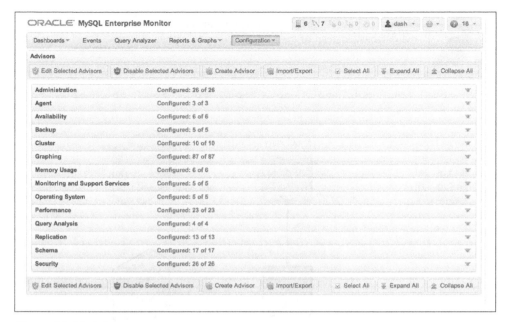

Figure 16-11. Advisors

Perhaps the most useful feature of this page is adding your own advisors. This feature allows you to expand the MEM to meet your specific needs. It also gives you the one thing you need most when migrating from a manual monitoring solution: the ability to preserve your hard work.

For example, if you create a reporting mechanism that monitors a custom application, you can create an advisor for it and add alerts to the Dashboard. The specific details of how to add new advisors and alerts are covered in the MySQL Enterprise Monitor manual on the MySQL Enterprise Edition documentation site (*http://bit.ly/ent-prods*). This customization feature is one the most powerful and underutilized features of MySQL Enterprise Edition.

Query Analyzer

One of the most powerful features of MEM is the Query Analyzer. The Query Analyzer works by intercepting SQL commands using MySQL Proxy and processing them, then passing them on to the local server for execution. This allows it to record statistics so that you can view them at any time. The Query Analyzer also supports advisors that fire alerts for slow queries. Figure 16-12 shows a conceptual drawing of how MySQL Proxy intercepts queries and reports the statistics to the MEM.

Newer versions of the Query Analyzer can use the Performance Schema database instead of the MySQL Proxy to gather statistics.

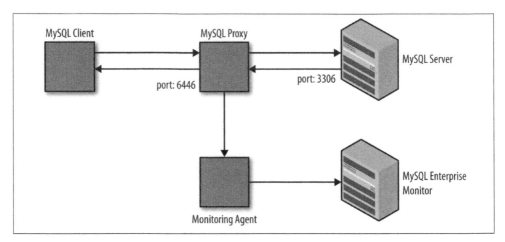

Figure 16-12. Using MySQL Proxy to collect data for Query Analyzer

 The Query Analyzer runs over the user-defined port 6446 (by default) and can introduce some performance delay. Thus, you should enable it only when you are searching for problems.

One nice thing about the Query Analyzer and the Dashboard is the tight integration among the tools. If you have an alert about a slow query or drill down into a CPU utilization report or other MySQL-based statistic, you will see the Query Analyzer page (which you can also access directly by clicking the Query Analyzer tab). Figure 16-13 shows an example of the Query Analyzer page on the Dashboard.

The Query Analyzer page displays a list of servers on the left. You can click a specific server to see a list of queries executed on that server, sorted by longest running query. You can also use the chart at the top to narrow the time window to see queries during a specific time period.

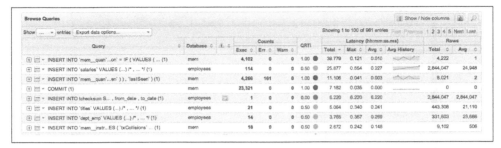

Figure 16-13. Query Analyzer display

You can sort the list on any column by clicking the column heading. This makes it a bit easier to see repetitive queries and diagnostics by sorting the rows with the longest-running queries at the top, showing the query statement, the amount of data manipulated, and more.

You can click any row to get a more detailed report on the query. Figure 16-14 shows a sample canonical query report. As with the other reports, you can get more detailed information, including the actual query on the Example Query tab, the output of the EXPLAIN command on the Explain Query tab (if you enabled that option), and graphs for execution time, number of executions, and number of rows returned on the Graphs tab.

MEM and Cloud Computing

MEM can also function well in a cloud computing environment. The same rules apply, however, regarding the persistence of the data and server instances. Just be sure to request a persistent IP address for your MEM server. Repeatedly starting and stopping your instances will cause no ill effects, but changing hostnames and some types of reconfiguration can cause the monitoring agents to stop reporting. The unique ID for each server is stored in the *mysql.inventory* table. Even though you change the IP address, it won't be re-added to the table because a previous incarnation (with the same unique ID) is already in the table. Thus, MEM may not be able to contact the server because it may be using stale data (the old IP address). Truncating the table typically solves this (because the server will be added to the table again), but it is best to use the same hostnames and IP addresses for all of your servers.

There is one excellent benefit of running MEM in a commercial provider's cloud: you pay only for computation and storage space. Data transfer within the cloud is usually free or much less than shipping data in and out of the cloud.

Figure 16-14. Canonical query report

This report presents details of the query captured, such as the canonical form of the query (a pictorial representation of the query as it was written), details of its execution (including time taken), and rows returned or affected.

Once again, the Query Analyzer component of MEM provides a monitoring tool that will save you a considerable amount of time diagnosing problems with MySQL. This component is a vital monitoring tool that will help you keep your servers running well and your queries executing efficiently.

Further Information

A complete and thorough description of the MEM and its many features is beyond the scope of this book. However, there is a great deal of information available on the Web. For more information about custom advisors and more, see the MySQL Enterprise Monitoring manual located on the MySQL Enterprise Edition documentation site. If you are an Oracle customer, you can check the knowledge base on the Oracle support website (https://support.oracle.com) for answers to common problems.

Conclusion

The MySQL server is the most popular open source database system for good reason. It is so versatile that any organization can use it, from a single self-contained web server providing content to users to online transaction processing systems (OLTPs) to highly available massively scaled-out data center infrastructures. MySQL can handle all of this and more. The MEM makes it possible to extend MySQL to large installations while preserving peak performance and reliability.

If you need high availability and want to build the best and most reliable data center based on MySQL, you should consider purchasing the appropriate MySQL Enterprise Edition licenses. Other solutions exist, but none have the depth of expertise for best practices offered by MySQL Enterprise Edition and none give you the sophistication of the advisors and Query Analyzer for a bargain price.

Joel was ready. He had sent his proposal to purchase the much-needed MySQL Enterprise Edition licenses to cover all of the company's servers. Mr. Summerson had a reputation for spending as little as possible, so Joel was ready to defend his proposal and had decided not to give up until Mr. Summerson had at least heard him out.

Each time he heard footsteps approaching, Joel would look up at his doorway. He knew his boss would stop by any moment. Another set of footsteps approached and he steeled himself once more. Mr. Summerson whisked by without a glance. "Wait for it," Joel whispered.

"Joel, I like this MEM thing. I want you to put together a cost estimate and…"

Joel interrupted his boss. "I already have a report for you, Bob."

Mr. Summerson raised his eyebrows and said, "Send it to me, and I'll get the bean counters to see if we can work it into the budget for next year." With that, Mr. Summerson was gone, on his way to his next victim.

Joel eased back in his desk chair and crossed his arms in satisfaction. "I'll take that as an 'attaboy,'" he said.

Managing MySQL Replication with MySQL Utilities

Joel was feeling pretty good about his job. Over the last few months he had conquered many tasks, including setting up replication and tuning MySQL. Most recently, his boss agreed to allow Joel to hire another MySQL administrator. Yes, Joel had finally made the job his own.

A familiar knock followed by an equally familiar intrusion by his boss broke Joel's revelry.

"Joel, I've got a few candidates I'd like to interview. Before you do that, I'd like you to write up a training manual. Make sure you include all of the tricks and tips as well as all of your administrative trickery so that our new employee can come up to speed quickly. Start with that replication thing. That worries me."

Not waiting for a reply, Joel's boss disappeared on his way to the next drive-by tasking. Joel chuckled as he considered his latest challenge.

Suddenly, Joel's boss thrust his head back into the doorway and said, "Be sure to use that DocBook format the documentation guys like so much."

"Great!" Joel said with a mock smile as his boss once again disappeared. "I guess I'll go visit the documentation team to see what tools they use to compile their DocBook files."

MySQL replication is a very sound and reliable server feature. As you have seen in previous chapters, initiating and configuring replication requires a certain amount of knowledge as well as a set of procedures tailored to your needs. Knowing what to do when is the key to managing MySQL replication well.

Many of the best practices for managing MySQL replication have been presented in previous chapters. Most have been presented in the context of learning replication and applying replication features for high availability solutions. However, we felt the book would be more complete if we devoted a special chapter to summarizing the common tasks involved with replication. We also highlight two important tools you can use to achieve high availability from MySQL right out of the box, without third-party tools or complicated installation steps.

In this chapter, we will examine the core replication administration tasks, best practices, and tools for managing multiple replication servers, including tools for performing failover and switchover. We begin with a short review of the common tasks that administrators of replication will encounter.

Common MySQL Replication Tasks

Managing a replication installation is thankfully very easy. There are a few things that must be done on a regular basis, but it is seldom necessary to change or tune the replication configuration. This section summarizes the common tasks that you are likely to encounter when managing MySQL replication.

We omit the obvious task—setting up replication—and instead refer you to Chapter 3 for a complete tutorial on setting up replication. However, we will show you a tool that you can use to make setting up replication a one-command endeavor.

Checking Status

Let's begin with the most frequent replication administration task you will likely perform: checking the status of your slaves for errors and other anomalies. This is the basic way to check the status of a replication. The key command to do this is SHOW SLAVE STATUS. This command displays a long list of information about the slave. We see an example of the output in Example 17-1.

Example 17-1. SHOW SLAVE STATUS example

```
mysql> SHOW SLAVE STATUS \G
*************************** 1. row ***************************
               Slave_IO_State: Waiting for master to send event ❶
                  Master_Host: localhost ❷
                  Master_User: rpl ❸
                  Master_Port: 13001 ❹
                Connect_Retry: 60
              Master_Log_File: clone-bin.000001 ❺
          Read_Master_Log_Pos: 594 ❻
               Relay_Log_File: clone-relay-bin.000002
                Relay_Log_Pos: 804
        Relay_Master_Log_File: clone-bin.000001
             Slave_IO_Running: Yes ❼
            Slave_SQL_Running: Yes ❽
              Replicate_Do_DB:
          Replicate_Ignore_DB:
           Replicate_Do_Table:
```

```
               Replicate_Ignore_Table:
              Replicate_Wild_Do_Table:
          Replicate_Wild_Ignore_Table:
                           Last_Errno: 0 ❾
                           Last_Error:   ❿
                         Skip_Counter: 0
               Exec_Master_Log_Pos: 594 ⓫
                    Relay_Log_Space: 1008
                    Until_Condition: None
                     Until_Log_File:
                      Until_Log_Pos: 0
                  Master_SSL_Allowed: No
                  Master_SSL_CA_File:
                  Master_SSL_CA_Path:
                    Master_SSL_Cert:
                  Master_SSL_Cipher:
                     Master_SSL_Key:
              Seconds_Behind_Master: 0 ⓬
     Master_SSL_Verify_Server_Cert: No
                      Last_IO_Errno: 0 ⓭
                      Last_IO_Error:   ⓮
                     Last_SQL_Errno: 0 ⓯
                     Last_SQL_Error:   ⓰
          Replicate_Ignore_Server_Ids:
                   Master_Server_Id: 101 ⓱
                        Master_UUID: aa73ae8c-2a9d-11e2-936b-7e5b4e755f7e  ⓲
                   Master_Info_File: /Volumes/Source/source/temp_13002/master.info
                          SQL_Delay: 0 ⓳
                SQL_Remaining_Delay: NULL ⓴
             Slave_SQL_Running_State: Slave has read all relay log; waiting
                                      for the slave ㉑ ㉒
                                      I/O thread to update it
                 Master_Retry_Count: 86400
                        Master_Bind:
            Last_IO_Error_Timestamp: ㉓
           Last_SQL_Error_Timestamp: ㉔
                     Master_SSL_Crl:
                 Master_SSL_Crlpath:
                 Retrieved_Gtid_Set: AA73AE8C-2A9D-11E2-936B-7E5B4E755F7E:1-2 ㉕
                  Executed_Gtid_Set: AA73AE8C-2A9D-11E2-936B-7E5B4E755F7E:1-2, ㉖
                                     BB8BF918-2A9D-11E2-936B-C5790DD70EC1:1
```

While this example contains a great many entries, there are a few critical lines you should examine when checking the status of a slave. We have highlighted these areas in the following groups:

❷ ❸ Check these entries for master connection information. You want to ensure the
❹ ❺ slave is connected to the correct master.
❻ ⓱

❾ ❿ Check these entries for errors. All of these entries should show 0 for error
⓭ ⓮ numbers, be blank for error messages, or not include any state that indicates an
⓯ ⓰ error.
㉒ ㉓
㉔

❶ ❼ Check these entries for state information. As we have seen in previous chapters,
❽ ㉑ there can be a number of different states. Usually you want to make sure there
are no states indicating the slave is encountering an error or has lost connection
with the master.

⓫ ⓬ Check for slave delay at these entries. You are looking for how far (seconds,
⓲ ⓳ transactions, etc.) the slave is from the master. Depending on your installation,
⓴ some delay may be acceptable.

⓲ ㉕ Check these entries for issues with GTIDs. Use the information here to diagnose
㉖ missing transactions on the slave.

See the online reference manual for more details about what each of these entries contain and what their normal values should be for a healthy slave.

Aside from the slave status, you can also glean some information from the SHOW PROC ESSLIST output on the master. Example 17-2 shows an excerpt of the command run on the master. This shows the typical state for a healthy slave connection as illustrated by the dump thread on the master.

Example 17-2. SHOW PROCESSLIST excerpt

```
mysql> SHOW PROCESSLIST \G
*************************** 1. row ***************************
     Id: 4
   User: rpl
   Host: localhost:51234
     db: NULL
Command: Binlog Dump GTID
   Time: 2623
  State: Master has sent all binlog to slave; waiting for binlog to be updated
   Info: NULL
*************************** 2. row ***************************
     Id: 7
   User: rpl
   Host: localhost:51374
     db: NULL
Command: Binlog Dump GTID
   Time: 4
  State: Master has sent all binlog to slave; waiting for binlog to be updated
   Info: NULL
[...]
```

In the example, we see one entry for the binlog dump thread for each slave attached. This master has two slaves attached and they are both healthy, because there's no indication of an error in the state field.

These commands are very good at giving all of the details about the slave and its connection with the master and are easy to issue from a *mysql* client. However, what if you have dozens of slaves or even hundreds of slaves, or better still a tiered topology with intermediate masters and thousands of slaves? Running these commands on each slave can get very tedious.

Fortunately, there are tools you can use to make life easier. For installations of many slaves and complex topologies, the MySQL Enterprise Monitor solution is most likely your tool of choice for its one-stop monitoring capabilities.

However, there is an alternative. Even if you have many slaves, you may want to check a few of them or perhaps check only the slaves for a particular master. In this case, you can use the `health` command of the *mysqlrpladmin* utility to generate a health report for a master and its slaves. We will see this utility in action later in this chapter.

Stopping Replication

The next most common replication administration task is stopping and restarting replication. We recommend doing these operations any time you need to do something to the slave: for maintenance reasons, to correct errors in the data, or perhaps for application specific changes.

The commands for starting and stopping replication include commands for resetting the replication configurations on the master or slave. We have seen these commands in previous chapters but summarize them here for convenience (we also include variants as separate entries for clarity):

STOP SLAVE
> Stops the replication threads (SQL, IO) on the slave. Use this command when you wish to disconnect the slave from the master and stop receiving updates.

STOP SLAVE IO_THREAD
> Stops the replication IO thread only. Use this command when you wish to stop receiving updates from the master but still want to process any events in the slave's relay log.

STOP SLAVE SQL_THREAD
> Stops the replication SQL thread only. Use this command when you wish to stop processing events in the relay log but do not want to stop receiving updates from the master.

START SLAVE
> Starts the slave's replication threads.

START SLAVE UNTIL SQL_BEFORE_GTIDS *gtid_set*

> Start the replication threads until both have reached the first GTID before the GTID in *gtid_set* is encountered, at which time the threads are stopped.

START SLAVE UNTIL SQL_AFTER_GTIDS *gtid_set*

> Start the replication threads until both have reached the last GTID before the GTID in *gtid_set* is encountered at which time the threads are stopped.

START SLAVE UNTIL MASTER_LOG_FILE='*file*', MASTER_LOG_POS=*position*

> Start the replication slaves until the master's log file and position are reached, after which the slave threads are stopped.

START SLAVE UNTIL RELAY_LOG_FILE='*file*', RELAY_LOG_POS=*position*

> Start the replication slaves until the slave's relay log file and position are reached, after which the slave threads are stopped.

RESET SLAVE

> This command causes the slave to delete the settings for connecting to the master. It is designed to be used for making a clean start of replication (e.g., when moving a slave from one master to another—also called pruning). The command also starts a new relay log ceasing any reads to existing relay logs.

RESET MASTER

> This command is issued on the master. It is used to delete all of the binary log files and the binary log index creating a new binary log and index. Clearly, this command is one you will want to use very sparingly and never in the normal course of replication management. For example, it will disrupt slaves (perhaps with data loss or inconsistency) when run on a master with active slaves connected. A case where you may use it is if you have a master that has been taken offline (or has failed) and you later wish to return it to service as a slave for another master.

> You can specify a thread type for the START SLAVE UNTIL command when used with SQL_BEFORE_GTIDS or SQL_AFTER_GTIDS. You can also specify only the SQL_THREAD option for the other START SLAVE UNTIL forms to act only on the SQL thread. See the online reference manual for a complete list of the options for the START SLAVE command.

If you need to stop, start, or reset a lot of slaves, connecting to each and every one may become time consuming if you haven't the time to write a script to repeat the command on a list (or something similar). Fortunately, there is a tool you can use to issue these commands to a list of slaves. We will see the *mysqlrpladmin* utility in more detail later in this chapter.

Adding Slaves

Aside from checking on the health of your slaves and the routine starting and stopping replication on slaves, the next most common replication administrative task is adding slaves to a topology. The purpose of doing so may be for scale out, making the data accessible to remote areas, or the normal maintenance process of removing a slave, making system changes, then returning it to the topology.

The most important element for this operation, and indeed the one that trips up most novice administrators, is getting the slave in sync with the master. This is particularly complicated when working with a slave that has older states of the databases. While the process is essentially the same, the case where you are adding a new slave with no data is a bit easer (only one data loading option to consider).

Before you add a slave to the topology, you must consider whether the slave has an older state of the data on the master. If this is true, you have several options.

- You can overwrite the data with a copy from the master. This would normally be applying a backup file taken from the master to the slave.

- You can attempt to roll forward the master's binary log from the last known master's binary log and position. This technique, called *point-in-time recovery* (PITR), has been mentioned elsewhere in this book. Depending on how far behind the slave is, this may be a faster option than waiting for the slave to catch up. Note that this requires you know the master's binary log file and position at the time the slave was taken out of the topology.

- You can connect to the master and let the slave catch up.

 You can discover the slave's last known master binary log file and position from the master information stored in the *master.info* file, for slaves started with the `--master-info-repo=FILE` option. You can also query the `mysql.slave_master_info`table for slaves started with the `--master-info-repo=TABLE` option.

The process of adding a slave involves deciding how to set up the data on the slave and then executing the plan using backups, file copies, or some other form of data recovery. Once the slave has data that is close to or the same as the master, you can then set up replication in the usual manner, as described in Chapter 3. The following list summarizes the steps for completeness:

1. If you're not using GTIDs, be sure the new slave's `--server-id` is set to a value that is unique among your master and its slaves.

2. Prepare the data on the slave.

3. Issue the `CHANGE MASTER` command on the slave. If using GTIDs, use `MASTER_AU TO_POSITION=1` instead of the master log file and position

4. Issue the `START SLAVE` command on the slave.

5. Check the slave's `SHOW SLAVE STATUS` for errors.

The preceding process is called *slave provisioning*. Although you can't perform all of these steps with a single command, there are helper utilities to make each of the steps easier. We will see these utilities in action later in this chapter.

MySQL Utilities

Oracle has included a set of very useful administrative tools called MySQL Utilities, which is a subproduct of MySQL Workbench. The utilities are written purely in Python and are all command-line based.

Included in MySQL Utilities are a number of helpful utilities for managing replication. Many of the tasks discussed in the previous section can be accomplished using these utilities. In addition to replication-specific utilities, there are a number of utilities that can be used in a variety of scenarios involving replication.

The following sections will present the utilities available. Rather than present an option-by-option discussion of each feature for each utility, we present the goals of the utilities along with discussions on how best to use them with replication. If you need more specific information about the utilities—the available options, features, and limitations—consult the online documentation for MySQL Utilities (*http://bit.ly/mysql-utils*). The documentation contains a number of additional example scenarios and in-depth description of all options.

Most utilities provide a verbosity option, `--verbose` or just `-v`, that can be specified multiple times to increase the amount of information printed. The highest level of verbosity is usually `--verbose --verbose --verbose` or `-vvv`, to indicate a verbosity of three.

Getting Started

MySQL Utilities are available via a direct download from the MySQL download site. To download from that site, visit the MySQL Developers' Zone download page (*http://dev.mysql.com/downloads*). You will find downloads for most popular platforms, including *.tar* and *.zip* files for those who wish to install the utilities using the traditional `python ./setup.py install` command.

The only installation requirements for installing and using MySQL Utilities are Python 2.7 or higher and the Connector/Python database connector. Connector/Python can also be found on the download site. The connector must be installed before running a utility but may be installed after MySQL Utilities.

Using the Utilities Without Workbench

To use MySQL Utilities outside of MySQL Workbench, you can open any terminal (console) and, if it is not already specified in your environment or profile, set the PYTHONPATH environment variable. It must include the locations of both MySQL Utilities and Connector/Python. If you installed both using a platform-specific installer or via the standard Python install command, both products were installed in your PythonXX folder.

Using the Utilities via Workbench

If you download and install Workbench version 6 and later, and you have installed MySQL Utilities, you can access MySQL Utilities from within Workbench. Versions of MySQL Workbench prior to version 6 include MySQL Utilities in the installation. MySQL Workbench version 6 and later do not.

To access MySQL Utilities from Workbench, open Workbench, then either click on the Plugins menu item and choose "Start Shell for MySQL Utilities" or click on the multi-tool icon. You may need to widen the display or click on the right arrow icon to see the Utilities plug-in icon. Figure 17-1 highlights both methods of accessing MySQL Utilities.

When the plug-in is launched, it will open a terminal (console) and print a list of the utilities available. Figure 17-2 demonstrates the results of launching the utilities plug-in.

 The development of MySQL Utilities and Workbench often result in new versions available several times a year. Be sure to check the downloads page for the latest version of MySQL Utilities and MySQL Workbench.

Figure 17-1. Accessing MySQL Utilities from Workbench

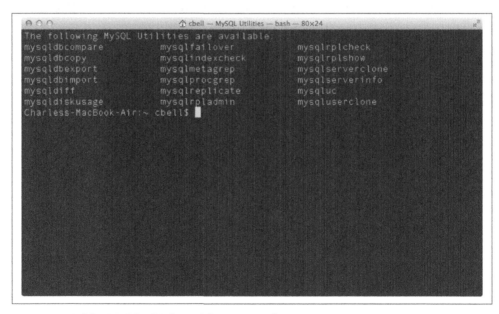

Figure 17-2. The MySQL Utilities Plugin Console

General Utilities

This section includes a brief overview of those utilities that are general purpose in nature. We describe each utility and present a brief example of its execution along with some ideas for how the utility can be used to help manage replication.

 While some utilities provide shortcuts such as `-s` for certain options, all utilities have the ability to use prefixes for option names provided the prefix matches a single option. For example, suppose there is a utility with an option named `--discover-slaves-login` and there are no other options that have similar prefixes. You can use `--discover=` or `--disco` instead of typing the entire option name. Clearly, this can be a huge time saver when entering many options.

Comparing Databases for Consistency: mysqldbcompare

Although data inconsistency is rare in a well-managed infrastructure, it is possible data can become corrupt. But it is not just data that could be inconsistent—the object definitions themselves can be inconsistent. Fortunately, the compare database utility is designed to compare both definitions as well as data.

In replication, it is less likely to encounter object definition differences. Most of the time, this is a result of user error but can be the result of errors occurring during the replication process. What is needed is a utility that allows you to compare two tables to determine any differences in the data.

Accidental or misdirected changes can cause data on a slave to become out of sync with the master. For example, if a user (or an application) writes to a slave, it has effectively introduced inconsistencies. Depending on the type of change, the inconsistency can go undetected for some time.

Data inconsistency can also occur if there are errors during transport of the changes from the master to the slave, or as a result of an unrelated failure of the slave during execution of events. In most cases, the error is detected right away, but it may be difficult to determine what inconsistencies exist or if any exist at all. Rather than take a chance that the data remains consistent after the slave is repaired, it is always a good idea to check for inconsistencies.

Checking for inconsistency is a non-trivial endeavor. There are also many ways one can determine inconsistencies. The *mysqldbcompare* utility builds checksums on a row-by-row basis, grouping them into chunks that are later compared to determine which chunk contains inconsistencies. While effective in identifying the exact rows that differ, due to the overhead involved in generating the checksums, running the utility against multiple databases or multiple tables with many rows may result in extended run times.

This utility is considered an offline utility due to the overhead required to execute it, which includes a potentially long lock on the tables. If you decide to run the utility while the database is available to users, try to do so when response time is not critical and you can hold up the database with the resource-intensive utility.

Use with replication

mysqldbcompare can be used during recovery from data corruption problems on the slave. Because the utility requires locking of the tables to be compared, it is considered an offline utility.

To minimize impacts to production applications and users, the best use case is to choose a slave among the active, viable slaves and compare the databases between the known good slave and the recovered slave. You don't have to take the servers offline, but it is best to suspend replication before running the compare to avoid the possibility of updates being blocked by the lock taken during the compare.

There are two uses of the utility for recovery. First, you can use the utility to compare the slave with the data issues with another slave to discover what has changed. Second, you can use the utility to determine whether the data recovery attempts were successful.

Once you have identified the rows that differ, you can begin efforts to correct the differences. There are many ways to go about this, from manual changes to the rows on the slave to running a data recovery process like backup or point-in-time recovery.

One feature makes this utility especially useful for recovery of data inconsistencies. It can generate the SQL commands needed to bring the databases into synchronization. This generates statements you can use on your slave to correct data inconsistencies.

Examples of mysqldbcompare

The following examples compare a database on two servers: two slaves in a replication topology. The first example detects missing views on `server2`. This may be OK for a slave. Some administrators will create views for application-specific features. Notice the data differences identified. Because we are running the utility on two slaves, we would expect the slaves to be identical, but clearly the row for the supplier table with id 2 was changed differently between the slaves. The good news is you now know which row to focus your attention to determine what changes are needed to bring the slaves into consistency.

```
$ mysqldbcompare --server1=root@slave1 --server2=root@slave2 \
  inventory:inventory --run-all-tests
# server1 on slave1: ... connected.
# server2 on slave2: ... connected.
# Checking databases inventory on server1 and inventory on server2
```

```
WARNING: Objects in server1:inventory but not in server2:inventory:
        VIEW: finishing_up
        VIEW: cleaning
                                            Defn    Row     Data
Type        Object Name                     Diff    Count   Check
-------------------------------------------------------------------
TABLE       supplier                        pass    FAIL    FAIL

Data differences found among rows:
--- inventory.supplier
+++ inventory.supplier
@@ -1,2 +1,2 @@
 code,name
-2,Never Enough Inc.
+2,Wesayso Corporation
```

In the next example, we run the same command, only this time we generate the data transformation statements needed to synchronize the databases and correct the data inconsistency. Compare this to the previous example. Notice the statements presented at the end of the listing. These are statements that can make your job of recovering from data inconsistency on a slave.

```
$ mysqldbcompare --server1=root@slave1 --server2=root@slave2 \
  inventory:inventory --run-all-tests --difftype=sql
# server1 on slave1: ... connected.
# server2 on slave2: ... connected.
# Checking databases inventory on server1 and inventory on server2

WARNING: Objects in server1:inventory but not in server2:inventory:
        VIEW: finishing_up
        VIEW: cleaning
                                            Defn    Row     Data
Type        Object Name                     Diff    Count   Check
-------------------------------------------------------------------
TABLE       supplier                        pass    FAIL    FAIL

Data differences found among rows:
--- inventory.supplier
+++ inventory.supplier
@@ -1,2 +1,2 @@
 code,name
-2,Never Enough Inc.
+2,Wesayso Corporation

#
# Transformation for --changes-for=server1:
#

UPDATE `inventory`.`supplier` SET name = 'Wesayso Corporation' WHERE code = 2;
```

Copying Databases: mysqldbcopy

There are times when you need to copy data from one server to another. Depending on the sizes of the databases you need to copy and the urgency or expediency of the copy, common offline solutions—a backup, file copy, or logical volume image—may be inconvenient to set up and execute. In these times, it would be easier to simply tell a utility to copy the databases. That is what the copy database utility, *mysqldbcopy*, is designed to do. *mysqldbcopy* copies all objects and the data in each database listed.

The copy database utility allows you to specify one or more databases to be copied from one server to another. There are options for renaming the databases on the destination server. You can also copy a database on the same server by specifying a different name for the database, thereby permitting you to rename databases without taking the original database offline.

Use with replication

One of the steps needed when adding a new slave is to load the slave with the data from the master, so you can then start replication without forcing the slave to read and execute many events from the master. Although it is often more efficient and faster to restore a backup from the master (or another up-to-date slave), it is sometimes necessary or convenient to copy a small amount of data. In this case, *mysqldbcopy* may be easier to execute than a partial restore.

Example of mysqldbcopy

The following example copies a single database from one server to another. Notice the messages printed as the copy executes. Not only are the objects and data copied, but the database-level grants are copied as well. Depending on your backup application, this last feature may make using this utility easier and faster than copying the data and then applying the grants manually.

```
$ mysqldbcopy --source=root@slave1 --destination=root@slave2 \
  util_test:util_test
# Source on slave1: ... connected.
# Destination on slave2: ... connected.
# Copying TABLE util_test.t1
# Copying table data.
# Copying TABLE util_test.t2
# Copying table data.
# Copying TABLE util_test.t3
# Copying table data.
# Copying TABLE util_test.t4
# Copying table data.
# Copying VIEW util_test.v1
# Copying TRIGGER util_test.trg
# Copying PROCEDURE util_test.p1
# Copying FUNCTION util_test.f1
```

```
# Copying EVENT util_test.e1
# Copying GRANTS from util_test
#...done.
```

Exporting Databases: mysqldbexport

Copying data using MySQL's database copy utilities involves two operations; reading the data from one server and writing the data to another server. There are times when you want or need to have copies of your data in a file for manipulation (correcting errors to many rows manually), for safekeeping, or for ingestion into analytical tools.

To meet these use cases, the copy operation was made into two utilities: *mysqldbexport* for exporting the data and *mysqldbimport* for importing it. The export and import database utilities are designed to perform a logical copy of the data. This means the utility will read tables one row at a time rather than reading the table data in binary form like a physical copy.

The export database utility is designed to copy object definitions, data, or both using the --export option. You can also specify which object types you want to include with the --skip option. Thus it is possible to export only the events for a given list of databases, only the data for a specific table, or all of the objects and data from a server.

Although the utility generates its output at the console (standard out), you can redirect the output to a file for use in other tools or for use by the import database utility.

One of the most powerful features of this utility is the ability to produce the output in one of several forms:

SQL
: Produce SQL statements for object creation (CREATE) and data (INSERT). This is the default output format.

GRID
: Display output in grid or table format like that of the *mysql* client.

CSV
: Display output in comma-separated values format.

TAB
: Display output in tab-separated format.

VERTICAL
: Display output in single-column format like that of the \G command option in the *mysql* client.

These formats are supported by a number of utilities, enabling you to pass the formats through further filtering to make the output easier to read or easier to use with external tools.

The export database utility is designed to support replication by adding the appropriate replication commands in the output stream. This permits you to use the output of the export as an import to a slave or a master depending on the option you specify. Use the --rpl option to instruct the utilty to add STOP SLAVE , CHANGE MASTER, START SLAVE commands to the output. For example, you can instruct the utility to include the replication commands for controlling a slave during import. To do so, use the --rpl=SLAVE option to copy data off of one slave with the goal of updating another slave that has fallen behind. The --rpl=SLAVE option adds a CHANGE MASTER command to the end of the output. When you import this file on another slave, the slave will connect to the same master as the slave where the export was run.

The --rpl=MASTER option also adds a CHANGE MASTER command to the end of the output. But this time, the master is the server where the export was run. This means when you import this file on another slave, the slave will connect to the slave where the export was run.

You can even tell the utility to generate both statements with the --rpl=BOTH option, allowing you to edit the import for use in different levels in your topology (slaves of the current server and peer slaves).

When replication statements are generated, they are always generated as SQL statements (regardless of the format chosen) and are written in the order they would be used during an import operation. The following shows the order of statements generated (the statements generated by use of the --rpl option are shown in bold):

1. **STOP SLAVE**
2. Object definitions
3. Data
4. **CHANGE MASTER ...**
5. **START SLAVE**

The utility also permits you to specify a separate file containing the replication commands. This lets you use the replication commands separately from the export. This may be most helpful when you use the replication mode to generate both forms of the CHANGE MASTER (current server as master or current servers master).

If you recall, the CHANGE MASTER command includes the replication user and password. You can specify this using the --rpl-user option in the form of *username:password*.

For example, the `--rpl-user=rpl:secret` option instructs the *mysqldbexport* command to use `rpl` as the replication user and `secret` as the replication user password in the `CHANGE MASTER` command as shown here:

```
CHANGE MASTER TO MASTER_HOST = 'localhost', MASTER_USER = 'rpl',
MASTER_PASSWORD = 'secret', MASTER_PORT = 13001,
MASTER_LOG_FILE = 'clone-bin.000001', MASTER_LOG_POS = 920;
```

If you omit the `--rpl-user` option, the `CHANGE MASTER` command will be generated with commented-out sections for the master user and password. This is because the information may not be known at the time the export is running. We show this in an upcoming example.

Another use for this utility with replication, perhaps the most useful, is during recovery of a slave from data corruption. When used together with the *mysqldbcompare* database consistency utility, *mysqldbexport* can be used to export the data from the known good slave. You then import it on the recovered slave to restore consistency.

The latest versions of both *mysqldbcopy* and *mysqldbexport* permit you to generate the correct GTID statements setting the `GTID_PURGED` list for use in importing the data on slaves. See the online reference manual for MySQL Utilities (*http://bit.ly/mysql-utils*) for more information.

Example of mysqldbexport

The following example shows an export of a database with replication statements and GTID statements. The format used is a comma separated file, but the replication commands are all SQL commands. Notice also the `CHANGE MASTER` command. To use this command, you need to provide the correct user and password for the replication user on the master.

Although the database in the example is trivial, the example illustrates the replication commands that enable the use of the utility in replication:

```
$ mysqldbexport --server=root:pass@localhost:13001 --export=both --rpl=master
--format=csv test_125
# Source on localhost: ... connected.
-- STOP SLAVE;
# Exporting metadata from test_125
# TABLES in test_125:
TABLE_SCHEMA,TABLE_NAME,ENGINE,ORDINAL_POSITION,COLUMN_NAME,COLUMN_TYPE,
IS_NULLABLE,COLUMN_DEFAULT,COLUMN_KEY,TABLE_COLLATION,CREATE_OPTIONS,
CONSTRAINT_NAME,REFERENCED_TABLE_NAME,UNIQUE_CONSTRAINT_NAME,UPDATE_RULE,
DELETE_RULE,CONSTRAINT_NAME,COL_NAME,REFERENCED_TABLE_SCHEMA,
REFERENCED_COLUMN_NAME
test_125,t1,InnoDB,1,a,int(11),YES,,,latin1_swedish_ci,,,,,,,,,,
test_125,t1,InnoDB,2,b,char(30),YES,,,latin1_swedish_ci,,,,,,,,,,
# VIEWS in test_125: (none found)
# TRIGGERS in test_125: (none found)
# PROCEDURES in test_125: (none found)
```

```
# FUNCTIONS in test_125: (none found)
# EVENTS in test_125: (none found)
# GRANTS in test_125: (none found)
#...done.
# Exporting data from test_125
# Data for table test_125.t1:
a,b
1,one
2,two
3,three
#...done.
# Connecting to the current server as master
# WARNING: No --rpl-user specified and multiple users found with
replication privileges.
-- CHANGE MASTER TO MASTER_HOST = 'localhost', # MASTER_USER = '',
# MASTER_PASSWORD = '', MASTER_PORT = 13001,
MASTER_LOG_FILE = 'clone-bin.000001', MASTER_LOG_POS = 920;
-- START SLAVE;
```

Notice the - - prefix for the replication commands. These are added to permit the *mysqldbimport* to import the file and identify the rows with replication commands.

Importing Databases: mysqldbimport

The import database utility, *mysqldbimport*, is designed to read a file formatted in any of the formats generated by the export database utility. This permits you to store or use copies of your data in the form most convenient to the task at hand and import the data without having to convert it.

The import database utility simply reads the file, parsing formats other than the SQL format by converting them to SQL statements, and executes the commands on the server.

You can use *mysqldbimport* to import your own files if they are formatted in one of *mysqldbexport*'s output formats.

One of the best features of this utility is the ability to import only the object definitions or the data. Use the - -import option to tell the utility to import the object definitions, the data, or both.

Another feature is the ability to change the storage engine of the tables when importing, thereby performing two operations in one pass. This can be very handy when importing data on servers that do not support the storage engines of the originating server. For example, you can use this feature to restore MyISAM tables, changing the storage engine to InnoDB in a single step.

Lastly, you can use the `--dryrun` option to validate the file but not actually execute the statements generated.

Use with replication

mysqldbimport is a key companion to *mysqleximport*, which we discussed previously, to support the use cases for replication. The import operation is the natural follow-up to an export: you read from one server and write to another. If the file to be imported contains replication commands, they are executed as they are encountered.

Examples of mysqldbimport

The following example shows the result of importing the data from the database export example shown in "Example of mysqldbexport" on page 627. In this case, we tell the import database utility to include both object definitions and data:

```
$ mysqldbimport --server=root:pass@localhost:13001 test_125.sql --import=both
# Source on localhost: ... connected.
# Importing definitions and data from test_125.sql.
#...done.
```

When you use the *mysqldbimport* utility to import output from the *mysqldbexport* utility that contains replication commands (via the `--rpl` option), you need do nothing extra to make these commands execute. The *mysqldbimport* utility is designed to identify these commands even if the format of the file is not SQL and execute them.

However, you can disable these commands by using the `--skip-rpl` option. You may want to do this if the export was saved to a file and you are using the file to import to a server that isn't or is not intended to be part of the topology. For example, if you want to generate a test server to test some application, you can use an export from a viable slave and skip the replication commands when importing the file on the test server.

Discovering Differences: mysqldiff

The database difference utility, *mysqldiff*, performs the object definition difference check required by *mysqldbcompare* data consistency utility and described in "Comparing Databases for Consistency: mysqldbcompare" on page 621. In fact, *mysqldiff* predates *mysqldbcompare*, which includes all its functionality. This shows an interesting consequence of the high degree of reuse in the MySQL Utilities supporting library.

Rather than replace the difference utility with the data consistency utility, it was decided to leave the utility for cases where users want to check object definitions only.

The output of *mysqldiff* is a difference report in one of several forms of your choice, including unified, context, differ, or SQL. The default is unified. The SQL mode can be valuable because it generates the transformation statements (ALTER statements) that can be used to transform the tables so that they are the same structure.

Use with replication

mysqldiff is very helpful with replication for detecting when objects have diverged. For example, one of your servers may fail to update data because one or more of the tables or dependent tables have changed in structure.

 MySQL replication permits you to have different columns on the master and slave. There are many legitimate use cases for these features. But *mysqldiff* does not currently recognize the valid forms of differences and instead identifies these cases as errors.

Example of mysqldiff

The following example demonstrates the use of the utility to detect differences in objects on two servers:

```
$ mysqldiff --server1=root:pass@localhost:13001
            --server2=root:pass@localhost:13002
diff_db:diff_db
# server1 on localhost: ... connected.
# server2 on localhost: ... connected.
# Comparing diff_db to diff_db                              [PASS]
# Comparing diff_db.table1 to diff_db.table1               [FAIL]
# Object definitions differ. (--changes-for=server1)
#

--- diff_db.table1
+++ diff_db.table1
@@ -1,4 +1,5 @@
 CREATE TABLE `table1` (
   `a` int(11) DEFAULT NULL,
-  `b` char(30) DEFAULT NULL
+  `b` char(30) DEFAULT NULL,
+  `c` timestamp NOT NULL DEFAULT CURRENT_TIMESTAMP
 ) ENGINE=InnoDB DEFAULT CHARSET=latin1
Compare failed. One or more differences found.
```

Detecting Misdirected Writes

One of the ways that replication can go wrong is if updates to data are misdirected to slaves instead of the master. If your slaves are not running in read-only mode, a user could issue an update to the wrong server. When this happens, it may go undetected for some time and can cause some frustrating side effects.

This could manifest as a slave that stops unexpectedly for queries that run correctly on other slaves or different data displayed by applications on some slaves and not others.

There is a trick that you can use to help identify the rogue updates. If your tables do not have any restrictions on using timestamps, add a timestamp column to the tables on your slave. By default, this value will not be updated for any replicated event but will be updated for a data change issued on the slave directly.

The following transcript demonstrates how to set up this configuration and how to use the data to identify the rows changed (we have annotated the listing, removing extraneous output for brevity; the commands were run on a simple replication topology of a master and a single slave):

```
# Executed on the master:
mysql> CREATE DATABASE diff_db;
mysql> CREATE TABLE diff_db.table1 (a int, b char(30));
mysql> INSERT INTO diff_db.table1 VALUES (1, 'one'), (2, 'two'), (3, 'three');
mysql> SELECT * FROM diff_db.table1;
+------+-------+
| a    | b     |
+------+-------+
|    1 | one   |
|    2 | two   |
|    3 | three |
+------+-------+

# Executed on the slave:
mysql> SELECT * FROM diff_db.table1;
+------+-------+
| a    | b     |
+------+-------+
|    1 | one   |
|    2 | two   |
|    3 | three |
+------+-------+

# Alter the table on the slave:
mysql> ALTER TABLE diff_db.table1
add column c timestamp default NOW() after b;

### Enter the rogue update ###
mysql> INSERT INTO diff_db.table1 VALUES (4, 'four', NULL);

mysql> SELECT * FROM diff_db.table1;
+------+-------+---------------------+
| a    | b     | c                   |
+------+-------+---------------------+
|    1 | one   | 0000-00-00 00:00:00 |
|    2 | two   | 0000-00-00 00:00:00 |
```

```
|    3 | three | 0000-00-00 00:00:00 |
|    4 | four  | 2012-11-14 15:34:08 |
+------+-------+---------------------+

# Executed on the master:
mysql> INSERT INTO diff_db.table1 VALUES (7, 'seven'), (8, 'eight');
mysql> SELECT * FROM diff_db.table1;
+------+-------+
| a    | b     |
+------+-------+
|    1 | one   |
|    2 | two   |
|    3 | three |
|    7 | seven |
|    8 | eight |
+------+-------+

# Executed on the slave:
mysql> SELECT * FROM diff_db.table1;
+------+-------+---------------------+
| a    | b     | c                   |
+------+-------+---------------------+
|    1 | one   | 0000-00-00 00:00:00 |
|    2 | two   | 0000-00-00 00:00:00 |
|    3 | three | 0000-00-00 00:00:00 |
|    4 | four  | 2012-11-14 15:34:08 |
|    7 | seven | 0000-00-00 00:00:00 |
|    8 | eight | 0000-00-00 00:00:00 |
+------+-------+---------------------+

# Query for detecting rogue updates:
mysql> SELECT * FROM diff_db.table1 WHERE c > 0;
+------+-------+---------------------+
| a    | b     | c                   |
+------+-------+---------------------+
|    4 | four  | 2012-11-14 15:34:08 |
+------+-------+---------------------+
```

Notice the last two queries issued on the slave. We see that the timestamp column was not updated by any row from the master (we show new rows being added for validation), but the row update on the slave is given a timestamp value. If you have reason to not make your slaves read only, you may want to consider a similar solution.

Showing Disk Usage: mysqldiskusage

The disk usage utility, *mysqldiskusage*, is one of several diagnostic utilities that report information about a MySQL server. This utility is designed to display the total size of each database as well as other file related information, such as names and sizes of logs and InnoDB configuration parameters.

Database sizes are calculated in one of two ways. If the user account has read access to the data directory, the sizes displayed reflect the total size of the files in the directory. If the user does not have read access to the data directory, the sizes are calculated based on metadata information about the tables, including row size and average row length. By default, the utility shows only the total size of the database, but the --verbose option shows the database size broken out by data and miscellaneous files.

The utility can also display the existing and number of binary logs with the --binlog option, relay logs with the --relaylog option, and slow and query logs with the --logs option. You can turn on all options with the --all option.

The output can be formatted in the GRID, CSV, TAB, or VERTICAL formats described in "Exporting Databases: mysqldbexport" on page 625.

 The utility must be run on the server hosting MySQL. You will also need read access to the data directory in order to display all of the information about logs and InnoDB data. As a result, you may need elevated privileges to run the utility.

Use with replication

Although *mysqldiskusage* does not apply directly to replication, it is useful when planning upgrades to replication servers to make sure you have sufficient disk space. You can also use the utility to check on the size of the log files and InnoDB files.

Example of mysqldiskusage

The following example shows a detailed list of the sizes of all databases on a server. We also show all information with all of the options enabled. Notice the information displayed for InnoDB. This could be helpful in diagnosing InnoDB configuration issues:

```
$ mysqldiskusage --server=root:root@localhost --binlog --logs --innodb --all
--empty -vvv
# Source on localhost: ... connected.# Database totals:
+--------------------+---------------+--------------+--------------+--------------+
| db_name            | db_dir_size   | data_size    | misc_files   |       total  |
+--------------------+---------------+--------------+--------------+--------------+
| oltp2              | 472,785       | 445,728      | 27,057       | 472,785      |
| frm_test           | 472,785       | 445,728      | 27,057       | 472,785      |
| compare_util_test  | 472,785       | 445,728      | 27,057       | 472,785      |
| bvm                | 15,129        | 6,080        | 9,049        | 15,129       |
| compare            | 97,924,346    | 97,897,677   | 26,669       | 97,924,346   |
| compare_employees  | 554,176,356   | 554,166,900  | 9,456        | 554,176,356  |
| db1                | 11,035        | 2,188        | 8,847        | 11,035       |
| db2                | 11,035        | 2,188        | 8,847        | 11,035       |
| emp1               | 17,517        | 81,920       | 17,517       | 99,437       |
| emp2               | 88,877        | 206,029,917  | 87,760       | 206,117,677  |
| emp3               | 27,989        | 33,885       | 26,872       | 60,757       |
```

```
| employees          | 88,892   | 206,029,917 | 87,775  | 206,117,692 |
| griots             | 14,415   | 5,288       | 9,127   | 14,415      |
| groits             | 9,045    | 16,384      | 9,045   | 25,429      |
| mysql              | 903,022  | 693,480     | 191,720 | 885,200     |
| oltp1              | 62,705   | 114,688     | 62,705  | 177,393     |
| sak1               | 411,538  | 6,887,232   | 143,442 | 7,030,674   |
| sakila             | 510,111  | 6,944,576   | 184,671 | 7,129,247   |
| test               | 580,636  | 74,029      | 506,607 | 580,636     |
| test123            | 17,343   | 32,768      | 17,343  | 50,111      |
| test_1             | 48,730   | 5,225       | 43,505  | 48,730      |
| test_cache         | 9,868    | 1,045       | 8,823   | 9,868       |
| test_trig          | 9,871    | 1,024       | 8,847   | 9,871       |
| util_test_clone2   | 36,709   | 50,269      | 35,592  | 85,861      |
| welford_kindle     | 59,058   | 48,896      | 10,162  | 59,058      |
| world              | 472,785  | 445,728     | 27,057  | 472,785     |
+--------------------+----------+-------------+---------+-------------+

Total database disk usage = 1,081,112,742 bytes or 1.00 GB

# Log information.
+------------------------+--------------+
| log_name               |        size  |
+------------------------+--------------+
| Chucks-iMac.log        | 829,601,162  |
| Chucks-iMac-slow.log   |      97,783  |
| Chucks-iMac.local.err  |     234,028  |
+------------------------+--------------+

Total size of logs = 829,932,973 bytes or 791.00 MB

# binary log information:
Current binary log file = my_log.000171
+-----------------+----------+
| log_file        | size     |
+-----------------+----------+
| my_log.000001   | 3527     |
| my_log.000002   | 785115   |
| my_log.000003   | 569      |
...
| my_log.000169   | 348      |
| my_log.000170   | 258      |
| my_log.000171   | 722      |
| my_log.index    | 2736     |
+-----------------+----------+

Total size of binary logs = 21,883,426 bytes or 20.00 MB

# Server is not an active slave - no relay log information.
# InnoDB tablespace information:
+--------------+----------+-------------------+-------------------------+
| innodb_file  | size     | type              | specification           |
+--------------+----------+-------------------+-------------------------+
```

```
| ib_logfile0 | 5242880   | log file          |                         |
| ib_logfile1 | 5242880   | log file          |                         |
| ibdata1     | 815792128 | shared tablespace | ibdata1:778M            |
| ibdata2     | 52428800  | shared tablespace | ibdata2:50M:autoextend  |
+-------------+-----------+-------------------+-------------------------+

Total size of InnoDB files = 889,192,448 bytes or 848.00 MB

Tablespace ibdata2:50M:autoextend can be extended by using ibdata2:50M[...]

InnoDB freespace = 427,819,008 bytes or 408.00 MB

#...done.
```

Notice the list of binary logs. We have cut a long section of the results for brevity, but it is clear from the listing that the server has never had its binary logs purged. This is one area that may be a concern for servers that have been running for extended periods.

Checking Tables Indexes: mysqlindexcheck

One of the most highly scrutinized areas for improving queries is indexing. The index check utility *mysqlindexcheck* examines tables to determine whether there are duplicate or redundant indexes. Duplicate indexes are those that match exactly, while redundant indexes are those that are subsets of others. For example, if you have one index on the id and title columns (in that exact order) and another index on just the id column, the index on the single column is not needed. You would be surprised to see how often this occurs.

mysqlindexcheck can generate SQL statements for the DROP command for all indexes identified. You can also show the statistics of the indexes identified. This may be helpful in performance tuning specific index parameters.

Perhaps the most useful options display a list of the worst (or best) performing indexes. This can be invaluable when tuning your databases for better query performance.

Use with replication

Although this utility has no direct application to replication other than improving the performance of queries, you would do well to use the utility to help you improve the performance of your applications that run on a replication system.

Example of mysqlindexcheck

The following example shows the result of checking for duplicate and redundant indexes on the sample Sakila database (while no duplicate or redundant indexes are found, we included the --worst option to show the worst performing index for each table; we omit some of the data for brevity):

```
$ mysqlindexcheck --stats -d -s --server=root:pass@localhost sakila --worst=1
--format=vertical
# Source on localhost: ... connected.
#
# Showing the top 1 worst performing indexes from sakila.actor:
#
************************      1. row ************************
  database: sakila
     table: actor
      name: idx_actor_last_name
    column: last_name
  sequence: 1
num columns: 1
cardinality: 200
 est. rows: 200
   percent: 100.00
1 rows.
...
#
# Showing the top 1 worst performing indexes from sakila.rental:
#
************************      1. row ************************
  database: sakila
     table: rental
      name: idx_fk_staff_id
    column: staff_id
  sequence: 1
num columns: 1
cardinality: 1
 est. rows: 16305
   percent: 0.01
1 rows.
```

Searching Metadata: mysqlmetagrep

The metadata search utility, *mysqlmetagrep*, is another diagnostic tool that can aid in
finding objects that match a given pattern. This can be helpful any time you need to
locate an object that matches a name or partial name.

The utility has unique search capabilities that permit you to search using POSIX regular
expressions (REGEX) or SQL patterns (e.g., LIKE). You can restrict the search to specific
object types using the --object-types option, which accepts a comma-separated list
of one or more of the following: database, trigger, user, routine, column, table,
partition, event, and view. The default is to search all object types. Although the
default is to search by name, you can also instruct the utility to search the body of
procedures using the --body option.

You can also generate a SQL statement for the search that you can use inside other
routines or scripts.

The output can be formatted in the GRID, CSV, TAB, or VERTICAL formats described in "Exporting Databases: mysqldbexport" on page 625.

Use with replication

You may need to find objects by name if you encounter errors in your application or binary log that result in partial statements or errors and warnings with partial information.

Example of mysqlmetagrep

The following example shows a metadata search for objects with that start with the letter "t" (we signify this by providing the underscore characer after the t):

```
$ mysqlmetagrep --server=root:pass@localhost --pattern="t_" --format=vertical
*************************    1. row *************************
  Connection: root:*@localhost:3306
 Object Type: TABLE
 Object Name: t1
    Database: example1
  Field Type: TABLE
     Matches: t1
*************************    2. row *************************
  Connection: root:*@localhost:3306
 Object Type: TABLE
 Object Name: t1
    Database: test
  Field Type: TABLE
     Matches: t1
2 rows.
```

Searching for Processes: mysqlprocgrep

The process search utility, *mysqlprocgrep* permits you to search the running processes on a server via the same search capabilities as the metadata search utility, *mysqlmetagrep*. In this case, you can match the user, host, database, command, info, and state fields of the SHOW PROCESSLIST output. You can also query for processes by age, permitting you to identify long-running queries or long-term connections. Once you have identified the processes you are interested in, the utility will also permit you to kill either the query or the connection matching the search terms.

 Run the utility with general search terms until you identify the exact processes you want. You can then run the utility again, specifying the --kill-query or --kill-connection option to kill either the query or the connection for processes that match.

Like the metadata grep utility, you can use the `--sql` option to generate SQL statements for use in procedures or scripts.

Use with replication

The process search utility can be helpful with replication by identifying the connections for each slave or for a specific slave by user or host. We will see a unique use of this utility in the example.

Example of mysqlprocgrep

The following example shows a topology map generated by one of the replication utilities we will discuss later (see "Showing Topologies: mysqlrplshow" on page 648). In this case, there is a slave that was started without the `--report-host` and `--report-port` options (required by all replication utilities). We first show the topology map, which depicts a master and three slaves. Notice the warning. The utility has detected more than the three slaves. Using the process search utility we can find the fourth slave.

```
$ mysqlrplshow --master=root:pass@localhost:13002 --disco=root:pass
# master on localhost: ... connected.# Finding slaves for master: localhost:13002
WARNING: There are slaves that have not been registered with --report-host or
--report-port.

# Replication Topology Graph
localhost:13002 (MASTER)
    |
    +--- slavehost1:13001 - (SLAVE)
    |
    +--- slavehost3:13003 - (SLAVE)
    |
    +--- slavehost4:13004 - (SLAVE)

$ mysqlprocgrep --server=root:pass@localhost:13002 --match-command="Bin%"
--format=vertical
************************         1. row ************************
  Connection: root:*@localhost:13002
          Id: 10
        User: rpl
        Host: slavehost1:56901
          Db: None
     Command: Binlog Dump
        Time: 258
       State: Master has sent all binlog to slave; waiting for binlog to be up
        Info: None
************************         2. row ************************
  Connection: root:*@localhost:13002
          Id: 8
        User: rpl
        Host: slavehost3:56898
          Db: None
```

```
      Command: Binlog Dump
         Time: 261
        State: Master has sent all binlog to slave; waiting for binlog to be up
         Info: None
*************************        3. row *************************
   Connection: root:*@localhost:13002
           Id: 6
         User: rpl
         Host: slavehost4:56894
           Db: None
      Command: Binlog Dump
         Time: 264
        State: Master has sent all binlog to slave; waiting for binlog to be up
         Info: None
*************************        4. row *************************
   Connection: root:*@localhost:13002
           Id: 19
         User: rpl
         Host: localhost:56942
           Db: None
      Command: Binlog Dump
         Time: 18
        State: Master has sent all binlog to slave; waiting for binlog to be up
         Info: None
4 rows.
```

Cloning Servers: mysqlserverclone

The server clone utility, *mysqlserverclone*, is the workhorse of the bunch. It provides the ability to create a new instance of a server, either by connecting to a running server or by launching a server from a MySQL installation (via the --basedir option).

When you use this utility, you specify a new data directory and a new port. You can also specify a server ID and a password for the root user, and pass any special options to the *mysqld* process that will be started. If you use the --verbose option, the utility will print the server messages on startup; otherwise these are suppressed.

The new server will be started with a new database with only defaults set. For example, you will only see the mysql database (along with the INFORMATION_SCHEMA and PERFORMANCE_SCHEMA). If you want to copy data to the new server, you can use the database copy or the database export and import utilities.

Use with replication

This utility is very handy when you need to create a new slave in a hurry. On most systems, the utility takes only a few seconds to create the new data directory and launch the server. This makes it very easy to quickly set up a new replication slave or even an entire topology on a single server.

When you are faced with difficult diagnostics of binary logs, replication errors, and data consistency issues, you can use *mysqlserverclone* to create and test a master and slave quickly. You can then use them to conduct a forensic investigation of problems by duplicating the server instances and re-creating the error on the instances. This in turn saves you from risking harm to your existing servers.

Example of mysqlserverclone

The following example shows how to start a new instance of a server that may be offline or unreachable. Run this command on the host where MySQL was installed. The options passed include a new data directory, the new port, the new server_id, and a root password:

```
$ mysqlserverclone --basedir=/usr/local/mysql-5.6 --new-data=../temp_13001 \
  --new-port=13001 --new-id=101 --root=pass123 \
  --mysqld="--log-bin --gtid-mode=on --log-slave-updates
  --enforce-gtid-consistency"
# Cloning the MySQL server located at ../mysql-5.6.
# Creating new data directory...
# Configuring new instance...
# Locating mysql tools...
# Setting up empty database and mysql tables...
# Starting new instance of the server...
# Testing connection to new instance...
# Success!
# Setting the root password...
# Connection Information:
#  -uroot -ppass123 --socket=../temp_13001/mysql.sock
#...done.
```

The following example shows how easy it is to launch a new instance of a running server. Notice the options passed to the server process (*mysqld*) using the `--mysqld` option. Notice as well that we used the `--delete-data` option to delete the data directory if it exists. The utility will not start unless the data directory is empty or this option is present:

```
$ mysqlserverclone --server=root:root@localhost:13001 --new-data=../temp_13002 \
  --new-port=13002 --new-id=102 --root=pass123 \
  --mysqld="--log-bin --gtid-mode=on --log-slave-updates
  --enforce-gtid-consistency" \
  --delete-data
# Cloning the MySQL server running on localhost.
# Creating new data directory...
# Configuring new instance...
# Locating mysql tools...
# Setting up empty database and mysql tables...
# Starting new instance of the server...
# Testing connection to new instance...
# Success!
# Setting the root password...
# Connection Information:
```

```
#  -uroot -ppass123 --socket=/Volumes/Source/source/temp_13002/mysql.sock
#...done.
```

Showing Server Information: mysqlserverinfo

The show server information command, *mysqlserverinfo*, is another diagnostic utility. It is used to present the basic information about a server. It displays the major settings for the server, such as the base directory, data directory, configuration file, and more.

There are options for displaying the defaults read from the configuration file as well as an option to display a list of any MySQL servers running on the host where the utility is running. The command can display the information in a variety of formats, as described in "Exporting Databases: mysqldbexport" on page 625: GRID, CSV, TAB, and VERTICAL.

Use with replication

Like any diagnostic tool, this utility is applicable to all forms of problem investigation in replication. If used in conjunction with the server clone utility, you can quickly discover any cloned server instances.

Example of mysqlserverinfo

The following example shows this utility running on a server installed on the local host. The chosen options output the servers running on this host along with the defaults from the configuration file:

```
$ mysqlserverinfo --server=root:root@localhost:13001 --show-servers
--show-defaults --format=VERTICAL
#
# The following MySQL servers are active on this host:
# Process id:   236, Data path: /Users/cbell/source/temp_13001
# Process id:   331, Data path: /Users/cbell/source/temp_13002
# Process id:   426, Data path: /Users/cbell/source/temp_13003
# Process id:   431, Data path: /Users/cbell/source/temp_13004
#
# Source on localhost: ... connected.
*************************        1. row *************************
        server: localhost:13001
       version: 5.6.6-m9-log
       datadir: /Users/cbell/source/temp_13001/
       basedir: /Users/cbell/source/mysql-5.6/
    plugin_dir: /Users/cbell/source/mysql-5.6/lib/plugin/
   config_file: /etc/my.cnf
    binary_log: clone-bin.000001
binary_log_pos: 853
     relay_log: None
 relay_log_pos: None
1 rows.
```

```
Defaults for server localhost:13001
        --port=13001
        --basedir=/usr/local/mysql
        --datadir=/usr/local/mysql/data
        --server_id=5
        --log-bin=my_log
        --general_log
        --slow_query_log
        --innodb_data_file_path=ibdata1:778M;ibdata2:50M:autoextend
#...done
```

 You must be running on the localhost (the server) to use the --show-defaults option.

Cloning Users: mysqluserclone

Database administrators working on MySQL have often commented on the inconvenience of creating multiple users with the same set of privileges. Savvy administrators often write scripts to do this, usually including the actual GRANT statements and just substituting the username and host for each user they need to create.

This can be error prone especially when the privileges change over time. If security is a top priority, the location and access to the script may require special handling.

This seems like a lot of extra work. Fortunately, there is a utility to make it easier to copy (clone) users privileges. The user clone utility, *mysqluserclone*, copies all of the privileges for one user to one or more users, either on the same system or on another system. You can even set the password for each user you create.

The utility has a number of interesting features, including the ability to include the actual SQL statements during the clone operation and the ability to include global privileges that match the *user@host* specified. You can also list all of the users and their privileges on the server with the --list option. The output can be formatted in GRID, CSV, TAB, or VERTICAL formats described in "Exporting Databases: mysqldbexport" on page 625.

Use with replication

One area where this utility can be helpful is during the provisioning of a slave. In this case, you may have a new slave that you need to re-create the accounts that exist on the master. The user clone utility makes this as easy as specifying the user on the master (or another active slave) you want to clone and providing the connection information for the master and the new slave. You can even use an option to clone all users. Thus, this utility is another convenience utility to make slave provisioning easier.

Example of mysqluserclone

The following example clones a user account and her grants from one server to another. The first command prints (dumps) the GRANT statements for the user. The second performs the clone operation. Notice that we specify the user twice in the second command. This is because the utility allows you to clone other users from a single user account. So in this command, the first instance is the one you want to copy and the second is the new user you wish to create with the same privileges. You may specify as many new users as you want, each one a clone of the existing one that you are copying:

```
$ mysqluserclone --source=root:root@localhost:13002 joe@localhost --dump
# Source on localhost: ... connected.
Dumping grants for user joe@localhost
GRANT SELECT ON *.* TO 'joe'@'localhost'

$ mysqluserclone --source=root:root@localhost:13002
--destination=root:root@localhost:13003 joe@localhost joe@localhost
# Source on localhost: ... connected.
# Destination on localhost: ... connected.
# Cloning 1 users...
# Cloning joe@localhost to user joe@localhost
# ...done.
```

Utilities Client: mysqluc

The MySQL Utilities client, *mysqluc*, is not a utility in and of itself. Rather, it is a wrapper that provides type completion for utility commands, options, and parameters. It also lets you specify user-defined variables that enable repeated reuse of a single value.

Perhaps the best feature of the utilities client is the ability to get help for any utility, including itself. This makes using any of the utilities much easier and more convenient.

Use with replication

While the client offers no administrative features related directly to replication, it can be a very handy tool for running replication utilities. This is especially true when user-defined variables are used to represent the master and slave connections. Type completion will also help you to remember the various options and is especially helpful for seldom used options.

Example of mysqluc

The following example executes several commands inside the utilities console. The commands demonstrate how to display the health of a simple replication topology. We will discuss the replication administration (mysqlrpladmin) utility in more detail in a later section:

```
$ mysqluc
Launching console ...
```

```
Welcome to the MySQL Utilities Client (mysqluc) version 1.1.0 -
MySQL Workbench Distribution 5.2.44
Copyright (c) 2000, 2012, Oracle and/or its affiliates. All rights reserved.

Oracle is a registered trademark of Oracle Corporation and/or its affiliates.
Other names may be trademarks of their respective owners.

Type 'help' for a list of commands or press TAB twice for list of utilities.

mysqluc> help rpladmin
Usage: mysqlrpladmin.py --slaves=root@localhost:3306 <command>

mysqluc> set $MASTER=root:root@localhost:13001
mysqluc> set $DISCOVER=root:root
mysqluc> rpladmin --master=$MASTER --disco=$DISCOVER health
# Discovering slaves for master at localhost:13001
# Checking privileges.
#
# Replication Topology Health:
+------------+--------+---------+--------+------------+---------+
| host       | port   | role    | state  | gtid_mode  | health  |
+------------+--------+---------+--------+------------+---------+
| localhost  | 13001  | MASTER  | UP     | ON         | OK      |
| localhost  | 13002  | SLAVE   | UP     | ON         | OK      |
| localhost  | 13003  | SLAVE   | UP     | ON         | OK      |
| localhost  | 13004  | SLAVE   | UP     | ON         | OK      |
+------------+--------+---------+--------+------------+---------+
# ...done.

mysqluc>
```

Notice the commands issued in the client. Another very convenient feature of the client is you don't have to type the *mysql* prefix in the utility commands. Notice also the use of the user-defined variables, $MASTER and $DISCOVER, and detailed help for the replication administration utility. Clearly, this is a very handy tool.

Replication Utilities

This section includes a brief overview of the MySQL Utilities that were designed specially for replicated environments.

Setting Up Replication: mysqlreplicate

We have discussed setting up replication in detail in Chapter 3. In summary, once the replication prerequisites are met, the steps involve the following general operations:

1. Create the replication user on the master.

---

2. If not using GTIDs, check the master's `SHOW MASTER STATUS` view and record the values.

3. Issue the `CHANGE MASTER TO` command on the slave.

4. Issue the `START SLAVE` command on the slave.

5. Check for errors on the slave with `SHOW SLAVE STATUS`.

While this is not a long list of operations, it does involve at least one trip to the master to issue at least two commands and at least three commands on the slave. If you consider needing to do this many times for a large scale out effort, the operations can become tedious.

This is where the replicate utility *mysqlreplicate* makes life much easier. Instead of issuing five commands over the master and its slave, the replicate command permits you to issue a single command where, at a minimum, you list the master and the slave. The utility takes care of the rest. There are options for setting the replication user, testing the replication setup, and most importantly, controlling how replication starts.

Replication can start from the beginning (where the slave requests all events from the master), start from the first event in a particular binary log file, or start from a specific binary log file and position. The utility provides sufficient options to cover many scenarios where you want to start replication.

Best of all, because this is a single command, you can script it for use in a large scale out operation where you simply use a variable populated by a list of values for the slave (or even the master).

Example of mysqlreplicate

The following example shows a simple replication setup using the default options:

```
$ mysqlreplicate --master=root:root@localhost:13001
--slave=root:root@localhost:13002
# master on localhost: ... connected.
# slave on localhost: ... connected.
# Checking for binary logging on master...
# Setting up replication...
# ...done.
```

The following example shows the previous command executed with the -vvv option to request a high level of verbosity. Notice that all of the commands needed for replication configuration are performed by the utility, as well as key prerequisite checks. If something goes wrong setting up replication with this utility, try rerunning it with verbosity and check the output for errors:

```
$ mysqlreplicate --master=root:root@localhost:13001
--slave=root:root@localhost:13002 -vvv --test-db=test_rpl
# master on localhost: ... connected.
```

```
# slave on localhost: ... connected.
# master id = 101
#  slave id = 102
# master uuid = 8e1903fa-2de4-11e2-a8c9-59dc46c8181e
#  slave uuid = 8a40ec3a-2ded-11e2-a903-0ca829d3a6c5
# Checking InnoDB statistics for type and version conflicts.
# Checking storage engines...
# Checking for binary logging on master...
# Setting up replication...
# Connecting slave to master...
# CHANGE MASTER TO MASTER_HOST = 'localhost', MASTER_USER = 'rpl',
MASTER_PASSWORD = 'rpl', MASTER_PORT = 13001, MASTER_AUTO_POSITION=1
# Starting slave from master's last position...
# status: Waiting for master to send event
# error: 0:
# Testing replication setup...
# Creating a test database on master named test_rpl...
# Success! Replication is running.
# ...done.
```

Notice that we also used the `--test-db` option to test replication between the master
and slave. This feature creates a new database specified by the option and ensures the
slave receives the update. Thus, the utility permits you to ensure replication is working
once the slave is started.

This utility is the most useful replication utility for configuring your replication topology. However, for situations where you may not know the full configuration of the slave
or have many masters and many more slaves, it can be tedious to check whether replication is configured correctly or whether two servers can be made master and slave.
Fortunately, the next replication utility fills this need.

Checking Replication Setup: mysqlrplcheck

One of the challenges for setting up replication is knowing when a master and slave
have all of the prerequisites for replication and are compatible. "Compatible," in this
case, means the slave has the correct settings so that it can either rejoin the master or
connect to the master for the first time.

The replication check utility, *mysqlrplcheck*, examines the master and slave to determine
whether each is configured properly for replication (e.g., the master has binary logging
enabled), whether they are compatible, and whether the slave has been connected or is
connected to this master. This last feature can be very handy if you are uncertain to
which master your slave is connected—especially if you have recovered the slave from
an error condition.

Because the utility accepts one master and one slave, it is well suited to diagnostic and
administrative work on replication. If you run the utility with verbosity turned on at
the `-vvv` level, you will see additional details including the actual values for the UUIDs,

slave status, and more. Verbosity also gives you more information about error conditions.

Example of mysqlrplcheck

Let's see an example where a master and slave are not connected and there are configuration conflicts. The following output shows a number of issues with replication between the chose master and slave (we use the verbosity option to see the additional details):

```
$ mysqlrplcheck --master=root:root@localhost:13001
--slave=root:root@localhost:13002 -vvv
# master on localhost: ... connected.
# slave on localhost: ... connected.
Test Description                                              Status
---------------------------------------------------------------------
Checking for binary logging on master                        [pass]
Are there binlog exceptions?                                 [pass]
Replication user exists?                                     [FAIL]

Slave is not connected to a master.

Checking server_id values                                    [FAIL]

The slave's server_id is the same as the master.

Checking server_uuid values                                  [pass]

  master uuid = 8e1903fa-2de4-11e2-a8c9-59dc46c8181e
   slave uuid = d722e59c-2de5-11e2-a8d1-3f758e665783

Is slave connected to master?                                [FAIL]

Slave is stopped.

Check master information file                                [pass]

#
# Master information file:
#
# Reading master information from a table.

Checking InnoDB compatibility                                [pass]
Checking storage engines compatibility                       [pass]
Checking lower_case_table_names settings                     [pass]

   Master lower_case_table_names: 2
    Slave lower_case_table_names: 2

Checking slave delay (seconds behind master)                 [FAIL]
```

```
The server specified as the slave is not configured as a replication slave.
```

```
# ...done.
```

Notice the problems revealed in the output. Because the slave is not connected to the master, a number of checks or tests fail, including the replication use check, whether the slave is connected, and the slave delay. But most importantly, we see that the server_ids are the same on the master and slave: a common problem that makes it impossible to set up replication.

 If the slave were connected to the master and there were errors, the verbosity option would display the output of the SHOW SLAVE STA TUS view.

The following example shows a successful execution of the utility (now we know that the master and slave are configured correctly, and that replication between them is working correctly):

```
$ mysqlrplcheck --master=root:root@localhost:13001
--slave=root:root@localhost:13002
# master on localhost: ... connected.
# slave on localhost: ... connected.
Test Description                                             Status
--------------------------------------------------------------------
Checking for binary logging on master                       [pass]
Are there binlog exceptions?                                 [pass]
Replication user exists?                                     [pass]
Checking server_id values                                    [pass]
Checking server_uuid values                                  [pass]
Is slave connected to master?                                [pass]
Check master information file                                [pass]
Checking InnoDB compatibility                                [pass]
Checking storage engines compatibility                       [pass]
Checking lower_case_table_names settings                     [pass]
Checking slave delay (seconds behind master)                 [pass]
# ...done.
```

Now that we have a nice replication setup and checking utility, it would be great if we could see our topology in a graph. The next utility was designed to allow you to discover your topology. Its core functionality is essential for the HA utilities, which we will discuss in the next section.

Showing Topologies: mysqlrplshow

Another useful utility for replication is the ability to see a graph of your topology. The show replication utility, *mysqlrplshow*, shows the slaves attached to a given master. Slaves must be started with `--report-host` and `--report-port` so that they show in the SHOW SLAVE HOSTS view.

If you provide the `--recurse` option, the utility will attempt to connect to each slave and display its slaves. In this manner, the utility can discover the topology for as many servers as can be reached with the credentials provided by the `--discover-slaves-login` option.

 You can use the `--prompt` option to prompt for the username and password for each slave that fails to connect with the default credentials provided.

The utility can also identify circular replication topologies. If you use the `--show-list` option, the utility displays a list of the servers in a variety of formats. The formats are the familiar GRID, CSV, TAB, and VERTICAL options. The output could be imported into another script of application for further analysis or reports.

Example of mysqlrplshow

The following example demonstrates the utility running on a simple tiered replication topology. Notice that there is an intermediate master on slavehost2.

```
$ mysqlrplshow --master=root:pass@masterhost:13001 --recurse \
  --discover-slaves-login=root:root --format=grid --show-list
# master on masterhost: ... connected.
# Finding slaves for master: localhost:13001
# master on slavehost1: ... connected.
# Finding slaves for master: localhost:13002
# master on slavehost2: ... connected.
# Finding slaves for master: localhost:13003
# master on slavehost3: ... connected.
# Finding slaves for master: localhost:13004

# Replication Topology Graph
masterhost:13001 (MASTER)
   |
   +--- slavehost1:13002 - (SLAVE)
   |
   +--- slavehost2:13003 - (SLAVE + MASTER)
       |
       +--- slavehost3:13004 - (SLAVE)

+------------------+------------------+
| Master           | Slave            |
+------------------+------------------+
| masterhost:13001 | slavehost1:13002 |
| masterhost:13001 | slavehost2:13003 |
```

```
| slavelhost:13002  | slavehost3:13004  |
+-------------------+-------------------+
```

High Availability Utilities

The MySQL Utilities project includes two utilities that are designed specifically for HA solutions. There is a general utility for performing routine, on-demand operations (*mysqlrpladmin*), and another designed to run continuously to monitor a master and its slaves (*mysqlfailover*).

The following sections present details of these utilities along with examples of their use and a discussion of scenarios for using the utilities.

Concepts

We begin with a discussion of the concepts used in the HA utilities. As with many specialized tools, there are often ideas or concepts that the user is expected to understand prior to using the tool. For example, the HA utilities are designed to perform two basic operations: switchover and failover. The following will help you understand the modes, commands, and output of the utilities and make your experience using them better. Some of these may be familiar but are included for review.

 We assume you have read the previous chapters on replication and high availability, including Chapters 4, 5, and 6, and have a good understanding of replication terminology.

Global Transaction Identifiers

A Global Transaction Identifier (GTID) is a special marker added to the binary log that includes a unique value to identify the origin of the event. These marks are added before each group of events (transactions) in the binary log and are composed of the Unique Universal Identifier (UUID) of the server and a sequence number. The sequence number is ordinal starting from 1.

GTIDs therefore enable a new replication protocol that permits the slave to request any GTIDs it has not executed from the master. The calculation of what GTIDs have or have not been applied is simplified and made accurate by the uniqueness of the GTID.

This new concept and the new protocol make it possible to take any slave of a downed master and make it the new master by collecting the GTIDs from the other slaves. Thus, for the first time, MySQL has a native mechanism to enable failover.

GTIDs must be enabled (the `gtid_mode=ON` option to *mysqld*) if you plan to run the *mysqlfailover* utility and to execute the failover command for the *mysqlrpladmin* utility.

Candidate slave

A *candidate slave* is a slave that has been chosen to replace the master when the master has gone down or is unreachable. The candidate slave can be chosen automatically from those meeting all the following criteria:

- The slave is running and reachable.
- GTIDs are enabled.
- The slave is not lagging behind the master.
- The slave's replication filters do not conflict. More specifically, the list of databases in the filters have matches. For example, if the master has *db1* and *db3* listed in `--binlog-do-db` and a slave had *db1* and *db2* listed in `--replicate-do-db`, these filters conflict because the data replicated to the slave is different from what the slave is filtering from the master.
- The replication user exists on the slave.
- Binary logging is enabled on the slave.

Slave election

This is the process of selecting a candidate slave for use in replacing the master. The utilities have a feature that includes this step as a precursor to failover.

Failover

Failover is the process of replacing the role of the master when the master is down or has become unreachable.

Switchover

Switchover is the purposeful switching of the master role from a live master to another slave. It is different from failover because in this case, the master is available and the new slave can be brought up to date with all events from the master. You may perform switchover, for instance, when you have to take the master offline for maintenance.

mysqlrpladmin

The *mysqlrpladmin* utility permits administrators to execute operations on MySQL replication resources on-demand (i.e., it executes a command and then exits). Available commands include:

`elect`
Elect the best slave and report the winner.

failover
Conduct a failover from the master to the best slave.

gtid
Show the status of Global Transaction Identifier variables, and display UUIDs for all servers.

health
Display the replication health for the master and its slaves.

reset
Issue the STOP SLAVE and RESET SLAVE commands to each slave.

start
Start all slaves.

stop
Stop all slaves.

switchover
Perform slave promotion.

The next section presents examples of the more frequently used commands and practical ways they can be used.

Examples of mysqlrpladmin

Let us begin the tour of the replication administration utility with the health command. This displays a list of the slaves connected to the master and a summary of the status for slave and replication health. The following example shows a master and its slaves. Notice we used the discovery option (-disco), passing the user and password to be used to connect to each slave. If you want to see more details for the health report, use the --verbose option:

```
$ mysqlrpladmin --master=root:pass@localhost:13002 --disco=root:pass health
# Discovering slaves for master at localhost:13002
# Checking privileges.
#
# Replication Topology Health:
+------------+--------+---------+--------+-------------+---------+
| host       | port   | role    | state  | gtid_mode   | health  |
+------------+--------+---------+--------+-------------+---------+
| localhost  | 13002  | MASTER  | UP     | ON          | OK      |
| localhost  | 13003  | SLAVE   | UP     | ON          | OK      |
| localhost  | 13004  | SLAVE   | UP     | ON          | OK      |
| localhost  | 13005  | SLAVE   | UP     | ON          | OK      |
+------------+--------+---------+--------+-------------+---------+
# ...done.
```

Remember that you must start your slaves with the `--report-host` and `--report-port` options to use the discover slaves feature.

If you want to use the failover command rather than the failover utility to conduct manual failover, the elect command permits you to look ahead to see which slave will be chosen for failover. This can be helpful when building a fault-tolerant application where you need to know specifics of the new master. The following example shows how to find out which slave will be chosen:

```
$ mysqlrpladmin --master=root:pass@localhost:13002 --disco=root:pass elect
# Discovering slaves for master at localhost:13002
# Checking privileges.
# Electing candidate slave from known slaves.
# Best slave found is located on localhost:13003.
# ...done.
```

The GTID command displays a list of all of the GTIDs in the topology. This can be a very long list if your master and slaves have been running for a long period with many transactions. You can use this report to help diagnose problems with transactions. The following shows an excerpt of the output of the GTID command:

```
$ mysqlrpladmin --master=root:pass@localhost:13002 --disco=root:pass gtid
# Discovering slaves for master at localhost:13002
# Checking privileges.
#
# UUIDS for all servers:
+-----------+--------+---------+--------------------------------------+
| host      | port   | role    | uuid                                 |
+-----------+--------+---------+--------------------------------------+
| localhost | 13002  | MASTER  | 673d40e4-32ac-11e2-87f6-419d4fb292c5 |
| localhost | 13003  | SLAVE   | 7cb05e3e-32ac-11e2-87f6-336560b463d4 |
| localhost | 13004  | SLAVE   | 940abcdc-32ac-11e2-87f7-9f158c80ded6 |
| localhost | 13005  | SLAVE   | a680695c-32ac-11e2-87f7-797d07ab4557 |
+-----------+--------+---------+--------------------------------------+
#
# Transactions executed on the server:
+-----------+--------+---------+--------------------------------------------+
| host      | port   | role    | gtid                                       |
+-----------+--------+---------+--------------------------------------------+
| localhost | 13002  | MASTER  | 0035A78A-32AF-11E2-8807-6F5662E76235:1-2   |
| localhost | 13002  | MASTER  | 42077312-32AC-11E2-87F5-4FD43CAEB376:1-2   |
| localhost | 13002  | MASTER  | 498880AE-32B1-11E2-8815-C19FD75A3D21:1-2   |
| localhost | 13002  | MASTER  | 4AA055C2-32AF-11E2-8808-366E88604744:1-2   |
| localhost | 13002  | MASTER  | 59D25A04-32AF-11E2-8809-6D4E4056F0AF:1-2   |
| localhost | 13002  | MASTER  | 5D3211AC-32B0-11E2-880F-F6735C743197:1-2   |
| localhost | 13002  | MASTER  | 673D40E4-32AC-11E2-87F6-419D4FB292C5:1-3   |
| localhost | 13002  | MASTER  | 74151132-32AE-11E2-8803-E93E7AABEB97:1-2   |
```

```
| localhost  | 13002  | MASTER  | 7CB05E3E-32AC-11E2-87F6-336560B463D4:1-3  |
...
| localhost  | 13005  | SLAVE   | 7CB05E3E-32AC-11E2-87F6-336560B463D4:1-3  |
| localhost  | 13005  | SLAVE   | 940ABCDC-32AC-11E2-87F7-9F158C80DED6:1-3  |
| localhost  | 13005  | SLAVE   | 9E6957E4-32AF-11E2-880B-C19ED44E0636:1-2  |
| localhost  | 13005  | SLAVE   | A680695C-32AC-11E2-87F7-797D07AB4557:1-3  |
| localhost  | 13005  | SLAVE   | C903D9AC-32AF-11E2-880C-6D4F415B0402:1-2  |
| localhost  | 13005  | SLAVE   | F37C4048-32AF-11E2-880D-CFD6C34C3629:1-2  |
+------------+--------+---------+-------------------------------------------+
# ...done.
```

The most popular command of the replication administration utility is the switchover command. This permits you to perform a controlled switch of the master role from the current master to a specified slave. We say "controlled" because the slave is allowed to catch up to the master before the change of role occurs.

A very handy option for this command is the --demote-master option. This tells the switchover command to make the old master a slave of the new master once the change of role is complete. This permits you to rotate the role of master among a set of slaves. The following example shows this command in action. Notice the health report at the end of the execution. You can use this to verify the change of role. Compare this to the health report from the earlier examples.

Take a moment and look through the output; all of the steps in the switchover process are documented with brief status statements.

```
$ mysqlrpladmin --master=root:pass@localhost:13003 --disco=root:pass failover
# Discovering slaves for master at localhost:13003
# Checking privileges.
# Performing failover.
# Candidate slave localhost:13002 will become the new master.
# Preparing candidate for failover.
# Creating replication user if it does not exist.
# Stopping slaves.
# Performing STOP on all slaves.
# Switching slaves to new master.
# Starting slaves.
# Performing START on all slaves.
# Checking slaves for errors.
# Failover complete.
#
# Replication Topology Health:
+------------+--------+---------+--------+------------+---------+
| host       | port   | role    | state  | gtid_mode  | health  |
+------------+--------+---------+--------+------------+---------+
| localhost  | 13002  | MASTER  | UP     | ON         | OK      |
| localhost  | 13004  | SLAVE   | UP     | ON         | OK      |
| localhost  | 13005  | SLAVE   | UP     | ON         | OK      |
+------------+--------+---------+--------+------------+---------+
# ...done.
```

We save the failover command for last to show you how it can be used manually in place of the failover utility, which is designed to support automatic failover. The following shows the results of running the failover command. Notice that this command also prints a health report at the end to confirm the operation.

Take a moment and look through the output; all of the steps in the failover process are documented with brief status statements.

```
$ mysqlrpladmin --master=root:pass@localhost:13003 --disco=root:pass failover
# Discovering slaves for master at localhost:13003
# Checking privileges.
# Performing failover.
# Candidate slave localhost:13002 will become the new master.
# Preparing candidate for failover.
# Creating replication user if it does not exist.
# Stopping slaves.
# Performing STOP on all slaves.
# Switching slaves to new master.
# Starting slaves.
# Performing START on all slaves.
# Checking slaves for errors.
# Failover complete.
#
# Replication Topology Health:
+------------+--------+---------+--------+------------+---------+
| host       | port   | role    | state  | gtid_mode  | health  |
+------------+--------+---------+--------+------------+---------+
| localhost  | 13002  | MASTER  | UP     | ON         | OK      |
| localhost  | 13004  | SLAVE   | UP     | ON         | OK      |
| localhost  | 13005  | SLAVE   | UP     | ON         | OK      |
+------------+--------+---------+--------+------------+---------+
# ...done.
```

mysqlfailover

The failover utility is not a run-once type of utility. Rather, it is a utility designed to run interactively. The failover utility is also called the *failover console*, but it is a command-line tool and purely text based.

The console can be run on any system but should be run on a system that can be monitored closely. It would not fare well for your failover strategy if the server on which the automatic failover utility runs happens to be offline should the master fail. Also, if you have multiple masters in your topology, you will need to run one (and only one) instance of the utility and connect each to one and only one master.

The console is also designed to be used with GTID-enabled servers and will not work with non-GTID enabled servers.

Because it is an interactive utility, there are a number of menu commands you can choose once the console is started. Let's take a look at what the console looks like when connected to master with four slaves:

```
$ mysqlfailover --master=root:pass@localhost:13001 --disco=root:pass
--log=failover_log.txt
# Discovering slaves for master at localhost:13001
# Checking privileges.
[...]
MySQL Replication Failover Utility
Failover Mode = auto    Next Interval = Mon Nov 19 20:00:49 2012

Master Information
------------------
Binary Log File    Position  Binlog_Do_DB  Binlog_Ignore_DB
clone-bin.000001   574

GTID Executed Set
42077312-32AC-11E2-87F5-4FD43CAEB376:1-2

Replication Health Status
+------------+--------+---------+--------+------------+--------+
| host       | port   | role    | state  | gtid_mode  | health |
+------------+--------+---------+--------+------------+--------+
| localhost  | 13001  | MASTER  | UP     | ON         | OK     |
| localhost  | 13002  | SLAVE   | UP     | ON         | OK     |
| localhost  | 13003  | SLAVE   | UP     | ON         | OK     |
| localhost  | 13004  | SLAVE   | UP     | ON         | OK     |
| localhost  | 13005  | SLAVE   | UP     | ON         | OK     |
+------------+--------+---------+--------+------------+--------+

Q-quit R-refresh H-health G-GTID Lists U-UUIDs L-log entries
```

 The [...] in the preceding listing represents a screen refresh. The failover console is designed to fill a text command window (terminal). Thus, the line that reads, "MySQL Replication Failover Utility" appears on the top line of the window.

The console displays the master information at the top, including the current log file and position as well as the GTID executed set. Below that is a health report—the same as the replication administration utility, *mysqlrpladmin*.

At the bottom of the screen is the menu. Select from the following items using the key specified as the capital letter preceding the label:

Quit

Exit the console.

Refresh

Refreshes the health report. Use this command while viewing the health report to refresh the data before the next interval.

Health

Displays the health report. Use this command to switch the view to the health report.

GTID Lists

Shows the GTIDs for the master's executed set, the slave's executed GTIDs, slave's purged GTIDs, and slave's owned GTIDs. Pressing G repeatedly will cycle through all of the lists. Use this command to switch the view to the list of UUIDs.

UUIDs

Shows the UUIDs for all servers. Use this command to switch the view to the list of UUIDs.

Log Entries

Read and display the rows in the failover log file. This item is displayed only if this log file is enabled.

The failover console is designed to check the status of the master at fixed intervals. The default is every 15 seconds. You can change this frequency using the `--interval` option.

One of the interesting features of the failover console is the ability to generate a log of the operations taking place. Each statement and status item is saved in the log. You can turn on the log with the `--log-file` option, specifying a path and filename for the log file. The log file is appended rather than rewritten by default, but you can use the `--log-age=N` option to tell the utility to overwrite entries older than *N* number of days.

The log file can be very useful in situations where you need to keep a permanent record of events or if you desire a higher level of audit capability.

Another useful option is the `--rediscover` option. This instructs the utility to rerun the slave discovery feature on each interval. Use this option if you want the failover console to detect when new slaves are added.

Failover modes

The failover console permits several modes of operation. This permits you to run the failover console in the manner most appropriate to your environment or requirements. The following describes each mode (the default mode is AUTO):

AUTO

Execute automatic failover to the list of candidates first. If no candidate slaves are viable, continue to locate a viable candidate from the list of slaves. If no slaves are found to be a viable candidate, generate an error and exit.

Once a candidate is found, the utility will conduct a failover to the best slave. The command will test each candidate slave listed for the prerequisites. Once a candidate slave is elected, it is made a slave of each of the other slaves, thereby collecting any transactions that were executed on other slaves but not the candidate. In this way, the candidate becomes the most up-to-date slave.

ELECT

This mode is the same as AUTO except that, if no candidates specified in the list of candidate slaves are viable, it does not check the remaining slaves, but generates an error and exits. Use this mode if you have a subset of slaves you want to use for failover, where the remaining slaves are not eligible. For example, you may want to exclude slaves with older or inferior hardware.

FAIL

Produces an error and does not failover when the master is down. This mode is used to provide periodic health monitoring without taking a failover action.

The failover event

A failover event occurs when the master can neither be reached via a database connection nor pinged. This check occurs once per interval. When both tests fail, the failover event is initiated.

The failover detection is also tunable. You can use the `--ping` option to tell the utility how many ping attempts to use before considering the master offline. You can use an external script to control the failover detection. "Extension points" on page 663 explains how to use an external script to initiate the failover event.

The following process summarizes the steps executed during the failover event. This is a generalized list based on the default failover mode. The process is slightly different for slave election depending on the mode (see "Failover modes" on page 657):

- A new candidate slave is elected as follows. If the `--candidate-slaves` option is specified, the slaves are tested in the order they appear. If none of these slaves meet the prerequisites in "Candidate slave" on page 651, and the `--slaves` option is specified, the slaves are tested in the order they appear. If none of these slaves are elected, the utility will test each slave it can discover. Because the prerequisites are not stringent, it is likely that the first candidate slave will be the first slave listed in the `--candidate-slaves` option.

- Once the candidate slave is elected, it is made a slave of every other slave. This utilizes the new replication protocol that ensures that the candidate slave retrieves any transactions that have executed on another slave but not this candidate slave.

- Now that the candidate slave is up to date with all transactions, it is made the new master.

- Lastly, the remaining slaves are connected to the new master and replication is restarted.

When this process runs, the failover console switches temporarily into a list mode where it lists status statements for each step of the process. If you use the --verbose option, the utility will display all of the details of the operations.

The following example shows a failover event in progress. Notice that you can see all of the GTIDs involved and even the CHANGE MASTER commands as they are run. If you turned on the log feature, all of these statements would appear in the log file as well:

```
Failover starting in 'auto' mode...
# Checking eligibility of slave localhost:13002 for candidate.
#   GTID_MODE=ON ... Ok
#   Replication user exists ... Ok
# Candidate slave localhost:13002 will become the new master.
# Preparing candidate for failover.
# LOCK STRING: FLUSH TABLES WITH READ LOCK
# Connecting candidate to localhost:13003 as a master to retrieve
unprocessed GTIDs.
# Change master command for localhost:13002
# CHANGE MASTER TO MASTER_HOST = 'localhost', MASTER_USER = 'rpl',
MASTER_PASSWORD = 'rpl', MASTER_PORT = 13003, MASTER_AUTO_POSITION=1
# UNLOCK STRING: UNLOCK TABLES
# Waiting for candidate to catch up to slave localhost:13003.
# Slave localhost:13002:
# QUERY = SELECT SQL_THREAD_WAIT_AFTER_GTIDS('0035A78A-32AF-11E2-8807-
6F5662E76235:1-2', 3)
# Return Code = 0
# Slave localhost:13002:
# QUERY = SELECT SQL_THREAD_WAIT_AFTER_GTIDS('42077312-32AC-11E2-87F5-
4FD43CAEB376:1-2', 3)
# Return Code = 0
# Slave localhost:13002:
# QUERY = SELECT SQL_THREAD_WAIT_AFTER_GTIDS('498880AE-32B1-11E2-8815-
C19FD75A3D21:1-2', 3)
# Return Code = 0
# Slave localhost:13002:
# QUERY = SELECT SQL_THREAD_WAIT_AFTER_GTIDS('74151132-32AE-11E2-8803-
E93E7AABEB97:1-2', 3)
# Return Code = 0
# Slave localhost:13002:
# QUERY = SELECT SQL_THREAD_WAIT_AFTER_GTIDS('7CB05E3E-32AC-11E2-87F6-
336560B463D4:1-3', 3)
# Return Code = 0
# Slave localhost:13002:
# QUERY = SELECT SQL_THREAD_WAIT_AFTER_GTIDS('9E6957E4-32AF-11E2-880B-
C19ED44E0636:1-2', 3)
# Return Code = 0
# Slave localhost:13002:
# QUERY = SELECT SQL_THREAD_WAIT_AFTER_GTIDS('F37C4048-32AF-11E2-880D-
```

```
CFD6C34C3629:1-2', 3)
# Return Code = 0
# LOCK STRING: FLUSH TABLES WITH READ LOCK
# Connecting candidate to localhost:13004 as a master to retrieve
unprocessed GTIDs.
# Change master command for localhost:13002
# CHANGE MASTER TO MASTER_HOST = 'localhost', MASTER_USER = 'rpl',
MASTER_PASSWORD = 'rpl', MASTER_PORT = 13004, MASTER_AUTO_POSITION=1
# UNLOCK STRING: UNLOCK TABLES
# Waiting for candidate to catch up to slave localhost:13004.
# Slave localhost:13002:
# QUERY = SELECT SQL_THREAD_WAIT_AFTER_GTIDS('0035A78A-32AF-11E2-8807-
6F5662E76235:1-2', 3)
# Return Code = 0
# Slave localhost:13002:
# QUERY = SELECT SQL_THREAD_WAIT_AFTER_GTIDS('42077312-32AC-11E2-87F5-
4FD43CAEB376:1-2', 3)
# Return Code = 0
# Slave localhost:13002:
# QUERY = SELECT SQL_THREAD_WAIT_AFTER_GTIDS('498880AE-32B1-11E2-8815-
C19FD75A3D21:1-2', 3)
# Return Code = 0
# Slave localhost:13002:
# QUERY = SELECT SQL_THREAD_WAIT_AFTER_GTIDS('74151132-32AE-11E2-8803-
E93E7AABEB97:1-2', 3)
# Return Code = 0
# Slave localhost:13002:
# QUERY = SELECT SQL_THREAD_WAIT_AFTER_GTIDS('940ABCDC-32AC-11E2-87F7-
9F158C80DED6:1-3', 3)
# Return Code = 5
# Slave localhost:13002:
# QUERY = SELECT SQL_THREAD_WAIT_AFTER_GTIDS('9E6957E4-32AF-11E2-880B-
C19ED44E0636:1-2', 3)
# Return Code = 0
# Slave localhost:13002:
# QUERY = SELECT SQL_THREAD_WAIT_AFTER_GTIDS('F37C4048-32AF-11E2-880D-
CFD6C34C3629:1-2', 3)
# Return Code = 0
# LOCK STRING: FLUSH TABLES WITH READ LOCK
# Connecting candidate to localhost:13005 as a master to retrieve
unprocessed GTIDs.
# Change master command for localhost:13002
# CHANGE MASTER TO MASTER_HOST = 'localhost', MASTER_USER = 'rpl',
MASTER_PASSWORD = 'rpl', MASTER_PORT = 13005, MASTER_AUTO_POSITION=1
# UNLOCK STRING: UNLOCK TABLES
# Waiting for candidate to catch up to slave localhost:13005.
# Slave localhost:13002:
# QUERY = SELECT SQL_THREAD_WAIT_AFTER_GTIDS('0035A78A-32AF-11E2-8807-
6F5662E76235:1-2', 3)
# Return Code = 0
# Slave localhost:13002:
# QUERY = SELECT SQL_THREAD_WAIT_AFTER_GTIDS('42077312-32AC-11E2-87F5-
```

```
4FD43CAEB376:1-2', 3)
# Return Code = 0
# Slave localhost:13002:
# QUERY = SELECT SQL_THREAD_WAIT_AFTER_GTIDS('498880AE-32B1-11E2-8815-
C19FD75A3D21:1-2', 3)
# Return Code = 0
# Slave localhost:13002:
# QUERY = SELECT SQL_THREAD_WAIT_AFTER_GTIDS('4AA055C2-32AF-11E2-8808-
366E88604744:1-2', 3)
# Return Code = 5
# Slave localhost:13002:
# QUERY = SELECT SQL_THREAD_WAIT_AFTER_GTIDS('59D25A04-32AF-11E2-8809-
6D4E4056F0AF:1-2', 3)
# Return Code = 0
# Slave localhost:13002:
# QUERY = SELECT SQL_THREAD_WAIT_AFTER_GTIDS('5D3211AC-32B0-11E2-880F-
F6735C743197:1-2', 3)
# Return Code = 0
# Slave localhost:13002:
# QUERY = SELECT SQL_THREAD_WAIT_AFTER_GTIDS('74151132-32AE-11E2-8803-
E93E7AABEB97:1-2', 3)
# Return Code = 0
# Slave localhost:13002:
# QUERY = SELECT SQL_THREAD_WAIT_AFTER_GTIDS('9E6957E4-32AF-11E2-880B-
C19ED44E0636:1-2', 3)
# Return Code = 0
# Slave localhost:13002:
# QUERY = SELECT SQL_THREAD_WAIT_AFTER_GTIDS('A680695C-32AC-11E2-87F7-
797D07AB4557:1-3', 3)
# Return Code = 0
# Slave localhost:13002:
# QUERY = SELECT SQL_THREAD_WAIT_AFTER_GTIDS('C903D9AC-32AF-11E2-880C-
6D4F415B0402:1-2', 3)
# Return Code = 0
# Slave localhost:13002:
# QUERY = SELECT SQL_THREAD_WAIT_AFTER_GTIDS('F37C4048-32AF-11E2-880D-
CFD6C34C3629:1-2', 3)
# Return Code = 0
# Creating replication user if it does not exist.
# Stopping slaves.
# Performing STOP on all slaves.
#    Executing stop on slave localhost:13002 Ok
#    Executing stop on slave localhost:13003 Ok
#    Executing stop on slave localhost:13004 Ok
#    Executing stop on slave localhost:13005 Ok
# Switching slaves to new master.
# Change master command for localhost:13002
# CHANGE MASTER TO MASTER_HOST = 'localhost', MASTER_USER = 'rpl',
MASTER_PASSWORD = 'rpl', MASTER_PORT = 13002, MASTER_AUTO_POSITION=1
# Change master command for localhost:13003
# CHANGE MASTER TO MASTER_HOST = 'localhost', MASTER_USER = 'rpl',
MASTER_PASSWORD = 'rpl', MASTER_PORT = 13002, MASTER_AUTO_POSITION=1
```

```
# Change master command for localhost:13004
# CHANGE MASTER TO MASTER_HOST = 'localhost', MASTER_USER = 'rpl',
MASTER_PASSWORD = 'rpl', MASTER_PORT = 13002, MASTER_AUTO_POSITION=1
# Change master command for localhost:13005
# CHANGE MASTER TO MASTER_HOST = 'localhost', MASTER_USER = 'rpl',
MASTER_PASSWORD = 'rpl', MASTER_PORT = 13002, MASTER_AUTO_POSITION=1
# Starting slaves.
# Performing START on all slaves.
#    Executing start on slave localhost:13003 Ok
#    Executing start on slave localhost:13004 Ok
#    Executing start on slave localhost:13005 Ok
# Checking slaves for errors.
# localhost:13003 status: Ok
# localhost:13004 status: Ok
# localhost:13005 status: Ok
# Failover complete.
# Discovering slaves for master at localhost:13002

Failover console will restart in 5 seconds.
```

Once the failover event is complete, the console is redrawn with the new master information and the updated list of slaves in the health report. Based on the previous examples, the resulting health report after failover follows:

```
MySQL Replication Failover Utility
Failover Mode = auto      Next Interval = Mon Nov 19 20:28:03 2012

Master Information
------------------
Binary Log File    Position  Binlog_Do_DB  Binlog_Ignore_DB
clone-bin.000001   7073

GTID Executed Set
0035A78A-32AF-11E2-8807-6F5662E76235:1-2 [...]

Replication Health Status
+------------+--------+---------+--------+-------------+---------+
| host       | port   | role    | state  | gtid_mode   | health  |
+------------+--------+---------+--------+-------------+---------+
| localhost  | 13002  | MASTER  | UP     | ON          | OK      |
| localhost  | 13003  | SLAVE   | UP     | ON          | OK      |
| localhost  | 13004  | SLAVE   | UP     | ON          | OK      |
| localhost  | 13005  | SLAVE   | UP     | ON          | OK      |
+------------+--------+---------+--------+-------------+---------+

Q-quit R-refresh H-health G-GTID Lists U-UUIDs L-log entries
```

Notice that the original master on port 13001 is no longer displayed and the elected slave has become the new master with all slaves connected.

Extension points

To make the failover utility more flexible, it supports four extension points that you can use to call your own scripts. This can be very helpful in tailoring your fault tolerant application to interact with the failover console. The following lists the extension points available and how each can be used (they are listed in the order in which they occur during a failover event):

`--exec-fail-check`
> This option permits you to provide an application-specific failover event. This replaces the default failover detection criteria (master cannot be reached and cannot be pinged) with your own event detection. A return code of 0 indicates that failover should not take place. A return code other than 0 indicates that failover should take place. The script is run at the start of each interval. The timeout option is not used in this case.

`--exec-before`
> The utility runs this script before the failover event occurs. You can use this to tell your application to halt all writes and prepare for changing the master.

`--exec-after`
> The utility runs this script after the failover event occurs but before the slaves are switched to the new master. You can use this to inform your application that the new master is ready.

`--exec-post-failover`
> The utility runs this utility after the slaves are redirected to the new master and the health report is generated. You can use this to inform your application that it can read from the slaves again.

Creating Your Own Utilities

Now that you know what the MySQL Utilities are and how they are used with replication, you may have ideas for new uses of these utilities or even new utilities that you would like to have that are specific to your environment. Fortunately, MySQL Utilities was designed with this kind of major extension in mind. This section covers the architecture and organization of the MySQL Utilities. We will also discuss an example of a custom utility that you can create yourself or use as a template for custom replication utilities.

Architecture of MySQL Utilities

Utilities are built using a single script responsible for defining and validating options and arguments. The script (also referred to by the name of the utility) references a series of modules that contain Python classes and methods for the operations they perform. These are called *command modules*. These are the interface to a larger set of Python classes and methods that are designed to model specific components or behaviors of the server. We call the files that contain these classes and methods *common modules*. Both command and common modules use the Connector/Python connector to connect to a MySQL Server.

The MySQL Utilities library therefore is the collection of all of the command and common modules. These files are stored together under the same folder. If you were to download the MySQL Utilities source code, you would see folders named */scripts*, */mysql/utilities/command*, and */mysql/utilities/common*.

Figure 17-3 shows the relationships between the parts of MySQL Utilities and therefore how each utility is built. For example, the *mysqldbcopy* script is implemented in the */scripts/mysqldbcopy.py* file and calls a command module named */mysql/utilities/command/dbcopy.py*, which calls several modules such as *server.py*, *options.py*, and *database.py* located in the */mysql/utilities/common* folder.

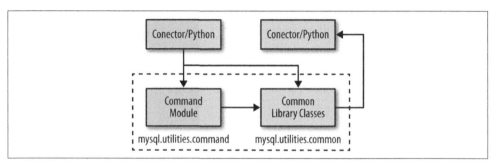

Figure 17-3. Architecture of MySQL Utilities

Custom Utility Example

This section contains an example of a custom utility built by combining features from existing utilities. Suppose you want a utility that copies all of the databases and users from one server to another. Furthermore, you want the utility to create a new instance of the server and use that as the destination for the copy. This utility can be very handy for creating test environments for development and diagnosis of data problems.

We will begin with a brief list of operations needed and a detailed look at the code for each operation. We conclude with a complete listing of the resulting source code.

Operations

If we skip the housekeeping operations, such as defining options and validating parameters and values, we can create a simple list of operations for the new utility. These can be combined into three major sections. First, we need to connect to the server and discover what needs to be copied. Second, we need to create a clone of that server. Lastly, we need to perform the copy to the new server. We can expand this list of operations into the following eight steps:

1. Set up the parameters.
2. Connect to the original server.
3. Find all of the databases.
4. Find all of the users.
5. Make a clone of the original server.
6. Connect to the new server.
7. Copy all of the databases.
8. Copy all of the users.

If you consider the available utilities, you'll find a utility that can copy databases, a utility that can copy (clone) users, and a server that can clone a running or offline server. Once you consider the architecture of the utilities, it is easy to see that our solution is a mash-up of these three utilities. In fact, we can study those utilities and discover the command modules they use, then re-create the same calls in our new utility.

The following section explains each of the operations in more detail.

Sample code

We begin with setting up the parameters for the utility. Because we are reusing parts of other utilities, we can identify the options we need to use from studying how the utilities are created.

If you set aside those options that are provided for additional elective features, we find we need only a few options. If we minimize the list, we find that not many options are needed. From the server clone utility, we see we need `--new-data`, `--new-port`, and `--new-id`. From the database copy utility, we need to list the databases with `--databases`. All of the utilities have the `--server` option in common, which we need in order to connect to the original server for the copy and clone operations. We also need the `--users` option to identify the users we want to copy.

Now that we have a list of options, we can start a new file named *cloneserver.py* and copy the options from the other utilities. The following shows the options needed:

```
parser = optparse.OptionParser(
    version=VERSION_FRM.format(program=os.path.basename(sys.argv[0])),
    description=DESCRIPTION,
    usage=USAGE,
    add_help_option=False)
parser.add_option("--help", action="help")

# Set up utility-specific options:
```

```
# Connection information for the source server
parser.add_option("--server", action="store", dest="server",
                  type="string", default="root@localhost:3306",
                  help="connection information for original server in " + \
                  "the form: user:password@host:port:socket")

# Data directory for new instance
parser.add_option("--new-data", action="store", dest="new_data",
                  type="string", help="the full path to the location "
                  "of the data directory for the new instance")

# Port for the new instance
parser.add_option("--new-port", action="store", dest="new_port",
                  type="string", default="3307", help="the new port "
                      "for the new instance - default=%default")

# Server id for the new instance
parser.add_option("--new-id", action="store", dest="new_id",
                  type="string", default="2", help="the server_id for "
                      "the new instance - default=%default")

# List of databases
parser.add_option("-d", "--databases", action="store", dest="dbs_to_copy",
                  type="string", help="comma-separated list of databases "
                  "to include in the copy (omit for all databases)",
                  default=None)

# List of users
parser.add_option("-u", "--users", action="store", dest="users_to_copy",
                  type="string", help="comma-separated list of users "
                  "to include in the copy (omit for all users)",
                  default=None)
```

 The current release of MySQL Utilities uses a module named opt-parse, which will eventually be replaced by argparse.

The next operation, connecting to the server, can be accomplished as follows. Notice we must import a helper method to parse the server option value, then import the Server class, build a dictionary of the options, and finally call the connect() method. The use of a Python dictionary to contain options is a common practice in all utilities:

```
# Parse the connection information
from mysql.utilities.common.options import parse_connection
  try:
    conn = parse_connection(opt.server)
  except:
    parser.error("Server connection values invalid or"
```

```
                    " cannot be parsed.")

    # Connect to original server
      from mysql.utilities.common.server import Server

      server_options = {'conn_info' : conn, 'role' : "source"}
      srv1 = Server(server_options)
      srv1.connect()
```

Now that we have a connection to a MySQL server, we can build a list of databases. If we consider the case where the user may want to copy all of the databases, we can check the database option and, if none are listed, get a list of all of the databases on the server. We can do the same for users. The following shows one example of how we can accomplish this:

```
    # Get list of databases from the server if not specified in options
    print "# Getting databases..."
    db_list = []
    if opt.dbs_to_copy is None:
        for db in server1.get_all_databases():
            db_list.append((db[0], None))
    else:
        for db in opt.dbs_to_copy.split(","):
            db_list.append((db, None))

    # Get list of all users from the server
    print "# Getting users..."
    user_list=[]
    if opt.users_to_copy is None:
        users = server1.exec_query("SELECT user, host "
                                   "FROM mysql.user "
                                   "WHERE user != 'root' and user != ''")
        for user in users:
            user_list.append(user[0]+'@'+user[1])
    else:
        for user in opt.users_to_copy.split(","):
            user_list.append(user)
```

The next major operation is to clone the server. Because we have minimized the options, we'll make a few with specific defaults. It would not be difficult to make these into options if desired. The following shows the code needed to make the clone. Because this is the first operation that calls the command modules, we would expect a bit of complexity. However, the opposite is true. Utility command modules are a very high level (sometimes called macro-level) of encapsulation, making the command modules very powerful and the script file very simple.

As you may suspect, this code is very similar to the connection code for the original server. The following shows the code for this operation:

```
    # Parse source connection values
    try:
```

```
    conn = parse_connection(opt.server)
except:
    parser.error("Server connection values invalid or cannot be parsed.")

# Get a server class instance
print "# Connecting to server..."
server_options = {
    'conn_info' : conn,
    'role'      : "source",
}
server1 = Server(server_options)
try:
    server1.connect()
except UtilError, e:
    print "ERROR:", e.errmsg
```

You might be wondering how we handle errors. The utilities make extensive use of exceptions. For normal operations that have known errors, command modules return typical return codes of False or True, but when a catastrophic error occurs, like invalid user credentials, the library modules throw an exception.

Now we are ready to copy the database and users identified previously. As you may expect, there are command modules for each of these operations that accept a server connection:

```
print "# Copying databases..."
try:
    dbcopy.copy_db(conn, dest_values, db_list, options)
except exception.UtilError, e:
    print "ERROR:", e.errmsg
    exit(1)

# Build dictionary of options
options = {
    "overwrite" : True,
    "quiet"     : True,
    "globals"   : True
}

print "# Cloning the users..."
for user in user_list:
    try:
        res = userclone.clone_user(conn, dest_values, user,
                                   (user,), options)
    except exception.UtilError, e:
        print "ERROR:", e.errmsg
        exit(1)
```

And that's all of the code for the new utility! Lets take a look at the completed code and see an example of its execution.

Putting it all together

Now that you have seen the code involved with each operation, let's take a look at the completed source code. Example 17-3 shows all of the sample code plus the typical housekeeping and setup code for managing a typical utility.

Example 17-3. Completed source code

```python
import optparse
import os
import sys

from mysql.utilities import VERSION_FRM
from mysql.utilities.command import dbcopy
from mysql.utilities.command import serverclone
from mysql.utilities.command import userclone
from mysql.utilities.common.server import Server
from mysql.utilities.common.options import parse_connection
from mysql.utilities import exception

# Constants
NAME = "example - copy_server "
DESCRIPTION = "copy_server - copy an existing server"
USAGE = "%prog --server=user:pass@host:port:socket " \
        "--new-dir=path --new-id=server_id " \
        "--new-port=port --databases=db list " \
        "--users=user list"

# Setup the command parser
parser = optparse.OptionParser(
    version=VERSION_FRM.format(program=os.path.basename(sys.argv[0])),
    description=DESCRIPTION,
    usage=USAGE,
    add_help_option=False)
parser.add_option("--help", action="help")

# Setup utility-specific options:

# Connection information for the source server
parser.add_option("--server", action="store", dest="server",
                  type="string", default="root@localhost:3306",
                  help="connection information for original server in " + \
                  "the form: user:password@host:port:socket")

# Data directory for new instance
parser.add_option("--new-data", action="store", dest="new_data",
                  type="string", help="the full path to the location " 
                  "of the data directory for the new instance")

# Port for the new instance
parser.add_option("--new-port", action="store", dest="new_port",
                  type="string", default="3307", help="the new port " 
                      "for the new instance - default=%default")
```

```python
# Server id for the new instance
parser.add_option("--new-id", action="store", dest="new_id",
                  type="string", default="2", help="the server_id for "
                      "the new instance - default=%default")

# List of databases
parser.add_option("-d", "--databases", action="store", dest="dbs_to_copy",
                  type="string", help="comma-separated list of databases "
                  "to include in the copy (omit for all databases)",
                  default=None)

# List of users
parser.add_option("-u", "--users", action="store", dest="users_to_copy",
                  type="string", help="comma-separated list of users "
                  "to include in the copy (omit for all users)",
                  default=None)

# Now we process the rest of the arguments.
opt, args = parser.parse_args()

# Parse source connection values
try:
    conn = parse_connection(opt.server)
except:
    parser.error("Server connection values invalid or cannot be parsed.")

# Get a server class instance
print "# Connecting to server..."
server_options = {
    'conn_info' : conn,
    'role'      : "source",
}
server1 = Server(server_options)
try:
    server1.connect()
except UtilError, e:
    print "ERROR:", e.errmsg

# Get list of databases from the server if not specified in options
print "# Getting databases..."
db_list = []
if opt.dbs_to_copy is None:
    for db in server1.get_all_databases():
        db_list.append((db[0], None))
else:
    for db in opt.dbs_to_copy.split(","):
        db_list.append((db, None))

# Get list of all users from the server
print "# Getting users..."
user_list=[]
```

```
if opt.users_to_copy is None:
    users = server1.exec_query("SELECT user, host "
                               "FROM mysql.user "
                               "WHERE user != 'root' and user != ''")
    for user in users:
        user_list.append(user[0]+'@'+user[1])
else:
    for user in opt.users_to_copy.split(","):
        user_list.append(user)

# Clone the server
print "# Cloning server instance..."
try:
    res = serverclone.clone_server(conn, opt.new_data, opt.new_port,
                                   opt.new_id, "root", None, False, True)
except exception.UtilError, e:
    print "ERROR:", e.errmsg
    exit(1)

# Set connection values
dest_values = {
    "user"    : conn.get("user"),
    "passwd" : "root",
    "host"    : conn.get("host"),
    "port"    : opt.new_port,
    "unix_socket" : os.path.join(opt.new_data, "mysql.sock")
}

# Build dictionary of options
options = {
    "quiet" : True,
    "force" : True
}

print "# Copying databases..."
try:
    dbcopy.copy_db(conn, dest_values, db_list, options)
except exception.UtilError, e:
    print "ERROR:", e.errmsg
    exit(1)

# Build dictionary of options
options = {
    "overwrite" : True,
    "quiet"      : True,
    "globals"   : True
}

print "# Cloning the users..."
for user in user_list:
    try:
        res = userclone.clone_user(conn, dest_values, user,
```

```
                              (user,), options)
    except exception.UtilError, e:
        print "ERROR:", e.errmsg
        exit(1)

print "# ...done."
```

Example 17-4 shows the output of this example. Here we see the new utility is used to copy two databases, all of the users, and create a new server.

Example 17-4. Example execution

```
$ copy_server --new-port=3307 --server=root:pass@localhost \
  --new-data=/Volumes/Source/testabc -d db1,db2
# Connecting to server...
# Getting databases...
# Getting users...
# Cloning server instance...
# Cloning the MySQL server running on localhost.
# Creating new data directory...
# Configuring new instance...
# Locating mysql tools...
# Setting up empty database and mysql tables...
# Starting new instance of the server...
# Testing connection to new instance...
# Success!
# Setting the root password...
# Connection Information:
#   -uroot -proot --socket=/Volumes/Source/testabc/mysql.sock
#...done.
# Copying databases...
# Cloning the users...
# ...done.
```

Suggestions

The example project is very helpful in producing a running clone of an existing server. However, if we consider how this can be used in replication, we may consider it would be more useful if it had the ability to optionally make the new server a clone of the original server. This would, in effect, create a new utility that can be used to provision slaves. How cool is that?

To do this, you would need to use the command module for the replication utility described in "Architecture of MySQL Utilities" on page 663. The following example gives a hint of the code you will need to use. We leave this modification for you to explore as an exercise. Start by identifying the required options and adding them to the file:

```
from mysql.utilities.command.setup_rpl import setup_replication

...
```

```
res = setup_replication(m_values, s_values, opt.rpl_user,
                        options, opt.test_db)
```

Conclusion

MySQL replication is a powerful feature that is easy to set up and administer for a small number of servers. When the topology grows to many servers or acquires complexity such as tiered servers, geographically remote sites, or configuration for data segregation via filtering, managing replication can become a challenge.

In this chapter, we presented a set of utilities you can use to manage your replication servers for operations like copying databases, cloning users, and setting up and checking replication. We also presented two powerful utilities designed to make switchover in a single command and to provide automatic failover.

Now that you know how to achieve high availability with MySQL, you can use MySQL Utilities to further enhance your MySQL installation.

Joel clicked the key sequence to save his latest version of his manifesto of managing MySQL replication. "That's done," he said with the satisfaction of a job completed.

Joel's new email tone chimed. With some trepidation, he glanced at his inbox. As he suspected, his boss was asking about the status of his writing project. He clicked on Reply and composed a simple response, then attached the new file.

A knock on his doorjamb distracted him before he could hit Send. "Joel, I've got a candidate on line 4 who knows MySQL. Why don't you check him out and quiz him on replication with that new document you've written?" As his boss hurried off, Joel sent the email and then reached for his phone. "How does he do that?" Joel wondered.

Replication Tips and Tricks

This appendix is a collection of useful tips and tricks for running, diagnosing, repairing, and improving MySQL replication. They are supplemental material and, as such, may not contain all of the details needed for a full tutorial. Consult the online MySQL Reference Manual (*http://bit.ly/sql-rep*) for more details about MySQL replication.

The last few sections of this appendix describe features that will be offered by MySQL soon, but are not officially available at the time of this writing.

Examining the Binary Log with Verbose

If you are using row-based logging, you can use the `--verbose` option to see a reconstruction of the queries in the event. The following shows what this looks like when run on a binary log with row-based logging:

```
$ mysqlbinlog --verbose master-bin.000001
BINLOG '
qZnvSRMBAAAAKQAAAAYCAAAAABAAAAAAAAAABHRlc3QAAnQxAAEDAAEDAAE=
qZnvSRcBAAAAJwAAAC0CAAAQABAAAAAAAAAEAAf/+AwAAAP4EAAAA '/*!*/;
### INSERT INTO test.t1
### SET
### @1=3
### INSERT INTO test.t1
### SET
### @1=4
```

Notice that the values are given using @*n*-style names for the columns. This is because row-based replication is transferring the record and applying it by column position, but ignores the names of the columns.

Using Replication to Repopulate a Table

If a table on your slave becomes corrupt either through error or accident (e.g., a user deletes the data), you can use replication to recover the data. Do so by creating a temporary table on the master that is a copy of the original table, dropping the original table, and then re-creating it from the copy. This works very well as long as you do not have any column data types that this could affect (e.g., `autoincrement`). You are using the power of replication to reproduce the table on the slaves. There are two forms of this process, based on which form of logging you are using.

Statement-Based Logging

If you are using statement-based logging, run the following for each table:

```
SELECT * INTO OUTFILE 't1.txt' FROM t1;
DROP TABLE IF EXISTS t1;
CREATE TABLE t1 ...;
LOAD DATA INFILE 't1.txt' INTO TABLE t1;
```

Row-Based Logging

If you are using row-based logging, the temporary table is not transferred to the slave. Therefore, send only the data that is necessary to bootstrap the table using the INSERT INTO command as follows:

```
CREATE TEMPORARY TABLE t1_tmp LIKE t1;
INSERT INTO t1_tmp SELECT * FROM t1;
DROP TABLE IF EXISTS t1;
CREATE TABLE t1 SELECT * FROM t1_tmp;
```

Using MySQL Proxy to Perform Multimaster Replication

No slave can have more than one master, but a master can have many slaves. This isn't an issue for most installations, but what if you need to combine data from two different masters and replicate the combined data to your slaves?

One way to do this is to use MySQL Proxy as an intermediate slave. Figure A-1 shows a conceptual drawing of this configuration.

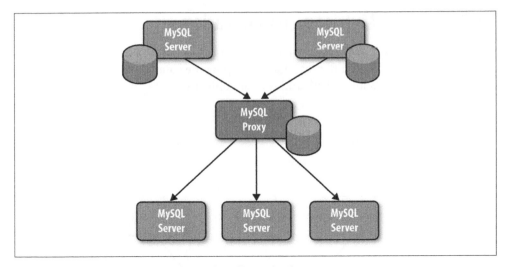

Figure A-1. Using MySQL Proxy to handle multiple masters

MySQL Proxy will receive changes (events) from both masters and write a new binary log without saving the data (writing it to a database). Your slaves use MySQL Proxy as a master. This has the effect of combining data from two masters and replicating to a set of slaves. This effectively implements multimaster replication.

For more information about MySQL Proxy, see the section on MySQL Proxy in the online MySQL Reference Manual.

Using a Default Storage Engine

If you use a default storage engine on your master by issuing the `SET GLOBAL STORAGE ENGINE` command, this command is not replicated. Therefore, any `CREATE` statement that does not specify a storage engine will get the default storage engine as it was set on the slaves. Thus, it is possible that your InnoDB tables will be replicated to MyISAM tables. If you ignore the warnings when this occurs, you can encounter a scenario in which replication stops due to some incompatibility.

One solution is to ensure the global storage engine is set on each slave by including the `default-storage-engine` option in the configuration file. However, the best practice is to specify the storage engine on the `CREATE` statement.

This does not prevent issues in which a storage engine used on the master does not exist on the slave. In this case, you may encounter problems that can be solved only by installing the missing storage engine on the slave.

MySQL Cluster Multisource Replication

You can set up multisource replication using MySQL Cluster (Figure A-2). To do so, set up the masters to replicate different data. By keeping the data on different masters, you avoid cross-contamination of keys and similar context-dependent values.

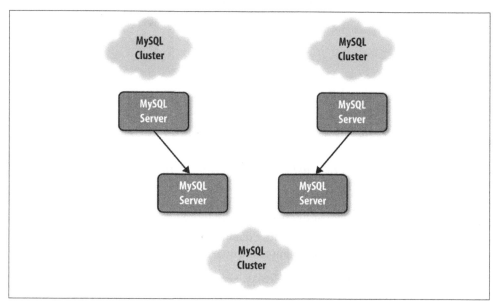

Figure A-2. Multisource replication

Multichannel Replication with Failover

For greater reliability and rapid recovery, you can use a dual replication setup (Figure A-3), in which two sets of replication topologies replicate from one cluster to another. If one stream goes down, you can fail over to the other stream quickly.

Notice that server names are of the form *mysql.X* and saved positions are of the form *mysql.X.savepos*.

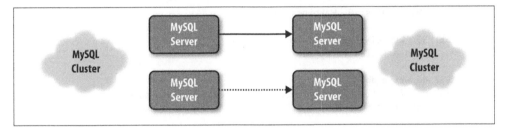

Figure A-3. Multichannel replication

Using the Current Database to Filter

The binlog filters can be quite convenient for eliminating statements for particular purposes.

For example, some statements may be meant only for the server, such as setting the engine of a table where you want the engines to be different on the master and the slave. There are many reasons to use a different engine on the slave, including the following:

- MyISAM is more suitable for reporting, and because the binary log contains complete transactions, you can use InnoDB on the master for transactional processing and MyISAM on slaves for reporting and analytical processing.
- To save memory, you can eliminate some tables on a slave used for analytical processing by replacing the engine with Blackhole.

You can suspend writing to the binary log by setting the SQL_LOG_BIN server variable to 0. For instance, Example A-1 turns off logging (SQL_LOG_BIN = 0) before changing a table to the MyISAM engine, so that it takes place only on the master, then turns logging back on (SQL_LOG_BIN = 1). However, setting SQL_LOG_BIN requires SUPER privileges, which you probably don't want to grant to regular database users. Therefore, Example 6-8 shows an alternative way to change an engine on the master without logging it. (In the example, it is assumed that the table my_table resides in a database my_db.) Create a dedicated database (in this case, we use the name no_write_db). Then, any user who wants to execute a statement that should not be replicated can USE the no_write_db database, and the statement will be filtered out. Because using a database requires access privileges, you can control who has the privileges to hide statements without providing the SUPER privilege to an untrusted user.

Example A-1. Two different ways to filter a statement from the binary log

```
master> SET SQL_LOG_BIN = 0;
Query OK, 0 rows affected (0.00 sec)

master> ALTER TABLE my_table ENGINE=MyISAM;
Query OK, 92 row affected (0.90 sec)
```

```
Records: 92  Duplicates: 0  Warnings: 0

master> SET SQL_LOG_BIN = 1;
Query OK, 0 rows affected (0.00 sec)

master> USE no_write_db;
Reading table information for completion of table and column names
You can turn off this feature to get a quicker startup with -A

Database changed
master> ALTER TABLE my_db.my_table ENGINE=MyISAM;
Query OK, 92 row affected (0.90 sec)
Records: 92  Duplicates: 0  Warnings: 0
```

More Columns on Slave Than Master

If you need to include additional columns on the slave that the master doesn't have—
for example, to record timestamps or add routing or other localized data—you can add
columns to a table on a slave without having to add the columns on the master. MySQL
replication supports this scenario by ignoring the additional columns. To actually insert
data into the extra columns on the slave, define them to accept default values (an easy
way to insert timestamps, for instance) or use a trigger defined on the slave to provide
the values.

For statement-based logging, you can create the columns as follows:

1. Create the table on the master:

   ```
   CREATE TABLE t1 (a INT, b INT);
   ```

2. Alter the table on the slave:

   ```
   ALTER TABLE t1 ADD ts TIMESTAMP;
   ```

3. Sample insert on the master:

   ```
   INSERT INTO t1(a,b) VALUES (10,20);
   ```

For row-based logging, you must make the new columns appear at the end of the row
and have default values. Row-based replication will fail if you add columns in the middle
or at the front of the row. As long as you add columns at the end of the table and give
them default values, no special consideration needs to be taken regarding which statements to use when replicating, because row-based replication will extract the columns
directly from the row being updated, inserted, or deleted.

Fewer Columns on Slave Than Master

If you need to have fewer columns on the slave than the master—for example, to protect
sensitive data or to reduce the amount of data replicated—you can remove columns

from a table on a slave without having to remove the columns on the master. MySQL row-based replication supports this scenario by ignoring the missing columns. However, the missing columns on the slave must be from the end of the master's row.

For row-based replication, you can drop the columns as follows:

1. Create the table on the master:

   ```
   CREATE TABLE t1 (a INT, b INT, comments TEXT);
   ```

2. Alter the table on the slave:

   ```
   ALTER TABLE t1 DROP comments;
   ```

3. Sample insert on the master:

   ```
   INSERT INTO t1 VALUES (1,2,"Do not store this on slave");
   ```

For row-based replication, you can replicate an arbitrary set of columns of a table without regard to whether they are at the end or not by using a trigger on the master to update the table from a base table in a separate database so that only the columns in the slave's database are replicated. Figure A-4 shows a conceptual drawing of this solution. Here, a table with three columns is transformed using a trigger to a table in the replicated database.

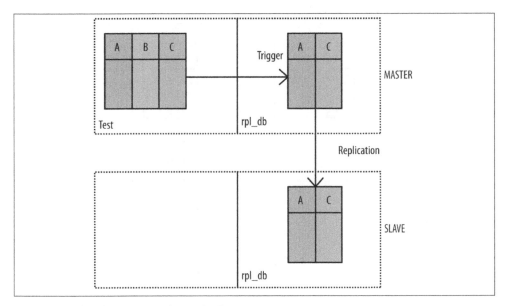

Figure A-4. Replicating a subset of columns

An example follows of how you can use a trigger to update the table in the replicated database. On the master, execute the following:

```
CREATE DATABASE rpl_db;
USE test;
CREATE TABLE t1 (a INT, b BLOB, c INT);
CREATE TRIGGER tr_t1 AFTER INSERT ON test.t1 FOR EACH ROW
INSERT INTO rpl_db.t1_v(a,c) VALUES(NEW.a,NEW.c);
USE rpl_db;
CREATE TABLE t1_v (a INT, c INT);
```

When executing a normal insert, the trigger will extract a subset of the columns and write it to the table in the rpl_db database. This database will then be replicated, but the original table will not:

```
USE test;
SET @blob = REPEAT('beef',100);
INSERT INTO t1 VALUES (1,@blob,3), (2,@blob,9);
```

Replicate Selected Rows to Slave

You can also segment replication so that only rows satisfying a certain condition are replicated. This technique uses a special database that is replicated from the master to the slave (this is accomplished by setting up a filter) and a trigger to determine which rows are to be replicated. The trigger determines which rows are to be replicated by inserting them into the replicated table (Figure A-5).

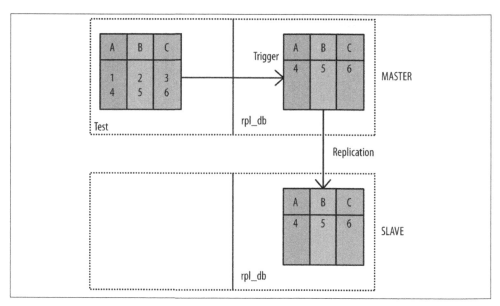

Figure A-5. Replicating a subset of rows

An example follows of how you can use a trigger to update the table in the replicated database with only rows having an odd value in column a inserted:

```
# Just replicate rows that have odd numbers in the first column.
USE rpl_db;
CREATE TABLE t1_h (a INT, b BLOB, c INT);
--delimiter //
CREATE TRIGGER slice_t1_horiz AFTER INSERT ON test.t1
FOR EACH ROW
BEGIN
  IF NEW.a MOD 2 = 1 THEN INSERT
    INTO rpl_db.t1_h VALUES (NEW.a, NEW.b, NEW.c);
  END IF;
END//
--delimiter ;
```

Replication Heartbeat (5.4.4 or Later)

It is possible to improve the reliability of replication and improve failover using the replication heartbeat mechanism. When the heartbeat is turned on, the slave will periodically challenge the master. As long as the slave gets a response, it will continue as usual and challenge the master again at the next interval. The server maintains statistics of the number of heartbeats received, which can help to determine whether the master is offline or not responding. Figure A-6 shows a conceptual drawing of the heartbeat mechanism.

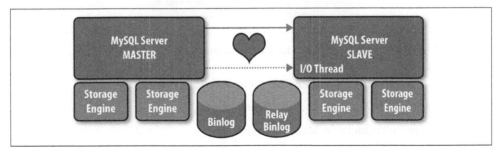

Figure A-6. Heartbeat during replication

The heartbeat mechanism allows the slave to detect when the master is still responding, and has the following advantages and capabilities:

- Automatic checking of connection status
- No more relay log rotates when the master is idle
- Detection of master/slave disconnect, configurable in milliseconds

Thus, you can use the heartbeat mechanism to perform automatic failover and similar high availability operations. Use the following command to set the heartbeat interval on the slave:

```
CHANGE MASTER SET master_heartbeat_period= val;
```

The following commands allow you to check the settings and statistics of the heartbeat mechanism:

```
SHOW STATUS like 'slave_heartbeat period';
SHOW STATUS like 'slave_received_heartbeats';
```

Ignoring Servers in Circular Replication (5.5 or Later)

If you have a circular replication topology and one of the servers fails, you must change the topology to exclude the failed server. In Figure A-7, server A has failed and you must remove it from the circle. In this case, you can set server B to terminate server A's events in the new circle.

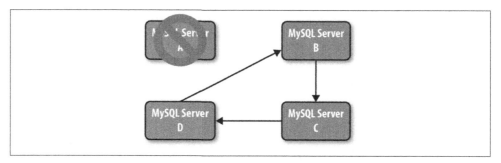

Figure A-7. Replacing a server in circular replication

You can do this by issuing the following command on server B:

```
CHANGE MASTER TO MASTER_HOST=C ... IGNORE_SERVER_IDS=(A)
```

This feature was introduced in MySQL version 5.5.

Time-Delayed Replication (5.6 or Later)

There is sometimes a need to delay replication—for example, when you want to ensure slaves are not overloaded with changes. This feature provides the ability to execute replication events on a slave so that it is *n* seconds behind the master at all times. You can set this parameter as shown:

```
CHANGE MASTER TO MASTER_DELAY= seconds
```

seconds is a nonnegative integer less than MAX_ULONG number of seconds for the slave to wait (attempts to set the number higher will be rejected with an error).

You can verify the delayed setup by running the SHOW SLAVE STATUS command and examining the Seconds_behind_master column of the output.

You can read more about time-delayed replication in the MySQL Reference Manual (*http://bit.ly/delay-rep*).

Shell Commands for Common Tasks

The set of shell functions in this section will add a lot of power to your shell scripts. The library is intended to be included from the script file and will parse the command-line options from the command line:

```
set -- `getopt 'S:u:P:h:p:' "$@"` ❶
while [ x$1 != x-- ]
do
    case $1 in
        -S) opt_sock=$2 ; shift 2 ;;
        -u) opt_user=$2 ; shift 2 ;;
        -P) opt_port=$2 ; shift 2 ;;
        -h) opt_host=$2 ; shift 2 ;;
        -p) opt_pass=$2 ; shift 2 ;;
    esac
done

connect_param () { ❷
    echo --user=$opt_user ${opt_pass:+--password="$opt_pass"} \
        ${opt_sock:+--socket="$opt_sock"} \
        ${opt_host:+--host="$opt_host"} ${opt_port:+--port="$opt_port"}
}

mysql_exec () { ❸
    echo "$@" |
    mysql `connect_param` --vertical --batch
}

stop_slave () {
    mysql_exec STOP SLAVE $2
}

start_slave () {
    mysql_exec START SLAVE $2
}

change_master () {
    host=${1:+MASTER_HOST=\'$1\'}
    port=${2:+MASTER_PORT=$2}
    user=${3:+MASTER_USER=\'$3\'}
    pass=${4:+MASTER_PASSWORD=\'$4\'}
    file=${5:+MASTER_LOG_FILE=\'$5\'}
    pos=${6:+MASTER_LOG_POS=$6}
    mysql_exec CHANGE MASTER TO \
        $host ${host:+,} $port ${port:+,} \
        $user ${user:+,} $pass ${pass:+,} \
        $file ${file:+,} $pos
```

```
    }

fetch_slave_exec_pos () {
    mysql_exec SHOW SLAVE STATUS | ❹
    grep '\<Relay_Master_Log_File\|\<Exec_Master_Log_Pos' |
    cut -f2 -d:
}

fetch_slave_read_pos () {
    mysql_exec SHOW SLAVE STATUS |
    grep '\<Master_Log_File\|\<Read_Master_Log_Pos' |
    cut -f2 -d:
}

fetch_master_pos () {
    mysql_exec SHOW MASTER STATUS |
    grep '\<File\|\<Pos' | cut -f2 -d:
}


slave_wait_for_empty_relay_log () {
    stop_slave IO_THREAD
    fetch_slave_read_pos | {
        read file pos
        mysql_exec "SELECT MASTER_POS_WAIT('$file',$pos)"
    }
    stop_slave SQL_THREAD
}
```

❶ Options are read using the standard *getopt* UNIX command. The intended usage of this library is to use *source* to pull it in, and it will then read the options from the command line. It accepts -h for specifying the hostname, -P for specifying the port, -u for specifying the user, and -p for specifying the password.

❷ Function that prints the connection parameters necessary to use for the *mysql* command. All the commands that accept the same parameters as *mysql* can use this function as well, so you can issue a mysqladmin connection_param shut down to shut down the server (for example).

❸ Helper function to simplify execution of SQL commands. The command is using the connection information set up previously and assumes that all the arguments provided makes up the command.

Because this function is intended to be used from other shell functions, the column names are skipped and the output is a simple columnar output written to standard output. To process the result further, you will have to split on columns using, for example, *cut*.

❹ Here you see an example of how to handle the result set. In this case, the lines containing the file and position of the last executed transaction are filtered out, and then cut is used to extract the columns with the value.

Multisource Replication in a Shell Script

A MySQL slave cannot be set up to read changes from multiple masters, but it is possible to simulate it by using time-sharing where a client issues SQL commands to the slave in a round-robin fashion, as in Figure A-8.

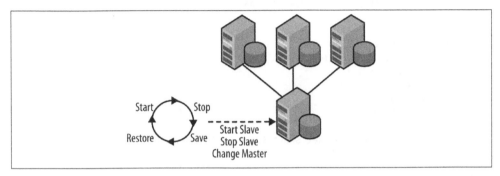

Figure A-8. Multi-master using round-robin

The procedure can be implemented in a few different ways, depending on what language you want to use and to some extent also what versions of the server you have. The general procedure is:

1. Initialize the procedure by storing the log position and the log file for all the masters. This position should be where you want to start replication.

2. Select one of the masters as the *current master*.

3. Repeat the following steps:

    a. Set the slave to read from the current master using CHANGE MASTER.

    b. Start the slave using START SLAVE.

    c. Let replication run for a while to replicate from the current master.

    d. Stop replication using STOP SLAVE.

    e. Save away information about the current position of replication by using SHOW SLAVE STATUS.

Implementing the client using our library of shell functions from "Shell Commands for Common Tasks" on page 685 and a few extra functions demonstrate an easy implementation using a shell script. This procedure can, of course, be implemented in a number of other languages. The code saves the position data in files, where each file is numbered sequentially and is based on the name of the slave server:

```
fetch_host_and_pos () {   ❶
    mysql_exec $1 SHOW SLAVE STATUS |
    grep '\<Master_\(Host\|Port\|Log_File\)\|\<Read_Master_Log_Pos' |
    cut -f2 -d:
}

stop_and_save () {   ❷
    sock="/var/run/mysqld/$1.sock"
    stop_slave $socket
    fetch_host_and_pos $sock >$1.savepos
}

restore_and_start () {   ❸
    socket="/var/run/mysqld/$1.sock"
    cat $1.savepos | {
        read host
        read port
        read file
        read pos
        change_master $socket $host $port $file $pos
        start_slave $socket
    }
}

cnt=1
while true   ❹
do
    stop_and_save mysqld.$cnt
    cnt=`expr $cnt % 5 + 1`
    restore_and_start mysqld.$cnt
    sleep 60
done
```

❶ This is a helper function to fetch the host and position so that it can be saved to the file. Because the data is retrieved in column format, it is possible to grep for the lines containing the position information, and then cut out the column names.

❷ This function stop the slave using STOP SLAVE, fetch the position of the current master using the fetch_host_and_pos function, and save it to the file provided as argument. This should be the file used for the current master.

❸ This file restore the position from the given file, uses CHANGE MASTER to set the slave to the correct position, and then starts the slave using START SLAVE.

❹ Here the loop shown in Figure A-8 is executed repeatedly and switches between the masters.

Stored Procedure to Change Master

When writing stored procedures for performing various tasks, it is quite useful to be able to supply declared variables or user variables instead of constant values. Unfortunately, this is not the case for all commands in MySQL. For example, CHANGE MASTER does not accept parameters, so in order to be able to use parameters for the command, it is necessary to be a little creative.

A statement can be prepared from a string, so by constructing a string containing the statement, it is possible to execute any statement you like. This trick can be used to construct any statement you fancy:

```
delimiter $$ ❶
CREATE PROCEDURE change_master(
    host VARCHAR(50) NOT NULL, port INT NOT NULL,
    user VARCHAR(50) NOT NULL, passwd VARCHAR(50) NOT NULL,
    file VARCHAR(50), pos LONG) ❷
BEGIN
    SET @cmd = CONCAT('CHANGE MASTER TO ',
                      CONCAT('MASTER_HOST = "', host, '", '),
                      CONCAT('MASTER_PORT = ', port, ', '),
                      CONCAT('MASTER_USER = "', user, '", '),
                      CONCAT('MASTER_PASSWORD = "', passwd, '"')));

    IF name IS NOT NULL AND pos IS NOT NULL THEN
        SET @cmd = CONCAT(@cmd,
                          CONCAT(', MASTER_LOG_FILE = "', name, '"'),
                          CONCAT(', MASTER_LOG_POS = ', pos));
    END IF;
    PREPARE change_master FROM @cmd; ❸
    EXECUTE change_master;
    DEALLOCATE PREPARE change_master;
END $$
delimiter ; ❹
```

❶❹ To be able to define the body of stored routines, it is necessary to change delimiter from a semicolon to something else. In this example, $$ is used as the delimiter. It is convenient because it does not normally occur inside the body of stored procedures, but you can of course use any delimiter you like. Just make sure that it does not appear inside the body of the stored routine.

❷ The position given by a file and a position within the file can be NULL. In that case, no file or position will be given to the CHANGE MASTER command, so replication will start from the beginning.

❸ The prepare statement accepts only a user variable, so it is necessary to store the string in a user variable. It would be convenient to be able to use a declare local variable but, alas, the syntax does not support it.

Implementing Multisource Replication in Pure SQL (5.6 or Later)

As you saw in the section "Multisource Replication in a Shell Script" on page 687, a slave can currently not replicate from multiple master (*multisource replication*) at the same time, but it is possible to replicate from multiple masters by using a time-sharing scheme where the current master is switched at regular intervals.

The solution in "Multisource Replication in a Shell Script" on page 687 used a separate client—implemented there in the Bourne shell—to work as scheduler and change the master for the server regularly. Wouldn't it be neat if there were a way to have the server change master itself? The good news is that it is possible... if you are using MySQL 5.6. By using the tables that were introduced in MySQL 5.6 to handle transactional replication (see "Transactional Replication" on page 270) it is possible to implement a time-share multisource entirely in SQL by creating an event (as in CREATE EVENT) to perform the master change.

To implement this, it is necessary to have a list of masters to traverse. The list need to contain all the necessary connection information, as well as the position where replication left off before switching to the next master. To keep track of the masters easily, there is also a column containing a server number (it is not the server ID, just a number used in the algorithm). In addition, it would be convenient if masters could be added and removed from the from the list without having to stop the event scheduler.

Table A-1. Definition of Table My_Masters

Field	Type	Null	Key	Default
server_id	int(10) unsigned	NO	PRI	NULL
host	varchar(50)	YES		NULL
port	int(10) unsigned	YES		3306
user	varchar(50)	YES		NULL
passwd	varchar(50)	YES		NULL

The table described in Table A-1 suits the purpose well. In order to keep track of the current master, a Current_Master table is introduced as well, holding the index of the currently active master. To be able to support addition and removal of masters, both tables have to be transactional because we will update the information in both tables as a single transaction. In this case, it would have been convenient if a session variable could be used to keep track of the index of the current server, but each time an event is started, a new sessions is spawned, so the value of the session variable is not kept between invocations of the event; therefore we have to store the value in a table.

Here is the complete definition of the event that switches the master (followed by a step-by-step explanation):

```
delimiter $$
CREATE EVENT multi_source
    ON SCHEDULE EVERY 10 SECOND DO
BEGIN
  DECLARE l_host VARCHAR(50);
  DECLARE l_port INT UNSIGNED;
  DECLARE l_user TEXT;
  DECLARE l_passwd TEXT;
  DECLARE l_file VARCHAR(50);
  DECLARE l_pos BIGINT;
  DECLARE l_next_idx INT DEFAULT 1; ❶

  SET SQL_LOG_BIN = 0; ❷

  STOP SLAVE IO_THREAD; ❸
  SELECT master_log_name, master_log_pos
    INTO l_file, l_pos
    FROM mysql.slave_master_info;
  SELECT MASTER_POS_WAIT(l_file, l_pos);
  STOP SLAVE;

  START TRANSACTION; ❹
  UPDATE my_masters AS m, ❺
        mysql.slave_relay_log_info AS rli
    SET m.log_pos = rli.master_log_pos,
        m.log_file = rli.master_log_name
  WHERE idx = (SELECT idx FROM current_master);

  SELECT idx INTO l_next_idx FROM my_masters ❻
  WHERE idx > (SELECT idx FROM current_master)
  ORDER BY idx LIMIT 1;

  SELECT idx INTO l_next_idx FROM my_masters ❼
  WHERE idx >= l_next_idx
  ORDER BY idx LIMIT 1;

  UPDATE current_master SET idx = l_next_idx;
  COMMIT;

  SELECT host, port, user, passwd, log_pos, log_file
    INTO l_host, l_port, l_user, l_passwd, l_pos, l_file
    FROM my_masters
  WHERE idx = l_next_idx;

  CALL change_master(l_host, l_port, l_user, l_passwd, l_file, l_pos); ❽
  START SLAVE;
END $$
delimiter ;
```

❶   Note that this variable is declared with a default of 1. We will use that in ❽.

❷ This disables the binary log, as we don't want to write any of the statements to the binary log. Because this is an event, the variable will automatically be reset at the end of the execution and not affect anything else.

❸ The next part of the event stop the slave I/O thread and empty the relay log before switching the master. This is done by reading the last seen position from the Slave_Master_Info table and then use `MASTER_POS_WAIT` to wait until the end of the relay log is reached.

❹ Because we want the changes to both the update of the My_Masters and Current_Master table to be performed atomically, we wrap the code to update the tables in a transaction.

❺ The position where the old master stopped is saved away in My_Masters.

❻ Finding the next master in turn, is necessary to do as a two-step procedure. This `SELECT` picks the next master according to the index. Recall that you can add and remove masters while the scheduler is running, so there can be gaps in the sequence of indexes.

❼ Wrap-around is handled by relying on the default of 1 used in **❶**. However, if there were a wrap-around, the master with index 1 (the default for `l_next_idx`) might not exist. In that case, we do a scan and find the first existing index that is equal to or greater than `l_next_idx`.

❽ After fetching information about the new master, we issue a `CHANGE MASTER` using the stored procedure introduced in "Stored Procedure to Change Master" on page 689.

A GTID Implementation

With MySQL 5.6, global transaction identifiers were introduced to provide a way to uniquely identify a transaction regardless of what server it is executed on. Handling failovers with a 5.6 server is very easy, and you can find a description of that in "Failover Using GTIDs" on page 263. But if you do not have a 5.6 server and still need to perform failover, you can use the methods described in this appendix, basically by implementing your own global transaction identifiers and writing them to the binary log. The goal is to implement the features necessary to perform slave promotion.

Adding GTIDs to a Server

To match the latest transaction on each of the slaves with the corresponding event in the binary log of the promoted slave, you need to tag each transaction. The content and structure of the tags don't matter; they just need to be uniquely identifiable no matter who executed the transaction so each transaction on the master can be found in the promoted slave's binary log. These tags are the *global transaction identifiers* that we are going to implement in this appendix.

The easiest way to accomplish this is to insert a statement at the end of each transaction that updates a special table and use that to keep track of where each slave is. Just before committing each transaction, a statement updates the table with a number that is unique for the transaction.

Tagging can be handled in two main ways:

- Extending the application code to perform the necessary statements
- Calling a stored procedure to perform each commit and writing the tag in the procedure

Because the first approach is easier to follow, it will be demonstrated here. If you are interested in the second approach, see "Stored Procedures to Commit Transactions" on page 698 later in this appendix.

To implement global transaction identifiers (GTIDs), create two tables as in Example B-1: one table named Global_Trans_ID to generate sequence numbers and a separate table named Last_Exec_Trans to record the GTID.

The server identifier is added to the definition of Last_Exec_Trans to distinguish transactions committed on different servers. If, for example, the promoted slave fails before all the slaves have managed to connect, it is very important to distinguish between the transaction identifier of the original master and the transaction identifier of the promoted slave. Otherwise, the slaves that didn't manage to connect to the promoted slave might start to execute from a position that is wrong when they are redirected to the second promoted slave. This example uses MyISAM to define the counter table, but it is possible to use InnoDB for this as well.

In this section, to keep code simple and familiar, we show the operations as plain SQL. In later sections, we show sample code that illustrates how to automate the operations as part of your applications.

Example B-1. Tables used for generating and tracking global transaction identifiers

```
CREATE TABLE Global_Trans_ID (
    number INT UNSIGNED AUTO_INCREMENT PRIMARY KEY
) ENGINE = MyISAM;

CREATE TABLE Last_Exec_Trans (
    server_id INT UNSIGNED,
    trans_id INT UNSIGNED
) ENGINE = InnoDB;

-- Insert a single row with NULLs to be updated.
INSERT INTO Last_Exec_Trans() VALUES ();
```

The next step is to construct a procedure for adding a global transaction identifier to the binary log so that a program promoting a slave can read the identifier from the log. The following procedure is suitable for our purposes:

1. Insert an item into the transaction counter table, making sure to turn off the binary log before doing so, because the insert should not be replicated to the slaves:

   ```
   master> SET SQL_LOG_BIN = 0;
   Query OK, 0 rows affected (0.00 sec)

   master> INSERT INTO Global_Trans_ID() VALUES ();
   Query OK, 1 row affected (0.00 sec)
   ```

2. Fetch the global transaction identifier using the function LAST_INSERT_ID. To simplify the logic, the server identifier is fetched from the server variable server_id at the same time:

```
master> SELECT @@server_id as server_id, LAST_INSERT_ID() as trans_id;
+-----------+----------+
| server_id | trans_id |
+-----------+----------+
|         0 |      235 |
+-----------+----------+
1 row in set (0.00 sec)
```

3. Before inserting the global transaction identifier into the Last_Exec_Trans tracking table, you can remove its row from the transaction counter table to save space. This optional step works only for a MyISAM table, because it internally tracks the latest autoincrement value and keeps autoincrementing from the value of the removed row. If you use InnoDB, you have to be careful about leaving the last used global transaction identifier in the table. InnoDB determines the next number from the maximum value in the autoincrement column currently in the table.

```
master> DELETE FROM Global_Trans_ID WHERE number < 235;
Query OK, 1 row affected (0.00 sec)
```

4. Turn on the binary log:

```
master> SET SQL_LOG_BIN = 1;
Query OK, 0 rows affected (0.00 sec)
```

5. Update the Last_Exec_Trans tracking table with the server identifier and the transaction identifier you got in step 2. This is the last step before committing the transaction through a COMMIT:

```
master> UPDATE Last_Exec_Trans SET server_id = 0, trans_id = 235;
Query OK, 1 row affected (0.00 sec)

master> COMMIT;
Query OK, 0 rows affected (0.00 sec)
```

Each global transaction identifier represents a point where replication can be resumed. Therefore, you must carry out this procedure for every transaction. If it is not used for some transaction, the transaction will not be tagged properly and it will not be possible to start from that position.

To define these tables and configure a server to use these GTIDs, you can use the Promotable class (shown in Example B-2) to handle the new kind of server. As you can see, this example reuses the _enable_binlog helper method introduced in "Server Roles" on page 19, and adds a method to set the log-slave-updates option. Because a promotable slave requires the special tables we showed earlier for the master, the addition of a promotable slave requires you to add these tables as well. To do this, we write a function named _add_global_id_tables. The function assumes that if the tables already exist, they have the correct definition, so no attempt is made to re-create them. However, the Last_Exec_Trans table needs to start with one row for the update to work correctly, so if no warning was produced to indicate that a table already exists, we create the table and add a row with NULL.

Example B-2. The definition of a promotable slave role

```
_GLOBAL_TRANS_ID_DEF = """
CREATE TABLE IF NOT EXISTS Global_Trans_ID (
  number INT UNSIGNED NOT NULL AUTO_INCREMENT,
  PRIMARY KEY (number)
) ENGINE=MyISAM
"""

_LAST_EXEC_TRANS_DEF = """
CREATE TABLE IF NOT EXISTS Last_Exec_Trans (
  server_id INT UNSIGNED DEFAULT NULL,
  trans_id INT UNSIGNED DEFAULT NULL
) ENGINE=InnoDB
"""

class Promotable(Role):
    def __init__(self, repl_user, master):
        self.__master = master
        self.__user = repl_user

    def _add_global_id_tables(self, master):
        master.sql(_GLOBAL_TRANS_ID_DEF)
        master.sql(_LAST_EXEC_TRANS_DEF)
        if not master.sql("SELECT @@warning_count"):
            master.sql("INSERT INTO Last_Exec_Trans() VALUES ()")

    def _relay_events(self, server, config):
        config.set('mysqld', 'log-slave-updates')

    def imbue(self, server):
        # Fetch and update the configuration
        config = server.get_config()
        self._set_server_id(server, config)
        self._enable_binlog(server, config)
        self._relay_event(server, config)

        # Put the new configuration in place
        server.stop()
        server.put_config(config)
        server.start()

        # Add tables to master
        self._add_global_id_tables(self.__master)

        server.repl_user = self.__master.repl_user
```

This routine configures the slaves and the master correctly for using global transaction identifiers.

Transaction Handling Using GTIDs

You still have to update the Last_Exec_Trans table when committing each transaction. In Example B-3 you can see an example implementation in PHP for committing transactions. The code is written using PHP, because this is part of the application code and not part of the code for managing the deployment.

Example B-3. Code for starting, committing, and aborting transactions

```php
function start_trans($link) {
  mysql_query("START TRANSACTION", $link);
}

function rollback_trans($link) {
  mysql_query("ROLLBACK", $link);
}

function commit_trans($link) {
  mysql_select_db("common", $link);
  mysql_query("SET SQL_LOG_BIN = 0", $link);
  mysql_query("INSERT INTO Global_Trans_ID() VALUES ()", $link);
  $trans_id = mysql_insert_id($link);
  $result = mysql_query("SELECT @@server_id as server_id", $link);
  $row = mysql_fetch_row($result);
  $server_id = $row[0];

  $delete_query = "DELETE FROM Global_Trans_ID WHERE number = %d";
  mysql_query(sprintf($delete_query, $trans_id),
          $link);
  mysql_query("SET SQL_LOG_BIN = 1", $link);

  $update_query = "UPDATE Last_Exec_Trans SET server_id = %d, trans_id = %d";
  mysql_query(sprintf($update_query, $server_id, $trans_id), $link);
  mysql_query("COMMIT", $link);
}
```

We can then use this code to commit transactions by calling the functions instead of the usual COMMIT and ROLLBACK. For example, we could write a PHP function to add a message to a database and update a message counter for the user:

```php
function add_message($email, $message, $link) {
  start_trans($link);
  mysql_select_db("common", $link);
  $query = sprintf("SELECT user_id FROM user WHERE email = '%s'", $email);
  $result = mysql_query($query, $link);
  $row = mysql_fetch_row($result);
  $user_id = $row[0];
```

```
$update_user = "UPDATE user SET messages = messages + 1 WHERE user_id = %d";
mysql_query(sprintf($update_user, $user_id), $link);

$insert_message = "INSERT INTO message VALUES (%d,'%s')";
mysql_query(sprintf($insert_message, $user_id, $message), $link);
commit_trans($link);
}

$conn = mysql_connect(":/var/run/mysqld/mysqld1.sock", "root");
add_message('mats@example.com', "MySQL Python Replicant rules!", $conn);
```

Stored Procedures to Commit Transactions

The main approach shown here to sync servers is to implement the transaction commit
procedure in the application, meaning that the application code needs to know table
names and the intricacies of how to produce and manipulate the global transaction
identifier. Once you understand them, the complexities are not as much of a barrier as
they might seem at first. Often, you can handle them with relative ease by creating
functions in the application code that the application writer can call without having to
know the details.

Another approach is to put the transaction commit logic in the database server by using
stored procedures. Depending on the situation, this can sometimes be a better alternative. For example, the commit procedure can be changed without having to change the
application code.

For this technique to work, it is necessary to put the transaction identifier from the
Global_Trans_ID table and the server identifier into either a user-defined variable or a
local variable in the stored routine. Depending on which approach you select, the query
in the binary log will look a little different.

Using local variables is less likely to interfere with surrounding code because user-
defined variables can be viewed or changed outside the stored procedure. This is known
as "leaking".

The procedure for committing a transaction will then be:

```
CREATE PROCEDURE commit_trans ()
  SQL SECURITY DEFINER
BEGIN
  DECLARE trans_id, server_id INT UNSIGNED;
  SET SQL_LOG_BIN = 0;
  INSERT INTO Global_Trans_ID() values ();
  SELECT LAST_INSERT_ID() INTO trans_id,
         @@server_id INTO server_id;
  SET SQL_LOG_BIN = 1;
  INSERT INTO Last_Exec_Trans(server_id, trans_id)
       VALUES (server_id, trans_id);
```

```
    COMMIT;
  END
```

Committing a transaction from the application code is then simple:

```
CALL Commit_Trans();
```

Now the task remains of changing the procedure for scanning the binary log for the global transaction identifier. So, how will a call to this function appear in the binary log? Well, a quick call to *mysqlbinlog* shows:

```
# at 1724
#091129 18:35:11 server id 1  end_log_pos 1899  Query    thread_id=75
  exec_time=0      error_code=0
SET TIMESTAMP=1259516111/*!*/;
INSERT INTO Last_Exec_Trans(server_id, trans_id)
  VALUES ( NAME_CONST('server_id',1),  NAME_CONST('trans_id',13))
/*!*/;
# at 1899
#091129 18:35:11 server id 1  end_log_pos 1926  Xid = 1444
COMMIT/*!*/;
```

As you can see, both the server identifier and the transaction identifier are clearly visible in the output. How to match this statement using a regular expression is left as an exercise for the reader.

Finding Positions of GTIDs

When connecting a slave to the promoted slave and start replication at the right position, it is necessary to find out what position on the promoted slave has the last executed transaction of the slave. This is done by scanning the binary log of the promoted slave to find the GTID.

The logs of the promoted slave can be retrieved using SHOW MASTER LOGS, so you can scan them for global transaction identifiers. For instance, when you read the *slave-3-bin.000005* file using *mysqlbinlog*, part of the output will look like that shown in Example B-4. The transaction received by slave-3 starting at position 596 (highlighted in the first line of the output) has the global transaction identifier received by slave-1, as shown by an UPDATE of the Last_Exec_Trans table.

Example B-4. Output from the mysqlbinlog command for one transaction

```
# at 596
#091018 18:35:42 server id 1  end_log_pos 664  Query    thread_id=952   ...
SET TIMESTAMP=1255883742/*!*/;
BEGIN
/*!*/;
# at 664
#091018 18:35:42 server id 1  end_log_pos 779  Query    thread_id=952   ...
SET TIMESTAMP=1255883742/*!*/;
```

```
UPDATE user SET messages = messages + 1 WHERE id = 1
/*!*/;
# at 779
#091018 18:35:42 server id 1  end_log_pos 904  Query   thread_id=952   ...
SET TIMESTAMP=1255883742/*!*/;
INSERT INTO message VALUES (1,'MySQL Python Replicant rules!')
/*!*/;
# at 904
#091018 18:35:42 server id 1  end_log pos 1021  Query   thread_id=952   ...
SET TIMESTAMP=1255883742/*!*/;
UPDATE Last_Exec_Trans SET server_id = 1, trans_id = 245
/*!*/;
# at 1021
#091018 18:35:42 server id 1  end_log_pos 1048  Xid = 1433
COMMIT/*!*/;
```

Example B-4 shows that the trans_id 245 is the last transaction seen by slave-1, so now you know that the start position for slave-1 is in file *slave-3-bin.000005* at byte position 1048. So to start slave-1 at the correct position, you can now execute CHANGE MASTER and START SLAVE:

```
slave-1> CHANGE MASTER TO
    ->      MASTER_HOST = 'slave-3',
    ->      MASTER_LOG_FILE = 'slave-3-bin.000005',
    ->      MASTER_LOG_POS = 1048;
Query OK, 0 rows affected (0.04 sec)

slave-1> START SLAVE;
Query OK, 0 rows affected (0.17 sec)
```

By going backward in this manner you can connect the slaves one by one to the new master at exactly the right position.

This technique works well if the update statement is added to every transaction commit. Unfortunately, there are statements that perform an implicit commit before and after the statement. Typical examples include CREATE TABLE, DROP TABLE, and ALTER TABLE. Because these statements do an implicit commit, they cannot be tagged properly, hence it is not possible to restart *just after* them. Suppose that the following sequence of statements is executed and there is a crash:

```
INSERT INTO message_board VALUES ('mats@sun.com', 'Hello World!');
CREATE TABLE admin_table (a INT UNSIGNED);
INSERT INTO message_board VALUES ('', '');
```

If a slave has just executed the CREATE TABLE and then loses the master, the last seen global transaction identifier is for the INSERT INTO—that is, just before the CREATE TABLE statement. Therefore, the slave will try to reconnect to the promoted slave with the transaction identifier of the INSERT INTO statement. Because it will find the position in the binary log of the promoted slave, it will start by replicating the CREATE TABLE statement again, causing the slave to stop with an error.

You can avoid these problems through careful design and use of statements that perform implicit commits. For example, if CREATE TABLE is replaced with CREATE TABLE IF NOT EXISTS, the slave will notice that the table already exists and skip execution of the statement.

The first step is to fetch the binlog files remotely, similar to the method used in Chapter 3. In this case, we need to fetch the entire binlog file, as we do not know where to start reading. The fetch_remote_binlog function in Example B-5 fetches a binary log from a server and returns an iterator to the lines of the binary log.

Example B-5. Fetching a remote binary log

```python
import subprocess

def fetch_remote_binlog(server, binlog_file):
    command = ["mysqlbinlog",
               "--read-from-remote-server",
               "--force",
               "--host=%s" % (server.host),
               "--user=%s" % (server.sql_user.name)]
    if server.sql_user.passwd:
        command.append("--password=%s" % (server.sql_user.passwd))
    command.append(binlog_file)
    return iter(subprocess.Popen(command, stdout=subprocess.PIPE).stdout)
```

The iterator returns the lines of the binary log one by one, so the lines have to be further separated into transactions and events to make the binary log easier to work with. Example B-6 shows a function named group_by_event that groups lines belonging to the same event into a single string, and a function named group_by_trans that groups a stream of events (as returned by group_by_event) into lists, where each list represents a transaction.

Example B-6. Parsing the mysqlbinlog output to extract transactions

```python
delimiter = "/*!*/;"

def group_by_event(lines):
    event_lines = []
    for line in lines:
        if line.startswith('#'):
            if line.startswith("# End of log file"):
                del event_lines[-1]
                yield ''.join(event_lines)
                return
            if line.startswith("# at"):
                yield ''.join(event_lines)
                event_lines = []
        event_lines.append(line)

def group_by_trans(lines):
    group = []
```

```
    in_transaction = False

for event in group_by_event(lines):
    group.append(event)
    if event.find(delimiter + "\nBEGIN\n" + delimiter) >= 0:
        in_transaction = True
    elif not in_transaction:
        yield group
        group = []
    else:
        p = event.find("\nCOMMIT")
        if p >= 0 and (event.startswith(delimiter, p+7)
                        or event.startswith(delimiter, p+8)):
            yield group
            group = []
            in_transaction = False
```

The last step is to implement the function to actually scan the binary logs of a server and locate the position given a GTID. This is done by scanning the binary log files starting with the most recent one and and processing older ones. The files are scanned in this order because the function assumes it is used for slave promotion, and here the most recent binary log should contain the GTID.

Example B-7. Finding file position from GTID

```
_GIDCRE = re.compile(r"^UPDATE Last_Exec_Trans SET\s+"
                     r"server_id = (?P<server_id>\d+),\s+"
                     r"trans_id = (?P<trans_id>\d+)$", re.MULTILINE)
_HEADCRE = re.compile(r"#\d{6}\s+\d?\d:\d\d:\d\d\s+"
                      r"server id\s+(?P<sid>\d+)\s+"
                      r"end_log_pos\s+(?P<end_pos>\d+)\s+"
                      r"(?P<type>\w+)")

def scan_logfile(master, logfile, gtid):    ❶
    from mysql.replicant.server import Position
    lines = fetch_remote_binlog(master, logfile)
    # Scan the output to find GTID update statements
    for trans in group_by_trans(lines):
        if len(trans) < 3:
            continue
        # Check for an update of the Last_Exec_Trans table
        m = _GIDCRE.search(trans[-2])
        if m:
            server_id = int(m.group("server_id"))
            trans_id = int(m.group("trans_id"))
            if server_id == gtid.server_id and trans_id == gtid.trans_id:
                # Check for an information comment with end_log_pos. We
                # assume InnoDB tables only, so we can therefore rely on
                # the transactions to end in an Xid event.
                m = _HEADCRE.search(trans[-1])
                if m and m.group("type") == "Xid":
                    return Position(server_id, logfile, int(m.group("end_pos")))
```

```
    return None

def find_position_from_gtid(server, gtid): ❷
    # Read the master logfiles of the new master.
    server.connect()
    logs = [ row["Log_name"] for row in server.sql("SHOW MASTER LOGS") ]
    server.disconnect()

    logs.reverse()
    for log in logs:
        pos = scan_logfile(server, log, gtid)
        if pos:
            return pos
    return None
```

❶ This function scans the *mysqlbinlog* output for the GTID. The function accepts a server from which to fetch the binlog file, the name of a binlog file to scan (the filename is the name of the binary log on the server), and a GTID to look for. It returns either a position of the end of the transaction containing the GTID, or None if the GTID cannot be found in the binlog file.

❷ This function iterates over the binlog files in reverse order and looks for a GTID. It starts with the most recent one and continue with older ones until either the GTID is found in a file, or all binlog files have been processed. If the GTID is found, the position of the end of the transaction containing the GTID is returned. Otherwise, None is returned.

Index

Symbols

(hash mark), 108
* (asterisk), 110
--log-slow-queries startup option, 408
_ (underscore), 175

A

acceptable downtime, 315
active binlog file
    described, 33, 53
    switching, 102
Activity Monitor, 361–365
administrative tasks
    adding slaves, 617–618
    checking slave status, 612–615
    load balancing functions, 165
    managing replication, 11–15, 160
    MySQL Workbench, 392–400
    performing common, 42–49
    stopping replication, 615
advisors
    described, 585, 594
    MEM support, 594–595
after image (column bitmaps), 282
agents
    described, 585
    fixing problems, 588–590
    installing, 587

ALTER statement
    binlog events and, 53
    logging transactions, 86
ALTER TABLE statement
    changing tablespaces, 450
    hierarchal replication, 172
    logging, 59
    MySQL Cluster and, 305
    ORDER BY clause, 470
    transactional replication and, 272
    troubleshooting, 465
    usage example, 438
ANALYZE TABLE statement
    best practices, 443
    described, 431–434
    repairing tables, 468
Append_block event, 65
apply-incremental-backup command, 550
apply-log command, 550
archival plans
    defined, 546
    forming, 546–547
Archive storage engine
    described, 440
    repairing tables, 468
asterisk (*), 110
asynchronous replication
    MySQL support, 6
    value of, 156–158

We'd like to hear your suggestions for improving our indexes. Send email to index@oreilly.com.

autoextend option, 450
automating
    backups, 579–581
    monitoring with cron, 356
AUTO_INCREMENT attribute
    bidirectional replication, 143
    context events, 62
    data sharding and, 193
    loading multiple tables, 99
    logging queries, 60
    usage example, 252
auto_increment_increment option, 143, 518
auto_increment_offset option, 143, 518

B

backup command, 549
backup-and-apply-log command, 549–554
--backup-dir option, 554
backup-dir-to-image command, 550
backup-to-image command, 550
backups, 546
    (see also specific backup tools)
    automating, 579–581
    cloning slaves and, 39
    cloning the master and, 36
    data sharding and, 203, 222
    expectations for, 544
    FLUSH TABLES WITH READ LOCK state-
        ment and, 40
    forming archival plans, 546
    high availability and, 295
    importance of, 5, 542–544
    InnoDB tables, 40
    logical versus physical, 545
    LVM support, 564–568
    method comparisons, 569
    MySQL Cluster and, 304
    MySQL Enterprise Backup, 36, 41, 94, 548–
        559
    mysqldump utility, 560–562
    online methods, 129
    physical file copy, 562–564
    PITR and, 571
    procedure overview, 575
    replication and, 571
    scaling out and, 155
    schema, 225
    snapshots and, 566
    system availability and, 7

terminology, 542
    XtraBackup, 569
bandwidth, replication monitoring and, 478,
    495
baselines, forming, 335
before image (column bitmaps), 282
BEGIN statement, 86, 280
Begin_load_query event, 65
benchmark function, 406, 444
benchmarking, 405–407
best practices
    checking configuration, 524
    checking logs, 523
    checking server status, 523
    common procedures, 526–528
    connection pools, 327
    constraint usage, 442
    data nodes, 327
    database optimization, 435–443
    hardware, 328
    high performance, 326
    for improving performance, 444–446
    indexes, 435, 442
    memory, 328
    nontransactional tables, 526
    normalization, 435
    operating systems, 328
    orderly restarts, 525
    orderly shutdowns, 525
    queries, 327, 444, 526
    query cache, 441
    replication, 445
    storage engines, 436–441
    topologies, 521–523
    transactional tables, 526
    troubleshooting, 521–528
    views, 441
bidirectional replication, 140–144, 190
binary log, 105
    (see also logging statements; mysqlbinlog
        utility)
    binary log group commit, 94–97
    cloning masters and, 37
    cloning slaves and, 39
    content considerations, 33–35, 52
    crash safety and, 100
    described, 25, 29, 52, 571
    execution order and, 249
    filtering, 67–69

--no-connection option, 559
node ID, 318
node recovery, 295, 318
nonhierarchal deployment, 178–180
nontransactional changes
  avoiding problems with, 89
  best practices, 526
  data consistency problems, 100
  error handling and, 83–86
  implicit commits and, 86
  logging, 88–89
  protecting, 274
  row-based replication and, 97
  statement execution and, 88–89
  troubleshooting, 507–509, 515
NoOptionError exception, 15
normalization, 435
NOT NULL option, 443
NotMasterError exception, 16
NotSlaveError exception, 16
NOW function, 60, 61
NO_WRITE_TO_BINLOG keyword, 434

O

ONLINE keyword, 305
online operations, 296, 304
operating systems, 340
  (see also specific systems)
  best practices, 328
  class methods, 16
  monitoring solutions, 340
  MySQL Replicant Library and, 12
  node recovery and, 319
OPTIMIZE TABLE statement
  best practices, 443
  defragmenting tables, 471
  described, 434
  myisam_recover_options option and, 474
  repairing tables, 468
ORDER BY clause
  ALTER TABLE statement and, 470
  LIMIT clause and, 507
  partial execution of statements and, 287
ORDER BY RAND() clause, SELECT statement,
  164
overall transfer rate, 338

P

paging technique, 337
partitioning
  data sharding and, 190, 197–205, 210–215
  described, 565
  events to slaves, 176
  MySQL Cluster and, 296, 303
passwords
  master log information file, 231
  MEM installation and, 588
  security considerations, 72
  user account, 28
Patriot Act, 534
pausing replication, 527
peak loads, handling, 159
per-process transfer rate, 338
Percona open source provider, 569
performance considerations, 326
  (see also monitoring)
  best practices, 326, 444–446
  data sharding and, 191
  data-mining queries, 43
  database, 423–443
  database object manipulation, 59
  described, 380
  diagnosing performance problems, 420
  high performance, 325–326
  InnoDB storage engine, 448
  MyISAM storage engine, 467
  MySQL Cluster and, 324
  MySQL servers, 381–419
  optimizing views and, 143
  Performance Monitor, 375–377
  proxies and, 160
  replication and, 477
  report generation, 24, 155
  synchronous replication, 157
Performance Monitor, 375–377
Performance Schema feature
  described, 409–412
  diagnosing performance problems, 420
  getting started, 412
  InnoDB storage engine and, 462–464
--performance-schema startup option, 412
Perl programming language, 405
PHP programming language, 162, 180
physical backups, 545
physical file copy, 562–564, 569
physical volumes, 565

best practices, 327, 444, 526
cross-schema, 202
data sharding and, 193, 195, 202, 215, 218–220
data-mining, 43
distributing, 160
EXPLAIN statement and, 596
indexes and, 387
manually executing, 526
map-reduce execution and, 193
shard IDs and, 218
slave lag and, 498
troubleshooting, 505, 507, 511–512
Query Analyzer
described, 595, 605–608
enabling, 596
query cache
best practices, 441
described, 387
server variables, 388
status variables, 388
query events
binlog event structure, 55
context events and, 251
current database and, 116
described, 32
execution contexts, 59–64
interpreting, 114–115
logging, 59–65
mysqlbinlog support, 110
post header and body, 115
reading remote files, 111
row-based replication and, 280
statement-based replication and, 278
thread IDs and, 65, 254
Q_AUTO_INCREMENT status variable, 116
Q_CHARSET status variable, 116
Q_SQL_MODE_CODE status variable, 116

R

RAID (redundant array of inexpensive disks), 534
Rand event, 62, 252
RAND function
context events, 61
described, 60
Rand event and, 252
range mapping (data sharding)
adding new shards, 211

creating index tables, 211
described, 210
fetching shards, 212
reactive monitoring, 335
READ COMMITTED isolation level, 184
read-only option, 120
reading data
avoiding stale data, 183
load balancing and, 154
from raw binary log files, 112
on remote files, 111
scaling out and, 155
thread-local objects, 253
recovery images, 573, 577
recovery point objective (RPO), 542, 546
recovery time objective (RTO), 542, 547
redundancy (high availability)
MySQL Cluster and, 296–298, 324
principle overview, 6, 124–126
redundant array of inexpensive disks (RAID), 534
relay log
configuring slaves, 27
fsync calls and, 269
inspecting for slaves, 491
maintaining replication positions, 246–248
row event execution, 283
structure of, 229–232
troubleshooting, 515
relay log information file
described, 230, 232
fsync calls and, 269
manipulating slave threads, 234
replication status information, 246
storing replication information, 271
thread syncing and, 269
transactional replication and, 272
troubleshooting data loss, 514
relay servers
adding in Python, 172
handling failures, 127
hierarchal replication, 170
setting up, 171–172
synchronizing with, 181
relay-log option, 27
relay-log-index option, 27
relay-log-info-file option, 230
relay-log-space-limit option, 246
relay_log_info_repository option, 271

transaction_allow_batching option, 327
tree topology, 12, 158
triggers
    creating, 72
    DEFINER clause, 117
    events and, 284–286
    invoking, 75
    logging statements, 70–75
    security considerations, 72
troubleshooting
    best practices, 521–528
    binary log, 506
    binary log events, 503–505
    data loss, 514
    detecting misdirected writes, 630
    error handling, 517
    I/O threads, 515
    InnoDB storage engine, 464–467
    master servers, 503–509
    memory, 513
    memory tables, 503
    nontransactional changes, 507–509, 515
    queries, 505, 507, 511–512
    relay log, 515
    replication, 510, 517–521, 527
    server IDs, 510
    slave servers, 509–517
    storage engines, 511
    synchronization, 513
    tables, 465, 505, 513–514
    temporary tables, 513
    threads, 516
    transactions, 515
    unsafe statements, 507–509
two-phase commit, 156

U

UAC (User Account Control), 48, 366
UDFs (user-defined functions), 97, 252
umount command, 566
--uncompress option, 554
underscore (_), 175
UNIV_DEBUG directive, 453
Unix operating system
    automated monitoring, 356
    disk usage, 350–353
    general system statistics, 355–356
    memory usage, 347–349
    monitoring, 334, 341–356

MySQL Replicant Library and, 12
    network activity, 353–355
    process activity, 342–347
    scheduling tasks on, 48
UNIX_TIMESTAMP function, 60–61
UNLOCK TABLES statement, 568
UPDATE statement
    invoking triggers, 72
    LIMIT clause, 97, 287
    logging, 58
    nontransactional changes and, 275
    stored procedures and, 76
    troubleshooting memory tables, 513
    WHERE clause, 52, 59
Update_rows event, 279, 283
uptime command, 340, 341, 355
USE statement
    current database, 69
    usage example, 108
User Account Control (UAC), 48, 366
user accounts
    cloning users, 642
    connecting master and slave, 28
    MEM installation and, 588
    MySQL Workbench and, 397
User class, 16
USER function, 97, 99
user-defined functions (UDFs), 97, 252
User_var event
    described, 62, 251
    mysqlbinlog support, 108–110
UUID, 194, 260
UUID function, 99, 507

V

Vagabond role, 20
validate command, 550
variables
    configuring servers, 381
    password considerations, 72
    query events and, 59
    thread-specific results, 254
variables command, 390
--verbose option, 618, 675
verification procedures, 539
vgcreate command, 566
vgscan command, 566
views
    best practices, 441

optimizing, 143
virtual shards, 202–205
vmstat command, 341, 353, 355
volume groups, 565
Volume Shadow Copy, 564

W

wait_for_pos function, 179, 184
wait_for_trans_id function, 184
WAIT_UNTIL_SQL_THREAD_AF-
    TER_GTIDS function, 187, 264
WHERE clause
    DELETE statement, 52, 275
    EXPLAIN statement and, 426
    SELECT statement, 441
    UPDATE statement, 52, 59
wildcards
    mysqlbinlog support, 110
    slave filters and, 175
Windows Experience report, 366
Windows operating system
    Cygwin and, 563
    Event Viewer, 369–372
    monitoring, 334, 365–377
    MySQL Replicant Library and, 12
    Performance Monitor, 375–377
    Reliability Monitor, 372–374
    scheduling tasks on, 48
    System Health Report, 366–369, 374
    Task Manager, 374
    Volume Shadow Copy, 564

Windows Experience report, 366
worst case scenario, 538
Write_rows event, 279, 283
writing data
    data sharding and, 156
    detecting misdirected writes, 630
    load balancing and, 154
    scaling out and, 155
    thread-local objects, 253

X

X/Open Distributed Transaction Processing
    model, 91–94
XA protocol, 91–94, 101
Xid event, 91, 110
XtraBackup
    backup comparisons, 569
    cloning slaves, 41
    described, 569
    snapshot support, 129
XtraDB storage engine, 569

Z

Zaitsev, Peter, 8
Zawodny, Jeremy D., 403
ZFS filesystem
    backup comparisons, 569
    performing backups, 568
    snapshot support, 40, 129

About the Authors

Dr. Charles A. Bell is a Senior Software Engineer at Oracle. He is currently the lead developer for backup and a member of the MySQL Backup and Replication team. He lives in a small town in rural Virginia with his loving wife. He received his Doctor of Philosophy in Engineering from Virginia Commonwealth University in 2005. His research interests include database systems, versioning systems, semantic web, and agile software development.

Dr. Mats Kindahl is principal senior software developer in the MySQL team at Oracle. He is the main architect and implementor of MySQL's row-based replication and several other replication features and is currently architect and project lead for the MySQL High Availability team that is developing MySQL Fabric. Before starting at MySQL, he did research in formal methods, program analysis, and distributed systems, the area where he earned his doctoral degree in computer science. He has also spent several years developing C/C++ compilers.

Dr. Lars Thalmann is the development manager for MySQL replication and backup. He is responsible for the strategy and development of these features and leads the corresponding engineering teams. Thalmann has worked with MySQL development since 2001, when he was a software developer working on MySQL Cluster. More recently, he has driven the creation and development of the MySQL backup feature, has guided the evolution of MySQL replication since 2004, and has been a key player in the development of MySQL Cluster replication. Thalmann holds a doctorate in computer science from Uppsala University, Sweden.

Colophon

The animal on the cover of *MySQL High Availability* is an American robin (*Turdus migratorius*). Instantly recognizable by its distinctive appearance–dark head, reddish-orange breast, and brown back–this member of the thrush family is among the most common American birds. (Though it shares its name with the European robin, which also has a reddish breast, the two species are not closely related.)

The American robin inhabits a range of six million square miles in North America and is resident year-round through much of the United States. Commonly considered a harbinger of spring, robins are early to sing in the morning and among the last birds singing at night. Their diets consist of invertebrates (often earthworms) and fruit and berries. Robins favor open ground and short grass, so they are frequent backyard visitors, and they are often found in parks, in gardens, and on lawns.

The cover image is from *Johnson's Natural History*, Volume II. The cover fonts are URW Typewriter and Guardian Sans. The text font is Adobe Minion Pro; the heading font is Adobe Myriad Condensed; and the code font is Dalton Maag's Ubuntu Mono.

Get even more for your money.

Join the O'Reilly Community, and register the O'Reilly books you own. It's free, and you'll get:

- $4.99 ebook upgrade offer
- 40% upgrade offer on O'Reilly print books
- Membership discounts on books and events
- Free lifetime updates to ebooks and videos
- Multiple ebook formats, DRM FREE
- Participation in the O'Reilly community
- Newsletters
- Account management
- 100% Satisfaction Guarantee

Signing up is easy:

1. **Go to: oreilly.com/go/register**
2. **Create an O'Reilly login.**
3. **Provide your address.**
4. **Register your books.**

Note: English-language books only

To order books online:

oreilly.com/store

For questions about products or an order:

orders@oreilly.com

To sign up to get topic-specific email announcements and/or news about upcoming books, conferences, special offers, and new technologies:

elists@oreilly.com

For technical questions about book content:

booktech@oreilly.com

To submit new book proposals to our editors:

proposals@oreilly.com

O'Reilly books are available in multiple DRM-free ebook formats. For more information:

oreilly.com/ebooks

O'REILLY®

Spreading the knowledge of innovators   oreilly.com